JAMES III
A Political Study

*To my father
and in memory of my mother*

JAMES III
A Political Study

NORMAN MACDOUGALL

Lecturer in Scottish History,
University of St Andrews

JOHN DONALD PUBLISHERS LTD
EDINBURGH

The publishers acknowledge the
financial assistance of the Scottish
Arts Council in the publication
of this volume

Exclusive distribution in the
United States of America and Canada
by Humanities Press Inc., Atlantic
Highlands, NJ 07716, USA.

ISBN 0 85976 078 2

Phototypesetting by H.M. Repros, Glasgow
Printed in Great Britain by Bell & Bain Ltd., Glasgow

Acknowledgements

FOR a variety of reasons, most of them good ones, this book has been a long time coming, and my indebtedness to a host of friends and mentors stretches back the greater part to two decades. However, pride of place must go to my parents, whose enthusiasm and practical support throughout have been boundless. To both of them, with deep gratitude, I dedicate this book.

My initial commitment to the subject met with a remarkable response from all whom I approached, and without their continuing encouragement little or none of this would have appeared in print. I owe a large debt to members of staff in my alma mater, Glasgow University, especially Professor A. A. M. Duncan, Dr I. B. Cowan, Dr J. A. F. Thomson, Dr John Durkan and Professor A. L. Brown. In particular, I should like to thank Dr Jenny Wormald, whose assistance extended far beyond her constructive criticism of the early chapters of this book; she will doubtless be relieved to discover that my tally of derogatory adjectives to describe James III greatly exceeds her own remarkable 1972 total. As in Glasgow, so also at St Andrews University, friends and colleagues have been extremely generous with their time, knowledge and advice since my arrival in 1979. I am grateful to Dr Ronald Cant, Dr Barbara Crawford, Mr Chris Upton and Miss Isobel Guy for information on a wide range of topics, and to Professor Christopher Smout for consistent encouragement and very practical support. Above all, I am indebted to Mr Roger Mason, the Glenfiddich research fellow in Scottish history at St Andrews, who not only read most of the book in typescript and pronounced it intelligible, but also added substantially to my understanding by imparting some of his extensive knowledge of the political thought of the period. Every tutor learns something — often a great deal — from his students, and I was extremely fortunate in my first James III Special Subject group, an inspired and inspiring class of three — Lindsay Beaton, Jenny Kinnear and Tyrrell Young. Their successors in the same class — Garry Cameron, Susan Hill, Christine McGladdery, Sandy Paul, Kevin Philpott, Elspeth Reid, and Suzanne Vestal — are already displaying a similar zeal.

My gratitude to many present and past members of Scottish Medievalists' Conference is expressed elsewhere in the text, but I should like to record a particular debt to Dr Rod Lyell, Dr Ranald Nicholson, Dr Ian Rae, Dr Leslie Macfarlane, Dr Athol Murray, Professor Donald Watt, Mr Geoffrey Stell and Mr Trevor Chalmers. The kindnesses shown to me in the early stages of my research by the late Dr Annie Dunlop, one of the pioneers of Scottish historical research and a great human being, deserve more space than they can possibly receive here.

Much more recently, I have enjoyed the final stages of writing not only because of the unfailing courtesy and efficiency of the St Andrews University library staff, but also because in Glasgow I have had the run of the excellent Baillie's Library, presided over by Mrs Manchester and possessing a uniquely quiet yet friendly atmosphere. John Tuckwell of John Donald Publishers has shown throughout an enthusiasm and consideration for the problems involved which any beleaguered author might well envy. The task of deciphering and typing the greater part of my manuscript was undertaken by Mhorag McBain (now Mrs Mhorag Dick), who managed it all with exemplary patience and remarkable accuracy. A close friend, Cary Richardson, not only typed the first chapter, read chapters seven and eight, and pestered me for years to get on with writing the book, but in March 1980 also shared with me the singularly appropriate experience of being trapped at Lauder, not by the Earl of Buchan, but by snow. Finally, I must record the contribution of my labrador Bonnie, whose almost constant desire for exercise involved me in long walks on St Andrews and Elie beaches where, for better or worse, many of the views advanced in this book were first formulated.

Contents

Preface

AROUND 1820 the Edinburgh antiquary George Chalmers sat down and tried to assemble materials for a history of the reign of James III. It was never completed; but the attempt itself places Chalmers among the many unsung heroes of Scottish historical literature, for in the early nineteenth century, before the publication of the majority of Scottish public and private records, and in the face of a formidable corpus of already established and largely mythical tales about the reign, such a task was daunting if not wholly impossible. Chalmers' memorial is some hundred pages of manuscript in the National Library of Scotland; this book is an attempt, more than a century-and-a-half later, to finish what he started.

The scholar of the 1980s has two inestimable advantages over Chalmers. First and most obvious, the nineteenth and early twentieth century mania for editing has made accessible in print the public records of Scotland; while the publishing clubs and societies of the same era have produced a vast body of family archive, monastic, and diplomatic material and infinitely eased the task of the historian. Secondly, the last twenty years have seen the appearance of a wealth of scholarly literature on fifteenth century Scottish government and society, above all a questioning of traditional views of the relationship between Crown and nobility and an effort to reinterpret the major political crises of the period. This activity has in turn generated extensive and frequently acrimonious debates about the nature of Scottish government during the century, and these show every sign of continuing and indeed developing over the next generation.

This healthy state of affairs owes much to the work of a few pioneers. In 1972 Dr. Jennifer Brown, in a short but devastating article, destroyed once and for all the myth of the fifteenth century as an unending series of Crown-magnate confrontations, and stressed the remarkable stability of Scottish central and local government between 1424 and 1488.[1] Subsequently she developed this theme with the assistance of a number of scholars working in specialist areas, and produced a volume of essays on a wide variety of aspects of government and society from which a clear picture of fifteenth century Scotland began to emerge for the first time.[2] Finally, in 1981 she contributed a penetrating analysis of post-1470 government and politics in a general history covering the period 1470-1625.[3] In all these works James III emerges as the most unpopular of the fifteenth century Stewarts, a man who conspicuously failed to do his job yet was able to survive a vast conspiracy against his government in 1482 and might well have done the same in 1488. Dr. Wormald's intriguing argument throughout is that fifteenth century monarchical government in Scotland required the maintenance of a delicate Crown-magnate

1

balance, the former acting as the source of justice and patronage, the latter supporting the royal house as lawgivers and leaders in war in their own localities; in a remote and relatively impoverished country, in which the Crown could not afford a contract army, delegation of royal authority in this way was essential. James III, by upsetting this balance, is in Dr. Wormald's view the exception who proves the rule; yet at the end, in 1488, he was opposed in the field by only two earls and two bishops, an indication that Scottish magnates took up arms even against an impossible king with extreme reluctance.

Professor Duncan is even more forceful in discussing the personality of James III and its influence on events. The king, he claims, 'was a calamitous failure who always took the easy way out', 'a hoarder who raised cash by demoralising methods', 'capable of the wildest suspicions of, and acts against, his own family'.[4] His pungent analysis of the problems of the reign is the best introduction to James III, provocative and stimulating, and disposing in short space of a large number of the myths surrounding King James's government.

Dr. Nicholson, employing a much broader canvas, is understandably more cautious, and he is not without praise for James III's political skill; broadly, however, his conclusions on James III's character are similar to, if slightly anticipating, those of Wormald and Duncan, and he rightly stresses the king's failure to attend adequately to the administration of justice. His chapters on James III provide the fullest modern treatment of the reign and are a model of painstaking scholarship.[5]

In the face of all this recent scholarly activity, it may well be asked whether a political study of James III is really necessary. There are at least three answers to this question. Firstly, there is the curious fact that in spite of modern efforts to explain the king's failure in terms of personality — in one glorious page Dr. J. M. Brown describes him as 'a man of grandiose and exalted ideas of kingship', 'lazy', 'remote, uninterested, and ineffective', 'personally disastrous', 'high-handed', 'whimsical', 'double-dealing', and 'impossible to serve'[6] — that personality remains remarkably elusive. This study cannot provide a definitive answer; but by tracing the king's acts from the end of his minority to 1488, and relating them to those of his father and his father's counsellors, it attempts to supply pointers to an understanding of a complex character whose actions produced two of the three major political upheavals of the century.

Secondly, it is undoubtedly true that the reign witnessed considerable development in Scottish royal government and the institutions associated with it, above all parliament and the royal council meeting as a civil court. The three estates met in parliament almost every year during this reign — a remarkable contrast with the following one — and James's concern to attract to his council appeals from the localities in civil actions is the subject of some of the last legislation of the reign. A radical change in Scottish foreign policy came with the English alliance of 1474, a piece of diplomacy for which the king was largely responsible, setting a pattern in which he persisted until his death. If this may perhaps be regarded as his most solid achievement, other aspects of his personal policy are more controversial and require examination — his efforts to centralise royal government in Edinburgh, his drastic solution to financial problems in time of crisis, and his remarkably arbitrary treatment of many of his most powerful magnates.

Thirdly, in spite of much recent work on the period, a proper understanding of the character and policies of James III is still impeded by the existence of a sixteenth century legend which bears little resemblance to the statements of contemporaries about the king or the evidence of official records. King James is portrayed as a recluse with no interest whatever in war or government, dominated by low-born favourites who turned him against his family and his nobility. This legend may be traced to its sources, and can be shown largely to be myth, remarkably similar in some respects to the English Tudor myth of Richard III.[7] English historians have long since come to terms with the wilful bias of Tudor writers in describing Richard III as a monster of iniquity; but some Scottish historians still subscribe to the sixteenth century myth of James III.[8]

Despite the advances of a century-and-a-half since Chalmers' day, the difficulties facing the biographer of James III are still very considerable. As Professor A. L. Brown has convincingly shown,[9] Scottish historians writing about the fifteenth century cannot hope to emulate their English colleagues in approaching the study of royal administration and government by way of privy council records, household accounts, and a vast array of royal letters and charters. The paucity of such evidence in Scotland makes certainty about the day-to-day running of the administration impossible. For example, council records bearing sederunt lists survive only for four years out of a possible nineteen, and these are restricted to the work of the council in its judicial function; the Treasurer's accounts, providing vital information about the royal household, its composition, expenditure, and movements, exist for a mere sixteen months of the entire reign. For much of the time, we cannot be certain of the king's movements. Small wonder that many have turned with relief to the narratives of the sixteenth century chroniclers for information. Yet this is a dangerous path to tread, for it may produce only an unsatisfactory blend of myth and fact, with the former predominating whenever official records are lacking. Throughout this study, therefore, James III's career is explained — in spite of the fragmentary nature of the sources — in terms of the evidence to be found in contemporary 'official' records — royal charters and letters, parliamentary acts, lords of council business, Treasurer's accounts, exchequer accounts, collections of diplomatic material, monastic cartularies, and family charters in private archives. Reference is made to the narratives of the sixteenth century chroniclers — Abell, Lesley, Ferreri, Pitscottie, and Buchanan — only where their statements can be corroborated by, or serve to illuminate, contemporary record evidence. Finally, in Chapter Twelve, these narratives are discussed in detail, with an assessment of their probable sources, general reliability or lack of it, and — latterly — their post-Reformation bias; and their contribution to the legend of James III is explained.

As this is essentially a political study, certain important themes — the peerage, the church, the development of the royal council, patronage of the arts, and finance — are dealt with only in passing; but these are well served by other scholars. In particular, the appearance of lords of parliament under James II, and the significance of this major new peerage group, are the subjects of a stimulating article by Dr. Sandy Grant;[10] Dr. Leslie Macfarlane, whose forthcoming biography of Bishop Elphinstone is eagerly awaited, is the acknowledged expert on the struggles between Crown and papacy over the creation and status of the archbishopric of St. Andrews;[11] and Dr. I. B. Cowan has recently produced an important article on a neglected but vital ecclesiastical topic, the role of the Church in fifteenth century Scottish society.[12] Dr. A. L. Brown's analysis of the council in a masterly lecture[13] provides the introduction to a huge topic currently being studied by Mr. Trevor Chalmers; while James III's patronage of the arts, a subject much discussed but little written about, is touched on by Dr. Jenny Wormald,[14] receives brief but fascinating treatment from Professor John MacQueen,[15] and is the subject of a forthcoming book by Dr. Rod Lyall. Dr. A. L. Murray's understanding of fifteenth century royal finances and financial officers is unparalleled, and his studies of the offices of Comptroller and Clerk Register are happily in print.[16] The coinage, a subject of major importance for the political history of this reign, has received dedicated and masterly treatment from Mr. Ian Stewart[17] and Mrs. Joan Murray.[18]

These important studies reflect a growing scholarly interest in fifteenth century Scotland. It is to be hoped that this biography of the most elusive of that century's monarchs will add to an understanding of late medieval Scottish royal government. It should at least provide an insight into the political machinations of an exceedingly unpleasant man.

NOTES

1. J. M. Brown (now Wormald), 'Taming the Magnates?' in G. Menzies (ed.) *The Scottish Nation* (BBC, 1972), 46-59.

2. J. M. Brown (now Wormald), *Scottish Society in the Fifteenth Century*, (Lond., 1977).

3. Jenny Wormald, *Court, Kirk, and Community: Scotland 1470-1625*, (London, 1981), Chapter 1.

4. W. C. Dickinson, *Scotland from the Earliest Times to 1603*, revised by A. A. M. Duncan (3rd edn., Oxford, 1977), Chapter 21, and esp. 243-4, 248.

5. R. G. Nicholson, *Scotland: The Later Middle Ages: 1286-1513*, (Edinburgh, 1974), Chapters 14-16.

6. Brown, 'Taming the Magnates?', 56.

7. The growth of the legend in the sixteenth century is discussed by N. A. T. Macdougall, 'The Sources: A Reappraisal of the Legend', in Brown, *Scottish Society in the Fifteenth Century*, 17-32. It receives broader treatment in Chapter 12 below.

8. Traces of the myth — especially regarding the identities of, and the part played by, the royal familiars — are to be found in Nicholson's otherwise excellent survey of the reign: *Nicholson, op.cit.*, 501-2, 530. Much more serious is Professor Donaldson's uncritical acceptance of Robert (*sic*) Cochrane as the architect who designed the Great Hall at Stirling: Gordon Donaldson, *Scottish Kings*, (London, 1967), 109, 113.

9. A. L. Brown, 'The Scottish "Establishment" in the later Fifteenth Century', in *Juridical Review*, 23 (1978).

10. A. Grant, 'The development of the Scottish peerage', *S.H.R.*, lvii, (1978), 1-27.

11. L. J. Macfarlane, 'The Primacy of the Scottish Church, 1472-1521', *Innes Review*, xx, 111-29.

12. I. B. Cowan, 'Church and Society', in J. M. Brown (ed.), *Scottish Society in the Fifteenth Century*, (London, 1977), 112-135.

13. *A. L. Brown, op.cit.*

14. *Wormald, op.cit.*, Chapter 4.

15. John MacQueen, 'The literature of fifteenth-century Scotland', in J. M. Brown (ed.), *Scottish Society in the Fifteenth Century*, 184-208.

16. A. L. Murray, 'The Comptroller, 1425-1488', *S.H.R.*, lii (1973), 1-29; 'The Lord Clerk Register', *S.H.R.*, liii (1974), esp. 128-133.

17. I. H. Stewart, *The Scottish Coinage* (2nd edn., London, 1967), Chapter VIII.

18. Joan Murray, 'The Black Money of James III', in *British Archaeological Reports 45*, (1977), 115-130.

1

Born into Crisis: 1437-55

JAMES STEWART, the eldest son of James II of Scotland and Mary of Gueldres, was born towards the end of May 1452 at St. Andrews, in Bishop Kennedy's episcopal castle where the queen had gone for her confinement, and probably also for her safety.[1] The news of the birth of a son and heir was quickly brought to the king at Edinburgh by Robert Norry;[2] and both Norry and Bishop Kennedy were speedily rewarded by the relieved monarch, Norry with lands in Menteith and the bishop with a charter confirming all lands which he had formerly received in regality from the Crown, with immunity from tolls and levies, and the right of minting money.[3]

The king's relief and immediate expression of gratitude are understandable. He had married Mary of Gueldres in 1449, and two earlier pregnancies had produced, first, a premature birth in May 1450, a child which lived only six hours, and secondly, a daughter, Princess Mary, born in the spring or early summer of 1451.[4] The birth of a son in May 1452 not only ensured the succession, but also gave James II an enormous psychological lift during the most serious crisis of the reign. Only three months before the prince's birth, James had murdered the eighth Earl of Douglas, the most powerful Scottish magnate, at Stirling, and the entire spring and early summer was taken up with the royal struggle against the Black Douglases and their allies, justifying the murder in parliament, and obtaining the approval and support of the three estates. In fact, the first six months of 1452 may be regarded as the second phase of a major civil war between James II and the Black Douglases which flared up on three occasions between 1451 and 1455, which ended in the ruin of the Douglases and, as a result, in an impressive extension of royal power and prestige.

Why such a civil war occurred at all requires closer examination. The maintenance of political and social stability in fifteenth century Scotland depended on cooperation between the Crown and the greater magnates, and the traditional picture of king and nobility in endless confrontation has long since been shown to be a myth.[5] There were frequent rebellions by isolated families wishing to make a particular grievance public, but these hardly constituted a major threat to the Crown. Much more typical was a tacit understanding between king and nobility to cooperate in advancing their interests, an understanding which worked in practice because each side had something to gain from, and to offer, the other. The king had enormous prestige and could exercise considerable patronage, but his power was always restricted by his income, which was small and which could be augmented by taxation only very rarely. His traditional obligations were to provide justice for his

7

subjects and — much more costly — act as a leader in war. Yet he could not afford a contract army; so in time of war he relied heavily on the greater magnates whose supporters would form the backbone of any Scottish army, or who, if local rebellion threatened, might act on the Crown's behalf by crushing the opposition themselves. In time of peace, the king needed magnate support even more, to exercise justice and maintain law and order in the localities; for there was no question of the Crown having the wealth to pay judges or lawyers, or even give proper remuneration to important officials such as wardens of the marches.[6] The answer to this problem, generally accepted throughout the century, was delegation of authority to responsible magnates who alone could represent the central government effectively in the localities.

For their part, the nobility had good reason to cooperate with the king. For most of them, success lay in enriching themselves by acquiring more land, which might be achieved through a fortunate marriage, but was more likely to come as the reward for service to the Crown. A Scottish monarch might be regarded as poor in comparison with his English and French neighbours, but compared with his own nobility, he had enormous wealth, sufficient for example to spend large sums on artillery, on a navy, on patronage of the arts, and on building projects. Above all, he could exercise patronage through grants of land or office, or remission of customs dues. In short, there were good practical reasons why the nobility wished to serve, rather than challenge, the Crown.

This acceptable, if at times rather uneasy, equilibrium of service balanced against reward was upset only twice before 1460. Between 1424 and 1437, James I deliberately and vindictively embarked on a campaign to wipe out the Stewart earls; and he almost succeeded.[7] No doubt he was motivated by fear of such a concentration of power in the hands of a family close in blood to the Crown; but his ruthlessness and greed led many to regard him as a tyrant, and as one commentator remarks on the king's assassination: 'There was no support of any kind for the tiny group of men who took this desperate step; but some men may have given a private sigh of relief when they heard of it.'[8]

A second upheaval of this kind occurred in the major confrontation between James II and the Black Douglases in the early 1450s, with the difference that the king not only succeeded in crushing the opposition ruthlessly and illegally, but got away with it to the extent that he was ultimately praised for doing so. In the eyes of contemporaries such as the Auchinleck Chronicler, or later writers including Boece, Major, Abell, Lesley, and Pitscottie, this was the great crisis of the reign, and according to at least one modern historian, a triumph for monarchy in general and the Stewart dynasty in particular.[9] The whole affair may only be understood by reference to the events of James II's minority, and to the character of the king himself.

James II was the younger of twin sons born on 16 October 1430 at Holyrood.[10] The elder twin, Alexander, died in infancy, and the murder of James's father at the Blackfriars of Perth in February 1437 thrust James into the kingship at the age of only six.[11] The minority which followed lasted about twelve years, and is one of the most obscure periods of the century, largely because of the lack of contemporary narratives and the scarcity of official records.[12] What is indisputable, however, is the rise to a position of remarkable power, in spite of many setbacks, of the Black Douglas family. The source of this power was the ambition of Sir Archibald 'the Grim', lord of eastern Galloway, who in the late fourteenth century had steadily increased the Black Douglas estates. In addition to Galloway, Archibald fell heir to the Douglas lands proper, including Douglasdale, Lauderdale, Eskdale, and the forest of Selkirk; and he became third Earl of Douglas.[13]

Archibald the Grim's power had been centred on Galloway and his tower house of Threave, where he died in 1400. His elder son, Archibald, fourth earl of Douglas, added the lordship of Annandale with rights of regality to the Black Douglas lands, and shortly before his death at Verneuil in August 1424, fighting for Charles VII of France, he had been made Duke of Touraine.[14] His son Archibald, who succeeded as fifth earl of Douglas, had already acquired, or at any rate assumed, the title of Earl of Wigtown;[15] and apart from a brief period of imprisonment in 1431,[16] he was left untouched during James I's active rule, when the king was preoccupied with a wholesale onslaught on the Stewart nobility. Thus the Black Douglases were already a formidable power, in terms both of land and prestige, at the outset of James II's minority in 1437; and their strength was reflected in the appointment of Earl Archibald as lieutenant-general in the shortlived triumvirate which governed the country between 1437 and 1439.[17]

Then came a major setback. The fifth earl died in 1439, and his successor William, who was only 14 or 15 years of age, was suddenly put to death, together with his younger brother David, following a feast at Edinburgh Castle — the 'Black Dinner' — in November 1440. One perpetrator of this judicial murder — for both young men were executed as traitors — appears to have been the Chancellor, Sir William Crichton; and the motive for the killings may have been young Earl William's desire to succeed his father as lieutenant-general, and a widespread fear amongst those controlling the young king about the extent of the Douglas power.[18] Another more sinister possibility, but for which there is no real evidence, is that the young earl and his brother were executed to make way for the advancement of another Douglas, the brother of the fourth earl, James Douglas of Balveny and Abercorn, who now succeeded as seventh earl of Douglas because his grand-nephews had died without issue. In support of this view, it has been argued that, although executed as traitors, the sixth earl and his brother were not forfeited, so that the entailed Douglas estates passed naturally to their grand-uncle James; and because there appears to have been no violent Douglas reaction to the 'Black Dinner', some writers have assumed that James Douglas, as the main beneficiary of the executions, must have had a hand in planning them.[19] Undoubtedly the new seventh earl — James 'the Gross' as he was colourfully described in the following century[20] — was a man of considerable ambition, both for himself and his five sons; and in view of the fact that four of them subsequently became earls, it is tempting with the benefit of hindsight to cast their father in the role of wicked uncle, conspiring to destroy his brother's grandchildren in order to advance his own family.

Tempting, perhaps — but the issue was not a simple one. As earl, James the Gross did not succeed to the vast Douglas inheritance built up over three generations, but only to the entailed estates. The dukedom of Touraine and other French lands acquired by the fourth earl lapsed to the French crown because there were no Douglas heirs male in the direct line. For the same reason, the lordship of Annandale lapsed to the Scottish crown. The lordships of Bothwell and Galloway — the latter the original centre of Douglas power — went to the suriving sister of the 'Black Dinner' victims, Margaret, the 'Fair Maid' of Galloway.[21] Consequently, Earl James was faced with the task of reuniting the dismembered Douglas estates, and recovering for himself and his family what had been temporarily lost. That his ambitions went further need not surprise us. In addition to the inherited Douglas territory, he hoped to extend his own lands, which included not only Avondale and his castle of Abercorn on the Forth, but also lands in the north, in Banffshire, Inverness-shire, Buchan, and Moray.[22] In short, James the Gross's ambitions were typical of a powerful fifteenth century Scottish magnate in that they were territorial. No doubt he was taking advantage of the weakness of central government during a long minority; but neither he nor his successor represented a threat to the crown in the sense that they tried to monopolise the major offices of state. Such manoeuvrings were much more typical of the Crichtons and Livingstons, hungry for advancement through service in central government and the royal household.

In terms purely of territorial aggrandisement, however, Earl James was spectacularly successful. He himself survived as earl for only three years, dying at Abercorn in March 1443;[23] but before his death he had acquired the earldom of Moray for his third son Archibald; he was temporarily successful in having his second son James — the future ninth earl — provided to the bishopric of Aberdeen; and to recover Galloway and Bothwell, James the Gross arranged the marriage of his son and heir William with the Fair Maid of Galloway, the marriage taking place in the kirk of Douglas in 1443 or 1444.[24] Subsequently, in the parliament of June 1445, James the Gross's fourth son Hugh appeared for the first time as earl of Ormond, the lands of this earldom being mainly in Inverness-shire and Aberdeenshire.[25] The fifth son John appears to have been much younger than his four brothers; but he received the lands of Balveny in Banffshire.[26] Thus by July 1449, when James II married and began to intervene actively in Scottish politics, the Black Douglases had established themselves in three of the eight existing earldoms; and with extensive lands in Inverness, Moray, Banffshire, Aberdeenshire, and much of southern Scotland, they were by far the most powerful magnate family in the country, enjoying a concentration of power painstakingly built up over three generations.

The minority of James II saw the rise of another family, the Livingstons, whose advancement in the 1440s was based not on the acquisition of land but on office-holding. The head of the family, Sir Alexander Livingston of Callendar, had begun this process when in 1439, as Keeper of Stirling Castle, he obtained possession of the person by the young king by forcibly removing him from the keeping of his mother, Joan Beaufort, subsequently reaching a temporary agreement with the Chancellor, Sir William Crichton, and acquiring for himself the office of justiciar by 1444.[27] His son and heir, James Livingston, succeeded his father as Keeper of

Stirling, from 1444 he was described as 'keeper of the royal person', and in the summer of 1448 he became chamberlain. Three other Livingstons, Alexander, Robert and John, received the custody of the castles of Methven, Dumbarton and Dunoon, and Doune respectively, while the justiciar's cousin, Sir Robert Livingston of Linlithgow, became comptroller in 1448.[28] In short, the rise of the Livingstons was concentrated in a single decade, was based on the acquisition of the major royal household offices, control of certain castles, and above all, the possession of the person of the young James II. Advancement of this kind would have been impossible for a small baronial family except during a period of royal minority, and the foundations of the Livingston power were at best shaky, based as they were in the seizure and coercion of the king's mother in 1439, a criminal act which might be held against them at any time.

Thus it was natural that the Livingstons, in order to protect and extend their newly acquired eminence in Scottish politics, should seek powerful allies, and the Black Douglases, as the most powerful magnate family in Scotland, were an obvious choice. From 1443 we may date a Douglas-Livingston alliance, which in the crises of the ensuing two years was directed with much success against two powerful opponents, the Chancellor, Sir William Crichton, and Bishop James Kennedy of St. Andrews. Crichton had been Chancellor since May 1439, and his earlier career had included the office of master of the royal household under James I, sheriff of Edinburgh, and keeper of Edinburgh castle.[29] Like Livingston, Crichton rose to prominence through office-holding, and he was similarly concerned to advance the fortunes of his kin. Thus his cousin, Sir George Crichton, became sheriff of Linlithgow and Admiral of Scotland before 1444.[30]

Crichton's principal ally, James Kennedy, bishop of St. Andrews, was soon to emerge as one of the most prominent ecclesiastical statesmen of the period; but his early career had been unpromising.[31] A nephew of James I, and educated at St. Andrews and Louvain, Kennedy was thrust into the bishopric of Dunkeld in January 1437 against the wishes of the Dunkeld chapter and the Pope, Eugenius IV, who had reserved to himself the provision of the see.[32] The pope, preoccupied with the European problems created by his conflict with the Basle conciliarists — the so-called 'Little Schism' — was prepared to accept Kennedy's promotion against his wishes in return for the new bishop's loyalty, and Kennedy speedily emerged as the leader of the papalist party in Scotland. Rapid promotion and honours followed. In September 1439, Eugenius IV conferred on Kennedy the abbey of Scone, to be held *in commendam*; and the following year, when Bishop Wardlaw of St. Andrews died, Kennedy was at once translated to St. Andrews. In spite of his control of the revenues of both Dunkeld and Scone, Kennedy was unable to raise the 'common services' of 3,300 gold florins payable on admission to the see, and he should have incurred excommunication for this reason. The fact that he was absolved and allowed to remit only half the fixed sum is an indication of how rapidly he had managed to acquire the pope's favour and patronage, taking advantage of the European ecclesiastical schism to advance his own career in Scotland.[33]

However, Kennedy's position as the leading papalist in Scotland had its dangers in the early 1440s, because the Black Douglases and the Livingstons were initially committed to the conciliarist side. Earl James the Gross's second son James had been promoted to the bishopric of Aberdeen by the conciliarist pope Felix V in May 1441; and at the same time Kennedy's old bishopric of Dunkeld was given to Thomas Livingston, abbot of Dundrennan and kinsman of the justiciar.[34] These appointments did not last, the 'Little Schism' itself was eventually terminated by the abdication of Felix V in 1449, and Bishop Kennedy has been rightly praised for attempting to restore harmony to the Scottish church once the schism was over; but in 1444 he faced the crisis of his career. This was no less than a struggle for control of royal government, taking the form of a civil war lasting more than a year, summer 1444 to summer 1445. Evidence is lacking as to the exact motives of the parties involved, but the origins of the war are probably to be found in the Douglas-Livingston alliance in the late summer of 1443. Kennedy was originally a party to this, and may even have benefited from it by briefly acquiring the Chancellorship from which Sir William Crichton was thrust later in the year. But if he did so, he must have resigned it very quickly, because the post went to James Bruce, bishop of Dunkeld.[35] For whatever reason, Kennedy had aligned himself with the opponents of the Douglas-Livingston faction before the autumn of 1444, and by thus changing allies found himself on the losing side. In July 1444, William, eighth earl of Douglas, appears to have been styled 'lieutenant-general'; in August he attacked and destroyed Admiral Crichton's house at Barnton; and in spite of retaliation by both Crichtons, the Douglas-Livingston alliance was strong enough to have a General Council, meeting at Stirling in October 1444, denounce the Crichtons as rebels.[36] More significantly, the same General Council declared the young king to be of age.

On 16 October 1444, James II was fourteen; and a charter of the following month referred to his revocation of all alienations of crown rights 'on his majority at the last general council at Stirling'.[37] This was the real foundation of the Douglas-Livingston monopoly of power. With the king officially declared of age, yet in Livingston custody, crimes committed during the minority by other families could now be described as treasons; and as the king had attained his majority, the queen mother, Joan Beaufort, could not claim tutelage of her son. This shrewd grasp of the realities of power by the Black Douglases and Livingstons did not bring the civil war to an end; but it made the position of their opponents, including Kennedy, much more difficult.

Kennedy himself, threatened with the loss of his command of the abbey of Scone and effectively prevented from exercising any political power, naturally inclined to an alliance of all those who had suffered from the Douglas-Livingston control of the king. His allies were hardly an impressive combination: the queen mother, her husband Sir James Stewart of Lorne, James Douglas, earl of Angus, and the outlawed Chancellor Crichton, who clung tenaciously to his keepership of Edinburgh castle as a bargaining counter in recovering his lost influence in the government. Kennedy's political weakness was apparent when, in November 1444, he attempted to have the magistrates of Aberdeen refuse payment of revenue to the party currently holding the king. The magistrates prudently decided to wait until some legislation was passed on the subject by the three estates.[38]

In effect, the Aberdeen burgh council, presumably like many others, was awaiting the result of an impending civil war between those who had possession of the king, and their opponents. They did not have long to wait. At the end of November, 1444, the young king came in person to the siege and capture of Methven castle; and members of the court party, including Livingston, the earl of Crawford, the Ogilvies, Robertson of Struan, and Sir James Hamilton of Cadzow, went on to ravage Kennedy's lands in Fife.[39] The following summer saw the sieges of Edinburgh and Dunbar castles, the former defended by Crichton, the latter by Joan Beaufort and Sir Adam Hepburn of Hailes. Joan Beaufort died during the siege, on 15 July 1445, her husband Sir James Stewart went into exile, and Dunbar was eventually surrendered by Hepburn.[40] Of the other rebels, Angus hastened to come to terms, and Crichton, in return for yielding up Edinburgh castle, recovered much of his former influence, acquiring not only a place on the council but an increase in his former allowance of 700 marks to £700.[41]

Crichton was the only member of the defeated faction who came reasonably well out of the struggle of 1444-1445. Even before he surrendered Edinburgh castle on terms, the victorious Livingstons, Douglases and their allies felt confident enough to hold a parliament in the burgh of Edinburgh to confirm their victory in the field and reward both active supporters and friendly neutrals. Two new earldoms were created, Sir Alexander Seton of Gordon becoming earl of Huntly, and Hugh Douglas, fourth son of James the Gross, receiving the title earl of Ormond. For the first time, James I's concept of 'lords of parliament' was put into practice, and Sir James Hamilton of Cadzow, who had played a prominent part in harrying Bishop Kennedy's lands, was given the heritable title of Lord Hamilton.[42] For the Livingstons, success in 1444-5 was the springboard to high office for members of the family, the first to benefit being Alexander, a younger son of the justiciar, who became captain of the recently captured Methven castle.[43]

Bishop Kennedy had reached the nadir of his political fortunes. His allies had either deserted him or were dead, and the victors in the parliament of June 1445 seem to have considered seriously the possibility of depriving him of his bishopric, citing as a precedent for such action Bishop Finlay of Argyll's rebellion against James I, deprivation following. In the event, Kennedy was not deprived, possibly because he was in favour with Pope Eugenius IV; but his total exclusion from central government for the next four-and-a-half years tells its own story. For a man of Kennedy's ambition, it can have been small consolation that the earl of Crawford, whom he had cursed solemnly for a year for harrying his lands in Fife, was killed in a skirmish at Arbroath in January 1446.[44]

The political situation changed dramatically in 1449 with the emergence of James II as an adult sovereign, rapidly followed by his assault on the entire Livingston family. The latter is a mysterious affair, partly because there survives no indictment of the family, and we have to speculate as to their treasons; and partly because there is a remarkable paucity of surviving official record evidence for the years 1445-49. There are a mere six charters registered under the Great Seal during these years of Livingston-Douglas ascendancy; and between June 1445 and January 1450 the three estates appear to have met only once, in a General Council at Stirling in April 1449, for which neither sederunts nor proceedings survive.[45] All that can be said with certainty is that the Livingstons who appear as royal charter witnesses during this period are Sir Alexander, the justiciar, and his son, James Livingston, the Chamberlain, keeper of the royal person and captain of Stirling castle. Their ally, William, eighth earl of Douglas, witnesses the 1445 and 1446 charters, and all Great Seal Charters were drawn up at Stirling until December 1449, when the court had clearly moved to Linlithgow.[46]

The fall of the Livingstons closely followed the marriage of James II to Mary of Gueldres in July 1449 and may indeed be connected with this event.[47] Mary of Gueldres was the niece of Philip the Good, Duke of Burgundy, and the marriage alliance, apart from bringing Scots merchants trading privileges in the Burgundian dominions, called for perpetual peace and friendship between Scotland and Burgundy. Probably more important from the Scottish king's point of view were the financial clauses of the treaty, for Duke Philip promised to pay his niece's dowry of 60,000 crowns within two years, and to send her to Scotland at his own expense. She arrived in a fleet of fourteen vessels, escorted by the Bishop of Dunkeld, John Ralston, and Chancellor Crichton, and the marriage took place at Holyrood on 3 July 1449.

Thereafter the Livingstons survived in power for less than three months. According to Auchinleck, the exact date of their arrest was 23 September 1449, and those imprisoned included Sir Alexander Livingston, the justiciar; his son and heir, James Livingston, the chamberlain, keeper of Stirling castle and of the royal person; his younger brother Alexander, captain of Methven; Robert Livingston, the comptroller; and two Livingston supporters, James Dundas and Robert Bruce of Clackmannan. Only the chamberlain's daughter, Elizabeth Livingston, was able to escape from Dumbarton to Kintyre and marry the young earl of Ross.[48]

After the passage of some four months, the Livingstons were duly tried before a parliament which opened in the tolbooth of Edinburgh on 19 January 1450. As all those arrested were forfeited in lands and goods, we may assume that the Livingstons were indicted for treason, and this is suggested by a statute of the same parliament which warns against 'crimes committit agaynis the king or again his derrest modir of gud mynde'.[49] Yet if treason was the Livingstons' crime, one would expect that the principal sufferers in 1449-50 would have been the justiciar, Sir Alexander, and his eldest son James. These were the men who had imprisoned the king's mother, Joan Beaufort, as early as 1439, had been prominent in a civil war against her in 1444-5, had seized the major royal household offices and the person of the king, and had appeared as royal charter witnesses between 1445 and 1449. From a royal standpoint, their treasons were blatant and long-standing. Yet their imprisonment and forfeiture was shortlived. Although Sir Alexander Livingston died in 1451, his son James not only avoided persecution for the remainder of the reign, but was restored to favour and raised to the peerage as Lord Livingston of Callendar as early as 1455.[50] The conclusion must be that the charge of treason concealed James II's other motive for attacking the Livingstons, namely finance.

The truth was that the Burgundian marriage alliance was not all gain for the Scottish monarch. Certainly the dowry which James would receive was enormous by Scottish standards; but the treaty also required the Scottish king to provide adequately for his wife, and fixed her dower at ten thousand French écus, a sum roughly equivalent to £5,000 Scots. To a monarch who was already embarrassed by a much smaller debt — £930 which he owed to Comptroller Livingston — the problem of providing for the queen must have loomed very large. There was the added difficulty that, as Burgundy was paying the dowry for Mary of Gueldres in two instalments, part of it might be withheld if James defaulted.[51] Thus there were pressing financial motives for the king's attack on the Livingstons and the rapid forfeiture of the entire family. Only two Livingstons were executed, the Comptroller and the justiciar's second son Alexander, who had been captain of Methven castle since 1444-5. Both men were beheaded on the Castle hill of Edinburgh on 21 January 1450, for crimes which may have amounted to nothing more than being owed money by the king, or possessing lands which James II wished to reassign to his wife. Thus the Comptroller's death immediately cancelled the king's debt of £930; and as Livingston had also been Custumar of Linlithgow, it was now possible to make the great customs of Linlithgow part of the queen's endowment. Similarly, Methven castle, held by the executed Alexander Livingston, had been assigned to the queen in the original marriage treaty of June 1449, so that the king had an obvious motive for recovering the castle as swiftly as he could. In the event, Menteith was substituted for Methven as part of the queen's settlement; but there is a clear connection between the two executions on 21 January, and James II's confirmation of his wife's marriage portion on the very next day.[52]

Little evidence exists as to the attitude of the Douglases when their former allies were brought down by the king. Possibly they approved of James's action, for relations between Douglas and Livingston seem not always to have been friendly in the years of their ascendancy. In 1447 Justiciar Livingston had become involved in a struggle with the earl of Douglas over the keepership of the castle of Lochdoon;[53] and it has been suggested that the two families became further estranged in 1448, when James Livingston became chamberlain rather than Sir John Forrester of Corstorphine, whose patron was the earl of Douglas.[54] In any event, Douglas seems to have made no attempt to save the Livingstons in 1449-50; indeed, Earl William benefited directly by their fall, acquiring some forfeited Livingston and Dundas lands and receiving royal permission to erect his town of Strathaven into a burgh in barony.[55]

Yet if Douglas and his brothers were happy to see the Livingstons brought down by the king, they were surely drawing the wrong conclusions from the events of autumn 1449. Nicholson suggests that the Douglases 'smiled when James II wrecked a new kind of power complex', and explains this by saying that the Livingston faction 'was one of lairds rather than lords', the implication being that the Douglases resented the Livingstons as low-born upstarts, and felt themselves secure because of their status as earls.[56] It is, of course, possible that the Douglases were confident that their power would protect them, and indeed force the king to favour them with further grants of offices and land; but if they thought in this way, they must have been remarkably naïve. No Stewart king hesitated to attack a member of his nobility if he stood to gain by doing so, and if he reckoned he could get away with it. James I had almost succeeded in wiping out the Stewart earls in a protracted policy of vindictiveness in the 'twenties and 'thirties, and often his victims seem to have committed no crime other than to bear the name Stewart.[57] This aggressive confidence was undoubtedly inherited by James II; and it seems highly probable that, by 1449, he felt that the Black Douglases had acquired far too much power.

Apart from assisting the Livingstons in 1444-5, however, Douglas had not committed any specific crimes which would justify an attack on his position by the Crown. There is therefore something very ominous about the statute of 19 January 1450 — in the same parliament as forfeited the Livingstons — warning individuals against rebellion. In future, so runs the statute, rebels would be punished according to the 'qualite and quantite' of the rebellion, and by the advice of the three estates. Anyone rebelling, or assisting rebels, or making war on the king's lieges 'agayn his forbiding', would be dealt with by the king, who would summon 'the hail lande' to punish them. Finally, the act laid down that if anyone should assist in any way 'thai that ar justifiit be the king in this present parliament or sal happyn to be justifiit in tym cummyn for crimes committit agaynis the king or again his derrest modir of gud mynde', they were to be dealt with in the same way as the principal trespassers.[58]

No names are given, either of the Livingstons condemned and executed two days later, or of their allies; but the statute clearly suggests that the king might proceed against other families in the future for crimes committed against himself and his late mother — that is, crimes at least five years old, as Joan Beaufort had died in 1445. This implies that there was to be no indemnity for those who had profited by the crises of the 1440s; and apart from the forfeited Livingstons, the Black Douglases fell most obviously into this category. Worse still from the Douglas point of view, the king had been declared of age as early as October 1444, so that support for the Livingston court party after that date could easily be interpreted as treason against an adult king. There was therefore no need for James II to find new crimes to lay against the Black Douglases, because the statute of 1450, broadly interpreted, provided him with the backing of the three estates for drastic action against the earl and his brothers. It may have been an awareness of the weakness of his position which led the eighth earl to join Chancellor Crichton, Bishop Kennedy, and the merchants of Edinburgh in making sizeable loans to the king — for all of them a means of emphasising their loyalty.[59]

Much more certain of continuing royal favour was William Turnbull, bishop of Glasgow, whose political and ecclesiastical career throughout the reign overshadows that of Kennedy. Keeper of the Privy Seal for twenty years, and at one time also royal secretary, Turnbull had been employed on diplomatic missions as early as the 1430s, stood high in favour with James II, and was a regular charter witness from 1428 onwards.[60] Towards the end of the minority, Turnbull received his major promotions — to the bishopric of Dunkeld in 1447, and later in the same year, following the death of James Bruce, bishop of Glasgow, the Chancellor, Turnbull was translated to the bishopric of Glasgow. This appointment was clearly backed by the king, who raised a loan from Scottish merchants in Aberdeen, Dundee, and Edinburgh to pay for the delivery of Turnbull's bulls of Glasgow. Turnbull was first among the witnesses to James II's marriage contract in June 1449, at which time Bishop Kennedy was apparently still out of favour.[61]

It may therefore be unrealistic to assume that central government after the fall of the Livingstons was largely dominated by a triumvirate consisting of Chancellor Crichton, Bishop Kennedy, and the earl of Douglas, rewarded by the king and high in favour at court.[62] Both Kennedy and Douglas appeared in the parliament of January 1450, and intermittently as charter witnesses or beneficiaries until the summer; but thereafter both went on pilgrimage to Rome to take part in the jubilee celebrations proclaimed by Pope Nicholas V. Kennedy, having emerged from relative obscurity for under a year, disappeared completely from Scottish public life between 28 August 1450 and 18 April 1452; and he may be located in Rome in January 1451, and Bruges at the beginning of May 1451.[63] Douglas's pilgrimage to Rome began, like Kennedy's, in the autumn of 1450; but the earl, returning home via England, had reached Scotland by April 1451.[64] But the absence of these powerful men did not create a vacuum at court. According to Law's manuscript, the dominant group consisted of Chancellor Crichton, his cousin George Crichton, the Admiral, and Bishop Turnbull; and all three incited James II to attack the earl of Douglas.[65]

This statement has the ring of truth about it. Bishop Turnbull was a former Keeper of the Privy Seal and firm supporter of the king; Chancellor Crichton had opposed the Livingston-Douglas faction in 1444-5; and Admiral Crichton had no love for the earl of Douglas, having had his house at Barnton destroyed by the earl in 1444.[66] These three men, with their formidable combination of long service in government office and fear and dislike of the Black Douglases, were most likely to urge James II to take advantage of Douglas's absence abroad to launch an attack on his lands. Nor can the king have needed much prompting. Apart from the great accumulation of Black Douglas territories before 1449, which James II undoubtedly feared, there was also the matter of finance. The king was short of money, and yet was expected to provide adequately for Queen Mary of Gueldres. Nicholson plausibly suggests that James may have been counting on his wife's dowry arriving sooner than it did. By 1 May 1450, he had received 20,000 écus of the dowry, but that left 40,000, of which 35,000 were still owing as late as January 1452. The comptroller's account for 27 August 1450 reveals a deficit of £1,315 15/10½d, in spite of which James II was expected to provide Mary of Gueldres with an enormous annual income — £5,000 — from her dower lands. So far his only provision for the queen had been the revenues of the earldoms of Atholl and Strathearn in January 1450, together with miscellaneous smaller sums, but these amounted only to a fraction of the expected dower. Indeed, the Duke of Burgundy may well have been delaying payment of the balance of the queen's dowry on the ground that James had not fulfilled his obligations in providing the queen with the income specified in the 1449 treaty.[67] A swift solution to James's financial difficulties lay in an attack on Black Douglas lands in the south, and there can be little doubt that the two Crichtons and Bishop Turnbull would encourage the king in such a course. The earl himself was abroad; and a pretext for a royal expedition against his lands could easily be found.

The immediate cause of the civil wars which followed was the possession of the earldom of Wigtown and the lordship of Western Galloway. Early in 1450, Margaret Stewart, widow of the fourth earl of Douglas and the eight earl's aunt, died, having previously resigned her rights in Galloway to earl William.[68] By 1451, however, James II had clearly ignored this resignation, granting the sheriffship of Wigtown to his 'familiar esquire' Andrew Agnew in May 1451, and in the following month describing himself as lord of Galloway.[69] The sequence of events in the spring and early summer of 1451 is not clear; but what is indisputable is that the king took the offensive. Probably he could not tolerate a further increase in the already imposing Black Douglas strength; and he had to build up his own resources if the queen's dower of £5,000 was to be assigned. So, according to Law's manuscript, the king assembled an army, attacked the castle of Craig Douglas on the Yarrow, and razed it to the ground.[70] Douglas, who had returned to Scotland by April 1451, was probably taken completely by surprise by the royal attack, and early in July he made a token submission to the king in parliament at Edinburgh. This took the form of a resignation of all his lands into the king's hands, whereupon James II restored them in a series of eighteen charters. These, however, contain no mention of the earldom of Wigtown, which apparently remained in the king's hands, a point confirmed by the contemporary Auchinleck chronicler, who adds that the crown also retained the lordship of Stewarton in Ayrshire.[71] The king was now able to repeat his promise to endow the queen with lands to the annual value of £5,000;[72] and by July 1451, the issues of royal authority and resources appeared to have been settled in his favour.

However, within three months a dramatic change had taken place. In another parliament, held at Stirling in October 1451, James II confirmed to earl William the earldom of Wigtown and the lordship of Western Galloway, in spite of crimes committed by Douglas's ancestors 'up to the present day', and notwithstanding any acts of parliament or general council to the contrary.[73] This grant, witnessed as it was by committed opponents of Douglas, including Bishop Turnbull, Chancellor Crichton, and Andrew, Lord Gray, marks a temporary reversal in the royal fortunes. We can only speculate as to why the king failed to retain the gains he had made during the summer; clearly he felt it necessary to make immediate concessions to Earl William, and he may have been motivated by the dangers of rebellion in the north. Perhaps significantly, Alexander, fourth earl of Crawford, who had been present at the June parliament, was absent from that held in October. Like Douglas, Crawford was one of the beneficiaries of the fall of the Livingstons, having been granted some lands in Perthshire as recently as 6 July 1451.[74] He may on that occasion have formed an unfavourable impression of the king, whose record of aggression since he had come to power, especially against the Black Douglases, who were powerful but not treasonable, provided an alarming precedent for possible further action of the same kind. The Lindsay earls of Crawford and the Black Douglases had been on terms of close friendship since the 1440s,[75] and a royal assault on the one might well be regarded as the prelude to an attack on the other. Crawford was certainly in rebellion in the spring of the following year; his motive was probably fear of royal aggression, and he may indeed have been planning rebellion as early as October 1451, when he was absent from the Stirling parliament.

On the king's side, the realisation that grants of forfeited Livingston lands had not guaranteed Crawford's loyalty must have come as an unpleasant shock, because he was faced with a potentially formidable coalition of northern earls. Apart from Crawford himself, there were the two Black Douglas earls, Moray and Ormond, brothers of earl William; and there was John, earl of Ross and Lord of the Isles, who had married Elizabeth, daughter of James Livingston, the chamberlain, just before the fall of the Livingstons in 1449.[76] The result was that Elizabeth had no dowry, the Crown would not grant him forfeited Livingston lands, and Ross could only take what lands he wanted by force. An alliance of Crawford, Moray, Ormond, and Ross in the north with Douglas in the south would have produced a difficult if not impossible situation for the Crown in the autumn of 1451; and James II's concessions to Earl William in the October parliament at Stirling may well be regarded as a strategic retreat on the part of a monarch who was temporarily unsure of his own strength. At the same time, however, the king forfeited a familiar of Douglas, William Lauder of Hatton, later granting Lauder's lands to the queen — an ominous pointer to the future.[77]

For the truth was that the complex political and military manoeuvres of 1451 had solved nothing. The king continued to regard the Black Douglas concentration of power as a menace, and royal financial problems were pressing. For the Crown, the solution lay in choosing a suitable time to launch another attack on the Black Douglases, and this was preceded by the murder of Earl William by James II himself at Stirling in February 1452. This notorious crime produced a spate of stories which contemporary and sixteenth century chroniclers used in an effort to provide a motive for the assassination. Three of these tales, recounted respectively by the Auchinleck chronicler, Boece, and Pitscottie, deserve some attention because they contributed to a false picture of events which vindicated the king and discredited the Douglases.

The Auchinleck chronicler casually records the killing of John Sandilands of Calder and two others on 16 August 1451; but he neither names the killers nor produces any motivation. Boece and Pitscottie embellish the bald facts by suggesting that Sandilands of Calder and one of his murdered friends, Allan Stewart, were adherents of the king; and both name the killer, Patrick Thornton (or 'Crichton' in a later manuscript of Pitscottie's *History*), who was apparently one of the Douglas faction.[78] These later embellishments provide motivation for the king's murder of Douglas, but they are most unconvincing. Apart from the garbling of the story in transmission over more than half a century, there remains the awkward fact that, according to the contemporary Auchinleck, Sandilands of Calder was killed in August 1451; and the sequel to this was not the murder of the Earl of Douglas by the king, but the restoration of his earldom of Wigtown in full parliament within two months.

The second story, told by both Boece and Pitscottie and lacking any reference to contemporary written sources, concerns Sir John Herries of Terregles. Herries' lands having been harried by adherents of the Earl of Douglas, he attempted to secure redress, failed, and sought revenge instead. Captured in Annandale, Herries was brought before Earl William, condemned and hanged, in spite of the king's commands to the contrary. No such execution can be identified in any written record, and indeed the history of the lairds of Terregles suggests close friendship with the Black Douglases during the first half of the century. If a member of the Herries family was hanged by Douglas, it was certainly not the head of the family, John Herries, who survived, although insane after 1459, well into the following reign.[79] It might have been one of Herries' many kinsmen in Wigtownshire, upset by the struggle between the king and Douglas for possession of the earldom; but with the chroniclers disagreeing over the Christian name of the victim, little can be made of the story.[80]

The third tale is related by Pitscottie alone, and has become the most popular because of its wealth of colourful detail. This is the story of Maclellan, tutor of Bombie, who according to Pitscottie refused to take the part of the Earl of Douglas against the king. He was imprisoned in Douglas castle, and his uncle Patrick Gray, Lord Gray's son and heir, came directly from the king with letters under the signet requiring Douglas to deliver Maclellan. Gray was entertained to dinner by Douglas, but on enquiring after Maclellan, he was told that he had come a little too late; the tutor of Bombie 'wantis the heid', as Douglas remarked, Maclellan having just been beheaded outside. This picturesque tale lacks any solid factual foundation. The earliest mention of a laird of Bombie, to whom Maclellan was supposedly tutor or guardian, occurs in 1467, and although the Maclellans were a prominent family in Carrick and Kirkcudbright, no evidence can be produced to show even the existence of Maclellan, tutor of Bombie, far less his relationship to Lord Gray.[81]

All these stories have one feature in common. They reflect the effort in the sixteenth century by Boece and Pitscottie to cast discredit on the Douglases, to suggest that Earl William was an obvious menace to the good king, and to drive home the message that the Douglases — not the king — provoked the events which followed. The tales of the fates of Herries and Maclellan probably have a common origin in stories passed on about the struggle between James II and Douglas for control of Wigtown and Galloway. Significantly, however, the contemporary Auchinleck chronicler and the official records leave little doubt that the king was the prime mover in all that occurred; and the dispute which led directly to Earl William's death does not seem to have involved Wigtown and Galloway at all.

The Register of the Great Seal records that Earl William was to be found at court in Edinburgh, witnessing royal charters, as late as 13 January 1452.[82] Yet little over a month later, he required a safe-conduct when summoned to James II's presence at Stirling. Pitscottie tells an almost plausible tale of an attempt by Douglas to waylay Chancellor Crichton, frustrated by Crichton's arrival in Edinburgh with a large company of friends and supporters, and Earl William's subsequent flight.[83] But such a story is unnecessary to explain Douglas's reluctance to come to Stirling without a safe-conduct. The Chancellor's cousin, Sir George Crichton, was keeper of Stirling Castle,[84] and bitter rivalry between the families of Crichton and Douglas went back at least as far as 1444. Furthermore, both Crichtons had advised the king to launch an attack on Douglas lands the previous spring.

Probably more important than all this was the attitude of the king himself. If the Auchinleck chronicler is to be believed, the subject of the discussions between James II and Earl William at Stirling seems to have been an alliance made by Douglas with the rebellious Earls of Crawford and Ross. Auchinleck describes it as a band or bond, and this term must apply to something more specific than a general bond of manrent or friendship. Probably a military commitment of some kind was involved. If so, the king, in spite of his concessions to Douglas the previous October, must have reckoned himself challenged by a powerful coalition which would include the three Douglas earls, Crawford and Ross. How serious a threat to James II such an alliance really represented is impossible to say, and no evidence of treason on the part of the Douglases, Crawford and Ross can be produced before the murder of Earl William by the king. But James II clearly felt himself severely threatened, he himself had initiated the civil wars in the previous year, and the situation early in 1452 was sufficiently serious for him to consider further drastic action.

The contemporary account of the murder, given by the Auchinleck chronicler, is straightforward enough. He begins with the bald statement that the earl was slain in the castle of Stirling by James II 'that had the fyre mark in his face'. Then he goes on to give details: the king sent William Lauder of Hatton (a familiar of Douglas, forfeited the previous October) to Douglas with 'a special assouerans and respit' under the privy seal and his own signature, and all the lords with him at court gave oaths to observe this safe-conduct. (Unfortunately the chronicler does not name any of these lords.) Earl William arrived on Monday 21 February and had talks with the king 'that tuke richt wele with him be apperans'. On the following day, the king and the earl took dinner and supper together, and it was at supper that the supposed band between Douglas, Crawford and Ross was discussed. After supper, at seven in the evening, the king and earl being 'in the inner chalmer', James II demanded that the earl should break his band. Douglas refused, whereupon the king stabbed him with a knife in the neck and body. Sir Patrick Gray then struck Douglas on the head with a pole axe, striking out his brains, and six other courtiers and lords attacked him with knives. All are named — Sir Alexander Boyd, Lord Darnley, Sir Andrew Stewart, Sir William of Grahamston, Sir Simon Glendinning, and Lord Gray. The earl's corpse had twenty-six wounds.[85]

No other chronicle account is contemporary, nor tells us so much. John Major, whose *History* was published in 1521, does not mention a safe-conduct and quotes a rumour that Douglas planned to usurp the crown with the assistance of his brothers Moray and Ormond; the earl was slain 'by the king and those that were about him'. This is not much help. Major's knowledge of the reign was clearly sparse; for example, he confuses the fall of the Livingstons in 1449 with the 'Black Dinner' of 1440. Lesley, whose vernacular history appeared in 1568, repeats the story that the king feared Douglas because the earl 'wes preissand to the crown'. He mentions a safe-conduct, and explains the murder by saying that the earl answered the king 'owre frilie and bauldlie', whereupon 'he was presentlye in the castell of Striveling slane at fastransevin 1451'. Pitscottie, the last to write and the most colourful of all, includes the details already familiar in Major and Lesley — the safe-conduct, the entertaining of Douglas after supper, the quarrel over Douglas's bands and leagues with other nobles — and suggests that the king was moved to stab Earl William because the earl both refused to break his band and complained about great offences committed by the Crown against the house of Douglas. Thereupon Jammes II 'tuik ane heigh anger', pulled out a sword, and struck Douglas through the body. The royal guard, hearing the tumult, rushed into the chamber and 'slew the Earle out of hand'. None of the killers is named, and Pitscottie concludes his account of the murder with the date 20 February 1452.[86]

The sixteenth century chroniclers of the Douglas murder are all concerned to justify the king's action by making Earl William the aggressor to the end, goading the king into passionate and ill-considered retaliation. But the contemporary Auchinleck, giving far more detail than the rest, suggests a very different course of events — that is, that the king made the first really ominous move by sending a forfeited friend of Earl William, William Lauder of Hatton, to summon Douglas to Stirling; that James's intentions, though obscure, clearly involved coercion of the earl and possibly extended to premeditated murder; and that the final conference between king and earl does not appear to have been private, but was attended by the courtiers who assisted the king in the murder. Dr. Dunlop is surely right when she points out the ominous nature of the entire episode.[87] Douglas was being summoned to Stirling by a former adherent whom the king had forfeited only four months before; the Crichtons, in attendance on the king, were traditional enemies of Douglas; and James II himself was incensed at what he must have regarded as Earl William's treachery in plotting rebellion even after the concession to him, the previous October, of the much disputed earldom of Wigtown.

The courtiers who, according to Auchinleck, joined the king in killing Earl William, were to become men of some consequence. Andrew, Lord Gray, a fairly regular royal charter witness from January 1452 onwards, was to become Master of the Royal Household by 12 April 1452, less than two months after the murder; Patrick Gray, who struck the first blow, was presumably Lord Gray's son and heir.[88] Sir Alexander Boyd of Drumcoll, knighted only three years previously, was to become warden of Threave castle for the king after the final collapse of the Black Douglases in 1455.[89] Lord Darnley, or Sir John Stewart of Darnley as he was in 1452, was, like Boyd, an Ayrshire man who had a charter of the lands of Dreghorn in May 1450, and another of the lands of Galston, confirmed by the king on 27 June 1452. Probably created first Lord Darnley at the coronation of James III in August 1460, he was later to become the first Stewart Earl of Lennox.[90] Even more impressive was the career of the fourth named assassin, Sir Andrew Stewart, who seems to have occupied a modest post in James II's household and had received a knighthood from the king; but in 1456, after the fall of the Black Douglases, he received the barony of Avandale, was made a lord of parliament in the same year, Warden of the West Marches by 1459, and finally Chancellor by 6 July 1460, within a month of James II's death. He was to hold this, the highest office of state, for no less than twenty-two years.[91] Rather less can be said about the remaining two assassins: Sir William Grahamston (or 'of Grahamston') is no more than a name, though Sir Simon Glendinning, whose lands lay in Westerkirk parish in north-east

Dumfries-shire, was at court in Edinburgh witnessing royal charters as early as August 1451, and his public career continued later in the reign as a Scots commissioner negotiating over breaches of the English truce on the borders in September 1458.[92] In short, these seven men, as might be expected, had a strong interest in the success of the king and the elimination of the Black Douglases. With the exception of the Grays, they all hailed from the south and west; they clearly expected, and received, rewards from the Crown for their loyalty, for they included a future Chancellor, Master of the Household, and Earl of Lennox.

The murder inevitably precipitated a further outbreak of civil war. James II had acted in such a way as to outrage large areas of Scottish opinion, even amongst those who had little sympathy with the Black Douglases. Yet translating outrage into positive action against the Crown would take time, was an extremely perilous business, and was unlikely to attract a great deal of support. Indeed, James II's position after the murder of Earl William may not have been as difficult as is sometimes suggested. From his own point of view, the king had removed an active and aggressive earl. He knew Earl William's brother and successor, James, ninth earl of Douglas, whom he had met at Stirling in February 1449,[93] and he may have formed the impression that James was a less able man. Certainly events were to show that the Black Douglas reply to the murder of Earl William was remarkably ineffective.

Indeed, the contrast at this time between the sound and fury of the Douglases and the resolute vigour of the king is striking. On St. Patrick's Day, 17 March 1452, James, the new earl of Douglas, together with his brother Hugh, earl of Ormond, and James, Lord Hamilton, came to Stirling with a force reckoned by the Auchinleck chronicler at no more than 600, sounded twenty-four horns, openly denounced the king and privy council as forsworn and perjured, and directly accused James II and his associates of the murder of Earl William. Auchinleck remarks that they brought with them the notorious safe-conduct, dragged it through the streets of Stirling at the tail of a horse, and then burned and looted the burgh.[94] But the king was not apparently in Stirling at the time. He had left the town immediately after the murder, was at Lochmaben and Jedburgh by the beginning of March, and on the 17th, according to Auchinleck, he was in Perth, on his way to meet the rebel Earl of Crawford. By 24 March, James II was probably back in Edinburgh.[95] This royal itinerary, no doubt undertaken to combine justice ayres with raising support in the south and to open the offensive against the rebel coalition, makes it clear that there was little or no delay on the king's side in launching an assault on Earl William's kin and supporters following the February murder. The first royal success came with the siege and surrender of the castle of Hatton in Midlothian, formerly held by the forfeited William Lauder of Hatton, in late March or early April.[96] During the crisis the king had the active support of the Crichtons, the earls of Huntly, Angus, and Orkney, Bishop Turnbull of Glasgow — who lent James II 800 marks from the proceeds of the 1450 jubilee indulgence — and even the Bishop of St. Andrews, James Kennedy, who after his second long absence from public life (and, for at least part of the time, from Scotland itself), reappeared in Edinburgh on 18 April 1452, and lent the king £50 about this time.[97]

c

The return of Bishop Kennedy and his subsequent assistance to the king may be the origin of Lesley's tale, unsupported by any contemporary record or chronicle source, that James II thought his position so serious that he considered fleeing to France, and that Kennedy dissuaded him from doing so.[98]

The truth was that in spite of, or perhaps even because of, the February murder, the king's fortunes were rapidly improving from April 1452 onwards. Grants were made to royal supporters at Edinburgh during that month, including Admiral Crichton, the Earl of Angus, and Bishop Turnbull of Glasgow; and in May, Queen Mary triumphantly ended her third pregnancy by producing a son and heir, James, at St. Andrews. About the same time, on 18 May, an army led by the royalist Alexander Gordon, earl of Huntly, defeated the rebel Earl of Crawford at Brechin, in spite of Pitscottie's remark that Crawford had assembled 'the haill folkis of Angus' in rebellion. Probably more realistic is the statement by Auchinleck that 'thair was with the erll of huntlie fer ma than was with the erll of craufurd becauss he displayit the kingis banere and said It was the kingis actioun and he was his luftennend'.[99]

In fact, the only area in which the rebels achieved any success was the north-west, where the third member of the Douglas-Crawford-Ross band, John, earl of Ross and Lord of the Isles, had already seized the castles of Inverness, Urquhart, and Ruthven. Ruthven he destroyed; the keepership of Urquhart he gave to his father-in-law, the deposed James Livingston; and apparently after an interview in Knapdale with the Earl of Douglas, whose family interests might have been better served elsewhere, Ross appears to have acquired the support of the naval forces of the Isles under the command of Donald Balloch, and launched an attack on the Clyde. Inverkip was burned on 10 July; subsequently Bute, the Cumbraes and Arran were also attacked, and Brodick Castle was taken and destroyed.[100]

No doubt such assaults added to the problems of Bishop Turnbull of Glasgow, who as recently as 14 April had been given the privilege of levying the crown rents of Bute, Arran, and Cowal, together with the customs of Ayr, Irvine, and Dumbarton.[101] But rebel maritime ventures in the west came too late to affect the position of the king, who had already summoned parliament to meet in Edinburgh on 12 June. Not surprisingly, those who attended were committed supporters of the king; and the principal object of a meeting of the three estates at this point was to clear the king's name. This was achieved by an investigation into the circumstances of Earl William's death in February, the findings to be recorded in an official document. The problems of the safe-conduct and the possibility that the earl had been the victim of premeditated murder were easily glossed over, and a dubious statement was issued to the effect that if Earl William had been protected by any securities on the day of his death, he himself had renounced these 'before a multitude of barons, lords, knights and nobles'. The parliamentary apologia then turns to the main charges against Douglas — that he had made leagues and conspiracies with certain magnates against the crown and together with his brothers was the frequent author of rebellions. On the day of his death, the eighth earl had refused to be persuaded by the king and his nobles to join them in attacking the rebels — presumably Crawford and Ross. All these offences provided ample justification for Earl William's death.[102]

Parliament then went on to punish the vanquished and reward the victors, albeit somewhat prematurely. The Earl of Crawford was forfeited, and James, ninth earl of Douglas, and his adherents were summoned to parliament to answer charges of treason. By this time, the new earl had rashly provided James II with some justification for the charges. Apart from his incitement to rebellion of Ross and Donald Balloch in May, Douglas had apparently been prepared to do homage to Henry VI of England at the beginning of June; and it seems likely that the safe-conduct obtained by his mother, Countess Beatrice, widow of James, the seventh earl, to go abroad for a year with her daughter-in-law, Margaret, the 'Fair Maid' of Galloway, to visit the shrine of St. Thomas of Canterbury, was politically motivated, and that the real aim of the visit was to negotiate with the English.[103] Thus the king's appalling treatment of the Black Douglases in 1451-2, and his outrageous justification of his acts in the June parliament of 1452, could now, with the discovery of real rather than imagined treasons, be accepted much more readily.

Douglas and his supporters did not, of course, appear at this time to answer the parliamentary charges, though Auchinleck suggests that a letter bearing the seals of Douglas, Ormond, and Sir James Hamilton was affixed to the parliament house door on the night of 12 June; all three withdrew their allegiance and condemned both king and privy council, describing the latter as traitors.[104] They had good reason to be concerned. Even before the June parliament, James II had been sending out summonses 'for the assembly of the king's lieges to his host'; and he clearly intended to attack the Douglas faction as soon as he had justified himself before the three estates. He paused only to reward his supporters. Admiral Crichton was made Earl of Caithness, William Hay, the Constable, Earl of Erroll, and James Crichton, son and heir of Chancellor Crichton, Earl of Moray in place of Archibald Douglas. James II's grant of the earldom of Erroll to William Hay, in fact the only one of the three 1452 creations to survive, may have been inspired partly by the fact that Hay's wife Beatrice was the daughter of the Black Douglas Earl James the Gross; and while appreciating the value of having in Hay a staunch royalist to offset the Black Douglas power in the north, the king may have been concerned to reward the Constable liberally so that his ties of kinship with the Douglases did not influence him to desert the royal side. The services of other royalists were recognised by the creation of seven lordships of parliament, conferring status — if not wealth — on Sir John Stewart of Darnley, Sir Patrick Hepburn of Hailes, Sir Robert Boyd of Kilmarnock, Sir Robert Fleming of Cumbernauld, Sir William Borthwick, Sir Robert Lyle of Duchal, and Sir Alan Cathcart. The first to be rewarded by the king was Bishop Kennedy, who on 14 June, within two days of the opening of parliament, was given a charter which reflects James II's relief at the birth of his first son at St. Andrews by confirming earlier royal grants to the bishopric and annexing lands to its regality. For the first time in his career, Kennedy was at last assured of royal favour and support.[105]

There followed the second royal attack of the year on the Black Douglas lands.

Assembling an army on Pentland Moor, James II moved rapidly south through Peebles, Selkirk and Dumfries, ruthlessly harrying Douglas territories and apparently making little distinction between friend and foe. Artillery was used on the royal side, the campaign was short, and the king was back in Edinburgh by early August, granting and confirming charters. It is in describing this campaign, however, that the Auchinleck chronicler makes his first strong criticism of James II's policies. The royal army 'did na gud bot distroyit the cuntre richt fellonly baith of cornes medowis and wittalis and heriit mony bath gentillmen and utheris that war with him self'.[106] The king, perhaps, had gone too far, and had forfeited too much support in his savage pursuit of the Black Douglases. In any event, the parliament of 26 August did not proceed with the forfeitures of the Earl of Douglas, his kin and adherents; there was instead a compromise settlement.

This was an agreement between king and earl, known as the 'Appoyntement', and dated at Douglas Castle on 28 August 1452. Both sides gave ground in vital areas of dispute. Douglas and his supporters forgave the assassins of the eighth earl, and guaranteed not to involve themselves in rebellious leagues. Douglas himself would show the king 'honour and worship' and faithfully perform his traditional duties of keeping the truce with England or, in time of war, defending the borders. He would not, however, attempt to obtain possession of the lands of the earldom of Wigtown without written permission from Queen Mary of Gueldres, nor would he try to recover the lordship of Stewarton without permission from the king — a sore point, as James II had already granted part of the Stewarton lands to Sir Gilbert Kennedy of Dunure on 30 June. The king's only concession seems to have been to abandon — for the time being — his intended forfeiture of the earl. The entire agreement was hollow and insincere, a truce between two implacably opposed enemies, the stronger looking for a breathing space before delivering a knockout blow to the weaker.[107]

The king's position did not, apparently, improve for some time to come. On 16 January 1453, Douglas made a bond of manrent with James II at Lanark, an astonishing document in view of the royal concessions contained in it. Douglas bound himself once more to renounce all leagues against James II, to render him full manrent and service, and to make a declaration to this effect in parliament. But such a declaration depended on the king granting Douglas re-entry into the disputed lands of Wigtown and Stewarton. Presumably Mary of Gueldres and Sir Gilbert Kennedy of Dunure, so recently installed in Wigtown and Stewarton respectively, raised strong objections to their surrender in the Black Douglas interest, and the king fell back on a scheme binding himself to promote the marriage of Earl James to his dead brother's widow. Margaret, the 'Fair Maid' of Galloway. A marriage dispensation for this purpose was quickly obtained, and the king, having dismembered the Black Douglas territories by murder and invasion only the previous year, now found himself in the galling position of having to reunite the families, and therefore the lands, on which the Douglas strength in the southwest was based.[108]

Why did James II act in this apparently contradictory fashion? It seems highly unlikely, in view of later events, that he had abandoned his determination to break the Black Douglases, and so both the 'Appoyntement' and the bond of manrent of 1453 must be regarded as tactical devices to gain time. The truth may simply have been that, as Nicholson suggests, the events of spring and summer 1452 had not really settled anything, and that the king's vigour and ruthlessness had provoked a reaction strong enough to make him reconsider the forfeiture of Earl James. Once James II had stopped short of this ultimate step, he was faced with the problem that the Douglas allies, Crawford and Ross, were active in the north, and that the rebellious band which had supposedly led to the February 1452 murder was still effectively in force. In his brief obituary of Crawford, Auchinleck describes him as 'a rigoruss man and ane felloun' who was 'richt Inobedient to the king'. Crawford's defeat by Huntly at Brechin in May 1452 probably did little to alter his character or attitudes, yet James II appears to have pardoned him to the extent that, together with Douglas and Moray, Crawford appeared as conservator of a new truce with England in May 1453. In any event, his death in September 1453 removed any menace which he might have posed to the royalist party.[109]

The king's conciliatory attitude towards his enemies may well have been extended throughout 1454 because of the sudden weakening of his own support through a series of rapid deaths. Two of James's 1452 creations, Admiral Crichton, earl of Caithness, and James Crichton, earl of Moray, died in August 1454 without apparently having enjoyed more than their titles; Chancellor Crichton, the most tenacious officer of state since the early days of the minority, was already dead, some time before July 1454. Finally, in September 1454, Bishop Turnbull of Glasgow, James's most trusted ecclesiastic, also died.[110] In only a few months, the king's principal supporters had been eliminated, including all the men who, back in 1451, had advocated the royal attack on the Black Douglases. The king seems to have been affected deeply by these sudden losses; according to the Auchinleck chronicler, James Crichton's death 'was haldin fra the king a litill quhile and syne gevin till him'. In any event, an immediate reconstruction of the royalist party was essential before any further assault on the Douglases could take place; and in the meantime, conciliation of former rebels continued. The illegal seizure by the Earl of Ross of the royal lands and castle of Urquhart and Glen Moriston during the 1452 crisis was tacitly accepted by James II because he had no choice in the matter. But in 1454 the king became reconciled to James Livingston, Ross's father-in-law and former royal chamberlain and keeper of the king's person during the latter stages of the minority. Livingston, perhaps the most surprising of the survivors of his family's fall in 1449-50, had regained his office of chamberlain by 1 July 1454.[111]

By October 1454, a new group of royal supporters had been rewarded with titles and offices. The most prominent of these was William Sinclair, earl of Orkney, who in addition to receiving the vacant earldom of Caithness, was made Chancellor. Of almost equal importance was George Schoriswood, a political churchman strongly committed to both James II and Mary of Gueldres, who served as an auditor of exchequer, diplomat, and royal charter witness from 1454 inwards; he was a royalist in the troubled area north of the Tay; and he was to be rewarded with the office of Chancellor — succeeding Orkney — in 1456. James had already secured the election of his old tutor Thomas Lauder to the bishopric of Dunkeld in 1452; and further south, he could count on the continuing loyalty of James Kennedy, bishop of St. Andrews. Bishop Turnbull's place at Glasgow was taken by Andrew Durisdeer or Muirhead, who, described as 'clerk and counsellor' to James II, had already been appointed procurator for the king at the papal court of Nicholas V in the jubilee year of 1450. A prominent diplomat, Durisdeer was to be absent in Rome during the final Douglas crisis of 1455; but thereafter he played an important role in Scottish government until his death in 1473.[112] As for the lay magnates, James II could rely on the earls of Huntly and Angus, and on his new creations as lords of parliament, two of whom — Hailes and Borthwick — figure in the witness lists to royal charters at this time.

Within a matter of a few months, therefore, the king was strong enough to embark on the third, and what was to prove the final, phase of the civil wars with the Black Douglases and their allies. A great number of reasons have been advanced for the final breakdown of relations between king and Douglases, ranging from their support for opposing factions in the struggle for governmental power in England, to the release from captivity in England, after twenty-six years, of Malise Graham, earl of Menteith, the last of the hostages for payment of James I's ransom. It seems unlikely, however, that official or unofficial negotiations with England on the part of the Black Douglases, for whatever purpose, were the source of the 1455 conflict. James II himself had commissioned Douglas, in April 1453, to negotiate in England for a renewal of the Anglo-Scottish truce; and there is probably nothing sinister to be read into the fact that Douglas, his three brothers, and Lord Hamilton all obtained English safe-conducts a month later, ostensibly for a journey to Rome. Certainly events in England changed dramatically with the admission of the Lancastrian Henry VI's temporary insanity and the Duke of York's assumption of the protectorship on 27 March 1454; there were now two English factions, Lancaster and York, with whom the Scottish rivals might negotiate. In this situation James II naturally began by supporting the royal house of Lancaster, and his uncle, Edmund Beaufort, duke of Somerset. The Black Douglases petitioned for and obtained a safe-conduct in June 1454, valid for two years, to allow Douglas's mother Countess Beatrice, his wife Margaret, and his youngest brother, Lord Balveny, to travel within England, the purpose of their visit supposedly being a pilgrimage to the shrine of Thomas Becket at Canterbury. The Duke of York was protector when the Douglas safe-conduct was issued; but this does not necessarily mean that the Douglases were indulging in treasonable dealings with him, or that they were in any sense committed Yorkists. If any such intrigues took place — and there is no evidence of any before 1455 — Nicholson is surely right in suggesting that these were probably of a defensive rather than offensive nature. After all, James II had attacked the Black Douglases both in 1451 and 1452; their search, above all, must have been for security.[113]

Even less likely, therefore, is the suggestion that the release of the last of the James I hostages, Malise Graham, in 1453, at the instance of Douglas and his ally Lord Hamilton, was part of a deliberate attempt by Douglas to revive the hoary old question of the royal succession occasioned by the two marriages of Robert II (1371-90).[114] No-one at the time seems to have questioned royal Stewart legitimacy for a moment, far less suggested that Malise Graham was a suitable alternative candidate for the Scottish throne. Not even James II, amongst the vast range of treasons with which he credited the Douglases after their defeat in 1455, accused them of this; and Malise Graham remained a remarkably obscure figure in national politics until his death in 1490.

The truth would appear to be much more straightforward, namely that the struggle in Scotland was renewed because the king was determined to crush the Black Douglases and found himself strong enough to do so. England was involved only to the extent that the imminence of civil war there probably affected the Scottish king's timing. In February 1455, the apparent recovery of Henry VI, and the restoration of a Lancastrian administration headed by his determined wife Margaret of Anjou, involved the fall from power of the Duke of York and produced a struggle for governmental power which could only be resolved by force.[115] The overall result was English weakness, however temporary, and inability to intervene in Scottish affairs. This was the ideal time for James II to resolve all his own outstanding problems — royal resources and authority, the accumulation of Black Douglas power, and the disputed earldom of Wigtown.

The campaign which followed illustrates strikingly the speed and determination of the king, and the indecision and weakness of the Douglases. Possibly they were taken by surprise by James II, who in March 1455 began his assault by attacking and destroying the Douglas castle of Inveravon. Gathering support as he went, the king crossed to Glasgow, moved south to Lanark and Douglas, and burned and harried Douglasdale, Avondale, and the lands of Douglas's ally Lord Hamilton. After a brief return to Edinburgh, James set out with a fresh force to conduct a ruthless raid on the forest of Ettrick, taking the goods and burning the property of all those who would not support the royal cause. This initial campaign seems to have taken about a month, and by the beginning of April, James had laid siege to the Douglas castle of Abercorn, using siege machines and artillery including 'the gret gwn the quhilk a franche man schot richt wele'. In a letter to Charles VII of France, the Scots king reported that Abercorn was taken by storm, its chief defenders were hanged, and the castle itself demolished.[116]

These royal successes produced a rapid collapse in the rebel leadership. It would appear that Lord Hamilton had not been in Scotland when the king harried his lands, but had made an unsuccessful journey to England to try to enlist aid, or raise supplies, for the Douglas cause. On his return, realising that the game was up, he made his submission to the king, possibly through the mediation of Sir James Livingston, the new chamberlain. This submission, which took place sometime in April during the early stages of the Abercorn siege, deprived Douglas of his most useful ally in the south; and Douglas's own leadership had so far been conspicuous by its absence. As Auchinleck tersely remarks: 'Men wist nocht grathlie quhar the douglass was all this tyme'.[117] He may already have fled to England, leaving his three brothers, the Earls of Ormond and Moray and Lord Balveny, to carry on the struggle. Certainly he was not present at the final collapse of the Douglas faction on May 1, at Arkinholm on the River Esk near Langholm. This skirmish appears to have taken place when Moray, Ormond, and Balveny were attempting to plunder the borders with a view to bringing spoils to their mother, the Countess Beatrice, in Carlisle, and it may be that the Douglases, recognising that the fight was lost for the time being, were trying to reach the comparative safety of England. Only a week before, on 24 April, almost two months after the opening of his own campaign, James II had taken the belated and cynical step of declaring war on the Douglases, appointing James Livingston as sheriff of Lanark to summon them on charges of treason. But the war was already nearly over, and at Arkinholm the three Douglas brothers were easily defeated by a combination of border lairds, Johnstones, Maxwells, and Scotts, with a force of only two hundred men. Moray was killed, Ormond captured and beheaded, and only Balveny succeeded in escaping to England to join the remnant of the Black Douglas family.[118] Potentially the greatest combination of magnates in Scotland had forfeited support and respect to the extent that, after two months' undistinguished struggle, they could be destroyed by a handful of southern lairds. The king was not even present.

James II opened parliament at Edinburgh on 9 June 1455, little more than six weeks after his summonses of treason. Not surprisingly, the entire Black Douglas family, including Earl James, Countess Beatrice, and Lord Balveny, was found guilty and forfeited.[119] But the king was concerned to follow up his victory, and parliament was rapidly prorogued to 4 August to allow time for yet another royal army to attack the remaining Douglas castles in the south. Before 8 July, Douglas, Strathaven, and other unspecified castles had surrendered to the king and been demolished. There remained only the great stronghold of Threave, on an island in the River Dee in Kirkcudbright, the original centre of Douglas power in the south-west. From the safety of England, the forfeited Earl James made a final effort to save Threave by granting it to Henry VI; and he was paid £100 sterling to help raise a force to relieve the castle. More money, in the shape of an English annual pension of £500, was given to Douglas at the beginning of August, in return for services which would be expected of him by the English crown.[120]

It was all too little and too late. James II devoted an immense amount of energy, time and expense to the siege of Threave, taking part personally while staying in the area, in the nearby monasteries of Tongland and Dundrennan. 'The great bombard', already used in the siege of Hatton in 1452, was dragged all the way to Galloway accompanied by the Chancellor, William, earl of Orkney. Its progress was slow, and the exchequer rolls record the breaking of the gun on Crawfordmuir and the wrecking of a gate through which it was hauled at Linlithgow, presumably on the return journey. In fact, Threave does not appear to have been battered into submission; its defenders surrendered, and there is some evidence that they were bribed by the king. Probably because of its strategic position in Kirkcudbright, close to the Solway ports and the border, Threave was not demolished but put in charge of a royal keeper, first Sir Alexander Boyd, and later Bishop Kennedy's half-brother, William Edmonston of Culloden.[121]

With the fall of Threave, the king's success was complete. It was, perhaps, also inevitable. Throughout the entire period of the civil wars, 1450-55, James II had acted with energy, determination and duplicity to secure the ruin of the Black Douglases. He had never gone so far that he was deprived of support, not even after the murder of Earl William in 1452. Personally, he took part in harryings and in sieges such as those of Hatton, Abercorn and Threave; but he was not involved in battles such as Brechin, which he could safely leave to the Earl of Huntly, nor in the skirmish at Arkinholm. At no time in the entire struggle does the king's crown, far less his life, seem to have been aimed at by the Douglases. Even in March 1452, Earl James's dramatic appearance in Stirling to confront James II with treachery and to renounce his allegiance lost its point because the king was not there to be confronted. Indeed, the remarkable ineptitude of Earl James and his supporters after 1452 is the most consistent theme of the ensuing years. Faced with a ruthless monarch, the Black Douglas position was certainly unenviable; and the earl's grievances against the king were either personal — the murder of his brother — or territorial, as in the royal seizure of Wigtown and Stewarton. Once the king had survived the consequences of the first, and made a show of negotiating over the second, Earl James's position became much weaker. His own belief that such was the case may have accounted for his total lack of leadership, and early flight, in 1455. Even luck seemed to be against him, with the earlier death or defection of his allies, Crawford and Ross, leaving James II free to launch a full-scale campaign in the south in the spring of 1455.

The king had taken risks, had stepped outside the law, and had acted not only aggressively but outrageously. Yet, as Dr. J. M. Brown points out, 'in terms of royal power, James was right to be confident. The Scottish monarchy was strong because of what it had to offer — political and social stability. It alone could keep a balance of power in the state, could bring to an end too great a concentration of power in the hands of one family, Stewarts or Douglases.'[122] It was this well-established monarchical strength which ensured, not only James II's survival, but his spectacular success by 1455.

NOTES

1. *S.H.R.*, xxx, (Oct. 1951), Notes and Comments, 199-204: 'The Date of the Birth of James III', a dispute between Wm. Angus and A. I. Dunlop over the date. Angus suggests 1451, but Dunlop's arguments for 1452 are much more convincing; *E.R.*, v, 685 (giving the dates 26 May-29 August 1452 for the Queen's residence at St. Andrews).

2. *R.M.S.*, ii, No. 566.

3. *Ibid.*, No. 1444.

4. *Asloan MS.*, i, 236; *E.R.*, v, 447, 537. The Queen's concern that she should achieve a successful birth in 1451 is illustrated by her sending to the Isle of May for the shirt of St. Margaret, thereby invoking the aid of the Saint in childbed: *E.R.*, v, 447, 512; Dunlop, *Bishop Kennedy*, 420.

5. J. M. Brown, 'Taming the Magnates?' in *The Scottish Nation*, edited by G. Menzies (London, 1972), esp. 57-59.

6. A detailed discussion of the power and problems of both Crown and magnates is to be found in J. M. Brown, 'The Exercise of Power', in *Scottish Society in the Fifteenth Century*, edited by J. M. Brown (London, 1977).

7. For details see J. M. Brown, 'Taming the Magnates?', 49-52.

8. A. A. M. Duncan, *James I, 1424-1437*, (University of Glasgow, Scottish History Department Occasional Papers, 1976), 26.

9. R. G. Nicholson, *Scotland: The Later Middle Ages*, (Edinburgh, 1974), 373-4.

10. Bower, *Scotichronicon*, xvi, 16.

11. *Ibid.; E.R.*, v, 33, 35. The motives of James I's assassins have been interpreted in many different ways. See, for example, E. W. M. Balfour-Melville, *James I, King of Scots*, (London, 1936), 243-247; Nicholson, *op.cit.*, 320-324; J. M. Brown, 'Taming the Magnates?', 51-52; Duncan, *James I*, 23-26.

12. The only contemporary chronicler, described by Thomas Thomson in 1819 as Thomas of Auchinleck, wrote 'Ane schorte memoriale of the Scottis corniklis for addicoun', which is printed in *Asloan MS.*, i, 215-244. An excellent unravelling of the tortuous political manoeuvres of James II's minority is to be found in Nicholson, *op.cit.*, 325-348.

13. *A.P.S.*, i, 557-8; *Scots Peerage*, iii, 159-60. For the details of Archibald the Grim's struggles against rival claimants to Douglas estates, see Nicholson, *op.cit.*, 201-3. Earl Archibald, an illegitimate son of the 'Good' Sir James Douglas (died 1330) was the first of the 'Black' Douglas earls. His father had been styled 'the Black Douglas' by the English, and he himself was described as 'Archibald the Black' by the Pluscarden chronicler (*Pluscarden Book*, i, 339).

14. *R.M.S.*, i, No. 920; *Scots Peerage*, iii, 166.

15. Nicholson, *op.cit.*, 249-250.

16. *Ibid.*, 317.

17. The others were Joan Beaufort, the Queen Mother, who had custody of her son and his sisters, and Bishop Cameron of Glasgow, the Chancellor: *A.P.S.*, ii, 54.

18. Bower, *Scotichronicon*, ii, 514; *Asloan MS.*, i, 233-4; Dunlop, *Bishop Kennedy*, 33; Nicholson, *op.cit.*, 330.

19. *See*, for example, Dunlop, *Bishop Kennedy*, 33-4.

20. Pitscottie, *Historie*, i, 46.

21. *Scots Peerage*, iii, 171, 176; *E.R.*, v, lvii.

22. *Scots Peerage*, iii, 173.

23. Fraser, *Douglas*, i, 442-3, n.1.

24. For details, see Nicholson, *op.cit.*, 332, 335. Earl James was taking advantage of the papal schism at the Council of Basle. Pope Eugenius IV had provided Ingeram Lindsay to the see of Aberdeen; but the Douglases adhered to the conciliarist Pope, Felix V, who provided Earl James's second son. With the ultimate collapse of the conciliarists, Ingeram Lindsay eventually obtained the see.

25. Some of these lands were transferred to Hugh by his elder brother, William, 8th earl of Douglas: *A.P.S.*, ii, 59.

26. *Scots Peerage*, iii, 174.

27. *Ibid.*, v, 427-8; *E.R.*, v, 249.

28. *R.M.S.*, ii, No. 286; *Scots Peerage*, v, 429; *E.R.*, v, lxxx, n.4; Nicholson, *op.cit.*, 349.

29. Fraser, *Douglas*, iii, 424 (first reference to Crichton as Chancellor, 4 May 1439); *Scots Peerage*, iii, 52-8; *E.R.*, iv, 607.

30. Nicholson, *op.cit.*, 339.

31. By far the most extensive treatment of Kennedy's life and political career is to be found in Annie I. Dunlop, *The Life and Times of James Kennedy, Bishop of St. Andrews* (Edinburgh, 1950). Although Dr. Dunlop's enthusiasm for Kennedy's statesmanship leads her on occasions to exaggerate his influence on vital events, her work is a classic of painstaking scholarship, indispensable to all those working on the period.

32. Dunlop, *Bishop Kennedy*, 19.

33. *Ibid.*, 39-41.

34. *Ibid.*, 40-42; Nicholson, *op.cit.*, 335.

35. *Ibid.*, 340.

36. *Asloan MS.*, i, 217-8 (incorrectly dating the General Council of October 1444 as October 1443); Nicholson, *op.cit.*, 339.

37. *H.M.C. Rep. XII,* pt. viii, pp. 114-115; Dunlop, *Bishop Kennedy*, 308, n.1.

38. *Extracts from the Council Register of the Burgh of Aberdeen* (Spalding Club, 1844), i, 399. It seems unlikely that Aberdeen was the only burgh to which Kennedy wrote appealing for support.

39. *R.M.S.*, ii, No. 283; *E.R.*, v, 186-7, 230; *Asloan MS.*, i, 220.

40. *Asloan MS.*, i, 219 (for death of Joan Beaufort and surrender of Dunbar); *E.R.*, iv, 620 (for Hepburn's keepership of Dunbar); *Rot. Scot.*, ii, 327, 331, 347 (for English safe-conducts for Stewart of Lorne).

41. Nicholson, *op.cit.*, 342, *E.R.*, v, 180, 221; *Asloan MS.*, i, 219.

42. *A.P.S.*, ii, 59. In the same Edinburgh parliament there appear the names of other lords of parliament for the first time — Campbell, Graham, Somerville, Maxwell, Montgomery — and Archibald Douglas makes his first parliamentary appearance as Earl of Moray. The emergence of this new peerage group is discussed by A. Grant, 'The development of the Scottish Peerage, *S.H.R.*, lvii (1978).

43. Dunlop, *Bishop Kennedy*, 63 and n. 3.

44. For Kennedy's movements 1445-9, see Dunlop, *Bishop Kennedy*, 432-3 (Kennedy Itinerary). For death of Crawford, see *Asloan MS.*, i, 220. According to the Auchinleck chronicler, the battle of Arbroath — dated 23 January 1446 — was a fight between the Lindsays and Ogilvies over the office of bailie or justiciar of the regality of Arbroath. Crawford was killed by accident, and his corpse remained unburied until Kennedy sent the prior of St. Andrews to remove the curse.

45. *R.M.S.*, ii, Nos. 284-289. Six more registered charters survive for December 1449, *after* the arrest of the Livingstons: *R.M.S.*, ii, Nos. 290-296; *A.P.S.*, ii, 60-66.

46. *R.M.S.*, ii, Nos. 287-293.

47. For details of negotiations leading to the royal marriage, see J. H. Baxter, 'The Marriage of James II', in *S.H.R.*, xxv, 69-72.

48. *Asloan MS.*, i, 236.

49. *A.P.S.*, ii, 33-35.

50. *Scots Peerage*, v, 429-430.

51. Dunlop, *Bishop Kennedy*, 106-109.

52. *Ibid.*, 108; *E.R.*, v, 479; *A.P.S.*, ii, 61.

53. Dunlop, *Bishop Kennedy*, 107-8.

54. Nicholson, *op.cit.*, 352.

55. *R.M.S.*, ii, Nos. 316, 317, 340.

56. Nicholson, *op.cit.*, 352.

57. *See above*, p.   .

58. *A.P.S.*, ii, 35. c. 3.

59. *E.R.*, v, 393. Douglas contributed £100, Chancellor Crichton £500, Bishop Kennedy £200, and the merchants of Edinburgh £131.

60. For Turnbull's career, see *R.M.S.*, ii, Nos. 116-28 (Privy Seal and royal Secretary). As diplomat, see Dunlop, *Bishop Kennedy*, 12, 116 n. A modern biography of Turnbull is: John Durkan, 'William Turnbull, Bishop of Glasgow',*Innes Review*, vol. ii (1951).

61. John Dowden, *The Bishops of Scotland* (Glasgow, 1912), 322; *E.R.*, v, 306, 310, 370; Dunlop, *Bishop Kennedy*, 102.

62. Nicholson, *op.cit.*, 353.

63. Dunlop, *Bishop Kennedy*, 135, 433.

64. *Cal. Docs Scot.*, iv, No. 1231; Nicholson, *op.cit.*, 355.

65. Law's MS., cited in *E.R.*, v, lxxxv, n. 2.

66. *See above*, p. 12. Admiral Crichton recovered his lands of Barnton by royal charter on 1 April 1450 (*R.M.S.*, ii, No. 334).

67. *R.M.S.*, ii, No. 345; Dunlop, *Bishop Kennedy*, 135 n. 3 (for the dowry); *E.R.*, v, 397 (for the royal deficit); *R.M.S.*, ii, No. 306 (for Atholl and Strathearn).

68. *A.P.S.*, ii, 64.

69. *R.M.S.*, ii, Nos. 447, 453.

70. *E.R.*, v, lxxxv, n. 2.

71. *R.M.S.*, ii, Nos. 463-482 (6-8 July 1451); *Asloan MS.*, i, 239.

72. *R.M.S.*, ii, No. 462.

73. *R.M.S.*, No. 503; *A.P.S.*, ii, 71-72.

74. *R.M.S.*, ii, No. 465.

75. Dunlop, *Bishop Kennedy*, 130 and 130 n. 3.

76. *Asloan MS.*, i, 235; Dunlop, *Bishop Kennedy*, 69n., 109, 110 n.2.

77. *E.R.*, v, xcviii; *R.M.S.*, ii, No. 544.

78. *Asloan MS.*, i, 225; Pitscottie, *Historie*, i, 126.

79. Boece, *History*, 372-3; Pitscottie, *Historie*, i, 88; *Scots Peerage*, iv, 401-3.

80. Godscroft, *History of the Houses of Douglas and Angus*, 186, giving Christian name 'William' to Herries. Boece and Pitscottie both call him John.

81. Pitscottie, *Historie*, i, 89-92; *Scots Peerage*, v, 257-8.

82. *R.M.S.*, ii, Nos. 522, 533. In No. 522, Douglas is described as Earl of Wigtown.

83. Pitscottie, *Historie*, i, 85-7.

84. *E.R.*, v, 458, 478, 596.

85. *Asloan MS.*, i, 239-241.

86. Major, *History*, 382; Lesley, *History*, 22; Pitscottie, *Historie*, i, 92-94.

87. Dunlop, *Bishop Kennedy*, 132-3.

88. *R.M.S.*, ii, No. 533; *Scots Peerage*, iv, 274-275.

89. *Ibid.*, v, 141-2; *E.R.*, vi, 208.

90. *Ibid.*, v, 348-9.

91. *Ibid.*, vi, 509-10.

92. *R.M.S.*, ii, Nos. 490-492; Dunlop, *Bishop Kennedy*, 203 n. 3.

93. *Asloan MS.*, i, 227. According to Auchinleck, James and two of his kin fought against Burgundian knights in the lists at Stirling, in the presence of James II, on 25 February 1448-9.

94. *Asloan MS.*, i, 241. Nicholson, *op.cit.*, 360, suggests that this dramatic scene was a ceremony of 'diffidatio', whereby a vassal renounced his fealty to his lord.

95. *R.M.S.*, ii, Nos. 529, 530, 532; *Asloan MS.*, i, 241.

96. *T.A.*, i, ccxvii.

97. *R.M.S.*, ii, No. 544; *E.R.*, v, 604.

98. Lesley, *History*, 23.

99. *R.M.S.*, ii, Nos. 533-551; *E.R.*, v, 685; Pitscottie, *Historie*, i, 96-9; *Asloan MS.*, i, 238.

100. *Asloan MS.*, i, 221, 222, 224-5. A different view of the Lord of the Isles' revolt and its connection with the Douglas murder appeared too late to be considered in this Chapter: *see* A. Grant, 'The Revolt of the Lord of the Isles and the Death of the Earl of Douglas, 1451–1452', in *S.H.R.*, lx, 2: No. 170 (October 1981), 169-174.

101. *R.M.S.*, ii, No. 542.

102. *A.P.S.*, ii, 73.

103. Rymer, *Foedera*, xi, 310-11; *Rot. Scot.*, ii, 357; Dunlop, *Bishop Kennedy*, 140.

104. *Asloan MS.*, i, 242. This story is remarkably similar to the tale of Douglas's arrival in Stirling in March 1452, condemning the king and privy council, dragging the safe-conduct through the streets, and withdrawing his allegiance (*Asloan MS.*, i, 241). As it would be unnecessary for the new earl to go through this performance twice, it is possible that Auchinleck has created two separate dramatic occasions out of a single event.

105. *E.R.*, v, 607 (for royal summons of the host); *Asloan MS.*, i, 243 (for parliamentary creations of 1452); *R.M.S.*, ii, No. 1444 (for royal charter to Kennedy).

106. *Asloan MS.*, i, 242; *E.R.*, v, xcvii-xcix (mentioning use of artillery); *R.M.S.*, ii, Nos. 588, 589. (Charters granted at Edinburgh on 9 July and 5 August 1452 respectively, with gap of 4 weeks during which the royal campaign took place).

107. The full text of the 'Appoyntmente' is printed in P. F. Tytler, *History of Scotland*, vol. i, part ii, Notes and Illustrations, pp. 386-7; *R.M.S.*, ii, No. 583 (for Stewarton grant).

108. Fraser, *Douglas*, i, 483-4 and n. 1 (for bond of manrent); *Calendar of Papal Registers*, x, 130-131 (for marriage dispensation); Dunlop, *Bishop Kennedy*, 142-3.

109. *Asloan MS.*, i, 225-6; Rymer, *Foedera*, xi, 334.

110. *Asloan MS.*, i, 226; *E.R.*, v, cvii. For Turnbull's death, the Auchinleck chronicler gives the wrong date, 3 December 1456: *Asloan MS.*, i, 228.

111. Nicholson, *op.cit.*, 366-7.

112. *R.M.S.*, ii, No. 680; Dowden, *Bishops of Scotland*, 185-6, 324-7; Dunlop, *Bishop Kennedy*, 152-3.

113. *Cal. Docs. Scot.*, iv, Nos. 1249, 1257, 1261; *Rot. Scot.*, ii, 362; Dunlop, *Bishop Kennedy*, 156 n. 1; Nicholson, *op.cit.*, 369.

114. Dunlop, *Bishop Kennedy*, 146 n. 2; *E.R.*, vi, xxvii.

115. E. F. Jacob, *The Fifteenth Century*, 509-11.

116. *Asloan MS.*, i, 243-4; Pinkerton, *History of Scotland*, i, 486-8 (for James II — Charles VII letter); *E.R.*, vi, 12.

117. *Asloan MS.*, i, 244.

118. Dunlop, *Bishop Kennedy*, 156 and n. 1; Nicholson, *op.cit.*, 370; *R.M.S.*, ii, No. 772; Chalmers, *Caledonia*, v, 90.

119. The forfeitures included Earl James, the Dowager Countess Beatrice, Archibald Douglas, 'pretended earl of Moray' (killed at Arkinholm), John Douglas of Balveny, and four of their adherents. Hugh Douglas, earl of Ormond, was not forfeited in this parliament; presumably he had been forfeited before his execution; *A.P.S.*, ii, 41-2, 76-7; *E.R.*, vi, xxxvii; Nicholson, *op.cit.*, 371.

120. *Cal. Docs. Scot.*, iv, No. 1272; Rymer, *Foedera*, xi, 367; Dunlop, *Bishop Kennedy*, 157.

121. *E.R.*, vi, 203, 207 (for royal residence at Tongland and Dundrennan); *ibid.*, 200, 201-2, 204, 209 (for artillery in Galloway); *ibid.*, 161, 293 (for progress of 'the great bombard'); *ibid.*, 203, 209 (for keeperships of Threave).

122. J. M. Brown,'The Exercise of Power', in J. M. Brown (ed.)), *Scottish Society in the Fifteenth Century*, 50.

2
The Legacy of James II: 1455–60

THE extent of the royal success produced an immediate reaction in the parliament of August 1455, and this probably explains the Act of Annexation passed on the first day, August 4. The preamble to the act includes the famous remark that 'the poverte of the crowne is oftymis the caus of the poverte of the Realme', and the act itself appears to be an attempt on the part of the three estates to ensure that the king, with his new-found wealth in forfeited Black Douglas lands, lived of his own and did not tax regularly.[1] This was to be avoided by annexing to the Crown certain lordships and castles in each part of the realm, and these could not be granted without consent of the entire parliament. A clear distinction was made in the act between annexed and unannexed lands, and the result should have been to give the crown a permanent cash endowment of £6050 per annum from annexed lands and customs, while annual rents of unannexed lands — those which the king might dispose of freely without parliamentary approval — appear to have exceeded £3500.[2] With its efforts to put checks on the king's disposal of lands and castles, the Act of Annexation implies criticism of James II. Financial difficulties had been partly responsible for the king's attack on the Livingstons in 1449-50, and had played a great part in his continual assaults on the Douglases. These had not been popular, and the Auchinleck chronicler reminds us that the king's raid on Peebles, Selkirk, and Dumfries in the summer of 1452 'did na gud bot distroyit the cuntre richt fellonly baith of cornes medowis and wittalis'.[3] In 1455, with the return of peace following more than five years of intermittent upheaval, there was an understandable desire to ensure that the Crown was not led into more civil wars on account of its poverty.

A further step in the same direction was taken by an act of 1455 condemning the royal practice of making grants of regalities. In future, these private jurisdictions might only be granted with the approval of parliament. A similar act had been introduced in the parliament of January 1450, no doubt with the same purpose, namely to acquire more wealth for the Crown through the extension of its judicial activities. Nicholson demonstrates convincingly that the royal profits of justice in ayres held in forfeited Douglas jurisdictions — Wigtown, Kirkcudbright, and Dumfries — were spectacular.[4]

Finally, the same parliament of August 1455 made impossible any future comeback of the Douglases by passing an act ordaining that no descendant of those forfeited in June would be permitted to succeed to, or even lay claim to, any lands or possessions in Scotland; while any persons giving aid or comfort to the Black

Douglas survivors would themselves be regarded as guilty of treason and liable to forfeiture of life, lands, and goods. The wealth and security of the Crown now seemed ensured. On 16 October 1455, James II was twenty-five; and when he came to pass his Act of Revocation a month later, he was already imbued with the confidence which his political and military successes had helped to create.[5] The queen's regular pregnancies had produced two surviving sons, James andAlexander, and a daughter, Mary; and some time in 1455 or very early in 1456 she was to give birth to a third son, David. The succession was secure, the king's enemies were dead or in exile, and, partly as a result of this, the resources and authority of the monarch had considerably increased.

In fact, the king had less than five years to live; and for the remainder of his short life he acted with an arrogance and — on occasions — disregard for the law which caused parliamentary concern long before the end. He showed a certain amount of diplomatic skill, and some of his creations — notably the earldom of Argyll in 1457 — were statesmanlike and necessary, producing loyal adherents of the Crown in troubled localities. Against this must be set the wilfullness which caused James II to dismiss two Chancellors, quite arbitrarily; to step outside the law in seizing the earldoms of Moray and Mar for his sons in the teeth of opposition from the rightful claimants; to attempt to conquer the Isle of Man and to demand cession to Scotland of the French county of Saintonge. Worse still, the royal record after 1455 is not only one of wilfullness but also of failure. The king failed to take Berwick in 1455, and he was killed trying to take Roxburgh in 1460.

If the Act of Annexation of 1455 may in some sense be regarded as a mild parliamentary admonition to James II, the king soon showed that he intended to disregard its terms. In 1456 he granted the liferents of Urquhart and Glenmoriston, both of them annexed lands, to the Earl of Ross, together with the custody of Urquhart castle; and by the following year, the king appears to have granted the forms of Ballincrieff to Bishop Kennedy.[6] Both these grants can be justified in terms of building up royal support and rewarding loyalty. As a former adherent of Douglas and a magnate of great power in the north-west, Ross's support for the Crown had to be bought; Bishop Kennedy, on the other hand, had been consistently royalist throughout the Black Douglas crises, and the farms of Ballincrieff may represent royal payment of a debt, or simply a reward for loyalty. In both cases, it seems clear that the king was not going to be bound by the 1455 act.

Much more serious was James II's intervention in the north to seize the earldoms of Moray and Mar. The king's attitude to the former was simple: it fell into Crown hands following the death and forfeiture of Archibald Douglas in 1455. On 12 February 1456 the earldom of Moray was bestowed on the infant David Stewart, the king's third son, and although the child died before 18 July 1457, James II retained possession of the Moray estates. This was to ignore not only the Crichton claim to the earldom, but also that of George Gordon, Master of Huntly, who within three weeks of Arkinholm had contracted to marry the widowed Countess of Moray, Elizabeth Dunbar.[7] There was a reasonably good case for a Huntly succession to the earldom of Moray. Alexander, earl of Huntly, had not only won for the king at Brechin in 1452, but had been consistently loyal throughout the crisis, while James Crichton, the former earl created by James II himself in 1452 and now dead, had been Huntly's brother-in-law. Furthermore, there was the question of fairness on the part of the Crown in balancing service and reward. The Earl of Ross, a former rebel, had been confirmed in the liferents of Urquhart and Glenmoriston, both of which he had seized; it was only natural for Huntly as the king's ally to expect to do rather better.

The king, however, not only ignored the Huntly claim, but treated the earl very shabbily. Huntly had been promised the island castle of Lochindorb, but instead it was demolished on the orders of the king in 1456. At about the same time, James relieved Huntly of his keepership of Kildrummy castle, replacing him with Alexander, Lord Glamis, who became one of four royal commissioners to revise the rentals of the earldom of Moray. One of the others was John Winchester, bishop of Moray since 1437, a confirmed supporter of James II, ambassador, royal charter witness, and parliamentarian, whose town of Spynie the King had made into a burgh in barony in July 1451, and a regality a year later — in spite of an act of 1450 oondemning the practice of granting regalities.[8] In short, whatever services Huntly had performed for James II in the past, these were not now to be recognised, and in addition to retaining the earldom, the king took care to build up support for the Crown in Moray, excluding Huntly in the process. His close personal interest in the area is shown in his visits to the north in 1457 and 1458, when he visited Inverness, Elgin, Spynie Castle, and the monastery of Kinloss. Apart from having his commissioners revise the rents of the earldom, the king sat on justice ayres in Inverness and Elgin, and continued the building of the hall in Darnaway Castle, started by the forfeited earl, Archibald Douglas.[9] All this is evidence of determination on the part of the king to consolidate Stewart power in the north; and Huntly, his hopes dashed, probably retaliated by devastating the lands of Mar, for which he had to receive a royal remission on 7 March 1457. The Master of Huntly was consoled — not, one feels, very adequately — with the offer of a marriage to James II's sister Annabella, the cast-off betrothed of Louis of Savoy.[10]

The same arbitrary royal actions, in many ways more blatant, can be seen in James II's treatment of the claimants to the earldom of Mar. The problem went back at least to 1435, when the liferenter of the earldoms of Mar and Garioch, Sir Alexander Stewart, had died, leaving the widowed Isabel, countess of Mar in her own right before she had married Stewart, and her heirs of line, Sir Robert Erskine and his son Thomas. James I had simply ignored the Erskine claims and annexed Mar to the royal domains; as for Garioch, he granted it to Elizabeth Douglas, widowed countess of Buchan, who later married William Sinclair, earl of Orkney. Thus the situation facing the government of James II in the late 1430s was that there were rival claimants to the crown in both Mar and Garioch. Sir Robert Erskine even went so far as to have himself served heir to the countess Isabel of Mar, infeft in half the earldom, and styled Earl of Mar from 1438. The royal government seems to have accepted at least his claim to the title, as the exchequer audits of 1446 refer to Erskine's son and heir Thomas as Master of Mar. But the Erskines do not appear to have enjoyed the lands of Mar at any time during the minority, and even when James II took control of the government in 1449-50, they

were told to wait for a Privy Council decision following the king's coming of age —
presumably his legal majority of twenty-five, on 16 October 1455.[11]

Long before 1455, however, the Crown's determination to retain both Mar and
Garioch had been made clear. When the Countess of Orkney, who had the liferent
of Garioch, died in 1452, the earldom was promptly bestowed on the queen, Mary
of Gueldres. Appeasement of the disappointed widower, William Sinclair, earl of
Orkney, followed at a later date, and his appointment as Chancellor and creation as
earl of Caithness[12] may well be regarded as part of the king's policy to retain
Orkney's support. In any event, royal favour to Orkney was shortlived; and Sir
Robert Erskine, the Mar claimant, was ignored for years and then cheated. There
would be no parliamentary or Privy Council hearing of his case; instead the king
would sit in judgement on his next visit to the north. This occurred in the autumn
of 1457, by which time James II had prepared the way for the overthrowing of the
Erskine claim. Orkney, with his own embarrassing claims to Garioch, was removed
from the Chancellorship, and in his place the king appointed the loyal George
Schoriswood, bishop of Brechin. James II himself was present when, in the
Tolbooth of Aberdeen, Schoriswood acted as his advocate in an Assize of Error,
rejecting Sir Robert Erskine's claims to Mar and declaring that the lands of the
earldom were rightfully vested in the Crown. Apart from Schoriswood, the king was
supported by George, Lord Leslie, who held some lands in the earldom, and who
was duly rewarded by being made Earl of Rothes three months later, with his lands
of Ballinbreich erected into a barony and his town of Leslie Green made a burgh in
barony. In short, Leslie was bribed; the Aberdeen jurors appear to have been
intimidated; and the Erskines were simply robbed. The king, however, had
achieved his objective of retaining the earldom, and some time before June 1459 his
youngest son John was made Earl of Mar.[13]

If the king had flouted the law in his efforts to retain the earldoms of Moray and
Mar, he had done so with some degree of political skill and forcefulness. Thus when
he ignored the Huntly claim to Moray, James II took care to show favour to other
prominent individuals in the area, especially Lord Glamis and John Winchester,
bishop of Moray; similarly while offending the Earl of Orkney and the Erskines
over the Mar claims, the King safeguarded himself by promoting other interested
parties, making the Bishop of Brechin Chancellor and creating Lord Leslie Earl of
Rothes. One may deplore the royal ingratitude to Huntly in the case of Moray, and
the bribery and intimidation used to secure the earldom of Mar; but it must be
conceded that the king recognised the political need, if he took with one hand, to
give with the other — especially when he could do so at little cost to himself.

James's other new creations were less controversial than that of Rothes. The
Gordon earldom of Huntly had been created during the minority, in 1445; and
James's first adult grant of the earldom of Erroll to William Hay in 1452 survived
the Douglas crises and the act of revocation of 1455. In 1457-8, however, came a
spate of new creations. Colin, Lord Campbell, became Earl of Argyll; James
Douglas, fourth lord of Dalkeith, was made Earl of Morton; and William, Lord
Keith, became Earl Marischal.[14] As for the redistribution of already existing
earldoms, with the exception of Caithness — which had already gone to William

D

Sinclair, earl of Orkney — these became a royal Stewart family monopoly. As we have seen, Moray and Mar went respectively to the king's youngest sons, David and John. James's second son Alexander, probably born in 1454, had been made Earl of March before 8 July 1455, and Duke of Albany three years later; and the earldom of Atholl, in the crown's hands since 1437, was bestowed on James's half-brother, the young Sir John Stewart of Balveny, in 1457.[15] Thus by 1458 James II had built up a body of loyal nobility, with a special emphasis on rewarding royalists in the west — Argyll — and north and north-east — Rothes, Marischal, and Erroll. The Earl of Huntly, in spite of his past service, was a significant exception to this rule but, surrounded by newly ennobled neighbours and royal Stewart earldoms, there was little he could do.

The king, however, did not wholly escape censure from the three estates. On 6 March 1458, parliament assembled in Edinburgh and produced a spate of legislation, forty clauses in all covering a vast range of subjects including civil and criminal justice, the money, agricultural improvements, the relief of poverty, the slaughter of wolves, and the condemnation of 'lesing makars' — those who told tales with the purpose of inciting discord between king and people. Much of the legislation was not new, and a great deal of it — for example the statute 'crying doune' football and golf in favour of regular archery practice — was probably ignored. However, the main concerns of the three estates are clearly illustrated by the sheer volume of statutes on civil and criminal justice, the subject of no fewer than nine acts. Very detailed instructions for the holding of three 'sessions', each lasting forty days, at Aberdeen, Perth and Edinburgh respectively, are set out, and nine lords of session, three from each estate, appointed to each. A similar attempt to make the sessions work had been made in 1456, when elected representatives of the three estates had been called upon to sit for a month at a time; probably this was a failure, and the extensive legislation of March 1458 was the result. The competence of the lords of session would extend to cases of spoliation, and to all civil actions except those involving fee and heritage. But if hopes were raised that a supreme civil court functioning in regular sessions might at last be established as an alternative to the lords of council, they were surely dashed by the stipulation that the lords of session would not be paid; and perhaps more significantly, the fifth clause of the 1458 acts laid down that after the conclusion of the Aberdeen, Perth and Edinburgh sessions, new lords of session would be chosen not by the three estates, but by the king and council 'at tymis and placis sene speidfull to him and his saide consale'.[16] Royal control of the sessions was thus assured; and no further reference to them is to be found until the parliament of 1471.

As for criminal justice, three statutes affirm the need for regular justice ayres, though they do not specifically insist that the king should be present when they met. Certainly, James II rode the ayres in the north-east in 1457-8; but his personal interest in the area was probably associated with his seizure of the earldoms of Moray and Mar. Furthermore, his concern to build up support in that area may well explain the two hundred remissions listed in the accounts of the royal chamberlains north of Spey for the exchequer year 1457-8; this practice was to be condemned roundly in the following reign.[17] As it was, the parliament of 1458 suggested that the ayres might be made to work more efficiently, with sheriffs ensuring that no intimidation took place through powerful men in the localities arriving at court with armed retainers. All this reads very much like wishful thinking; and there is an almost despairing ring to the penultimate clause of the parliament, an appeal to the king to command sheriffs and commissioners of burghs to come to the clerk register and copy down all the 1458 articles, acts and statutes, subsequently proclaiming them openly throughout shires and burghs so that no lieges could allege ignorance of the law'

However, the most quoted of all the articles of this parliament is the last, frequently regarded as a commentary on the entire reign. It runs as follows:

> And that attour sene God of his grace has send our soverane lorde sik progress and prosperite that all his rebyllys and brekaris of his Justice ar removit out of his Realme and no maisterfull party remanande that may caus ony breking in his Realme sa that his hienes be inclynit in himself and his ministeris to the quiet and commoune profett of the Realm and Justice to be kepit amangis his liegis his thre estatis with all humilite exhortis ande requiris his hienes to be inclynit with sik diligence to the execucione of thir statutis actis and decretis abone writtyn that God may be emplesit of him and all his liegis spirituale and temporale may pray for him to Gode and gif thankyng to him that sende thame sik a prince to thir governor and defendor.[18]

This final clause is not, surely, a simple compliment to the king, because it suggests criticism as well as praise. As all the king's rebels — presumably the Black Douglases — had been defeated and peace and order had returned, James II should now apply himself to observing the statutes of the 1458 parliament so that his people would have cause in the future to thank God for sending them such a good prince. The implication is that there was an underlying fear amongst members of the estates as to what policies the king might follow. The Douglases had been crushed in 1455; but James II's arbitrary actions, including his disregard of the Act of Annexation, his extensive remissions in the north-east, and his seizure of Moray and Mar, had continued unchecked, and must have worried many more than those who suffered directly in consequence. So in March 1458, parliament gently reminded the king of his duties, above all of the need to observe the 'statutis, actis and decretis' of the three estates.

How effective this parliamentary admonition might have been is impossible to judge, because James II was dead little more than two years later. There are signs that he was prepared to accept parliament's advice in some areas, for example in giving an example to his lieges by introducing feu-farm tenure on some royal lands, especially Falkland; but this policy was largely abandoned in the next reign, and not indeed vigorously pursued by James IV until after 1508.[19] Furthermore, there were no obvious changes in the style of royal government and justice. The ayres continued at infrequent intervals, the sessions probably never met at all; and the king continued to act with aggressive confidence to the very end of his life.

Royal aggression is most marked in James II's foreign policy. Between 1455 and 1460, the king undertook a number of ambitious foreign schemes, ranging from the attempted recovery of Berwick and Roxburgh from the English — apparently a popular policy in Scotland — to the abortive invasion of the Isle of Man and demands for the cession to Scotland by the French of the county of Saintonge.

The first assault on Berwick, which James II described as 'our town, long wrongfully detained by the English', occurred in the summer of 1455, when the king diverted part of the army engaged on the siege of Threave to make a surprise attack on the town and castle. This occurred before 3 July 1455, by which date the Bishop of Durham was able to inform the Archbishop of Canterbury that the Scots had been rebuked and departed. On 8 July, James II wrote to Charles VII of France about the siege, blaming the Scots' failure to take the town on leakage of information; but his letter also makes clear that, without French assistance, the Scots would not be able to storm Berwick with much hope of success.[20] This was a realistic viewpoint; but the truth was that Charles VII, in spite of subsequent appeals from the Scots for military aid to take Berwick, or even for a French diversionary raid on Calais, had his own domestic troubles and in any case had no real desire to make trouble for Henry VI's French queen, Margaret of Anjou, by allying with the Scots.[21]

Denied French assistance, James II did not abandon his efforts to acquire Berwick. Throwing caution to the winds, he renounced the Anglo-Scottish truce in May 1456 and invaded the lands subject to the English garrison at Roxburgh two months later. No doubt he hoped to take advantage of English governmental weakness during the conflict between Henry VI and Richard, duke of York, and he transferred his support to the latter at the same time. But James's second attack on Berwick, in February 1457, also failed, and the Scots king was forced to conclude a two-year truce with England in June 1457, including a clause upholding the maintenance of the status quo regarding Berwick and Roxburgh.[22]

Even more dubious was James II's attempt to conquer the Isle of Man. This was blatant aggression, because the lordship of the island, together with the patronage of the bishopric and other ecclesiastical benefices, had been vested in the Stanley family as early as the reign of Henry IV. James used the provision of an English bishop to the see of Man in 1455 as an excuse for his political ambitions. Claiming that Man was in fact part of the old diocese of Sodor, or the Isles, and that it was a Scottish bishopric, he sent an expedition to the island and invested his second son, Alexander, duke of Albany, in the political lordship. There is little evidence of the struggle that followed. The Galloway accounts of 1456 mention the sending of a ship to Man while the king's army was there; and in 1457 compensation was paid for the wreck of a ship while at the Isle of Man on the king's service. At some time in the same exchequer year, a courier was given five shillings for carrying letters from Dundrennan to James II at Falkland 'with news of the ships'.[23]

Retaliation by the Stanleys against the Scots makes more convincing reading. Ignoring the Anglo-Scottish truce of July 1457, young Stanley crossed by sea from Man to Kirkcudbright, plundered and burned the town and raided the West Marches. This was a blow to James II, who had made Kirkcudbright a royal burgh after the Douglas forfeitures of 1455, immediately using it as the seaport from which his expedition to Man had sailed.[24] The lesson for the Scots king was clear: short of a total governmental collapse in England, or the unlikely possibility of

French military assistance, raids on English-controlled territory on the Borders or Man were a very dangerous game to play, inviting immediate and devastating retaliation. If the king failed to realise this, his attitude contrasts very sharply with the caution of the three estates, whose concern was that an English invasion via Roxburgh or Berwick might well be disastrous. This caution is reflected in the acts of the Stirling parliament of October 1455, in which no fewer than thirteen ordinances were on the subject of the defence of the borders. The estates stipulated exactly how the Marches were to be guarded. In the east, 'betuix Roxburghe and Berwik', Scottish sentinels were to watch the fords, and light beacons in the event of an English invasion. There were to be three garrisons on the borders, two hundred spearmen and two hundred archers on the East March, the same number on the Middle March, and a force half that size on the West March — a total of 1000 men.[25]

Such provisions are a clear indication of parliament's concern; but they do not by themselves represent a really effective defence policy. Thinly scattered garrisons throughout the Marches, with a mere 400 men in the East March between Roxburgh and Berwick, where invasion was most to be feared, were a pitiful response to English border organisation, which allowed £2000 sterling per annum in time of war for the defence of a single stronghold like Roxburgh.[26] All this suggests that the Scottish king, short of mustering an army for some urgent and specific purpose, could offer little more than token resistance to an English invasion, especially in a year in which he had already had to call extensively on local support, as well as a royal army, to end the civil wars against the Black Douglases. On the other hand, James II's constant desire to recover Berwick and Roxburgh and thereby provide a positive solution to parliament's fears of English invasion from these strongpoints is quite understandable. He simply lacked the means to achieve success.

In other areas of foreign policy, James II behaved like a powerful and wealthy European monarch with a major role to play. It is understandable that he should have had a more active interest in foreign affairs than his father; he had, after all, family ties through marriage to the houses of Burgundy and Gueldres. Four of his sisters had been married in France, Brittany, Veere, and Austria respectively by the end of the 1440s; and that the king was known abroad is shown by his appearance in the long 'Testament' of the French poet Francois Villon. His reputation, founded perhaps on the 'fiery face' which Villon and Auchinleck both describe, must have been that of a tough and unscrupulous negotiator, showing little or no regard for his family in his efforts to increase his wealth and authority, at home as well as abroad. His cynicism is seen at its most blatant in his dealings with his second sister Isabella, married to Francis, duke of Brittany, in 1442. The duke had died in 1450, and the Scottish king, in spite of the fact that he had never paid his sister's dowry to the Bretons, soon opened negotiations with Charles VII of France to help Isabella find a suitable remarriage which would be financially and politically profitable. The problem for the Scottish king was that Isabella had no wish to fall in with his schemes. As early as 1453 she complained that James had never paid her dowry, showed considerable hostility towards her brother's ambassadors, and refused to come home from Brittany. She repeated her refusal in 1455; and it seems possible that James had in mind for her a political alliance in Scotland of the kind inflicted on her sisters Annabella and Joan, both of them failures in the European marriage market.[27] In fact, Isabella was not forced to return to Scotland, and James II's policy with regard to her future was not realised; but his interest in his widowed sister's position was undoubtedly the fact that it gave him some claim to Brittany, a claim which was to be revived by his son, James III, in 1472.

Towards the end of the reign, James II's foreign schemes multiplied, and between 1458 and 1460 he was involved in extensive negotiations with Henry IV of Castile, Christian I of Denmark-Norway, and Charles VII of France. The Castilian agreement was logical enough, given the state of the Anglo-Scottish truce. Both Scotland and Castile were concerned about English privateers acting for the Earl of Warwick and attacking the shipping of both countries; and the Scots were seeking redress for inevitable breaches of the truce. There might be commercial advantages for Scotland in a Castilian alliance; and above all, there were diplomatic considerations. Charles VII of France was concerned about the future attitudes of the Scottish and Castilian kings because both had interceded for the rebellious Dauphin — the future Louis XI — when he had fled to Burgundian territory in August 1456. The French king was clearly concerned to have James II and Henry IV as allies rather than enemies if at all possible; and he was probably impressed by the fact that, in the former case, the Scottish king's wife was the Duke of Burgundy's niece.[28]

The main motives governing James II's negotiations with Christian I of Denmark-Norway seem to have been financial and territorial. In 1266, the Scots had pledged themselves to the payment of 100 marks each year in perpetuity, the so-called 'annual', for the transfer of the Western Isles to Scotland; and this agreement was renewed in 1312. Thereafter payments appear to have lapsed until 1426, when a further treaty requiring Scots payment of the 'annual' was drawn up. The Scots again defaulted, neither making regular annual payments nor apparently considering any payment of arrears. In 1456 the Scots added insult to injury. Some time before May of that year, James II was responsible for, or was at least a party to, the imprisonment in Orkney of the governor of Iceland and his wife, at the same time seizing all the royal and ecclesiastical revenues which they were carrying to Denmark. Orkney was still technically Norwegian territory; and King Christian I of Denmark-Norway, already in serious financial difficulties at home, alleged that James II was directly responsible and submitted the entire dispute to the arbitration of Charles VII of France. The Danish king's real aim was to obtain regular Scottish payment of the 'annual'; but Christian's desperate need of money meant that James II, though one of a long line of defaulters, could turn the situation to his own advantage. The issue dragged on through 1459 and into 1460, with Christian I looking for a treaty which, as Dr. Crawford puts it, would 'mask the ignominy of having to admit that he was no longer the recipient of the "annual" and that he could not force the Scottish kings to continue paying it'.[29]

James II, for his part, hoped for a Danish marriage treaty and remission of the 'annual'; and in the spring of 1460, the Scottish and Danish kings were invited to send representatives to Bourges, where Charles VII would act as mediator in negotiations for an agreement and marriage alliance. Bishop Kennedy, accompanied by the young Duke of Albany, had departed on this errand by 17 June 1460, but he fell ill at Bruges, so the Scots ambassadors at Bourges were Sir Wiliam Monypenny and Patrick Folkart, Captain of the Scots Guards. James II, taking advantage of Christian I's financial problems, made excessive demands: not only the remission of all arrears of the 'annual', but also a Danish marriage which would bring the Orkney and Shetland islands to the Scottish Crown in full sovereignty. The Danes, no doubt taken aback if not appalled, claimed that they lacked sufficient powers to conclude such a treaty, demanded settlement of the 'annual', and the issue remained unresolved, probably because of James II's death on 3 August. The Scottish king's aggressiveness was to pay off early in the reign of his son, when the demands made at Bourges were fully met by the Danes.[30]

The wildest of all James II's abortive continental schemes was his claim to the French county of Saintonge in 1458. Scottish ambassadors were sent to demand sasine of Saintonge in James II's name, justifying the claim in terms of a treaty made thirty years before in 1428, when Charles VII, hard pressed by the English in France and desperate for Scottish assistance, had promised James I and his heirs the county of Saintonge as part of a marriage treaty between the Scottish king's daughter Margaret and the Dauphin Louis. It was also stipulated, however, that the Scots would assist the French with an army of six thousand; this had never materialised, and so Charles VII withheld Saintonge. In 1458 as in 1428, nothing came of the Scots demands; and Dr. Dunlop may well be correct in suggesting that claiming Saintonge was simply James II's method of putting pressure on the French king to be more accommodating in other areas of diplomacy — for example the Denmark-Norway question and the perennial problem of England.[31] On the other hand, such an idea may be paying too high a tribute to the Scottish king's diplomatic abilities. It would certainly be consistent with James's confidence and high-handedness at home and abroad at this time for him to have expected the cession of Saintonge to Scotland. He had, after all, failed in Man, at Berwick and Roxburgh, and the Denmark-Norway negotiations were unresolved; so the king may have felt that an easy foreign success would help to boost his prestige at home and abroad. Charles VII of France did not even consider ceding Saintonge to Scotland; but the issue was not dead, for James III was to renew it in the 1470s.

The most convincing demonstration of a successful foreign policy could, however, be made much nearer home, by the capture of Berwick, or Roxburgh, or both. Although the Anglo-Scottish truce had been extended from 1459 to 1463, there was little doubt that James II would violate it if there appeared any chance of success on the East Marches. Such an opportunity arrived on 10 July 1460, when the battle of Northampton signalled not only the start of a protracted period of civil war in England, but also the falling into Yorkist hands of the Lancastrian Henry VI. Only such disruption in England made a Scottish assault on Berwick and Roxburgh a practical possibility, and James II was quick to take advantage of the new situation. He may indeed have been planning invasion for some time — the Scottish host could not after all be called out overnight — and in July 1460 a rumour was already circulating in Bruges that the Scottish king was about to invade England with an army of 30,000 men, and that he had married one of his daughters to a son of the Duke of York. In England itself, within 10 days of the battle of Northampton, it was reported that 'the King of Scots with all his power is expected to lay siege "eftsones" to the town and castle of Berwick-on-Tweed'; and the Scottish exchequer audit of 1460 reveals James II's interest in Berwick.[32] The king preceded his invasion by sacking the Chancellor, George Schoriswood, bishop of Brechin, perhaps because the bishop had been used the previous year as an ambassador to the then Lancastrian government.[33] The new Chancellor, the fourth in six years, was Andrew Stewart, Lord Avandale, whose political fortunes were based on his earlier support of James II against the Black Douglases; and he was to remain Chancellor for the remarkable period of 22 years.

The king may have intended to attack both Roxburgh and Berwick; but his initial target was Roxburgh. There was a long history of Scottish attempts to recover this fortress from the English, including an abortive raid by James II himself in the summer of 1456, on the lands subject to the English garrison. But the most recent full-scale assault had been that made by James I in August 1436, with a large army, the entire Scottish host reinforced by artillery. Yet the attack had been a total failure within a fortnight, the army dispersed and siege engines abandoned to the enemy, a bitter disappointment to James I, who in anticipation of success had included the legend 'Marchmont' (Roxburgh) on the royal signet.[34] Like his father, James II summoned what the Auchinleck chronicler describes as 'ane gret ost' to the 1460 siege. The same narrator, our only contemporary source for the siege, goes on to describe the death of James II on Sunday 3 August 1460. The king 'unhappely was slane with ane gun the quhilk brak in the fyring for the quhilk was gret dolour throu all Scotland and nevertheless all the lordis that war thar remainit still with the oist and on the fryday efter richt wysly and manfully wan the forsaid castell and tynt nocht a man may In the wynnyng of It'. Only after the king's death, in Auchinleck's account, did the queen with her eldest son, some bishops and other nobles, come south to Kelso, arriving there on Friday 8 August and taking part in the coronation of the new king two days later.[35]

All subsequent accounts of the siege of Roxburgh are of much later date, and their detailed information must be treated with caution' Thus the 'Extracta' chronicler adds the information that the Earl of Angus was wounded in the same explosion which killed the king; and he comes into direct conflict with Auchinleck by suggesting that Mary of Gueldres was present at the siege, and that it was in honour of her arrival that James II fired the fatal salvo. John Major, briefly describing the siege in his *History*, published in 1521, follows the 'Extracta' in referring to the wounding of the Earl of Angus in the fatal explosion, but otherwise gives no detail at all, merely remarking unhelpfully that the king's death was 'a lesson to future kings that they should not stand too close to instruments of this sort when these are in the act of being discharged'. In his vernacular history published in 1568, Bishop Lesley includes the wounding of the Earl of Angus, but suggests that the siege was brought to a successful conclusion by the queen, who was apparently present throughout and who was responsible for the winning of both Roxburgh and Wark.

The fatal salvo, according to Lesley, was not therefore fired in honour of the queen's arrival, but was directed at Roxburgh itself, from the Scottish trenches, and a wedge flying out of one of the cannon mortally wounded the king.[36]

The most elaborate — and probably the least trustworthy — account of the king's death is that of Lindsay of Pitscottie, whose *Historie*, continuing and amplifying that of Boece, was published in 1579. Pitscottie alone places the Lord of the Isles, whom he mistakenly calls 'Donald', in James II's 'gret ost' at Roxburgh. The Lord of the Isles, in this account, came to the royal camp at the siege of Roxburgh, bringing with him a large Highland force; he was well received by the king, and used by James to harry the surrounding country, because the siege was proving much more difficult than the besiegers had expected. More reinforcements arrived with Alexander, earl of Huntly, 'quhilk maid the King so blytht that he commandit to charge all the gunnis to gif the castell ane new wollie. Bot quhill this prince mair curieous nor becam him or the maiestie of ane King did stand neir hand by the gunneris quhen the artaillzerie was dischargand, his thie bone was doung in tua witht ane peace of ane misframit gune that brak in the schutting, be the quhilk he was strikin to the ground and dieit haistelie thairof'. There is no mention here of the Earl of Angus being wounded, and the Earl of Huntly takes the place of the queen as the immediate cause of James's discharging the fatal salvo. Thereafter, according to Pitscottie, the queen brought her eldest son up to the siege, and he puts in her mouth a long speech exhorting the Scottish besiegers to persist in the assault in spite of the king's death.[37]

These conflicting accounts — the result no doubt of stories of the siege becoming garbled through oral transmission — have a few common features. All are agreed that Roxburgh was a very tough nut to crack; all suggest that James II needed or received reinforcements; all agree on the actual manner of his death. Bearing in mind these facts, and that James was dead a week before Roxburgh was taken, we may speculate as to the size of his 'gret ost'. There is no reason to suppose that the army of 1460 was larger than that of 1436, though the failure of the earlier siege can probably be attributed as much to the unpopularity of James I as any other single factor. The general popularity of James II's last campaign must however also be questioned, for much of the praise of the king's ability to command support from all over Scotland at this time is based on Pitscottie's unsupported statement that the Lord of the Isles was present at Roxburgh with a Highland contingent. There must be considerable doubt about this, for within two years he is to be found conspiring with the exiled Earl of Douglas and Edward IV of England. If he was present, he may have been moved by fear of the king. He was, after all, the last survivior of the Douglas-Crawford-Ross bond of 1452, and James II's recognition of his seizure of the royal lands and castle of Urquhart and Glen Moriston in 1452 had been made while the king was under extreme pressure. James's unscrupulous seizures of the earldoms of Moray and Mar in the late 'fifties can have left the Lord of the Isles with little confidence as to his own future, and it is possible that he turned up at Roxburgh in an effort to ingratiate himself with the king.

It remains difficult, if not impossible, to arrive at a satisfactory estimate of the character and policies of James II. His years of active rule were short, a mere eleven years; and his death at the age of twenty-nine left unanswered a host of questions as to how he might have developed as a ruler. In some respects he was undoubtedly a success. He was a vigorous and courageous military leader, tenacious enough to conduct civil wars at home and consider the recovery of border territory lost to England at one and the same time. His reign saw a strengthening of the already powerful Stewart monarchy in Scotland, reflected not only in the creation of a new peerage — the lords of parliament — but in the conferring of earldoms on magnates on whose support the Crown depended in the west and north, notably Argyll and Huntly. The monarchy was further strengthened, in terms of both authority and finance, by the Livingston and Black Douglas forfeitures of 1450 and 1455 respectively. James II himself travelled extensively throughout Scotland, not only on military expeditions, but on justice ayres and for pleasure; and he must have been personally known to a fair number of his subjects. Even at the very end, the fact that the Scottish host remained to take Roxburgh after the king's death illustrates James's popularity with the army.

There is, however, a darker side to his character. James's military prowess was undoubted; but the wars which he undertook were, on the whole, started by himself, and in many cases avoidable. Thus there is no clear dividing line between war and peace in the period 1449-60. James II summoned either local or national forces to support royal policies in 1451, 1452, 1455, 1456, 1457 and 1460. The year 1455 alone included full-scale war against the Isle of Man. Hence the note of caution, if not genuine alarm, sounded by parliaments from 1455 onwards — at Edinburgh in August 1455, when the Act of Annexation attempted to ensure that the Douglas forfeitures were not frittered away; at Stirling in October of the same year, when provision was made for the defence of the borders in expectation of a retaliatory English invasion; and finally at Edinburgh in March 1458, when the estates petitioned the king, following the defeat of all his traitors and rebels, to observe parliament's statutes and ordinances so that his reputation with his subjects might stand high in the future.

NOTES

1. Nicholson estimates that in all, forfeited Black Douglas lands brought the King gross cash rents of at least £2000, or about one third of the total for all the crown lands: Nicholson, *Scotland: The Later Middle Ages*, 378.

2. *A.P.S.*, ii, 42-3; Nicholson, *op.cit.*, 379. Lordships and castles annexed to the crown were: Ettrick, Galloway, Redcastle (Ross), forfeited Douglas lands north of the Spey, the castles of Edinburgh, Stirling and Dumbarton with the royal domains around them, Ballincrieff and Gosford (Lothian), the castles of Inverness and Urquhart, the earldoms of Fife and Strathearn, and the lordship of Brechin.

3. *Asloan MS.*, i, 242.

4. Nicholson, *op.cit.*, 377-8.

5. *A.P.S.*, ii, 42, 43-4; Dunlop, *Bishop Kennedy*, 176.

6. Dunlop, *Bishop Kennedy*, 162 n.3, 177 n.2; *E.R.*, vi, 119, 359.

7. *E.R.*, vi, cxxvi n., 280, 291, 355; *Spalding Miscellany*, iv, 128-30.

8. Dunlop, *Bishop Kennedy*, 178 (for Lochindorb demolition); *E.R.*, vi, cxxvii, 269 (for Kildrummy); Dowden, *Bishops of Scotland*, 159-60 (for career of Winchester).

9. *E.R.*, vi, 380, 468, 469, 475, 487; for building operations at Darnaway, *E.R.*, xi, 220, 380, 482.

10. Dunlop, *Bishop Kennedy*, 178 n.4, 179.

11. *Ibid.*, 183 and n.1.; *E.R.*, vi, 235; *A.P.S.*, ii, 62-3.

12. Although the formal grant to Orkney of the earldom of Caithness was only made in parliament on 4 August 1455, in exchange for the earl's surrendering to the Crown his rights in the lordship of Nithsdale and sheriffdom of Dumfries, in fact Orkney is already described as Earl of Caithness in the autumn of 1454: *R.M.S*, ii, No. 680.

13. *Spalding Miscellany*, v, 275-6; Dunlop, *Bishop Kennedy*, 185-6 (for the Aberdeen Assize of Error); *E.R.*, vi, 516 (for creation of John, earl of Mar).

14. *Scots Peerage*, i, 332 (for Argyll); *Reg. Honor. de Morton*, i, xlii; *A.P.S.*, ii, 78 (for Morton); *Scots Peerage*, vi, 40, *R.M.S.*, ii, No. 62 (for Marischal).

15. *E.R.*, vi, 44, 63 (for Albany and March creations); *Scots Peerage*, i, 441 (for Atholl). Sir John Stewart of Balveny was the son of James I's queen dowager, Joan Beaufort, and Sir James Stewart, the Black Knight of Lorne. Sir John Stewart was born about 1440, and had two younger brothers James (later Earl of Buchan) and Andrew (later Bishop of Moray). All three were to play a vital part in the political events of the next reign.

16. *A.P.S.*, ii, 47-52.

17. *E.R.*, vi, 485-6; Nicholson, *op.cit.*, 384.

18. *A.P.S.*, ii, 52.

19. For a full discussion of feu-farm tenure, its advantages and disadvantages, *see* Nicholson, *op.cit.*, 381-3.

20. Pinkerton, *History*, 487-8; Dunlop, *Bishop Kennedy*, 157 n.4.

21. Ramsay, *Lancaster and York*, ii, 198.

22. *Rot. Scot.*, ii, 378-83; Dunlop, *Bishop Kennedy*, 171.

23. *E.R.*, vi, 204, 349; Dunlop, *Bishop Kennedy*, 176-7.

24. *Ibid.*, 202.

25. *A.P.S.*, ii, 44-5.

26. *Rot. Scot.*, ii, 360-1. £2000 sterling was the equivalent of $\frac{1}{3}$-$\frac{1}{2}$ the Scottish king's annual income from normal sources.

27. A full discussion of James's manipulation of his sisters' marriages is to be found in Dunlop, *Bishop Kennedy*, 147-8, 181, 182, 185, 185 n.3; Annabella was returned to Scotland against her will and married to the Master of Huntly, following the dissolution of her marriage contract with Louis of Savoy, for which James II received 25,000 crowns as damages in 1456 (*R.M.S.*, ii, No. 745; Dunlop, *Bishop Kennedy*, 181 n.3). Joan had been sent abroad in 1445-6, but no husband had been found for her, and she was returned to Scotland with Annabella in the spring of 1458 and given in marriage to the king's newest creation, James Douglas, earl of Morton, whose position James II wished to strengthen (*E.R.*, v, 225; vi, lvii; *A.P.S.*, ii, 78; *R.M.S.*, ii, No. 699). On the whole, James's dealings with Isabella, Annabella, and Joan suggest that his relationships with his sisters were governed by political cynicism and the prospect of financial advantage.

28. *Cal. Docs. Scot.*, iv, No. 1295; Ramsay, *Lancaster and York*, ii, 210; Dunlop, *Bishop Kennedy*, 195 n.5.

29. Barbara E. Crawford, 'Scotland's foreign relations: Scandinavia', in J. M. Brown (ed.), *Scottish Society in the Fifteenth Century*, 87-88.

30. *See below*, Chapter 3. A full discussion of the negotiations leading up to the Bourges conference in 1460 is to be found in Crawford, *op.cit.*, 87-88; Dunlop, *Bishop Kennedy*, 197-201. It is not clear why the Duke of Albany, who was only six, accompanied Kennedy abroad. Presumably his destination was not the conference at Bourges, unless he was the prospective bridegroom.

31. *Spalding Miscellany*, ii, 181-6; Dunlop, *Bishop Kennedy*, 196-7.

32. *Cal. State Papers (Milan)*, i, 27; *Cal. Docs. Scot.*, iv, No. 1307; *E.R.*, vi, 581.

33. *Rot. Scot.* ii, 391.

34. *Scotichronicon,* xvi, 26; *Pluscarden Book,* xi, 7; *Extracta ex Cronicis Scotiae,* ed. Turnbull, (Abbotsford Club, 1842), 235; Balfour-Melville, *James I,* 230. Significantly, the *Extracta* — possibly the work of Alexander Myln, abbot of Cambuskenneth, author of the 'Lives of the Bishops of Dunkeld' who died in 1548 — contains the remark that the siege of Roxburgh broke up on the appearance of the queen, who took away the king, and the rest followed (p. 235). Later in the same work, referring to the *1460* siege of Roxburgh, the chronicler remarks that James II ordered his artillery to discharge a salvo on account of joy at the arrival of the queen, and so received his death wound (pp. 243-4). Can this be a confusion of the two sieges by the 16th century chronicler, attributing to the arrival of two different queens a similar tragic result?

35. *Asloan MS.,* i, 229-30.

36. *Extracta,* 244; Major, *History,* 386; Lesley, *History,* 31-2.

37. Pitscottie, *Historie,* i, 143-4.

3

Pragmatism versus Tradition: The Queen Mother and Bishop Kennedy: 1460–65

THE nine years of James III's minority produced a political situation which later writers were quick to compare with the similar period during the previous reign; and indeed many contemporaries must have made the comparison, for only eleven years separated the end of James II's minority and the beginning of that of his son. Undoubtedly there were superficial similarities — a king cut off in his prime, leaving a minor to succeed him, a queen mother whose position as guardian of her offspring gave her a central position in any council of regency, and an ambitious family — in the case of James II the Livingstons, James III the Boyds — whose elevation to a dominant position in royal household and central government was based on possession of the person of the young king.

Closer examination of the two minorities, however, reveals that the differences are more striking than the similarities. In the former case James I, an unpopular king, had been assassinated, and his queen had remarried, producing a difficult political situation which was exacerbated by the deaths of the other members of the council of regency, the Bishop of Glasgow and the Earl of Douglas. A major struggle for power was therefore inevitable in the 1440s, and was resolved by the Douglas-Livingston alliance and the dubious expedient of declaring the young king of age in 1444. Nothing of the sort occurred in the early 1460s. The king had been killed accidentally. and his popularity had been such that the Scottish host remained to take Roxburgh a week after his death. His son was immediately crowned at Kelso in what appears to have been an impressive ceremony, attended by the queen mother, bishops, and other nobles; and a hundred knights were created. It may be that they were immediately used to help take the castle of Wark, which was seized and demolished.[1] On the whole, the new government seems to have acted with vigour and determination to mitigate the effects of James II's early and unexpected death, and too much should not be read into the remark by the author of the Brief Latin Chronicle that, following the death of the king, there was 'tumult in Edinburgh'.[2] This probably refers to the popular reaction to the news of James II's death; it hardly indicates a breakdown in central government.[3]

Some ten years later, recalling the political situation at the outset of the reign, James III remarked that parliament — presumably the first parliament of the reign, in February 1461 — had confirmed an act of the previous reign making it high treason to lay hands on the sovereign without parliamentary consent; and the custody of the young king had been given to his mother, Mary of Gueldres, and the

51

lords of her council.[4] This is confirmed by the Auchinleck chronicler, who states that parliament 'left the king in keeping with his modere the qwene and gouernyng of all the kinrik'.[5] Mary of Gueldres was clearly a capable and determined politician, and she made a number of new appointments early in 1461. She put in her own men as keepers of Edinburgh, Stirling, and Dunbar castles immediately after the conclusion of the parliament. These were Andrew Keir in Edinburgh, Lord Hailes in Dunbar, and Robert Liddale in Stirling.

However, the queen's most controversial appointment was that of James Lindsay, provost of the collegiate church of Lincluden, as Keeper of the Privy Seal. Auchinleck, cryptic as ever, remarks that Lindsay also became the queen's 'principal counsellor', 'nochtwithstanding that she said master James was excludit fra the counsall of the forsaid King (James II) and fra the court and for his werray helynes and had bene slane for his demeritis had nocht bene he was redemit with gold'. We can only speculate about the events which had caused Lindsay's earlier disgrace; but it may well be significant that he first appears in official records as Keeper of the Privy Seal on 12 January 1453, that is, during the period of James II's temporary reconciliation with the ninth earl of Douglas. As provost of Lincluden, in the heart of the Black Douglas estates, Lindsay must have had a keen personal interest in the civil war between the king and the Douglas earls; and as a supporter of the queen, he may well have reacted strongly against James II's bond of manrent with the ninth earl of 16 January 1453, by which the king promised to give Douglas re-entry into the earldom of Wigtown and thereby deprive the queen of a large part of her dower.[6] Resistance to this bond was sufficiently strong to frustrate James II's policy, and Lindsay may well have been dismissed for opposing his sovereign on a matter of principle. Certainly his tenure of the Keepership of the Privy Seal was short, probably a mere six months from January to July 1453; and it may be that it was the queen who 'redemit' Lindsay with gold. Whatever the details of his disgrace, however, there is no doubt that Lindsay was no mere timeserver, but a capable administrator who continued in office after Mary of Gueldres' death, and was made Treasurer in 1468.[7]

In spite of her vigour and determination — or perhaps because of it — the queen mother was criticised both for her policies and her personality. The Auchinleck chronicler sourly remarks that 'thai did littill gud in the forsaid parliament' (the parliament of February 1461) and 'the lordis said that thai war littill gud worth, bath spirituale and temporall, that gaf the keping of the kinrik till a woman'.[8] Such statements possibly reflect the male chauvinism of the politically active nobility of the day, but more specifically they may be taken to refer to the breach between Mary of Gueldres and Bishop James Kennedy. With his almost unfailing political instinct for being in the wrong place at the wrong time, Kennedy was abroad, either in France or the Low Countries, when James II was killed at Roxburgh. He does not appear to have returned to Scotland until sometime in 1461, and was probably not present at the parliament of February 1461.[9] In short, he returned to a Scotland in which the queen mother had already managed to acquire the lion's share of power in the royal government, and had appointed her own supporters to important posts. Friction between Kennedy and Queen Mary was therefore inevitable, the more so because they held conflicting views on Scottish foreign policy. The queen mother, as niece of the Duke of Burgundy, was naturally reluctant to commit herself to the Franco-Lancastrian axis favoured by Kennedy, and inclined more to her late husband's policy of playing off both sides in the English civil war to Scotland's advantage on the borders. Kennedy, on the other hand, was pro-French by conviction, and while lying ill at Bruges sometime in 1460 he had been exhorted by Charles VII of France to return to Scotland and use his influence on the Scottish council in favour of the Lancastrian Henry VI.

Long after the bishop's final return to Scotland, he was to be found fulminating against Mary of Gueldres in a despatch to the French king, explaining that he had 'found a great division in the country caused by the Queen, whom God pardon, from which there resulted a great dissension between the said Queen and me and great likelihood of slaughter between the kinsmen and friends of either party'. This statement simply reflects the factions inevitable in royal government during a minority; and Kennedy, by his own admission, was clearly the leader of a group opposed to the queen, and therefore contributed to the divisions about which he was complaining. Yet in the same despatch Kennedy was able to boast that it was his patience and skill in diplomacy which secured Mary of Gueldres' support for a pro-Lancastrian policy, remarking with engaging naivety that 'the great lords of the realm' were against such a policy, designed as it was simply to please the king of France.[10]

The truth may have been that much of Kennedy's complaint was the sour grapes of the disappointed office seeker; because from James II's death in August 1460 until the autumn of 1463 — that is, until the last months of Mary of Gueldres' life — it is impossible to ascribe to him a major role in Scottish politics. He returned home late, possibly as late as the spring of 1461; he was not made an officer of state, and very rarely appears as a charter witness before September 1463. He was not appointed as an auditor of exchequer until 1464, after the queen's death, and he does not appear to have been present at the Edinburgh parliament of October 1462. As primate of Scotland, and a man with powerful family connections, Kennedy must have had some political influence; but government was clearly in the hands of the queen and counsellors appointed either by her or by James II towards the end of his life.

These appointments, for three of which the queen was personally responsible, in fact created a remarkable stability and continuity of service on the royal council. James Lindsay, the Privy Seal, had been employed by James II and was to continue in that office until 1468, when he was appointed Treasurer. Andrew Stewart, Lord Avandale, made Chancellor by James II in 1460, held the office for the remarkable period of 22 years. Most striking of all, however, was the career of Archibald Whitelaw, humanist, diplomat, and tutor to the young James III. Clerk Register between 1461 and 1462, by August 1462 he had been promoted to Royal Secretary, a post which he was to hold for over 31 years, until October 1493.[11] To these names may be added David Guthrie of Kincaldrum, later Sir David Guthrie of that ilk, who began his public career as Treasurer in 1461, was Comptroller during the period of the Boyd ascendancy after 1466, Clerk Register between 1468 and 1473, and close enough to James III to be appointed Captain of the royal guard in 1473-4.[12] Among the higher nobility, by far the most significant politically was Colin Campbell, earl of Argyll, already a charter witness in the latter years of James II's reign, a constant attender of parliaments in the 1470s and 1480s, a royal councillor during the same period, Master of the Royal Household from 1465 to 1482, Chancellor from 1483 to 1488 and again at the beginning of James IV's reign. Rightly described by Professor A. L. Brown as '*the* man of business at this period', Argyll first came into prominence when, together with Lindsay, Avandale, Whitelaw, Guthrie and the Bishops of Glasgow and Galloway, he served as an exchequer auditor in July 1462.[13]

In short, these men, the dominant personalities in the government of Mary of Gueldres, were to continue in office throughout much of the reign of her son; and with the exception of Lindsay, who died too early, they were to be close to James III not merely in the sense that they were key political figures, but also because they were attached to the royal household, as in the case of Argyll, Guthrie, and Whitelaw, or received remarkable gifts from the king, Avandale above all. Thus the counsellors on whom James III was to rely when he entered upon his adult rule in 1469 had been chosen for office either by his father towards the end of his reign, or his mother as the young king's guardian in the early 1460s. This argues the wisdom of both, especially Mary of Gueldres, and makes it impossible to regard the minority as a period of chaos, faction, and governmental instability.

That it has been viewed in this way is attributable to three factors — first, the concern of the new government that the queen 'suld nocht intromit with his (the king's) profettis bot allanerlie with his person', that is, that she should have the keeping of her son but not the royal revenues; secondly, later stories, perhaps inspired by Kennedy's despatch and the wild tales of the Lancastrian Duke of Somerset, successfully besmirched Mary of Gueldres' reputation for centuries; and third and most important, the queen's shift from an apparently pro-Lancastrian to a pro-Yorkist foreign policy by 1462 was viewed with disfavour by Kennedy and his supporters.

Each of these factors, however, admits of a different interpretation than that of the queen's public and private wilfulness. First, it was hardly surprising that the first parliament of the new reign should seek to distinguish very clearly between the queen's dower lands and revenues and the royal income, as the former had been one of the principal causes of the civil war between James II and the Douglases, while the latter had been the subject of legislation — the Act of Annexation — as recently as 1455, when parliament had complained that the poverty of the crown was the direct result of too many alienations of royal lands.[14] In 1461, therefore, there would be a natural concern not to slip back into the situation which had provoked the political struggles of the '50s; and it is likely that Mary of Gueldres, in an uncertain situation after her husband's death, was concerned to have parliament guarantee her wealth, and was herself one of the prime movers in making a clear distinction between her own revenues and those of the Crown.[15]

Secondly, the queen's bad reputation in her private life, a favourite theme of sixteenth century writers and still confidently accepted as fact, can be shown to be myth. As recently as 1974, Dr. Nicholson collated the tales about the queen mother which were circulating by the early sixteenth century, and in accepting all of them, helped to perpetuate the legend of a neurotic and unstable woman who caused sorrow to the wise Bishop Kennedy and aroused contempt amongst the Scottish nobility' 'The queen's policy,' we are told, 'was perhaps not uninfluenced by personal factors. For it was rumoured that she had had a love affair with the refugee Lancastrian Duke of Somerset, that he had spread abroad the news of his amorous conquest, and that Mary, finding herself scorned, had in a fit of repugnance urged Patrick Hepburn, Lord Hailes, to try to slay the duke. If he tried he failed, but his son, Adam Hepburn, was to replace the duke in the queen's affections. Adam, the Master of Hailes, was seeking a divorce from his wife, and the queen's relationship with him 'caussit hir to be lichtlieit (scorned) witht the haill nobilietie of Scotland'. (A quote from the chronicler Pitscottie.) 'Mary of Gueldres ensconced herself in Dunbar castle, of which her lover's father, Lord Hailes, was keeper, and was doubtless the source of the 'evil and peril' and 'great division' of which Bishop Kennedy complained'.[16]

Such a story is of course convenient in that it explains in the crudest terms Mary of Gueldres' shift in foreign policy from Lancaster to York. The Lancastrian Somerset was no longer her lover, so the queen responded by rushing to Dunbar castle and Hepburn of Hailes, and could later be consigned to that curious group in later medieval Scottish history — the parade of promiscuous queen mothers, widows of James I, James II, and James IV, who lacked the good taste to die before their husbands and whose amorous exploits once they were free of them blackened their reputations and provided wonderful copy for the chroniclers. In the case of Mary of Gueldres, however, the problem is that there is no convincing contemporary evidence for the queen's frenetic changing of lovers. The earliest appearance of the story is in the 'Annals' of William Worcester, who as a servant of Sir John Fastolf was at least contemporary with the events of the 1460s.[17] But Worcester's 'Annals' do not really place us on very safe ground, partly because he did not write them, but merely added interpolations to a manuscript already in his possession; and partly because, as K. B. MacFarlane points out,[18] the handwriting in the 'Annals' covering the period 1459 to 1463 is the same as that at the end of the work, which describes an event — the death of Stillington, bishop of Bath — in 1491. In short, it seems very likely that the part of Worcester's 'Annals' relating to the early 1460s is of late 15th century date rather than strictly contemporary, and that there exists no surviving written tale of Mary of Gueldres' fornication with Somerset and Hepburn until a full generation after it supposedly occurred. The story as it appears in Worcester includes the queen's affair with Somerset, and recounts that he offended her by making it public later, telling, among others, Louis XI of France, whereupon Mary reacted by urging Patrick Hepburn, Lord Hailes, to try to kill Somerset.

Subsequent stories are all of sixteenth century date, and presumably include borrowings from Worcester or Worcester's source. Thus in 1521 John Major, in his 'History of Greater Britain', adds the information that after the Somerset affair, the queen transferred her affections to Adam Hepburn, son of Patrick, Lord Hailes, who was seeking a divorce from his wife at the time; and in 1579 Lindsay of Pitscottie included the colourful detail that the queen's relationship with Hailes led to her being scorned by the entire Scottish nobility. There is even a variation of these tales by the sixteenth century antiquary John Leland, who in his *Itinerary* remarks that Mary of Gueldres was suspected of adultery with one of the Greys of Northumberland. Grey is rumoured to have come to Edinburgh to challenge his accuser, but no combat took place.[19]

None of these stories appears in the only contemporary Scots chronicle of the period, the Auchinleck chronicle, in spite of the fact that the author gives lengthy descriptions of the death of James II and the problems of the queen mother's government in the early years of the minority. This is not simply caution on the part of a contemporary who did not wish to offend Mary of Gueldres, for Auchinleck's sour remarks about the government of women in general, and about the queen's choice of Privy Seal and keepers of the principal royal castles, make it clear that he did not sympathise with the queen.[20] This makes his omission of awful revelations of adultery the more surprising, and prompts the question as to the validity of the source or sources on which later chroniclers relied.

It may be added that the sixteenth century chroniclers do not all blacken the queen's reputation. Bishop John Lesley, whose vernacular *History of Scotland* appeared in 1568, hopelessly confused the events of Mary of Gueldres' regency in the 1460s, but says nothing at all about adultery, remarking simply that the queen mother died in 1463 and was buried in her own foundation, the Church of the Holy Trinity in Edinburgh. It is not altogether surprising that Lesley, one of the foremost defenders of Mary Queen of Scots, has nothing to say on the subject of the adultery of queens; but even George Buchanan, who suffered from no such inhibitions, is vague about Mary of Gueldres, saying that 'by giving ear to flatterers, she flung herself to her ruin upon unsafe and craggy precipices'. No details are given; but Buchanan was certainly able to distinguish between flattery and fornication, and one feels that he would have done so in no uncertain terms if the necessary stories had been available to him.[21]

Herein lies the key to the problem. For the one thing which links all these chroniclers — with the possible exception of Worcester — is their lack of motivation in producing stories of this kind. If blackening the queen's name had an immediate political purpose in the early 1460s — as it had, for example, for Kennedy and Worcester's source — that purpose was long since gone by the third and later decades of the following century. It follows that the sixteenth century chroniclers simply did not know what had happened during the early minority of James III; but stories would certainly be passed on about his mother as head of the government, the founder of Trinity College, Edinburgh, and the builder of Ravenscraig castle in Fife. Oral tradition is not a good source for the accurate transmission of information in any age, and the Scottish parliament's concern about the activities of 'lesing makars' — professional tale-bearers whose chief crime was in stirring up trouble between sovereign and lieges — is the subject of repeated legislation in the fifteenth and sixteenth centuries. Thus it is understandable that Worcester's annalist, Major and the rest received a garbled version of the events of the early 1460s, and the variety of stories about the queen's adultery is hardly surprising. The recurrent leitmotif, however, is that her lovers were Somerset and Adam Hepburn of Hailes, the place Dunbar castle.

It is of course possible that the Duke of Somerset, finding himself very clearly on the losing side in the English civil wars by 1462, and blaming this on Mary of Gueldres' desertion of the Lancastrian cause, was the originator of the assault on the queen's reputation. But it seems much more likely that there is a simpler explanation. In his history, John Major, after remarking that Mary of Gueldres had not kept her chastity, but 'dealt lewdly' with Adam Hepburn of Hailes, a married man, continued pompously: 'Now I say that this woman was herein exceeding careless, for she should rather have taken a lord who had no wife, or the heir of some lord; and she thus acted more wickedly than did the wife of James the First'.[22] The wife of James I was the Duke of Somerset's daughter, Joan Beaufort, who died in 1445, that is only eighteen years before Mary of Gueldres. Having survived James I by over eight years, Joan Beaufort remarried, her new husband being James Stewart, 'the Black Knight of Lorne', but far more remarkable are the circumstances surrounding her death. On the losing side in a political power struggle during the minority of James II, she took refuge in Dunbar castle, whose keeper was Sir Adam Hepburn of Hailes, and died there on 15 July 1445.[23] Herein surely lies the explanation for the garbled sixteenth century tales. Two queen mothers have obviously been confused; and the association of Joan Beaufort, *not* Mary of Gueldres, with Adam Hepburn and Dunbar is supported by contemporary chronicle and record evidence. The fact that Joan Beaufort remarried after her husband's death was the starting point for later stories of adultery, and the Duke of Somerset, dragged in as Mary of Gueldres' lover, was in fact Joan Beaufort's father. So much for oral evidence and the passage of time; for entirely understandable reasons, the chroniclers of later generations have attacked the reputation of the wrong queen mother.

It remains to consider Mary of Gueldres' foreign policy, described by a recent writer as 'wayward'. This presumably means that the queen mother negotiated with, or lent support to, both Lancastrians and Yorkists in the English civil war, inclining towards the winning side as far as possible; and such a policy might perhaps be described as intelligent rather than wayward. The years 1460–63 saw a number of startling political upsets, and the appearance of a new dynasty, in England; and a rigid approach to English affairs by the Scots — Bishop Kennedy consistently advocated support for the Lancastrians and alliance with France — would hardly have been in Scotland's best interests.

In fact, Mary of Gueldres inherited and continued — arguably more ably — her husband's policy of playing off Lancaster and York in order to make territorial or diplomatic gains for Scotland. Roxburgh had been taken by the Scots in August 1460; and in the same autumn there followed the curious compromise whereby the Duke of York was recognised as the heir of the Lancastrian Henry VI. Margaret of Anjou, Henry's wife, was outraged by this settlement because it disinherited her son Prince Edward, and she came to Scotland in the early winter of 1460 to ask for an alliance and military assistance against the Duke of York. There were good reasons for Mary of Gueldres' interest in such a scheme at the time. The Lancastrians had considerable strength in the north, and it was not at all clear that the Yorkist government in London could survive for any length of time. So a conference was held between the two queens in the collegiate church of Lincluden, probably in December 1460; Auchinleck records that it lasted ten or twelve days and that the proposals included a marriage between Edward, Prince of Wales, and young King James's elder sister Mary.[24] These proposals, and the later overtures to the Yorkists in April 1462, show Mary of Gueldres' concern to acquire the firm friendship of the English government of the day, and strikingly anticipate her son's pro-English policies after 1474. The queen mother, as the niece of the Duke of Burgundy, may have been initially reluctant to commit herself to the English Lancastrian cause and the French alliance which it might involve; but she was realistic enough to appreciate that substantial gains might be made through such a policy. Margaret of Anjou and the Lancastrian cause appeared to be in the ascendant when in the same month as the Lincluden conference, on 30 December 1460, Richard, Duke of York, was defeated and killed at Wakefield. The Lancastrian queen, with a large army which included Scots, Welsh, and English Northerners, hurried south and won a further battle at St. Albans in February 1461. The total collapse of the English Yorkist faction seemed imminent; and it appeared that Mary of Gueldres, at this stage doubtless with the backing even of Bishop Kennedy, had chosen the right course.[25]

However, Lancastrian successes were remarkably shortlived. On 4 March, within only a fortnight of St. Albans, Richard duke of York's son Edward had proclaimed himself king as Edward IV, and before the end of the month had confirmed his new status with a shattering victory at Towton. Thus when Margaret of Anjou returned to Scotland in April she came as a refugee, bringing with her the deposed and feeble-minded Henry VI, her son Prince Edward, and the Dukes of Exeter and Somerset. Her bargaining position was clearly much weaker, and she began by surrendering the coveted burgh of Berwick to the Scots, at the same time promising also to cede Carlisle. Berwick was still strategically important as the gateway to the East March; but economically the burgh had seen a sharp decline from its prosperity in the early fourteenth century, before the English occupation.[26] However, the recovery of Berwick must have given a considerable psychological lift to the new Scots government. Some doubt must remain as to whether the Lancastrian fugitives handed the burgh over because it had become indefensible; certainly there exists a reference in the exchequer accounts of the Earldom of March for the year ending 1461 to a payment made for bringing a gun known as the queen's bombard from Berwick to Trinity College in Edinburgh, which would suggest that the Scots were ready to attack, or had attacked, Berwick before it was surrendered to them. Carlisle was a different proposition. A combined Scottish and Lancastrian army laid siege to the town in May 1461, a month after the surrender of Berwick, but were repulsed with heavy losses by the Yorkist Lord Montagu.[27]

By this stage, of course, the object of the Lancastrian exercise was to acquire not only Scottish hospitality but also armed assistance to recover their position in England. Mary of Gueldres, clearly assessing the English situation accurately, was prepared to grant the Lancastrian fugitives accommodation for a full year, first at

Linlithgow and later at the Dominican convent in Edinburgh; but she recognised them at this stage for what they were — refugees who might be politically useful to bring pressure to bear on the new Yorkist government, but not allies whom the Scots might assist militarily with any prospect of gain. There is something rather pathetic about Margaret of Anjou's pledging of a gold cup to the Scottish queen mother in return for a gift — or loan — of 100 crowns, while at about the same time Mary of Gueldres was displaying her political realism by sending an embassy headed by Lord Hamilton to explore the possibility of a truce with the Yorkist government of Edward IV.[28]

It took time for the queen mother's overtures to meet with any success, and both sides spent much of 1461 and early 1462 assessing each other's strength and ability to make trouble. The Scottish government had the Lancastrian fugitives as useful pawns in this diplomatic game; as for Edward IV, his obvious course was to make use of the disinherited ninth Earl of Douglas and such highland allies as Douglas might muster. In fact remarkably little came.of this scheme, which Andrew Lang erroneously describes as an attempt 'to stab Scotland in the back with the Celtic dirk'. The truth was that there was already considerable unrest in the West Highlands, part of a local feud between Colin Campbell, earl of Argyll, on the one hand, and John Macdonald, earl of Ross, and his kinsman, Donald Balloch, on the other. Ross had already been summoned to appear before parliament as a defendant — doubtless at Argyll's instigation — in February 1461, and negotiations for an understanding between Ross and the government were still in progress in June, when a deputation headed by the Bishops of St. Andrews and Glasgow interviewed him in Bute.[29] Whether any accommodation was arrived at is not recorded, but we know that Ross eventually joined with Donald Balloch and Douglas in making an indenture with Edward IV in February 1462, in which there was laid out a grandiose scheme whereby all three would become the liegemen of the English king and assist him in his wars in Scotland and Ireland. If Scotland should be conquered, it would be divided among all three as vassals of Edward IV, with Douglas acquiring the lion's share, the whole of Scotland south of Forth.[30]

Too much should not be made of this. It was common practice for exiled and forfeited Scots to become pensioners of the king of England, and to be used by him to join any disaffected Scottish lords to cause trouble for the Scots government. The London indenture should be judged by its effect rather than its avowed intentions, and the principal result of it was to produce a repeat performance of Ross's 1452 treasons, when he had seized the royal lands and castle of Urquhart and Glen Moriston in Inverness-shire. In the late spring or early summer of 1462, with the same allies as he had used a decade before, Ross attacked Crown lands near Inverness, and when he met with resistance the following year, laid them waste by fire.[31] This was serious enough because the royal government was not immediately in a position to cope with it;[32] but it hardly constituted more than a local threat, and had little effect on negotiations between the government of Mary of Gueldres and the Yorkists, which by the winter of 1461–2 were already well advanced.

In September aand again in November 1461 safe-conducts were issued by Edward IV for Scottish embassies to come south to discuss a truce; and included among the ambassadors was the queen mother's own choice as Privy Seal, Master James Lindsay. If common sense alone had not dictated such a policy, Mary of Gueldres' position as the niece of Duke Philip of Burgundy, the powerful and disaffected vassal of the king of France, would probably have contributed to produce it. The duke had already sent an ambassador, the Sieur de la Gruythuse, to Scotland in the winter of 1460–1 to encourage the queen mother to support the Yorkists,[33] and when she started to incline towards them as the victors of spring 1461, using the resources of the Scottish government for the purpose, the pro–French and –Lancastrian Kennedy was naturally alarmed. By March 1462 Mary of Gueldres had paid considerable sums to be rid of Margaret of Anjou, who sailed from Kirkcudbright to Brittany in April to plead her doubtful cause before Louis XI. In the same month the Scottish queen mother met the Yorkist Earl of Warwick at Dumfries, and discussed a long truce which would be sealed by royal marriages, perhaps even between the queen mother herself and Edward IV. Further talks followed at Carlisle in June 1462, but it seems clear that the Scots were divided on the subject of peace with England, and that Bishop Kennedy had by this stage emerged as the main opponent of Mary of Gueldres.[34]

There followed a year of complex diplomatic negotiations, alarms and excursions, in which the queen mother's pro-Yorkist policy was thwarted partly by Kennedy, who managed to hold up the sending of envoys to England, and partly by the third arrival of Margaret of Anjou in Scotland, in October 1462. The Lancastrian queen's interview with Louis XI of France had been partially successful, and with some French aid she was able to recover the northern castles of Alnwick, Bamburgh and Dunstanburgh. But the Yorkist retaliation reversed this result, and Queen Margaret, Henry VI and Pierre de Brezé, seneschal of Normandy, escaped to Berwick and once again became refugees in Scotland. Clearly they were an acute embarrassment to the government, and their promises to the Scots in return for assistance had become increasingly preposterous as their chances of success in England diminished. Thus the Earl of Angus was offered an English dukedom in return for armed assistance to restore Henry VI; English rumours circulated to the effect that Margaret of Anjou had promised the young James III seven English sheriffdoms and a marriage alliance, and even that Kennedy was to be rewarded with the archbishopric of Canterbury.[35]

The sequel to all this was the rescue of the Lancastrian garrison at Alnwick in January 1463, the result of a raid into Northumberland by the Earl of Angus and de Brezé; and in July 1463 a full-scale military operation, involving the refugee Lancastrian king and queen, Mary of Gueldres, and James III, was mounted, the object being the capture of Norham castle. The project was ill-conceived from the start, and it must be doubted whether the queen mother wholeheartedly supported it. After all, she had recently negotiated personally with Warwick, the Yorkist commander in the north of England; and there was the practical consideration, as Scofield puts it, that 'no-one who did not wilfully shut his eyes to the truth could fail to see that the king of France had practically abandoned Henry (VI) and Margaret (of Anjou) to their fate'.[36] It is probable that this apparent contradiction in the queen mother's policy is to be explained by the growing influence of Kennedy.

We may date his dominance in public affairs from the autumn of 1463; and this may coincide with a decline in the health of Mary of Gueldres, who died before the end of the year.[37] Her premature death has tended to obscure the fact that the foreign policy being pursued late in 1463 was not hers but Kennedy's; and it was neither successful nor realistic. The attack on Norham proved a total failure, the Scots retreating when the Earl of Warwick approached; and the subsequent devastation of the borders by Warwick and Douglas was regarded as serious enough to require Kennedy and the young king to consider taking the field against the Yorkists. In fact the danger soon passed; and the Black Douglas family lost another of its male members, Lord Balveny, who was captured during a raid on the borders, taken to Edinburgh and executed.[38] This was, however, small consolation for the Scots failure at Norham; and Margaret of Anjou, perhaps seeing the writing on the wall at last, left her feeble husband in Scotland and sailed from Bamburgh with her son to plead her cause before Duke Philip of Burgundy. This move speaks eloquently of her awareness of her position as a refugee looking for help in any quarter, even that of an enemy. She did not find that help, nor did she return to Scotland.

It is, perhaps, one of the greatest ironies in the political history of the period that when Bishop Kennedy had at last acquired the dominant role in government which he had been seeking for so long, his foreign policy collapsed almost at once, and that of his rival Mary of Gueldres was vindicated. On 8 October 1463, Louis XI of France and Edward IV agreed to a truce, and the French king casually omitted to include Scotland in its provisions.[39] Well might Kennedy remark that 'the whole of the said realm was much dismayed'; but he himself was the cause of that dismay. His wholehearted commitment to France and the House of Lancaster had left Scotland in a dangerous position, and his maladroit diplomacy was redeemed only by the skill of Mary of Gueldres in setting a firm precedent for negotiations with the victorious Yorkists.

Close examination of Mary of Gueldres' career after James II's death, therefore, shows that her foreign policy was shrewd and realistic, anticipating that of her son; that her sexual misadventures may be consigned to the realm of myth; and that her choice of royal counsellors was wise and enduring. We may assume that, as guardian of her son, she had a great influence on the young James III, who was already eleven-and-a-half when his mother died. The queen mother's considerable wealth is reflected in her building projects between 1460 and 1463. The royal carpenter worked for eighty days constructing a new chamber, fireplace and stable for Queen Mary at Falkland palace; but far more impressive was the queen's interest in Ravenscraig castle at Dysart in Fife. This was a new project, a powerful fortress on the Fife coast designed for use with artillery and involving payments of £600 to David Boys, the royal master of works, for building operations there in 1462 and 1463. Mary of Gueldres' keen interest throughout extended from her acquisition of the necessary land for building Ravenscraig in the spring of 1460 to her death in December 1463, when payments for the castle's construction abruptly cease.[40]

The queen mother's greatest expenditure, however, went on her collegiate church foundation on the southern slopes of the Calton Hill in Edinburgh, Holy Trinity Church. This was to comprise a provost, eight prebendaries, and two choristers, and attached to it would be a hospital for the support of thirteen persons. Holy Trinity is first mentioned in a Bull of Pope Pius II, dated 23 October 1460, authorising the annexation of the Hospital of Soutra to the new foundation; and this early date in the minority makes it likely that the idea had originally been that of James II.[41] The queen mother's expenditure on the planning and building of Holy Trinity was enormous, a total of almost £1100 in under three years; but in spite of this, and further building by James III throughout his reign, only the choir and transept of the church were completed by 1488, after which work on the building was probably abandoned. An impression of the interior of Holy Trinity is to be found in R. W. Billings' *Baronial and Ecclesiastical Antiquities of Scotland;* and it seems likely that the church has also bequeathed to us portraits by the Flemish painter Hugo Van Der Goes, not only of James III and his queen, Margaret of Denmark, but also of Trinity College's first provost, Sir Edward Bonkil, all of which probably formed parts of an altarpiece. It has even been suggested that in the portrait of Bonkil, the angel sitting behind him playing the organ is intended to represent Mary of Gueldres herself, though this view does not appear to rest on any documentary evidence and has subsequently been disputed. The queen mother's personal interest in her foundation — other than financial — is however recorded in her insistence that 'no prebendary shall be appointed unless he shall be capable of reading and singing in plain chant and descant'; and all the prebendaries were required, every day in the year, 'to sing matins, high mass, vespers, and compline, with notes'.[42]

The death of Mary of Gueldres on 1 December 1463 removed Bishop Kennedy's major rival from the political scene and left the bishop, for the last eighteen months of his life, as the dominant figure in the Scottish government. His achievement during this period was necessarily limited; in foreign policy he was forced into a complete reversal of his former pro-Lancastrian position into an early acceptance of a lengthy truce with Yorkist England. The urgent necessity of immediate peace with England was underlined by a rumour, current in Scotland in 1464, that the cynical Louis XI might join forces with Edward IV to conquer Scotland — in fact a highly unlikely project, but one which emphasised Scotland's vulnerability when deserted by the French. Seven Scots commissioners were sent to York to negotiate a fifteen years' truce, ratified by the English king on 3 June 1464. Kennedy, who had been involved in many diplomatic missions during his career, was not one of the seven. Possibly he was unable to accept the collapse of his foreign policy with a good grace; but he was not sufficiently stricken to ignore the offer of a pension from Edward IV. Indeed, both Kennedy and Bishop Spens of Aberdeen soon became the recipients of annual pensions, totalling £366, from the English king.[43]

These pensions to Kennedy and Spens have been the subject of conflicting opinions among modern historians. Dr. Dunlop assumes that they were paid by Edward IV as compensation for an act of piracy which occurred some time before 8 July 1464. Returning home from Gueldres in a Scottish carvel, the young Duke of Albany and Bishop Spens — who had an English safe-conduct — were nevertheless captured by an English barge and held in England, either as prisoners or hostages to ensure the total abandonment of the Lancastrian cause by the Scots. Dunlop suggests that the English pensions to Kennedy and Spens were paid because the outraged Kennedy was prepared to withhold ratification of the truce of York unless compensation were made and the prisoners returned to Scotland. However, it seems at least as likely that the seizure of Albany and Spens occurred before, rather than after, the truce, for the English safe-conduct was issued on 20 April, six weeks before the York negotiations were concluded. Furthermore, Albany and Spens were not sent back to Scotland for over a year, by which time Kennedy was dead.[44] The truth may well have been that by 1464 Kennedy found his options in foreign policy closed. He had been abandoned by Louis XI of France, and to secure peace he was forced to accept whatever terms the Yorkists offered, even if they flagrantly violated both truce and safe-conduct. There is indeed something rather unconvincing about Kennedy's despatch of Sir William Monypenny to France to announce to Louis XI that suspicions were circulating about his good faith, that other European princes were courting the alliance of Scotland, that in particular both Burgundian and English marriage alliances had been proposed, that the French king should therefore hasten to send an embassy to Scotland, and that in the meantime he should write speedily to reassure the Bishop of St. Andrews of his goodwill. Louis probably assessed Kennedy's claims as little more than bluster, and there was no reply from France.[45]

If Kennedy's diplomatic position was so weak, it may be asked why Edward IV should bother to offer him a pension at all. The answer probably lies, as Nicholson suggests, in the only bargaining counter which the Scots retained, their threat of assistance to the Lancastrians, and particularly Henry VI, who had only recently left Scotland and whose whereabouts in the north of England, even after the defeat of his followers at Hexham in May 1464, were uncertain. It was certainly worth a few hundred pounds to Edward IV to ensure that Henry VI did not once again find a refuge in Scotland; and in addition to his pension to Kennedy, the English king applied pressure to the Scottish government not to support the fugitive Lancastrian ruler by holding the heir presumptive to the Scottish throne and the Bishop of Aberdeen in England for over a year. In the circumstances, it is difficult to agree with Dr. Dunlop's suggestion that Kennedy saw peace with England as 'the pivot of Scottish policy', or that he was enthusiastic about the truce. Although designed to last for fifteen years, it had done nothing to stop the cold war in the classic areas of friction between the two countries, on the borders and at sea; and it is probably significant that proposals for an Anglo-Scottish marriage alliance were made only after Kennedy's death. The bishop's English pension may therefore represent an attempt by Kennedy to save something from the wreck of his foreign policy; and such behaviour, as Nicholson mildly remarks, 'was not altogether irreproachable even by the standards of the time'.[46] Kennedy's death, in May 1465, eased the path towards better relations between Scotland and England. A month later, proposals for a much longer truce included the prospect of a marriage alliance between James III and an unnamed English bride; first Spens, and then Albany, were released to return home to Scotland; the fugitive Henry VI was captured by the Yorkists at

Bungerley Hippingstones in Lancashire in July; and finally an indenture made at Newcastle in December 1465 ambitiously prolonged the existing fifteen-year truce by another forty years, to terminate only in 1519.[47]

Kennedy's record in internal affairs in 1464–5 was much more impressive than his foreign policy. He had the good sense to recognise that the custody of the young king was vital to his domination of the royal government; and if James III himself is to be believed, a meeting of the estates, probably early in 1464, gave Kennedy the authority he sought.[48] Following the exchequer audit at Perth on 28 May 1464, the bishop accompanied the young king on the first of the reign's two royal progresses north of Forth. This was an elaborate visitation, lasting three months and involving the entire court in an itinerary which included Dundee, Aberdeen, Inverness, Elgin, and a second visit to Dundee on the return journey in September 1464.[49] The progress had two obvious functions — to show the royal government's concern to enforce law and order in the localities, and to bring the twelve-year-old king before his people more or less for the first time. Before 1464, we catch only occasional private glimpses of James III in one or other of the royal palaces, generally in the company of his brothers and sisters, at Stirling, Doune, and Falkland; and the premature death of his father at Roxburgh had necessitated James's hastily improvised coronation at Kelso, hardly in the public eye. A royal progress may have been planned for 1461–2, when the king was expected at both Aberdeen and Kildrummy, but these visits failed to take place. James III appears to have been present at the exchequer audit at Stirling on 6 July 1462, though this is hardly surprising as much of his youth seems to have been spent either in Stirling or Edinburgh.[50] Thus the progress of summer 1464 took the young king through parts of Scotland which he had never visited, and with him went all the big names in the government of the day — apart from Kennedy, described throughout rather pretentiously as 'uncle of the king', there were Chancellor Avandale, Colin, earl of Argyll, Master of the Royal Household, David, earl of Crawford, John Stewart, Lord Darnley, Secretary Whitelaw and Treasurer Guthrie; and during the fortnight which the king and court spent in Inverness in July, the Bishops of Moray, Ross, and Caithness came to the burgh, no doubt to affirm their loyalty to the new regime.

This lengthy progress was followed by further peregrinations by king and court during the winter of 1464–5. By October, they had returned to Edinburgh; but by late November, the entire court had moved to St. Andrews. Christmas was spent at Stirling; and by mid-March 1465, James III and his household had returned to St. Andrews, where they remained until June of that year, about a month after Kennedy's death.[51] Altogether this itinerary provides a remarkable contrast with the static royal administration of the 'seventies and 'eighties; in a single year, the king, his officers of state and household, had journeyed to the extreme limits of effective Stewart power in the north.

Beyond these limits lay the north-west, the domain of the chronic rebel John Macdonald, earl of Ross and Lord of the Isles. His defiance of the crown in 1452 and 1462 had passed temporarily unchallenged; but by 1464, the royal government apparently felt strong enough to take action against him. The prime mover in demanding this action must have been Colin Campbell, earl of Argyll, whose kinsman John Stewart, Lord Lorne and Innermeath, had been killed by Alan McCoule, one of Ross's tenants and supporters. The same 1464 parliament which gave Kennedy custody of the king also demanded that McCoule should be put to the horn, and accused Ross of ignoring royal letters on the subject. Indeed, one of the main reasons for the court's visit to Inverness in July 1464 may have been to force Ross to submit. Nothing so dramatic happened. The earl had to admit that, in 1463, in the course of laying waste Crown lands near Inverness, he had also seized £74 12/3d. from the burgh customs; but no severe punishment was meted out by the king and council, and a determined royal assault on Ross was delayed until the mid-1470s.[52]

Much of the business transacted by the royal administration during Kennedy's last winter concerned efforts to increase the resources and authority of the crown. The death of Mary of Gueldres and the subsequent recovery of her dower lands by the Crown produced an enormous increase — more than £4000 a year — in royal rents; and a general council meeting in Edinburgh on 11 October 1464, soon after the court's return from the north, provided for the immediate resumption of annexed crown lands which had been illegally alienated by James II. This general council, which was made up of clergy and nobility, but did not include the third estate, also made pious noises about securing 'the peace and tranquillity of the realm and doing justice', doubtless a reference to the holding of sessions in Edinburgh, Perth, and Aberdeen, a course already recommended twice by parliament, in 1461 and 1464.[53]

On 24 May 1465, Bishop Kennedy died at St. Andrews. His reputation with Scottish historians stands high, and rightly so, for he was far more than a political bishop. The breadth of his interests was remarkable. His concern for his diocese, most clearly seen in his foundation and endowment of St. Salvator's College, forms a sharp contrast with his cosmopolitan career as conciliarist, as diplomat throughout western Europe, and more prosaically, as merchant trading with the Hansa towns on the North Sea coast and in the Baltic. His political career within Scotland itself is altogether less remarkable, for in spite of a constant struggle to advance himself and his family, Kennedy was quite eclipsed by Bishop Turnbull of Glasgow as James II's most trusted ecclesiastic in the 1450s, and by Mary of Gueldres as head of the minority government of James III until 1463. Indeed, most of Kennedy's active political life was marred by blunders, such as backing the wrong side in the civil war of 1444–5, bad luck, seen in his absence abroad in the critical years 1452 and 1460, and intransigence, most clearly illustrated in his insistence on a Franco-Lancastrian alliance for Scotland long after it made any political sense. Ultimately it was only the deaths of luckier, or more able, people which gave Kennedy his dominant role in government between 1463 and 1465.

Even in this period we must be careful not to assume too much from the scanty evidence available. It was not until much later that John Major, in his *History* of 1521, remarked that Kennedy had charge of 'the whole government of Scotland' during James III's minority;[54] and there are clear contemporary indications that although he was the elder statesman of the period simply through having stayed the course, he did not have things all his own way even at the end. Kennedy himself, with remarkable frankness, more or less admits as much in his French despatch when he says that 'the great lords' of Scotland were opposed to his pro-French policy before 1463. Furthermore, there was no question of Kennedy making major changes in the royal administration after the queen mother's death. The same men remained in key offices throughout the '60s, and in some cases, very much longer — Avandale as Chancellor, Lindsay as Keeper of the Privy Seal, Whitelaw as Secretary, Guthrie as Treasurer, and the two 'political' earls, Crawford and Argyll, the latter as Master of the Royal Household, constantly present at court. Kennedy's name heads the list of witnesses to charters under the great seal during this period simply because he was the foremost ecclesiastic in the country, not because he was the only maker of policy. It seems likely, for example, that others were responsible at least for the act of resumption of October 1464; for in 1457 Kennedy himself had been one of the early beneficiaries of James II's illegal alienation of annexed crown lands.[55]

In the last analysis, therefore, Bishop Kennedy was not the force in Scottish politics of the '50s and '60s that he probably imagined himself to be, or at any rate that later writers have suggested he was. His acceptance of an English pension, the ostentation of his tomb, and the calculated magnificence of his barge, the 'Salvator', further point to a character who was worldly rather than saintly, attempting to impress contemporaries with his wealth and influence in the manner of a secular prince. In one area at least — control of the person of the young king — he was successful both for himself and his family. James III had after all been born at St. Andrews, probably in the episcopal castle, during the crisis of 1452; and this had given Kennedy a special claim on the gratitude of James II. After 1460, he had temporarily lost control of the new king, who seems to have been in the care either of Mary of Gueldres or the Earl of Orkney;[56] but in 1464, the estates had formally granted him the position of guardian of the king; and the bishop in turn placed James III in the care of his brother, Gilbert, Lord Kennedy, keeper of Stirling castle.[57]

On his deathbed, Kennedy must have had the satisfaction of being the centre of attention amidst a very distinguished company, for the king and the entire court were staying in St. Andrews at the time. One may speculate that James III was genuinely sorry to lose a loyal servant in whose castle he had been born almost exactly thirteen years before; but in no real sense was this the end of an era, nor can one agree with Dr. Nicholson that James was left 'at the mercy of lesser politicians'.[58] Quite apart from the fact that the officers of state and household remained unchanged after the bishop's death, his place as premier ecclesiastical statesman was rapidly taken first by Andrew Muirhead, bishop of Glasgow, and subsequently by Thomas Spens, bishop of Aberdeen, the latter's release from captivity in England and return to court occurring at the latest by 2 July 1465. Kennedy himself had tried to ensure that his family would retain political influence after his death when he lent his support to his nephew and eventual successor at St. Andrews, Patrick Graham, in elections to the see of Brechin in March 1463;[59] and more important, the person of the adolescent king was committed to the late bishop's brother, Gilbert, Lord Kennedy. There was therefore no obvious threat to the continuity or stability of the royal government in 1465.

NOTES

1. *Asloan MS.*, i, 230.

2. *Transactions of the Society of Antiquaries*, xxviii.

3. Both Dunlop, *Bishop Kennedy*, 213, and Nicholson, *op.cit.*, 398 (following Dunlop) make much of the gap in official records for some months, and claim this as 'evidence that chaos reigned'. This is hardly convincing; the gap in the Great Seal Register (1460-63) probably simply means that part of the register has been lost. There are similar gaps in James II's reign — for example, only one registered charter for 1440, none at all for 1443; but Mr. W. Scott has identified a very large number of royal charters for this period which are not to be found in the register. Similarly, although its statutes are not recorded in *A.P.S.*, the first parliament of the reign of James III was held in February 1461; and there is no gap at all in the Exchequer records.

4. C. A. J. Armstrong, 'A Letter of James III to the Duke of Burgundy', *S.H.S. Misc.*, viii, 19-32.

5. *Asloan MS.*, i, 232.

6. *See above*, Chapter 1.

7. *R.M.S.*, ii, Nos. 594-598 (for Lindsay as Privy Seal 1452-3); *ibid.*, Nos. 756-954 passim (for Lindsay as Privy Seal 1463-8).

8. *Asloan MS.*, i, 231-2.

9. Dunlop, *Bishop Kennedy*, 435 (Kennedy grants charter at St. Andrews, 2 May 1461); and *see above*, Chapter 2.

10. Kennedy's despatch, in Jehan de Waurin, *Anchiennes Cronicques D'Engleterre* (ed. Dupont, Société de l'Histoire de France, 1863), vol. III, 166. This despatch is discussed in Dunlop, *Bishop Kennedy*, 219-20, where the author interprets it rather differently.

11. *Handbook of British Chronology*, passim.

12. *Ibid.; R.M.S.*, ii, Nos. 1132, 1137, 1140-2, 1144-1152, 1155-1160, 1165-6, 1169-75 (for Guthrie as Captain of the royal guard).

13. Alfred L. Brown, 'The Scottish "Establishment" in the later 15th century', in *Juridical Review*, 1978, pt. 2, 96; *E.R.*, vii, 107.

14. *See above*, Chapter 2.

15. The queen's wealth was very considerable. Her own exchequer audit — at Edinburgh in July 1463 — shows almost £4,000 forthcoming from her dower lands, and there were in addition large quantities of victuals which may have brought the total real income of the queen to something like the £5,000 bestowed on her at the time of her marriage to James II: *E.R.*, vii, 161-200; Nicholson, *op.cit.*, 398-9.

16. *Ibid.*, 403-4.

17. *D.N.B.*, lxii, 441.

18. K. B. MacFarlane, 'William Worcester: A Preliminary Survey', in *Studies presented to Sir Hilary Jenkinson*, ed. J. Conway Davies (Oxford, 1957), 196-221.

19. Major, *History*, 388; Pitscottie, *Historie*, i, 158; Leland, *Itinerary*, v, 58.

20. *Asloan MS.*, i, 231-2.

21. Lesley, *History*, 36; Buchanan, *History*, ii, 133.

22. Major, *History*, 388.

23. For details, *see above*, Chapter 1.

24. *Asloan MS.*, i, 230-1.

25. For a detailed description of the complex manoeuvres of 1460-1, see Nicholson, *op.cit.*, 398-406, where however the author takes a rather different view of the actions of the Scottish queen mother.

26. The first accounts of the Berwick custumars after the Scottish reoccupation of the burgh were made at the Exchequer in 1465. Dr. Nicholson shows that the total customs amounted to only £31 5/1½d. See Nicholson, *op.cit.*, 400.

27. *E.R.*, vii, 99; *ibid.*, xxxviii.

28. *E.R.*, vii, xxxvi-xxxvii, 49, 145 (for reception of Henry VI and Margaret of Anjou); *ibid.*, 62, 80 (for the pledging of the gold cup); *Rotuli Scotiae*, ii, 402 (for Hamilton's mission to England, dated April 1461).

29. Andrew Lang, *History of Scotland*, i, 336; *Asloan MS.*, i, 231-2; *R.M.S.*, ii, No. 1196. Kennedy's presence in Bute on royal business in June 1461 is his first recorded employment by the new government; perhaps significantly, the mission appears to have been a failure.

30. *Rot. Scot.*, ii, 405-7. This indenture, dated London, 13 February, 1462, is sometimes referred to as the treaty of Westminster — Ardtornish.

31. *A.P.S.*, ii, 108-9; *E.R.*, vii, 347, 357.

32. Ross had been summoned to answer charges of treason in parliament; he did not appear, and the case was continued to 24 June 1462, when it was to be tried in parliament at Aberdeen. This however was adjourned because the king did not come: *Asloan MS.*, i, 232; *E.R.*, vii, 143.

33 Dunlop, *Bishop Kennedy*, 214-5.

34. This is clear from his 1463 despatch, in which he describes himself as a leader of a faction at odds with the queen, 'whom God pardon'. This despatch is cited in Jehan de Waurin, *Anchiennes Cronicques d'Engleterre* (ed Dupont, Société de l'Histoire de France, 1863), vol. III., 166.

35. Nicholson, *op.cit.*, 405.

36. Scofield, Edward IV, i, 274.

37. Dunlop, *Bishop Kennedy*, 435; *E.R.*, vii, liv-lv

38. Nicholson, *op.cit.*, 405.

39. Dunlop, *Bishop Kennedy*, 238.

40. *E.R.*, vii, 75, 78, 79, 106 (for Falkland); *ibid.*, 1, 78, 86; *R.M.S.*, ii, Nos. 746, 747 (for Ravenscraig).

41. Augustin Theiner, *Vetera Monumenta Hibernorum et Scotorum historiam illustrantia* (Rome 1864), 439, 442. As Soutra was held *in commendam* by the Cathedral of St. Andrews as the benefice of the Chancellor, Bishop Kennedy, Kennedy's attitude to its annexation to the queen mother's new foundation in Edinburgh may have been less than cordial, especially as his own collegiate church of St. Salvator in St. Andrews was not yet completed in 1460. It seems possible, therefore, that Mary of Gueldres' visit to St. Salvator's in Lent of 1461, when she made an offering in the cathedral and gave gifts to the masons, was designed to appease the bishop, and perhaps also heal the political breach which had divided them since his return to Scotland: cf. *E.R.*, vii, lii-liv, where the problems presented by this curious relationship are examined at greater length.

42. R. W. Billings, *The Baronial and Ecclesiastical Antiquities of Scotland*, (1845-52), vol. ii, plate 29; for the most modern and complete examination of the Trinity Panels by Van der Goes, see Colin Thompson and Lorne Campbell, *Hugo van der Goes and the Trinity Panels in Edinburgh* (National Gallery of Scotland, HMSO, 1974); for the more traditional view that the Bonkil portrait includes Mary of Gueldres, see David Laing's paper in *Proceedings of the Society of Antiquaries of Scotland*, iii, 8. For a general history of the church, see J. D. Marwick, *The History of the Collegiate Church and Hospital of the Holy Trinity and the Trinity Hospital, Edinburgh, 1460-1661* (S.B.R.S. publication, Edinburgh 1911).

43. Scofield, *Edward IV*, i, 349-50 (for the rumour of 1464); Rymer, *Foedera*, xi, 525 (for the truce of York); *Cal. Docs. Scot.*, iv, No. 1360 (for the English pensions).

44. Dunlop, *Bishop Kennedy*, 244-5 and 245 nn. 1, 2. For the return to Scotland of Spens, see *R.M.S.*, ii, No. 837 (2nd July, 1465). Albany's return was delayed (*E.R.*, vii, 401) beyond the start of exchequer year 1465-66, though he can be shown to be in Scotland some time during the same exchequer year (25 June 1465 to 9 July 1466), when he is to be found both at Falkland and on justice ayres (E.R., vii, 383, 384).

45. Dunlop, *Bishop Kennedy*, 246-7.

46. Dunlop, *Bishop Kennedy*, 245-6, 248; Nicholson, *op.cit.*, 406.

47. Rymer, *Foedera*, xi, 546; *Cal Docs. Scot.*, iv, Nos. 1362, 1363; *Rot. Scot.*, ii, 418-20.

48. Dunlop, *Bishop Kennedy*, 241 and n. 6. There is no reference either to a meeting of parliament or General Council in the printed *A.P.S.*

49. *R.M.S.*, ii, Nos. 796-810.

50. *E.R.*, vi, 3, 116, 280, 425, 583; vii, 143, 160, 223.

51. *R.M.S.*, ii, Nos. 821-834.

52. *A.P.S.*, xii, 31: 'Minutes of Parliament'; Nicholson, *op.cit.*, 406-7; *E.R.*, vii, 296-7.

53. Nicholson, *op.cit.*, 408-9; *A.P.S.*, xii, 31: 'Minutes of Parliament'.

54. Major, *History*, 387.

55. Dunlop, *Bishop Kennedy*, 162 n. 3; and *see above*, Chapter 2.

56. *Records of the Earldom of Orkney*, ed. J. Storer Clouston (S.H.S., 1914), 54; cited in Dunlop, *Bishop Kennedy*, 220.

57. *E.R.*, vii, 346, 392.

58. *R.M.S.*, ii, Nos. 831, 832; Nicholson, *op.cit.*, 409.

59. Dunlop, *Bishop Kennedy*, 251-2.

4

The Rise and Fall of the Boyds: 1466–69

TOO much has probably been made of the notorious Boyd coup — the seizure of the young king by the Boyds of Kilmarnock on 9 July 1466, just after the exchequer audit at Linlithgow — and of its effect on the last three years of the minority. Little more was involved than a struggle between the Kennedy and Boyd factions at court for possession of the person of the king, with the remainder of the politically active nobility and clergy looking on. Neither of the rival groups was new to the business of government, and there was no question during the three years of Boyd ascendancy of domestic or foreign policy being neglected or subverted in the interests of a solitary power group.

Nevertheless the coup itself was bound to create a considerable stir, if only because the Kennedy faction held the king before it, the Boyds after it. The prime mover in thus advancing his family's fortunes in the shortest possible time was Robert, Lord Boyd. Time was to show that he was a totally unscrupulous political gambler, but his career before 1466 was distinguished by fourteen years of loyal service to the crown. Created a Lord of Parliament by James II — probably in June 1452 — Boyd had sat in the parliament of 1455 which forfeited the Black Douglases, was subsequently used as an envoy to England in 1459 and 1464, and in the early years of the new reign he was much at court.[1]

Although his services had been rewarded with a lordship of parliament, Boyd was quite eclipsed, in terms of influence at court, by his younger brother, Sir Alexander Boyd of Drumcoll who, although only a knight, had honours showered on him throughout the early sixties. His success may have originated in his committed support of James II against the Black Douglases, for Auchinleck names him as one of the assassins of the eighth earl at Stirling in 1452. In the 1460s, Sir Alexander was not only a fairly regular royal charter witness, but acted as an auditor of exchequer on two occasions, sat in parliament, was made captain of Edinburgh Castle in 1464, and sometime before 1466 acted as the young king's instructor in chivalric exercises. Most important of all, by March 1466 he had become chamberlain of the royal household, and was thus in a unique position to help further the ambitions of his elder brother.[2]

Whether relations between the Boyd brothers were good at this time is impossible to say. Robert, Lord Boyd, may well have resented his younger brother's greater influence at court; at any rate, his plan for acquiring control of the king seems to have been based on using Sir Alexander to defeat the Kennedy faction, and then discarding him once the coup had been accomplished. Long and careful planning seems to have been involved, and a great deal of dissimulation on the part of Robert, Lord Boyd, in order to acquire his brother's support. We may trace some of this planning in two surviving bonds of friendship, made in January and February 1466, which point directly ahead to the Boyd coup in July.

The first of these, made by Robert, Lord Boyd, with Gilbert, Lord Kennedy, in Edinburgh on 20 January, departs from the usual form of such bonds by stating its purpose precisely. Lord Boyd promised to support Gilbert, Lord Kennedy, 'for als lang as he sal haf the kepyng of our soverane lordis persoun', and to prevent anyone else from removing the young king from Kennedy's keeping — a clear indication that James III was at Stirling during this period, the castle there being in Kennedy's custody. In the same agreement, Boyd mentioned bonds which he had already made with John, Lord Darnley, James, Lord Hamilton, Alexander, Lord Montgomery, Alexander, son and heir of Robert, Lord Lyle, and his own brother, Sir Alexander Boyd of Drumcoll — all west of Scotland men, and the sort of list likely to impress Kennedy. Finally, the bond was to be strengthened by a marriage alliance between 'James Boid my son and appeirand air, and Marioune, dochter to the said Lord Kennedy', the wedding to take place as soon as possible 'eftir the hame cumyng of the princhess' — presumably an early reference to the proposed Danish marriage for James III.[3]

Three weeks later, on 10 February 1466, evidence of this Kennedy-Boyd alliance is provided by a second bond of friendship, made this time at Stirling between Sir Alexander Boyd and Gilbert, Lord Kennedy, on the one hand, and Robert, Lord Fleming, on the other. Once again, possession of the person of the young king was the key issue. Fleming agreed that he would be 'of special service, and of cunsail to the Kyng, als lang as the saidis lordis Kenedy and Sir Alexander are speciall servandis and of cunsail to the Kyng'; and he promised not to remove James III, nor allow him to be removed, out of the keeping of Lord Kennedy and Sir Alexander Boyd. The parties then listed indentures which they had already made with other influential men: Lord Fleming had bonds with Lords Livingston and Hamilton; while Kennedy and Sir Alexander Boyd could list bonds not only with those two, but also with Patrick Graham, the new bishop of St. Andrews, David, earl of Crawford, and Lords Maxwell, Cathcart, and Boyd.[4]

It remains something of a mystery why Lord Kennedy and Sir Alexander Boyd felt it necessary to win the support of Robert, Lord Fleming, for the latter was not a man of any great political importance, his only known office having been a brief tenure of the Stewardship of the Royal Household in 1454.[5] An expression of Fleming's immediate gratitude was his promise to infeft his 'weilbelouit cousing' Gilbert, Lord Kennedy, and his heirs, in the lands of the barony of Thankerton in Lanarkshire; and Kennedy reciprocated by promising Fleming some lands in the barony of Lenzie in Dunbartonshire. This latter agreement was witnessed by Colin, earl of Argyll, William, Lord Forbes, Sir Alexander Boyd of Drumcoll, Sir John Colquhoun of that ilk, the Comptroller, Secretary Whitelaw, and three notaries, an indication that king and court were still at Stirling; and Fleming probably reckoned that he would do himself no harm in court circles by attaching himself to Kennedy and Sir Alexander Boyd, men who had 'arrived' and whose power seemed to be on the increase. Like Sir Alexander, Fleming had miscalculated and was soon to become one of the dupes of the Boyd coup.[6]

Thus by February 1466, the real instigator of the king's seizure in July, Robert, Lord Boyd, had carefully prepared the way by building up temporary support in the Edinburgh and Stirling indentures. The only reason for negotiating with Kennedy at all was that the latter had possession of the king at Stirling castle, and he was therefore inaccessible; and it seems highly unlikely that Boyd had any intention of marrying his son — whose name was not James, as the indenture states, but Thomas — to Lord Kennedy's daughter. His ambitions for his heir were much more exalted; but in the meantime the existence of the Kennedy-Boyd alliance would greatly increase Boyd's chances of securing the king, and his temporary ally was lulled into a false sense of security. On the other hand, Sir Alexander Boyd presumably knew what his brother intended, and was a party.to the coup in July; but he can have had no idea that his elder brother planned to discard him as soon as he had served his purpose.

The outcome of all this was the seizure of James III by the Boyds on 9 July 1466, a confusing affair about which there survive four accounts, three of them contemporary. First, three months after the event, a statement was made about it in parliament on 13 October 1466; secondly, the seizure is referred to twice in the parliamentary forfeiture of the Boyds on 22 November 1469; thirdly, in a letter written to the Duke of Burgundy, probably in 1471, James III described his abduction at some length. Finally, the only sixteenth century chronicler to describe the capture of the king was George Buchanan; and his account of the event, though often confused and inaccurate, contains some points of interest.[7]

The Boyd explanation of the coup, ratified and approved by parliament in Edinburgh in October 1466, understandably makes the least convincing reading. In what must have been a pre-arranged scene, Robert, Lord Boyd, appeared before the estates, knelt in front of the young king and enquired whether he bore any ill-will towards those who had taken him on horseback from his palace of Linlithgow, 'post scaccarium', to Edinburgh. Thereupon the king stated in a clear voice that this had been done at his command, and that consequently he would bear no rancour or malice, either at that time or in the future, towards those who were responsible. Four of those involved are named — Robert, Lord Boyd himself, Adam Hepburn, son and heir of Patrick, Lord Hailes, John, Lord Somerville, and Andrew Ker, son and heir of Andrew Ker of Cessford.[8]

Not surprisingly, the Boyd coup was described rather differently after the fall of the family three years later. Robert, Lord Boyd, and his son Thomas, according to the parliament of November 1469, had committed treason by removing James III, who was then 'in scaccario nostro apud burgum nostrum de Lynlythgw nono die mensis Julii (1466) contra nostre voluntatis libitum et in contrarium acti Parliamenti'. Thereupon, the indictment runs, they treasonably seized control of the government and assumed permanent authority over the actions of the king and his brothers. At the same time, Sir Alexander Boyd was accused of the treasonable seizure of the king, but significantly his indictment did not associate him with any of his brother's and nephew's acts after the 1466 coup.[9]

On 14 February of an unspecified year — probably 1471 — James III himself gave his own account of his seizure by the Boyds. The occasion was a letter written at Holyrood in reply to a request by Charles the Bold of Burgundy that Robert, former Lord Boyd, and his son Thomas might be pardoned for their treason committed against the person of the Scottish king. James described their crimes at length in his reply. Defying the law and the estates, Robert and Thomas Boyd had dared with a large armed band to fall upon him when, scantily attended, he was enjoying the pleasures of the chase. They carried him away whither they pleased despite his tears and without consulting him or the estates, governed the kingdom by themselves and, moreover, corruptly. Had Duke Charles known of their crimes, doubtless he would neither have intervened on their behalf nor admitted them to his territory, for one of their accomplices, Sir Alexander Boyd, had suffered execution and forfeiture, while a parliamentary sentence of death and confiscation had been passed on Robert and Thomas. James III concluded by refusing Burgundy's request for clemency for the Boyds and suggested that the duke ought no longer to favour traitors.[10]

The description of his seizure by the Boyds in James's letter to Burgundy differs somewhat from the parliamentary forfeiture of 1469, but is not in serious conflict with it. In 1469, parliament had accepted that the king had been abducted when he was sitting 'in scaccario', during the annual season of the auditors of exchequer — that is, during a council meeting — rather than on a hunting party after the exchequer audit; this served the function of making the occasion of the crime more serious, and from a legal point of view was more likely to secure a conviction in 1469. But the seizure of the king cannot have occurred during the meeting of the auditors; and the parliament of October 1466, only three months after the event itself, had accepted that James III was removed by the Boyds 'post scaccarium' at Linlithgow. This was no doubt the truth; out hunting after the close of the annual audit of the royal accounts, the king was captured and taken to Edinburgh.

It was understandable that the royal government, and the king personally, should seek to make the Boyd coup appear a heinous crime, and exaggerate its detrimental effect on the administration in the years following the family's fall. Yet the whole episode evoked remarkably little response from the later chroniclers, who had much to say about other episodes in this reign. Only one of them, George Buchanan, writing more than a century later, mentions the seizure of the king in 1466; and much of what he has to say is inaccurate. Thus he describes Gilbert, Lord Kennedy, throughout as John Kennedy; and he misdates the death of Bishop Kennedy of St. Andrews by one year, so that he appears to be alive at the time of the Boyd coup in July 1466. Buchanan's story of the seizure begins by stating that Lord Kennedy and Sir Alexander Boyd were the royal guardians, and the latter was the king's instructor in the rudiments of military tactics. Gradually, according to Buchanan, Sir Alexander acquired influence with James III, and suggested that he should free himself from Kennedy's tutelage. The actual seizure of the king took the form only of a quarrel between Lord Kennedy and Sir Alexander Boyd. The young king having gone off from Linlithgow to hunt without Kennedy's knowledge, he was pursued by Kennedy, who took the King's horse by the bridle and instructed him to return to the town, as he lacked a sufficient retinue for his protection; but at this point Kennedy was felled by a blow from Sir Alexander Boyd, and the hunting party continued on its way. The physical removal of the king to Edinburgh, in Buchanan's account, did not occur that day at all, but much later, as the result of a quarrel between the Kennedys and the Boyds, the former wishing to take the king to Stirling, the latter to Edinburgh. The Boyds having more power at the time, James III was led to Edinburgh without the authority of parliament, ostensibly to assume control of the government. Buchanan notes that the king's companions on the journey, apart from the Boyds, were Adam Hepburn, John Somerville, and Andrew Ker, each the chief of his family. He misdates the king's removal by one day, ascribing it to 10 July 1466, and concludes by stating that the Kennedys — the bishop and his brother — returned to their lands determined to revenge themselves on the Boyds.[11]

Despite the many inaccuracies, there are obviously elements of truth in all this. In broad outline, Buchanan's story is that the seizure of the king arose out of a dispute between the Kennedy and Boyd factions as to which should have control of the royal person; and this is probably the case. Gilbert, Lord Kennedy, prominent at court up to and including 1466, disappears from charter witness lists after the July coup, was replaced as Keeper of Stirling castle by Chancellor Avandale, and was even imprisoned in the castle for a time during the exchequer year 1466-7.[12] Buchanan is also able to name accurately those lords who assisted the Boyds in abducting the king from Linlithgow to Edinburgh; and his story of the hunting party is corroborated by James III's letter to Burgundy in 1471. The fact that the hunting party and the seizure are described by Buchanan as two separate events suggests that his information was derived from two independent sources, one of which, a parliamentary record for October 1466, supplied him with the names of Hepburn, Somerville, and Ker.

Thus the late Bishop Kennedy's promotion of his brother to ensure that the Kennedy faction would retain possession of the king, and considerable influence on the council, collapsed in little over a year. With remarkable cynicism, both Boyd brothers ignored the bonds which they had made in January and February, and acted together to abduct the king to Edinburgh before he could return to Kennedy's keeping at Stirling after the Linlithgow audit. This purpose accomplished, Sir Alexander Boyd now found to his cost that his unscrupulous elder brother had no further use for him. Sir Alexander's name vanishes from the witness lists to charters under the great seal after 13 August 1466, just over a month after the Boyd coup; he does not reappear as an auditor of exchequer after June-July 1466; nor is he to be found sitting in parliament. Most significant of all, he was relieved of the office of Keeper of Edinburgh castle after the first term of the exchequer year 1466-7, and replaced by his brother, Robert, Lord Boyd.[13] The conclusion is inescapable that Lord Kennedy and Sir Alexander Boyd were used throughout by Robert, Lord Boyd, on account of their intimacy with the young king and their positions as Keepers of Stirling and Edinburgh castles, and the final twist to the devious Boyd plot was the discarding of Sir Alexander once he had taken on the Kennedy faction and acquired the person of the king. In a sense, Sir Alexander Boyd, not James III, was the principal victim of 1466.

On the other hand, it may well be asked what made the victor, Robert, Lord Boyd, think that he could get away with all this. Even in Scotland, the abduction of kings during a minority was a dangerous business for those directly involved, and any temporary gains made were liable to be reversed — or worse — when the monarch came of age. Yet the wisdom of hindsight was not possible for Boyd in 1466, or the Douglases in 1526, or for that matter the Ruthven Raiders in 1582. Robert, Lord Boyd, could certainly remember the Livingston ascendancy during the minority of James II, and its abrupt termination with the disgrace of the family in 1449-50.[14] Yet James Livingston, who as Keeper of Stirling castle had had direct control of the person of the young James II, had soon been restored to his lands, had been made a lord of parliament in 1455, and by 1466 he was Chamberlain. So if Boyd was in any sense modelling himself on Livingston, the precedent was not one which suggested that his 1466 coup would necessarily lead to ruin later.

The difference between Livingston and Boyd, though this was not immediately apparent, lay in the latter's greed. He was already a lord of parliament; and the same October parliament which declared him guiltless of the abduction of James III from Linlithgow also created him governor of the person of the king and of his two brothers until James should reach the age of twenty-one, made him responsible for the execution of the royal authority and justice, and keeper of the royal castles. These enactments, made at Edinburgh on 13 October 1466, were rapidly confirmed by royal charters granted at Stirling on the 25th of the same month.[15] So far so good; Boyd had not upset the equilibrium of the royal government. In a sense he had done its chief men a service by breaking the Kennedy hold on king and court, and by taking on the thankless task of governor of the royal person. Service merited reward, and the fees which Boyd would receive from his keeperships of the royal castles were not an excessive price to pay. Thus both Chancellor Avandale and Colin, earl of Argyll, Master of the Royal Household, had no reason to oppose the Boyd coup; they probably yawned all through it. Boyd's control of the royal castles was in any case tenuous at best. Certainly his kinsman Archibald Boyd received the captaincy of Dunbar, formerly held by Gilbert Kennedy of Kirkmichael; but this was the property of James III's younger brother Albany, who held it as Earl of March. The vital stronghold of Stirling was promptly transferred from Lord Kennedy, not to Boyd, but to Chancellor Avandale.[16] In short, the acquisition of power by the Boyd family did not create a Boyd faction at court; Robert, Lord Boyd, had been able to act as he did in seizing the king due to the apathy of many and the benevolent neutrality of a few; and he would have been wise, after the parliamentary remission of October 1466, to proceed with caution.

Instead, he threw caution to the winds and embarked on a policy of aggrandisement for his family as well as for himself. Before 22 February, 1467, his eldest son Thomas had been created Earl of Arran, and in support of the dignity was granted extensive lands in Bute, Roxburghshire, Perthshire, and Forfar, as well as the Island of Arran and the barony and castle of Kilmarnock; and probably at about the same time the royal marriage which his father had arranged for him, to James III's elder sister Mary, was celebrated.[17] Shortly afterwards, on 4 March 1468, Lord Boyd's eldest daughter Elizabeth was married to Archibald Douglas, the young earl of Angus, receiving as tocher the lands of the lordship of Abernethy on 21 May of the same year.[18] Following the death of the Chamberlain, James Lord Livingston, some time after 26 April 1467, Lord Boyd added this office to the others which he had already acquired.[19] It was perhaps fitting that the new Chamberlain, like the old, should base his fortunes on the possession of the person of the monarch.

These Boyd elevations, however, increased the vulnerability of the family to attacks from other members of the politically conscious nobility. If they had been able thus far to regard Boyd simply as a useful dogsbody who would remove the Kennedy influence and shoulder the responsibility of guarding the king, his actions in 1467-8 must have given them cause for concern. His daughter's marriage to the powerful Earl of Angus was overambitious; but his son's alliance with the king's sister, Mary, uniting the Boyds with the royal family, put the entire Boyd enterprise at risk. Nicholson suggests that as the marriage was arranged by a parliamentary commission appointed in October 1466, the idea may have been to marry off the Princess Mary relatively cheaply within Scotland — her dowry was a modest thousand marks — and to concentrate on achieving continental alliances for the king and his brothers. This is possible; but the remit of the commission from the full body of parliament was to sit for three months, until February 1467, to consider the marriages of the king, his brother (presumably Albany) and sister, together with other weighty matters such as the payment of the Norwegian 'annual' and the securing of the royal castles.[20] It seems likely that, when the commission's powers expired, its business was unfinished, for there is no record of any marriage being arranged for Albany. This is not surprising, as a continental alliance for the king would obviously take precedence, foreign diplomacy is rarely accomplished within three months, and indeed a further commission to consider a marriage abroad for James III had to be appointed in 1468. Lord Boyd may therefore have been in a position, when the first commission ran out of time in February 1467, to hurry through both his son's elevation to the earldom of Arran and his marriage to the Princess Mary. The precedents of James II's six sisters, all of whom were sent abroad and four of whom achieved foreign marriages, suggest that in normal circumstances Princess Mary would have been treated in a similar way, that is, as a potential asset in the foreign marriage market. The speedy Boyd marriage must have made the family many enemies, including James III himself, who if his later letter to Burgundy is to be believed, wept at the wedding.[21]

It it clear from all this that the power of the two Boyds, almost from the outset, was more ephemeral than real. They never controlled the royal government in the sense that they were able to make or break officers of state. Avandale remained Chancellor, Whitelaw Secretary, and Argyll Master of the Household throughout; and James Lindsay was Privy Seal until his death in 1468, when he was replaced by Bishop Spens of Aberdeen, who was an experienced ecclesiastical statesman and certainly not an adherent of the Boyds. It is probably significant that the only office Boyd obtained for himself after the initial adjustments of 1466 was that of Chamberlain, not through supplanting someone, but by the death of the incumbent, Lord Livingston. There was also the very considerable problem of retaining control of the person of the king. Boyd had solved this initially by taking

James from Linlithgow to Edinburgh, where the king was presumably lodged in the castle; but he could hardly feel safe until parliament had legalised his coup and approved his seizure of the king, and this did not happen for three months. Before the October parliament, king and court, including Robert Lord Boyd, and his brother travelled south on an extensive progress, probably on justice ayre, reaching Lochmaben by 13 August[22] and returning to Edinburgh only in time for the meeting of the estates two months later. Protected by their parliamentary remission on 13 October, the Boyds may have felt that a close watch on James III was no longer necessary. Certainly it would have been difficult, if not impossible, to achieve. Between October 1466 and the early months of 1469, king and court travelled more frequently and further afield than at any other period of the reign, visiting Stirling, Linlithgow, Falkland, Jedburgh, Perth, Kirkcudbright, and Peebles; and James III himself is to be found hunting in Balquhidder and Glenfinglas, probably in the early summer of 1467, and in the forest of Mamlorne in the following exchequer year.[23] Under the circumstances, Robert, Lord Boyd, could only cling to his parliamentary remission, hope for royal and other goodwill, and involve himself and his son as much as possible in the business of government.

One of the most pressing items of business was essentially the legacy of James II, the unsolved problem of the Norwegian 'annual', that payment of 100 marks which the Scots had pledged for the transfer of the Western Isles from Norway in 1266 and, in spite of many adjustments to the original treaty, had rarely paid. Shortly before his death in 1460, James II had sent ambassadors to Bourges with the demand, not only that Christian I of Denmark-Norway would remit all arrears of the 'annual', but that a Danish marriage alliance would bring to the Scottish Crown not only a sizeable dowry, but also the Orkney and Shetland islands in full sovereignty.[24] Such aggression had been possible only because the Danish king was financially embarrassed; even so, the Danes refused to consider the Scottish proposals at Bourges, and the issue was again deferred. Christian I's need of money and prestige did not, however, diminish, and he had to accept the fact that his hold on Orkney was tenuous at best; the bishops of Orkney, although still recognising Nidaros as their metropolitan, had been Scottish for generations, and as Dr. Crawford shows, by the mid-fifteenth century there may not have been a single Norse or native ecclesiastic in Orkney.[25] Likewise William Sinclair, earl of Orkney, had never done homage to Christian I of Denmark, whereas his contacts with the Scottish royal house were so close that he had probably been entrusted with the care of James III during part of Mary of Gueldres' regency. A crisis arose in 1466-7, when Christian I, having tried but failed to obtain Earl William's homage, turned instead to Bishop William Tulloch of Orkney for support, and the result was a brief struggle within Orkney itself, culminating in the temporary imprisonment of the bishop by the earl's eldest son.[26] King Christian, faced with rebellion in Sweden and opposition in Denmark, not to mention continuing financial problems which had already forced him to mortgage large parts of his kingdom, wisely decided to temporise with the Scots.

Thus it was that the Scottish government was able to turn to its advantage the diplomatic situation in 1468, and in spite of its two centuries of defaulting on the 'annual' payments, to drive what appears a very hard bargain with the Danish king. A parliamentary commission, meeting at Stirling on 12 January 1468, the second of its kind in little over a year, decided to finance an embassy to Denmark by a levy of £3000 drawn equally from the three estates; the embassy's business was to arrange as quickly as possible the long delayed royal marriage, and also to settle 'the mater of Noroway'.[27] At the beginning of August 1468, the ambassadors departed on their mission.[28] They included Chancellor Avandale, Andrew Muirhead, bishop of Glasgow, William Tulloch, bishop of Orkney, and the new Earl of Arran, Thomas Boyd. The resulting treaty of Copenhagen was achieved with remarkable speed; on 8 September, Christian I ratified an alliance between the two countries which included an agreement that each king and his successors would assist the other against all parties except existing allies. However, the more important part of the treaty linked the problems of the 'annual' and the proposed royal marriage; James III was to marry Christian's only daughter Margaret, and part of her dowry was the ending of the Norway 'annual' and a quitclaim for all arrears. The remainder of the dowry — an impressive remainder — was to be 60,000 Rhenish florins, ten thousand of these to be paid before the Scots embassy left Denmark, while the Scottish king was to have all the lands, rights and revenues pertaining to the Norwegian crown in Orkney until the remaining fifty thousand had been paid by the Danes. The principal Scottish concession was the queen's dower — one third of the royal revenues together with Linlithgow palace and Doune castle.[29]

This treaty, in theory the realisation of so much of James II's ambition, was sufficiently hedged round with written and unwritten qualifications as to make all its benefits for the Scots not immediately apparent. The business of the 'annual' was at last settled to their advantage; but it does not appear that the pawning of Orkney, ultimately the most significant feature of the treaty from a Scottish point of view, was intended by Christian I to be permanent.[30] In fact, as Dr. Nicholson has recently pointed out, there was one specific provision written into the treaty for the restoration of the Norwegian Crown's lands and rights in Orkney; if Margaret of Denmark were to outlive her husband — a not unlikely contingency — she would have the option, within three years of his death, of leaving Scotland, at which point she would lose her dower, but receive as compensation from the Scots the sum of 120,000 Rhenish florins, less the 50,000 which would be deducted as the residue of her dowry. Thereupon Orkney would revert to the control of the King of Denmark-Norway. The Scots not only accepted this provision in the 1468 treaty, but gave it additional ratification in the parliament of May 1471.[31]

The reality of the situation, however, was that whatever King Christian's hopes, his financial position was deteriorating rather than improving. In spite of the speed with which the terms of the marriage treaty had been agreed and ratified, the Scottish embassy remained in Denmark for a further ten months. The delay was caused by Christian's inability to raise more than two thousand of the promised ten thousand florins of Margaret's dowry; and the Danish king's ultimate solution, at the end of May 1469, was to grant James III a wadset of the royal lands, rights and revenues in Shetland until the balance of eight thousand florins was paid.[32] Once again, there was no question that Christian I intended to redeem Shetland at the earliest possible opportunity; but only a few months after taking personal control of the Scottish government, James III was to act decisively to secure the northern isles permanently for the Scottish crown, a process which was complete within three years of his marriage.

The year which included the Danish marriage treaty and the royal wedding also saw the overthrow of the Boyds, father and son; but signs of their impending fall had been apparent from as early as the spring of 1468. In an attempt to secure general acceptance of the rapid elevation of himself and his son, Boyd acted as one of the signatories to an agreement, probably drawn up by himself, made at Stirling on 25 April 1468. The others involved were Andrew Muirhead, bishop of Glasgow, Thomas Spens, bishop of Aberdeen, Colin, earl of Argyll, Boyd's son Thomas, earl of Arran, James Lindsay, Keeper of the Privy Seal, Secretary Whitelaw, and the young king himself.[33] This agreement declared that the signatories 'sal remayn and abide with oure Soverane lord the King and Ilkane with uther in the furthputting of his autorite and ministracioune of Justice till all his lieges and rewling and governyng of his persoun autorite landis and gudis according til his estate Worschip and honour at all thare power bathe with thare personys and gudis againe ony personys that wald tend in the contrare thereof'. None of the seven signatories was to conclude 'ony great materis concernyng the King the gude of the Realme or Justice' without consulting 'the Remanent of the Lordis being present for the tyme'. Also, those involved promised that they would 'with all thare diligens assist to Robert Lord Boid and supple him in the governyng of the Kingis persone strenthis castels housis and all uther thingis grantit to him be our soverane lord in his parliament contenit in the letres under the grete sele maid to him therapon' — clearly a reference to Boyd's appointment as Governor of the king's person in parliament on 13 October 1466, and to the charters issued on the 25th day of that month confirming him in this office and that of Keeper of the royal castles. The agreement goes on to request that the signatories 'sal Induce and persuaid oure soverane lord to hald and schew his hart lufe favouris and singulare tendernes to the said Robert lord Boid'. This last statement suggests that James III, now aged almost sixteen, resented being dominated by Lord Boyd; and such an assumption is amply borne out by the king's letter to Burgundy three years later, in which he states that Robert and Thomas Boyd governed corruptly, consulting neither monarch nor estates; and that James's sister, whose hand was sought by many princes, was married to Thomas Boyd in spite of the king's tears at the wedding. If this letter, written of course long after the flight and forfeiture of the Boyds and pleading a special case, is to be believed, James was merely deferring taking revenge on the Boyds until he and his brothers were safely out of their grasp.[34]

Thus the agreement of 25 April 1468 is, in fact, a confession of insecurity on the part of the Boyds, an attempt to maintain the status quo in the face of mounting opposition. If Robert, Lord Boyd, had still possessed widespread support, he would surely have repeated the device of October 1466 of having parliament approve of his actions; for if the estates had laid down that the seven signatories should remain with the king and take joint decisions, this would have carried much more weight than a private agreement like that of April 1468. The conclusion must be that Boyd dared not call parliament for fear of being overthrown. It had been possible to do so in October 1466 when he had newly come to power; but by the spring of 1468 he had thrust his family into such prominence — particularly by the royal marriage he had acquired for his son — that he would have been inviting his own ruin if he had pressed the estates for an endorsement of his position and policies.

In the event, the ruin of the Boyds was merely delayed, and like many earlier bonds which Robert, Lord Boyd, had broken, the Stirling agreement of April 1468 was set aside in little more than a year. When Boyd and his son Thomas, earl of Arran, were forfeited in November 1469, all the other living signatories to the agreement sat in the parliament which condemned their former colleagues. Also present in that parliament were Boyd's nephew, the Earl of Angus, and — surprisingly — John, Lord Somerville, who had assisted the Boyds in abducting the king from Linlithgow in July 1466.[35] This raising up and casting down of a single family, essentially by the same men sitting in parliament, may be explained partly by resentment at the rapid elevation of the Boyds after the initial coup, but also perhaps by Lord Boyd's breaches of faith with his former allies. In a society in which written bonds were increasingly being used to forge desirable alliances between men of substance, what was to be said for a man who could not be trusted even when making a bond with his own brother?

The actual details of the Boyd collapse are soon described. The departure on embassy to Denmark of two of the seven men — the Bishop of Glasgow and Thomas Boyd, earl of Arran — who had made the bond of April 1468 concerning the keeping of the king must have weakened Lord Boyd's position, especially as the ambassadors' return was so long delayed. In the spring of 1469 Lord Boyd himself, together with Thomas Spens, bishop of Aberdeen, went on embassy to England, and there then ensued a period during which both Boyds were absent from Scotland.[36] If James III's later letter to Burgundy is to be believed, it was for such an opportunity that the young king had been waiting to rid himself of the Boyds without danger to himself or to his brothers. Certainly the protracted Boyd absence seems like remarkable folly at a time when the king needed more rather than less surveillance, though the departure of Lord Boyd to England could also be construed as intelligent anticipation of his impending overthrow. It seems unlikely that he was naive enough to believe by this time that his parliamentary remission of October 1466 would protect him if the king turned against his family.

In any event, by the spring of 1469 only three of the seven signatories to the bond of April 1468 confirming Boyd's governorship remained in Scotland — Colin, earl of Argyll and Master of the Royal Household; James Lindsay, Keeper of the Privy Seal; and Archibald Whitelaw, the royal secretary. Of these three, by far the most powerful was Argyll, who as Master of the Household presumably had James III in his keeping. Already a political earl of considerable experience, Argyll's influence was to increase after the fall of the Boyds, when we find him a constant attender at parliament, a judge in sittings of the Lords of Council and Lords Auditors, and ultimately Chancellor in 1483. So his favour with the young king did not begin in the spring of 1469, but he was probably quite ready to win James III's gratitude by helping to supply the gentle push necessary to topple the Boyds.

As for Secretary Whitelaw, it is impossible at this time — or indeed at any time — to determine his political opinions. For over thirty years he remained in the same post, apparently neither supporting nor resisting insurrections: the royal civil servant par excellence. But he was, or had been, the king's tutor,[37] and as part of James's household would have been likely to join Argyll in taking the king's side in the overthrow of the Boyds. In the case of James Lindsay, provost of Lincluden and Mary of Gueldres' choice as Privy Seal, he seems to have resigned his office late in 1468, probably on account of ill health, as he was certainly dead by June 1469.[38] In short, by the spring or early summer of 1469, of the original seven men who were supposed to control the king under Boyd's governorship, and had made the April 1468 bond to that effect, four — including Robert and Thomas Boyd — were abroad, two were probably in the act of changing sides to support the young king against the Boyds, and one was dead.

The crisis was reached when the Scottish embassy returned to Leith with James's twelve-year-old bride, Margaret of Denmark. Buchanan places the arrival of the fleet bringing over the queen in the spring; but he gives the wrong year, 1470 instead of 1469, and his chronology throughout this crisis period is sadly askew.[39] In fact, the queen's arrival cannot have taken place before 12 June 1469, on which date the names of the principal Scottish ambassadors who were also regular charter witnesses — Chancellor Avandale and the Bishop of Glasgow — are still absent from the witness list to a charter granted under the Great Seal at Edinburgh.[40] But their return must have occurred shortly after that date; for the surviving fragment of a near-contemporary chronicle which is, in general, extremely accurate as regards dates, states that the royal wedding took place at Holyrood on 13 July 1469. John Major, the first of the sixteenth century chroniclers to describe the event, places it on 10 July; while much later, John Lesley and Giovanni Ferreri, the latter probably following Lesley's account, add the colourful story that when the Scottish fleet arrived at Leith, James III's sister Mary, the wife of Thomas Boyd, earl of Arran, warned her husband not to disembark with the queen and the remainder of the Scottish embassy.[41] Husband and wife then fled abroad, and had arrived in Bruges early in 1470. At some time during the same year Robert, Lord Boyd — who had prudently not returned to Scotland from his English embassy with his fellow ambassador, the Bishop of Aberdeen[42] — joined his son and daughter-in-law at Bruges.[43]

Thus the overthrow of the Boyds must have taken place rapidly in the summer of 1469; and a gap of ten months — between February and November 1469 — in the Register of the Great Seal suggests that not much important royal business was being transacted, and that changes were underway in the spring. They were accomplished with remarkable ease because of the flight of Robert, Lord Boyd, and his son; and on 22 November 1469 parliament dutifully forfeited and passed sentence of death on all three Boyds — that is, not only Lord Boyd and his son Thomas, earl of Arran, but also Sir Alexander Boyd of Drumcoll — for their treason in seizing the king in 1466 in all three cases, and in the case of Lord Boyd and his son, for following this up with three years' corrupt government of the realm.[44] Only Sir Alexander Boyd remained in Scotland to answer the charges. Although he denied his guilt, he was not even protected by a royal remission for the abduction of 1466. The outcome of this trial, conducted by an assize of fifteen lords headed by David, earl of Crawford, was inevitable; and Boyd was immediately beheaded on the castle hill of Edinburgh.[45] A pathetic figure, he paid for his elder brother's ambition, as well as for his own deceit in 1466, with his life.

Apart from the Boyd forfeitures, no other punishments were meted out in November 1469. Lord Boyd's three accomplices in carrying off the king from Linlithgow to Edinburgh on 9 July 1466 did not suffer at all; indeed one of them, John, Lord Somerville, sat in parliament to condemn his former ally. Of the other two, Adam Hepburn of Hailes, who had become sheriff of Berwick on 7 April 1467, retained this office after the fall of the Boyds; and Andrew Ker, son and heir of Andrew Ker of Cessford, also went unpunished. His father was tried for his complicity with the Boyds — surprisingly as late as 5 March 1471 — but acquitted.[46] The specific charges brought against Andrew Ker the elder are, however, of interest in that they shed some light on the Boyd collapse. Apart from the accusation that he assisted in the seizure of the king at Linlithgow in 1466, Ker was charged with giving aid to Robert, Lord Boyd, after he had been declared a rebel — that is, after 1469 — with the treasonable inbringing of James Douglas, the forfeited ninth earl, living in exile in England, and with giving his counsel and consent to the proposed killing of Lord Avandale, Chancellor of Scotland. An assize headed by the Earls of Angus and Crawford acquitted Ker on these charges; but there is no doubt that his son was involved in the 1466 seizure of the king, and father and son are among the few committed Boyd supporters for whose actions evidence survives. It seems likely, therefore, that the belated trial of Ker the elder — whether or not he was innocent — reflects an abortive attempt by Robert, Lord Boyd, between his embassy to England in 1469 and his flight to Bruges in 1470, to reinstate himself in Scotland with English help and the forfeited Earl of Douglas. If there was indeed a plot to kill Avandale, it suggests strongly that the Chancellor remained firmly committed to James III throughout the period of the Boyds' ascendancy, and probably helped to engineer their overthrow. This may also be inferred from the fact that Avandale did not associate himself with the Stirling bond of April 1468, confirming Boyd's governorship, although he was in Scotland and at court about this time; and also from James III's subsequent extensive favours showered upon his Chancellor from 1471 onwards.

Quite apart from Avandale, however, a large number of the politically active nobility must have been happy to see the removal of the Boyds; and many of them no doubt played an active part, or at any rate cheerfully acquiesced, in the family's fall. Three of those who sat on the parliamentary assize which condemned Sir Alexander Boyd in November 1469 — David, earl of Crawford, James, earl of Morton, and George, Lord Gordon — can be shown to have held aloof from the Boyd government and benefited by their fall.

David Lindsay, fifth earl of Crawford, was the most prominent of the three. Aged about thirty, an earl for sixteen years, Crawford had already appeared prominently in the service of the Crown as charter witness, parliamentarian, and ambassador. He was particularly associated with embassies to England, being granted safe-conducts to travel south on embassy in the autumn of 1465 and the winter of 1466. On 11 March 1466 he had been included in a safe-conduct to travel to England, issued at Westminster, and he may have been out of Scotland at the time of the Boyd coup.[47] Almost a year later, yet another English safe-conduct included not only Crawford but Lord Boyd and his son; but Crawford did not go to England in their company, nor is he to be found as a royal charter witness more than twice during the three years of their ascendancy.[48]

The contrast between the relative inactivity of the Earl of Crawford — clearly a man with political ambitions before 1466 — during this period, and his subsequent career of constant loyalty to, and lavish reward from, James III is both striking and suggestive. From June 1470 he reappears as a charter witness, and is to be found in this capacity almost without a break till the end of the reign. A constant attender at parliaments, ambassador and royal counsellor, Crawford was successively rewarded with the lordship of Brechin in 1473, the office of Chamberlain in 1483, and — most remarkable of all — the dukedom of Montrose in May 1488, thus becoming the first non-royal duke in Scottish history.[49] No other magnate during the reign was to match Crawford's record of committed and unswerving loyalty to James III; and there can be little doubt that, when the king wished to rid himself of the Boyds in 1469, Crawford gave him his full support.

Rather different was the case of James Douglas, earl of Morton, the king's uncle and the only other earl on the assize. Morton was not a 'political' earl — he did not often come to parliament or court — but he was allied to the Kennedy faction shortly before the Boyd coup of July 1466. Indeed, on 30 June 1466, only nine days before the seizure of the king and the eclipse of the Kennedys, Morton entered into a contract with Patrick Graham, nephew of bishop Kennedy and the new bishop of St. Andrews, and Graham's father and brother, for the marriage of the bishop's niece to his son John.[50] As the bishop already had bonds with Lord Kennedy and Sir Alexander Boyd, this marriage contract with Morton may be seen as an attempt to draw the earl into the Kennedy faction. Their timing could not have been worse. The immediate seizure of the king and the ousting from power of both Lord Kennedy and Sir Alexander Boyd must therefore have come as a blow to both Patrick Graham and the Earl of Morton; it placed Morton firmly in the camp of those who had held power before the Boyd coup, and he doubtless resented the pre-eminence of the Boyds and their control of his nephew, the king.

George, Lord Gordon, the fifth-named of the 1469 assize, may more obviously be numbered amongst the opponents of the Boyds. He was to succeed his father as second Earl of Huntly the following summer; but while still Lord Gordon, on 7 February 1470, he had conferred on him by James III, for faithful service to the monarch, extensive lands which had fallen into the hands of the king through the forfeiture of Robert, formerly Lord Boyd.[51] This grant reflects both Gordon's dislike — or perhaps envy — of the Boyds and his favour with the young king; and as Earl of Huntly he was to pursue a policy of consistent — if geographically somewhat remote — loyalty to James III over much of the remainder of the reign.

The prospect of reward may also have moved James Stewart of Auchterhouse, the king's half-uncle, to attack the Boyds. This enigmatic individual, the source of two of the major mysteries of the later stages of the reign, was the second son of James I's queen Joan Beaufort by her marriage to James Stewart, the Black Knight of Lorne, about 1439. His elder brother John had already been created Earl of Atholl by James II; but James Stewart owed his advancement entirely to James III. In his late twenties in 1469, he acquired the office of Chamberlain on the fall of the Boyds; and some time between April and September 1470, he was created Earl of Buchan.[52] Together with his elder brother Atholl, Buchan appears as a royal charter witness occasionally after the forfeiture of the Boyds; but it is his elevation to the peerage and assumption of high office which marks him out as a beneficiary of the change of government. The nickname 'Hearty James'[53] appears singularly inappropriate in describing the man who was the probable instigator of yet another seizure of the king, at Lauder in 1482, and whose role in the major Stewart crisis of 1482-3 has sinister overtones. In 1469-70, however, Buchan had good cause to be well satisfied with his advancement, probably the reward of a grateful nephew for support in crushing the Boyds.

Another beneficiary of the revolution of 1469, though in rather a different way, was James, Lord Hamilton, a veteran of Scottish political infighting and firm supporter of the Crown since at least 1455, when he had deserted the Black Douglases and made James II's efforts to crush them much easier. A regular parliamentarian and frequent royal charter witness throughout the '60s, including the Boyd period, Hamilton received the most striking marks of royal favour in the '70s, once James III had taken control of the government. Not only did his parliamentary and charter witness activities increase, but he was almost constantly elected to the Committee of the Articles, and was a member of the Lords of Council till his death in November 1479.[54] Most remarkable of all, by 1474 Hamilton had been permitted to marry James III's sister, the errant Mary who had fled abroad with her husband Thomas Boyd, the forfeited earl of Arran, and subsequently returned alone to Scotland in 1471, leaving her refugee spouse either divorced or dead. Mary can hardly have been popular with her brother the king on her return; she had borne two children, James and Margaret, to Thomas Boyd, both of them born in exile in Bruges, and a potential source of trouble for the future;[55] and she was now presumably useless as a marriage prospect in the international market. Her misfortune, however, was the making of Lord Hamilton and, even more, of the Hamilton family in the following century; and the marriage, clearly arranged by the king, was a signal mark of royal favour which suggests that James III had reason to be grateful for Hamilton support, possibly in 1469.

Finally, it is possible that family feud had some bearing on the fall of the Boyds. Early in 1439, according to the Auchinleck chronicler, Sir Thomas Boyd, father of Robert, Lord Boyd, killed Sir Alan Stewart of Darnley, father of John, Lord Darnley, near Falkirk, as part of an old feud between the two families. In retaliation, Alexander Stewart, brother of Sir Alan, killed Sir Thomas Boyd in battle — the late and unreliable Pitscottie places the fight at Craignaught Hill in Renfrewshire — on 9 July 1439.[56] It is clear from this that the two families, Boyd and Lennox Stewart, both with extensive adjoining lands in Ayrshire, were at feud. A generation later, in 1466, the eldest son of the slain Sir Thomas Boyd was in control of the king; Stewart of Darnley's son, John, Lord Darnley, was governor of Rothesay castle and one of the claimants to the title of Earl of Lennox. If family feud had persisted for a generation, as seems likely, Darnley probably thought it hopeless attempting to press his claim to the earldom while Robert, Lord Boyd, was governor. Thus he had a positive motive throughout the three years 1466-69 for working for a change of government and ingratiating himself with James III. In the event, Darnley would not only be disappointed, but very shabbily treated by the king, who rapidly — and illegally — conferred the liferent of the Lennox on Chancellor Avandale;[57] but in the late '60s Darnley may well have reasoned that support of James III against the Boyds would earn him the earldom.

In the last analysis, whatever the complexities of individual magnate alliances for or against the Boyds, the events of 1469 are simply explained. Except during a royal minority, it was impossible for a single family to dominate Scottish royal government for any length of time. The Boyds had thrust themselves into power by a coup for which Lord Boyd sought not only a parliamentary remission but subsequent written royal approval, a sure sign that he had failed to pacify the king. The royal marriage for Boyd's son earned the family James's hatred; the broken bonds of friendship with many lords, to say nothing of his brother, made Boyd himself peculiarly vulnerable; and whatever their record, the Boyds had the misfortune to be in power at a time when the young king was about to emerge, at the age of seventeen, from nine years of tutelage, during which time he had been successively in the keeping of his mother, the Earl of Orkney, Bishop Kennedy, Gilbert Lord Kennedy, and Robert Lord Boyd.

Yet in spite of the various palace revolutions of the 1460s, the outstanding overall impression conveyed by the records of the nine years of James III's minority is of governmental stability and continuity. There were no dramatic changes in officers of state, such as were to occur during the crisis of 1482; death removed the Chamberlain, James, Lord Livingston, and the Privy Seal, James Lindsay; and that was all. It may be argued that continuity in the royal administration does not necessarily prove much in the case of someone like Archibald Whitelaw, the royal secretary; governments may come and go, but the civil service goes on for ever. However, the men who mattered, the real makers of policy, were clearly magnates like Chancellor Avandale and Colin, earl of Argyll, Master of the Royal Household, latterly joined by Thomas Spens, bishop of Aberdeen, as Privy Seal, and David, earl of Crawford, as Chamberlain. All these men had begun their public careers under James II; and their experience of government, coupled with their unswerving loyalty to the Crown, made them admirable counsellors for his son. After the latter-day excesses of James II, the minority of James III had indeed produced a necessary period of calm. It remained to be seen whether the new king, on assuming full governmental responsbility himself, would understand and profit from the lessons of the minority.

NOTES

1. *A.P.S.*, ii, 77; *Cal. Docs. Scot.*, iv, Nos. 1301, 1341.

2. *Asloan MS.*, i, 239-241; *E.R.*, vii, lvii, 284, 302, 362, 380, 422; *R.M.S.*, ii, No. 867; *A.P.S.*, ii, 84.

3. S.R.O. Ailsa Charters, No. 96 (Copy of original).

4. N.L.S. MS. Acc. 3142. No. 33, 18.

5. *E.R.*, v, 609.

6. S.R.O. Ailsa Charters Nos. 97, 99.

7. *A.P.S.*, ii, 185, 186; *S.H.S. Misc.* viii, 19-32; Buchanan, *History*, ii, 126.

8. *A.P.S.*, ii, 185.

9. *Ibid.*, 186.

10. C.A.J. Armstrong, 'A Letter of James III to the Duke of Burgundy', *S.H.S. Misc.* viii, 19-32.

11. Buchanan, *History*, ii, 126.

12. *E.R.*, vii, 441, 443, 458.

13. *Ibid.*, 500.

14. *See above*, Chapter 1.

15. *A.P.S.*, ii, 185; *R.M.S.*, ii, Nos. 891, 892.

16. *E.R.*, vii, 494; *Ibid.*, 441, 443, 458.

17. *Cal. Docs. Scot.*, iv, No. 1368; *R.M.S.*, ii, Nos. 912-15.

18. *Scots Peerage*, v, 146; *R.M.S.*, ii, No. 945.

19. *Ibid.*, Nos. 912, 932.

20. Nicholson, *op.cit.*, 413; *A.P.S.*, ii, 185.

21. *S.H.S. Misc.* viii, 30.

22. *R.M.S.*, ii, No. 884.

23. *R.M.S.*, ii, Nos. 885-975; *E.R.*, vii, 488, 512, 533, 560, 569.

24. *See above*, Chapter 2.

25. Barbara E. Crawford, 'The pawning of Orkney and Shetland', *S.H.R.*, xlviii, 40.

26. *Ibid.*, 41, 42, 44 and n. 3.

27. *A.P.S.*, ii, 90-91.

28. See *R.M.S.*, ii, No. 962 (30 July 1468) and No. 963 (9 August 1468). In the former, Chancellor Avandale and the Bishop of Glasgow are witnesses; in the latter, their names are absent from the witness list, and do not reappear until 27 November 1469; *R.M.S.*, ii, No. 986.

29. *E.R.*, viii, lxxvii-lxxxvii.

30. For discussion of this question, see Barbara E. Crawford, *op.cit.*, 45-51.

31. Nicholson, *op.cit.*, 416; *A.P.S.*, ii, 187-8.

32. Barbara E. Crawford, *op.cit.*, 52-3.

33. Boyd Papers No. 1, in *Abbotsford Miscellany*, i, 5-7.

34. *S.H.S. Misc.* viii, 32.

35. *A.P.S.*, ii, 93.

36. Boyd's name vanishes from the Register of the Great Seal, in which he had been a regular witness to charters, after 18 February 1469 (*R.M.S.*, ii, No. 983); and he had arrived at the English court by 28 April 1469. (*Cal. Docs. Scot.*, iv, No. 1383).

37. Dunlop, *Bishop Kennedy*, 205 n. 4.

38. The last date on which Lindsay may be found as provost of Lincluden is 19 November 1468 (Vat. Reg. Supp. 633, f.22). He appears to have resigned as Privy Seal between 10 August and 7 November 1468, as by the latter date the office had been assumed by Thomas Spens, bishop of Aberdeen (*R.M.S.*, ii, Nos. 964, 965). In the Linlithgow accounts for the two years ending in June 1469, he is described as 'quondam magistro Jacobo Lindesay' (*E.R.*, vii, 656).

39. Buchanan, *History*, ii, 133.

40. Atholl Charters (Blair Castle), Box 24, Parcel 1, No. 2.

41. B.M. Royal MS 17 Dxx, f.307r.; Major, *History*, 389; Lesley, *History*, 37-8; Ferrerius, *Appendix to Boece*, f.388v.

42. Thomas Spens, bishop of Aberdeen, was back in Edinburgh by 12 June 1469 (Atholl Charters, Box 24, Parcel 1, No. 2).

43. W. H. Finlayson, 'The Boyds in Bruges', in *S.H.R.*, xxviii (1949), 195-6.

44. *A.P.S.*, ii, 186.

45. *Ibid.*, 187.

46. *Ibid.*, 93; *Scots Peerage*, ii, 148; *E.R.*, viii, 2; *H.M.C. Rep. xiv*, App. iii, 27-8 (for trial of Ker).

47. *R.M.S.*, ii, Nos. 788-848; *A.P.S.*, ii, 84; *Rot. Scot.*, ii, 418, 420-1; *Cal. Docs. Scot.*, iv, No. 1366.

48. *Ibid.*, No. 1368; *R.M.S.*, ii, Nos. 938, 978.

49. *R.M.S.*, ii, No. 1111 (Brechin); *Ibid.*, No. 1565 (Chamberlain); *Ibid.*, No. 1725 (Montrose).

50. *Morton Registrum*, ii, 213-4.

51. *Scots Peerage*, iv, 526; *R.M.S.*, ii, No. 988.

52. *R.M.S.*, ii, Nos. 989, 996.

53. *Scots Peerage*, ii, 266.

54. *R.M.S.*, ii, Nos. 1177, 1178; *Glasgow Registrum*, ii, 616.

55. Nicholson, *op.cit.*, 420.

56. *Asloan MS.*, i, 215; Pitscottie, *Historie*, i, 23-4.

57. *R.M.S.*, No. 1018.

5

Aggression and Illegality: 1469–74

IN November 1469, James III was seventeen-and-a-half, a year younger than his father had been when, only twenty years before, he had assumed control of the government. Like his father, however, he showed an immediate determination to be an effective-sovereign in spite of his youth; but his respect for James II was unfortunately reflected in a desire to emulate that ruler's later excesses, above all in his efforts to play a major role in northern European politics, and in dubious, or openly illegal, distribution of lands and offices. However, James III had also revered his mother, Mary of Gueldres, who had died when he was eleven; and he sought to honour her memory by continuing the building of her foundation, Trinity College, in Edinburgh, by retaining her ministers, and by praising her virtues in a letter to the Duke of Burgundy written years after her death. Thus the five years which followed, until the English alliance of 1474, were to witness James III following a wayward course which displayed rather more of the aggression and ruthlessness of his father than the moderation and political good sense of his mother.

Lacking benefit of hindsight, James III may of course have viewed his position in 1469 in a less favourable light than later historians. Quite apart from the problem of dealing effectively with elder statesmen competing for his favour, the king had inherited the nobility largely created by his father. The earldoms of Huntly, Erroll, Argyll, Rothes, Morton, and Marischal were all new, occupied by men who had served James III's father but were the better part of a generation older than the new king. Nearer to home, there was the recurrent problem of the royal Stewart family; James III was the first Scottish king since Robert III to have surviving brothers, and close to him in age. The earldoms of March and Mar were in the hands of his younger brothers; the earldom of Atholl had been held since 1455 by the King's eldest half-uncle, John Stewart; Atholl's younger brother James expected — and received — the earldom of Buchan in 1470; and there was also a third Stewart half-uncle who expected to make a career in the church. James III may therefore have felt hemmed in, like his grandfather, by a concentration of Stewart males close to the throne, offering no immediate threat but expecting rewards commensurate with their status; and when one of his three brothers, David, died in infancy, James's sorrow may have been tempered with relief; for in 1456 David had been given the title Earl of Moray by his father, and on his death the earldom reverted to the Crown.[1]

The most pressing household problem, however, concerned James III's sister Mary, an exile abroad with her forfeited husband Thomas, earl of Arran. If they had fled first to Denmark, as Lesley and Ferreri suggest, husband and wife cannot have remained there longer than a few months, for by February 1470 they are to be found living in Bruges as the guests of Sir Anselm Adornes. Adornes' connections with Scotland had begun at least as early as 1468, when he had visited the country as an envoy; and his local power and influence with Charles the Bold must have been the means through which the Boyds now received the Duke of Burgundy's patronage. Indeed, Margaret, Duchess of Burgundy, acted as godmother to Arran's son James; and Robert, Lord Boyd, appears to have joined his family in Bruges sometime in 1470. While staying in the town, the exiled Boyds must have been heartened by the arrival of the Duchess of Burgundy's brother, Edward IV of England — temporarily supplanted at home by the feeble Henry VI — and his swift departure in March 1471 to recover his throne. James III must have been alarmed by the prospect of the Boyds obtaining Burgundian or Yorkist support for a restoration, and his letter to Charles the Bold condemning the family undoubtedly exaggerates their crimes in order to rule out the possibility of clemency.[2] Undeterred, the Boyds set out for Scotland in the company of Anselm Adornes at the beginning of October 1471, but had the good sense to travel first to England and ingratiate themselves with the restored Edward IV. Only James's sister Mary came on to Scotland with Adornes, presumably to ask for the restoration of her husband and father-in-law. Not only was this withheld, but Mary herself was detained in Scotland by the king and subsequently married to James, Lord Hamilton.[3] With his sister no longer a potential pawn on the chessboard of European diplomacy and with her husband Arran dead, probably by 1474, the king could afford to ignore Robert Lord Boyd, allowing him to join the forfeited James, earl of Douglas, as Edward IV's pensioner, rapidly forgotten men who re-emerged briefly in the crises of the 1480s, when many must have believed them long dead.

The part played by Adornes in the return of Princess Mary to her brother was a curious one. If his aim was really to plead with James III for a Boyd restoration, he must have changed his mind rapidly; for the king granted him the liferent of Cortachy, and forfeited Boyd lands in Forfar and Perthshire, by April 1472; and shortly afterwards, on 10 June, Adornes was made Conservator of the Privileges of the Scots in all the domains of the Dukes of Burgundy.[4] It must be concluded that Adornes regarded the Boyds as expendable if James III's terms were right; and greater issues may have been involved than the straightforward bribery of the Flemish ambassador. Scottish trade was highly valued by the city of Bruges; but continual strife over the respective privileges of Scots and Flemish merchants had led the Scots government in 1467 to forbid all Scottish subjects to trade with Sluys, Damme, or Bruges. In the protracted negotiations which followed, Adornes was three times the envoy of Charles the Bold and the city of Bruges to Scotland — in 1468, 1469, and 1471. He was already in favour with James III before his third mission, bringing home the Princess Mary in 1471; and his main task at that time was probably to settle trade disputes between Scotland and Flanders rather than try to retrieve the fortunes of a forfeited family. Thus Adornes' rewards — the liferent of Cortachy and the rest — may well have been granted for his services as trade ambassador; and James III's favour towards him was possibly based partly on a common interest in art.[5]

Thus the settlement of James III's immediate family problems took up the first two years of his personal rule. During the same period, the king was taking trouble to make himself and his queen known throughout Scotland; in the summer of 1470 they made a progress throughout the north, staying in Inverness for a month, from 23 July to 24 August, and the queen's itinerary also included Aberdeen, Fyvie, Banff, and Wrangham in the Garioch. There are no entries in the Great Seal Register between 12 July and 17 September 1470, which suggests that the royal progress lasted about two months.[6] Clearly it was a less elaborate, and less formal, occasion than the progress of 1464, which had involved the granting of charters at the various burghs visited en route. It was also the last occasion on which James III would travel so far afield.

Just before setting out for the north, on 25 June 1470, the king showed that — like his father — he did not intend to be bound by parliamentary annexations of lands to the Crown, territories which might not be alienated without the consent of the three estates. The lands in question were those forfeited by the Boyds in November 1469, including Bute, Cowal, Dundonald, Renfrew, Arran, Stewarton, Kilmarnock, and Sir Alexander Boyd's lands of Drumcoll. Parliament had laid down that these former Boyd lands were to be annexed to the 'principality' of Scotland, to be bestowed on the first-born son of the king; but James ignored the estates and granted the lands of Kilmarnock to the queen, as a free barony, for life, a gift which was to have significant consequences over a decade later, during the crisis of 1482–3.[7] The gift was made, according to the king, to pay for the queen's gowns and the ornaments of her head. This would suggest that she had expensive tastes, and the surviving Treasurer's account for 1473–4 helps to confirm as much, containing as it does payments of £757 9/10d for the queen's clothes and other expenses.[8] On the whole, however, James III had got Margaret of Denmark on the cheap. There was no rush to invest her in her dower lands, as there had been in the case of Mary of Gueldres in 1450; but Mary of Gueldres had been better placed, the niece of the powerful Duke of Burgundy. Margaret of Denmark, as the daughter of the impecunious Christian I, merited no such immediate consideration. A substantial gift — the liferent of the barony of Kilmarnock — would suffice in the meantime, even though it involved flouting the law.

The balance of the queen's dowry — the pawned Orkney and Shetland Isles — was another matter. It became clear within a year of his assumption of power that James III was determined to acquire the Northern Isles on a more permanent basis than the treaty of Copenhagen and its later appendages allowed. His method was to reach an agreement with William Sinclair, earl of Orkney and Caithness and Lord Sinclair, whereby Sinclair, in return for substantial compensation, would convey to the Crown the Earldom of Orkney with its castle of Kirkwall, and presumably also its dependency of Shetland. Sinclair was probably not coerced into this resignation of Orkney by James III; part of his compensation included the substantial concession that he was henceforth exempted for life from attending in person at parliaments or general councils, on embassies and expeditions, justice ayres and sheriff courts, and from royal offices and service in general, a sure sign that Sinclair had no personal interest in the business of government and wished to opt out of his responsibilities. He retained the titles of Earl of Caithness and Lord Sinclair, and the remainder of his compensation was impressive — the new castle of Ravenscraig in Fife, together with other lands in the vicinity, and a life pension of 50 marks, dramatically increased to 400 marks in the following year, from the great customs of Edinburgh. Furthermore, the king promised not to revoke these grants to Sinclair, although they had been made before he reached twenty-five, the legal age of majority.[9]

What James III had acquired from Earl William in return for this compensation was the comital rights in Orkney and Shetland. He already held a wadset of the royal rights; and to ensure his complete control, he referred the matter to parliament. On 20 February 1472 the three estates approved the annexation of Orkney and Shetland to the crown, not to be alienated unless to legitimate male issue of the king.[10] In theory, Christian I or his successors could still redeem the Northern Isles by paying the balance of Queen Margaret's dowry; but in practice, the Scottish Crown's control of Orkney and Shetland had become so strong that the recovery of the islands by Denmark-Norway, whatever the Danish King's intentions, was a highly unlikely contingency. It is clear that the whole operation was carried through by James III mainly in order to enhance his prestige, for in financial terms he gained remarkably little. William Tulloch, bishop of Orkney and Keeper of the Privy Seal, was granted a tack of the Northern Isles in return for a yearly rent of £466 13/4d; and by 1476 the assessment had been reduced, so that the total annual rent dropped by £100.[11] Bearing in mind the high cost to the king of buying off the Earl of Orkney — not only an annual 400 marks but Ravenscraig and the rest — the royal determination to secure Orkney and Shetland for the crown, and to involve parliament in the transfer, must be seen as Stewart territorial aggrandisement for its own sake. For the next ten years, James III could boast that Scotland's boundaries, stretching from Shetland to Berwick, had reached a greater extent than at any time in the country's history.

Stewart prestige was also involved in foreign proposals advanced in the parliament of May 1471. Almost the first business of the estates was an agreement to send a Scottish embassy to France and Burgundy to try to establish peace between the two powers; and perhaps as reward for playing the role of mediator, James III hoped to negotiate a marriage alliance with the French or Burgundians for his younger sister Margaret.[12] Parliament was summoned because taxation was involved; as in the case of the king's Danish marriage, the estates were to pay the expenses of the embassy, a total of three thousand crowns, by midsummer. Thus the estates were required to pay, but the ambassadors' instructions were not their business; instead, 'the lordis of the secret consal and utheris lordis the vil cheiss tharto to have powar of this hail parlyament to mak the instruccionis concernyng the materis of the kynge of France and the duc of burgunze whitht powar to commounce aviss and conclude eftir as thai fynde the materis disposit'. Unfortunately the lords of the Privy Council are not named; but it is likely that some of them also sat as Lords of the Articles. This is in fact suggested by the phrase 'to have powar of this hail parlyament', which was normally used to refer to the committee appointed to deal with unfinished business following the adjournment of parliament.[13]

Nothing seems to have come of the whole scheme, either mediation or marriage alliance; and this may have been because Edward IV was already sounding out James III with a view to a treaty within two months of the 1471 parliament. The Yorkist king was no doubt anxious to avoid trouble on his northern frontier; the battles through which he had recovered his throne, at Barnet and Tewkesbury, had been fought as recently as April and May, and he had still to consolidate his position in the south. James III showed some interest, and by 7 August an English safe-conduct had been issued for Bishops Muirhead, Spens and Tulloch, the Earls of Argyll, Crawford and Caithness, Lords Hamilton and Borthwick, Archibald Crawford, abbot of Holyrood, Secretary Whitelaw, and Masters Reau and Gilbert Rerik, archdeacon of Glasgow, to come to Alnwick on 23 September to meet Edward IV's commissioners and treat with them for redress of offences committed on the Marches.[14] No peace treaty, or even prolonged truce, was concluded as a result of these preliminary feelers; but it is noteworthy that — although the Scots were interested — the initiative came from England, and came when it did probably because James III was toying with the idea of a Burgundian or French alliance.

In the following year the Scottish king may again be found playing the part of intermediary between two European nations, Denmark and France. Christian I, still embroiled in a struggle with rebels throughout his dominions, looked to Louis XI of France for a treaty of friendship and a marriage alliance for his son Prince Hans and Louis' daughter Jeanne. Most of the groundwork appears to have been done by James III, who not only acted as host to the French and Danish embassies, but even provided the Danish ambassadors himself — William Tulloch, bishop of Orkney, and John Hawden. The Scottish king's position as mediator is referred to throughout the treaty, the clauses of which are mainly concerned with mutual support in the event of either ruler facing rebellion. The treaty failed in its objects, as no French support was forthcoming for Christian I, nor did his son Hans marry the French Princess Jeanne;[15] but the role played by James III indicates his determination to have a voice in European affairs. This should not surprise us; James II had behaved in a similarly confident manner in 1458, joining Henry IV of Castile in interceding with Charles VII of France for clemency for the rebellious Dauphin who had fled for safety to Burgundy.[16] In each case the voice of the Scottish king carried some weight because, although only the rulers of a relatively poor and remote European country, James II and James III were linked by marriage to Burgundy and Denmark respectively; and as the first Scottish rulers to marry abroad since the thirteenth century, both made the most of the diplomatic advantages which such a position afforded them.

James III's continental interests, however, went far beyond mediating between rival foreign rulers. In 1472-3 he involved himself in no fewer than three continental schemes — the invasion of Brittany, the acquisition of the Duchy of Gueldres, and the cession to Scotland of the French county of Saintonge. In the process, he alarmed not only the Duke of Brittany, Edward IV of England, and the

Burgundians, but also the Scottish estates; and in the event all three schemes proved abortive.

The projected invasion of Brittany formed part of the business of the parliament of February 1472. Naturally taxation was required, and the proposed levy was five thousand pounds for the passage to Brittany of an army of six thousand men, which the king planned to lead in person. It was probably the controversial nature of this proposal which produced a large turn-out, including thirty-four lairds and eleven burgh commissioners. 'To the King to the passage of 6,000 men in France to put thaim to the see', the clergy granted £2,000, the barons £2,000, the burgh commissioners £1,000.[17] The object of the expedition was to seize part of Brittany from its duke, the instigator being Louis XI of France. According to Dupuy,[18] Louis sent William, Lord Monypenny and Lord of Concressault, to Scotland to offer James III a part of Brittany in exchange for the services of a Scottish army. Certainly Monypenny is to be found in Scotland, and in favour with the king, at this time. On 8 October 1471, for praiseworthy and loyal service, he was granted the royal lands of Kirkandrews in Galloway; in the same month or the following one, he acquired a confirmation of more Galloway lands; on 26 February 1472, the lands of Kirkandrews, which Lord Hamilton had resigned, were confirmed to Monypenny in parliament; and on 31 August and 13 September 1472, he received further grants in Galloway and Stirlingshire respectively.[19]

The dispensing of such extensive rewards makes it clear that James III was enthusiastic about the scheme for the invasion of Brittany, and this is borne out by the parliamentary records. Apparently also on 20 February, three days after parliament met in Edinburgh, it was announced that the king intended to head the expedition in person, whereupon the clergy present in parliament protested vigorously, on three grounds. First, the king should not leave his realm open to English attack; secondly, in the event of his demise, he had no issue to succeed him; and thirdly, he should avoid levying taxation upon the estates.[20] This protest forced the king to delay, and later abandon, his invasion plans; but there can be no doubt that he was in earnest. Duke Francis of Brittany was sufficiently alarmed by the prospect of a Scottish army descending upon him to ask Edward IV for support in the shape of six thousand archers. These were not forthcoming, but Edward IV was concerned enough to send Earl Rivers, Sir Edward Woodville, a few ships and a small force to Brittany to lend support to the duke.[21]

It is curious that expostulation on the part of the clergy should have put an apparently successful check on James III's continental aspirations, particularly as they had already allowed their part of the tax for the transport of the army. It is an odd example of opposition in parliament to the ruling party, opposition more explicit than that directed at James II in 1458; and it is particularly unfortunate that the names of the Lords of the Articles, who presumably prepared the ground for the imposition of this tax between 18 and 20 February, are unknown to us. It may be that there was extensive opposition throughout the estates, and that many of those present knew before they attended that part of the business of the parliament would be to impose a tax. This might account for the presence of an unusually large number of lairds. However, all the record shows is that the clergy present — four bishops, six abbots, and four priors — petitioned successfully against the expedition.

In 1473, the king's continental interests seem to have taken a different turn. At the beginning of May, he sent Sir Alexander Napier of Merchiston on embassy to Burgundy, providing him with an elaborate series of instructions signed by himself.[22] Part of these related to the Duchy of Gueldres, in which James III had an interest as the son of Mary of Gueldres, herself the eldest daughter of the reigning Duke Arnold. It appears from Napier's instructions that Arnold had been deposed by his son Adolphus, who had imprisoned him until Charles the Bold, on his accession to the dukedom of Burgundy in 1467, had demanded that the old duke be released. In view of his son's treachery, Duke Arnold wished to disinherit him; but the probable result of this would be that Charles the Bold would succeed him in Gueldres. Arnold, therefore, looked to Scotland, where his daughter had borne three sons — James III and his two brothers. He appears to have written to the king asking him, or Albany or Mar, to come to Gueldres to take possession of the duchy, which Adolphus had forfeited by his treason. However, in February 1473, presumably not long after having written to Scotland about the succession, Duke Arnold died.

James III, though clearly attracted by the prospect of securing Gueldres for Scotland, was faced with a major difficulty. Charles the Bold of Burgundy, the man on the spot, intended to acquire the duchy himself; and on 30 December 1472 he had forced the old and ailing Duke Arnold to grant a cession of his territory to Burgundy, reserving to himself only a liferent possession.[23] As Charles the Bold also had in his power the person of Arnold's son Adolphus, James III's chances of asserting his claim to the duchy on the basis of a plea from the late duke seemed slim. However, the king sent Napier to inform Burgundy that though he was clearly the rightful heir to Duke Arnold of Gueldres, nevertheless he would 'nocht labour na put his hand to the said matter withoute counsale and aviss of his said cousing, the Duc of Burgunze, traisting verraly to have throu him supportatione, aide, and supplie in the said matter, and in the recovering of his richt'.

As is apparent from Napier's safe-conduct,[24] these instructions were issued by the king about the beginning of May 1473. Less than a fortnight later, on 12 May, Christoforo di Bollati, Milanese ambassador at the French court, which was then at Tours, wrote to his master, the Duke of Milan: 'The ambassadors of the King of Scotland have been here some time, with offers to wage active war on the King of England, if he chooses to land in this kingdom, and they promise his Majesty (Louis XI) that they will adhere to their ancient league and confederation, but that they must have what his precedessors have received from the Crown of France in the past, to wit, a pension of some 60,000 crowns a year, so that they may be able to oppose the King of England in favour of his Majesty'.[25] This is interesting in the context of James III's determination to lead an army abroad in person. What was to be its destination? Some light on the problem is shed by the articles of the parliament of July 1473.

The estates assembled in Edinburgh on 23 July, and moved quickly to the most urgent business, the king's desire to go abroad. At great length, they advised against the scheme, 'considering that he [the king] is unprovidit or furnyst of his expenss'. It would seem therefore that James's attempt the previous year to raise a tax of £5,000 with parliamentary approval had either been unsuccessful, or else the money had been appropriated to some other purpose. Parliament's advice to the king was to stay at home and execute justice in Scotland; however, if James 'standis uterly determyt to pas in uthir countries', the most useful role he could perform would be to act as mediator between the Duke of Burgundy and Louis XI of France. This would mean great saving of Christian blood, and might eventually result in a united crusade against the infidel Turk. In this manner, James III would gain considerable honour in Christian Europe, and might be in a better position to press his claims 'nocht alanerly to the counte of xanctone bot als of the duchery of gillire'. As a first step towards achieving all this, the estates advised that an embassy should be sent at once to Burgundy, and then France, and if it should appear that Louis XI was unwilling to put the Scots in possession of the County of Saintonge, then the Dukes of Burgundy and Brittany ought to be informed of the injustice to James III and his ambassador, who is named as Sir David Guthrie.[26]

Scottish demands for the cession of Saintonge, and French refusals to oblige, stretched back forty-five years to November 1428, when Charles VII, at the lowest ebb in his fortunes, had conferred the county on James I and his heirs in return for the services of six thousand Scots troops. These had never been sent, and so in 1436 the French king repudiated the cession of Saintonge. James II had demanded that the county be handed over in 1458, and the minority government of James III had made the same appeal in 1465, both to no avail. It is possible, of course, that in each case the call for the surrender of Saintonge had been little more than a diplomatic move on the part of the Scots to alarm the French king; but the end result was the same, a French refusal.[27]

In 1473, however, it seems clear that James III was considering active steps to acquire Saintonge, either as a reward for assisting Louis XI against Edward IV, or by direct invasion. The parliamentary protest against the king's leaving the realm in person, however, suggested that Saintonge might be acquired peaceably, as the king's price for acting as mediator between Burgundy and France. First of all, however, the estates insisted that James III should 'send and stop the lettre quhilk is ordanit to pass to the King of France sene na mater can be convoyit to the honour worschip and proffit of his hienes without cessing of the said lettre'. Finally, parliament suggested that a Scots embassy should refer James III's right to Gueldres to Charles the Bold, and it was hoped that Louis XI might also look favourably on a Scottish succession to the duchy. In any event, 'in this sesone' the king should stay at home 'and travel throw his Realme and put sic Justice and polycy in his awne realme that the brute and the fame of him mycht pas in utheris contreis'. This effort to flatter the king ended with the enticing prospect that James, through following the estates' advice, 'mycht be grace of God be callit to gretare thingis than is yit expremit'. Dr. Nicholson has ingeniously suggested that this was a hint that James III might eventually be elected emperor.[28]

What emerges from this lengthy protest is, first, that parliament was principally concerned to keep the king at home; secondly, that if the king remained 'uterly determyt' to go abroad in person, it should be as an ambassador rather than a military leader; thirdly, that the parliamentary petitioners had considerable understanding, even at this early stage, of the character and ambitions of James III; and finally, that James's foreign policy in the first half of 1473, of which this protest was in fact an indictment, does seem to have been extremely devious. On 25 March, at Burgundy's request, the king had confirmed a truce made with England, to last for two years from 10 April.[29] Yet at the beginning of May, according to Sir Alexander Napier's instructions, the king was adopting a much less friendly attitude towards Edward IV. He complained to Burgundy that the Scottish ambassadors had exceeded their commission by concluding a treaty of mutual defence with the duke which introduced an exception in favour of the king of England, the only king, as James pointed out, who made war on him. Only his affection and respect for Burgundy could have induced him to consider a truce with England, and he expected a favour in return, namely that Burgundy should send ambassadors to Edward IV to demand compensation for Scottish grievances, particularly in the case of the Bishop's Barge, Kennedy's famous 'Salvator', wrecked at Bamburgh. Finally, to put pressure on Burgundy and perhaps to make his claim to Gueldres seem more reasonable, James III complained that Scots merchants were not being well treated in Bruges, and that they should have freedom to choose their staple in whichever of Burgundy's towns they pleased.

At about the same time, James's embassy in France was assuring Louis XI of the Scottish king's adherence to the Franco-Scottish alliance and promising — for a large annual pension — to make active war on Edward IV. Another Scots ambassador, sent to Louis to press for a reply to this offer, arrived at the French court at Tours on May 27.[30] Finally, there is the 'lettre' sent to Louis by James III which, according to the July parliament had to be stopped. There is no indication of what it contained, but judging by the lengthy parliamentary remonstrances, it is quite likely to have been an offer by James to go campaigning abroad, possibly resurrecting his earlier plans for an invasion of Brittany. Obviously, therefore, the king had been conducting a foreign policy contrary to that favoured by the estates. His interest in warlike ventures, whether involving Brittany, Gueldres, or Saintonge, produced a crisis which ended in a parliamentary confrontation; and in the end it was parliament's view which prevailed.

Who was responsible for the eloquent and successful parliamentary appeal against James III's continental schemes? As in 1472, there is no sederunt list of the Lords of the Articles, but it is clear from the preamble to the parliamentary record of July 1473 that the system was in operation, and that the Articles were elected.[31] It was not, of course, customary to reveal to the entire body of the estates the instructions given to an ambassador, and so presumably the precise details of Napier's mission to Burgundy in May (for which he was granted a Scottish safe-conduct under the privy seal), and the later embassies to France, were worked out by the king and privy council. Yet evidence available for the following year suggests that the council and the Lords of the Articles included much the same personnel.[32] If this is true also of 1473, then it poses the problem why the same men as would be expected to advise the king, in privy council, on foreign policy, should be found preparing parliamentary articles in direct opposition to a policy on which they had previously agreed. It may well be that they had been misled in council, or had not been party to James's French 'lettre' and other embassies; certainly the parliamentary record suggests this. Between Napier's instructions in May and the meeting of parliament in July, something happened to cause the estates considerable alarm, and as it was in some way connected with James's desire to go abroad in person, it seems likely that the king was carrying on secret and urgent negotiations with Louis XI.

The ultimate result of the conflict seems to have been something of a stalemate. James did not go abroad; he was, after all, 'unprovidit or furnyst of his expenss'. Indeed, his secret negotiations with the French king in the late spring of 1473 were most likely the result of his financial frustration in Scotland. In three successive years, he had asked parliament for taxation, either to finance embassies or military expeditions, and he doas not appear to have received much, if any, of the money he required. If, therefore, he became the pensioner of Louis XI — something which Edward IV of England was to do only two years later — he would have a certain independence of Scottish parliamentary subsidy. Hence the alarmed reaction of the estates, trying to achieve a balance between flattery of the king on the one hand, and schooling him in his business on the other.

However, the schemes suggested to James III by parliament as alternatives were, if anything, less profitable and realistic than his own. In fact they borrowed the king's own policy in suggesting that he should mediate between France and Burgundy; James III had proposed this in 1471, and asked for three thousand crowns from the estates, which may have made them less enthusiastic at the time. Nor was the role of mediator between Louis XI and Charles the Bold likely to win either Gueldres or Saintonge for the Scottish king. Sir David Guthrie, described in the parliamentary protest as the king's ambassador 'send to the King of France for the Recovering of the said counte' (Saintonge), did not in fact go abroad at this time at all;[33] and parliament's suggestion that an embassy to France and Burgundy should press the King's claim to the Duchy of Gueldres — virtually a repetition of Napier's instructions in May — indicates that the king had meantime set in motion more extreme policies without consulting the Lords of the Articles. If these policies indeed involved military assistance to France in return for a sizeable pension, they were in essence more realistic than the parliamentary alternatives. Louis XI of France, faced with hostility from both Yorkist England and Burgundy, might well have paid handsomely for an effective Scottish alliance.

The concern of the politically active in Scotland, it would seem, was not so much with the details of one foreign policy as opposed to another, but rather with the character of the man who was responsible for them all. To many of them who remembered the 1450s, the foreign ambitions and arbitrary acts of James III must have seemed all too familiar. Indeed, the mild parliamentary injunction to James II in 1458, requiring him to observe parliamentary statutes so that his lieges might thank God for sending them such a worthy ruler,[34] strikingly anticipates the flattery with which the estates, in 1473, attempted to turn James III from his purpose, so that 'he mycht be grace of God be callit to gretare thingis'.

They knew their man. From the start of his active rule in 1469, King James had displayed an alarming belief in the sanctity of his office, and it is not at all inconceivable that he thought in imperial terms. In an act of 1469 James claimed 'ful jurisdictioune and fre impire within his realme', including the right to create notaries public, formerly appointed only by the pope or the emperor. Nor was this all. Notaries created by the emperor would in future have no authority in Scotland.[35] The implication that the Scottish king recognised no external jurisdiction within the 'empire' of Scotland was reinforced by a further act of 1472, by which the royal arms of Scotland were no longer to bear the fleurs de lys which might suggest, in heraldic terms, a subordinate relationship to the Crown of France.[36] These imperial pretensions, a dangerously exalted view of Scottish kingship, may in part have been based on the Stewart-Habsburg alliance of 1449, when Eleanor, James III's aunt, had married Duke Sigismund, who subsequently became Archduke of Austria and later emperor. Ties of friendship between James III and Sigismund appear to have been strong enough for the latter to send the Scottish king a gift of artillery in 1481, during the Anglo-Scottish war;[37] and in the last silver coinage of the reign, minted about 1485, James III's portrait would show him to be wearing an imperial crown rather than a coronet.[38]

These delusions of grandeur were clearly already apparent in July 1473; and a direct assault on James's royal dignity was craftily avoided by the prelates' suggestion that his showing himself an able ruler by restoring law and order and justice within Scotland was the most effective way of securing European fame. A year later, the king was further flattered by the estates by the suggestion that he should use his father-in-law, Christian I of Denmark, to help secure for Scotland an alliance with Emperor Frederick III.[39]

Much more alarming to the estates than King James's imperial pretensions, however, was his record of arbitrary and, on occasions, illegal acts within Scotland itself, coupled with an apparent disregard for the monarch's recognised duty of maintaining law and order. It is difficult to assess how much justification there was for the latter complaint. As early as November 1469 a parliamentary commission had been instructed to consider the production of a book of laws drawn from many sources — 'the Kingis lawis, Regiam Majestatem, actis, statutis and uther bukes' — so that the lieges, and the judges, might have no doubt as to what the law laid down; but this had clearly not been done by 1473.[40] It is not clear whether this failure was the result of lack of royal interest, or pressure on the commissioners of other business. Undoubtedly a great and increasing burden of governmental committee work was being shouldered by remarkably few individuals about this time. The Committee of the Articles, so prominent in James III's very frequent parliaments, had the task of preparing statutes and articles — often, though not always, introduced by the Crown — for enactment in full parliament. Although its members seem to have been elected by the three estates when they assembled, they always included a number of royal counsellors. The same men, or some of them, might well also serve on the committee of the lords auditors for causes and complaints, the civil court which met while parliament was in session; and with the total disappearance of judicial sessions after 1468, the lords of council, appointed by the king rather than parliament, acted as the supreme civil court, settling all cases which had been left undecided in parliament.[41] Again, the same men might be involved; and it was not uncommon for certain royal counsellors, such as Argyll and Crawford, to serve on all three committees. Under the circumstances, and bearing in mind the absence of a salaried and professional judiciary, the failure to produce a digest of Scottish law is not altogether surprising.

This was after all a time of significant change in the operation of civil law. An act of November 1469, reaffirmed six years later, laid down that litigants must first take their cases to the judges ordinary — that is, justiciars, sheriffs, stewards, bailies, barons, provosts or bailies of burghs. If, however, they failed to obtain what they regarded as an adequate or fair judgment, they might appeal beyond the ordinaries to the king and council, who would not only judge the case but, if necessary, suspend from office the corrupt or inefficient judge ordinary.[42] We possess no records of the work of the lords of council until 1478; but it is clear that from the time of its inception it was an enormously popular court — far too popular by May 1474, when parliament exhorted judges ordinary to do their jobs properly so that litigants would not continually be troubling the king and council with appeals.[43] Clearly, therefore, the five years following 1469 saw an increase in royal intervention in civil justice, though how far this reflects the personal interest of the king is difficult to say. Certainly the early '70s saw the beginnings of a problem for the royal counsellors involved in civil justice — a heavy and increasing load of work and a backlog of unfinished cases for which James IV was still trying to find a solution early in the following century.

More serious was the apparent lack of royal concern for the proper execution of criminal justice. Too much, perhaps, should not be made of the parliamentary exhortation to James to travel through the realm 'in his awne persone in the execucioune of justice' — that is, on justice ayre — for the same demand had been made of James II in 1458. But the remainder of the estates' complaint in July 1473 reveals concern at the king's too ready granting of remissions and respites for serious crimes, including murder. Here, as perhaps also in his use of the lords of council in civil cases, James III was primarily motivated by greed; and although the parliamentary record of 1473 includes an appeal for an end to remissions 'for a certane tyme',[44] the king appears to have disregarded the estates' advice. By May 1474, parliament would again be condemning those who showed 'gret derisione and skorne of justice' by buying remissions cheaply rather than answering charges in the justice ayre; and the situation was apparently worse in 1478.[45]

From the beginning of James III's personal rule, we may trace the growth of a party of royal familiars whose favour with the king was demonstrated in a remarkable series of royal grants. Thus, on 12 February 1471, James confirmed his 'familiar squire' David Guthrie and his heirs in possession of the barony of Guthrie in Forfarshire;[46] and sometime between 14 May and 4 July 1473 — about the time of his twenty-first birthday — the king made Guthrie captain of the royal guard. He continues to be described in this way for about a year, the last reference to the post being on 21 June 1474.[47] The office of 'Capitaneus Garde Regis' was in itself highly unusual; Pinkerton claims that it was not new, and citing Lindsay of Pitscottie, he finds the origins of the royal guard in the reign of James II, when the post was apparently held by Sir Patrick Gray. In fact, however, Sir Patrick Gray is described by Pitscottie simply as 'the Kingis principall captaine and secreit serwant and familiar to his graice'; there is no specific mention of a royal guard.[48] In any event, Pinkerton states that in 1473 David Guthrie was captain, and George Bell lieutenant, of the King's guard. That Guthrie was captain is borne out by the records; and George Bell appears to have been an archer of the guard before October 1474. It is possible that Bell is to be identified with the 'hensman' of the king for whose clothes and other necessities the Treasurer's accounts supply some information in the autumn of 1473. There would seem to have been five 'hensmen' — that is, pages or close attendants — and Bell is the most frequently mentioned, described sometimes as 'litil Bell'. One of his duties was to sleep in the king's chamber.[49]

As for Guthrie himself, his career is well known, and it is certainly not that of a royal favourite pushed into undue prominence by the king. Treasurer from 1461 to 1468, Clerk Register from 1468 to January 1473, and with two periods as Comptroller, from July 1466 to March 1468, and again from April 1470 to February 1471, Guthrie had been knighted early in 1473.[50] In 1468 he had received a licence from the Crown to erect and fortify a tower at Guthrie; he was one of the Lords of the Articles in 1471 and 1474, and by 18 May 1474, if not before, a member of the royal council.[51] His appointment as captain of the royal bodyguard may therefore be regarded as reward for a long and successful administrative career, but it is possible that he became unpopular with other members of the council as a result.

Why should James III have created a royal bodyguard in the early summer of 1473, and having done so, apparently abandon the idea about a year later? It is possible that he was influenced by the French kings, Charles VII and Louis XI, both of whom had bodyguards of Scots mercenaries; and James III, conscious not only of his status but of growing opposition to his foreign policy between May and July 1473, may have feared for his personal safety. If so, his fears may have come to an end by the summer of 1474, when the office of 'Capitaneus Garde Regis' disappears from witness lists and is not heard of again. The office and the bodyguard may of course have remained in existence; but it is significant that after the summer of 1474 Sir David Guthrie appears only infrequently as a royal charter witness, does not sit again on the Committee of the Articles, and is not to be found in parliament. He was still alive in 1479, when he founded the collegiate church at Guthrie for a provost and three prebendaries;[52] but it is difficult to escape the conclusion that about the middle of 1474 his favour at court, and his tenure of the captaincy of the royal guard, both came to an end. Possibly his fellow councillors believed that he had acquired too many offices too swiftly; until 1473, after all, he was only a laird. Alternatively, it may be that the innovation of a royal bodyguard was itself contrary to the wishes of some members of the council, and that, when Guthrie was removed, the institution lapsed. But according to the sixteenth century chronicler Giovanni Ferreri, the guard reappeared in the 1480s under the command of an undoubted royal favourite, John Ramsay, Lord Bothwell;[53] so it may in fact have been maintained after 1474, possibly with different personnel. The subject is of some importance in any estimate of the king's character, for it was not until Ferreri's narrative a century later that the royal bodyguard was associated with favourites and the estrangement of James III from his nobility; what contemporary records show is that the office of captain went in 1473 to a distinguished administrator, a man of business of long standing.

While we may therefore speculate about the king's elevation of Guthrie, no such doubt surrounds the favour shown to Andrew Stewart, Lord Avandale, Chancellor since 1460. On 4 April 1471, Avandale was given the liferent of the earldom of Lennox, in spite of the fact that there were three claimants to the earldom, that the Lennox was not in Crown hands and therefore not in the king's gift. This grant, which must rank as the most scandalous of the reign, was followed on 28 August 1472 by the issue — somewhat belatedly — of letters of legitimation to Avandale and his brothers Arthur and Walter; and further immediate grants to the Chancellor included a confirmation of his lordship of Avandale, and the lands of Easter Leckie in Stirlingshire, both in September 1472.[54]

The sequel to James III's illegal gift of the liferent of the Lennox to Avandale in 1471 occurred two years later. On 6 August 1473, the king, who after a long delay had conferred on John Stewart, Lord Darnley, the title of Earl of Lennox, granted Darnley a confirmation of his lands in Renfrewshire and Ayrshire; and in a letter under the privy seal, dated 10 October 1473, King James commanded the tenants of Lennox to obey Darnley as earl, because the earldom had now been conferred on him 'with the avis and delyuerance of the Lordis of oure Consaile' for long and true service on Darnley's part to the king and his predecessors.[55] The situation was bizarre in the extreme. Chancellor Avandale, the recipient of the king's gift of the Lennox liferent, no doubt sat in the council meeting at which Darnley was given the title; and he may have reflected that he had done considerably better as a courtier than Darnley, who had launched his career in the royal service on the same day twenty-one years before, when both men had thrust their daggers into the body of the eighth Earl of Douglas. Darnley can hardly have been happy with the title alone; and in any case, as he was painfully aware, he was only one of three claimants. His two opponents, John Haldane of Gleneagles and John Napier of Merchiston, were both to be found at court and in favour with the king in the spring of 1473; and Darnley was forced to fight for his rights.

On 4 March he had appeared before the privy council and protested his right to the earldom, claiming that the lands of the Lennox were in the king's hands by reason of ward (since the death of Earl Duncan in 1425), and that his opponent John Haldane could not therefore have been granted the lands by royal gift as he claimed. This argument does not appear to have been accepted, for on 28 March Haldane was granted, for faithful service, a quarter of the earldom; and Darnley had to wait till 27 July for an instrument of sasine in his favour, granting him half the lands and the title.[56] Even the royal confirmation, on 6 August, of Darnley's own Renfrewshire and Ayrshire lands, was made only on condition that, as Earl of Lennox, he would admit Avandale's liferent of the earldom 'als frely and in siclyk forme as our forsaid chancelar had the samyn landis of us of before'; and he was also required to accept William Edmonstone of Duntreath in certain Lennox lands which had been granted to him by James II.[57] This tenuous and unsatisfactory position — Darnley with the title and half the lands, Avandale with the liferent, and Haldane with a quarter of the lands and a claim to the title — was to endure for only another two years, when a further arbitrary act of James III would rob Darnley even of his title. The entire episode is illustrative of the king's disregard of the rights of the senior co-heir in preference to those whom he chose to favour. Hence Avandale's belated letters of legitimation; and in the case of the familiar Haldane, James III was flouting the law by treating the earldom as a forfeited possession and therefore in his gift.[58]

In the early 1470s, royal favour extended also to men who had still to make their careers at court, above all Dr. William Scheves, the future archbishop of St. Andrews, who is to be found in 1471 receiving his first annual pension — a modest £20 — for his services as a physician. Possibly the son of John Scheves, clerk register in the early minority of James II, William Scheves had been educated at St. Andrews University, where by April 1460 he was a resident master. He was still there on March 9, 1470, when he signed a conclusion of the Faculty; and he presumably entered the royal service shortly afterwards. George Buchanan claims that Scheves studied for several years at Louvain under 'John Spernic, a celebrated physician and astrologer'.[59] This individual can be identified as John Spierinck, who was rector of the University of Louvain in 1457, 1462, and 1479. There is no doubt that Scheves was interested in astrology, as a book on the subject was dedicated to him in 1491 by Jaspar Laet de Borchloen. In the early 1470s, however, his duties at court were severely practical rather than esoteric; apart from acting as physician, he obtained drugs from Bruges for the king, prescribed green ginger for David Kirkcaldy and Will Pringill, two servants of the king's chamber, made payment for 'the sewing of the King's sarks', bought velvet for the king and looked after the silver for the harness of three of the royal horses. All in all, this suggests a minor official in the royal household, of no more importance than Rob Scheves, a servant in the wardrobe who was presumably a relation. The spectacular career of William Scheves as the principal royal favourite of the '70s had still to come.[60]

As in secular affairs, so in the church, James III pursued an arbitrary and wilful course; but in taking part in the general European struggle between crown and papacy for control of provisions to important benefices, he was following a well-trodden path, already associated in Scotland with his grandfather and with the royal administration during his own minority. Successive rulers, attempting to protect the resources and authority of the Scottish Crown against what they regarded as papal encroachment, had resisted papal claims both to provisions and to annates. However, by the 1440s, following the success of the papacy in mastering the reforming council of Basle, there had come a lull in the struggle, at least over provisions, and what followed was a reversion to what Dickinson describes as 'the comfortable working relationship' between papcy and monarchy which had existed before the Great Schism — that is, that the pope would provide to vacant bishoprics or abbeys men certain to be acceptable to, and generally nominated by, the king.[61] In practice, therefore, the monarch had a good chance of controlling appointments to important benefices, which were often conferred on officers of state as rewards for loyalty. He also ran the risk of upsetting local vested interests by appointing someone who was regarded as unsuitable — or, in the case of James III, by attempting to suppress an existing foundation.

The critical year was 1472, when the king intervened in the affairs of the abbeys of Dunfermline and Paisley and the priory of Coldingham. In the former case, James III was simply overturning an election to the vacant abbacy of Dunfermline by the monks there, installing instead his own candidate Henry Crichton, abbot of Paisley, with the approval of the pope. The resulting vacancy at Paisley was filled by another royal nominee, Robert Shaw, parson of Minto. A century later, Bishop Lesley would condemn the king's actions at Dunfermline and Paisley as the beginning of the degradation of Scottish monastic life; but in fact it was nothing of the kind. The truth was that the 'godlie electiones' so dear to Lesley were far from universal long before 1472; that king and pope were closely interested in — if frequently at odds over — appointments to the major benefices; and that, as Nicholson points out, free elections by monastic chapters had long been frustrated by papal reservations, provisions, and grants in commendam.[62] Thus the election of the king's candidate was not necessarily detrimental to the spiritual health of a religious house; as long as the crown used its extended patronage responsibly, excellent appointments — such as Lindsay at Lincluden or Lichtoun at Arbroath — might be made.

Coldingham, however, came into a different category, for here the issue from the beginning was not one of spirituality but of wealth. This rich Benedictine priory, lying on the North Sea coast in the extreme south-eastern corner of Scotland some ten miles north of Berwick, had until 1462 been a dependency of the English priory of Durham; but in May of that year, the Scots had taken advantage of the English civil wars to eject the last of the Durham monks from Coldingham and from Scotland.[63] An act of parliament of 1466 confirmed the seizure of 1462 by declaring 'that na Inglis man have na benefice, seculare nor religouss, within the realme'.[64] In spite of continuing efforts by the Durham monks to recover their property, the priory of Coldingham soon became the centre of a purely local struggle between members of the Scottish baronial family of Hume. Patrick Hume, archdeacon of Teviotdale, attempted to obtain the priory in commendam in 1461; but his claims were thrust aside by Sir Alexander Hume of that ilk, who as bailie of Coldingham since 1442 wanted his son John appointed as prior so that his family could continue to enjoy the revenues of the priory. In 1464 John Hume was duly provided to Coldingham, and Hume control remained unchallenged for eight years.[65]

In 1472, however, the Prior of Durham made the tactical mistake of petitioning James III to promote the reoccupation of Coldingham by Durham monks. Typically, the Scottish king used the situation to attempt to enrich himself; disregarding the Durham appeal and ignoring the Humes, on 6 April 1472 King James petitioned Pope Sixtus IV to suppress the priory of Coldingham and reallocate its revenues to his own chapel royal of St. Mary of the Rock, St. Andrews. The royal supplication to Rome was successful; but the result was a long struggle between James III and the Humes for possession of the priory and its revenues; it was resolved only in 1488 when the king was killed.[66]

H

However, the event which provoked the greatest opposition from the Scottish ecclesiastical hierarchy was one which the wily king was able to turn rapidly to his advantage. This was the erection of St. Andrews into an archiepiscopal see, by Pope Sixtus IV, on 17 August 1472, at long last providing Scotland with a metropolitan in the shape of Bishop Patrick Graham. Three centuries earlier, such a move would have been welcomed as an obvious means of terminating the persistent efforts of the archdiocese of York to assert metropolitan status over the entire Scottish church; but by the fifteenth century such considerations were no longer relevant, and indeed the Scottish clergy relished their position as part of a church which was a special daughter of the Holy See. As Macfarlane convincingly shows, such an arrangement allowed local ordinaries to run their own affairs without too much interference from Rome or from one of themselves, while at the same time any Scottish bishop who felt that his rights were being violated might appeal directly to Rome rather than having to refer his plea to a metropolitan. Likewise Scottish kings had little need for metropolitans or primates, because they could resist papal claims more effectively without them. Indeed, 'the last thing the crown and episcopate wanted of the Scottish church was the possibility of an awkward or intransigent primate, bent on enforcing dubious papal policies'.[67]

Into this ecclesiastical minefield stumbled the unfortunate Patrick Graham, bishop of St. Andrews. The son of Sir Robert Graham of Fintry, Graham had been born about 1435; as the grandson of Robert III's daughter Mary and the nephew of Bishop Kennedy, he could expect rapid preferment within the church. When he was fifteen, canonries and prebends at Glasgow and Aberdeen were reserved for him; five years later he was dispensed to receive two further benefices. In 1456 he graduated in arts at St. Andrews University, and by 1457 had become Dean of the Faculty of Arts and an examiner of bachelors the year after. In March 1463, Graham was provided to the See of Brechin, probably at the instance of his uncle Bishop Kennedy; and his royal blood and Kennedy connections doubtless earned him the bishopric of St. Andrews after Kennedy's death. Subsequently he acquired the abbey of Paisley and the priory of Pittenweem in commendam.[68]

Such a rapid rise — Graham was only thirty when he was provided to St. Andrews — inevitably provoked jealousy and some justifiable anger amongst other members of the Scottish hierarchy. In particular, Bishops Muirhead of Glasgow and Spens of Aberdeen, in view of their seniority and proven administrative ability, would have been better suited to the task of running the country's senior diocese. Nevertheless, as Macfarlane suggests, Graham was probably a conscientious and hard-working bishop, attending parliaments regularly, taking seriously his duties as Chancellor of St. Andrews University, and legislating for his diocese.[69] Yet if he had been a saint, he would still have found his position precarious in the extreme.

This was partly, though not entirely, because Graham had acquired his ecclesiastical preferment during James III's minority, so that in practice the king had had little or nothing to do with it. In addition, he faced the problem of having to pay to the Apostolic Camera over 3,000 gold florins for his common services for Brechin, St. Andrews, Paisley, and Pittenweem; and he was clearly in financial difficulties, which involved him in litigation and quarrels over the first three of these benefices.[70] Further troubles for Graham followed the king's assumption of power in 1469. There already existed a statute, dating from 1466 and perhaps made with Graham in mind, threatening any holder of a commend with the loss of his temporality and the penalties of rebellion;[71] and although the bishop had prudently resigned his commend of Paisley, he still held Pittenweem in commendam in 1469. James III soon showed that he intended to use the three estates — no doubt with the clergy well to the fore — to limit papal provisions within Scotland, and that he expected Graham to support him. Thus in November 1469 parliament passed an act reviving an indult of Nicholas V to the late Bishop Kennedy, whereby the Bishop of St. Andrews was allowed to confirm elections in the monastic houses of his diocese. This was a substantial concession, involving as it did eleven abbeys and four priories, and James III wanted to revive the indult so that papal patronage could be largely excluded from the most important Scottish diocese.[72]

Whatever his ambitions, Graham now found himself a pawn in the struggle for control over provisions being waged by King James and Pope Paul II. The pope, determined to make a fight of it, further embarrassed the bishop by announcing that the St. Andrews indult had been revoked; and the Scots parliament of May 1471 responded to this challenge by reasserting the right of 'fre elecioune', at the same time using threatening language about annexations and unions of benefices made since the king's accession. These were now to be annulled, and no papal collector was to levy taxes on the Scottish clergy higher than those customary in the past. There was much fulmination about 'the gret dampnage and skaith' done to the realm by the continual referral of ecclesiastical appeals to Rome, with the outflow of money to the curia which this involved.[73] In short King James, with the backing of the Scottish estates, was openly challenging papal authority; and in June 1471 he appointed Henry, abbot of Cambuskenneth, to act as his procurator on a mission to the Roman curia, possibly, as Nicholson suggests, to bargain with the pope for a settlement of the dispute over provisions.[74]

However, Patrick Graham reached Rome before James III's procurator, gained the ear of the new pope, Sixtus IV, and concocted with him a totally new settlement of the Scottish church, one which was at odds with the policies of both king and hierarchy. The result was the bull of 17 August 1472, erecting the bishopric of St. Andrews into an archbishopric with metropolitan authority; the other twelve Scottish bishops were to be suffragans, owing obedience to the new archbishop. The bull took note of the Scottish criticisms of constant appeals to Rome by suggesting that the existence of a metropolitan would help to reduce the number, a remarkably ill-informed view of the true situation in Scotland. But it also accepted the need to include within Scottish ecclesiastical jurisdiction the bishoprics of Galloway — still technically subject to York — the Isles and Orkney, removed from the theoretical control of the Norwegian archbishopric of Nidaros. This was the only realistic part of a proposed settlement whose main provisions were bound to be rejected by James III and the Scottish bishops. Indeed, the bull commented on the tendency of the Scottish ordinaries to abuse their power, and suggested that a metropolitan would bring some discipline to the church, a prospect which undoubtedly served to unite the Scottish hierarchy with remarkable speed, though not in the way that was intended.[75] The vital issue of ecclesiastical patronage, the source of the dispute, was not mentioned in the bull, though it might safely be assumed that with Graham as metropolitan the pope would recover some of his control in Scotland. Perhaps to be sure of his man, Sixtus IV heaped further honours on Patrick Graham. The unfortunate archbishop found himself invested with powers and offices which he would never be able to exercise — legate a latere; Apostolic Internuncio for the purpose of collecting money and levying men for a crusade against the Turks, with the power to exact a tithe of the incomes of the Scottish clergy; beneficiary of the revenues of the priory of Pittenweem and seven parish churches in spite of the parliamentary statute of 1471 forbidding such unions; monastic visitor; and commendator of the Abbey of Arbroath for five years.[76] Patrick Graham has sometimes been described as insane, but it is surely proof of his sanity that he delayed his return to Scotland until at least September 1473.

His long absence gave his incensed sovereign time to act; and it is quite unnecessary to follow Buchanan's sixteenth century story of William Scheves as the evil genius who brought about Graham's fall. Many, if not most, of the clergy, and certainly the king, must have favoured it. Graham had after all gone to Rome without the royal licence and in direct contravention of an act of parliament of 1471, and had returned archbishop, legate a latere, and papal collector. A General Council, of which no official report survives, was summoned in November 1473, and it would appear that as a result of this the king, by February 1474, had ordered the seizure of the temporalities of the diocese of St. Andrews.[77]

Throughout the entire affair, the king had been careful to seek the widest possible support for his actions against the archbishop. The period of three months between the original summons and the final judgment of the General Council gave time, even allowing for Christmas and the possibility of inclement weather, for a fairly full representation of the estates, including those who had a considerable distance to travel. General letters were sent out to the various regions, to the north, to Galloway, to Angus, Fife and Lothian, rather than special letters summoning a few important magnates;[78] the business was after all important, involving the resumption of a powerful vassal's lands by the Crown. Where the king spent Christmas 1473 is not recorded, but he was probably still in Edinburgh on 18 December, when he granted to James of Menteith some lands in Menteith as a reward for the slaughter of Patrick Stewart, a rebel.[79] Thereafter there is no suggestion as to James III's whereabouts until 18 January 1474, when he is once again to be found in Edinburgh.[80] It is therefore probable that the General Council took place in January 1474, possibly in the latter half of the month; this would be consistent with its judgment being delivered before 4 February.

The results of this judgment, and the subsequent career of Patrick Graham, are unfortunately contained at length only in the sixteenth century narratives of John Lesley and George Buchanan, and the records shed very little light on royal action taken against the archbishop. Some time between 3 and 13 April, 1474 a payment was made to Andrew Mowbray for 'the solisting of the Kingis materis in the Court of Rome' — presumably a justification of James's seizure of the temporalities of the

See of St. Andrews and a supplication that Graham's bulls be rescinded.[81] Buchanan includes the story that the king accepted a gift of twelve thousand marks from the Scottish bishops for his support against the archbishop, and then offered to come to terms with Graham in return for a money payment by his friends.[82] The sum involved may be exaggerated by Buchanan; but such duplicity and venality would not be inconsistent with what we know of James III's character at this time; and it may well be significant that the king wrote to Robert Grahame, the archbishop's kinsman, in October 1473, though it is not known on what subject.[83]

Whatever the details, the undoubted beneficiary of Graham's deposition was the king himself. He had successfully used the Scottish clergy to frustrate Graham's ambitions and bring about the archbishop's ruin, and in doing so had increased his authority over the church at the expense of Pope Sixtus IV. It was a political triumph, if hardly an edifying one; and James III was able to use it to retain the office of archbishop and to confer it on his favourite, William Scheves, in 1478. There is, however, something very disagreeable about the sustained attacks on the deposed Patrick Graham by both king and clergy after 1473. By August of that year his goods and money had been restrained; in February 1474, following the General Council's judgment against him, his temporalities were seized; and by September 1476 Graham, discredited and deeply in debt, suffered a complete breakdown in his health, and the king's man Scheves was appointed to deputise for him as coadjutor. Not until three months after this, in December 1476 — by which time the issue had been dragging on for over four years — was a papal commission set up to enquire into Graham's irregularities, and the wretched man was confronted with charges which included blasphemy and heresy, a remarkable advance on the more obvious bureaucratic abuses of simony and pluralism for which most, if not all, of the Scottish hierarchy might have been condemnded. But the bull of condemnation, followed by the official deprivation of Archbishop Graham in January 1478, simply put a formal end to a process which was long since over in Scotland. It was not, in the last analysis, the papacy or the Apostolic Camera which had broken Graham, but a greedy and vindictive monarch and a jealous Scottish ecclesiastical hierarchy; and the public occasion of his fall was the meeting of the General Council at the beginning of 1474.[84]

Dr. Macfarlane suggests that the affair of Patrick Graham produced at least two long-term effects — 'that no prelate, however well born and supported by the papacy, could ever again successfully oppose the Scottish crown and hierarchy together, and that by 1478 James III was able to manipulate and over-ride papal provisions at will'.[85] This is perhaps paying too high a tribute to James's political acumen; and at the same time it exaggerates the overall results of Graham's fall. In the '80s, the king was to lose two major battles with the papacy and recalcitrant churchmen over appointments to the bishoprics of Glasgow and Dunkeld, failures on his part which duly produced two rebel bishops in 1488. Yet it cannot be denied that King James, like other European monarchs of his day, was steadily winning the struggle with the papacy for control of important church benefices, and that the deposition of Archbishop Graham was in that sense a royal victory. If, as Macfarlane suggests, the ultimate loser was the Scottish church, in the short term certain individuals within the hierarchy did remarkably well for themselves through their support for crown policies. Prominent among these was Thomas Spens, bishop of Aberdeen, already a politician of considerable experience, who in February 1474 was given complete exemption for himself and his diocese from the jurisdiction of Archbishop Graham.[86] Spens had already served as Keeper of the Privy Seal between 1468 and 1470, and was a constant member of the Committee of the Articles throughout the '70s. Above all, as a frequent ambassador to England and a pensioner of Edward IV, he was a protagonist of firm peace and alliance with the English king, a policy which James III was to follow from 1474 onwards.[87] Spens's vast experience of government should have made him the most prominent ecclesiastical statesman of his day, and he was probably regarded in this way by many in the royal administration and in parliament; but it may be doubted whether his industry, experience, and long service to the Crown necessarily made him a close friend of King James. That role was reserved for William Scheves, the future archbishop.

By 1474, therefore, the career of James III bore a striking resemblance to that of his father — the same wilful arbitrariness, the same desire to contemplate foreign invasion schemes and to play a major diplomatic role in northern Europe, and the same kind of opposition from the estates, mildly suggesting that the king ought to get on with his job as they understood it. Both kings were well served by able and long-suffering counsellors, in a few cases the same men; and both ignored conciliar and parliamentary advice when it suited them. The evidence available, however, suggests that James III was a more devious character than his father, capable of more sustained duplicity, as in his illegal interference in the Lennox disputes and his very secret negotiations with Louis XI in 1473. But he still had the intelligence to reward service on the part of the greater nobility. On 26 February, 1474, Colin Campbell, earl of Argyll, already Master of the Royal Household and a Privy Councillor, was given a royal grant of the office of justiciar, chamberlain, sheriff, and bailie within the bounds of the regality of Cowal, with the power to hold justice and chamberlain ayres and sheriff courts therein; and on 17 July of the same year the loyal David, earl of Crawford, was given custody of the castle of Berwick-on-Tweed, a burgh of which the king was to show himself inordinately proud.[88]

Grants like these to loyal servants cannot, however, obscure the fact that the king's treatment of lands and offices was arbitrary in the extreme, and that he displayed a confidence in this respect which suggests an unshakeable belief in the exalted status of a Stewart monarch. Thus parliamentary admonitions such as those of 1473 might prove a temporary irritant, but they did not radically alter royal policies. The king advanced foreign schemes after 1473 as before; and much more important, his wilful interference in the distribution of lands and offices continued unchecked. One such act was typical of James III's arbitrariness and ability to make implacable enemies with remarkable speed. On 20 March 1474 he conferred upon John Drummond of Cargill the offices of Steward, Coroner, and Forester of the earldom of Strathearn, apparently already resigned into Drummond's hands by Maurice Drummond.[89] Yet only the previous year, in August 1473, Sir William

Murray of Tullibardine had obtained a charter from James III granting him the same office.[90]

It appears that the Drummonds and Murrays, who were neighbours in Perthshire, were at feud; and we do not necessarily need to believe Pitscottie's colourful account of the burning to death of six score Murrays in Monzievaird church in a fire started by the Drummonds. Rather more prosaically, the two families are found appearing in an action heard before the Lords Auditors on 18 July, 1476, Sir William Murray complaining of the spoliation by the Drummonds of thirty kye and oxen from his lands of Orchell in Strathearn.[91] Thus we are faced with the curious fact that James III appointed two feuding lairds to the same profitable office more or less at the same time; and it is not clear which of them actually enjoyed the fruits of the office. Having fostered the local feud, the king at last made up his mind about the Stewartry of Strathearn on 19 September 1475. On that date he announced that the resignation of the Stewartry by Maurice Drummond into the hands of John Drummond of Cargill was invalid, because the office had in fact been in Crown hands 'past memory of man'; and he went on to revoke Drummond's charter only eighteen months after it had been granted, 'charging his sheriffs in that part to make proclamation at the burgh of Perth and at Uchterardour (Auchterarder) of the King's taking into his own hands the said office; and none of the lieges to obey the said John of Drummond in the office till further commandment'.[92] By this seizure of the Stewarty of Strathearn and its profits for himself, James III made an enemy of Drummond of Cargill for life. Later concessions to him, including a lordship of parliament, did nothing to heal the breach; and in fact the king made matters worse when he granted the Stewartry of Strathearn to Drummond's rival, Sir William Murray, during the crisis of 1482-3.[93]

Why did King James act in this wilful manner? He may of course have been moved purely by greed, which would suggest this simple and arbitrary solution to the Drummond-Murray dispute in Strathearn. But royal authority was also involved, and it seems likely that the king believed that he could strengthen his position and resources by acts which were doubtful or openly illegal. Royal action over the Stewarty of Strathearn falls into a category which also includes the annexation of the Coldingham revenues in 1472 and the partition, and seizure of the liferent, of the Lennox between 1471 and 1475. In none of these cases was the king apparently at all interested in doing justice to the litigants involved; and the price which he paid was the creation of specific enemies without at the same time adding to the number of his friends. In the last analysis, the issues of Coldingham, the Lennox and the Stewartry of Strathearn remained unresolved until the following reign;[94] for James III himself, they constituted a nagging political ulcer which finally burst in the spring of 1488.

In 1474, however, King James was as yet untroubled by these problems; indeed, he probably viewed his first five years' active rule with some satisfaction. Certainly there had been setbacks. He had been checked in his desire to appear a leader in war on the continent; and he had discovered for himself that extraordinary taxation provoked opposition in parliament. Yet the strictures of the July parliament of 1473 may not have worried the king unduly. His first son, the future James IV, had been born at Stirling on 17 March;[95] and it is likely that James III accompanied Queen Margaret on a pilgrimage to the shrine of St. Ninian at Whithorn, presumably to give thanks for the birth of a son, at the end of July. By late August both king and queen were to be found hunting at Falkland, returning to Edinburgh some time before 16 September.[96] King James was perhaps right to be confident, even arrogant, about the future; for the birth of a son had not only secured the dynasty, but also provided him with the family necessary to negotiate his most profitable diplomatic achievement — the English alliance of October 1474.

NOTES

1. *See above*, Chapter 2.

2. In general, see W. H. Finlayson, 'The Boyds in Bruges', *SHR*, xxviii, 195-6; and for James III's letter, *S.H.S. Misc.* viii, 19-32.

3. Nicholson, *op.cit.*, 420.

4. *R.M.S.*, ii, Nos. 1060, 1123; *S.H.S. Misc.* viii, 26-7.

5. Nicholson, *op.cit.*, 442-3.

6. *E.R.*, viii, 85, 80; *R.M.S.*, ii, Nos. 995, 996.

7. *A.P.S.*, ii, 187; *R.M.S.*, ii, No. 992.

8. *T.A.*, i, 29-39, quoted in Nicholson, *op.cit.*, 421.

9. *R.M.S.*, ii, Nos. 996-999; and see Nicholson, *op.cit.*, 417 n. 149, where the author suggests that the increase in Earl William's pension from 50 to 400 marks may have been the result of a transaction conveying the lordship of Shetland to James III.

10. *A.P.S.*, ii, 102.

11. Nicholson, *op.cit.*, 417-8.

12. *A.P.S.*, ii, 99. Margaret is not named in the parliamentary record, but as Mary had fled to Burgundy with her husband and had not yet returned to Scotland, it was clearly Margaret who was intended as the prospective bride.

13. *See*, e.g., *A.P.S.*, ii, 97, 101.

14. *Cal. Docs. Scot.*, iv, Nos. 1394, 1395, 1397; *Rot. Scot.* ii, 429-30. It is curious to find the Earl of Caithness named in this safe-conduct, as only a year before he had obtained a royal exemption from attendance on embassies or expeditions.

15. Barbara E. Crawford, 'Scotland's Foreign Relations: Scandinavia', in J. M. Brown (ed.), *Scottish Society in the Fifteenth Century*, 89.

16. *See above*, Chapter 2.

17. *A.P.S.*, ii, 102.

18. A. Dupuy, *Histoire de la Réunion de la Bretagne a la France*, i, 302.

19. *R.M.S.*, ii, Nos. 1041, 1043, 1055, 1073, 1079; *A.P.S.*, ii, 188.

20. *A.P.S.*, ii, 102.

21. Scofield, *Edward IV*, ii, 31.

22. Mark Napier, *Memoirs of John Napier of Merchiston* (Edinburgh, 1834), 512-14. Original in N.L.S.

23. *Ibid.*, 33.

24. B.M. Add. MS. 43496, f. 1.

25. *Cal. State Papers (Milan)*, i, 174-5.

26. *A.P.S.*, ii, 103-4.

27. G. du Fresne de Beaucourt, *Histoire de Charles VII* (Paris 1881–1891), ii, 496; and *see above*, Chapter 2.

28. Nicholson, *op.cit.*, 475.

29. Rymer, *Foedera*, xi, 772.

30. *Cal. State Papers (Milan)*, i, 175.

31. *A.P.S.*, ii, 103.

32. *A.D.A.*, 18 May 1474; *A.P.S.*, ii, 106. Thomas Spens, bishop of Aberdeen, Secretary Whitelaw, the Earl of Argyll and Sir David Guthrie were common to both bodies.

33. *A.P.S.*, ii, 104; and *R.M.S.*, ii, Nos. 1125-1155, in many of which Guthrie appears as a charter witness.

34. *See above*, Chapter 2.

35. *A.P.S.*, ii, 95.

36. *Ibid.*, 102. The political theory on which King James's claims to imperial status were based — consciously or unconsciously — was the Bartolist 'rex in regno suo est imperator'. *See* Quentin Skinner, *The Foundations of Modern Political Thought* (Cambridge, 1978), i, 9-12.

37. Innsbruck, Landesregierungsarchiv, Sigismund ivc/180/9. I am indebted for this reference to the late Dr. A. I. Dunlop.

38. Stewart, *The Scottish Coinage*, 67; and see jacket illustration.

39. *A.P.S.*, ii, 106.

40. *Ibid.*, 97, 105.

41. The Lords of the Articles, whose membership varied between nine and sixteen, always contained representatives from each of the three estates, and met on at least fourteen occasions between 1467 and 1485. For typical personnel, see e.g. *A.P.S.*, ii, 121. The Committee for Causes and Complaints (Civil actions) usually numbered nine, three from each estate, e.g. *A.P.S.*, ii, 124. The Lords of Council, royal nominees, did not always include members of the third estate: *A.D.C.*, i, 3-79; and see discussion in Nicholson, *op.cit.*, 425-7.

42. *A.P.S.*, ii, 94, 111.

43. *Ibid.*, 107.

44. *Ibid.*, 104.

45. *Ibid.*, 118.

46. *R.M.S.*, ii, No. 1011.

47. *Ibid.*, Nos. 1125, 1132, 1175.

48. J. Pinkerton, *The History of Scotland from the Accession of the House of Stuart to that of Mary, with Appendices of Original Papers* (London, 1797), i. 322; Pitscottie, *Historie*, i, 91.

49. *R.M.S.*, ii, No. 1186; *T.A.*, i, 15, 16, 55, 56. On p. 16, the reference is to 'x elne of canves to mak Nikky and Bell a bed to ly on in the Kingis chalmire'.

50. *R.M.S.*, Nos. 1102, 1104.

51. *H.M.C.*, *Rep. ii*, App. 197; *A.P.S.*, ii, 93, 106; *A.D.A.*, 34.

52. *H.M.C. Rep. ii*, App. 197.

53. Ferrerius, *Appendix to Boece*, f. 398 v.

54. *R.M.S.*, ii, Nos. 1018, 1066, 1067, 1068, 1076, 1080.

55. *Ibid.*, No. 1136; Lennox Charters No. 68, printed in Fraser, *Lennox*, ii, 101-2.

56. *R.M.S.*, ii, No. 1116; Lennox Charters No. 66, printed in Fraser, *Lennox*, ii, 97-100.

57. Fraser, *Lennox*, ii, 94-6; and see transumpt of privy seal letter of James III to Darnley, 21 June 1473: Lennox Charters, No. 64.

58. Fraser, *Lennox*, i, 288-311: 'Partition of the Earldom of Lennox'.

59. Buchanan, *History*, ii, 137.

60. Scheves' career forms a chapter in Herkless and Hannay, *Archbishops of St. Andrews*, i, 80-149; but this contains a number of omissions. I am indebted to Dr. Rod Lyall for drawing my attention to John Scheves as the probable father of William. For Scheves' early duties at court, see *T.A.*, i, 18, 21, 23, 28.

61. W. C. Dickinson, *Scotland from the Earliest Times to 1603* (3rd edition, revised and edited A. A. M. Duncan, 1977), 272-3.

62. Lesley, *History*, 39-40; Nicholson, *op.cit.*, 459.

63. For a full discussion of the pre-1462 Coldingham disputes, see R. B. Dobson, 'The Last English monks on Scottish soil', *S.H.R.*, xlvi, 1-25.

64. *A.P.S.*, ii, 86.

65. R. B. Dobson, *op.cit.*, 6-7, 13-15.

66. *C.P.L.*, xiii, 14; Cameron, *Apostolic Camera*, 172; and for a full discussion of the Coldinghan dispute, see N. Macdougall, 'The Struggle for the Priory of Coldingham 1472-1488', *Innes Review*, xxiii, (1972), 102-114.

67. Leslie J. Macfarlane, 'The Primacy of the Scottish Church, 1472-1521', *Innes Review*, xx, No. 2, 111-12.

68. *Ibid.*, 112-113.

69. *Ibid.*, 114.

70. *Ibid.*, 113-114.

71. *A.P.S.*, ii, 85.

72. Nicholson, *op.cit.*, 460.

73. *A.P.S.*, ii, 99.

74. Nicholson, *op.cit.*, 461.

75. A. Theiner, *Vetera Monumenta Hibernorum et Scotorum* (Rome, 1864), 465-468.

76. Herkless and Hannay, op.cit., i, 50; J. A. F. Thomson, 'Some New Light on the Elevation of Patrick Graham', *S.H.R.*, xl, 83-88; R. K. Hannay, *The Scottish Crown and the Papacy* (Historical Association Pamphlet), 8-9.

77. *T.A.*, i, 47.

78. *Ibid.*, 46.

79. Fraser, *Menteith*, ii, 300.

80. Fraser, *Keir*, 247.

81. *T.A.*, i, 48.

82. Buchanan, *History*, ii, 137-8.

83. *T.A.*, i, 46.

84. L. J. Macfarlane, *op.cit.*, 114.

85. *Ibid.*, 115.

86. *Ibid.*, 114.

87. *R.M.S.*, ii, Nos. 965-1006; *A.P.S.*, ii, 93, 98, 106, 111, 117, 121, 124; *Rot. Scot.*, ii, 432, 436, 439, 441, 443, 444; *Cal. Docs. Scot.*, iv, Nos. 1360 and 1383.

88. *R.M.S.*, ii, Nos. 1110, 1133.

89. *R.M.S.*, ii, No. 1160.

90. Atholl Royal Letters No. 1 (Blair Castle).

91. Pitscottie, *Historie*, i, 237; Atholl MSS., Box 1, Parcel I, 1 (Blair Castle).

92. Atholl Charters, vol. 1, No. 47 (Blair Castle).

93. Atholl Royal Letters, No. 2 (Blair Castle).

94. In May 1491 James IV was still trying to arbitrate between Drummond and Murray concerning the Stewartry of Strathearn: *A.D.A.*, 150-1.

95. The date of the birth is inferred from the date of James IV's general revocation on reaching the age of 25.

96. *T.A.*, i, 44; *E.R.*, viii, 215-6; *T.A.*, i, 29; *R.M.S.*, ii, No. 1140.

6

The Price of Peace: 1474–80

PEACE and alliance with England was not an obvious policy for a fifteenth century Scottish king to pursue. Indeed, with the possible exception of the Treaty of London in 1423 — which came into rather a different category as it involved the release of James I from eighteen years of confinement in England and the payment of a substantial ransom by the Scots — there had been no such alliance during the century. Instead there had emerged a familiar pattern of short truces subject to constant abuse by both sides, especially on the borders and at sea, an almost interminable cold war whose continuation seemed guaranteed by the frequent renewal of the Franco-Scottish alliance.

This diplomatic pattern had been modified to some extent in the early 1460s, when Mary of Gueldres had looked more than once to England for a marriage alliance for herself or her two eldest sons; and the truce of York of 1464 was optimistically designed to last for fifteen years. In the event, however, James III had been married in Denmark rather than England, and his military projects of the early 1470s must have caused Edward IV much concern. But King James's schemes of foreign aggrandisement seem to have foundered on the rock of Scottish parliamentary opposition in 1473, and out of the ensuing diplomatic confusion there finally emerged the English alliance of 1474, a definite break with tradition and the first of many similar schemes which James III was to pursue energetically until the end of his life.

Such a policy was not however adopted until the possible alternatives had been explored. Indeed, in April 1474, war between Scotland and England appeared imminent. On 27 April, proclamation was made for the lieges to assemble to resist a projected raid by the Duke of Gloucester in the West and Middle Marches; and a gathering under James III's brother Albany, as Warden of the Marches, was apparently assembling at Lauder at the end of the month to oppose Gloucester.[1] Nothing seems to have come of this, and there is no suggestion of a threatened invasion in the articles of the parliament which met less than a fortnight later. The rumours of war, however, rapidly spread abroad. At Noyon on 17 June, Christoforo di Bollati, the Milanese ambassador to the French court, reported that 'this year the King of Scotland and the King of England are preparing to have war together, and it has already been declared and the first of July next appointed as the day of battle'.[2] He added, however, that this was merely a general rumour of which Louis XI had at that time no confirmation.

Nevertheless it may have been King Louis' belief that an Anglo-Scottish war was imminent which prompted him to reply to a communication from the Scottish king, in the spring of 1474, in somewhat uncooperative terms. James had sent as his ambassador to the French king one 'Jehan amorray', who is almost certainly to be identified with John Murray, the king's 'familiar squire' who received, possibly by way of reward, the lands of the barony of Touchadam in Stirlingshire the following year,[3] and who remained a loyal servant of the king throughout the reign. King Louis describes Murray as 'Capitaine de sa (i.e. James's) garde', and it may be that Murray had succeeded Sir David Guthrie in that post; alternatively, and probably more likely, the French were unfamiliar with the offices in the Scottish royal household, and expanded the fact that Murray was a court servant and familiar of the Scottish king into the statement that he was captain of the guard. In fact, the post appears to have been held by Guthrie as late as 21 June 1474, by which time Murray had probably departed for France.[4]

In any event, the purpose of Murray's mission to France was threefold — to impress upon Louis XI the fact that the Scottish king was being pressed by Edward IV of England to break the Franco-Scottish alliance and negotiate instead a treaty with England, but that he was resisting Edward IV's offers; to inform Louis that James III intended to make a pilgrimage to the shrines of St. Peter and St. Paul in Rome; and to discover the reaction of the French king to James's intention to travel through France on his way.[5] The warning that Scotland and England might conclude an alliance should have been taken more seriously by King Louis; but his information, faithfully reported by the Milanese ambassador, was that war between the two countries was likely.

The ambassador employed by Louis XI to carry his reply to James III was Alexander Monypenny, son of William, first Lord Monypenny, like his father an expatriate Scot in the service of the French Crown. William, Lord Monypenny, is also to be found in Scotland about the same time as his son. On 20 March 1474 he was in Edinburgh witnessing a royal charter; and he had returned to the French court by September of the same year.[6] Lord Monypenny had already acted as Louis' ambassador to James III in 1472, and on 10 October 1473 the French king made him Seneschal of Saintonge.[7] Already Monypenny held the lordship of Concressault and was in receipt of an annual pension of 1200 livres from Louis XI.[8] The name of his son Alexander, Louis' ambassador in 1474, does not appear so frequently in the French official records; occasionally he received a gift from the French king; and ultimately, before 1491, he was to succeed his father as Lord of Concressault. Alexander's brother, George Monypenny, was also employed by Louis XI; described as a Doctor of Laws, he is to be found travelling to England on embassy in 1470.[9]

It was perhaps because his reply was far from satisfactory, from the Scottish king's point of view, that Louis used the son of a trusted Scottish lord of parliament as his mouthpiece; and doubtless William, Lord Monypenny, was also on hand to present the French king's answer in the best possible light. Nevertheless, it was unattractive. On the subject of James III's proposed pilgrimage, Louis XI equivocated; on the one hand he stated that he would be delighted to receive the Scottish king in France en route to Rome; but on the other, he suggested that James should stay at home, as considerable hazards would attend a journey across Europe and the king's business required his remaining in Scotland. There was much to be said for the latter view as wise advice, though Louis was of course acting purely out of self-interest. The absence of the Scottish monarch from his own country would greatly weaken the government there, and might even result in Edward IV — feeling his northern frontier secure — pressing home his much heralded scheme for the invasion of France. At the same time, Louis had no desire to see a Scottish army on French soil. So he endeavoured to steer the middle course by offering James III 10,000 crowns if he could keep Edward IV at home, either by launching an attack on him and so diverting the army which he proposed to lead to France, or by assisting the English king in the event of a rebellion within his own country. The money, however, would only be paid 'au cas que ladit armee d'Angleterre seroit rompue par le moyen dudit Seigneur Roy d'Escosse et empeschee de venir en france et apres que la Chose seroit seure qu'elle ny viendroit point et non autrement'.[10] Louis' instructions to his ambassador concluded by adopting a high moral tone; in the event of a peace being negotiated with England, it did not seem honest or reasonable to the French king that either ally, France or Scotland, should conclude a treaty without including the other.

Louis XI had miscalculated seriously in not offering more encouragement to James III to preserve the Franco-Scottish alliance; mistakenly believing that England and Scotland were on the brink of war, he had adopted a high-handed manner in dealing with the Scottish king. Thus his offer to pay for Scots armed assistance was hedged round with so many conditions that James presumably doubted whether he would ever see his money; and ten thousand crowns was, after all, only a sixth of what the Scottish ambassadors had demanded — as an annual pension, not merely a lump sum — in their offer to provide an army to attack Edward IV the year before. It is true that Louis' appointment of Lord Monypenny as Seneschal of Saintonge in the autumn of 1473 suggests that the French king was trying to raise James III's hopes that he would ultimately receive the county to which he, his father, and grandfather, had laid claim in vain for almost half a century; but no definite promise appears to have been made.

For King James, the obvious alternative to fighting against the English in the interests of France with no definite prospect of gain was a marriage treaty with England, and sometime in the late summer of 1474 Louis XI must have learned that his embassy to Scotland had failed and that negotiations between England and Scotland were proceeding apace. On 17 September 1474 he was making use of William, Lord Monypenny, father of Alexander, in an attempt to interest the Duke of Milan in a marriage alliance between one of his daughters and the Prince of Scotland. On 3 October the Duke, writing from Pavia, caustically replied that though he was willing to oblige the French king by opening negotiations, Louis knew well enough that his eldest daughter was already married, and that in any case he would not wish to marry any of his daughters 'so far off as Scotland would be'. In this he was only echoing his ambassador, who on 27 September had described Scotland as 'in finibus orbis'.[11] In any event, less than a month later the Anglo-Scottish alliance rendered obsolete these eleventh-hour proposals on the part of the French king.

Less than a month after the war scare of April 1474, which had brought Albany to the muster point at Lauder, we find the Scottish parliament recommending the sending of an embassy to England to obtain redress for breaches of the truce, and this proved to be the start of Anglo-Scottish diplomatic moves which produced far more than Louis XI could have anticipated. The principal Scots grievance, which had undermined relations between Scotland and England for over a year, was the seizure of the late Bishop Kennedy's famous barge, the 'Salvator', by an Englishman, James Ker, following her shipwreck, laden with merchandise, near Bamburgh, in March 1473. One of her passengers, the Abbot of Inchcolm, had been taken prisoner and only released on payment of eighty pounds, and Scottish demands for compensation had dragged on throughout 1473 and the early months of 1474 without any success.[12] Finally, however, Edward IV responded satisfactorily; on 25 October 1474, James III declared himself quit of all claims against the king of England or his lieges for the spoliation of the 'Salvator' following her wreck; and payment of five hundred marks, by way of restitution, was finally received by Thomas Spens, bishop of Aberdeen, on behalf of the Scots merchants who had suffered loss, on 3 February 1475.[13]

However, the main task of the ambassadors who complained of the wrecking of the bishop's barge was to negotiate with a view to a marriage between Prince James of Scotland and Edward IV's daughter Cecilia. On 25 June 1474, James III appointed Thomas Spens, bishop of Aberdeen, the Chamberlain Sir John Colquhoun of Luss, James Shaw of Sauchie, and Lyon King of Arms, for this purpose. On 29 July, Edward IV appointed his own commissioners, the Bishops of Durham and Carlisle, Sir John Scrope and Sir John Dudley, and Master John Russell, archdeacon of Berkshire and Keeper of the Privy Seal.[14] These commissioners conducted the preliminary negotiations; but the bodies which agreed on the final treaty were rather different in personnel. On the Scottish side they were John Laing, bishop of Glasgow, William Tulloch, bishop of Orkney and Keeper of the Privy Seal, the Earls of Argyll and Crawford, Archibald Crawfurd, abbot of Holyrood, and the ubiquitous royal secretary, Archibald Whitelaw. It is curious that Thomas Spens is absent from this group, as his whole career was taken up with achieving and maintaining peace with England. His name is absent from the Great Seal Register — where he is almost always to be found as a witness — during October 1474, when the final negotiations and settlement took place in Edinburgh. He may have been ill or on a visit to his Aberdeen diocese; but if the latter was the case, he chose a curious time to leave the vicinity of the court.

The four English ambassadors, the Bishop of Durham, Lord Scrope, Privy Seal Russell, and Robert Bothe, arrived in Edinburgh on 8 October; and at noon on 26 October the betrothal was solemnised in the Blackfriars of Edinburgh. As Prince James and Princess Cecilia, the prospective groom and his bride, were respectively aged one and five, they took no part in the ceremony, with the Earl of Crawford and Lord Scrope standing in as proxies. On the same day the alliance was concluded, and it was ratified by James III about a week later, on 3 November.[15]

Amongst other advantages, the treaty of October 1474 brought James III the prospect of rapid financial gain. Cecilia's dowry was fixed at twenty thousand marks of English money, to be paid in instalments, two thousand marks a year for the first three years, and thereafter at a rate of one thousand a year. Payments were to begin on 3 February 1475, in St. Giles, Edinburgh; and James was assured that, even if Cecilia or Prince James were to die before they reached marriageable age, and no alternative marriage could be arranged, he would be able to retain all the dowry money paid to him up to two thousand five hundred marks.[16] In the event, James III was later to retain eight thousand marks of Edward's money, despite the non-fulfilment of the marriage.

Provided that Prince James and Cecilia were married within six months of their reaching marriageable age, the treaty was intended to bind England and Scotland together in everlasting friendship. During James III's lifetime, Cecilia was to be endowed with all the lands, rents and revenues of the 'olde heritage of the prince sone and heire of Scotland' — the duchy of Rothesay, the earldom of Carrick, and the lordships of the Stewart lands of Scotland — and to be entitled, on the accession of her husband to the throne, to a third part of his property.[17]

The treaty was a statesmanlike measure which preserved the peace between the two countries, if not perpetually, at least for five years; and it is difficult to agree with Dr. Nicholson's dismissive remark that 'for a small outlay Edward had neutralised Scotland'.[18] Greater issues were at stake than Scotland's neutrality in the event of Edward IV's invading France. The Scottish king had shown that he had the measure of Louis XI's devious and unrealistic diplomacy of the previous year, and had an answer to it. He had clearly learned from his projected continental expeditions of 1471-3 and the Scottish estates' unfavourable response to them; and a sound answer to his diplomatic problems, bringing both tangible financial gain and a friendly southern neighbour, was alliance with the king of England, the only king, as James himself had remarked to the Duke of Burgundy the year before, who made war on him. The English treaty of 1474 was in fact the beginning of a consistent and realistic policy of Scottish friendship and alliance with England, a policy which James III was to further personally, often under extremely difficult circumstances and with one disastrous exception, to the very end of his reign.

It is hardly surprising that such a break with the past in foreign policy was unpopular in some quarters. Dr. McDiarmid has convincingly argued that the epic poem *The Wallace* dates from this period, and that its opening lines, like the rest of the poem full of vituperation against the English, are a condemnation of the 1474 marriage treaty.[19] The author was not a court poet,[20] but he must have been patronised — perhaps indeed commissioned — by Scotsmen who approved of his violent anti-English bias. These would not be found amongst the merchant classes, who stood to gain by a period of prolonged peace; indeed, some of them benefited immediately when the English paid compensation for the wreck and spoliation of the bishop's barge. Nor was this class confined to prosperous burgesses whose wealth was accumulated through foreign trade; certain of the nobility and smaller barons, and the king himself, engaged in overseas trading ventures, and had been severely impeded in their business by English attacks. Thus in February 1475 we find Edward IV making restitution for the capture of James III's *Yellow Carvel* by the Duke of Gloucester's *Mayflower*, and also of a ship belonging to Sir John

Colquhoun of Luss, captured by a vessel of Lord Grey.[21] Scotland was rarely fortunate in hostile encounters at sea with the English, and English restitution for the bishop's barge, the *Yellow Carvel* and Colquhoun's ship would probably never have been made at all but for the 1474 treaty.

Nor do we find any evidence of anti-English feeling amongst the nobility north of Forth. Indeed, the reverse is true of the two most prominent 'political' earls, Crawford and Argyll, both of whom were actively involved in furthering the alliance of 1474. Further north, the Earls of Ross and Huntly seem to have been preoccupied with their own quarrels; and royal letters were sent to both in March 1474, 'for stanching of the slachteris and herschippis committit betuix thare folkis'.[22] Quarrels between William Hay, earl of Erroll, and Lord Forbes were the subject of similar royal letters despatched the previous year.[23] It seems highly unlikely, therefore, that the author of the 'Wallace' found either support or patronage amongst the northern magnates.

The south, however, was another matter, for there the English alliance meant an end to the intermittent border warfare to which many had long been accustomed; and those southern lords and their adherents who now faced the prospect of strong action against them by their own monarch if they continued making raids into England must have viewed the diplomatic revolution of 1474 with alarm. Significantly, two of 'Blind Hary's' authorities are southern knights, Sir William Wallace of Craigie in Ayrshire and Sir James Liddale of Halkerston, steward of the Duke of Albany.[24] The young and powerful Archibald, earl of Angus, can have had little regard for the alliance. Like his father before him, he thrived on border warfare; and when the English peace eventually collapsed in the spring of 1480, he at once laid waste parts of Northumberland.[25]

There is even a hint that to this period can be ascribed the beginnings of animosity between James III and his brother Alexander, duke of Albany, earl of March, and the most powerful of the southern nobility. On 26 July 1475, Giovanni Pietro Panicharolla, Milanese ambassador at the Duke of Burgundy's court, wrote from Arras to his master to the effect that 'the king of England has received news that the king of Scotland, his ally, has been poisoned by his brother at the instigation of the king of France, and the brother has made himself king, driving out the sons of the late king and the queen from the realm. He seems inclined to make trouble on the English frontier in order to fetch back the English'.[26] This strange rumour is, of course, highly inaccurate. Quite apart from the fact of James III's survival, there is the objection that in 1475 he had only one son. Furthermore, such a highly coloured tale may have been invented by the French, and may simply reflect the devious diplomacy of Louis XI only days before the Anglo-French treaty of Picquigny. But it is an indication, although an extremely fanciful one, of rapid and violent opposition to the English marriage alliance; it is the first suggestion of Albany's later aspirations; and it indicates that border warfare would be the first result of the breakdown of the alliance.

Thus the author of *The Wallace* would most likely find his audiences and patrons amongst the southern lords, Albany, Angus and their supporters in particular. This is in part confirmed by John Major, who states that 'Blind Hary' led the life of a wandering minstrel, passing from one lordly hall to the next reciting romantic legends.[27] Extensive opposition to the new royal policy of peace with England, therefore, may well have been fostered throughout the south by the rampant, aggressive patriotism of the author of *The Wallace*, and once the king's character had been attacked on account of the marriage alliance, further criticism would follow, stories would be embellished and passed on. Thus almost a century later, Lindsay of Pitscottie describes Albany as 'hardie and manlie', loving 'abill men and goode horse', and for his singular wisdome and manheid . . . estemed in all contrieis aboue his brother the Kingis grace'; whereas James III 'desyrit never to heir of weiris nor the fame tharof . . . for he delyttit mair in singing and playing upoun instrumentis nor he did in defence of the bordouris or the ministratioun of justice'.[28] This is surely an exaggerated way of saying that Albany was popular with a section of the nobility because in 1474 he was not in favour of a peace which in part robbed them of their occupations, while the king, because on this occasion he concluded a treaty with England, was therefore unmanly and unwarlike. This was far from the truth, as King James's bellicose behaviour between 1471 and 1473 had already amply demonstrated; but unpopularity in the south and south-east was part of the price which the king had to pay in return for the advantages of the 1474 alliance. Perhaps in an effort to conciliate the Earl of Angus, on 7 June 1475 the king confirmed to him his possession of the castle and lands of Tantallon in East Lothian, for unspecified faithful service.[29]

Conciliation of potential enemies, however, does not appear to have been a striking feature of royal policy. After 1474 as before it, James III continued to act in the most arbitrary manner, above all in the distribution of lands and offices; he either ignored or despised the caution which a more prudent ruler might have adopted after embarking on an untried and unpopular foreign policy. Thus the king's wilful acts over the next six years were accompanied by a failure to reward adequately active friends of the Crown; and the same period witnessed the elimination, through flight abroad and death respectively, of the king's brothers.

It was this last feature of the late 1470s — the struggle between James III, Albany and Mar — which caught the attention of the sixteenth century chroniclers, and which they sought to explain by emphasising the role of royal favourites, by contrasting the weak and indolent king with his manly brothers and loyal nobility, and by suggesting a steady build-up of baronial opposition to unpopular royal policies. Contemporary records reveal little of this, but they are as deficient as those in the first half of the decade — indeed more so, for the Treasurer's Accounts, which survive for some sixteen months of 1473-4, are totally lacking for the late '70s. Yet what remains is quite sufficient to raise serious doubts about the validity of the popular notion that James III was a lazy king whose alienation from his family and his nobility was the result of his inactivity. On the contrary, it was the king's furious pursuit of unpopular and often arbitrary policies which caused increasing alarm amongst many of the politically conscious. It is not, after all, an indolent ruler who provokes opposition, but rather an active and innovatory one.

Thus a century later, when Giovanni Ferreri remarked that James III was hardly an energetic ruler,[30] what he had presumably absorbed was a tradition widely

J

circulating in Scotland that the king was not doing his job as was expected of him. It was not a matter of laziness, but rather of attempting too many changes at once. Some of these, such as the granting of remissions for serious crimes in order to make money, indicate royal activity of the wrong kind and were rightly condemned by successive parliaments. Likewise in the sphere of civil justice, the king's legislation on the subject's right of appeal to the lords of council laid an increasingly heavy burden on these officials and probably offended a number of the ordinaries at the same time. Foreign policy changed rapidly from projected royal expeditions or pilgrimages to Brittany, Gueldres, Saintonge and Rome, to equally determined efforts to make the most out of the 1474 English alliance; and the future was to show that James III hoped to use this rapprochement with Edward IV to enhance his prestige and travel abroad on pilgrimage. At home, the extension of royal influence over church appointments, together with the deposition of Patrick Graham, was followed after 1474 by the completion of the archbishop's ruin and the appointment of the royal favourite, William Scheves, as his successor. By the end of the decade the king had added the earldom of Ross to his earlier seizures of the Boyd lands, the Stewartry of Strathearn and the Lennox.

Furthermore, the records reveal that during the '70s James III travelled extensively throughout his realm. Apart from the royal progress of 1470, he appears to have travelled to Whithorn and Fife in the autumn of 1473 and 1474, and had intended to hold a parliament at St. Andrews in the latter year. Isolated entries in the Exchequer Rolls indicate that the king visited Linlithgow, Perth and Stirling in the mid-70s; and it is possible that his presence in many other parts of the country would be proved if the major portion of the Treasurer's Accounts were still in existence. Like David II more than a century before, James III conducted his administration from Edinburgh, where he spent the greater part of his adult life; but an emergency, such as that of the long delayed attack on Ross in 1476, or the much more celebrated crises of 1482 and 1488, would take him away from Edinburgh for long periods at a time.

In the middle and late '70s, however, activity on the part of the king frequently involved aggression and sharp practice in the distribution of lands and offices. Thus on 18 September 1475 Archibald, earl of Angus, resigned into James's hands his barony of Cluny, the lordship of which was conferred three months later on David Crichton of Cranston, the king's 'familiar squire'. As recently as August of the same year, Angus had attempted to sell to Crichton the lands of the barony; so the king's prompt recovery of Cluny and granting of it to Crichton as a gift may well be regarded as royal coercion, with Angus as the victim.[31]

Worse still was the king's further dismemberment of the Lennox early in the following year. On 12 January 1476, John Haldane of Gleneagles was recognised by James III as senior co-heir to the earldom of Lennox.[32] The brieves and service of John Stewart, Lord Darnley, in this dignity, were revoked and annulled, on the ground that Haldane had been out of the country on embassy for the king when they were granted, and that this advancement of Darnley constituted an infringement of the conditions of the letters of protection with which Haldane had been issued before he left Scotland. Yet less than three years before, in 1473, Darnley had been forced to accept Avandale as liferenter of the lands of the earldom as a condition of the king's recognising his right to the Lennox inheritance. Now even his right to the title was being denied him in favour of someone whom the king wished to reward. Darnley sat in the November 1475 parliament as Earl of Lennox, and he was named as Earl of Lennox in a commission of lieutenancy from the king on 4 December,[33] but thereafter he was not to reassume the title until the death of Avandale and the accession of James IV. James III's letter revoking Darnley's grant of the title of earl must have caused him considerable bitterness. In it, it is stated that Haldane 'evir claimit the said superiorite be resson of his spouse (Agnes Menteith), and optenit oure favouris tharto as principal be oure charter and seisin'. Furthermore, 'the richt of the successione pertaining to the said John's spouse [is] undemandit by ony of our lieges'. This was manifestly untrue.

John Haldane's claim to be recognised as heir to the title was based on the contention that he was descended, through his wife Agnes Menteith, from Margaret, sister of the Countess Isabella, eldest daughter of Duncan, eighth earl of Lennox, and next to her in seniority; Darnley, according to Haldane, was descended from Elizabeth, the younger sister.[34] Yet when arbitrators were finally appointed in June 1477 to decide which of the two men had the senior claim — that is, of the two sisters from whom they were descended, whether Margaret or Elizabeth was the elder — they arrived at no satisfactory conclusion.[35] Thus in January 1476, on very doubtful legal grounds, James III had broken his word to Darnley by going back on an agreement less than three years old, an agreement, moreover, which had only given Darnley the title of earl, the liferent being retained by Chancellor Avandale. Under the circumstances the king probably realised that he would have to pay for Darnley's future loyalty, and he attempted to do so by granting him the keepership of Dingwall castle in 1476, and that of Rothesay the following year.[36]

On one major item of royal business, however, king and magnates were at one — the forfeiture of John Macdonald, earl of Ross, in the parliament of November-December 1475. On 16 October, Unicorn pursuivant had summoned Ross, both at his castle of Dingwall and at the market crosses of Dingwall and Inverness, to appear in parliament on 1 December to answer charges of treason. The indictment makes formidable reading. The earl is accused of treasonable dealings with England, of making 'ligis and bandis' with Edward IV, and of assisting the forfeited James, ninth earl of Douglas, with supplies and counsel — a reference to the Treaty of Westminster-Ardtornish of 1462. He had usurped royal authority by making his bastard son a lieutenant to himself, giving him power to 'justify to the dede' such of the king's lieges as would not obey him. Finally, Ross was accused of conducting a siege of Rothesay castle and laying waste the island of Bute.[37] In effect, from a royal standpoint, Ross's unpunished treasons stretched back as far as 1452, and his major opponents in the west — the Earl and Bishop of Argyll, and the Earl of Atholl — all assembled in parliament to condemn him. Not surprisingly, Ross did not appear before the parliamentary court on the appointed day, 1 December, and sentence of forfeiture was immediately pronounced by Chancellor Avandale.[38]

Prompt action was taken to make this sentence effective. On 4 December the Earl of Argyll was given a commission of lieutenancy by James III, tenable within the bounds of Argyll and Lorne, and to be exercised with Laurence, Lord Oliphant, John Drummond of Stobhall, William Stirling of Keir, and Argyll's servants and tenants in Strathearn, to execute the forfeiture pronounced by parliament on John of the Isles, formerly Earl of Ross and Lord of the Isles, 'traitor and rebel'. The commission included the power to raise the lieges of Lennox, Menteith, Strathgartney and Balquhidder in the king's service, and to pursue John of the Isles to the death, invading his territories with fire and sword. On the same day, similar commissions were given to John, earl of Atholl, and George, earl of Huntly. In the south, John Stewart, Lord Darnley, described as Earl of Lennox for the last time for thirteen years, was given a commission of lieutenancy covering the sheriffdoms of Renfrew, Ayr, and Wigtown, the Stewartry of Kirkcudbright, part of Clydesdale and the islands of Bute and Arran.[39]

By 8 February 1476 preparations for dealing with the Earl of Ross were sufficiently far advanced to allow James III to make a grant of lands in Carrick, Buchan and Ross to Elizabeth, countess of Ross, wife of the rebel Macdonald. These lands were given to the countess for life, because, as the royal charter explains, she was innocent of her husband's treason. The first lands mentioned in the grant are those of Greenan, the teinds of which had been given by the forfeited earl to a local esquire, John Davidson, the previous April.[40]

Over the details of the royal expedition to subdue Ross, the sixteenth century chroniclers are somewhat at odds with the surviving record evidence. Ferreri misdates the parliamentary forfeiture of the earl, placing it in January 1476 instead of the month before; and, together with Lesley, he names Crawford and Atholl as the prime movers in bringing the Earl of Ross to submission. By these accounts, Crawford was appointed commander of the royal fleet, while Atholl took charge of the army; and in the month of May 1476 the king himself crossed the estuary of the Forth, moving north against his rebel.[41] Some of this may well be true. A gap of over a month in the Great Seal Register — from 16 April to 20 May 1476 — suggests that the king was away from Edinburgh, probably campaigning, between these dates. As to Crawford's active participation, there exists no evidence; but Atholl was certainly involved. Apart from his commission of lieutenancy, he received a royal grant of the forest of Cluny and park of Laighwood on 3 March 1481, expressly for his trouble and expense in suppressing the rebellion of John of the Isles.[42] Unfortunately the seventh Duke of Atholl, in recounting the history of the earldom, is unable to be more explicit about his ancestor's part in the expedition than to relate tales of the creation of the family motto, 'Furth fortune and fill the fetters' (by tradition the words used by James III on despatching Atholl to the north) and the invention of Atholl brose![43]

In fact, one of the first of the king's lieutenants to take the field was George, earl of Huntly. As early as 28 March 1476 James III wrote to Huntly, thanking him for 'the recouer of our castell of Dingwall, and specialy now of laite of the invasioun that ye have maid uppone our rebellis in Lochquhabir, till oure singular and gret emplezer'; and he promised to reward the earl for his services. It is clear from the letter, however, that much remained to be done, as Huntly is exhorted to be 'of gude perseuerance and continuance in the invasion of our said rebellis'.[44]

It may be, however, that King James did not rate Huntly's services to him in the north as highly as he suggested. To give him a commission of lieutenancy in Inverness-shire was, after all, simply to take sides in the feud which had been going on between Ross and Huntly at least since the spring of 1474;[45] and Huntly had naturally been quick off the mark in taking advantage of a royal admonition to make war on his rival. The king probably appreciated this; and so, although he made promises to Huntly, he produced nothing substantial by way of reward. Indeed, the earl was not even allowed to retain Dingwall castle, which he had taken for the king; the keepership went instead to Darnley. As James deviously remarked in explaining this to Huntly, 'had it saa bene that ye at your last being with us had dissirit the keping of our castell, we suld hawe preferrit you therin befor all wtheris'.[46] Not until October 1476 was Huntly to receive any kind of reward from the king, and then it took the form of a mere hundred marks worth of land 'in the north partis of our realme'.[47] Like his father before him, James III was beginning to display that most dangerous of characteristics amongst medieval rulers, failure to recognise and reward service.

On the face of it, however, the royal expedition against Ross appeared wholly successful. On 10 July 1476, before a very full assembly of parliament in Edinburgh, John of the Isles appeared and submitted to the royal will. He was stripped of the title of Earl of Ross, the earldom being annexed to the domains of the Crown; and Knapdale and Kintyre were also withdrawn from his authority, together with the sheriffship of Inverness and the castles of Inverness and Nairn. On the same day, however, apparently on the intercession of Queen Margaret, he was created a lord of parliament as Lord of the Isles, a concession made presumably on account of his submission. Significantly, the sovereign was to have the liberty to grant the annexed earldom to his second son.[48]

How effective all this was in practice must remain a matter of some debate. From the point of view of royal authority, the king had certainly shown that he could make his presence felt in the north and west, and his personal intervention had been made effective through the cooperation of three or four of his most powerful magnates. Further, he had put a stop to a number of Ross's illegal acts in the north, of which the seizure of the farms of the burgh of Inverness in the early 1460s is one example.[49] But the 1476 settlement was hardly a lasting one; as early as 7 April 1478 the Lord of the Isles was once more summoned to appear before parliament on charges of treason. On this occasion he was charged with giving aid to rebels and traitors in Castle Sween in Argyllshire, and for supporting Donald Gorme and Neil MacNeil and their accomplices, 'the quhilkis dali Invadis the Kingis lieges and distrois his landis'.[50] Clearly Colin Campbell, earl of Argyll, royal lieutenant in the area, was already finding that the submission of Ross in 1476 had not produced more than a temporary respite.

The problem of subduing the west and north was complicated by the fact that John Macdonald, Lord of the Isles, seems to have been a most ineffective leader. Perhaps his position following 1476 was an impossible one, attempting as he was to control vast territories as a vassal of the Crown; while in the eyes of his kin and neighbours his recent surrender of the earldom to the Stewart monarchy can hardly have enhanced his prestige. His wife Elizabeth, long estranged from her husband, went so far as to complain to the pope that her husband was trying to poison her;[51] and Macdonald's illegitimate son and only offspring, Angus of Islay, clearly held his father in contempt and acquired considerable local support for resistance to Crown authority in the west. Thus the Lord of the Isles, trapped between local and central government pressures, dithered unhappily from one alliance to the next in an unsuccessful attempt to prove himself an effective clan leader and Crown servant at one and the same time. Not surprisingly, he failed, and in addition suffered the ignominy of being summoned by the king to answer for treasons perpetrated by his bastard son.

However, by the end of 1478 the Lord of the Isles was once more at the king's peace, for on 16 December he received confirmation of his lordship of parliament and his lands in the isles, regranted to him following the royal act of revocation of 1476.[52] No reference is made in this regrant to Macdonald's treasonable behaviour of the previous spring, which suggests that the royal government had now come to appreciate that the major threat to its authority in the west came not from the Lord of the Isles himself, but from Angus of Islay. The parliamentary record of March 1479 makes mention of 'the gret trubill that is in Ross cathness and suthirland';[53] but this cannot be connected with the activities of the forfeited earl. Indeed, one indication that Crown authority was increasing in Ross is that a series of Crown accounts of the earldom begin to be rendered from 1479 onwards; and the gross farms for two years amounted to £546 13/4d., together with a large revenue in kind.[54]

Thus these events of 1476-9 may be regarded as a qualified success for the Crown. James III had benefited substantially in terms of finance; and he would have no further trouble with John Macdonald. Indeed, the Lord of the Isles had the wisdom to support King James, albeit in a rather lukewarm fashion, following the outbreak of the Anglo-Scottish war of 1480-2.[55] But in the longer term, as Nicholson reminds us, Macdonald's submission 'opened the far north and west to the Lowland influences that were bound to follow, sooner or later, in the wake of crown control'.[56] Most important of all, royal authority in the west Highlands was now exercised directly by Colin Campbell, earl of Argyll, who combined in his person the attributes of a shrewd and hardworking royal counsellor and the ambitions of an immensely powerful Highland clan chief. He was still faced with an uphill struggle to avoid failing, as John Macdonald had failed, in the north and west. But within a few years Argyll would have succeeded, by a combination of aggression, marriage alliance and kidnapping, in adding to his own power as royal lieutenant the authority formerly possessed by the Lord of the Isles in the west; and once he had achieved this position of pre-eminence in the Highlands, even the king would be taking a very rash step if he attempted to encroach upon it.

Such subtleties are not reflected in Hector Boece's estimate of James III's achievement in the north and west. Although not conspicuous for his general accuracy, Boece was nevertheless writing in the early 1520s, when he had the examples of James IV's successful Highland expeditions of the 1490s with which to compare those of his father. Referring to James III, Boece wrote: 'While still a mere boy, he subdued the Highlanders, a fierce race, ever delighting in intestine feuds and sedition; he gave the whole country a well-established peace; no dangers threaten it, no fear of enemies'.[57] This is undoubtedly an exaggeration, and to describe the king as a 'mere boy' when he was in his twenty-fifth year is something of a distortion. However, Boece's statement has value in that it predates by more than a generation the sixteenth century histories which cover the reign; and in his lavish praise of James III's Highland policy, the author destroys the unanimity of later chroniclers in condemning the king at this period.

Apart from the forfeiture of the Earl of Ross, the main business of the Edinburgh parliament of July 1476 was to approve King James's act of revocation. On 10 July, the last day of the parliament, all alienations, or gifts prejudicial to James's Crown, or to his heirs, were solemnly revoked, together with grants of the custody of royal castles held otherwise than during royal pleasure. The king was in his twenty-fifth year, though about ten months short of twenty-five, the accepted age of complete majority of a Scottish monarch.[58]

The act of revocation does not seem to have affected the nobility adversely, and for more than three years after 1476 we find a continuing flow of regrants of lands and offices which had been conferred during the official minority and which had been resigned into the king's hands by the holders. The earliest of these regrants was made on 12 October 1477, more than fifteen months after the act of revocation, by which time the king had undoubtedly passed the age of twenty-five. Before the end of the same year, the Earl of Buchan, the Countess of Ross, John Ross of Montgrenan and the Earl of Atholl had all had confirmation of grants of land made to them during the minority.[59] In the first two months of 1478 there was a spate of confirmations — to the queen, for the barony of Kilmarnock, forfeited by Robert, Lord Boyd; to John Reid, a clerk in the secretary's office, a continuing annual pension of £20; to John Stewart of Fothergill and his son and heir Nigel, of lands in Perthshire; to Marchmond and Ross heralds, of lands in Fife; to David Crichton of Cranston, of the lands of Cranston-Riddell in the sheriffdom of Edinburgh, forfeited during the minority by William Murray; to Thomas Smyth, royal apothecary, who had treated both the king and queen, a continuing annual pension of £20; and to the queen, fulfilling the Scottish part of the 1468 marriage treaty, one third of the property and income of the crown.[60]

This last grant, an enormous one, included the lordship of Galloway with the customs and farms of the burghs of Kirkcudbright and Wigtown, and the castle of Threave; the lordship of the forest of Ettrick with the tower, fortalice and manor of Newark; lands of the lordships of Stirlingshire and Tillicoultry, with the castle of Stirling and the customs and farms of the burgh; the lordship of Strathearn, with the customs of the burgh of Perth; the lordships of Menteith, Strathgartney and Balquhidder, with the castle of Doune; the lordships of Kinclaven and Methven, with the castle of Methven; and the lordship of Linlithgowshire, with the palace, lake and ward of Linlithgow, the customs and farms of the burgh, justice and chamberlain ayres, and the right of patronage of all benefices and churches within these lands. These concessions were made to the queen for life; small wonder that James III, like his father and for the same reason, rapidly found himself financially embarrassed, to the extent that within a year he could not afford even a modest dowry for the projected English marriage of his sister Margaret and had once again resorted to taxing the lieges.

Associated with the king in this taxation was the individual whose spectacular advancement during the 1470s was based entirely on his intimacy with James III, and who is, perhaps, the only readily identifiable royal favourite of the period — William Scheves. His career as a minor court official between 1471 and 1474[61] was rapidly transformed after the latter date, and by 1479 he had emerged as one of the most powerful men in the kingdom. With the king's support, Scheves obtained the revenues of the Hospital of Brechin and, by 15 April 1474, the archdeaconry of St. Andrews.[62] On 13 July 1476 a bull of Sixtus IV appointed Scheves coadjutor of the see of St. Andrews on account of Patrick Graham's excommunication and insanity.[63] Three days previously Scheves, already styled vicar-general of St. Andrews, was appointed to the parliamentary committee set up to continue the business of the July parliament;[64] and by this time his name was appearing with increasing regularity in the records. On 28 March 1476 his signature appears together with that of the king on a signet letter thanking the Earl of Huntly for recovering Dingwall castle from the rebellious Earl of Ross.[65] On 24 October Scheves joined the king in signing a privy seal letter granting Huntly a hundred marks for recovering Ross;[66] and two days later his name again appeared alongside that of James III on a signet letter ordering William, Lord Crichton, to desist from interfering with Edward Livingston of Bowcastell's tenure of his lands in Dumfriesshire.[67]

Scheves' rapid elevation does not appear to have affected his interest in the routine business of government. From 1475 to 1479 he is to be found sitting annually as an auditor of exchequer, and from the beginning of the Lords of Council records in October 1478 he is frequently, though not constantly, to be found sitting in judgment with them.[68] A prominent parliamentarian, Scheves was elected to the Committee of the Articles in October 1479 and March 1482.[69]

One could, of course, produce a similar record of service for other royal servants at this time, Argyll and Thomas Spens, bishop of Aberdeen, in particular. But what marks Scheves out from the rest is his close relationship with the king, remarkable in view of James III's aloofness and keen sense of the royal dignity. Thus there survive no fewer than nine royal letters, issued between March 1476 and August 1479, which bear Scheves' signature as well as that of the king; at no other period of the reign is a letter under the privy seal or signet, signed by the king, to bear anyone else's signature. Furthermore, the letters which Scheves prepared or signed during these three years cover a great variety of topics — relations with England, royal gifts and admonitions, local affairs and finance. On 28 April 1477, he signed a receipt acknowledging the third instalment of 2,000 marks of Princess Cecilia's dowry;[70] on 3 October of the same year, his signature is found with that of the king on a privy seal letter ratifying statutes made by Edinburgh town council on the subject of markets within the burgh.[71] On 19 February 1478, he signed a signet letter of James III informing Alexander Legh, Edward IV's almoner, that Lord Hume would meet him and escort him from the marches to Edinburgh;[72] and on 18 July of the same year, Scheves' signature is on a letter from James III to his uncle James, earl of Morton, acknowledging a payment of one hundred pounds Scots.[73]

Finally, in 1479 Scheves' signature is to be found on two royal letters. On 4 March, he put his name to James III's receipt for the fifth payment of Cecilia's dowry money; and on 18 August, together with the king, he signed a signet letter ordering the sheriff of Edinburgh to raise the first payment of the tax to provide for the expenses of Princess Margaret's wedding.[74]

The period of all these signatures — March 1476 to August 1479 — was that of Scheves' rise from archdeacon to coadjutor, and from coadjutor to Archbishop of St. Andrews. His consecration as archbishop, which occurred some time between 17 June and 16 October 1478,[75] probably took place at Holyrood with the king present; and at least one disappointed candidate for the office may be identified at once in James Livingston, bishop of Dunkeld.[76] But it was Scheves alone who continued to enjoy the rewards of intimacy with, and service to, the king. On 9 March 1479, parliament had ratified the act of 1469 giving the Bishops of St. Andrews the confirmation of appointments of abbots and priors within the diocese; and on 7 October of the same year James III, with the consent of the three estates, confirmed all gifts and grants from his predecessors to the see of St. Andrews.[77] Then on 9 July 1480 a royal charter renewed a grant of James II, ratifying gifts to the church of St. Andrews and confirming to Scheves and his successors the privileges which he and all previous bishops had enjoyed.[78] On the same day the king confirmed all grants and annexations, and all indults made in favour of the see of St. Andrews, particularly that of Pope Nicholas V to Bishop Kennedy, and all other liberties granted by Sixtus IV to Scheves. The new archbishop is described in effusive terms by the king as 'our dear and intimate counsellor', and the grant is made 'propter sua merita servitia gratuita atque fidelia nobis nostra tenera in aetate et longo tempore impensa'.[79]

Scheves, then, fills the role of royal favourite, as envisaged by the later chroniclers, in almost every particular. A minor court official in 1471, in the space of only a few years he had been elevated to the archbishopric and had become one of the king's most intimate counsellors, at the same time acquiring a hold on many aspects of royal business, judicial, financial and diplomatic. In one respect, however, Scheves does not measure up to the popular concept of a favourite; he was too old, already about forty when he became archbishop.[80] Now this is far too elderly to allow him to be accounted amongst the royal favourites as conceived both by contemporary and sixteenth century writers. The anonymous author of *The Thre Prestis of Peblis* complains that the king

luifit nane was ald or ful of age,
Sa did he nane of sad counsel nor sage.[81]

Almost a century later the colourful Pitscottie remarked that 'wyse lordis . . . desired him (the king) to leive young counsall'.[82] In neither description does the ageing Scheves qualify; and it may be added that, despite his rapid rise to power, he emerges as rather a colourless person, a far cry from the glamorous and elusive

Cochrane, whose largely fictitious career was the product of lively imaginations in a later age.

There is therefore something of a paradox in the fact that William Scheves, the most obvious candidate for the title of royal favourite during the late '70s, is almost completely neglected by the later chroniclers, who concoct a list of names of individuals about whom the record evidence has little or nothing at all to say. It is of course possible that the archbishop was too well known a figure for his origins or his favour with the king to be closely investigated in the following century; after all, he sat in parliament and the Lords of Council together with such established figures as Argyll, Crawford, and Avandale, none of whom appears to have resented his presence. Indeed, there exists a bond of friendship, dating from 31 October 1477, made between Scheves and William Hay, earl of Erroll and Constable of Scotland.[83] This bond, which follows the usual form — Scheves promising to take the earl's part in all lawful and honest actions, saving his allegiance to the king — illustrates that the archbishop had been accepted as of equal standing with one of the most prominent of the northern nobility. That he also had his enemies, especially amongst the bishops, is obvious from the attitude of Livingston of Dunkeld; and during the crisis of 1482 Andrew Stewart, bishop-elect of Moray, would try to depose Scheves in order to secure the archbishopric for himself.[84]

The subject on which all the sixteenth century chroniclers concentrate when discussing the late 1470s is not, however, the remarkable rise of Scheves, but the spectacular fall of the king's two brothers, Albany and Mar. Albany, the luckier of the two, fled to France in the spring of 1479, while Mar was dead and forfeited by the following winter. Where facts are few, legends abound; and one would never guess from the confident stories related by the chroniclers that there is, in fact, very little record evidence for the fall of Albany and Mar, and still less for the reasons which prompted James III to take action against them.

It is, of course, tempting to judge Albany by his later treasons, to regard him as a Scottish Clarence, shifty, untrustworthy and with an eye to the main chance. But the truth is that remarkably little is known of his career before his indictment for treason in 1479. We catch sight of him only occasionally, going to the Low Countries in 1460 at the tender age of six, returning and being captured by the English in 1464, released and taking part in at least one justice ayre in exchequer year 1465-6; then, as an adult, emerging as Admiral of Scotland and a March Warden who was expected to resist an English invasion in the spring of 1474, and who is to be found attending parliament in Edinburgh in May 1471, February 1472, and July 1476.[85] These scraps of information indicate that Albany eventually obtained a position of considerable trust on the Scottish Marches, and that he took some part in public affairs; but he was not a regular parliamentarian, nor is he to be found on the Council or more than occasionally at court. As for contemporary and later estimates of his character, both are extremes of opinion. Thus in July 1475 the Milanese ambassador to Burgundy passed on the rumour that James III had been poisoned by Albany, who had subsequently driven out the remainder of the royal family from Scotland and was preparing to make war on England in the interests of Louis XI of France.[86] By the following century, however, Albany's reputation had been rescued and he emerged in Abell's and Pitscottie's histories as the main prop supporting King James's shaky throne.[87] Faced with these conflicting views, we are forced to examine what record evidence there is for Albany's sins.

A certain amount may be learned from the indictment of treason brought against Albany in the parliament of October 1479. The treasons of which he was accused were 'the tresonable stuffing providing and fortifying of the castell of dunbar with man vitals herness gunnis apparalingis pulderis and artilzeary ganing for weire contrar the maieste and Autorite Riale of oure souuerain lord'; assisting known rebels; deliberately violating the truce with England 'be slauchteris Reffis and hereschippis tresonable committit contrar to the King and the comone gud of his Realme', and thereby abusing his office of Warden of the Marches; and finally, 'the cruell slauchter of Johne of skougale'.[88]

These charges have some substance, though whether they amount to treasonable activity, for which no forgiveness was possible, is questionable. It is quite likely that Albany was abusing his position as March Warden and was responsible for serious violations of the Anglo-Scottish alliance. In 1480 Edward IV was to condemn the Scots for invasion and harrying of the English north-east, and the failure of the wardens to intervene;[89] and it may be significant that Albany was later in close and treasonable association with Archibald, earl of Angus, who in the spring of 1480 led a raid into Northumberland lasting three days and nights.[90] Collaboration between the two nobles in border raids may well have begun in the late '70s, if not before, and such activity would reflect the intense dislike of the 1474 alliance on the part of the southern nobility, an attitude immortalised by 'Blind Hary' when he remarked: 'Till honour ennymyis is oure haile entent'.[91]

The other principal charge in Albany's indictment, the treasonable defence of Dunbar castle against the king, is rather less convincing, because there would have been no need for defence had James III not first attacked his brother. Unfortunately, the sources which describe Albany's arrest and dramatic escape from Edinburgh castle are all late, ranging from Adam Abell of Jedburgh in 1533 to Lindsay of Pitscottie a generation later;[92] but they do at least provide some motivation for the siege of Dunbar in the late spring of 1479, and for Albany's subsequent flight to France. Ferreri claims that he escaped by sea to Dunbar, and thence to France, though he first made an effort to defend the castle against the king. Subsequently he remarks that during the siege of Dunbar by the royal forces, the laird of Luss was among those killed on the king's side.[93] This would appear to be true. The laird of Luss, Sir John Colquhoun, was alive on 18 April 1479, but dead before 21 June, when his son and heir Humphrey was granted a remission of payment of relief on his father's lands because Sir John had fallen at the siege of Dunbar Castle.[94] So the siege must have been conducted some time between these dates and it was probably over by 24 May, the first occasion on which Albany was summoned to appear before parliament to answer charges of treason, including the defence of Dunbar against the king.[95]

In any event, even if he had been personally present for a time, Albany had escaped by sea to France when the castle fell. Not only was he received at court by Louis XI, but in January 1480 he married Anne de la Tour, daughter of the Count of Auvergne and Bouillon.[96] In his absence, some of his Dunbar associates and supporters, including John Ellem of Buttirdene, captain of Dunbar, were forfeited in the parliament of October 1479.[97] But no sentence of forfeiture was passed against Albany himself; instead, the summons calling on him to appear to answer the various charges was continued again and again over the next two-and-a-half years. In the first instance, the continuation was made 'at the gret raquest, instance and supplicacioune' of the three estates in parliament.[98] This would seem to suggest that the estates regarded forfeiture as appropriate for those who had held Dunbar castle against the king, but that such a sentence was too severe if directed at Albany himself. Alternatively, the king may well have wished to leave open the possibility of a reconciliation with his brother, or at least a voluntary submission by Albany, similar to that made by Macdonald of the Isles in 1476; and he can hardly have been unaware of the diplomatic implications of the duke's flight. Albany in France, enjoying the favour of Louis XI, was a potential menace, especially since the Anglo-French rapprochement of 1475, which left Scotland without a committed ally. This fact could well explain the repeated adjournments of meetings of commissioners with the full power of parliament to pronounce sentence on Albany right through to February 1482,[99] after which the events of that year of crisis made the original summonses rapidly obsolete. Significantly, as late as the spring of 1483, by which time Albany's treasons were blatant and he had lost most of his support, James III was still trying to reach an agreement with his brother which would avoid the formal process of forfeiture.[100]

Even more problematic than the summons of Albany for treason is the imprisonment, death and forfeiture of his younger brother, John, earl of Mar, which occurred about a year later, late in 1479 or early in 1480. If we know little of Albany's earlier career, Mar is even more enigmatic, making isolated appearances in the pages of the exchequer rolls during his early youth, represented in parliament by procurators in November 1469 and May 1471, and personally present there on only two occasions — July 1476 and March 1479.[101] This is remarkably slender evidence on which to base any estimate of Mar's character; certainly to speak of his 'conventional tastes and extrovert character'[102] is to fall victim to the sixteenth century legend. All that the official records tell us is that Mar sat in the parliament of March 1479; thereafter his name vanishes until 14 July 1480, when he is described as dead and his earldom forfeited.[103] There is not even a hint as to the reasons for his imprisonment; and his attainder is not to be found in the parliamentary records.

Deprived of official sources, we may nevertheless acquire some information from chronicle narratives, most of which include a version of Mar's imprisonment and death. A near-contemporary chronicle of Scottish history from its mythological beginnings down to the year 1482 laconically records that in 1479 'was mony weches and warlois brint on crag gayt and Jhone the erle of mar the kingis brothir was slayne becaus thai said he faworyt the weches and warlois'.[104] Abell, writing in 1533, says that Mar was slain on the advice of 'ane trucur callit Cochrene'; while a few years later John Bellenden, in his translation and expansion of Boece's *History*, adds the detail that Mar 'was slane in the Cannongait, in ane baith fatt'; that is, in a bathing vat.[105] A generation later, Pitscottie would seem to have seen Bellenden, as his tale of Mar's death is almost identical; the earl was 'murdrest and slaine in the Cannongait in ane baith fatt . . . be quhose persuasion or quhat cause I can not tell'.[106] The last of the sixteenth century histories to appear, that of George Buchanan in 1582, states that Mar was condemned on charges of witchcraft and executed by having a vein opened. Buchanan adds that twelve old women were burnt as witches at this time; no date is given, but Mar's death is erroneously placed before Albany's arrest and confinement.[107]

The narratives of Ferreri and Lesley, both published in the 1570s, add some detail not given by the others. Ferreri's story is that Mar was arrested in the night and taken to Craigmillar, where he was imprisoned. Finally convicted of conspiring against the king by invoking magic arts, he was executed 'in vico Canonicorum juxta Edimburgum' by having a vein opened and bleeding to death; at the same time a number of men and women suspected of dealing in the magic arts were burnt. The date given, December 1480 — a year late — is also to be found in Lesley's story of Mar's death. This is very similar in detail; Mar was imprisoned in Craigmillar and bled to death in the Canongate, having had one of his veins deliberately cut. The crime of which he was convicted was a conspiracy of witchcraft against the king; and at the time of his execution, many witches and sorcerers, men and women, were burnt for the same crime at Edinburgh.[108]

Four of these accounts, including the earliest, mention Mar's complicity with witches and sorcerers. The vat appears in only two narratives, those of Bellenden and Pitscottie, the latter probably deriving his information from the former. Much later, in the 1650s, William Drummond of Hawthornden further obscured the events surrounding Mar's death by putting a new interpretation on them. According to Drummond, Mar was committed to Craigmillar castle where, believing that he was in a prison, he developed a fever. He was moved to the Canongate by the solicitous king, who sent his physicians to try to cure Mar; in order to try to restore the earl's reason, they opened some veins of his head and arms, and losing too much blood, Mar fainted and died 'amongst the hands of his best friends and servants. Those who hated the king, gave out that he was taken away by his command, and some writers have recorded the same.' Drummond, however, claims that he has advantage over these writers in that he has followed the records of B.W.E. (presumably Bishop William Elphinstone, whom Drummond believed had written a history), who was alive at the time and would tell the truth. He goes on to add that Mar was implicated with certain witches and sorcerers in an attempt to destroy the king by framing his image in wax and then burning it.[109]

Superficially, this seems a much more balanced and believable account than the bizarre stories of the sixteenth century. Yet there are grave objections to it. Drummond very mildly states that Mar 'surmised' that he was in a prison. Surely this was the case; after all, there is evidence that he was ultimately forfeited.[110] Furthermore, Drummond not only leaves his very detailed story undated, but follows it with the statement that Albany, claiming that the royal favourites had brought about his brother's death, was betrayed and imprisoned while preparing his revenge. In fact, by the winter of 1479, the probable season of Mar's death, Albany had already been in France for about six months; and this is surely something which Elphinstone would have known.

Stripped of its novel interpretation, therefore, Drummond's account of Mar's death reads like a conglomeration of the sixteenth century narratives with portions taken from each. The witchcraft and sorcery, Craigmillar and the Canongate, can all be found elsewhere; and Drummond's caution in not suggesting a date is perhaps attributable to the fact that the earlier narratives give a choice of three — 1475, 1479 and 1480. As an apologist for Charles I and royal absolutism in his own day, Drummond attempts a similar rescue exercise by playing down James III's responsibility for Mar's death; his account reads simply like a quarrel between the two brothers, and there is no mention of the forfeiture of the earldom of Mar. As the normal life expectancy of someone forfeited for treason was not very great, it seems just as likely that Mar was executed as that he died in the hands of physicians, as Drummond suggests. Significantly, only one chronicler — Pitscottie — refers to Mar's death as murder.[111]

The stories of witches and warlocks, and Mar's complicity with them, appear very soon after the earl's death, in the contemporary short chronicle appended to the British Museum Royal Manuscript of Andrew Wyntoun; and the writer, who rarely enlarges on the events which he includes, mentions that the witches were burnt at Crag Gate.[112] While a witch-burning in fifteenth century Scotland seems highly improbable, Crag Gate may possibly be identified with Cragingalt, the name given to the Calton Hill at this period; and the chronicler may have known of executions which had taken place at this spot, and incorporated a variant of these into the Mar story. However that may be, his tale of Mar's conspiring with witches and sorcerers, which was to be embellished by the sixteenth-century writers, probably obscures more substantial charges of plotting against the Crown. A striking parallel to Mar's death and forfeiture is to be found almost a year earlier in England, in the proceedings leading up to the execution of Edward IV's brother George, duke of Clarence; and in Clarence's case, his attainder is extant.[113] It includes stories of the duke's conspiracy with necromancers and witches, described at such length as to obscure the real charges of treason and projected rebellion. Furthermore, the story that Clarence was drowned in a butt of malmsey wine in February 1478 — first related by Dominic Mancini who completed his chronicle in France in the winter of 1483,[114] and later to be found in a number of the London chronicles — is parallelled by Bellenden's comment that Mar was slain in a bathing vat. It is probable that the Clarence story, which was later well known in England and abroad, was simply copied by Bellenden when he mentioned the death of Mar, and that this bizarre tale obscures the fact that Mar, like Clarence, was executed for treason.

In the face of an almost total lack of official evidence, there must of course remain some doubt about this. However, it should not surprise us that no evidence for Mar's condemnation, or indeed for the sitting of a commission of parliament or general council to try him for treason, survives. In a reign in which annual meetings of the three estates had become the norm, no parliament is recorded in the printed acts as having taken place in 1480. Yet it seems highly likely that the estates met to discuss such vital matters as the defence of the realm against impending English invasion and the renewal of diplomatic links with France; and such a sitting of parliament, in the spring of 1480, would provide the opportunity for an assize to deal with Mar. He may indeed already have been dead, in which case the king would undoubtedly have found it easier to secure his forfeiture.[115] Mar seems to have been childless when he died, so that his earldom would in any event revert to the Crown; but King James, faced with a fugitive and hostile Albany in France, the breakdown of his schemes to marry his sister Margaret in England, and the ruin of his Anglophile foreign policy, must have been anxious to ensure that his condemnation of Mar had the full support of an assize drawn from the three estates. Some indication that the king had gone too far, had condemned his youngest brother on inadequate grounds, and required to salve his conscience, is to be found in his gift to St. Salvator's College in July 1480, stipulating that, in return, masses should be said for Mar's soul.[116]

King James's relations with his family, whether or not his fears of their ambitions were justified, can hardly have endeared him to his lieges, and as the 1470s neared their close, he made some attempt to heed the frequent parliamentary admonitions to provide firm justice throughout his realm. Thus the parliament of March 1479 saw a royal promise 'that our souuerain lord Is of gud mynd and dispositioune to the putting furthe of Justice throwout all his Realme, And sall god willing in tyme tocum with the avis of the lordis of his counsale attend deligently tharto'.[117]

Specific problems are then detailed — 'the gret brek' in Angus between the earls of Buchan and Erroll, and between Alexander Lindsay, Master of Crawford, and Alexander Lyon, second Lord Glamis; also in Nithsdale and Annandale between Robert, Lord Maxwell, and William Douglas of Drumlanrig; and in Teviotdale between the Rutherfords and the Turnbulls, and between the sheriff of Teviotdale — William Douglas of Cavers — and his relatives, and the laird of Cranston.

There is evidence that royal action promptly followed in the case of the problems in Angus. On 11 March 1479 the Earl of Buchan appeared on behalf of himself and his brother Atholl in an action before the Lords of Council, the details of which are unspecified, but in which Erroll was the other party.[118] Unfortunately we have no record of the outcome; but the king and council moved swiftly to curb the lawlessness of Alexander Lindsay, Master of Crawford, son and heir of the loyal fifth earl. On 22 April 1479, the Lords of Council summoned Lindsay and a number of accomplices on charges of attacks made on the abbot and convent of Coupar Angus. They had seized two monks, stolen horses, and molested the abbey servants. Lindsay was ordered to enter his person in ward at Blackness castle within twelve days, to remain there at his own expense until freed by the king; his accomplices were respectively ordered to Dumbarton and Berwick within twelve days, and to various unspecified castles within eight days. So that there would be no opportunity for the offenders to ignore the court's sentence, the sheriffs were to be provided with letters from the captains or constables of the various castles involved, intimating the arrival of the persons sentenced into ward 'under the pain of Rebellioun and putting of thaim to the horne'.[119]

This is a good example of royal justice in action; and there are a few others. On 6 August 1479 Thomas Joffrasone, who had committed the crime of seizing royal letters, was ordered to ward in Blackness in more stringent conditions than Lindsay, as letters were to be written to the captain and constable of the castle to receive him 'and keip him in prisone in a cloiss hous quhill he be fredde be the King'.[120] This case, and that of Lindsay, is a criminal action, although classified as business appropriate to the Lords of Council in Civil Causes; and both emphasise the diversity of actions with which the Council was burdened. On 13 August 1479 Alexander Hume was ordered to ward in Blackness for 'the distrubling done be him' in the sheriff court of Berwick in presence of the sheriff, Sir Patrick Hepburn; and two months later Alexander Seton was sent to Lochleven for striking a royal servant.[121] In both cases, letters were to be delivered to the captain or constable responsible for receiving the offenders into ward, a condition which is not always specified and which may well reflect the gravity of the offences.

Such actions indicate that James III did not always turn a deaf ear to the admonitions of the estates on the subject of maintaining justice; but his interests were closely involved. If royal letters were seized, royal servants struck, and royal sheriffs defied in their own courts, the king was bound to show greater concern than he would in the case of a local feud in Teviotdale. The records of the Lords of Council also reveal that the king had not abandoned his policy of arbitrary seizures of lands and goods, using the act of revocation of 1476 as a convenient excuse.

The most important and protracted action of this kind began on 13 March 1479, when Walter Stewart was summoned before the king and council to answer for 'the wrangwiss occupacioune' of the lands of the town of Cluny in Perthshire, which it was claimed belonged to the king. Stewart duly produced a charter of James II, made on 16 April 1452, granting the lands in dispute to Sir Patrick Gray; but this was rejected on the ground that it 'was made and gevin in our souuerain lordis tendir age' — an understatement, as James III was not born until the following month. At any rate, because the charter produced by Stewart had been made long before the revocation of 1476, it was declared null and void unless new ratification of the gift of Cluny had been made since then; and Stewart was ordered to produce a charter of confirmation if he could. In August, after the case had been continued three times, he at length produced charters and infeftments under the great seal showing that the lands, town, loch, inch and meadow of Cluny belonged to him; but these documents, according to the court, were similar to the charter of 1452, if not identical with it, and the Lords of Council ordered Stewart to quit the property, which then reverted to the Crown.

James III showed a close personal interest in this case; and it did not end with Stewart's discomfiture in August 1479. On 27 October James Hering claimed to hold Cluny in feu farm of the king, and complained that he was prevented by royal letters from enjoying the fruits of the lands. Although it does not survive, such a charter did exist, as the Lords of Council admitted that they were shown it by Hering; and he was granted letters to force Walter Stewart to void the lands of Cluny — in other words, to make effective the Crown's order of August against Stewart, Hering clearly hoping that if he did so, the case would be decided in his favour by the king. But after another two months had elapsed, on 22 December 1479 James III ordered letters to be written to inform Hering that he had decided to continue the case of his right to the lands of Cluny until 14 April 1480; on that day, Hering should appear with his 'evidentis and Richtis' to the lands; in the meantime, he was not to enforce the royal letters of October accepting his tenure of Cluny.[122]

This reversal of the October judgment is an indication that the king was determined that the Cluny lands should revert to the Crown; and like the royal intervention in the Stewartry of Strathearn five years earlier, it shows King James at his worst. He had clearly used Hering to get rid of Stewart for him, then reversed a council judgment in the former's favour in order to acquire Cluny for himself. Hering does not appear to have risked a further appeal to the Lords of Council; and by 3 March 1481 we find the king making a belated gift of part of the disputed lands — the forest of Cluny and the park of Laighwood — to his uncle John, earl of Atholl, for his trouble and expenses in suppressing the rebellion of the Lord of the Isles in 1476.[123] The delay in making this gift was probably the result of the protracted litigation with Stewart and Hering.

In other instances — often quite minor ones — the king showed himself to be equally exacting. On 26 March 1479 Thomas Menteith was summoned before the council at the instance of the king to answer for the spoliation of a single ox from lands which had reverted to the Crown at the time of the revocation. About a month later, on 29 April, the Lords of Council decreed that the lands which Archibald Dundas of that ilk and John Stewart of Craigiehall held of Lord Seton should now revert to the king 'be Resone of warde nocht withstanding the gift of the said warde made of before to the Saidis Archibald and Johne be our souuerain lord in his tendir age quhilk is fallin undir the Reuocacion and Is now of na vale'.[124]

These actions, and the king's general behaviour throughout 1479-80, show a determination on the part of James III to increase his revenues, whether they involved the price of an ox or the revenues of the earldom of Mar. For the most part, he did not dispense rewards liberally amongst his familiars, indeed he may have felt that he was not secure enough financially to do so. Thus, apart from favours lavished on Scheves, the most noteworthy royal gift of the late '70s was that of the lands of Drumcoll, bestowed on John, Lord Carlyle, on 31 October 1477, and given the authority of parliament the following June.[125] The lands, which had formerly belonged to Sir Alexander Boyd of Drumcoll, executed in November 1469, were to be united in perpetuity to the barony of Carlyle; and the grant was made specifically to recompense Carlyle for his many expenses and great labours, and for exposing his person to danger in many places, serving the king abroad in France and elsewhere. This is an interesting gift, because Carlyle was a man whom James III held in high regard. A loyal supporter of James II, he had held such posts as Keeper of Threave and Lochmaben castles, Master of the Queen's Stable, and justiciar in Annandale for the young Duke of Albany. Created a lord of parliament between October 1473 and July 1474, Carlyle was thereafter a frequent attender of parliaments for the remainder of the reign, a regular member of the Lords of Council from the start of their records in 1478, and a frequent witness to royal charters from April 1477 to the end in May 1488.[126] In the winter of 1479-80, he was employed by James III as ambassador to Edward IV;[127] but it was for his services in France that he had been rewarded with Drumcoll in October 1477.

K

These services are not specified, but it seems likely that they involved Carlyle in the frustrating and delicate task of maintaining tenuous contacts with the court of France following the Anglo-Scottish alliance of 1474.

For the truth was that the pro-English policy of James III was visibly failing by 1479-80, and that the king needed whatever foreign assistance he could muster. He was unlikely to find committed support in Scotland in the event of war with England, because he had not paid the price of an unpopular peace — conciliation of the southern nobility, especially his brother Albany, and an even-handed distribution of rewards for his friends in the north and elsewhere. Instead, there was a series of arbitrary acts — the seizure of the Lennox, the Stewartry of Strathearn, Cluny, the attack on the royal brothers — which could only inspire uncertainty and fear amongst supporters and opponents alike. Thus the collapse of the Yorkist alliance in 1480 left the aloof and unpopular king peculiarly vulnerable, not only to English invasion, but to internal revolt.

NOTES

1. *T.A.*, i, 49.
2. *Cal. State Papers (Milan)*, i, 180.
3. *R.M.S.*, ii, No. 1195.
4. *Ibid.*, No. 1175.
5. B.N. MS. Lat. 10187, ff. 59r-62v
6. *R.M.S.*, ii, No. 1161; *Cal. State Papers (Milan)*, i, 186.
7. *Lettres de Louis XI*, iii, 157n.
8. B.N. MS. francais 10685, 542, 606, 625.
9. *Ibid.*, 482, 503, 767.
10. B.N. MS. francais 6981, f. 217r.
11. *Cal. State Papers (Milan)*, i, 186-8.
12. Lesley, *History*, 39; Ferrerius, *Appendix to Boece*, f. 392v. (giving the impossible date of 12 March 1473-4 for the wreck of the 'Salvator').
13. Rymer, *Foedera*, xi, 820-1; *Cal. Docs. Scot.*, iv, Nos. 1416, 1424.
14. *Ibid.*, No. 1414.
15. *Rot. Scot.*, ii, 446; *Cal. Docs. Scot.*, iv, Nos. 1417, 1418.
16. *Rot. Scot.*, ii, 447.
17. *Ibid.*
18. Nicholson, *op.cit.*, 479.
19. M. P. McDiarmid, 'The Date of the "Wallace", in *S.H.R.* xxxiv (April 1955), 26-31.
20. Not at any rate until the following reign. 'Blind Hary' was paid 18/- at the command of James IV on 27 April 1490; but this is his first appearance in the Treasurer's Accounts (*T.A.*, i, 133). Thereafter his name reappears until January 1492 (*T.A.*, i, 174, 176, 181, 184).
21. B. M. Cotton, MS. Vespasian Cxvi, ff. 118-120 (Edward IV's instructions to his almoner, Alexander Legh).
22. *T.A.*, i, 48.
23. S.R.O., Lord Forbes Collection, section c, Nos. 65, 66.
24. *Actis and Deidis of Schir William Wallace*, ed. Craigie (S.T.S., 1940), Book xi, lines 1443-6; *Yester Writs*, No. 170.
25. B. M. Royal MS. 17 Dxx, f. 307v.
26. *Cal. State Papers (Milan)*, i, 198.
27. Major, *History*, 205.
28. Pitscottie, *Historie*, i, 162-3.

29. Fraser, *Douglas*, iii, 104.

30. Ferrerius, *Appendix to Boece*, f. 391.

31. *R.M.S.*, ii, No. 1213; *H.M.C. Rep. iv*, App., 496.

32. Fraser, *Lennox*, i, 299.

33. *A.P.S.*, ii, 108; *R.M.S.*, ii, No. 1209.

34. *See* Fraser, *Lennox*, i, 288-311: *Partition of the Earldom of Lennox*.

35. *Ibid.*, 304.

36. *Spalding Miscellany*, iv, 133; Fraser, *Lennox*, ii, 115.

37. *A.P.S.*, ii, 109.

38. *Ibid.*, 111.

39. Argyll Charters, No. 270; *R.M.S.*, ii, Nos. 1210, 1211, 1212 (in No. 1212, Huntly is misnamed 'Alexander'). A summary of these royal commissions is to be found in *H.M.C. Rep. iv*, App., 487.

40. *R.M.S.*, ii, No. 1227; *H.M.C. Rep. v*, App., 614.

41. Ferrerius, *Appendix to Boece*, 393 r-v; Lesley, *History*, 41-2.

42. Atholl Charters, Box 13, Parcel vii (Blair Castle).

43. John, 7th Duke of Atholl, *Chronicles of the Atholl and Tullibardine Families* (1908), i, 27-30.

44. *Spalding Miscellany*, iv, 133. King James may have taken part personally in the early stages of the campaign to subdue Ross. No royal charters were issued at Edinburgh between 8 February and 6 March 1476; Dingwall had been taken before 28 March; and on that date, the king in his letter of thanks to Huntly refers to his having seen the earl recently.

45. *T.A.*, i, 48.

46. *Spalding Miscellany*, iv, 133.

47. *Ibid.*, 134.

48. *A.P.S.*, ii, 113.

49. *E.R.*, vii, 513.

50. *A.P.S.*, ii, 115.

51. *Highland Papers* (S.H.S., 1914-34), iv, 206-9.

52. *R.M.S.*, ii, No. 1410.

53. *A.P.S.*, ii, 122.

54. *E.R.*, viii, p. lxvii, 592.

55. *See below*, Chapter 7.

56. Nicholson, *op.cit.*, 481.

57. Boece, *Vitae*, 73.

58. *S.H.R.*, xxx, (Oct. 1957), 199-204, for debate as to the birth date of James III; and *see above*, Chapter 1.

59. *R.M.S.*, ii, Nos. 1314, 1318, 1325, 1331.

60. *Ibid.*, Nos. 1340, 1341, 1353, 1354, 1355, 1356, 1357, 1365.

61. *See above*, Chapter 5.

62. *R.M.S.*, ii, No. 1358; S.R.O., Airlie Charters, 29/1. Nothing is known of the circumstances in which the previous holder of the archdeaconry, Walter Stewart, resigned the office. It may have been royal coercion, to make way for Scheves' advancement.

63. *C.P.L.*, xiii, 555-6.

64. *A.P.S.*, ii, 114.

65. *Spalding Miscellany*, iv, 133.

66. *Ibid.*, 134.

67. Fraser, *Annandale*, i, 13-14.

68. *E.R.*, viii, 266, 326, 401, 476, 559; *A.D.C.*, 13, *et seq.*

69. *A.P.S.*, ii, 124, 137.

70. *Cal. Docs. Scot.*, iv, No. 1448.

71. *Edinburgh City Chrs.*, 140.

72. P.R.O. Scots Docs. E39 102/20 (summarised in *Cal. Docs. Scots.*, iv, No. 1451. However, Bain omits the fact that the letter is signed by the king *and* Scheves. Rymer prints it correctly, but puts it under the date 1503 (*Foedera*, xiii, 54)).

73. N.L.S. MS. 73, Morton Royal Letters (printed in *Morton Registrum*, ii, 243).

74. *Cal. Docs. Scot.*, iv, App. I, No. 30.

75. *E.R.*, viii, 476; *A.D.C.*, 13.

76. Ferrerius, *Appendix to Boece*, f. 398v; Myln, *Vitae*, 26.

77. *A.P.S.*, ii, 123, 128-9.

78. *R.M.S.*, ii, No. 1444.

79. *Ibid.*, No. 1443.

80. Herkless and Hannay, i, 89.

81. *Thre Prestis*, lines 459-60.

82. Pitscottie, *Historie*, i, 186.

83. S.R.O., Erroll Charters, No. 97.

84. *Edinburgh City Chrs.*, 154; and *see below*, Chapter 8.

85. Dunlop, *Bishop Kennedy*, 199 n. 5, 244-5, 245 n. 1; *E.R.*, vii, 383; *T.A.*, i, 49; *A.P.S.*, ii, 98, 102, 113.

86. *Cal. State Papers (Milan)*, i, 198.

87. NLS. MS. 1746, ff.111-112; Pitscottie, *Historie*, i, 162. The reasons for sixteenth century praise of Albany are discussed below in Chapter 12.

88. *A.P.S.*, ii, 126.

89. *Cal. Docs. Scot.*, iv, App. i, No. 28.

90. B.M. Royal MS. 17 Dxx, f.307v.

91. *Hary's Wallace*, i, Book I, line 5. Professor Duncan, in *Scotland from the Earliest Times to 1603* (W. C. Dickinson, rev. and ed. A. A. M. Duncan, Oxford 1977), 241, ingeniously suggests that the charges against Albany were more or less fabricated by the king and that 'intercommuning with England . . . was a vague charge and in any case part of Albany's duties as March Warden'. But in 1479 Albany was *not* accused of intercommuning with the English, but of slaughtering them. The distinction is surely important.

92. NLS. MS. 1746, f.111; Pitscottie, *Historie*, i, 186-8.

93. Ferrerius, *Appendix to Boece*, 392 r-v.

94. *R.M.S.*, ii, No. 1426; Fraser, *Colquhoun*, ii, 197.

95. *A.P.S.*, ii, 126.

96. *Scots Peerage*, i, 153-4.

97. *A.P.S.*, ii, 125-8.

98. *Ibid.*, 128.

99. *Ibid.*, 125, 128, 129, 130, 131, 132, 135, 136. It is a remarkable fact that the summons on Albany and his associates, in which the main charge is the breaking of the English truce on the borders, is repeated in exactly the same form even after Scotland and England had gone to war in 1480.

100. S.R.O. State Papers No. 19; and *see below*, Chapter 8.

101. *A.P.S.*, ii, 93, 98, 103, 120.

102. Nicholson, *op.cit.*, 484; and *see below*, Chapter 12.

103. *A.P.S.*, ii, 120; *R.M.S.*, ii, No. 1446.

104. B.M. Royal MS. 17 Dxx, f.307v.

105. NLS. MS. 1746 f.110v; Bellenden, *Chronicles*, ii, 267.

106. Pitscottie, *Historie*, i, 167-8.

107. Buchanan, *History*, ii, 141-2.

108. Ferrerius, *Appendix to Boece*, f.393v.; Lesley, *History*, 43-4.

109. Drummond, *History*, 137-8. For Drummond's 'Elphinstone' MS., *see* T. I. Rae, 'Historical Writings of Drummond of Hawthornden', *S.H.R.*, 29-30.

110. *R.M.S.*, ii, No. 1446. This is a charter confirming a grant of Fife lands to St. Salvator's College at St. Andrews, dated 14 July 1480, and stipulating that masses should be said for the souls of the king and queen, and for the late Earl of Mar, whose earldom had fallen into the king's hands by reason of the earl's forfeiture.

111. Pitscottie, *Historie*, i, 167. A different interpretation of Mar's death is to be found in Dickinson/Duncan, *op.cit.*, 247.

112. BM. Royal MS. 17 Dxx, f.307v.

113. *Rolls of Parl.*, vi, 193-5.

114. Mancini, *Usurpation of Richard III*, 76-7.

115. Lesley (*History*, 43-4) and Ferreri (*Appendix to Boece*, f.393v.) both suggest the month of December 1480 for Mar's death. If December *1479* is correct, then the king may well have been justifying his brother's death — whether executed or dying from natural causes — before the estates the following spring, and securing a sentence of forfeiture then. Lack of any evidence for the sitting of a parliamentary assize is no doubt due not only to gaps in the records of parliament, but also to the lack of Lords of Council records between 1480 and 1483, and the total loss of the Treasurer's accounts — which in 1473-4, alone amongst the official records, referred to the condemnation of Patrick Graham in a general council.

116. *R.M.S.*, ii, No. 1446. A similar gesture is to be found on the part of King James in 1487; his wife, Margaret of Denmark, from whom he had lived apart since 1482-3, died in 1486, and the king promptly attempted to secure her canonisation from Pope Innocent VIII.

117. *A.P.S.*, ii, 122.

118. *A.D.C.*, 21.

119. *Ibid.*, 29.

120. *Ibid.*, 31.

121. *Ibid.*, 31, 32.

122. *Ibid.*, 21-2, 31, 37, 46.

123. Atholl Charters, Box 13, Parcel vii, No. 1 (Blair Castle).

124. *A.D.C.*, 27-30.

125. *R.M.S.*, ii, No. 1327; *A.P.S.*, ii, 193.

126. *E.R.*, viii, 216; *A.P.S.*, *A.D.C,* and *R.M.S.*, ii, Nos. 1288-1730 *passim.*

126. *Cal. Docs. Scot.*, iv, No. 1436.

7

The Road to Lauder Bridge : 1480–82

'ANNO domini m° cccc° lxxx° thair raise ane gret were betwix Ingland and Scotland', comments the chronicler, without, however, supplying any reason for its outbreak.[1] The war to which he referred was to drag on for over two years in inconclusive fashion before it brought to a head the most serious crisis of the reign.

Responsibility for the outbreak of war was probably about equally divided on both sides of the border. James III, firmly committed to the alliance of 1474 although undoubtedly embarrassed by the hostility of some of his southern nobility, was also unfortunate in that the European diplomatic situation had altered to his disadvantage within a year of his treaty with Edward IV. From July 1475 the English king ceased to be Louis XI's enemy and became his pensioner; and the death of Charles the Bold of Burgundy in January 1477 upset the power structure in northern Europe and made James III's pretensions to act as mediator between France and Burgundy — a policy originally urged by parliament in 1473 — impractical if not absurd. Edward IV's enthusiasm for the Scottish alliance understandably waned once a secure northern frontier ceased to be a matter or urgency, and by the late 1470s he must have wondered when he was going to see any return on his outlay of cash each February, when the annual instalments of Cecilia's dowry were paid to the Scots.

Naturally the Scottish official viewpoint was rather different. Before 1474, James III had shown a shrewd grasp of diplomatic realities when he remarked that the king of England was the only monarch who made war on Scotland, and pressed for an alliance in the interests of security. At the same time he had favoured a more aggressive policy in north-western Europe, and the three estates, using their control of the purse strings, had dissuaded the king from undertaking foreign adventures and had substituted the less costly role of mediator between hostile foreign princes as a means of acquiring European fame.[2] Mediation between Louis XI of France and Charles the Bold of Burgundy had been considered first; and in the autumn of 1476 and opening of 1477 we find James, earl of Buchan, the king's half-uncle, on embassy to Burgundy and offering his services as mediator between the Burgundians and Sigismund of Austria.[3]

Two strands of this policy involved the king personally — the active pursuance of stronger ties with England through the marriage there of his sister Margaret, and his repeated efforts to travel abroad in the late '70s. The former scheme was first mooted in the parliament of November 1475, when it was recorded that Lady Margaret, James III's younger sister, then aged about thirteen, should be married 'in sum convenient place'. Details would be arranged by the king and council, and the estates informed how much they would have to pay for the dowry. Parliament responded cautiously to these proposals, and reminded the king of 'the gret chargeis that thai have borne of befor' — no doubt a reference to royal taxation of 1471-3.[4] The projected marriage was again considered by the estates in July 1476, and then referred to a parliamentary commission of forty, whose other tasks included the sending abroad of an embassy and unfinished judicial business.[5] Probably this ungainly body never met; and early in 1477, when Edward IV's almoner, Alexander Legh, came to Edinburgh to pay the third instalment of Princess Cecilia's dowry, James III again took the initiative by making two quite specific marriage proposals — that his sister Margaret should marry George, duke of Clarence, Edward IV's brother, and that his brother Albany should wed Mary, daughter of the widowed Duchess of Burgundy, Edward IV's sister. The Scottish king's information was at least up-to-date. The Duke of Clarence had been widowed as recently as December 1476, and Charles the Bold of Burgundy was killed at Nancy on 5th January 1477.[6]

Both marriage proposals, however, were speedily quashed. Edward IV offered as his reason for dismissing them the rather specious argument that no honourable person would consider marriage less than a year after bereavement, a state in which both Clarence and his Burgundian sister found themselves. It is probable, however, that he was moved by more material considerations, namely that he did not relish the idea of a Scottish-Burgundian marriage alliance on the one hand, and suspected Clarence of treasonable designs on the other. In April 1477, the month before King James's marriage proposals reached him, Edward had been incensed by Clarence's arbitrary seizure and execution of Ankarette Twynyho, whom he accused of having poisoned his wife. This action seems to have been inspired, in part at least, by Clarence's disappointment at his failure to marry Mary of Burgundy, his niece, and the knowledge that Edward IV had been opposed to the match.[7] Coming when they did, therefore, James III's marriage proposals were both unfortunate and unrealistic.

However, the king persisted, and again enlisting the aid of the estates in June 1478, reiterated that Margaret should be married in England.[8] On 14 December 1478 Alexander Inglis, dean of Dunkeld, and Lyon King-of-Arms were in London to negotiate a marriage for Margaret, the prospective bridegroom being Anthony, earl Rivers, Edward IV's brother-in-law. The marriage contract was drawn up and signed before the end of January 1479. James III was to pay a dowry of four thousand marks of English money, but as he could not afford to hand it over in cash, it was agreed that it would be deducted from the annual payments which Edward IV was making to the Scots for the dowry of the princess Cecilia.[9] This agreement is a revealing commentary on the financial position of the Scottish king at this time. Four thousand marks sterling, rather more than eight thousand pounds Scots, was an enormous sum, probably more than half the king's gross annual income.[10] In the face of such expenditure, the few hundred pounds acquired by the crown for two years' farms of the annexed earldom of Ross (the accounts of which do not begin until 1479 in any case) appear trivial indeed.

Pressing financial problems may explain why King James made no immediate effort to honour his agreement to pay off the dowry in the manner laid down in the

January marriage contract. Alexander Legh, Edward IV's almoner, arrived in Scotland as usual and by 4 March had paid the fifth instalment of Cecilia's dowry. Far from offering to reduce or refund this, King James showed his concern that it should be paid in English currency rather than Scots.[11] At the same time he turned to the three estates for financial help. The March parliament of 1479 voted the huge sum of twenty thousand marks to meet the expenses which the king would incur in sending the bride to England, as well as those connected with the actual occasion of the wedding. This sum was to be made up by a contribution of eight thousand marks by the clergy, eight thousand by the barons, and four thousand by the burghs; and it was to be paid in two instalments, half by the Feast of St John the Baptist (24 June), the other half within three years. The huge attendance of one hundred and four members of the estates, the long delay in organising taxation for Margaret's marriage — some three-and-a-half years since the issue had first been raised in parliament — and the size of the sum asked for by the Crown, all these facts taken together indicate that King James's demand for cash in 1479 was highly controversial and provoked much opposition.[12] Twenty thousand marks was, after all, more than double what the king had asked for to equip an army of six thousand to invade Brittany in 1472. He had failed to obtain the necessary money from the estates on that occasion, and he would fail again in 1479.

There is, however, evidence that some effort was made to bring in the tax. An extant taxation roll for the sheriffdom of Edinburgh shows that the values of its properties had been drawn up by 26 March 1479.[13] But it was not until 18 August that a royal order went out to the sheriff to raise, for the first payment, a tax of two shillings on every pound's worth of land. As the total value of the lands of the entire sheriffdom (including royal lands, which would not be taxed) amounted to £928 13/4d., the king would be lucky if the tax yield was as much as £80 or £90 from Edinburgh. So much for his ten thousand marks before 24 June.

Thus, by the autumn of 1479, James III must have been aware of the scanty return on his tax, and his desire to marry off his sister in England may well have been cooling as a result. On 23 January 1479 Edward IV had issued a safe-conduct for Margaret and a retinue of three hundred to come to England, at the expense of her brother, before 16 May.[14] Her failure to turn up may reflect a row over money between James III and the estates, or the king's preoccupation with Albany's treason, or both. The safe-conduct was renewed on 22 August 1479, the stipulation then being that the prospective bride should be in England before 1 November.[15] Again she did not appear; and James III thereafter abandoned his efforts to secure an alliance for her in the south.[16]

King James's failure to obtain most of his tax for Margaret's marriage in 1479 may well have been the result of a growing suspicion amongst members of the estates that he intended to divert the money to some other purpose; for the second area of his diplomatic activities in the late '70s was a renewal of his interest in foreign travel. It was, of course, unheard of for a fifteenth century Scottish king in his majority to go abroad in person; and parliament had made it clear to James III, in 1472 and 1473, that it did not wish him to travel to Europe, mainly because of the English threat and the king's lack of money.[17] By the middle of the decade, however, there was at least peace with England; and no fewer than three English safe-conducts were issued to King James to allow him to make a pilgrimage to the shrine of St. John at Amiens without risking a long sea voyage — on 15 May 1476, 17 March 1478, and finally on 23 November 1479.[18] Lack of money may have made the journey impossible in 1476, and fear of Albany and Mar could have been a motive in 1478. By the late autumn of 1479, however, Albany had fled, Mar was probably in custody, and some part of the tax granted by the March parliament must have come in. James III took the proposed visit to Amiens seriously enough to order the striking of a gold medallion, at Berwick, in honour of St. John the Baptist, whose shrine was at Amiens.[19] No other gold coinage was minted at Berwick during the reign; and James's sending of the medallion from Berwick to Amiens is clearly a public manifestation of his pride in the Scots acquisition of the burgh in 1461, at the expense of the English.

Why was King James so persistent in his efforts to travel abroad to Amiens? Presumably conventional piety was not the only, or indeed the main, reason; he must have had a political motive. In 1479 Louis XI of France once again began to make approaches to James III with a view to having the Scottish king break the English alliance. At some time during the year, Dr. John Ireland, an expatriate Scot, was sent by Louis to Scotland with the aims, according to Dempster, of composing the differences between James III and Albany and inciting the Scots to make war on Edward IV.[20] The Scottish king can hardly have been enthusiastic about the latter proposal; but with Albany in favour with Louis XI, and Edward IV visibly cooling towards Scottish diplomatic advances, King James must have considered negotiations with France desirable if not essential. So he was prepared to receive Dr. Ireland again in the spring of 1480; and more immediately, his intention to go to France in the late autumn of 1479 may have been part of an arrangement whereby he might meet Louis XI in person and discuss a renewal of the Franco-Scottish alliance.[21] He may specifically have hoped to obtain better terms by negotiating a French marriage for Princess Margaret; alternatively he may have been following his estates' advice of 1473 and putting himself forward as a mediator between King Louis and his Burgundian rivals. At the same time, he must have been anxious to impress Edward IV with a display of Scottish strength and political unanimity, hence his request for a safe-conduct through England with a retinue of no less than a thousand.

Edward IV was not impressed. Within only three months of James III's final safe-conduct, he issued instructions to Alexander Legh which indicated the total breakdown of relations between Scotland and England. The English king undoubtedly had his grievances — the instalments of Cecilia's dowry, paid each February without any return in terms of the fulfilment of the marriage, and the inevitable breaches of the truce by border Scots. In particular, Edward complained that they had murdered Robert Lisle and taken prisoner Sir Henry Percy and many other gentlemen, apparently with the connivance of the lieutenant of the Warden of the Marches.[22] But the Scots had similar complaints, and James III had recently sent Ross Herald to demand redress for breaches of the border truce on the English side.

In the circumstances, Edward IV's response seems excessive, his instructions to

Legh going far beyond the bounds of the normal give-and-take of diplomacy. He announced that he was going to make war on the Scots because he was not satisfied that James III was fulfilling 'his promised trewes'. The king of Scots had received 'grete and notable soumes of money' in anticipation of the marriage of his son to Princess Cecilia; but he had responded to this goodwill by allowing Edward's subjects on the borders 'to be invaded, murdred, and slayne without cause'; he was still in wrongful occupation of Berwick, Coldingham, Roxburgh and other towns; he had not done homage to Edward IV, 'as he oweth to doo and as his progenitours have doon in tyme passed'; and he had 'wrongfully disherited the earl of Douglas', whom Edward declared he intended to see restored. Finally, he demanded that Prince James should be sent to England, to be received by the Earl of Northumberland, before 1 May 1480. However, Edward ended by saying that if these four things could not be accomplished, he would be content with the handing over of Prince James and Berwick; only in this way could the spilling of Christian blood be avoided.[23]

These two final demands were of course quite unacceptable in Scotland, as Edward IV presumably knew they would be; and his adoption of such a belligerent attitude at short notice is possibly explained by his receiving definite intelligence that James III was once again negotiating with Louis XI, and that the outcome might be a Scottish invasion of the English north-east. On 29 October 1480, long after the outbreak of war between the two countries, Carlo Visconti, the Milanese ambassador at the French court, which was then at Tours, wrote an illuminating letter to the Duke and Duchess of Milan, in which he remarked: 'As I wrote before, the Scots have attacked the English, and I think it is the handiwork of the king here (Louis XI), in order that others may have to think more of their own affairs than of those of others. I am confirmed in this opinion because I chance to have seen a letter from the king of Scotland to the king here, in which he advises him that the English . . . had made an incursion into his country, but his people had forthwith cast them out, and they had done but little harm and had gone away with the worst of it. In conclusion, he asks for one or two gunners or bombardiers and some artillery, saying that he has need of both. This makes me practically certain that the king here has a hand in it, since he [James III] asks him for help against the English, who are in league and close affinity with his Majesty.'[24]

This letter is of particular interest in that it suggests that the Scots opened hostilities at the instigation of Louis XI; it reflects the French king's concern that Edward IV was being wooed by Maximilian of Austria to abandon his French pension and join Burgundy in a concerted attack upon France; and as Visconti had sent an earlier letter in which he also mentioned the Anglo-Scottish war, it must have been going on for some time. The English belligerence to which he refers is supported by the record evidence, as on 12 May 1480 Edward IV appointed his brother Richard, duke of Gloucester, Lieutenant-General of the North, to lead an army against Scotland.[25] Boece, Ferreri and Lesley all give the month of April 1480 as the date of the death of Bishop Spens of Aberdeen, and the cause of this, according to Lesley and Ferreri, was the bishop's grief and sorrow on hearing war — incited by Dr. Ireland — had once again broken out between England and

Scotland.[26] It would appear from the evidence, therefore, that war broke out in April or May 1480, and if Boece's precise date for Spens's death — 15 April — is correct, in early April.

James III's foreign policy now lay in ruins; and Visconti's letter gives some idea of the Scottish king's isolation and military weakness. However, beyond the very brief account of Angus's raid into Northumberland and the general excursions mentioned by the Milanese ambassador, no campaigns of any note can definitely be ascribed to the year 1480. A number of payments were made out of the English exchequer during the Michaelmas term to supply the army proceeding to Scotland; the forfeited ninth earl of Douglas was sent north to the Scottish Marches; and Richard, duke of Gloucester, who had received a hundred marks on 12 December 1479, for the repairing of the walls of the city of Carlisle, was granted a further fifty marks.[27] This last is of course a trifling sum when compared with the vast expenditure on the war against Scotland two years later; and it is probable that the hostilities of 1480 were confined to minor raids on both sides. Edward IV, however, spent much of the year making vigorous preparations for war, levying benevolences for the purpose from the towns of Salisbury and Canterbury, the city of London, and the counties; and the clergy of the province of Canterbury granted a tenth for the defence of the kingdom.[28]

In the campaigning season of 1481 the war was continued on a larger and more organised scale. Six of the seven statutes of the Scottish parliament of April 1481 were concerned with preparations for war. The lieges were to be ready to assemble at the king's bidding 'in thare best wise with bowis speris axis and uthir abilzementis of were' on eight days' notice, provided with victuals to last for twenty days. The length of spears and condition of armour were the subject of legislation; and in anticipation of invasion the king ordered that his castles of Dunbar and Lochmaben should be well provided with victuals and artillery. All lords, spiritual and temporal, with castles on the borders or the sea coast — St. Andrews, Aberdeen, Tantallon, Hailes, Dunglass, Hume, Edrington, 'and specealy the hermetage that Is in maste dangere' — were likewise instructed to 'stuff' them 'with men vitale and artilzery' and to carry out any repairs necessary for their defence. At about the same time James III sent a herld and pursuivant to Edward IV, offering to make redress for all breaches of the truce for which the Scots were to blame, if he could have peace with England. However the English king, after detaining the Scottish ambassadors for a considerable time, would neither see them nor give them any answer.[29]

The second phase of the war followed, with the English taking the initiative. In May 1481 Lord Howard and Sir Thomas Fulford were commissioned by Edward IV to keep the western seas, with power to take Scottish ships, mariners and supplies. According to Lesley and Ferreri, however, Howard appeared in the east, sailing into the Firth of Forth, taking as prizes eight ships lying at Leith, Kinghorn and Pittenweem, landing at Blackness, burning the town and seizing another large ship.[30] On 20 May Edward IV wrote to the pope, explaining that although he was enthusiastic about a crusade against the Turk, he was meantime compelled to remain at home 'to take necessary measures, on account of the fickle movements of the Scots'; and he went on to remark: 'We cannot abstain from asserting our primeval right [of overlordship], left dormant for a while for the sake of foreign affairs . . . For these reasons, we lead in person to Scotland, in the course of this summer, our army lately raised and so immensely burdensome to ourselves and to our subjects.' A letter written to the pope by Edward in the following year, however, admitted that he did not command in person, either in 1481 or 1482; he was prevented from doing so, in the former case, by 'adverse turmoil'.[31] Financial difficulties, combined with a very bad harvest in 1481, may have been to blame; certainly payments from the English exchequer towards the furtherance of the war, as compared with the following year, are meagre. The Duke of Gloucester, with Lords Dorset, Rivers and Stanley, was in the north;[32] but apart from the unsuccessful siege of Berwick, in October and November 1481, not much seems to have been attempted. Nor did Lord Howard emerge unscathed from his naval exploits on the east coast; on 18 March 1483 Sir Andrew Wood received a feu-charter of Largo from James III for his services and losses during the war on land and sea, and the grant makes it clear that he inflicted extensive damage on the English at sea.[33]

In the same year Edward IV also employed two indirect methods of attack, neither of which appears to have been successful. On 22 August he gave a commission to his brother Gloucester and to James, earl of Douglas, to extend assurances to all Scotsmen wishing to come into England, promising them lands, lordships, and other gifts for their services.[34] Already in June he had attempted to persuade John MacDonald, Lord of the Glens of Antrim, to rebel against James III; one Patrick Haliburton, chaplain, was sent to conclude an alliance with Macdonald and Donald Gorme.[35] However, treason in the north and west was no longer a serious threat to the Scottish Crown, because the Lord of the Isles had ceased to be the most powerful natural troublemaker in the area; that role had now devolved upon his illegitimate son, Angus Og of Islay, and Macdonald of the Isles had become a king's man, looking for royal favours and even petitioning Argyll for help against his own offspring. Thus in the Ayr customs account for 1483 we find an entry of £42 15/6d. arrears for furnishing and provisioning a ship sent by the king's command from Ayr to the Lord of the Isles to capture Master Patrick Haliburton, traitor.[36] Clearly, therefore, the struggle in the western Highlands, in itself the result of the 1476 Ross forfeiture, made support for Edward IV unlikely in that quarter; and John Macdonald thought it necessary to his own future not to rebel against his sovereign.[37]

On the Scottish side, however, the campaigning season of 1481 was even less successful. James III, determined to avenge the insult which Edward IV had inflicted on him by refusing to see the Scots ambassadors, assembled an army for the purpose, apparently both for defence of the realm and invasion of England. In view of Edward IV's intention to come north in person, expressed as recently as May, the Scottish preparations must have been mainly defensive; but little indication of this appears in the parliamentary records of the following year, which describe 'ane hoist of the hale grete powere of Scotland', gathered by James III 'to have past for the resistence and Invasion of oure ennemyis of Ingland'. The same source describes the sequel; the king, being shown papal bulls admonishing him to desist from bloodshed, disbanded his army, trusting that the English would do the same. However, they did not do so, and 'thare was incontinent gret byrnyngis hereschip and distructioun done apone oure saide souerain Lord his Realme and Liegis'.[38] This may well be a reference to Lord Howard's depredations in the Firth of Forth and on the Fife coast; and there is also some evidence to suggest papal intervention to try to end the Anglo-Scottish war. On 23 July 1483 there is royal authorisation, referring back to the events of 1481, for a payment of twenty pounds to 'Gelicane, nuncio apostolico'.[39]

The parliamentary account of King James's 'scaling' of the Scottish host in 1481 was greatly expanded by later writers. Thus Ferreri describes the king's intention to invade England with a large army; but when the troops had mustered, James was met by the envoy of a cardinal then in England, threatening him with excommunication if he did not disband his army; Christian princes must remain at peace, and reserve their forces for a crusade against the Turk. Dutifully, the king disbanded his army, whereupon the English fleet reappeared in the Forth, and there were serious English raids across the border. Lesley's story, which Ferreri may partially have copied, is similar; but in his account James III was dissuaded from invasion by a messenger of Edward IV, sent from the cardinal legate resident in England at the time, commanding the king by apostolic authority to cease the war under pain of interdict. When King James disbanded his army, Edward IV sent his navy to Inchkeith, where however it was repulsed 'be the cuntrey men'.[40]

Both these accounts contain information which may be verified, at least in part, from official records. But they also provided wonderful copy for Sir James Balfour, writing in the early seventeenth century in the knowledge that James III had been condemned by most earlier writers. So in his *Annales*, Balfour explains that Edward IV resorted to trickery by dressing up 'a knavish monk' as the pope's legate, sending this individual to the Scottish camp to thunder out excommunications and curses in the pope's name against James III and his entire host, should they make further war on England, and so hinder such pious work as a concerted Christian attack on the Turks and Moors. 'The facile king,' concludes Balfour, 'tooke all this trumprey for good coyne, and presently, without more enquyrey, licentiats his armey.'[41]

Thus, by the seventeenth century, the simple contemporary statement that the king, on being shown some papal bulls, disbanded his army, had been distorted and exaggerated to provide a tale of James III's stupidity and incompetence. In fact, it is not in question that Pope Sixtus IV, for his own ends, was attempting to secure peace in Europe, or that a papal messenger was in Scotland in 1481. But the parliamentary statement of 1482, praising the king for disbanding his army solely on the pope's instructions, reads suspiciously like propaganda, the Scots making out a case against 'the Revare Edward calland him king of Ingland';[42] and James III's reasons for 'scaling' the host were probably much more material ones. First, there was the ever-present difficulty of finance, of raising enough money to pay, equip and supply the army. Certainly a tax had been voted in parliament on 13 April 1481, a contribution of seven hundred marks to be raised by the three estates; but this was merely to provide for the victualling of Berwick for forty days.[43] The host itself had to be summoned in traditional fashion, the lieges to be ready for war at eight days' notice, bringing their own provisions to last twenty days — time, in fact, only for a very short defensive campaign. Secondly, the defence of Berwick, which was clearly the object of the exercise, was probably a priority, as a matter of prestige, for the king, but unpopular with the host and its leaders. Little or no profit and great risk was involved in military setpieces — battles, sieges or defences of strongpoints — on the borders; James I's siege of Roxburgh in 1436 had ended in total disaster, and James II had lost his life at the same place in 1460. Now in 1481, James III proposed not only to defend Berwick but to take the field against an army which the Scots presumed would be led by Edward IV in person. The lieges and their leaders may well have felt disinclined to risk their lives either for Berwick or for the insult perpetrated by the English king in refusing to give their unpopular sovereign's ambassadors an audience. So the Scottish host was disbanded. The entire episode was, perhaps, a warning to James III, an unpleasant rehearsal for Lauder Bridge.

The Scots, spared an English invasion in 1481, had little cause for relief or celebration. On 25 October, at Nottingham — the farthest north he travelled that year — Edward IV renewed the treaty he had originally made with Louis XI in July 1477; a truce between England and France was to continue for as long as Edward and Louis lived, and for a year after one or other of them died.[44] The French king, having achieved his diplomatic aim of embroiling Scotland in war with England while at the same time keeping Edward IV on a tight rein through payment of an annual pension, now withdrew from further involvement to watch the results of his policy. For the remainder of the war James III would call in vain on King Louis for assistance; indeed the parliament of March 1482 recorded that the Scottish king had 'divers tymes writtin to the King of France . . . and gottin nane answer'.[45]

The renewal of the Anglo-French peace meant that Edward IV would be freer to turn his attention to the Scots war in the spring of 1482; and James III had already begun to cast around for allies or practical assistance. Thus in the autumn of 1481 Duke Maximilian of Burgundy reported to Edward IV that the Scottish king had recently sent him an ambassador, a bishop, who offered him an alliance and asked for some bombards and other engines of war. Maximilian assured Edward that he had refused the Scottish offer, but had promised to do all he could to restore Anglo-Scottish amity.[46] As early as the autumn of 1480, James III had asked Louis XI to send him 'one or two gunners or bombardiers and some artillery'[47] — probably in vain; and we also find him making a similar request of his distant relative, Archduke Sigismund of Austria, during the period of hostilities with England. On 14 March of an unspecified year, James wrote to the archduke thanking him for a gift of some cannon, and saying that nothing would have given him greater pleasure than their safe arrival. Unfortunately they had been lost, together with the ship transporting them, in a violent storm.[48] The letter may tentatively be dated 1480–81, when according to the contemporary chronicler, 'ane gret storme began at new yeir day and lestyt quhill the xxvi day of Marche'.[49]

All these requests for assistance underline James III's unpreparedness for war and especially for its financial burdens; and it is hardly surprising that the Scottish parliament which assembled at Edinburgh on 18 March 1482 was concerned almost exclusively with the defence of the kingdom. There was a large attendance of seventy-five, including the archbishop, four bishops, nine abbots, five earls, seventeen lords of parliament, and twenty burgh commissioners. Perhaps significantly, the clergy who sat on the Lords of the Articles included not only Archbishop Scheves but three future chancellors, John Laing, bishop of Glasgow, James Livingston, bishop of Dunkeld, and William Elphinstone, bishop-elect of Ross. The stipulation was included that, should the archbishop be absent, the royal secretary, Archibald Whitelaw, would take his place.[50]

All efforts to secure peace with England had by this time been rejected as useless, the danger of invasion was fully appreciated, and many of the parliamentary articles read like a clarion call to arms. It was declared that 'the thre Estaitis . . . has undirstandin and knawis wele that this instant were Is movit apone oure souerane lord and his Realme again the will mynde and entencioune of his hienes'; James III was made out to be totally wronged by 'the Revare Edwarde' and still desirous of peace; and Edward IV was 'aluterly set to continew in this were that he has movit and begunnyn and be all his powere tendis and schapis to Invaid and distroye and in sa fer as he may to conquest this Realme'.

On this occasion there was an air of urgency about the preparations for defence. Letters were to be written to the sheriffs ordering the lieges to be ready, well armed and supplied with provisions for an unspecified number of days (as opposed to the twenty days required the previous year), to come to the king 'in all possible haist eftir as thai salbe chargit' (as opposed to the eight days' notice which they were to receive in 1481). Weapon-showings were to be held by the sheriffs every fifteen days; and the sea coasts were to be divided into sections, six miles in length and a mile in breadth, each section under the command of a captain 'to gadir the cuntre' to resist invasion by sea. The sloth which was apparently usual amongst couriers bearing royal letters to the sheriffs was to be amended by prompt payment of their expenses and the employment of 'autentik persones and wele horsit men to warne his lieges in the ferrest partis of the Realme before utheris that ar nerrare'. Finally, an interesting comment was made on the king's obligations in the coming war. If Scotland should be invaded by the English Wardens of the Marches, resistance to them should be made by their counterparts on the Scottish side of the border; if, however, Edward IV were to lead an invading army in person, he should be resisted by James III 'in propir persoune and with the hale body of the Realme to lyf and dee with his hienes in his defence'.[51] In fact James needed no inciting to turn out to oppose the English, nor did he observe the distinction between invasion by March Wardens or the English king in person. In 1481 he had been prepared to defend Berwick by personally calling out and leading the host; and in 1482 he was to attempt to do so again, although Edward IV once more failed to come north in person.

In fact, the defence of Berwick was an obsession with James III; and it is clear from the parliamentary record of March 1482 that he was far more enthusiastic about retaining the burgh than many of those present in the estates, for he had to pay for it himself. Parliament acknowledged that the king had already been 'honorable and curageous' in keeping Berwick at great cost, that he had fortified and strengthened the burgh walls and purchased artillery for its defence, and that he now proposed to pay for a garrison of five hundred men. In recognition of the king's commitment, the estates 'of thar ane free will' offered to pay the wages of another six hundred soldiers — not for Berwick, but to be garrisoned in various places on the borders. It seems clear from this that the estates were prepared to play their traditional part in defending the borders, but that Berwick's defence was James III's responsibility alone. Retaining Berwick was for King James a matter of prestige, for the burgh had been captured early in the reign, and the king had enhanced its status by siting there the royal mint which produced the Amiens gold medallion. But members of the estates do not seem to have considered the imperial pretensions and prestige of James III worth paying for.

The defence of the borders, however, was another matter. Of the six hundred soldiers provided by parliament, two hundred and forty were to be paid by the clergy, the same number by the barons, and the remaining hundred and twenty by the burghs; the entire six hundred were to arrive at their respective garrisons by 1 May, and were to remain there for three months. The king's Berwick garrison would begin its term of duty a month later, on 1 June;[52] and the dispersal of the total of eleven hundred men throughout the borders was meticulously worked out. In the east, of the Berwick five hundred, two hundred were constantly to be ready for the use of the Warden of the East Marches. The strongpoints of Blackadder, Wedderburn and Hume were entrusted to James Borthwick (a son of William, second Lord Borthwick), who was to choose two deputies to command the twenty-strong garrisons of Blackadder and Wedderburn, while he himself held Hume with sixty men. In the Middle Marches, the guardianship of which area was entrusted to James Stewart, earl of Buchan,[53] there was a divided command. The laird of Edmonstone was appointed captain of Cessford, Ormiston and Egarstone with garrisons of sixty, twenty and twenty men respectively. The same garrisons, in the same proportions, were to be received into Jedburgh, Cocklaw and Dolphinstoun respectively, under the captaincy of the laird of Cranstoun. Hermitage Castle, garrisoned by a hundred men, was to be held by the laird of Lamington. In the West Borders, the main strongpoint was Lochmaben castle, which was to be provided with a garrison of a hundred under the captaincy of the laird of Closeburn, Thomas Kilpatrick.[54] Robert Charteris, laird of Amisfield,[55] was to command the smaller garrisons of Castlemilk, Annan and Bell's Tower, a total of one hundred soldiers being involved. Finally, the king entrusted John Stewart, Lord Darnley, with the Wardenship of the West Borders.[56]

Other acts of this March parliament reflect the grave problems facing the country. An embassy was to be sent from the king and the three estates to the king of France and the Parliament of Paris, urgently requesting aid against 'thair commoun Inimie of Ingland', an optimistic or obsolete description by the Scots of France's ally. No help would come from Louis XI; and it was not until March 1483 that his successor Charles VIII made a peace treaty with James III,[57] by which time the Scottish king had extricated himself from his internal crisis by his own exertions. In the spring of 1482, however, the war had clearly been a disaster for Scottish trade and living conditions. The last statute of the parliament commands that aliens coming into Scotland with merchandise and victuals should be well received, 'considering that the merchandis of this realme ar throw weiris stoppit to exerce and use the cours of merchandice and specially to gar vittalis be brocht in sen thir is now skantnes thirof'. This gloomy economic picture is borne out by the writer of the contemporary short chronicle, who remarks that 'thir was ane gret hungyr and deid in Scotland for the boll of meill was for four pundis . . . And als was gret were betuix Scotland and Ingland and gret distruction throw the weris was of corne and cattell'.[58]

Yet 1482 was not primarily an economic, but rather a political, crisis. In spite of the apparent unanimity of king and lieges in the March parliament, in spite of the commitment of James III to the defence of Berwick and the estates to the garrisoning of border strongholds, in spite even of the noble statement that the lieges would 'live or die' with their king in defence of the realm, we find in the parliamentary records two ominous signs of impending crisis involving some of the most influential Scottish magnates.

The first of these was the trial, on 22 March 1482, of Robert, second Lord Lyle, on charges of having corresponded with the exiled earl of Douglas and other Englishmen 'in tressonable maner', and of receiving letters from Douglas and others in an effort to further the English cause. The trial, before a parliamentary assize, ended in an acquittal for Lyle; but it would be valuable to know the source of the charges against him, because his future career until 1488 was one of unswerving loyalty to James III. This in itself would suggest that Lyle's accuser was not the king; and indeed the charges are remarkably flimsy. Lyle was not accused of correspondence with Edward IV, a charge which would certainly have been levied if there had been any grounds for it. Correspondence with Douglas was a lesser matter, especially because, in spite of the English king's constant championship of the forfeited earl, Douglas did not in fact accompany the English invading army of 1482; and in any case the court acquitted Lyle of acting treasonably. The assize itself was composed of sixteen laymen over whom the king sat in judgment. None of the judges was a member of the committee of the Articles; but two of the king's uncles, John Stewart, earl of Atholl, and James Douglas, earl of Morton, headed the assize, which also included nine lords of parliament.[59] Later in the year, Atholl was to be closely involved with his brothers in the political revolution following Lauder; and Andrew, Lord Gray, who the following year, if not before, was to be found deep in treasonable negotiations with Albany, Angus and the English,[60] also sat on the Scottish tribunal which tried Lord Lyle for a very similar offence. Lyle was a king's man, and the presence of the king probably helped to secure his acquittal. However, the fact that he was accused at all is indicative of opposition to James III and his supporters in high places, an opposition stimulated, perhaps, by the king's Stewart half-uncles.

Indeed, the half-uncles were the cause of the second clear source of tension in the March parliament. In the presence of the three estates the king declared that 'anent the takin and Intrometting had of before of the Castel of Edinburgh be his unclis Johne erle of Athole and James erle of buchane in our souerane lordis tendir age was takin and done of the command of his hienes gevin to thaim thirapone'; the clause goes on to relate that Atholl and Buchan had immediately handed over the castle on being commanded to do so; and emphasised that the king made this declaration in his majority so that his uncles had 'nocht Inrunnyn ony crimez blame or offence in that mater agane his hienes bot in tyme tocum . . . salbe qwite of al dangere and perell . . . in thare lyfis landis and gudis anent the said accioune'.[61] Here is clear evidence that Atholl and Buchan required a parliamentary remission for substantial sins committed during the king's legal minority; and an earlier remission, granted before 1476, was now renewed with elaborate provisions for the making of an engrossment sealed by the king and the estates. In view of subsequent events, this act is highly significant; Atholl and Buchan had clearly tried to further their political ambitions by seizing Edinburgh castle sometime before 1476. It does not appear from the records that they acquired the annuity paid to the keepers of the castle, both of whom were men close to James III, the Earl of Argyll and David Crichton of Cranston.[62] But their action was clearly illegal and carried the gravest penalties; and it reflects the ambitions of men who must have felt that their kinship with the king, and their services to him, merited rewards which they had failed to acquire.

How reassured both men were by their parliamentary remission in March 1482 must remain a matter of doubt. Atholl may have felt that it represented an expression of the king's goodwill towards him, and such a view would be reinforced by his receiving another charter of his earldom from James III on 18 March.[63] Buchan was however less likely to be convinced. Unlike his elder brother Atholl, he owed his advancement to the dignity of earl to James III; and he had come to power on the ruin of the Boyds in 1469, when he had been made Chamberlain in place of the forfeited Robert Lord Boyd.[64] Buchan's remission for taking Edinburgh castle reads remarkably like the king's acceptance, in full parliament in 1466, of the Boyds' seizure of his person earlier that year; and as one of the principal beneficiaries of the Boyd collapse, Buchan must have been cynical about the permanence of parliamentary remissions for acts which incurred the displeasure of his nephew. James III, trying to foster national unity in the face of the threat from England, was prepared to make concessions to win support; but how would he act once the danger had passed? Buchan can hardly have felt that his position was secure, particularly in view of King James's treatment of other members of his kin; and it is likely that he was waiting for an opportunity to acquire allies to coerce the king.

Within a matter of weeks, such an opportunity appeared to have arisen; the projected English invasion was given a new dimension by the arrival in England, at the beginning of May, of the fugitive Alexander, duke of Albany. The duke had sailed from France in a Scottish carvel and landed at Southampton 'to serve . . . the King of England, as his liege subject, against his Scotch enemies and rebels'. At Edward IV's expense, he lodged in London between 2 and 4 May at a house called the 'Erber'; and it was clear from the start that he was going to serve the English king's ends by declaring himself king of Scotland.[65] On 10 May a royal proclamation ordered every man who had indented to go with the 'king of Scotland' to be ready to do so on fourteen days' notice.[66] A month later, at Fotheringhay castle, Albany, signing himself 'Alexander R' and styling himself King of Scotland, promised to do homage to Edward IV on obtaining the realm of Scotland for himself; in addition, he would break the alliance between Scotland and France and surrender the town and castle of Berwick within fourteen days of reaching Edinburgh.[67]

The following day, the treaty of Fotheringhay specified more exactly the terms of the contract drawn up by Albany and Edward IV. The English king, who had announced his intention to lead the army against Scotland in person, had arrived at Fotheringhay with Albany on 3 June, and they were joined there by Richard, duke of Gloucester.[68] The agreement itself takes the form of an indenture in which Albany is described as King of Scotland by the king of England's gift; Edward IV bound himself to assist Albany in obtaining the crown of Scotland, but he reserved to himself Berwick, Liddesdale, Eskdale, Ewesdale, Annandale, and Lochmaben castle. He also promised to give Albany his daughter Cecilia in marriage 'gif the said Alexander can mak hym self clere fra all othir women according to the lawes of Cristis chyrche withyn ane yere next ensuying or souner' — in short, if Albany could obtain an annulment of his recent French marriage. If not, Albany would marry his son and heir to some lady amongst Edward IV's relations, provided she were approved of by both parties. To the indenture was appended Albany's signet and the signature 'Alexander R'.[69]

Thus Edward IV, in the summer of 1482, was acting in a far more belligerent way than ever before. Gone was the policy of using the exiled Earl of Douglas or the Lord of the Isles as a fifth column to embarrass the Scottish government; gone, too, was the demand that the Scots fulfil the marriage of Prince James to Cecilia and hand over Berwick, essentially the policy of 1480. The English king, by the treaty of Fotheringhay, was committing himself to full-scale invasion of Scotland in the interests of a pretender, to the overthrow of the existing regime north of the border, and a measure of control in southern Scotland. As for Albany himself, it seems likely that he simply fell in with the Yorkist schemes to make him king rather than impressing Edward IV with his determination to depose James III. He may have felt that he had no option but to do so. Certainly he was not going to receive any practical assistance from Louis XI of France; and the English king was clearly not interested in him as another Douglas, an alien hanger-on to be put on show on expeditions to the Scottish Marches. So his choice lay between languishing in France or England — or risking a return to Scotland in very dubious circumstances, but backed by English military strength. He may have reasoned that the risk was worth taking because he had not yet been forfeited in Scotland, and because he could not afford to delay much longer if his cause was going to attract any support there.

Edward IV had intended to lead the army north himself, but possibly for reasons of ill-health[70] entrusted its command to his brother Richard, duke of Gloucester. The latter had recently returned from a military expedition into Scotland, probably about the middle of May, the purpose being to subdue 'the Kings greit enemye the King of Scotts and his adherents'.[71] This was clearly a border raid, and James III's probable absence from Edinburgh between 18 April and 13 June[72] suggests that the

Scottish king may have taken a force south to try to check the English incursions. But the English attack later in the summer was to be on a different scale altogether. On 12 June Edward IV renewed Gloucester's commission as lieutenant-general, and the conduct of the subsequent campaign was entirely in the duke's hands. It would appear that when Gloucester and Albany set out for the border, they were at the head of an army whose size exceeded all other English forces for over eighty years. During the Easter term of 1482, the English exchequer issued to Sir John Elryngton, Edward IV's Treasurer-at-War, the sum of £4,504 11/8½d 'in part payment of the wages of 20,000 men-at-arms, going upon a certain expedition with the Duke of Gloucester against the Scots'.[73] Ramsay, unconvinced by this very high figure, described twenty thousand as 'a number unheard of on record evidence', and showed that the total sum assigned by Edward IV for the wages of this force was about £6,092; 'at the established rate of sixpence a day, £6,000 would keep 20,000 men for just twelve days; not enough to take them to the border and back again'.[74] Scofield, however, pointed out that the £6,092 9/- assigned to Sir John Elryngton was intended specifically for 'the wages of divers men retained by him (Gloucester) for the war against the Scots for the space of 14 days'; and she noted *another* entry in the Exchequer records mentioning £7,000 assigned to Elryngton for the wages of twenty thousand men retained 'for the space of other 14 days immediately following the aforesaid 14 days'.[75] Thus it was intended to keep this enormous army in the field for only four weeks at most. At about the same time, during the Easter term of 1482, a payment of £595 was made out of the Exchequer, once again to Elryngton as Treasurer-at-War, but on this occasion 'for the wages of 1,700 fighting men, retained by the said Duke (Gloucester) to accompany him in the war against the Scotch; viz. from the 11 August until the end of fourteen days then next following'.[76]

This small army of seventeen hundred seems to have been intended to carry on the campaign for a fortnight after the vast force of twenty thousand, retained for a month, was disbanded. The York contingent left the city to join Gloucester's main army about 14 July,[77] so that their pay for twenty-eight days would run out on 11 August, precisely the date on which the duke was to be paid to retain a much smaller force for another two weeks. What these detailed preparations reveal, therefore, is Gloucester's intention to conduct the invasion of Scotland in the course of a month, from about mid-July to mid-August, with an army of twenty thousand, and using a force of seventeen hundred for a further fortnight in August, possibly to ensure the capture of Berwick. Thus in July 1482 the Scots, with their small Berwick garrison of five hundred, and their pitiful six hundred men scattered throughout the Marches in penny numbers, confronted a paid, well-equipped and well-led English army of enormous size; and James III was faced with the greatest crisis of his reign.

The extent of the English menace must have been well known in Scottish political circles, for Gloucester's army was mustered in the north of England. As early as 18 June, only a week after making the treaty of Fotheringhay, we find Gloucester and Albany in York on their way north. By 29 June the city had granted the dukes a hundred and twenty archers; and by 14 July the army had moved on,

Gloucester having reduced York's contribution to a hundred archers.[78] After this date, the English advance north was probably rapid, for the army would only be paid for a month's campaign. Thus Gloucester and Albany must have entered south-east Scotland via Berwick at the end of the third week of July, or the beginning of the fourth week at the latest. According to Edward IV, writing to the pope on 25 August, 'a small chosen band . . . received the surrender of the town immediately on sitting down before it, though the same was entirely surrounded with impregnable walls'.[79] If this account is substantially correct, it would appear that the main army simply bypassed Berwick, and that the town was in any case tamely surrendered. The English king went on to admit that the citadel held out until the army had returned from Edinburgh, 'when, not without some slaughter and bloodshed, it was reduced'.

Acts of gallantry by the defenders of the Berwick citadel — Sir Patrick Hepburn of Dunsyre, presumably assisted by the king's five hundred troops — had neither saved the town nor stopped the English advance. Indeed, the immediate surrender of the town raises the question of the loyalty of James III's commanders there, David, earl of Crawford, and Andrew Lord Gray.[80] The former had an outstanding record of loyalty and service to the king throughout the reign; but the latter's attitude is much more difficult to discern, as by February of the following year he would be found heavily involved in Albany's English treasons, treasons which included the cession to England of all right to the town and castle of Berwick.[81] It seems more than a possibility, then, that similar collusion between Lord Gray and the English army led by Albany and Gloucester existed in July 1482, and that Gray surrendered the town by arrangement.

Thus James III, as he summoned the Scottish host to Lauder, was calling up men who must have been aware that an enormous invading army was on its way, who may well have discovered on arrival at the muster point that Berwick town had fallen without a struggle and that the English were less than thirty miles away, and who were being asked to risk their lives in support of a monarch whose domestic policies were offensive to many and whose foreign policy had produced the almost certain military disaster which they now saw staring them in the face. Small wonder, then, that leaders and led amongst the Scottish host may have felt disposed to align themselves with any faction whose aim was to oppose the king and avert the impending calamity. In the event, no battle took place; and Gloucester and Albany — above all the latter — must have been much cheered by the news that James III was no longer free to oppose them. On 22 July he had been seized at Lauder and forcibly removed to Edinburgh.

NOTES

1. B.M. Royal MS. 17 Dxx, f.307v.
2. *See above*, Chapter 5.
3. Innsbruck, Landesregierungs-archiv, Sigismund IVc. 180.12.
4. *A.P.S.*, ii, 112.
5. *Ibid.*, 114.

6. B.M. Cotton MS., Vesp. C xvi, f.127.

7. Scofield, *Edward IV*, ii, 187.

8. *A.P.S.*, ii, 119.

9. *Rot. Scot.*, ii, 456; *Foedera*, xii, 171 (mistakenly dated 1482).

10. *E.R.*, ix, Pref., p. lxxvi. This is an estimate of royal income from crown lands, sheriffs, customs, and burgh farms for the year. A.L. Murray, in 'The Comptroller, 1425-1488', *S.H.R.*, lii, 1-29, suggests that the total annual figure of £16,380 is a considerable overestimate.

11. *Cal. Docs. Scot.*, iv, No. 1456.

12. *A.P.S.*, ii, 120-1, 122. An attendance of 104 in a fifteenth century Scottish parliament was exceptional; no other parliament of the reign (for which sederunt lists survive) can match this, and the average attendance appears to have been about 50-60.

13. *Bannatyne Miscellany*, iii, 427-31.

14. *Cal. Docs. Scot.*, iv, No. 1455.

15. *Rot. Scot.*, ii, 457.

16. Dr. Nicholson has suggested (Nicholson, *op.cit.*, 489) that it had become apparent by late 1479 that Margaret was pregnant; the father of her child, a daughter also named Margaret, was William, third Lord Crichton. I cannot agree that Crichton's liaison with Princess Margaret occurred at this time. For a full discussion of this point, *see below*, Chapter 9.

17. *A.P.S.*, ii, 102, 103-4.

18. *Rot. Scot.*, ii, 453, 455, 457.

19. *P.S.A.S.*, xcvii, (1964-6), 256-61.

20. Dempster, *Historia*, ix, 752. Ferreri mentions the sending of Dr. Ireland to Scotland, though he misdates it as 1471; but as it occurs in his account between the elevation of Archbishop Scheves and the death of the Earl of Mar, this is consistent with the year 1479: Ferrerius, *Appendix to Boece*, f.391r.

21. Louis XI was a frequent visitor to the shrine of St. John at Amiens, where he is known to have discussed matters of foreign policy while on pilgrimage.

22. *Cal. Docs. Scot.*, iv, App. i, No. 28 (mistakenly dated as February 1475-6).

23. *Ibid.*

24. *Cal. State Papers (Milan)*, i, 244-5.

25. *Foedera*, xii, 115.

26. Boece, *Vitae*, 53; Ferrerius, *Appendix to Boece*, f.394r.; Lesley, *History*, 44.

27. Devon, *Issues of the Exchequer*, 500-1.

28. Scofield, *Edward IV*, ii, 304-6. An excellent modern account of Edward IV's conduct of the war against Scotland in 1480-82 is to be found in Charles Ross, *Edward IV*, (Lond., 1974), 278-290.

29. *A.P.S.*, ii, 132, 133, 138.

30. Lesley, *History*, 44; Ferrerius, *Appendix to Boece*, f.394r.

31. *Cal. State Papers (Venice)*, i, 142-3, 145.

32. Davies, *York City Records Extracts*, 108 *et seq.*

33. *R.M.S.*, ii, No. 1563.

34. *Cal. Docs. Scot.*, iv, No. 1470. Only three men appear to have availed themselves of this offer — Alexander Jardine, Sir Richard Holland, and Master Patrick Haliburton, all of whom were declared traitors in the Scottish parliament of March 1482.

35. *Foedera*, xii, 140.

36. *E.R.*, ix, Pref., p.xl, 211; Nicholson, *op.cit.*, 481-2; *Highland Papers*, i, 48, 50.

37. Lesley and Ferreri both suggest that Macdonald remained loyal to James III during the Anglo-Scottish war, and even that he sent a contingent to support the royal forces in 1481: Lesley, *History*, 45; Ferrerius, *Appendix to Boece*, f.394.

38. *A.P.S.*, ii, 138.

39. *E.R.*, ix, 218.

40. Ferrerius, *Appendix to Boece*, f.394r.; Lesley, *History*, 45.

41. Balfour, *Annales*, i, 204.

42. *A.P.S.*, ii, 138.

43. *Ibid.*, 134.

44. *Foedera*, xii, 46.
45. *A.P.S.*, ii, 140.
46. Scofield, *Edward IV*, ii, 327-8.
47. *Cal. State Papers (Milan)*, i, 245.
48. Innsbruck, Landesregierungs-Archiv, Sigismund ivc/180/9. Sigismund was the husband of Eleanor Stewart, daughter of James I. He became Archduke of Austria in 1477.
49. B.M. Royal MS. 17 Dxx, f.307v.
50. *A.P.S.*, ii, 136-7.
51. *Ibid.*, 138-9.
52. *Ibid.*, 139-40.
53. *R.M.S.*, ii, No. 1418.
54. *Ibid.*, No. 1007.
55. *A.D.C.*, 60, 95.
56. *A.P.S.*, ii, 140.
57. B.M. Add. MS. 12,192, ff.58-71.
58. B.M. Royal MS. 17 Dxx, f.308r.
59. *A.P.S.*, ii, 138.
60. *Cal. Docs. Scot.*, iv, Nos. 1486, 1489.
61. *A.P.S.*, ii, 138.
62. *E.R.*, viii, 120, 189, 190, 253, 312, 390, 466, 547, 629-30; ix, 79.
63. *R.M.S.*, ii, No. 1503.
64. *See above*, Chapter 4.
65. Roll of Accounts, Easter 22 Ed. IV, in Devon, *Issues of the Exchequer*, 502-3.
66. *Cal. Patent Rolls, 1476–85*, 320.
67. P.R.O. Scots Doct. E 39/92 (17); in *Cal. Docs. Scot.*, iv, No. 1475.
68. Ross, *op.cit.*, 287.
69. P.R.O. Scots Doct., E39/92 (38); summary in *Cal. Docs. Scot.*, iv, No. 1476.
70. Ross, *op.cit.*, 287 and n.3.
71. *York Civic Records*, i, 54-5.
72. Inferred from gap of almost two months in granting charters at Edinburgh: *R.M.S.*, ii, Nos. 1510, 1511.
73. Devon, *Issues of the Exchequer*, 502.
74. Ramsay, *Lancaster and York*, ii, 442.
75. Tellers' Roll: Easter 22 Ed. IV, quoted in Scofield, *Edward IV*, ii, 344.
76. Devon, *Issues of the Exchequer*, 501.
77. *York Civic Records*, i, 58, 59-60.
78. *Ibid.*, 56, 59-60.
79. *Cal. State Papers (Venice)*, i, 145-6.
80. *E.R.*, ix, 433.
81. *Cal. Docs. Scot.*, iv, No. 1489.

8

Lauder, Edinburgh and Dunbar: The Great Stewart Crisis 1482-83

THE seizure of James III at Lauder in July 1482 was en event without parallel in fifteenth century Scottish political history. An adult king was seized by a group of magnates and his arrest was immediately followed by a remarkable revolution in governmental personnel and a period of intense, complex negotiations, during which various power groups struggled to take advantage of the abnormal situation and further their own interests in acquiring lands and offices. Not surprisingly, the crisis at Lauder became a feature of later accounts of the reign, with most writers seeking to explain it in terms of James III's failure to do his duty as a king and take proper counsel from his nobility — a curious verdict on a man who at Lauder was surrounded by magnates and was attempting to fulfil one of the vital tasks of a medieval king, acting as a leader in war.

Any analysis of Lauder is extremely difficult, for we possess only three contemporary references to the incident, all of them very brief. The king himself, in a letter to Lord Darnley on 19 October, described what had happened in only the most general terms: '. . . quhen our souerane lordis Hienes come fra Lawdir to Edinburgh, and was haldin and kepit in warde againe his will in the castele of Edinburgh . . . his Maieste dred and doutit that certane lordis and persounys that was than about him wald hafe slayne and undoune him' — an understandable fear, but no rebel names are specified.[1] Much later, in a signet letter of 23 July 1483, James III commanded the auditors of exchequer to allow to George Robison, custumar of Edinburgh, £146 'that he had in keping of ouris and that was takin fra him at Lawdre and withhaldin be Alexander Lawdre, of the quhilk we will have the saide George dischargit and the said Alexander callit to mak us payment tharof'.[2]

These comments do not help at all in solving the two principal problems posed by the Lauder crisis, namely, the reasons for the seizure of the king and the identities of the men who seized him. However, our third contemporary source, a brief chronicle which breaks off in 1482, goes some way towards explaining the motives of those involved. Apart from the devastation caused by two years of war, he claims that 'thir was blak cunzhe in the realme strikkin and ordinyt be King James the thred, half pennys and thre penny pennys Innumerabill of coppir . . . And thai twa thyngs [the war and the black money] causit baitht hungar and derth and mony pure folk deit of hungar.' Thereafter 'the lords of Scotland held their counsaill in the kirk of Lawder, and cryit downe the blak silver'.[3] This is a clear indication that the king had introduced a drastic debasement of the coinage, presumably to make a quick profit, and that the effects on Scots currency were disastrous. But the chronicler is inconsistent in his descriptions of the debased money, calling it first 'blak cunzhe', then 'half pennys and thre penny pennys . . . of coppir', and finally 'black silver'. There is a contradiction here, because 'black silver' is undoubtedly billion, not copper, and 'thre penny pennys' may possibly be identified with billon placks, but not readily with any copper coins; yet the chronicler states that the coins were of copper. The problem therefore is to identify the 'black money' of 1482, and its place in the king's monetary policy.

Superficially, the case for the royal black money being identified with billon placks appears a strong one. Probably first introduced in 1471, and current at sixpence, these coins had dropped to fourpence by 1473, the latter probably being their intrinsic value; so a baser issue of these placks early in the following decade might well explain the chronicler's reference to threepence. Also, there is evidence that billon placks were distrusted in 1485 and 1486, and in the latter year their value was fixed at twopence.[4] The argument is therefore that a new issue of placks, much debased, by James III about 1479 or 1480 was greeted with a similar lack of confidence.

There are, however, grave objections to this thesis. The fineness of the James III placks is against their ever being called black, even in the phrase 'black silver'. Specimens are admittedly comparatively few, but the fineness of the 1471–3 placks of James III was perhaps six-twelfths; the placks of James IV and James V were much less fine, the 1533 issue having a fineness of only two twelfths. A more serious objection is that the placks do not appear to have any relevance to the Lauder crisis. Introduced in 1471-3, they do not seem to have been withdrawn despite an act of parliament of 1473 ordering 'that the striking of thame be cessit';[5] they were still current in 1485, and there are no indications that the period 1479-82 saw a fresh issue of placks. While it is true that the word 'plack' is used by Pitscottie to describe the black money of this period,[6] this reference probably represents a confusion in popular tradition between the black money which was cried down in 1482 and the placks which were withdrawn at twopence in 1486. So the billon placks of 1471-1486 hardly qualify as James III's black money, and were most unlikely to have been one of the causes of a crisis in 1482.

There is no doubt, however, that royal issues of black money occurred in the early '80s, and that these were rapidly 'cryit downe'. In a signet letter dated 23 July 1483, and referring to the exchequer year 1482-3 — that is, including the Lauder crisis — the king authorised a payment of £180 16/- 'to the werkmen that wrocht the blac money of oure commande'.[7] Less than three months later, on 13 October, a case came before the Lords Auditors concerning an obligation on the part of the prior and convent of St. Andrews to pay one Marjory Kerkettle the sum of £96. It was pointed out that the obligation had been entered into 'befor the cours of ony blac mone', and yet the priory was now offering payment 'in blac mone lang eftir the termes of the said obligacioun'; and the Auditors ordained that payment should be made in money that had course at the time of the original contract, or in 'the mone that now rynnis', but not in black money. Allowing for the time taken for the plaintiff's case to come before the Auditors, especially in a period of crisis, the inference to be drawn is that the black money had been cried down a long time before this case was heard, probably as early as the previous year. There is no doubt that the black money to which Marjory Kerkettle refers was introduced by the king, for it is specifically stated that the matter 'concernis our souueran lord and the hale Realme'.[8]

Here, then, is record evidence to substantiate the chronicler's claim that the 'crying down' of the royal black money occurred shortly after the Lauder crisis. What this process involved is indicated by two exchequer accounts. First, the account of George Robison, custumar of Edinburgh, for the exchequer year 23 June 1483 — 6 July 1484 reveals that a small part of the burgh customs had been paid in 'nigra moneta'; therefore the king, considering that this black money had immediately ('subito') been cried down and was valueless, remitted part of the sum owed to him.[9] Similarly, in an account of 1487, reference was made to the fact that 'illa moneta' (the black money) 'erat declamata et sic deperdita'.[10] These references are not merely to a devaluation, but to a total demonetisation of the royal black money; and it follows that the 'nigra moneta' must have had a very brief life as legal tender.

It would appear, therefore, that the king was personally responsible for the issue of some form of black money other than the billon placks of the '70s; that he had to pay a considerable sum of money in 1482-3 to those who 'wrocht' the black money; and that it was swiftly demonetised after the Lauder crisis. All these facts suggest that James III had recourse to the desperate expedient of minting large quantities of very debased coins and putting them into circulation at a false value. A fair proportion of these, as the contemporary chronicler suggests, may have been of copper; and the minting of copper coins was not unprecedented in Scotland. In 1468 an account rendered by the moneyers Alexander Tod and William Goldsmyth indicates that between June 1466 and June 1467 a large amount of copper money had been coined; the profits from this activity, which went in theory to the king, but in fact more probably to the Boyds, are recorded as £650. A parliamentary act of 9 October 1466 had laid down that the coppers struck should be issued as farthings, but in fact the big profit was made by resorting to the expedient of issuing them at one halfpenny each, and the Lords of Council had to intervene to reduce them to their proper value of one farthing each.[11] Finally the parliament of 1467 ordered the cessation of the minting of the black farthings 'under the payne of dede', and an attempt was made the following year to fix their value in relation to the pound Scots.[12]

Here, then, was a precedent — albeit not such a drastic one — for a copper coinage, which in spite of its short period of issue remained in circulation for some years. But the term 'black money', as used by the Scottish parliament, clearly included base billon as well as copper. Thus an act of November 1469 complained of the existence of counterfeit black money circulating in Scotland, above all French deniers, and ordained that in future the only legal tender of this kind would be 'oure souerane lordis awne blac mone' produced by the royal mint.[13] The reference to French deniers, which are classified as black money, is significant because these coins included some silver. The conclusion must be that the general term 'black money', as used in the 1469 act, refers not only to the copper farthings but also to the base billon pennies current at the time; and we may not argue simply from the use of the expression 'black money' as applied to the later coinage of 1480-82 that this was wholly a copper issue. However, some of it may have been. In 1488 and 1489, there are references in the Treasurer's Accounts to payments made at the king's command to 'Willie Goldsmyth callit Halpenny man'.[14] Goldsmyth, who was one of the royal moneyers, had been responsible for the copper coinage of the 1460s; but he did not apparently acquire his nickname at that time. It seems likely, therefore, that he came to be described as 'Halpenny man' for striking, at the king's command, the notorious halfpennies mentioned by the chronicler as part of the discredited coinage of 1480-82. If this is the case, then considering Goldsmyth's earlier work in the same field, it would seem probable that the 1482 halfpennies were of copper. As for the rest of the 'black' coinage, the coins issued at threepence, it seems likely that they were of very base billon — hence the expression 'black silver' — and introduced at a highly inflated nominal value.

Certainty is, of course, impossible when we are dealing with scanty numismatic evidence and a coinage which, though described by the chronicler as 'innumerable', was totally demonetised in little over two years.[15] But there is sufficient evidence to suggest that James III indulged in a drastic debasement of the coinage over a period from about 1480 until 1482, producing very base billon coins and a large quantity of copper ones. That he did so at this time should not surprise us, for he must have been in desperate need of money. The estates had been prepared, in March 1482, to supply six hundred soldiers for the defence of the borders; but the king had to find the money for another five hundred to defend Berwick. In addition, he had to provide artillery, and for the 1482 campaign alone there was an outlay of £214 4/- 'to the makin of serpentynis and gunnys'.[16] His experiences of parliamentary reaction to proposed taxes to raise troops, in 1472 and 1473, had not been happy ones, and the collection of the other extraordinary grant, twenty thousand marks in 1479 for the expenses of his sister Margaret's proposed marriage with Earl Rivers, may not have progressed much farther than a belated valuation of the properties to be taxed.[17] Since then, there had been more than two years of war with England, and the resulting destruction of corn and cattle spoken of by the chronicler doubtless occurred on the royal lands as well as those of the nobility. As late as 1486 an exchequer account referred to the half-waste state of the granges of Dunbar as a result of the war in 1481.[18]

All these problems, together with the need to summon the Scottish host to confront the advancing Gloucester, led James III into a major debasement of the coinage, a quick but very dangerous way of making money for the Crown which, though it might meet the king's immediate needs, could not in the long run be successful. If the contemporary chronicler is to be believed, James started to introduce black money about 1480, the year that the Anglo-Scottish war broke out. Thus, by the summer of 1482, the debased money had been in circulation long enough for the king to have lost the support, not so much of the nobility, but rather of the merchant class and those lower in the social scale. As a result of the money, the chronicler reminds us, 'many pure folk deit of hungar'.[19] Thus the introduction of the 'black' coinage may be regarded as one of the causes of royal unpopularity and general reluctance to lend support to James III in 1482, but not specifically a reason for the seizure of the king at Lauder in the month of July. It is, after all, inherently improbable that the group of rebellious nobles who arrested the king, robbed him of at least £146, and imprisoned him in Edinburgh castle, did so in an attempt to improve Scotland's economic position.[20] But loss of confidence in royal coinage over two years may well have provided them with a popular cause to make their own.

Apart from the hunger and dearth produced by the black money, the Scots nobility, according to the contemporary chronicler, had another motive for their actions at Lauder. The king, he remarks, 'wrocht mair the counsaell of his housald at war bot sympill na he did of thame that war lorddis'; as a result 'the lordis of Scotland' (unspecified) 'slew ane part of the kingis housald and other part thai banysyt'. This theme of bad counsel given to King James by base-born familiars on whom he lavished favours and gave lands and offices as rewards to the exclusion of his 'natural' counsellors, the nobility, was to recur again and again in the works of the sixteenth century chroniclers Abell, Lesley, Ferreri, Buchanan and Pitscottie. To them the Lauder crisis could be explained as a conspiracy of a great multitude of lords with the single, and laudable, object of freeing the king from bad counsel and improving the governing of the realm. Thus with the exception of Abell, who like the contemporary chronicler cautiously describes the conspirators anonymously as 'the lordis', the later writers vie with each other in producing imposing — and inaccurate — lists of offended Scottish magnates, all working for the good of the country in ridding the king of his odious favourites.

Thus Lesley and Ferreri name the rebel lords as Angus, Huntly, Lennox (Lord Darnley), and Buchan, together with Lords Gray, Lyle, and many others;[21] Pitscottie goes even further, saying that twenty-four lords were chosen to protest to the king, and naming them as Angus, Annerdaill (presumably Avandale, one of James's most loyal supporters), Argyll, Huntly, Orkney, Crawford, Bothwell, Lords Hume, Fleming, Gray, Drummond, Seton, and certain bishops — in fact a conspiracy involving virtually every important magnate in the realm.[22] This is clearly pure invention; and two of the names on Pitscottie's list are patently wrong. The earldom of Orkney had been annexed to the crown in February 1472, and the earldom of Bothwell was not created until after James III's death in 1488. Even if Pitscottie was referring to Sir Patrick Hepburn, who became successively second Lord Hailes and first earl of Bothwell, it can definitely be proved that he was not involved in the Lauder crisis, as he was engaged in the defence of Berwick castle after the town had fallen to Gloucester and Albany.[23] Such discrepancies illustrate that the sixteenth century writers had no clear idea of what had happened at Lauder, or who had been responsible for it. Gleaning all they could from legends about James III which originated mainly in the early sixteenth century,[24] they all endeavoured to make the point that the nobility of Scotland, tired of the misgovernment of James's low-born familiars, took the law into their hands for the good of the kingdom. As a result of the deficiencies of their sources for the Lauder crisis, many of them no doubt oral rather than narrative, the chroniclers emphasised the hanging of the royal familiars, and so missed the point of the incident, which was the seizure of the king.

It is true that some royal servants, who happen to have been at Lauder with James III, appear to have been hanged. Three of them are known — Thomas Preston, Thomas Cochrane, and William Roger. The later chroniclers were to provide these men, especially the second-named, with a notoriety which was probably wholly undeserved; and in fact, remarkably little is known about all three. Thomas Preston, the favourite of good family described by Ferreri and Buchanan, is mentioned twice in the records. On 23 July 1483, James III ordered the payment of £90 to the custumar of Edinburgh, to reimburse him for granting that sum, on behalf of the king, to 'Thomas Prestoun quhen he past in Orkinnay for the hame bringin of the schip with wyne'.[25] The ship in question was an English prize. In the same account, Preston is described as 'quondam Thome Prestoun', a description which would fit the chronicle evidence that he was hanged at Lauder in July 1482. Even more significant, a great seal charter dated 25 December 1482, granting the lands of Middle Pitcairn in Perthshire to William Ruthven, explains that these lands had reverted to the Crown 'per forisfacturam quondam Thome de Prestoun'.[26] Thus we learn that, some time before Christmas 1482, one Thomas Preston had been forfeited and was now dead; and the fact that he was forfeited suggests that he was executed. So the accounts of Ferreri and Buchanan, which both describe Preston as one of the victims of the Lauder hangings, receive a certain amount of support from the record evidence. Buchanan names Preston first of all the royal familiars, the father-in-law of Cochrane, but gives no details of his position or character except that he was descended from an honourable family; Ferreri suggests that he was innocent of any crime when hanged at Lauder.[27] As to his status, the evidence of his services to the king in bringing in the English wine ship suggests that he may have been a well-to-do Edinburgh merchant burgess.

The only royal familiar whose career is described by all five sixteenth century chroniclers is Cochrane. Despite the elaborate tales of Pitscottie, the record evidence for the notorious favourite's existence is as scanty as that relating to Thomas Preston. Ferreri and Buchanan both state that Cochrane's Christian name was Robert; but the only Cochrane who can in any way be associated with the king during this period is one Thomas Cochrane, who is mentioned twice — if indeed both entries refer to the same man — in the records of the Lords of Council. Thomas is also the Christian name which Lesley supplies for Cochrane;[28] and it is therefore probable that Ferreri and Buchanan are in error.

The first of the relevant Lords of Council cases occurred on 22 January 1480, when Hugh Ross of Kilravock, William thane of Cawdor, Thomas Cumyn and Alexander Cumyn were ordered to pay to Thomas Cochrane sums amounting to £60; these payments had originally been promised to Sir John Colquhoun of that ilk, rather quaintly described as 'usher of our sovereign lord's chamber door', who had been killed at the siege of Dunbar castle in May 1479; and the king had now ordered that the money should be paid to Cochrane.[29] The assignment of these sums, formerly granted to an usher of the royal chamber, suggests that Cochrane may have held the same, or a similar, post after Colquhoun's death. The other civil action in which Cochrane's name appears came before the Lords of Council on 2 May 1483. This was a case arising out of a dispute between Archibald Preston and

William Lord Sinclair; Preston, as pursuer, claimed that he ought to be given sasine of £20 worth of the lands of Cousland near Dalkeith, these lands having been held by 'umquhile thomas of cochran, and eftir the dede and forfature of the said thomas, the said archbalde present be our souerane lorde to be tenant to the said william'.[30] Here is positive evidence that a Thomas Cochrane, presented by the king to the lands of Cousland, died and was forfeited some time before May 1483 — probably many months before, as a lengthy period would elapse before the new tenant would have his case heard before the council. It is therefore quite likely that Cochrane, like Preston, met his end at Lauder Bridge late in July 1482, his forfeiture following his death at a time when the king was a prisoner. In Cochrane's case, the records suggest that his death preceded his forfeiture; this would be consistent with a hasty hanging at Lauder, followed by an attempt to justify it.

It is reasonable to suppose that the Cochrane of both Lords of Council cases is the same man. The period is that assigned by the chroniclers to the familiars, 1479 until 1482; and in both actions Cochrane is associated with the king. The picture of Cochrane provided by the records, therefore, is that of a servant in the royal household — perhaps usher of the king's bedchamber, the post formerly held by Sir John Colquhoun — who had been granted a modest portion of land in the neighbourhood of Edinburgh by the king. No record source other than the *Acts of the Lords of Council* mentions Cochrane, a fact which suggests that his position at court was not of great importance.

In the case of William Roger, the English musician whose virtues are extolled by Ferreri, and who is also mentioned by Lesley and Buchanan,[31] his status as royal favourite and his death at Lauder are much less certain. Thus a William Roger, described as clerk of the chapel royal, is to be found receiving £20 from the customs of Haddington as early as 25 February 1467; and it is clearly the same man who is described as master of the hospital of St. Leonard near Peebles in the following two years.[32] Thus Roger's career in the royal service started during the minority, more than a decade before the period ascribed to the favourites; and the name reappears only once more in the records, in a great seal charter of 3 February 1479. This is a grant by James III to his half-uncle James Stewart, earl of Buchan, of the lands of Traquair in Peeblesshire, to be held by Buchan in free barony. Formerly the lands had been held by Robert Lord Boyd, but on his forfeiture in November 1469 the king, while still in his legal minority, granted them to his familiar squire William Roger, who resigned Traquair to the Crown after the general revocation of 1476.[33]

It seems likely that the William Roger of the 1479 charter is either the same man who is described as clerk of the chapel royal in 1467, or a close relative, possibly his son. Certainly intimacy with the king and a Peeblesshire location are common to both the 1460s and 1479. Yet the charter of 1479 is slender evidence on which to build the career of a favourite, for what it tells us is that a William Roger enjoyed the lands of Traquair for about seven years, resigned them to the king in or after 1476, and did not receive them back. For the 'classic' period of supposed domination of the king by the favourites, the years immediately preceding 1482, there is no indication of anyone surnamed Roger in any other record source who can in any way be connected with the king. It may be added that the charter of 1479 does not describe Roger as a musician, and makes no reference to the chapel royal.

We are therefore forced back to the statements on the later chroniclers, especially Ferreri, who makes a point of saying that Roger was the founder of a school of musicians who remembered him as late as 1529;[34] and as Ferreri had come to Scotland in 1528, spent some time at court, and was a teacher at Kinloss between 1531 and 1537,[35] his information may well have been first hand. Furthermore, Ferreri adds the interesting detail that Roger was innocent of any crimes when he was seized at Lauder,[36] a statement which suggests that he was not of any importance politically. The record evidence, such as it is, suggests a minor cleric modestly rewarded by the king, and only before 1476. It cannot be said for certain that Roger perished at Lauder bridge; unlike Preston and Cochrane, he does not appear in the records as deceased and forfeited.

The truth would seem to be that Cochrane, Preston and Roger had little or no influence on the king's actions; that they may have been, respectively, an usher, a merchant burgess, and a musician; that Cochrane and Preston (and possibly Roger) were hanged at Lauder because they had the misfortune to be there, and in the king's entourage. Indeed, stripped of the interpretations placed on it by the writers of the following century, the Lauder crisis becomes what the near-contemporary chronicler said it was: the hanging of one part of the king's household, the banishment of another, and the removal of the king to Edinburgh castle. Those hanged were insignificant; those banished were probably James's faithful administrators, Scheves, Avandale, and Argyll, whose names disappear from official records for the duration of the crisis; but those who removed King James from Lauder to Edinburgh castle are not identified in any reliable source.

Nevertheless they may with some accuracy be identified by reference to the political events immediately before and after the seizure of the king; for Lauder can surely be explained satisfactorily neither in terms of black money nor favourites, but only as a political coup engineered by men who feared James III, were thoroughly alarmed by the military situation in 1482, and reckoned that their best chance of survival, and perhaps advancement, was to coerce the king. The names of many of those involved are revealed at once by a glance at the witness lists to great seal charters before and after Lauder. On 17 June we find a list which includes many of the men whom James had used and trusted for a decade or more — Archbishop Scheves, John Laing, bishop of Glasgow, James Livingston, bishop of Dunkeld, Chancellor Avandale, the Earl of Argyll as Master of the Royal Household, David, earl of Crawford, John Lord Carlyle, Alexander Inglis, archdeacon of St. Andrews and Clerk Register, and the ubiquitous Archibald Whitelaw, archdeacon of Lothian, the royal secretary. By 25 August, with Lauder past and the king incarcerated in Edinburgh castle, there is a dramatic change in personnel. The names of Scheves and Avandale vanish, and the office of Chancellor has been conferred on Bishop Laing of Glasgow; Livingston of Dunkeld is still present, but then follow the king's three half-uncles, Andrew Stewart, bishop-elect of Moray, described for the first time as keeper of the privy seal, John Stewart, earl of Atholl, and James Stewart, earl of Buchan, the Chamberlain. These men, together with Archibald Crawfurd, abbot of Holyrood, the Treasurer, two lords of parliament,

Erskine and Borthwick, Secretary Whitelaw, and Master Patrick Leich, canon of Glasgow, the new clerk register, formed the administration after the seizure of the king.[37]

It is easy to understand the presence of the Bishops of Glasgow and Dunkeld in the August list; Laing of Glasgow became Chancellor, and Livingston of Dunkeld, if Myln is correct, may well have aspired to Scheves' archbishopric.[38] With Scheves excluded from government, the office of clerk register was transferred from the Archdeacon of St. Andrews, Alexander Inglis, to Patrick Leich, who as a canon of Glasgow was doubtless a nominee of the new Chancellor, Bishop Laing. The youngest of the Stewart half-uncles, Andrew, bishop-elect of Moray, became privy seal and it emerged later that, like Livingston, he had designs on the archbishopric of St. Andrews.

A list of those prominent in the new administration on 25 August does not of course reveal exactly who was present at Lauder on 22 July. But the conspiracy to seize the king at the muster must certainly have involved the other royal half-uncles, Atholl and Buchan, especially the latter. As Warden of the Middle Marches, Buchan was actually responsible for the defence of the Lauder area, and the leading magnate most likely to be present. With only a dubious parliamentary remission of March 1482 standing between him and James III's accusations of treason, Buchan may well be regarded as the prime mover in the seizure of the king. Certainly he subsequently behaved as though he had offended the king too grievously to be forgiven, and by the following year was to be found deep in treasonable negotiations with Albany and Edward IV, treasons for which he was exiled for three years. In the summer of 1482, however, Buchan probably reckoned that seizure of James III would avert a military disaster, secure his position in the royal household and perhaps lead to his acquisition of the earldom of Mar,[39] and give him, together with his Stewart brothers, a dominant role in government. The advent of Albany with the English invading force was therefore a godsend, in political terms, to the Stewart half-uncles, for it obscured the extent of their treasons — seizing the monarch in the face of an advancing enemy — and these could subsequently be regarded as an effort to reconcile the king and his brother and ensure efficient government in a time of national crisis.

The key factor in the Stewart half-uncles' bid for political power was possession of Edinburgh castle; and both Atholl and Buchan had seized the castle during the legal minority of the king — presumably from James III's own custodian, David Crichton of Cranston — in such a way as to render them liable to the penalties for treason.[40] Atholl appears to have repeated his earlier treason by taking over custody of the castle in the summer of 1482,[41] and his role after Lauder must have been that of gaoler of the king. Indeed, although they are not specified by name, Atholl and Buchan must be the men of whom James III subsequently said they 'would have slain and undone him'. If they or one of them had participated in the executions at Lauder and then removed James to Edinburgh, the fears of the king would be understandable.

The magnate on whom the later writers all concentrate when describing Lauder is, however, neither Atholl nor Buchan, but Archibald, earl of Angus. That he was there need not be doubted as the sixteenth century sources dwell on his presence, this is consistent with his other treasonable activities, and his castle of Tantallon lies within easy striking distance of the muster point at Lauder. But he can hardly have played a leading role in the affair; if he ever controlled the captive king, he was quickly ousted, for he does not appear at Edinburgh to take part in the critical events there between August and November. Indeed, he is lost to sight until the parliament of December 1482, a fact which suggests that neither James III, the rebel lords, nor Gloucester had cause to trust him or deal with him. Thereafter he supported Albany, and this may always have been his position. In February 1483, together with Lord Gray and Sir James Liddale, he renounced his allegiance to Scotland and became the liegeman of England; and all three were involved in Albany's schemes for obtaining the Scottish Crown, ceding Berwick to the English, and assisting the exiled James, earl of Douglas, to recover his estates in Scotland according to a convention, of which no record exists, made between Angus and Douglas.[42] Indeed, Angus's treasons continued well into the next reign; on 15 November 1491, he is to be found making a secret agreement with Henry VII, promising in the event of an Anglo-Scottish war to deliver into the English king's hands his castle of Hermitage, commanding the route into Scotland through Liddesdale, in return for compensation in England.[43] This repetition of his treasonable behaviour of 1482-3 is clear proof of the fact that Angus was a chronic rebel in the reigns of James III and his son, although he was not a planner of the calibre of Buchan, with political ambitions and intelligence. King James appears to have recognised as much in the spring of 1483, when he stripped Buchan of his offices and banished him for three years, but left Angus with much of his former power and influence in the south.

Other magnates and their supporters who were present at Lauder with Buchan and Angus cannot be identified. Lord Crichton, who with Buchan was exiled in March 1483, may have been there; and in 1483 the Earl of Argyll was apparently given a royal pardon, together with Sir Duncan Campbell of Glenorchy, for his part in 'the raid of Lauder'.[44] It is, in fact, hardly likely that Argyll, who was to be promoted to the office of Chancellor in 1483, had joined the rebel lords at Lauder. It seems more probable that he felt open to the charge that he had failed to help the king to the best of his power. Much depends on the size of the Scottish host mustered at Lauder when James III was seized, and on this subject we possess no reliable evidence at all. Pitscottie describes an incredible army of fifty thousand assembled on the Boroughmuir of Edinburgh; and Lesley suggests, perhaps with more chance of being correct, that after Lauder the Scottish nobles had assembled an army at Haddington, but that it 'wes nocht sufficient to resist the army of Ingland'.[45] It seems inherently likely that the king was arrested before large numbers of the host arrived at the muster, so that only a few unfortunate members of his household were there to provide resistance; and the later tales of armies on the Boroughmuir and at Haddington presumably reflect a tradition that the host had been summoned but that substantial parts of it had not reached Lauder when the king was seized. So any member of the nobility who was elsewhere might feel the need, like Argyll, to obtain an official pardon at a later stage. In any event, what seems clear is that the royal Stewart uncles were responsible for the removal of the king from Lauder to Edinburgh castle, where James continued to fear for his life.

At the beginning of August, less than a fortnight after the Lauder crisis, the largest English army to invade Scotland for over eighty years entered Edinburgh unopposed. Its able commander, Richard, duke of Gloucester, was however confronted with immediate problems. The principal objective of his expedition, according to the terms of the treaty of Fotheringhay, was to place Albany on the Scottish throne; but it must rapidly have become clear to him that the idea was not popular with the Scots. Polydore Vergil[46] remarks that James III's subjects were not prepared to support Albany, and Albany himself seems to have been ready to accept, with remarkable speed, a public agreement which would restore him to his lands and offices. A more practical difficulty for Gloucester was the inaccessibility of King James; as Edward IV remarked in a letter to the pope a few weeks later, on arriving in Edinburgh his brother had discovered 'the king with the other chief lords of the kingdom shut up in a most strongly fortified castle'.[47] A siege was out of the question because time was lacking; Gloucester could not retain his large army beyond 11 August, by which date they would have been in the field for a month. Furthermore, if he were to attempt to storm the castle, not only would he lay himself open to attack from such Scottish loyalists as had already assembled in arms, but he might find himself unable to recover Berwick castle, still held by Sir Patrick Hepburn for the Scots, on his way south. In Edinburgh, however, Gloucester's strength put him in a position to dictate terms if he could find a reasonably representative and responsible body of nobility with whom to confer.

In the event, this was not difficult. The Scottish king's displaced counsellors, loyal members of the host, and the provost and community of the city of Edinburgh were all at one in wishing to be rid of the English as swiftly as possible. Thus peace settlements were hurried through on three consecutive days, 2-4 August. The first of these, on 2 August, was an agreement between Archbishop Scheves, Andrew Lord Avandale — still described as Chancellor — Colin, earl of Argyll, and James Livingston, bishop of Dunkeld, on the one side, and Gloucester and Albany on the other. The former group bound themselves to secure for Albany a grant from James III, ratified by parliament, of all the lands and offices which he had held before his flight in 1479; he was also to receive a full pardon for his offences, including his 'aspiring and tending to the throne'.[48]

Three of the four Scots who signed and sealed this undertaking — Scheves, Avandale, and Argyll — were unquestionably committed supporters of James III; and it may be that they came to Edinburgh from Haddington where, as Lesley suggests, the loyalist Scottish army was to be found.[49] They must therefore have seemed to Gloucester the most obvious influential people with whom to reach a settlement; but the truth was that their power to dictate events in Scotland had been undermined. Avandale might still describe himself as Chancellor; but the agreement of 2 August does not bear the great seal, and later in the same month it became clear that possession of the royal seals had fallen to the Stewart half-uncles and their allies, who with the king in their power were the only men worth negotiating with at this stage. Clearly they had declined to do so, or their inaccessibility in Edinburgh castle forced Gloucester to turn to the James III loyalists.

Albany's attitude is harder to discern. On entering Edinburgh, he was probably surprised, and not a little alarmed, to discover that his brother was not available to be coerced. The Scots' open reluctance to have him as king must have caused him some embarrassment with his English allies, and he therefore settled on the agreement of 2 August as the best terms he could obtain for the time being. However, the following day, if Hall is to be believed, Albany pledged himself secretly to Gloucester to abide by the terms of the treaty of Fotheringhay, in spite of his temporary accommodation with the Scots.[50] These agreements were only the beginning of a winter of tortuous negotiations for Albany which ended in his losing the trust of all the parties with whom he dealt. He may not have wished to go so far as to replace his brother on the throne, but perhaps felt the need to comply with this English idea in return for English aid; however, events were to show that he expected more than restoration to his lands and offices.

Finally, on 4 August, the city of Edinburgh paid the price necessary to rid itself of the English. Walter Bertram, provost of the city, together with the merchants, burgesses and community of Edinburgh, promised, in the presence of Gloucester, Albany, the Earl of Northumberland, the Earl of Argyll, and Bishop Livingston of Dunkeld that if the marriage between Prince James and Cecilia was not accomplished, all the money which Edward IV had paid towards his daughter's dowry would be refunded in yearly instalments paid in the same manner in which the English king had paid James III.[51] The bond also committed the provost and community of Edinburgh to accepting Edward IV's ruling on whether or not the match should take place; and by 27 October King Edward had decided that he would settle for a refund of the money rather than the marriage.[52]

Shortly after concluding the agreement of 4 August, Gloucester moved south. The city's inhabitants would be enormously relieved to see him go, in spite of the price — some eight thousand marks of English money — which they had contracted to pay for their deliverance. On 11 August Gloucester duly dismissed his large army after their month's campaign, retaining only seventeen hundred men to take Berwick castle.[53] The siege which followed must have been short, for on 25 August Edward IV was able to send a letter from London to the pope announcing the capture of the castle. The English king's praise of his brother Gloucester was effusive. 'Thank God,' he wrote to Sixtus IV, '. . . for the support received from our most loving brother, whose success is so proven that he alone would suffice to chastise the whole kingdom of Scotland.'[54]

However, there is reason to suppose that Edward IV was not at all satisfied by the results of Gloucester's Scottish expedition; the continuator of the Croyland chronicle states that the king was far from happy, so little having been gained for the great sums of money which had been expended on the summer campaign.[55] King Edward's discontent can only have been caused by Gloucester's failure to set Albany on the Scottish throne, as in Albany he had hoped to have a Scottish king married to his daughter; and his support for Albany — not as a restored magnate of considerable influence but as a potential vassal king — was advanced once more early the following year. This was never a realistic scheme. If the Scots were not prepared to consider Albany as king even after the Lauder crisis and the coercion of James III, they were hardly likely to take up his cause the following spring, when the Scottish king had recovered much of his power. Indeed, throughout the war Gloucester seems to have looked at the Scottish problem much more realistically than his brother, and to have concentrated on the capture of Berwick. To add to this major prize, Albany had been restored to his estates with English aid, and might be expected to be heavily reliant on, and amenable to the wishes of, the English king. Gloucester could well argue that this was no mean achievement for the price of a six-week campaign in the north.

The departure of the English from Edinburgh early in August left the various Scottish factions to resolve their political problems without external pressure. Throughout the month, with King James incarcerated in Edinburgh castle and in fear of his life, real power was in the hands of the Stewart half-uncles, who controlled not only the king but also the royal seals. By 25 August they clearly felt strong enough to emerge from the castle — leaving the king there, still a prisoner, officially under the custody of Atholl — and to form a new government.[56] Significantly absent from their faction were King James's loyal supporters Scheves, Avandale, and Argyll, three of the four Scottish signatories to the agreement of 2 August; indeed their names thereafter vanish from official records until the following spring. The one survivor of the four was Bishop Livingston of Dunkeld, a man possibly envious of Scheves' position and undoubtedly seeking advancement as an officer of state.

The position of Alexander, duke of Albany, in August 1482 was in some ways as precarious as that of the king's displaced counsellors; for the truth was that no-one but the royal uncles, who had possession of James III, was in a position even to promise the duke the second best for which he had negotiated on 2 August, namely a restoration of his lands and titles. For more than a month, therefore, Albany moved restlessly about looking for allies. According to Lesley, he went to Stirling together with Scheves, Avandale and Argyll to obtain the advice and support of Margaret of Denmark, who was living there with her eldest son Prince James; following the queen's advice, Albany then returned secretly to Edinburgh and laid siege to the castle, which was surrendered because of the defenders' lack of provisions, and the king was set free.[57]

Much of this, including the queen's part in the crisis, may be substantially accurate. To protect his own position, Albany had thrown in his lot with the king's supporters, and together they turned to the queen and Prince James in order to gather assistance for James III. There was really no alternative as long as the king remained a prisoner in the hands of the Stewart half-uncles and they refused to negotiate. A much earlier authority than Lesley, the Bolognese Giovanni Sabadino degli Arienti, who produced a brief hagiography of Queen Margaret in 1492,[58] described the collusion between Albany and the queen; although the details are hopelessly wrong — Albany, for example, is credited not only with releasing the king from Edinburgh castle but also with imprisoning him there for the good of the kingdom — the queen is quite specifically associated with Albany in freeing James

III. Corroborative evidence of the queen's part in her husband's release is to be found in a royal charter of 17 January 1483, when James III, in rewarding John Dundas of that ilk, 'familiar squire of his chamber', with the barony of Bothkennar for his labours, assistance, and risk of life in liberating him from Edinburgh castle, remarked that the grant was made 'cum consensu et assensu carissime consortis nostre Margarete Regine Scocie'.[59] Further proof of the queen's involvement is provided by the exchequer records for the year 1482-3, which reveal that Margaret of Denmark paid Lord Darnley for the custody of Edinburgh castle.[60]

The circumstances of the siege of Edinburgh castle and the liberation of the king at the end of September are mysterious. We do not know if Scheves, Avandale and Argyll were with Albany at the time of the siege, or if the royal half-uncles were defending the castle. It is perhaps significant that none of the documents which mention the king's delivery refer to the castle being taken. It was besieged and the king was freed; and this makes it likely that Atholl, Buchan and the bishop-elect of Moray liberated James III on terms which left them considerable power in the royal government. Those conducting the siege, apart from Albany himself, included the provost of Edinburgh, Patrick Baron, three bailies, the dean of guild, the city treasurer, clerk, twelve councillors 'and the whole community' of the burgh; the event itself took place on 29 September; and on 16 November James III rewarded Edinburgh by granting the city the right to hold its own sheriff courts, specifically for the part the citizens had played in helping Albany with the siege and in freeing the king's person.[61]

The king's liberation did not however involve his restoration to a dominant position in government. It merely removed him physically from the control of a single faction; and while he himself later remarked that it was his wish to come out of the castle to be with his brother, there can be no doubt that he was forced to make concessions by the two major factions — led respectively by the Stewart uncles and Albany — until the end of the year. Some of these concessions were immediate; by 10 October, within a fortnight of the siege, James III showed his gratitude to Albany by bestowing on him the earldom of Mar.[62] Four days later a royal grant to James's elder sister Mary, widow of James, first Lord Hamilton, conferred on her the barony of Kilmarnock with its castle, the barony of Dalry, and other Ayrshire lands; these had belonged to the late Robert Lord Boyd and his son Thomas, the forfeited earl of Arran, Princess Mary's first husband. Mary was now to have the liferent of the lands, while her son James Boyd was to hold them in feu. He was in fact given sasine of the lands of Kilmarnock at the castle at eleven o'clock on the morning of 22 October 1482.[63]

This latter grant was a remarkable one, the swansong of the Boyds in Scotland, and it reveals in a striking way the breakdown of normal relationships amongst the royal Stewart kin. Thus James III's elder sister Mary, freed from the marriage to Lord Hamilton which her brother had forced upon her in 1474, reverted swiftly to her Boyd allegiance as soon as the king was seized and no longer his own master, and endeavoured to exploit the situation to recover for herself and her Boyd son James the territories from which the family had been thrust in 1469. James, aged fourteen at most in 1482, was clearly no more than a pawn in the territorial game being played by his mother; and as one of the Scottish disinherited, his advancement at this time would be understandable if he had arrived in Scotland with Albany and Gloucester late in July and was now the beneficiary of Albany's rapproachement with the Stewart half-uncles. Certainly the grant of Kilmarnock and Dalry was illegal; at the time of the Boyd forfeitures, in November 1469, parliament had enumerated the various lands which in future would be reserved to the first-born princes of the kings of Scotland, and the lordships of Kilmarnock and Dalry were amongst them; in the meantime, they formed part of Margaret of Denmark's dower.[64] Young James Boyd and his mother must have known that their titles were of doubtful value, and depended upon the maintenance of Albany's authority.

Finally, on 8 November 1482, the ambitions of another member of the Stewart kin were finally made explicit. Andrew Stewart, bishop-elect of Moray and youngest of James's half-uncles, spoke of the possibility of his promotion to the archbishopric of St. Andrews. William Scheves would in normal circumstances have been in a position to resist Stewart with the backing of the king; deprived of this support, he appears to have resigned his archbishopric, and the following March it was announced that he had done so under duress, and that the resignation was invalid.[65] In pursuit of his promotion, however, Andrew Stewart required not only to oust Scheves, but to find enough money to pay his common services and also persuade the Roman curia to accept Scheves' resignation as 'voluntary'. He had neither money nor credit, and so on 8 November he is found together with his two elder brothers, Sir John Ross of Halkhead, Dean of Glasgow, and John Stewart of Craigiehall, promising to reimburse 6,000 golden ducats to the burgh of Edinburgh, which had empowered four clergy to raise that sum from foreign bankers on the security of the burgh's property and revenue, to assist the promotion of the Bishop-elect of Moray to the archbishopric or any other benefice. On 16 November Edinburgh was given two royal charters, one confirming its property, the other giving the burgh the right to hold its own sheriff courts;[66] these are said to be rewards for the burgh's assistance in freeing the king from the castle, and they may in part be considered as such, but surely they were also granted in recognition of Edunburgh's financial backing, only eight days before, to the royal uncles — in effect a benevolence to the uncles, in Albany's name, at the king's expense!

These grants of October and November to Albany, James's sister Mary and the royal uncles show that the king had obtained his liberty, but not his freedom of action, at the end of September. The siege ended not with a general reconciliation of all factions and promises of future loyalty, but with a deal between Albany and the royal uncles which involved the betrayal of James III's loyal administrators Scheves, Avandale and Argyll; and Lesley is surely right in stating that at this point they fled.[67] Their bright hopes of recovering power through the August agreement with Albany and Gloucester had vanished, and the possibility that they would now be victimised must have been uppermost in their minds.

The king had been freed, and on the surface was reconciled to Albany. But Edinburgh castle was not surrendered until mid-October, probably about a fortnight after King James's release. On 7 October the king wrote to John Stewart,

Lord Darnley, ordering him to hand over the castle to the Earl of Atholl or his representative.[68] By this date the royal uncles must have left the castle — presumably coming out on 29 September with the king himself — and their rapprochement with Albany is revealed in the witness list to a royal charter of 10 October.[69] The royal letter to Darnley is revealing in that it suggests that James was still acting under duress; he did not have access to the privy seal, the keepership of which had gone to the Bishop-elect of Moray, nor even to the signet, which Secretary Whitelaw would have in his keeping. In the absence of both, he sealed the letter with a signet ring portraying a unicorn and bearing the legend 'Tout a Une', a method of authentication of which only two other instances are known.[70]

Why did Darnley continue to hold Edinburgh castle after the king's liberation? A remarkable letter written by James to Darnley on 19 October — after the castle had been surrendered — provides us with the answer, and with a fascinating insight into the king's devious policy and character. On being brought from Lauder and imprisoned in the castle, James III 'dred and doutit that certane lordis and persounys that was than about him wald hafe slayne and undone him; for the quhilk dreide, and for saufte of his life, and for the singler traiste that he had in the said Lord Dernlie, his Hienes baith prait and chargit him, with certane seruituris of his, to remayne and awayt apoun his persoun, baith nicht and day, for the keeping and defence of him as said is; and alsa that his Maieste chargit and gafe licence to the said Lorde Dernele to sele and subscrive with his hand certane endenturis, ligis, and bandis made be the remanent of the lordis; the quhilk he causit him to sele and subscrive, to eschew that tha Lordis sulk tak na suspicioun again the saide Lorde Dernelie be refusing thareof, and tharethrow have removit and put him fra the keping of the saide castell, and of oure Souerane Lordis persoun'.[71] Darnley's adherents in protecting the king are all named, and they number sixty-six, presumably the garrison of Edinburgh castle at the time.

On the evidence of this letter, Darnley must surely be regarded as someone who became a royal supporter, someone to whom the king was genuinely indebted for assistance during a period when he feared for his life. Although shabbily treated by King James over the Lennox in the '70s, Darnley had been thrown sops — the keeperships of Dingwall and Rothesay castles, the Wardenship of the West Marches — which may well have inclined him towards support for the king in a crisis in the hope of greater rewards in the future. He was presumably in the west borders when the Lauder crisis broke, arrived on the scene some time after the royal uncles had imprisoned James III in Edinburgh castle, acquired their trust and that of the king, and clearly decided to support the latter. James's account suggests that he was grateful to Darnley and placed considerable reliance on his protection, encouraging him to join the formal confederation of lords which was established while the king was still their prisoner in the castle. Darnley duly put on a show of friendship for the king's gaolers, and ended up as custodian of Edinburgh after James III had been freed. Thereafter he played no great part in the crisis, but was in favour with the king after James had recovered power the following year. A customs account for the exchequer year 18 August 1482–27 June 1483 records a payment made to John Lord Darnley by the queen, for the keeping of Edinburgh castle;[72] and he was confirmed as custc̣ ḍiaṛ of Rothesay castle for a further seven years in 1484.[73] Perhaps significantly, the last-named of Darnley's sixty-six adherents who were in charge of the king in Edinburgh castle is Rothesay Herald, and he was to be employed by James III in May 1483 to summon Albany for treason.[74]

Thus after the initial appalling shock of the Lauder seizure and understandable fears that his uncles were going to do away with him, the wily king was beginning to show signs of recovery. In some ways, his position was similar to that of Louis XI at Peronne in October 1468, when the French king had miscalculated and been incarcerated by a powerful enemy who was also his vassal and who undoubtedly considered regicide as a possibility. For both Louis at Peronne and James III at Edinburgh, the solution was the same — meet the enemy's demands, temporise, play for time and rely on the strength of the royal name to save the day. If we may extend the comparison a little further, the role of mediator, played in the former crisis by Philippe de Commynes, was performed in the latter by John Stewart, Lord Darnley.

The concern of both major factions to secure Edinburgh castle underlines its importance as the repository of the records and the hub of the king's administration. The king, though freed by Albany and the queen on 29 September, had no access to the royal seals on 7 October; and even as late as 19 October, when the king made his elaborate exculpation of Darnley, he had apparently no seal to put on it.[75] The conclusion must be that the royal seals were in Edinburgh castle, and that both factions badly needed them as the instruments of government. It is likely that they obtained the seals on 19 October, for the royal letter giving assurances to Darnley was probably his price for handing over the castle. Although the letter refers to the handing over as having taken place in the past, it is much more likely that it was given to Darnley before he surrendered the castle. It was a quid pro quo, but was written in such a way as not to appear so. This would strengthen its authority.

Thus the political situation in Edinburgh by mid-October 1482 was that the king was released yet was not free of his half-uncles, that the castle was not surrendered for more than a fortnight after his liberation, that compromises had to be made with the Bishop-elect of Moray, Princess Mary and her son James, second Lord Boyd, that Albany had not achieved complete ascendancy in running the administration, and that the government had become more respectable and attracted more widespread support by this time.[76] The one explanation which satisfies these apparently contradictory facts is that negotiations between James III, Albany and the half-uncles had not ended in a settlement, but with an agreement to reach a settlement in a full parliament. The surrender of the castle, if it occurred on Saturday 19 October 1482, would provide the interim government with the royal seals, and parliament could then be summoned officially at forty days' — that is, six weeks' — notice. Six weeks later fell on Saturday 30 November, St. Andrew's Day and a major holy day in the Scottish church. Parliament met on the first possible day thereafter, Monday 2 December.[77] The dates fit too neatly for them to be coincidence, and it may well be that Albany's intention all along, from the time of his liberation of the king at the end of September, had been to secure a meeting of the estates in order to safeguard his own position. Indeed, this may have been the only point for discussion. The duke may well have reasoned that James III would feel some gratitude to him for his liberation from Edinburgh castle, and that the king's main targets would eventually be the men who had seized him at Lauder. Some support for Albany from the estates in full parliament could still lead to his advancement. He was an incurable optimist.

The estates assembled at Edinburgh on 2 December, when the Lords of the Articles were elected. Twelve were chosen, four from each estate. The prelates were James Livingston, Bishop of Dunkeld, who was to become Chancellor on Laing's death the following month, and who was probably a lukewarm supporter of the king's half-uncles; Andrew Stewart, bishop-elect of Moray, who aspired to the primacy; James Lyndesday, dean of Glasgow, a supporter of Andrew Stewart;[78] and Secretary Whitelaw. The nobility were represented by two earls, Huntly and Crawford, neither of them directly involved in the Lauder seizure or its immediate aftermath; and Lords Borthwick and Cathcart. Of the four burgh commissioners, two were from Edinburgh, provost Patrick Baron and former provost Walter Bertram, the latter of whom had supported Albany in his siege of the castle at the end of September. Thus in this committee of twelve only the two non-Edinburgh burgesses and the Earl of Huntly had apparently been absent from Edinburgh and the court in November; and it would seem that the Articles were chosen largely because of the members' familiarity with recent political events. On the whole, however, those elected appear to have been moderate men. Angus, Buchan, and Gray, to say nothing of Albany himself, were all present in parliament but not chosen to be Lords of the Articles. There was a total attendance of fifty-eight, ranging in outlook from Albany and Angus to the Earl of Crawford and the Bishop-elect of Ross, William Elphinstone;[79] but none of the king's former administrators — Scheves, Avandale, or Argyll — was present, an indication that James III was still by no means a free agent.

The acts of this parliament are dated 11 December, when presumably they were presented by the Committee of the Articles to the remainder of the estates. Taken together they represent a remarkable collation of irreconcilable points of view; and in the end, none of the statutes or articles was to be implemented. In the first of them, reference is made to 'the kingis hienes, my lord of albany and the hale estaitis of the Realme'. This would suggest that Albany had attained a position of considerable political influence, almost on a par with that of the king. Doubtless he aspired to this at least; but the article itself orders the immediate resumption of negotiations with England for a truce, peace, and the marriage of Prince James. It represents therefore the king's policy and not that of Albany. Even more remarkable is the second article, which after complaining that the borders are being invaded daily by the English and insisting that the king should not put his person in danger by going to meet the threat, recommends that King James 'speke to his bruthir the duke of albany to take apone him to be lieutennant generale of the Realme and to defend the bordouris and resist his ennemyis baith of Ingland and utheris in al tymes of nede'; and advice is to be given by the estates on how Albany may bear the costs of his office.[80]

The precedents for appointments by the estates of lieutenants-general, in 1399 and 1438, are worth considering for their contrast with 1482. On 27 January 1399, in a General Council held at Perth, David, duke of Rothesay, was appointed 'the kyngis lieutenande generally throch al the Kynrike for the terme of thre yhere, hafand ful powere and commission of the kyng to governe the lande in all thyng as the kyng sulde do in his person gife he warre present'. These extensive powers were given to Rothesay because of the infirmity of Robert III.[81] Again, some time before 17 November 1438, the estates, meeting either in parliament or general council, had appointed Archibald, fifth earl of Douglas, lieutenant-general with the same extensive powers;[82] in this case, the reason for the appointment was the youth of the king, who was a boy of eight. In each case, however, the lieutenant-general was given royal powers, his appointment was made to meet a special need (Robert III was senile, James II a minor), and his powers were not confined to any specific sphere of government.

When we turn to the parliamentary article of December 1482, the differences are at once obvious. The king was neither senile nor a minor; and the long preamble about the need to defend the borders against English invasion suggests the appointment of a March Warden — an office already held by Albany — rather than a lieutenant-general. The wording, indeed, suggests that Albany's activities in his new role should be confined to defence of the borders against possible invasion. Nevertheless, the office would have made him second person in the realm, and would have given him direct control over the Scottish host. This was undoubtedly much further than James III, even in a weakened position, was prepared to go; and it is clear that the article of 1482 was not a parliamentary appointment of Albany as lieutenant, and this is the greatest difference between it and the earlier enactments of 1399 and 1438. Presumably parliament could not derogate from the authority of an adult king by transferring his powers. Only the king himself could appoint someone to act for him; so the parliament of December 1482 could do no more than invite James III to do this and to make suitable financial arrangements. Whether the mention of defence of the borders and protecting the king's person was an excuse suggested by the estates or a limitation bargained for by the king, we cannot know. For it seems that the office of lieutenant-general was not in fact conferred.

Why the estates should have proposed that the duke be given the office is perhaps easier to understand. Albany's negotiations with Edward IV and his treasonable behaviour during the autumn were temporarily forgotten, and he was praised for his loyalty to his brother, the king; but he was, to say the least, a curious choice as defender of the borders against English incursions. Probably, however, the great majority of those present in parliament were prepared to accept an uneasy alliance between the two brothers rather than face the prospect of immediate civil war. The Lothians and the south-east had already suffered greatly from two-and-a-half years of war with England, and it may have been thought by some that the appointment of Albany as lieutenant-general would force him to renew his allegiance to Scotland and commit himself openly to opposing Edward IV.

So the suggestion was made to the king that Albany should be promoted; but it seems nothing happened. On 25 December the duke was still at court, witnessing a charter, but described therein neither as lieutenant-general nor as Earl of Mar.[83] The latter omission may be a slip on the part of the chancery clerk, but hardly the former. Three months later, in an abortive agreement made between James III and Albany, the duke was again described as Earl of Mar and Garioch; this may be a royal restitution, or he may never have lost the title. But the summary of this document given in the preface to the ninth volume of the *Exchequer Rolls of Scotland* is inaccurate in stating as part of the agreement that Albany 'is relieved of his office of Lieutenant-General'.[84] In fact, the original statement is to the effect that 'in tym tocum he sall not use nor exerce in any wys the office of Lieutennent-General within the Realme but discharge him thereof now incontinent'.[85] This means that Albany had pretended to the office but clearly had no royal commission or other authority for it.

The third article of the December parliament provided for a proclamation to warn the lieges to be ready to come to the king and his Lieutenant for the defence of the realm. The fourth relates to the destruction on the borders and 'a grete parte Inwarde', and ordains the holding of warden courts and all other courts for the administration of justice. The remaining business presents no unusual features. There are eleven articles in all, and against each there is a marginal note. The third bears the comment: 'to be new proponit and apprevit; pronuncit', and a similar note — omitting the word 'new' — occurs against six other articles, while against the last there is the remark: 'this grant contenit in this writing is fulfillit be oure souerane lordis lettres direct of before'.[86] It is apparent from these notes that all the statutes and articles were submitted to a later session of parliament, presumably because the king was dissatisfied with the validity of the proceedings of December 1482.

Three of the parliamentary articles are in fact marked 'abrogate' — the first, concerning an English truce and the marriage of Prince James, was presumably rendered obsolete by Edward IV's death in April 1483; the second, concerning the lieutenant-generalship, was no longer relevant after Albany's fall; and the fourth, concerned with protection of, and justice on, the borders, was of less importance once the internal crisis of 1482-3 had been resolved. In fact, the fourth article came up again for reconsideration in the parliament of February 1484, when it was included in an act ordering the holding of justice ayres.[87] It is probable, therefore, that the later acts of the December 1482 parliament were 'new proponit' and in some cases 'apprevit' in 1484.

As a political settlement, however, the parliament of 2–11 December 1482 was a total failure. The king was apparently strong enough to ignore its main provision for an accommodation with his brother. There was no place in the state for Albany in James's view, and this view prevailed against the moderating advice of the Lords of the Articles that Albany should be given a commission of lieutenancy on the borders at least, if not become the second person in the kingdom. The excuse for the failure may have been the inability to reach agreement over the financial terms, for the cost of defending the borders was obviously considerable and Albany would need a generous income to meet it. This the king may have refused, and by Christmas no settlement was in sight. It is not clear how James recovered so much strength, for he was still without Scheves, Avandale and Argyll. On the other hand, Albany's bargaining strength was not impressive, for he could only reckon on the active support of those, like Buchan and Gray, whose treasons were unlikely to be forgiven by the king. For the rest, no matter how involved they might have been in feathering their own nests while James was a captive, their future now rested on displaying loyalty to the Crown.

Thus Albany, as he sat at the king's Christmas table, must have been a disappointed man. His political ineptitude was no match for the self-seeking greed of many of the nobility or his brother's cunning and evasiveness. By 30 December he had retired to his castle at Dunbar, but not simply to sulk. With him were Archibald, earl of Angus, James Stewart, earl of Buchan, Sir James Liddale (Albany's steward), and Alexander Hume of that ilk, grandson of the first Lord Hume and the future second Lord. Albany made a grant to Hume of twenty husbandlands in the town and territory of Letham, lying within the earldom of March and sheriffdom of Berwick, for faithful service done and to be done.[88] This gathering at Dunbar so soon after Albany's parliamentary failure earlier in the month undoubtedly represents an attempt on the duke's part to recruit support for his political aspirations; for the men involved were either his tenants or rebel leaders in the Lauder crisis.

The sequel was swift and dramatic: on Friday 3 January 1483, only four days after Albany's grant to Hume at Dunbar, James III wrote to Sir Robert Arbuthnot of that ilk to the effect that 'we ar sikkerly informit that certan persons, to grete nowmer, were gadderit tresonably to haf invadit our person this last Thursday'. Presumably the king is referring to the day before, Thursday, 2 January. He asks Arbuthnot for immediate armed support 'as ye lufe the welfar of owr persone, succession, realme, and liegis, and ye sal have special thank and rewards of us according to your merit'.[89] Arbuthnot was only a laird whose lands lay mainly in the Mearns rather than close to Edinburgh, so it is likely that his was only one of many royal letters, rapidly circulating, in which the king asked urgently for assistance. The treasonable gathering to which the letter refers must surely be the Albany faction assembled at Dunbar on 30 December, the men whom the duke hoped would support him in another Lauder Bridge.

The plot misfired badly, however, for instead of throwing in his lot with Albany, Hume appears to have gone directly to Edinburgh and revealed the conspirators' intentions to the king. Albany, who may well have brought Hume into the plot because of the long-standing battle between the Hume kin and James III over the revenues of Coldingham, must have been appalled at this betrayal; and he seems to have retaliated by arresting Hume and some of his friends and kinsmen for going over to the king, and indeed accused them of attempting to kill him on King James's orders. Evidence of this Hume volte-face is to be found not only in an indenture made between the king and Albany in March,[90] but also in later royal grants to the Hume family. Thus on 2 July 1483, while the parliament which ultimately forfeited Albany was in session, James III confirmed his brother's grant, made on 30 December 1482, to Hume, of lands in the town and territory of Letham.[91] On 11 January 1484 the king followed this up by granting to Alexander Hume, for unspecified faithful service, the lands of Chirnside in Berwickshire, which had fallen into his hands as a result of Albany's forfeiture.[92] The day before, the king had made a similar grant to his 'familiar household squire' John Hume (son and heir of George Hume of Aytoun, and therefore Alexander Hume's cousin) of twelve pounds' worth of the lands of Duns, in the earldom of March and shire of Berwick, forfeited by Albany the previous June.[93] These grants of land formerly held by Albany make it clear that James III had reason to be grateful to two of the Humes; and it seems probable that John Hume was one of the 'friends and kinsmen' of Alexander Hume, whom Albany complained had attempted to kill him on James's orders early in the new year.

In fact, Albany's abortive coup had ruined him simply because his intentions became rapidly known to the king. Henceforth none of the other parties in the government could trust him; and it is probable that the seizure of the king's person planned for 2 January 1483 was thwarted simply by being made common knowledge. Moderate men would realise that Albany's plans meant continued domestic upheaval, and the queen would have nothing further to do with him when it became apparent that his object was to seize her husband. Thus James III who, although he enjoyed some measure of personal liberty by this time, still had to find his allies amongst men like Atholl, the Bishop-elect of Moray, Chancellor Laing, and Bishop Livingston, was able to exploit the disunity caused by Albany's sudden treachery to recover his own position, appoint his own counsellors, and take over the government himself.

This change was not immediate. In Albany's absence, royal charters were witnessed by these same men who had assumed control of the offices of state after Lauder, together with the loyal Earl of Crawford in his capacity of Master of the Household. However, they were rapidly losing their political strength. It had been seriously weakened by Buchan's defection to Albany at the end of December 1482; and less than a fortnight later, on 11 January 1483, the Chancellor, John Laing, bishop of Glasgow, died.[94]

Within a week — either on or just before 18 January — King James felt strong enough to summon the estates to meet in Edinburgh on 1 March,[95] presumably to revise the provisions of the parliament of December 1482, or at least to eliminate the obligation imposed on the king there to consider making Albany lieutenant-general. This move was rapidly followed by others; between 20 and 22 January 1483, there occurred a change in court personnel which indicates the full recovery of control of the government by James III. On the 20th, Andrew Stewart, bishop-elect of Moray, is still described as keeper of the privy seal; but by the 22nd Master David Livingstone, rector of Ayr, had replaced him in that office. Andrew Stewart continued to witness royal charters for some time, but he is described only as the king's uncle. Even more significant, the name of Archbishop Scheves reappears in the records for the first time since 2 August 1482. Presumably James III had compelled his half-uncle to restore Scheves to St. Andrews, and at the same time punished Stewart by dismissing him from his keepership of the privy seal. Also on 22 January William Elphinstone, bishop-elect of Ross, a future Chancellor and firm supporter of the king, appears as an Edinburgh charter witness, as does the Earl of

Huntly, the most powerful magnate in the north-east.[96] Huntly, who had taken no part in the complicated political manoeuvres of the autumn of 1482, may have come to court at Edinburgh in response to a royal letter, similar to that received by Arbuthnot, urgently requesting assistance. The same men witnessed another charter granted at Edinburgh on 5 February, and from then on into March their names appear with increasing regularity.[97] Thus over a short period in January and February James III had been able to surround himself with men who had either been his supporters during the '70s or had had no connections with the post-Lauder government.

Once his treasonable intentions became widely known, Albany prudently remained at Dunbar; and he appears to have recognised within a matter of days that his projected coup had failed and that there was only one recourse left to him. On 12 January 1483, he sent the Earl of Angus, Andrew Lord Gray, and his steward Sir James Liddale to England as his commissioners; and on 11 February these three concluded a treaty with Edward IV's commissioners — Henry Percy, earl of Northumberland, John Lord Scrope, and Sir William Parre — at Westminster. Albany and his supporters renounced their allegiance to Scotland and became the liegemen of the king of England; Albany undertook to assist Edward IV in conquering Scotland, to cede all right to the town and castle of Berwick, to assist James, earl of Douglas, to recover his estates, and to take one of Edward's daughters in marriage without any charge to the English king. Edward IV promised, for his part, to assist Albany in the conquest of the Crown of Scotland.[98]

Ten days later, on 21 February 1483, in the comparative safety of Dunbar castle, those extremists who were still prepared to support Albany witnessed a charter granted by the duke to one of his followers. Prominent among the witnesses was James Stewart, earl of Buchan, the Chamberlain, who after displaying considerable shrewdness in shifting his allegiance at the right moment, finally found himself on the wrong side; and also present were William Lord Crichton, James Boyd, described as 'Lord Boyd', and Sir John Douglas, Master of Morton and sheriff of Edinburgh.[99] Archibald, earl of Angus, Andrew Lord Gray, and Sir James Liddale had presumably not yet returned from Westminster; so including them, the extremists consisted of one duke, two earls, and three lords of parliament, as well as the two knights, Liddale and Douglas, and a number of lesser men.

It may be doubted, however, that Albany and his supporters wished to advance his unpopular claim to the throne at this late stage. They must have known that it stood little chance of success, but found that Edward IV would offer help to a puppet king but not to a faction of rebel nobles. In the circumstances Albany would have no alternative but to renew the treaty of Fotheringhay. After all his agreements made and broken on all sides — with Edward IV, with Margaret of Denmark, with Scheves, Avandale, and Argyll, with the Stewart half-uncles, and with James III himself — Albany was back where he had started, skulking in Dunbar and committing himself once more to his English treasons. The wheel had come full circle.

NOTES

1. Lennox Chrs., No. 81, printed in Fraser, *Lennox*, ii, 121-3. The original is missing.
2. *E.R.*, ix, 218-9.
3. B.M. Royal MS. 17 Dxx, f.308r.
4. Stewart, *The Scottish Coinage*, 60; *A.P.S.*, ii, 172, 174' For the suggestion that the billon placks were introduced in 1471 — the new alloyed groats of that year — and for much that follows on the subject of the coinage, I am greatly indebted to Mrs. Joan Murray, who has made a close study of the numismatic evidence for the period. Cf. Joan E. L. Murray, *The Early Unicorns and the Heavy Groats of James III and James IV*, British Numismatic Journal, vol. xl (1972), 62-96, esp. 63-66; and for the black money itself, see the excellent paper by the same author, 'The Black Money of James III', delivered at the second Oxford Symposium on Coinage and Monetary History, and printed in *Coinage in Medieval Scotland (1100–1600)*, ed. D. M. Metcalf, *British Archaeological Reports 45* (1977), 115-130.
5. *A.P.S.*, ii, 105.
6. Pitscottie, Historie, i, 169.
7. *E.R.*, ix, 218-9.
8. *A.D.A.*, 122.*
9. *E.R.*, ix, 286.
10. *Ibid.*, 480.
11. *A.P.S.*, ii, 86; *E.R.*, vii, 580.
12. *A.P.S.*, ii, 88-9, 90. According to Stewart, *The Scottish Coinage*, 61, a second coinage of black farthings dates from the early '70s, but no reference to it has been preserved in contemporary documents.
13. *A.P.S.*, ii, 97.
14. *T.A.*, i, 94, 130.
15. B.M. Royal MS. 17 Dxx, f.308r.
16. *E.R.*, ix, 218-9.
17. *Bannatyne Miscellany*, iii, 427-431.
18. *E.R.*, ix, 431.
19. B.M. Royal MS. 17 Dxx, f.308r.
20. *E.R.*, ix, 219. The contemporary chronicler quotes the high price of the boll of meal — £4 before Lauder on 22 July, as a result of the black money, and only 22/- after demonetisation and the king's release on 29 September. But these are not exceptional prices, and may simply reflect the situation before and after the ingathering of the harvest, with grain prices falling in the autumn: B.M. Royal MS. 17 Dxx, f.308r.
21. Lesley, *History*, 48-9; Ferrerius, *Appendix to Boece*, f.394v.
22. Pitscottie, *Historie*, i, 173.
23. *E.R.*, ix, 433.
24. These legends are discussed in detail below, in Chapter 12.
25. *E.R.*, ix, 218.
26. *R.M.S.*, ii, No. 1533.
27. Buchanan, *History*, ii, 141; Ferrerius, *Appendix to Boece*, f.395v.
28. Lesley, *History*, 48-9.
29. Fraser, *Colquhoun*, ii, 297; *A.D.C.*, 49.
30. *Ibid.*, 82.
31. Ferrerius, *Appendix to Boece*, f.391r-v; Lesley, *History*, 49; Buchanan, *History*, ii, 141.
32. *E.R.*, vii, 507, 583, 666.
33. *R.M.S.*, ii, No. 1418.
34. Ferrerius, *Appendix to Boece*, f.391 r-v.
35. Ferrerius, *Historia*, p. vi.
36. Ferrerius, *Appendix to Boece*, f.395v.
37. *R.M.S.*, ii, Nos. 1514, 1517.
38. Myln, *Vitae*, 26.

39. The earldom of Mar had been seized by the Crown following the death of Earl Alexander Stewart in 1435; thereafter in 1457 the Erskine claim had been denied and James II had granted the earldom to his youngest son John. Following John's death by July 1480, the revenues of the earldom were not paid into the exchequer before the crisis of 1482. Historically, many families had an interest in the earldom of Mar: Albany, who briefly acquired it, the rejected Erskines, and Lord Lyle; and it is significant that Buchan, whose primary aim seems to have been to recover the territorial power in the north and north-east formerly vested in the Buchan earldom before 1424 (a policy he was to continue in the next reign), is to be found at feud with Lyle in the '80s: *Scots Peerage*, ii, 263-4, 266-7; *E.R.*, ix, xliii-xliv; *R.M.S.*, ii, No. 1617; *A.P.S.*, ii, 210-11.

40. *See above*, Chapter 7.

41. *E.R.*, ix, 219. Some time during exchequer year 1482-3, Atholl was paid £100 for the custody of Edinburgh castle. This was exactly three-quarters of the annual fee paid to David Crichton in the '70s: e.g. *ibid.*, 79.

42. *Cal. Docs. Scot.*, iv, No. 1489; printed in *Foedera*, xii, 173.

43. Gairdner, *Letters of Richard III and Henry VII*, i, 385.

44. *Origines Parochiales*, ii, 144. The reference is to Breadalbane Chrs. (S.R.O.), but the relevant document appears to have been lost.

45. Pitscottie, *Historie*, i, 172-3; Lesley, *History*, 49.

46. Polydore Vergil, *Historia Anglica*, (Camden Soc., 1844), 170.

47. *Cal. State Papers (Venice)*, i, 145-6.

48. *Foedera*, xii, 160.

49. Lesley, *History*, 49. Later in his account, however, Lesley states that after Gloucester had left Edinburgh to lay siege to Berwick, Albany pursued him with an army as far as Lammermuir. It seems likely that Lesley is referring on both occasions to the same army — the one led by James III's supporters — and that his confusion in placing Albany at its head is the result of his lack of understanding of the duke's role in the crisis. For Lesley's sources, *see below*, Chapter 12.

50. Hall, *Chronicle*, 334; but no contemporary source for this secret deed of 3 August is given.

51. *Foedera*, xii, 161; *Cal. Docs. Scot.*, iv, No. 1480.

52. *Ibid.*, Nos. 1481, 1482, 1483, 1484.

53. Devon, *Issues of the Exchequer*, 501.

54. *Cal. State Papers (Venice)*, i, 145-6. Both Hall (*Chronicle*, 334-5) and Lesley (*History*, 49-50) state that Berwick fell to Gloucester on 24 August. This date is obviously impossible if the evidence of King Edward's letter is accepted; alternatively Edward may have been anticipating the fall of the castle, or confusing it with the surrender of the town the previous month.

55. *Hist. Croy. Cont.*, 563.

56. *R.M.S.*, ii, No. 1517.

57. Lesley, *History*, 49-50.

58. S. B. Chandler, 'An Italian Life of Margaret, Queen of James III', in *S.H.R.*, xxxii, (1953), 52-7. This contains a full discussion of Sabadino's sources and the text of Margaret's biography.

59. *R.M.S.*, ii, No. 1539. The original is in N.L.S., Dundas Chrs., B 109. This association of the queen with her husband in a royal grant is unique for the whole reign.

60. *E.R.*, ix, 213. The queen paid Lord Darnley £145 16/11d. for the custody of the castle. The normal annual fee for Edinburgh's custodian was £133 6/8d.

61. *Edinburgh City Chrs.*, 157; B.M. Royal MS. 17 Dxx f.308r: the writer states that the king was in the castle 'fra the magdalyne day (22 July) quhill michaelmess' (29 September).

62. *R.M.S.*, ii, No. 1518 (10 October 1482) omits Albany's new title, but it is to be found in the MS. R.M.S. (xi, 33).

63. S.R.O., Inventory of Boyd Papers, 138-140 (originals missing); *R.M.S.*, ii, No. 1520.

64. *A.P.S.*, ii, 186.

65. *Edinburgh City Chrs.*, 154; S.R.O., State Papers No. 19.

66. *R.M.S.*, ii, Nos. 1525, 1526; printed in *Edinburgh City Chrs.*, 157, 165.

67. Lesley, *History*, 50.

68. *Lennox Chrs.*, No. 80; printed in Fraser, *Lennox*, ii, 121.

69. *R.M.S.*, ii, No. 1518.

70. *See* Hannay, *Early History of the Scottish Signet*, 19. James IV gave a charge under 'oure Signet of the Unicorn' at Perth in February 1509: *S.H.R.*, xxvi, (1947), 147-8.

71. Fraser, *Lennox*, ii, 121-3 (original lost).

72. *E.R.*, ix, 213.

73. Fraser, *Lennox*, ii, 124-6.

74. *Ibid.*, 123; *A.P.S.*, ii, 151.

75. The Great Seal charter dated 10 October (*R.M.S.*, ii, No. 1518) would not have passed the Great Seal on that day, which was the date of its originating warrant.

76. The reappearance of the name of David, earl of Crawford — the most consistently loyal earl of the entire reign — in charter witness lists from 10 October suggests a broadening of the administration to include some committed supporters of the king.

77. *A.P.S.*, ii, 142.

78. *Edinburgh City Chrs.*, 154.

79. *A.P.S.*, ii, 142.

80. *Ibid.*, 143.

81. *Ibid.*, i, 572-3.

82. *Ibid.*, ii, 31.

83. *R.M.S.*, ii, No. 1533; MS. Reg. vol. xi, 31. Albany is described in the witness list to this charter as Earl of March, Lord of Annandale and Man, and brother of the king.

84. *E.R.*, ix, p. li.

85. S.R.O. State Papers No. 19; printed in *A.P.S.*, xii, 31-3.

86. *Ibid.*, ii, 143-4.

87. *Ibid.*, 165.

88. *H.M.C. Rep. xii*, Part viii, App., 155.

89. Nisbet, *Heraldry*, ii, App., 83.

90. S.R.O., State Papers No. 19.

91. *H.M.C. Rep. xii*, Part viii, App., 155-6.

92. *R.M.S.*, ii, No. 1572.

93. *Ibid.*, No. 1571.

94. *Glasgow Registrum*, 615.

95. *A.P.S.*, ii, 145.

96. *R.M.S.*, ii, Nos. 1542 (20 January), 1544 (22 January).

97. *Ibid.*, Nos. 1551, 1558, 1560-63.

98. *Foedera*, xii, 172-3.

99. *R.M.S.*, ii, No. 1573.

9

King's Friends and King's Enemies: The Politics of the 1480s

JAMES III's recovery of power in January 1483 brought to an end a period of complex political manoeuvring unique in fifteenth century Scottish history. The king had been brutally humiliated by his kin; his brother had proposed to take his place and, in the early stages of the crisis, his uncles may have considered murdering him. The men in whom he had reposed his trust in the '70s had proved to be broken reeds; and even his elder sister had used his predicament to taunt him with the claims of the forfeited Boyds. All in all, it is a sorry tale, reflecting the general unpopularity of James III and, related to this, his inability to choose the right men as counsellors and his unwillingness adequately to reward loyal service.

Yet the crisis of 1482-3 also reveals the immense strength of the Stewart monarchy in Scotland. In spite of King James's unpopularity, in spite of the arrival of a pretender to his throne, in spite of hostile magnate factions joining together to coerce the king, in spite even of a background of a wrecked foreign policy and over two years of damaging war with England punctuated by plague and bad harvests, the truth was that there was no real alternative to James III. Once he had survived the early weeks of incarceration, he required to do little more than bide his time until his enemies overreached themselves and provoked a loyalist reaction in his favour. The power and prestige of the Crown were such that nothing short of murder could have removed King James; none of the factions were ultimately prepared to go so far, and even if they had, the precedent of James I's assassination in 1437 made it clear that the king's eldest son — not his brother Albany — would instantly be accepted as his successor.

Thus in January and February 1483 Albany in desperation made his worst mistakes; and James III, by publicising the treasons of the extremists, was provided with a pretext for rallying supporters, with whose assistance he was able eventually to dictate terms to Albany, and ultimately free himself not only from the duke and his associates but from the men who had run the government from August 1482 until January 1483.

This policy is seen at work on 1 March 1483, when the parliament summoned to Edinburgh in the third week of January finally met. Although there is no sederunt list for this parliament, the lords elected to the Committee of the Articles — the unusually large number of sixteen — were almost without exception loyal servants of the Crown. The clergy present were headed by the restored Archbishop Scheves, and included Robert Colquhoun, bishop of Argyll, brother of Sir John Colquhoun who had been killed fighting for James III at the siege of Dunbar castle in 1479; George Carmichael, the king's nominee for the vacant see of Glasgow; Archibald

Crawfurd, abbot of Holyrood, the Treasurer; Henry, abbot of Cambuskenneth, King James's procurator in Rome in the early '70s; and Secretary Whitelaw. For the barons, Andrew Lord Avandale re-emerges from obscurity, but no longer as Chancellor; three earls were elected — David, earl of Crawford, James's staunchest supporter throughout the reign; George earl of Huntly, the leading magnate in the conservative north-east; and Colin, earl of Argyll, who was to be the next Chancellor. Two lords of parliament — Robert Lord Lyle, James's ambassador to England the folldwing year, and John Lyon, Lord Glamis, whose loyalty to the king continues unbroken until Sauchieburn — complete the second estate. Among the burgh commissioners appears the name of Walter Bertram, who had not only assisted in freeing James from Edinburgh castle the previous September, but was also chosen as an ambassador to France, to settle disputes between Scots and French merchants, in the parliament of December 1482.[1] Perhaps significantly, Bishop Livingston of Dunkeld, the new Chancellor, was not elected to the Committee of the Articles although he acted fairly regularly as a royal charter witness at this time. He may have coveted Scheves' archbishopric,[2] he had taken a prominent part in government since the Lauder crisis, and he was not a James III man, having been made Chancellor before the king's full recovery of power.

The business of the March parliament was to find an acceptable political settlement, the major issue postponed in the abortive parliament of December 1482. With royalists packing the Articles, such a settlement would undoubtedly involve the public recognition of the recovery of power by the king, and the punishment of his enemies. In fact, however, no statutes were passed in March, and there followed a series of continuations through the spring and early summer until the estates finally reassembled in Edinburgh on 27 June. The reason for the long delay was undoubtedly Albany's fresh English treasons. On the one hand, the duke's renewal of the treaty of Fotheringhay destroyed his political credibility in Scotland; but on the other, he was inaccessible in Dunbar castle, and if he were to receive English support on anything like the scale of the previous year, James III might well find himself in the same vulnerable position as in July 1482. The uncertain diplomatic situation made some form of compromise with Albany, even at this late stage, the best policy for King James; while the duke himself, with his options rapidly closing, must have felt that an agreement with his brother would give him some protection in the event of further English support proving illusory.

Thus on 19 March 1483, at his castle of Dunbar, Albany signed an indenture with James III, from the terms of which it is clear that, though an element of compromise remained on the part of the king, he had undoubtedly recovered full control of the government.[3] King James undertook to receive his brother into favour, and to grant a full remission under the great seal, and with the authority of parliament, of all treasons and other misdeeds, to Albany and those of his accomplices whose names he would provide. Albany for his part was to declare in parliament that a rumour which had been going about that the king had been attempting to poison him 'in his presens and palace' was a groundless slander; and Alexander Hume, nephew[4] of Lord Hume, together with some of his friends and kinsmen, arrested by Albany because the duke had been informed that James III had ordered them to kill him, were to be released on the king's denial that he had given any such orders. Further, Albany was to renounce his treasonable bands with Edward IV, as were his supporters in this, who are named as the Earls of Angus and Buchan, Lords Crichton and Gray, and Sir James Liddale of Halkerston — all of them men who had either gone over to Albany at Dunbar or had been employed as his commissioners to Edward IV in January and February. Those who had made treasonable bands with Albany, but not with the King of England, are named as Andrew Stewart, bishop-elect of Moray, and John, earl of Atholl, the two remaining half-uncles, and Alexander Hume, Lord Hume's nephew; and all three are ordered to renounce these bands. Thus the indenture makes clear the distinction between those who had joined Albany after 30 December 1482 and were involved with Edward IV, and those whose alliance with him was earlier, presumably in the autumn of 1482.

The remaining terms of the agreement are still more extraordinary. Albany is ordered not to come within six miles of the king without special licence, is not to pretend to the office of lieutenant-general, but is permitted to retain that of March Warden. He is to endeavour to obtain peace with England and to achieve the marriage of Prince James, the heir apparent, with Edward IV's daughter Cecilia. The revival of this tarnished scheme illustrates clearly that James III had regained total control of policy making. During his incarceration in Edinburgh castle in August 1482, the city of Edinburgh had bound itself for the repayment of the sums already paid to the Scottish king by Edward IV towards Cecilia's dowry; and on 27 October of that year the English king had intimated that he wanted the money returned.[5] No repayments, however, had been made; the first would have been due early in February 1483, at the church of St. Nicholas in Newcastle,[6] but was probably delayed by the rapidly changing political situation in Scotland during that month. The attempt to resume the marriage negotiations and obtain more dowry money rather than submit to repayment of what had already been sent was clearly the handiwork of the king himself, the resumption of his former diplomatic schemes and the prelude to an even more vigorous policy of peace and marriage alliances with England throughout the '80s.

By not stripping Albany of all his offices, James seems to have been attempting, in the indenture of 19 March, to make his brother's position tolerable; though the agreement also required that 'the said noble prince (Albany) sal take in hertly favoris frendschip and tendirness all the lordis and persons of oure Souerane lordis counsail' — men like Scheves, Avandale and Argyll, whom Albany had thrust out of office during his brief tenure of power. Yet Albany had few reasonable complaints to level at the king. The rumour that James had intended to poison Albany — presumably at Christmas 1482 before the duke left court for Dunbar — is probably no more than a rumour; and the complaint that the king had hired Alexander Hume to kill Albany was probably an invention of the duke's, concocted in desperation when he realised that Hume had betrayed his treasonable intentions to his brother.

With the majority of Albany's accomplices, and with those who had held him in ward after the Lauder crisis, James took a firm line. None of them was to come within six miles of the king's residence except to his own dwelling place; but an exception was made in the case of Sir John Douglas, son of James, earl of Morton, who was to be allowed to visit his father at Dalkeith, an indication that Morton had remained loyal, or at least inactive, throughout the crisis. The king's half-uncle James Stewart, earl of Buchan, whose behaviour since the previous August must have terrified his nephew, was banished from Scotland for three years, together with Lord Crichton and Sir James Liddale; and Buchan was further ordered to resign the offices of Chamberlain, Warden of the Middle Marches, keeper of the castles of Newark and Methven, and bailie of Methven. Similarly, the Earl of Angus was to resign the offices of Justiciar south of Forth, Steward of Kirkcudbright, keeper of Threave castle, sheriff of Lanark, and his right to the wardship and marriage of the heir of Dalhousie; and the Earl of Morton's son, Sir John Douglas, was to give up the sheriffship of Edinburgh.

These sentences seem to have been in part effective. Buchan's office of Chamberlain had gone to the Earl of Crawford by April 1483; his keepership of Newark castle went to Angus — an extraordinary choice — before 3 June 1483; and Angus also received Buchan's forfeited office of Warden of the Middle Marches.[7] Buchan's name now vanishes from the records for four-and-a-half years, and he must have gone into foreign exile.[8] Angus lost at least the custody of Threave castle, which went to John Lord Carlyle, a loyal servant of the king;[9] but the earl's gains at the expense of Buchan, his former ally, left him in a remarkably strong position in the south of Scotland.

Finally, the indenture ordered Albany to take into favour the Archbishop of St. Andrews, and not to assist James's half-uncle, the Bishop-elect of Moray, in taking advantage of Scheves' pretended resignation of his see, an action which the primate had been 'throw force aw and dreid compellit and constitut to mak'. The king had succeeded in saving his archbishop's position; but Scheves would never again exercise the authority which his intimacy with the king had won for him in the late '70s.

On the whole, the agreement of 19 March displays not only James III's renewed strength but also a remarkable leniency towards rebels. It is extraordinary that, if the terms of the indenture had ever been implemented, both Albany and Angus would have been left as March Wardens, a fact which suggests that the king's initial desire was to heal the breach with Albany if the duke would accept a subordinate position. But there is another explanation. James III was determined that the agreement should be as widely publicised as possible — perhaps to guard against further treasons on the part of Albany and his supporters — and it was stipulated that some of the terms of the indenture should be carried out in parliament. Albany's public acceptance of his new status would effectively curb his ambition to achieve the office of lieutenant-general, and destroy his credibility with his English allies as pretender to the Scottish throne. He signed the indenture on 19 March, and parliament had been prorogued from the 10th to the 21st of that month, perhaps to give him a chance to appear. However, nothing happened beyond a further adjournment to 7 April, and then another to the 15th of the same month. On 15 April there followed yet another prorogation of parliament to 16 June; but on this occasion the reason given for the delay was 'pro non nullis arduis materiis dictum supremum dominum nostrum Regem et Rem publicam Regni concernentibus'.[10]

It seems likely that this weighty business concerning the welfare of the king and kingdom which caused the much longer prorogation of parliament on 15 April was news of fresh treasons on Albany's part. The duke had presumably hoped that the March agreement with James III would give him a powerful position in the state; this was not forthcoming, so Albany accepted the unfavourable terms of the indenture in order to play for time until English military assistance arrived. Hence James III's optimistic short prorogations of parliament until 15 April, and Albany's evasiveness. In June, the duke's forfeiture made mention of his reception and entertainment of an English pursuivant, Bluemantle, at Dunbar, and his admittance of an English garrison into Dunbar castle.[11] No date is given for this treason; but it is likely that, as Albany's commissioners had renewed the treaty of Fotheringhay as early as 11 February, the duke's negotiations with Bluemantle at Dunbar would follow shortly afterwards, perhaps in early March. Presumably there was then a delay while the English mustered and sent their troops to Dunbar. When Albany admitted them is unknown, but if it were between the parliamentary prorogations of 7 and 15 April, then this 'tresonable inbringing of Inglismen' would explain the long prorogation of the estates on the latter date.

Albany had finally committed himself to the wrong side, and his luck had run out. On 9 April 1483 — probably about the same time as he admitted the English into Dunbar — his patron, Edward IV of England, died in London.[12] From James III's point of view, this was an unexpected stroke of luck; the new English monarch, Edward V, was a boy of thirteen, and the establishment of a regency in England would mean a relaxation of the aggressive policy towards Scotland which Edward IV had pursued in his last years. Furthermore, any council of regency established in England for the boy king would inevitably include Richard, duke of Gloucester, and this would mean his recall from the north, where he had been by far the most effective of the English leaders.

Thus Albany's renewed negotiations with England, after he had been offered the alternative of the March indenture, not only proved abortive but made it clear to James III that he could never trust his brother; and on 8 July 1483, Albany and his steward, Sir James Liddale, were forfeited in parliament at Edinburgh.[13] Long before the final parliamentary doom, however, Albany had fled from Dunbar, presumably realising that his personal position in Scotland was hopeless. On 17 May, when Rothesay Herald went to Dunbar to summon the duke to appear before parliament on charges of treason, Albany had already left the castle. It appears from his forfeiture that he had been negotiating with Edward IV until the latter's death. He had sent Sir James Liddale of Halkerston into England 'with tressonable mandimentis and writingis to the tressonable confederacioune of inglis men contrar to our souuerane lord and his Realme'; this is clearly a reference to Albany's despatching Angus, Gray, and Liddale to England as his commissioners on 12 January 1483, with Liddale alone mentioned in Albany's forfeiture because only Albany and Liddale were forfeited in the summer of 1483. Then follows the charge that Albany had received Bluemantle at Dunbar and admitted an English garrison into the castle. Lastly, he was condemned for his 'tressonable passing in ingland without oure said souuerane lordis licence or leif to the tressonable destruccioun of our said souuerane lordis persoune his Realme and liegis'. This is clearly a reference to Albany's departure from Scotland, probably in April when he learned of Edward IV's death and realised to the full how precarious his position had become. He left Dunbar in the hands of an English garrison, and it was not to be recaptured for James III until the spring of 1486. On 8 July 1483, when Albany and Liddale had failed to appear before parliament, both were declared to have forfeited to the king their lives, lands, goods, offices and all other possessions within the realm of Scotland.[14] William, Lord Crichton, who under the terms of the March indenture had been banished for three years, was not as yet forfeited, but he seems like the others to have fled. In December 1483 he was living in sanctuary in Tain.[15]

The final collapse of Albany brought down others who had benefited by his temporary control of the government. After the duke was forced on to the defensive by James III in January 1483, James Boyd, son of the king's sister Mary who had thrust him illegally into the lordships of Kilmarnock and Dalry, had no recourse but to flee to Dunbar, where he had joined Albany by 21 February.[16] On the afternoon of 16 April the Lords of Council met to consider a complaint made by the queen 'anent the taking fra hir of the lordschip and landis pertening to umquhile Robert, Lord Boid . . . quhilkis war gevin of befor to a richt hie and michti prince, James, Duk of Rothissay . . . and thairefter to our said soverane Lady, for anourment of hir persoun quhil the age of our said Lord the Prince'. The Lords of Council ordained that the queen should immediately be restored to Kilmarnock, and that when Prince James came of age he was to enjoy the lands 'nochtwithstanding the pretendit gift made be our soverane lord to James Boid or ony utheris'.[17] Not surprisingly, the personnel on the Lords of Council who restored the status quo so convincingly were committed royalists, men who — with the exception of Bishop Livingston of Dunkeld — had taken no prominent part in government during the winter of 1482 — Argyll and Avandale, Andrew Painter, bishop of Orkney and keeper of the castle of Kirkwall, and John Ross of Montgrenan, the Lord Advocate. James Boyd's brief restoration had been overturned, and like Sir Alexander Boyd in 1469, he lacked the intelligence to realise that he had no future in Scotland. In 1484, aged only sixteen, he was killed by Hugh Montgomery of Eglinton, who was on the point of succeeding to a lordship of parliament and who may well have hoped that James III would reward him for the elimination of Boyd with a portion of the Kilmarnock or Dalry lands.[18] If he did, he was disappointed; the Boyd lands reverted to the Crown.

The recovery of royal power did not, however, produce an immediate crop of forfeitures of all those who had opposed the king in 1482. The two most obvious survivors of the king's wrath were the Lauder conspirators Archibald, earl of Angus, and Andrew, Lord Gray. Both sat in the parliament of June 1483 which condemned the man to whom both had been prepared to swear allegiance as King of Scotland only five months before. Angus, as we have seen, both gained and lost ground in terms of lands and offices; the Wardenship of the Middle Marches probably went a long way towards compensating him for the loss of the Stewartry of Kirkcudbright. Gray was not penalised at all, appearing once more in parliament in May 1484, by which time yet another of his former allies, William Lord Crichton, had been forfeited. Why did men who had been heavily implicated in the seizure of

James III and in negotiations with England in January and February 1483 fare so well when the king recovered control of the government? There was no question that their treason had remained undiscovered, as the indenture of 19 March had made clear. But the king may have appreciated, or been advised, that he could not indulge in the wholesale punishment of all those who had played a dubious role in the crisis of 1482; after all, he had been faced with a very serious rebellion which had involved, in greater or lesser degree, a fair proportion of the Scottish nobility and clergy — Albany, Angus, Atholl and Buchan, the Bishops of Glasgow, Dunkeld and Moray, Lords Crichton, Gray and Boyd, John Douglas, Master of Morton, and Sir James Liddale of Halkerston. The Bishop of Glasgow had died in January 1483; but it must have been clear to the king that he would require the services of at least some of the others. So he followed a policy of moderation, especially with Angus, at least for the time being.

The passage of five hundred years, and the fragmentary and sometimes contradictory evidence available to us, make any final judgment on the drama of 1482-3 impossible; and the motives of some of the principal actors can only be guessed at. But the behaviour of all of them surely casts a harsh light on the personality of James III, showing him to be a man who not only made enemies, but failed to display any consideration towards his friends. In a private individual, this unpleasant trait might be regarded as a serious flaw of character; in a king, it produced a full-scale confrontation with his subjects which might well have ended in disaster. A single example — the career of Sir Anselm Adornes — illustrates the difficulty of James's friends in serving such a master. Adornes, described by Dr. Nicholson as 'one of the more exotic of the king's familiars',[19] had first come to James's attention in the late '60s as a mediator in trade disputes; then, in the early '70s, he had acted as spokesman for, and protector of, the forfeited Boyds in Bruges, and latterly gained the king's approval by escorting James's sister Mary back to Scotland, where she could be married off to Lord Hamilton.[20] Rewarded with forfeited Boyd lands in Forfar and Perthshire, Adornes was also given the office of Conservator of the Privileges of the Scots in all the domains of the Duke of Burgundy.[21] There is also some evidence to suggest that Adornes and James III had a common interest in the arts. Adornes apparently dedicated his account of his travels in the east in 1470-71 to James III; and in 1472 James wrote to him asking him to have the playing of the lute taught to one John Broune, whom he was sending to Bruges, and to whom he gave a pension of £20.[22]

Thereafter royal favour towards Adornes appears to have come to an end; Adornes' interest in Scotland may have waned, for by 1475 he had become burgomaster of Bruges, and it is probable that his Scottish lands were simply a useful source of revenue to him, a reminder of his intimacy with the king. In the spring of 1476, Adornes resigned his Conservatorship, and James III did not make a regrant of the office at his revocation, conferring it instead on his 'familiar squire' Andrew Wodman.[23] Thereafter Adornes' movements are difficult to trace. He seems to have been infrequently in Scotland before 1476; and no Scottish source reveals his presence there until his death, sometime before 29 January 1483, when his Conservatorship, which he may eventually have had had restored to him, was conferred on the king's 'familiar servant' Thomas Swift.[24] Some time before his death Adornes had destroyed the East Mill of Linlithgow, which no doubt produced the confused story in Flemish sources that he had been made governor of Linlithgow by James III. Quoting the same sources, Dr. Nicholson ingeniously argues that he was killed by Alexander Jardine, a henchman of the forfeited earl of Douglas, one of those specifically exempted from royal forgiveness in March 1482.[25] This is possible; but why was Adornes in Scotland at all? Had his position in the Low Countries become untenable after the death of his master Charles the Bold in 1477? Or was he inspired to throw in his lot with James III in his hour of need in 1482, throwing away his life in a gesture of quixotic chivalry? There is also a third possibility. Adornes may well have resented James's failure to restore to him his Conservatorship in 1476, and responded by falling back on support for his former guests in Bruges and principal Scottish contacts, the Boyds, when James's sister Mary attempted a Boyd restoration in 1482. Adornes' death before the king's recovery of power leaves the issue in some doubt; but his career provides an excellent example of a royal familiar whose loyalty the king may have failed to retain. James III was certainly quick enough to transfer Adornes' office to two other familiars, in 1476 and 1483 respectively; and while there may be nothing sinister in this, the rapid changes display an arbitrary wilfulness which must have worried James's friends as much as his potential enemies.

However, at least two of James III's new appointments were above criticism, being conferred on men who could not be classed as familiars, both being drawn from the ranks of the 'natural' counsellors of the king, the greater nobility. On 28 August 1483, when death removed the Chancellor, Bishop Livingston, a man who had apparently been acceptable to all the parties throughout the crisis, King James was quick to confer the office on the Earl of Argyll, who had been appointed Chancellor by 6 September.[26] As a prominent royalist in the '70s, a royal lieutenant in 1476, a drudge on the Lords of Council and a former Master of the Household, Argyll was in many ways an obvious choice; but his appointment involved passing over the man who had been Chancellor for twenty-two years, Andrew Stewart Lord Avandale. Avandale had not been disloyal at the time of Lauder or afterwards; but it is possible that James was afraid of losing Argyll's support if he reappointed Avandale; and he may have regarded his thrusting into prominence of Avandale in 1471, at the expense of Darnley and contrary to earlier acts of parliament, as a rash measure which could now partly be redeemed by bestowing the Chancellorship on someone else.

The offices of Chamberlain — taken from Buchan — and Master of the Royal Household were now bestowed on a single individual, David Lindsay, earl of Crawford. Although he had taken some part in the government during Albany's ascendancy, and had indeed taken over the office of Master of the Household in October 1482,[27] Crawford's loyalty to the king was beyond question; and by heaping honours on the earl, James III made an exception to his general rule of failing to reward service. Indeed, his advancement of Crawford and Argyll throughout the '70s, and then subsequently in the '80s, is one of the most striking features of the reign, and is very much at odds with the later statements that James consistently advanced lesser men as part of a deliberate policy of curbing the power of the greater nobility. But Crawford and Argyll were exceptions within their class, men who were prepared to involve themselves regularly in the routine and often boring business of government in order to achieve advancement.

Very different in background and character was Scheves' successor as intimate familiar of the king, John Ramsay. His career is unusual in that the first chronological references to him occur in the accounts of the sixteenth century chroniclers; and all are unanimous in introducing him as a survivor of Lauder Bridge. Lesley states that he was an eighteen-year-old favourite of the king, and that when the rebel nobles attempted to seize him, he clung so tightly to James III for protection that he could not be removed without injuring the king.[28] Buchanan, who of course justifies the actions of the Lauder nobles in every respect, makes them appear very reasonable: 'the king only entreated that they would spare one young man, of honourable birth, John Ramsay, who clung to him, and his tender age furnishing his excuse, they readily complied'.[29] Apart from the detail that Ramsay was of honourable birth (which cannot be proved or disproved), this is the same story as that related by Lesley and Ferreri. Finally, there is the account of the notoriously inaccurate Pitscottie, who states that 'ane young man callit Schir Johnne Ramsay, was saiffit be the kingis request who for refuge lape on the horse behind the king for to saif his lyf. This Schir Johnne Ramsay was laird of Balmain and efterwart thesaurar of Scottland'.[30] Pitscottie is wrong in suggesting that Ramsay was a knight; he never occupied the office of Treasurer; and he was not described as laird of Balmain until 1510.[31]

What is significant, however, is that all four sixteenth century writers, with their very different backgrounds and accounts of the reign, tell virtually the same story by way of introducing Ramsay's career; namely, that the rebellious nobles at Lauder wished to put to death, among others, this insignificant young man, that he clung to the king for protection and thus saved his life. It is probable, therefore, that something of the kind happened; and if the Treasurer's Accounts had survived for the period, it is likely that Ramsay's name would figure in them before Lauder as a minor servant or groom in the royal household.

Surviving Lauder, Ramsay soon began to acquire rewards from the king. On 6 September 1483, James III, describing Ramsay as his familiar squire of his chamber, granted him all the lands and annual rents which had been held by the deceased Alexander Kennedy of Irwell, and which had come into the hands of the Crown by reason of Kennedy's bastardy.[32] Then, in parliament on 24 February 1484, the king bestowed the barony of Bothwell on Ramsay, together with forty marks' worth of land within the barony which had been occupied by William, first Lord Monypenny, before the general revocation. With the gift of Bothwell went the fishings and right of presentation to the collegiate church, its prebends and chapels.[33] The earliest reference in the records to Ramsay as 'Lord Bothwell' is in the sederunt list of the parliament of May 1485; so his creation as lord of parliament must have taken place on some date between July 1484 and the following May. On 20 July 1484, at Edinburgh, James III granted to Ramsay — described as 'oure lovit familiare squyar' — and his wife Isabel Cant, a nineteen years' lease of half the lands of the two Kinkells in the royal lordship of Strathearn.[34] Finally, in 1487, the farms of Caddon Lee in Selkirkshire, formerly taken up by the late queen, were assigned to Ramsay and one Patrick Crichton in steelbow.[35]

Together with grants of lands and a lordship of parliament went promotion to offices in the royal household and government. Ramsay acted as an auditor of exchequer from 1484 to 1487; in November 1486 he occupied the post of Master of the Household for a brief period; and in 1486 he acted as a commissioner for letting Crown lands in Ettrick and Menteith.[36] In June 1486, about six months after the capture of Dunbar castle from the English garrison which had occupied it since the flight of Albany in 1483, the custody of the castle was committed to John Ramsay, Lord Bothwell.[37]

Ramsay's brief career under James III, therefore, was one of steady advancement, as a result of royal favour, from September 1483 until James's death in June 1488. As Lord Bothwell he sat in the parliaments of May 1485 and January 1488.[38] On 24 July 1484 he witnessed a royal charter for the first time, and though it was not for more than two years that he acted in this capacity again, his absence may be explained largely by his participation in Scottish embassies to England in October 1485 and June 1486.[39] From early in 1487 to the end of the reign, however, Ramsay was a very frequent charter witness; and on 21 January 1488, together with Lord Lyle, he is described in a witness list as a royal justiciar.[40] This was a remarkable rise to prominence, for Ramsay was only twenty-four in 1488. But it was as one of James's most trusted ambassadors to England that the new Lord Bothwell spent much of his time in the '80s. On 30 October 1485, with English safe-conducts dating from 22 September, Ramsay, together with Bishops Elphinstone, Blacader, Browne, and the Abbot of Holyrood, represented James III at Henry VII's coronation at Westminster.[41] In May 1486, as Lord Bothwell, Ramsay, together with Elphinstone and Ross of Montgrenan, went on embassy to England to conclude a truce with Henry VII of England, and they were received by King Henry at Westminster on 5 June.[42] In November 1487, John Ramsay, Lord Bothwell, and Bishop Elphinstone were the two Scottish commissioners who negotiated with their English counterparts Richard Fox, bishop of Exeter, and Sir Richard Edgecombe, with a view to achieving an Anglo-Scottish peace treaty; and on 27 April 1488, Ramsay was at Windsor with Henry VII, again on embassy from James III.[43]

Sixteenth century writers tend to ignore Ramsay's career after his escape at Lauder, but two of them — Ferreri and Buchanan — mention him again. The former, after remarking that Ramsay was frequently used by King James in negotiations for peace with Edward IV, and that the king made him Earl of Bothwell — both of which statements, though incorrect, have a foundation of truth — goes on to say that Ramsay was the only man allowed to bear arms in the royal residence, all others being prohibited from doing so by edict, and that he commanded the new royal bodyguard.[44] Buchanan's story is similar; Ramsay, 'not satisfied with his fortune, obtained an order, that no-one except himself and his companions should carry arms in those places where the king lodged; that by this means he might protect himself and his faction against the nobility, who had frequent meetings among themselves, and paraded in armour'.[45] It may be that James III had once more created a royal bodyguard comparable with that known to exist in 1473-4, and that it comprised Ramsay and his adherents. Alternatively, as the safety of the king was one of the responsibilities of the Master of the Household, and as Ramsay held that post for a short time, allusions by Ferreri and Buchanan to an armed gang led by Ramsay being in constant attendance on the king may be no more than distorted references to his normal household duties. His youth, however, undoubtedly caused resentment amongst members of the nobility, including those who were normally to be found at court; and anger at his rapid elevation is reflected in the rebel propaganda sent to Denmark in 1488, about two years after Queen Margaret's death, claiming that the queen had been poisoned by Ramsay at the instigation of the king.[46] This tale, though obviously untrue, suggests that Ramsay was one of James III's closest and most influential friends, the obvious target of abuse which could not be levelled directly at the king. Ramsay is, in fact, the only example during the reign of the court favourite against whose type some contemporary, and a great deal of later, criticism was levelled, and whose existence and activities are clearly set out in official records. Scheves, Avandale and Ireland, who in a sense fall into the same category, were all mature men. Ramsay alone justifies the strictures which the anonymous author of the contemporary *Thre Prestis of Peblis* levelled at James III: the king, he said, 'luifit ouer weil yong counsel'.[47]

The beginning of the '80s also saw the king anxious to promote a more worthy individual — John Ireland, a Doctor of Theology of the University of Paris since 1476, ambassador for Louis XI to his native Scotland in 1479 and 1480, where he made such an impact on James III that he was sitting with the Lords of Council by 15 July of the latter year.[48] He appears thereafter to have returned to Paris, where he remained during the critical years 1480-83. But Louis XI's failing health probably made Ireland realise that he would have to look to his native land for a secure future, and it is significant that his *Tractatus de Immaculata Conceptione Virginis Mariae*, which was probably composed in the winter of 1480-81, was addressed to two royal patrons — Louis XI and James III.[49] Probably at the same time, and according to Ireland himself at James III's request, he wrote the treatise *De Speciali Auxilio*; and he also sent two Latin hymns from Paris to the Scottish king.[50]

Ireland's judicial and literary activity during these years suggests that James III was keenly interested in employing him in Scotland. Louis XI died on 30 August 1483; and less than three months later, Ireland was already in King James's service. The king's first aim was to find his new counsellor a remunerative ecclesiastical appointment; and as early as 29 November 1483 Ireland's name appears on a list of Scottish ambassadors to England under the designation of Archdeacon of St. Andrews.[51] But his appointment to that office was conditional on the promotion of the incumbent, Alexander Inglis, for whom the king hoped to secure the bishopric of Dunkeld. But the royal candidate was rejected and Sixtus IV nominated George Browne to Dunkeld;[52] although James III intended to contest this decision, some alternative appointment had meantime to be found for Ireland. Eventually, after the death of Alexander Murray, director of the royal chancery, sometime between 20

June 1485 and 1 March 1486,[53] Ireland took his place as rector of Ettrick and canon of Moray; and he may also have succeeded Murray as rector of Hawick.[54] Already on 28 December 1483, Ireland is described in a supplication to the pope as provost of the collegiate church of Crichton.[55] The supplication, which is a request for a dispensation to hold other benefices besides Crichton, also describes Ireland as 'Regis Scotorum consiliarius' — quick work for a man who had only been in the country for under four months.

The provostship of Crichton, a benefice with an annual value of £233, was a preliminary gift to Ireland by the king. The patron of Crichton collegiate church was William, Lord Crichton, who had been deeply implicated in Albany's treasons of 1482-3 and who was to be forfeited in the parliament of February 1484. Summonses had gone out to Crichton to appear in parliament to answer charges of treason in December 1483,[56] the same month as Ireland is described in the supplication as provost of Crichton; so it would appear either that the king had speedily annexed his rebellious subject's lands and offices without waiting for the parliamentary forfeiture, or else he was anticipating the event and allowing Ireland to describe himself as provost of Crichton before he was in possession of the office.

The promotion of Ireland by the king was clearly resented by the ecclesiastical favourite whose fortunes were visibly declining, William Scheves. On 9 March 1484, James III, in a supplication to the pope on Ireland's behalf, not only describes him as 'clerk, St. Andrews diocese, professor of theology', royal counsellor and ambassador, but includes the valuable information that Ireland aspires to the archdeaconry of St. Andrews, which it is hoped will fall vacant when Alexander Inglis is promoted to the bishopric of Dunkeld. This is the king's will, but not that of the Archbishop of St. Andrews, who against King James's wishes is attempting to assign the archdeaconry to another candidate allied to himself. The king therefore supplicated that Ireland might be exempted from Scheves' jurisdiction, and that he and his benefices might be taken under the protection of the Apostolic See. The bulls of exemption were duly obtained on 10 May 1484.[57]

There are a number of possible explanations of Scheves' intense dislike of Ireland, an antipathy which he was to carry on into the next reign. One suggestion is that, as Scheves had been a contemporary of Ireland's at St. Andrews, he would have been teaching there in 1459 when Ireland had a dispute with the university authorities and left without a degree.[58] The careers of the two men, however, cannot definitely be linked at this early date. Alternatively, Durkan suggests that if Scheves may be regarded as one of the precursors of humanism in Scotland, he may well have been out of sympathy with Ireland, whose intellectual interests would appear to have been traditional and scholastic.[59] However, it is probably the case that Scheves' resentment of Ireland was very largely the result of the latter's intimacy with James III. As a former recipient of the royal favour, Scheves probably found the king cooling towards him after his weak and ineffective role in the crisis of 1482-3. He may even have seen in Ireland's rapid rise a dangerous parallel to his own career during the '70s. Scheves had been provost of Crichton; now Ireland was provost of Crichton. Scheves had acquired the archdeaconry of St. Andrews through royal influence; now Ireland seemed about to take the same step. Even more ominous,

Scheves had acquired his archbishopric through the deposition of his predecessor Patrick Graham, and his intimacy with the king had been largely responsible for his promotion. Early in 1484 Scheves may well have asked himself whether Ireland, as the new candidate for royal favours in the ecclesiastical sphere, might not eventually replace him as archbishop as he himself had replaced Graham. Hence perhaps his open antagonism to Ireland, and his petulance in opposing the king's wishes; both suggest the resentment of the discarded favourite.

In the event, however, Ireland was not to obtain the archdeaconry of St. Andrews, because his promotion to the office depended on the king's securing the bishopric of Dunkeld for Alexander Inglis, and by the summer of 1485 James had dropped Inglis' candidature. Yet there can be no doubt as to Ireland's influence with the king. James IV was to describe him, in a letter to the pope in 1490, as 'one whom our father held dear, a Parisian professor of divinity . . . his ambassador to kings and princes abroad, and his counsellor at home — most admirable as his confessor'.[60] Ireland himself made much of his intimacy with James III. Addressing his son in the introduction to *The Meroure of Wyssdome* in 1490, he speaks warmly of 'thy fader of gud mynd, that j was orature and confessoure to and tendirlie lefit with'.[61] Ferreri, in fact, names Ireland as one of the royal favourites.[62] The records, although not so effusive, do indicate that he had an important place in court and government. He was present in the parliaments of February and May 1484, and his name appears in the sederunt lists of the Lords of Council in January, February and April 1485.[63] Ireland's claim that he acted as diplomatic agent for James III 'anens the kingis of fraunce, inglande and uthir princes'[64] is borne out to some extent by official records showing him as a member of the Scottish embassy sent to Paris in 1484 to renew the Franco-Scottish alliance with the new French king, Charles VIII; and he received safe-conducts in November 1483 and April 1485 to travel to England to discuss a truce and the maintenance of peace on the borders.[65] The latter safe-conduct may not have been used; for a month later, in the parliament of May 1485, it was proposed to send a delegation to Rome headed by Archbishop Scheves, and Ireland was to be a member.[66] Ireland did not, however, accompany the mission to Rome, probably because of his enmity with Scheves; for it was hardly to be expected that the latter would exert himself at the Roman curia to acquire for Ireland the archdeaconry of St. Andrews.

The remainder of Ireland's career under James III, as Burns points out,[67] is obscure. The records of the Lords of Council are lacking after 1485, and all that is known of Ireland is that he was at court on 19 April 1486.[68] He may have gone to France, where on 1 March 1488 the records of the University of Paris refer to him as having resigned his chaplaincy, a post which he had held for over twenty years.[69] This would suggest that he intended in future to confine his career to Scotland; and if Abell is to be believed, Ireland's last service to James III occurred little more than three months later, when he heard the king's confession before the fatal battle of Sauchieburn.[70] His patronage by the king in the last years of the reign provides the only striking example of James III as a devotee of the arts.

The '80s also saw the rise to prominence of another ecclesiastic who was to become even more influential under James III's successor — William Elphinstone. His career in the royal service had, it is true, begun long before James reasserted himself in 1483. As early as June 1478, Elphinstone sat in parliament as official of Lothian; and he was an almost constant member of the Lords of Council from the beginning of their records on 5 October 1478. On 4 December 1478 and 11 February 1480, he witnessed royal charters as Archdeacon of Lismore and official of Lothian.[71] In August 1481 he was promoted to the bishopric of Ross; and on 26 November of the same year is described as elect and confirmed of Ross.[72] Elphinstone sat in parliament before, during and after the crisis of 1482-3. In March 1482 he is described as 'elect confirmed of Ross'; in December 1482, as elect and confirmed once again; finally, and perhaps significantly, as 'bishop of Ross' in the parliaments of March and June 1483, after the king had regained power.[73] In the parliament of May 1484, however, Elphinstone is once more described as 'electus confirmatus Rossensis'.[74] On 27 July 1484, he is styled — for the first time — bishop of Aberdeen, to which see he had been translated more than a year before, on 19 March 1483.[75] Elphinstone was never consecrated as bishop of Ross; and in spite of royal influence securing him a better see, he was to wait four years before his consecration as bishop of Aberdeen.

Boece's highly colourful *Lives of the Bishops of Mortlach and Aberdeen*, which appeared in 1522, is largely a eulogy of Elphinstone; and the author regards the bishop as the most important influence on the king during the latter years of the reign. 'He was admitted,' says Boece, 'a member of the king's privy council. So much had he gained the king's confidence, that all his majesty's most important affairs were carried out under the bishop's direction and as he suggested.'[76] This is one of the more moderate exaggerations of Boece's work; but it is true that Elphinstone had an important place in the royal government, and like Thomas Spens, bishop of Aberdeen during the previous decade, he served the king frequently as an ambassador. During 1483 and 1484, Elphinstone received four safe-conducts to travel to England with a view to negotiating peace with Richard III — in November 1483, and March, April and August 1484; and he made use of the last of these to conclude an Anglo-Scottish truce at Nottingham in September 1484.[77] A year later, he was present at Henry VII's coronation as a representative of James III; and he was first among the Scottish commissioners who went to Westminster in June 1486 to conclude a truce with the English king. Finally, Elphinstone and John Ramsay, Lord Bothwell, were the Scottish commissioners who negotiated the English treaty of November 1487.[78]

In the field of domestic affairs, Elphinstone, apart from his regular work on the Lords of Council, sat as an auditor of exchequer in 1485, 1486 and 1487. This was a task which he had first undertaken in 1479 while still Archdeacon of Lismore and official of Lothian, sitting again in 1480 and 1481.[79] From 22 January 1483,[80] when James III was beginning to recover power, and for the remainder of the reign, Elphinstone is to be found as a regular witness to royal charters whenever he is not absent from the country on embassies. His is a remarkable career; at the age of over fifty, when it might have been expected that he would end his life as Spens had done, a trusted and efficient royal servant, he was suddenly precipitated into the Chancellorship and, eventually, into a long career as one of the principal counsellors of James IV.

By 1484, therefore, the king had replaced the familiars of the '70s — Scheves and Avandale — with Ireland and Ramsay, and had found a new pro-English ecclesiastical statesman in Elphinstone. At about the same time, he secured the forfeiture of another of Albany's principal supporters, William, Lord Crichton. Crichton had escaped the forfeiture of Albany and Liddale in June 1483, but had prudently retired to sanctuary at Tain, where at the market cross on 23 December 1483 he was summoned to appear in parliament the following February to answer charges of treason. These charges were identical with those for which Albany and Liddale had been forfeited, with two additions: Crichton was accused of 'stuffing' his castle of Crichton with men and provisions with a view to holding it against the king; and by means of a chaplain named Thomas Dicsoune, he had corresponded with Albany in England after the latter's forfeiture — that is, since July 1483.[81]

These charges alone were more than sufficient to condemn Crichton; but in addition, it is probable that the king had strong personal reasons for disliking him intensely. It must have been about this time that Crichton and James's younger sister Margaret had a child, a daughter first mentioned in the Treasurer's account for 1495-6 and described simply as 'Lady Margaretis dochtir'.[82] She was married about 1506 to William Todrik, a merchant and burgess of Edinburgh, and ultimately died some time before 1546 as Countess of Rothes.[83] The fact that Margaret's daughter is unnamed in the 1495-6 account, and that she was married to an Edinburgh merchant, suggests that she was illegitimate; and it is significant that, whereas Margaret's proposed marriage, in England and (possibly) France, had been one of the major items of Scottish foreign policy in the late 1470s, after 1483 she was never put forward as a potential bride in spite of many English marriage alliances proposed by her brother. So a liaison between Crichton and Margaret during or after the 1482-3 crisis, and an illegitimate child as a result, seems the most likely explanation.[84]

The only sixteenth century chronicler to comment on the affair is George Buchanan, who tells a scurrilous story about the animosity between James III and Crichton, part of which has the truth as its foundation. He claims that the king had seduced Crichton's wife — whom he names as Janet Dunbar — and that in retaliation Crichton formed a liaison with James's younger sister Margaret, by whom he had a daughter Margaret Crichton, 'who died not long ago'.[85] There is no corroborative evidence for the royal seduction of Crichton's wife; and Buchanan names her wrongly as Janet Dunbar. Crichton's mother, not his wife, was a Dunbar; his wife, whom he married before 1478, was Marion Livingston, daughter of James, Lord Livingston.[86] In his tale, Buchanan states that Crichton's wife died at his castle about the time of her husband's infidelity, that is about 1483; but as he thinks that she was Janet Dunbar, and no evidence exists for Marion Livingston's being dead by this time, his account is most unconvincing. Janet Dunbar died between 1494 and 1505.[87] Presumably Buchanan was drawing on the same, or a similar, source as that available to Lesley, who explained King James's unpopularity with his nobility as being caused by his consorting with a whore named Daisy.[88] In both cases the king's supposed lechery — or at least infidelity — provokes a fitting response, and provides both Lesley and Buchanan with a suitable moral tale.

Crichton was forfeited in parliament on 24 February 1484; and at the same time other minor supporters of Albany suffered the same fate. John Liddale, eldest son of Sir James Liddale of Halkerston, and David Purves were forfeited for assistance given to Albany at Dunbar the previous year; and Gavin and George Crichton, Lord Crichton's younger brothers, James Cockburn, and thirty-five adherents were similarly condemned for garrisoning Crichton castle against the king.[89] The subsequent career of William, Lord Crichton, is obscure, and he may have left the country. Buchanan states that he was partially reconciled to James III on his promising to marry Princess Margaret, and that he had a conference with the king at Inverness some time after 1485.[90] There is no record evidence for such a conference, however, and on the face of it it seems highly unlikely. In any event, Crichton died some time before 23 October 1493, when he is described as 'umquhile William, sumtyme Lord Creichton'.[91]

Crichton and his adherents were not however the last to suffer for their support of Albany during and after the 1482-3 crisis. As late as 26 May 1485, parliament passed sentence of forfeiture on James Gifford of Sheriffhall, whose treasons included assistance given to 'Alexander, formerly Duke of Albany' in 1483, by receiving an English pursuivant, Bluemantle, at Dunbar, and by admitting an English garrison into Dunbar castle; and finally, by taking up arms against the king with Albany, the English, and other Scottish traitors 'in die sancte marie magdalene' — a reference to Albany's attempted comeback in the south-west and the skirmish at Lochmaben on 22 July 1484. Gifford did not appear, and was sentenced to lose life, lands, goods and possessions, all of which were forfeit to the Crown.[92]

By the end of May 1485, therefore, all those who had taken Albany's part in 1482-3 were dead, forfeited, or banished, with two notable exceptions — Archibald, earl of Angus, and Andrew, Lord Gray. The continuing forfeitures, almost two years after the end of the crisis, must have alarmed them greatly; for at any time the king might turn against them both. There was even an act of February 1484 which, after stating that Albany's rebellion had been crushed and those guilty of treason brought to justice, went on to order enquiries to be made throughout the country 'to have knaulage quhat personis giffis assistance or favoris to the said tressoun and to mak thame be punyst with sic Rigor according to Justice in exemple of all utheris in tym tocum to commytt sa odious crime and offence aganis his maieste'.[93] This act, passed at the same time as a host of forfeitures gave a practical demonstration of what it implied, could be very widely interpreted by James III to bring within its scope not only the two survivors of the Lauder rebels, but anyone who had not actively assisted the king during the crisis. Thus fear of what the king might do may well have been fairly general; and Angus, who was present in parliament when the act was passed, must have wondered how long his power in the south-east would protect him from the royal displeasure.

He was right to be concerned. On 24 January 1485 the king appeared as pursuer in a case before the Lords of Council; Angus was accused of wrongfully assigning the lands of Balmuir in Forfarshire to Thomas Fotheringham of Powrie. James III claimed that the lands had belonged to the Crown since the forfeiture of Sir James Liddale of Halkerston in 1483; and the Lords of Council decreed that 'Archbalde erle of Angus has done wrang in the disponing of the said landis of balmure to the said thomas and decernis the Infeftmentis maid be him thirapoune of nane avale becaus thir was no thing schewin for the part of the said Archbalde that he is infeft with fee and forfatur'. A week later, on 31 January, Fotheringham of Powrie appeared before the Lords of Council charged with 'the wrangwis occupacioun manuring and intromettin with the landis of balmure' (assigned to him by Angus) and the uptaking of the mails and farms for the previous three terms. In cash, the sum involved was trivial — a mere £26; but the Lords of Council duly found in favour of the king, decreeing that the mails and profits of Balmuir belonged to the Crown 'sene the forfatur of Sir James of liddale and in tyme tocum ay and quhil the said landis be lauchfully recouerit fra his hienes'.[94]

These two cases are surely indicative of the king's continuing hostility towards the Earl of Angus. Sir James Liddale had held Balmuir of Angus. In law, when Liddale was forfeited, the lands reverted to the king unless Angus was enfeoffed by the Crown with the right to forfeitures of his vassals; this was something which he had to prove, and the lands were held by the Crown until he did, hence the reference in the second case 'quhil the said landis be lauchfully recouerit fra his hienes'. This aggressive assertion of royal rights, which James could easily have overlooked, is not paralleled in the records of the Lords of Council by similar cases involving any other important landowners. The king may well have been stung into action because Angus had ignored his right to the lands of Balmuir after Liddale's forfeiture; or he may merely have been looking for an opportunity to catch the earl out on legal technicalities. The fact that he took the trouble to bring both cases against Angus suggests that he was attempting to make an issue out of a triviality.

As early as February 1484, parliament expressed the pious hope that private enmities which had arisen out of the recent crisis might be ended. Concern was expressed over 'the devisioun debaitis and discordis that standis ymangis our souuerane lordis liegis barons and utheris'. Continuing feuds constituted danger to the kingdom, as it was then unprepared for attacks by 'oure Souuerane lordis Inymyis of ingland'. Therefore 'it is thocht expedient be the said lordis and counsalis oure souuerane lordis hienes to mak be callit before him and his consale the grete lordis and put thaim in friendschip and concord or thai depart fra his presens'.[95] It is noteworthy that this statute is the work of the council rather than the king. It represents a well-meaning but naive attempt on the part of the civil servants who did much of its work — men like Elphinstone, Whitelaw, Ross of Montgrenan, and Richard Lawson — to reconcile factious magnates by having them swear friendship in the king's presence; it strikingly anticipates similar efforts to achieve conciliation during the civil war in April 1488; and it contrasts strongly with James III's personal policy of gradual removal through forfeiture of all those who had actively supported Albany in 1482-3, and, on a smaller scale, his victimisation of Angus in the law courts early in 1485.

For the king was the problem, to his friends as well as to those who feared that he regarded them as potential enemies. The dramatic challenge to his authority in 1482 seems to have produced in James III a determination to ensure that such an event could never occur again. Hence probably his rapid reversion to a policy of peace and alliance with England as soon as it could be obtained. This made good sense, as it was essentially the breakdown of the English alliance in 1480 which had made possible the traumatic events of the autumn and winter of 1482. But the lessons which the king might have learned from these events — that he should conciliate as well as punish, that he should see to the proper administration of criminal justice, that he must reward his friends — seem to have been totally· ignored; and the internal policies of the '80s bear a striking resemblance to those of the '70s.

Thus we find royal concern, expressed in an act of February 1484, that some of the royal mails, rents and farms 'ar haldin fra his hienes', and it is thought expedient that the Master of the Household and Comptroller should conduct an immediate enquiry and bring defaulting officials before the Lords of Council.[96] It is unfortunate that the records of the Lords of Council do not go beyond 15 April 1485; fragmentary as they are, however, they provide ample testimony of James's efforts to secure obedience and to assert his rights in the localities. In August 1484 James wrote to Sir William Ruthven of that ilk, sheriff of Perth, indicating his displeasure: 'we marvel of the non execucion of our divers and mone lettres diretyt to you anent the prior and convent of the charterhous for the payment of thaim of certain duwetais, fermes and maills of the landis lyeing in Athole'. Ruthven was ordered to pay up or enter his person in ward at Dumbarton.[97]

However, it was James's selling of royal justice in criminal cases which provoked the most consistent opposition amongst the estates. In the same February parliament of 1484 it was stated that the king was determined to give no further remissions or respites, for a period of three years, to persons guilty of treason, slaughter, premeditated felony, or common theft. This act must represent pressure on James III by parliament, for he had no reason of his own volition to abolish a profitable source of royal revenue. In any event, the act appears to have remained a dead letter, for it was repeated in the parliament of May 1485.[98]

Even thereafter the king appears to have ignored his promises to the estates about withholding remissions. Boece relates a story, which may be dated 1485-7, in which James III, together with Elphinstone and the papal legate, James Pasarella, bishop of Imola, went on a short pilgrimage to Lestauream (presumably Restalrig, the king's new collegiate church). On the way, the royal party met a nobleman, who had been condemned for murder, going to execution. The condemned man appealed for mercy to the king on the ground that he was guilty of manslaughter rather than murder. 'Then the king, being naturally ready to pardon, turned to the legate, who, as it appeared, he wished should have the credit of suggesting pardon for the criminal, and said: 'What do you advise?'. The legate replied: 'Let justice be carried out'. Then the king, addressing William (Elphinstone), whose countenance he observed had fallen at the legate's remark, and who was far from approving the answer given, said: 'Is this the compassion of Italian churchmen? You used to give me far different advice'. And protesting against the legate's ruthless sentence, mindful, too, of the clemency which befits kings, he said: 'Let mercy prevail'. So he discharges the criminal. By this decision he showed both that kings should be merciful and that it was wicked to advise them not to be so'.[99]

Boece, writing in the 1520s, regards the royal pardon in this case not as an example of James III's weakness (a view adopted by at least one modern writer[100]), but as a proper instance of royal clemency. Yet he has probably made a virtue out of one of the king's undoubted vices by omitting the vital factor of payment for royal forgiveness. His sources must have been oral tales of the king's granting of remissions even for murder, tales which he could use to illustrate the wisdom and mercy of the sovereign when properly advised by the subject of his biography, the good Bishop Elphinstone. Contemporaries may perhaps be forgiven if they did not view James's venality in quite the same light; to them, the selling of royal pardons for serious crimes interfered with the proper execution of criminal justice and undermined respect for the law in the localities. James III was not of course the first king to make money through granting of remissions, nor would he be the last. The anonymous poet of the early 1460s who complained in *The Harp* that the king, having ordained 'strate justice na man to spair', nevertheless changed his mind in a remarkably short time, so that 'al the warld murmuris that thou are bocht', must have been referring to James II; and indeed the parliament of March 1458 had sought in vain to curb that king's enthusiasm for remissions.[101] Throughout the reign of James IV, considerable sums were to be made for the Crown through royal acceptance of compositions for varied crimes, only arson, rape and treason against the king's person being excluded.[102] But both these rulers, and especially James IV, went out on justice ayres in person, so that 'strate justice' was directly associated with the king; James III, sitting in Edinburgh remote from areas where royal authority and law and order were difficult to maintain, was understandably more roundly and consistently condemned for making cash through the selling of remissions.

In the '80s, complaints about royal venality and its consequences reached a climax in the parliament of October 1487. James III promised that for the next seven years he would give no pardons for criminal actions, 'that is to say for tresoun murther birning revissing of wemen violent reif slauchter of forthochtfellony commoun thift and resset of commoun thift and fals cuinyeing' — a fairly comprehensive list of crimes. Such royal action was necessary, according to the statute, because the realm was 'greitlie brokin ... throw tresoun slauchter reif birning thift and oppin heirschip throw default of scharp execucion of justice and ouer commoun granting of grace and remissiounis to trespassouris'.[103] We have no means of knowing if the king intended to observe this act, couched as it was in stronger language, and embracing more crimes, than those of 1484 and 1485; for he had less than a year to live. After James's death, however, the new government indicted his favourite, John Ramsay, for assisting him in the oppression of his prelates, barons, burgesses and lieges by the common selling and buying of justice.[104] While such a complaint may be regarded partly as propaganda to justify rebellion and the coming to power of successful rebels following James III's death, and though it is couched in conventional language which prudently shifts the blame from the king to an evil counsellor, it undoubtedly contains an element of truth.

However, if James III may rightly be criticised for indolence and irresponsibility in the administration of criminal justice, the royal attitude to civil justice comes into an altogether different category. A generation ago, the late Professor Dickinson argued that king and council were very much concerned with the extension of royal justice, to the extent indeed that they were causing offence by encroaching on feudal jurisdictions.[105] In support of this view, Dickinson cited statutes of 1469, 1471 and 1487, all of them concerned with the subject's right of appeal in civil cases beyond the court of his judge ordinary to the king and council. Thus at the outset of James III's active rule, in November 1469, an act provided not only for complaints to be laid against an erring or corrupt local judge, but the judge himself could be summoned to answer for his actions before the council. In May 1471 a further act provided for direct appeal to king and council against an ignorant or malicious local jury.[106] In October 1487, however, there was a retreat from this position. Litigants in civil actions were instructed that they must first take their cases before their judges ordinary, so that the king's council would be burdened only with royal actions, and with complaints made by kirkmen, widows, orphans and strangers; however, it was still conceded that complaint could be made direct to the king and council in any case in which 'it beis fundin that the officiaris has procedit wrangwisly or unordourly'.[107]

The advantage of the procedures suggested in the statutes of 1469 and 1471, as Dickinson shows, was speed, a method whereby the litigant could avoid the long process of falsing the doom of the ordinary courts. Instead, he had direct access to the king's own council without waiting for a formal sitting of the high court of parliament to give its 'doom law'. Yet the parliament of 1487 attempted to reverse the process, or at least to restrict the number of cases coming before the king's council. Such action requires explanation. It may be that the Lords of Council, increasingly overburdened with appeal cases, requested that some form of restriction be placed on civil complaints to prevent the council becoming as slow in hearing cases as the ordinary courts. Pressure may also have been brought to bear on the king by politically active members of his nobility — Chancellor Argyll, Crawford, the Chamberlain, or William Lord Borthwick, Master of the Royal Household — to desist from encroaching on the rights of the ordinary courts. As magnates with an interest in, and a duty to exercise, the law in their own localities, they may well have had mixed feelings about the king's enthusiasm to attract cases to his own court.

So much is theory, unsupported by adequate evidence. Records of the Lords of Council for this reign cover seven years, from 1478 to 1485, but over this period there are few instances of cases being referred from local courts to the king and council, or of iniquitous judges ordinary being summoned to Edinburgh for their misdeeds. There is no evidence at all of any of the nobility being cited to appear before the council for miscarriages of justice in the localities. However, there are examples of the Lords of Council taking action in cases which appear to be quite trivial. On 9 November 1479, the alderman and bailies of Dundee who had held office in 1478 were cited to appear for withholding £5 from one David Scrymegeour and for disobeying royal letters ordering them to appear before the Lords of Council. All of them were to enter their persons in ward at Blackness castle and to remain there at their own expense until freed by the king. Scrymegeour was to be paid thirty shillings costs, and the aldermen and bailies holding office in 1479 were held responsible for paying the earlier debt of £5.[108] This is a clear example of a subject in a civil action appealing to the king and council on being denied justice in a local court; and there are a few others. None of them involves anyone of political importance; but it may well be the case that after 1485, when the records are lacking, the king had recovered sufficient power and confidence to encroach more and more on local jurisdictions. This would explain the parliamentary complaint of October 1487, and the effort to restrict the numbers and types of appeal cases coming before the Lords of Council.

In little over three months, on 29 January 1488, James III showed that he intended to reverse the October legislation regarding appeals. On the final day of the January parliament, an act was passed by the king, 'with avise of his estatis', commenting that, because of the recent legislation, many litigants would find that justice would be deferred or postponed indefinitely if they had to refer cases first to their judges ordinary; therefore the king ordered that 'It sall be lefull to all partijs in tym tocum to raiss and persew summondis before oure souerane lord and his consale like as thai were wont in tymes bigane nochtwithstanding the said statute'.[109] This was nothing less than a total reversal of very recent legislation in order to restore the subject's right of appeal to king and council as it had been established in 1469; and it must have been carried through only in the face of extensive opposition, especially from the second estate, some of whom served as Lords of Council. Dickinson is probably over-simplifying when he suggests that 'the struggle which ended at Sauchieburn was partly one of an old order striving to maintain itself against an order that was new — a struggle . . . of feudal lords striving to preserve their feudal jurisdictions against new encroachments by the 'chosen council' of the king'.[110] The problem was more complex, for the 'chosen council' included feudal lords, three of whom — Argyll, Drummond and Oliphant — found their only solution in immediate rebellion against a master whose arbitrary behaviour and exalted view of kingship were becoming unacceptable to many.

NOTES

1. *A.P.S.*, ii, 145.

2. Myln, *Vitae*, 26.

3. S.R.O. State Papers No. 19; printed in *A.P.S.*, xii, 31-3. On the same day (19 March 1483), the records of the Lords of Council begin after a gap of about two-and-a-half years, and the personnel include Scheves, Elphinstone, Argyll, Crawford, Erroll, Avandale, Glamis, Alexander Inglis, archdeacon of St. Andrews, and John Ross of Montgrenan — all firm supporters of the king: *A.D.C. (1496–1501)*, p. cxix.

4. Alexander Hume was in fact Lord Hume's grandson.

5. *Cal. Docs. Scot.*, iv, No. 1483.

6. *Foedera*, xi, 820 *et seq.*

7. Fraser, *Douglas*, iii, 115; *E.R.*, ix, 271.

8. Possibly he spent part or the whole of his exile in Austria with his half-sister Eleanor, wife of Sigismund, archduke of Austria, whom he had visited while on embassy abroad in 1476-77.

9. *E.R.*, ix, 583.

10. *A.P.S.*, ii, 145.

11. *Ibid.*, 151.

12. *Hist. Croy. Cont.*, 564.

13. *A.P.S.*, ii, 151-2.

14. *Ibid.*

15. *Ibid.*, 159.

16. *R.M.S.*, ii, No. 1573. The note on Boyd in *Scots Peerage*, v, 149-50, confuses the witness list to the royal confirmation of 1484 with that of the original charter issued by Albany in February 1483.

17. *A.D.C. (1496-1501)*, p. cxxxii.

18. *Scots Peerage*, iii, 434; v, 150.

19. Nicholson, *op.cit.*, 514.

20. *See above*, Chapter 5.

21. *R.M.S.*, ii, Nos. 1060, 1123; *S.H.S. Misc.* viii, 26-7.

22. W. H. Finlayson, 'The Boyds in Bruges', in *S.H.R.*, xxviii, (1949-50), 196; Comte Limbourg Stirum, 'Anselme Adornes, ou un voyageur brugeois au XVe siecle', in *Messager des sciences historiques*, 1881, 15-16; *T.A.*, i, 43.

23. *R.M.S.*, ii, 1234.

24. *Ibid.*, 1548.

25. *E.R.*, ix, 400; Limbourg Stirum, *op.cit.*, 37; Nicholson, *op.cit.*, 514 n. 294.

26. Myln, *Vitae*, 26; *R.M.S.*, ii, No. 1565.

27. *Ibid.*, No. 1518.

28. Lesley, *History*, 49; Ferreri follows Lesley exactly at this point: Ferrerius, *Appendix to Boece*, f.395v.

29. Buchanan, *History*, ii, 147.

30. Pitscottie, *Historie*, i, 176.

31. *R.M.S.*, ii, No. 3460.

32. *Ibid.*, No. 1565.

33. *A.P.S.*, ii, 153.

34. *E.R.*, ix, 255-6.

35. *Ibid.*, 468.

36. *Ibid.*, 232, 298, 437, 459, 405, 636.

37. *Ibid.*, 523.

38. *A.P.S.*, ii, 169, 180.

39. *R.M.S.*, ii, Nos. 1589 (24 July 1484), 1666 (1 November 1486).

40. Atholl Chrs., Box 7, Parcel ii (4) (Blair Castle).

41. *Rot. Scot.*, ii, 469.

42. Leland, *Collectanea*, iv, 203.

43. *Rot. Scot.*, ii, 480; Leland, *Collectanea*, iv, 240.

44. Ferrerius, *Appendix to Boece*, ff. 397v, 398v.

45. Buchanan, *History*, ii, 155.

46. Danske Rigsarchiv T.K.U.A., Skotland, A.1., 1.

47. *Thre Prestis*, line 457.

48. *A.D.C.*, 78.

49. *Meroure*, i, 48, 165.

50. *Ibid.*, 48.

51. *Rot. Scot.*, ii, 461.

52. *See below*, Chapter 10.

53. *E.R.*, ix, 198, 611.

54. Crawfurd, *Officers*, 45.

55. Vat. Reg. Supp. 832, f. 113 r.

56. *A.P.S.*, ii, 159.

57. Vat. Reg. Supp. 833, f. 92 r–v; Cameron, *Apostolic Camera*, 212.

58. Herkless and Hannay, i, 81.

59. *Innes Review*, iv, (1953), 5.

60. *Cal. State Papers (Venice)*, i, 199.

61. *Meroure*, i, 15.

62. Ferrerius, *Appendix to Boece*, f. 391.

63. *A.P.S.*, ii, 153, 167; *A.D.C.*, 101, 105, 109-118.

64. *Meroure*, i, 83.

65. *Rot. Scot.*, ii, 461, 467-8.

66. Campbell, *Materials*, i, 44. The embassy was postponed, and Ireland's name does not appear in the renewed safe-conduct of 7 July 1486: *Cal. Docs. Scot.*, iv, No. 1522.

67. J. H. Burns, 'John Ireland and "The Meroure of Wyssdome" ', *Innes Review*, vi, part ii, (1955), 86.

68. *E.R.*, ix, 612.

69. *Auctarium*, iii, 166.

70. N.L.S. MS. 1746, f. 111 r.

71. *A.P.S.*, ii, 116; *R.M.S.*, ii, Nos. 1408, 1439.

72. *Eubel*, ii, 248; *Laing Charters*, No. 184.

73. *A.P.S.*, ii, 136, 142, 145, 146.

74. *Ibid.*, 166.

75. *A.D.C.*, 84; *Eubel*, ii, 87.

76. Boece, *Vitae*, 75.

77. *Rot. Scot.*, ii, 461, 462, 464; *Bannatyne Misc.*, ii, 37-40.

78. *Rot. Scot.*, ii, 469, 480-1; Leland, *Collectanea*, iv, 203; and *see below*, Chapter 10.

79. *E.R.*, viii, 559; ix, i, 92, 298, 437, 459.

80. *R.M.S.*, ii, No. 1544.

81. *A.P.S.*, ii, 159, 160.

82. *T.A.*, i, 265.

83. *Ibid.*, Pref., App., ccxc, ccxci-ii.

84. Andrew Lang (*History*, i, 359 n. 88) suggests that Crichton and Princess Margaret may have been married, but cites no evidence in support of this view. Nicholson, *op. cit.*, 489, suggests an early date — 1479 — for the discovery of Margaret's pregnancy and the breakdown of Anglo-Scottish marriage negotiations as a result. But this is probably too early a date, as the daughter subsequently born of the union was not married until about 1506; and James III would surely have condemned Crichton immediately in 1479 if Margaret's pregnancy had occurred in that year.

85. Buchanan, *History*, ii, 151-2. The original Latin is 'quae non adeo pridem decessit' (Buchanan, *Rerum Scoticarum Historia*, (edn. 1582), Lib. xii, f. 141 r.). As Margaret Crichton died sometime before 1546 (*T.A.*, i, Pref., App., pp. ccxci-ii), Buchanan's statement that her death was a recent event suggests that this part, at least, of his *History* was written long before the publication of the entire work in 1582.

86. *A.D.C.*, 15.

87. *Scots Peerage*, iii, 66-7.

88. Lesley, *History*, 48; and *see below*, Chapter 12.

89. *A.P.S.*, ii, 161-4.

90. Buchanan, *History*, ii, 152.

91. *A.D.C.*, 311.

92. *A.P.S.*, ii, 173-4.

93. *Ibid.*, 165.

94. *A.D.C.*, 98-9, 105. Although the records of the Lords of Council end in April 1485, the Register of the Great Seal reveals that on 7 December of the same year a council decreet ordered the apprising of a number of the titles to annual rents held by Angus, raising for the Crown the sum of about £50 (*R.M.S.*, ii, No. 1664). As in the Balmuir case in January, the king appears to have been harassing Angus on minor matters, using the law to weaken the earl's position.

95. *A.P.S.*, ii, 165.

96. *Ibid.*

97. Atholl Chrs., Box 6, Parcel iv, No. 6 (Blair Castle).

98. *A.P.S.*, ii, 165, 170. In a period of seventeen months between August 1473 and December 1474, James III had acquired almost £550 as the price of remissions granted to over 60 people: Nicholson, *op.cit.*, 499.

99. Boece, *Vitae*, 76-7.

100. Mackie, *James IV*, 32.

101. *Liber Pluscardensis*, i, 392-400; *E.R.*, vi, 485-6; *A.P.S.*, ii, 50.

102. Nicholson, *op.cit.*, 569.

103. *A.P.S.*, ii, 176.

104. *Ibid.*, 201.

105. W. C. Dickinson, 'The Administration of Justice in Medieval Scotland', *Aberdeen University Review*, xxxiv, (1952), 348-51.

106. *A.P.S.*, ii, 94, 100; and *see above*, Chapter 5.

107. *A.P.S.*, ii, 177-8.

108. *A.D.C.*, 43.

109. *A.P.S.*, ii, 183.

110. Dickinson, *op.cit.*, 351.

10

The Gathering Storm: Foreign and Ecclesiastical Diplomacy 1483–87

IN spite of the royal recovery of power in the spring and early summer of 1483, there remained unanswered a number of important questions as to the future direction of foreign and ecclesiastical policies. In the case of the former, healing the breach with England was no longer an easy task, for Dunbar and Berwick were in English hands, and Albany a fugitive in England and a continuing menace for as long as the Yorkists considered him worthy of armed support. In the sphere of important ecclesiastical vacancies, the deaths of the Bishops of Glasgow and Dunkeld, during and immediately after the crisis of 1482–3, produced a number of internal tensions which not only divided the higher clergy but made a number of them committed opponents of the king; and James III's failure to settle the outstanding problem of the revenues of Coldingham priory was to tell heavily against him in the rebellion of 1488, when Hume support for the rebel cause may well have been the decisive factor.

Nevertheless, there can be no denying the diplomatic skill shown by the king in the years following 1483. Like all successful diplomats, he was aided throughout by luck. The death of Edward IV on 9 April 1483 had enabled him to complete the ruin of Albany in Scotland; and in less than four months, on 26 June, Richard, duke of Gloucester, usurped his nephew's throne and thereby produced a sharp reaction to his government in southern England. Richard's subsequent search for security in the north soon removed from King James's mind the fear of another 1482 and allowed him to press ahead with his own very personal policy of renewed peace and alliance with England. However, the necessary conditions for a prolonged settlement would include the restoration to Scotland of Dunbar and Berwick.

The resumption of negotiation with England began soon after James's recovery of power. On 16 August 1483 the king wrote to the new English monarch Richard III, proposing to send an embassy south to discuss the re-establishment of peace between the two realms. Richard III replied rapidly from York on 16 September, regretting the recent war and asking James to send him a list of names of ambassadors to negotiate a peace, to whom he would gladly grant a safe-conduct.[1] On 6 November James III responded with another letter carried south by Dingwall pursuivant, to whom he gave the names of his proposed ambassadors; but he also tried to step up the pace by asking King Richard to observe a truce on land and sea until the following 15 March, so that peace negotiations might be carried on in a more friendly atmosphere.[2] Richard III was not impressed by this suggestion. Replying to James from London on 2 December, he thanked him for supplying the names of the Scottish ambassadors, but remarked that the Scottish king had sent no-one to him with authority to discuss the proposed truce; and he continued by saying that the March Wardens and their lieutenants had neither the power nor the means to make it effective.[3]

It is noteworthy that in this first exchange of letters both kings make the distinction between peace and truce. James's long-term objective, as events were to show, was a peace treaty based on the restoration of Dunbar and Berwick; and in the late autumn of 1483, with Richard III acutely embarrassed by a number of simultaneous rebellions in the nine southern counties, the Scottish king probably rated his chances of recovering the two lost strongholds by negotiation to be fairly good. As a usurper of only four months' standing, King Richard would surely be prepared to make sacrifices in order to ensure a Scottish peace while he strengthened his own position in the south. Richard's evasive reply at the beginning of December, however, must have made it clear to James that he was not going to achieve a swift end to hostilities; and so, in the parliament of February 1484, the Scottish king reverted to making warlike noises, and in particular to planning the siege of Dunbar.

Thus we find letters patent under the privy seal being sent out to sheriffs, bailies and other officers, ordering the lieges to be ready for war, that is if necessary to muster to the king or his lieutenant upon eight days' warning. Those assembling were to carry provisions and money to last twenty days; and sheriffs were to hold weaponshowings to ensure that the lieges were well provided with arms. Furthermore, the sheriffs and bailies were to inform the king on what day the weaponshowings were being held, 'that he may send certane servandis of his avne to se that his liegis be bodin and that the said shireffis and baillies do thir office as efferis'. As usual, the sheriff was ordered to make a roll of the number of spears, bows, axes, and 'defensible personis' within his shire, and to bring it to the muster, sealed with his own seal and those of four of the barons within his sheriffdom.[4] This parliamentary article of February 1484 suggests Scottish belligerence; and this would first take the form of an assault on Dunbar castle. Indeed, preparations for its siege, to begin on 1 May 1484, are fully set out in the following article. Yet Richard III's refusal to consider an immediate truce also made defence of the borders a matter of urgency; and parliament made much of the need for 'the defens of the Realme and resisting of his [the king's] Inymyis'.[5] The correspondence between the two kings came to an end until the following July, and when it was resumed, it was with the limited object of initiating negotiations for a truce.[6]

In the meantime, the Scots busied themselves with the recovery of Dunbar. In February 1484 the estates provided that 'the said castell salbe closit and assegit the first day of the moneth of maij nixt tocum be the kingis liegis and hoist of the south part the watter of forth', and they were ordered to appear at Dunbar on 1 May, well armed and carrying provisions for a twenty-day siege. All those whose names had been taken at the weaponshowings were expected to turn up, under pain of having their possessions confiscated and handed over to sustain the besiegers. It was further provided that the lieges north of Forth should appear at the siege on 18 May on the same conditions.[7] Presumably the intention was to provide, if necessary, for a siege of about six weeks, carried on by two separate bodies for spells of twenty days each.

It is probable, however, that this was an attempt to make proper provision for the conduct of a siege which had already begun. The exchequer account for the earldom of March for the three years between May 1483 and July 1486 includes a payment made to John Dundas of that ilk 'tempore obsedionis de Dunbar anno octuagesimo tercio'. Mention is also made of the besiegers of Dunbar castle destroying the grain crop in the granges of West Barns, Newton Lees, and Oswaldsdean — all in the Dunbar area — in 1483.[8] Either the siege was not being conducted with great vigour, or the Scots found it impossible to prevent the garrison being supplied by sea — a further reason for Richard III's reluctance to consider an immediate cessation of hostilities on land and sea — for Dunbar was still in English hands in the autumn of 1484, when a truce was finally made with the English king. One of its stipulations was that the siege of Dunbar should be suspended for six months;[9] and so it dragged on through 1485.

Faced with an English ruler reluctant to negotiate, James III reverted to the classic pattern of Scottish diplomacy. In the early spring of 1484 two ambassadors arrived in Edinburgh, sent by the new French government acting for the adolescent Charles VIII, and seeking a renewal of the Franco-Scottish alliance of 1448–9 between Charles VII and James II. One of these men was Bernard Stewart, Lord of Aubigny, like the Monypennys an expatriate Scot in the service of the king of France. With remarkable speed, on 13 March 1484, James III confirmed the 1448 alliance at Edinburgh: that is, a pact of friendship between France and Scotland, an offensive and defensive treaty directed against England. Neither French nor Scottish king was to shelter the rebels of the other. The treaty was signed by King James in the presence of Bernard Stewart and Master Pierre Milet, Charles VIII's ambassadors, and was ratified by the French king on 9 July 1484.[10]

It would appear that James III now sent Charles VIII material assistance in the shape of 'bon nombre de gens de Guerre conduits par Messire Bernard de Stuard apelle en France le seigneur d'Aubigny'.[11] This is also suggested by Sir James Balfour, who states that, on concluding their business in Edinburgh, the ambassadors from France took back with them eighteen companies of Scots foot under the command of one Donald Robertson. A Donald Robertson appears as a tenant of James III in 1480; and this may be the same man.[12] Both Balfour's account and the French one quoted above are admittedly of seventeenth century date, and probably contain a fair amount of embroidery. There is no reason to doubt, however, that King James sent some soldiers back to France with the embassy.

From the point of view of Richard III, the renewal of the Franco-Scottish alliance was an alarming turn of events. Of three safe-conducts which he had issued to Scottish ambassadors to come to England in November 1483, and March and April, 1484,[13] not one had been taken up; and the reason for this must have become clear to the English king when, in March 1484, James III renewed the Franco-Scottish alliance at the suggestion of the French. If King James also sent some troops to France, the situation must have appeared extremely ominous to Richard III. The previous autumn, he had been fortunate enough to quell a serious uprising — known as Buckingham's rebellion — in the southern counties; but only bad weather had prevented the landing in England of Henry Tudor, pretender to the throne, who was being harboured by Charles VIII of France. The renewal of the Franco-Scottish alliance, therefore, meant for Richard III the prospect of an imminent war on two fronts, as well as the possibility of rebellion at home.

One of his responses to the problem was to resurrect the Scottish fifth column. In July 1484, Albany made a last effort to recover his position in Scotland; with English support, he entered the south-west in the company of James, the forfeited ninth earl of Douglas, and James Gifford of Sheriffhall, the man responsible for admitting an English garrison to Dunbar the previous year.[14] Of the sixteenth century chroniclers, Buchanan alone mentions the battle which followed. According to his account, 'Alexander, duke of Albany, and James Douglas, desirous of trying the affections of the people towards them, having selected five hundred horsemen, proceeded to Lochmaben on St. Magdalen's day, when a great fair used to be held; where, from some sudden quarrel, a battle arose, which was fought with various success, according as assistance was brought to the one side or the other from the neighbourhood, and continued to hang in doubt from mid-day till night, when a bloody victory remained with the Scots, who lost a great number of their friends. Douglas was taken prisoner, and sent by the king to the monastery of Lindores. Alexander escaped on horseback to England, but did not long remain there'.[15] Buchanan's tale, closely followed by Drummond of Hawthornden in the seventeenth century, is plausible enough, and the date he gives for the battle — St. Magdalen's day, 22 July — is correct. There is also a fair amount of record evidence to add detail to his story. The royal army consisted of a number of local lairds, Robert Crichton of Sanquhar, Cuthbert Murray of Cockpool, John Johnstone of that ilk and his eldest son James.[16] The statement that John, Master of Maxwell and Steward of Annandale, was killed at Lochmaben fighting on the royal side[17] would appear to be incorrect; on 4 September 1487 Murray of Cockpool mortified an annual rent to the High Altar of the Blessed Virgin Mary in the church of Carlaverock for the souls of James III and John, Master of Maxwell, whom Murray had slain in a feud with that family.[18] There is, in fact, no evidence to suggest that there were any Maxwells present at Lochmaben.

The fight at Lochmaben cannot have involved great numbers on either side; but it was decisive enough, ending in the rout and final flight of Albany and the capture of Douglas. James III's reward, originally offered in the parliament of March 1482, of a hundred marks' worth of land and a hundred marks of money for the man who captured Douglas, was at last claimed by one Alexander Kirkpatrick, who acquired the lands of the town of Kirkmichael in Dumfriesshire, together with other lands in Annandale and Berwickshire forfeited by Lord Crichton and Albany respectively. Robert Crichton of Sanquhar was rewarded by the king with a confirmation of his barony of Sanquhar, and of the hereditary sheriffship of Dumfries; and his younger brother Edward, who had also fought on the royal side at Lochmaben, received a confirmation of the lands of Kirkpatrick in Dumfriesshire, and other lands in Dumfries and Lanark.[19]

Albany's career was at an end, and he fled to France. Presumably such reputation as he had managed to maintain in England was finally destroyed by the fight at Lochmaben. In country where he and the Earls of Douglas had formerly ruled virtually as kings, he had been defeated by a small gathering of local lairds, and clearly he had no future anywhere in Scotland. The following year, in Paris, at the age of thirty-one, he was killed by a lance splinter at a tournament and buried in the church of the Celestins.[20] His career in many ways resembled that of Edward IV's brother George, duke of Clarence. From his early 'twenties he had shown himself to be totally untrustworthy, and in his attempts to increase his own power and influence he had been prepared to ally himself with anybody — with two kings of England, Edward IV and Richard III; with Louis XI of France in 1479; with Margaret of Denmark in the autumn of 1482; with James III himself in October 1482 and March 1483; and with two separate groups of rebellious Scottish nobles during the crisis of 1482–3. His ambitions had varied from a desire to extend his power by adding the earldom of Mar to his possessions to securing for himself the office of Lieutenant-General and ultimately, at the instigation of Edward IV, the Scottish throne. The many alliances he made only served in the end to undermine any trust that might have remained in his motives and ability. The lairds of Lochmaben had demonstrated clearly what the Scots thought of Albany; and the country was well rid of him. It may be added that, according to the terms of the Franco-Scottish alliance of March 1484, Albany should not have been allowed to land in France, far less be given asylum there and an honourable burial; and James III must have appreciated that, in practical terms, parts of the French treaty were of little value to him.

The capture at Lochmaben of the forfeited Earl of Douglas was also an event of much significance. For thirty-two years, since the so-called treaty of Westminster-Ardtornish in the spring of 1462, he had acted as an English agent in every treasonable activity directed against Scotland by Edward IV and Richard III. From Michaelmas 1461 he had received a pension of £500 per annum from Edward IV, and there is evidence that Richard III intended to give him an annuity of at least £200 for life.[21] His capture by the royalists at Lochmaben put an end to a long era of harbouring of Scottish traitors by English kings. The Boyds were dead; Albany had fled; and now the last of the Earls of Douglas was imprisoned for the remainder of his life. Buchanan names the monastery of Lindores as the place of his imprisonment.[22]

If Lochmaben was therefore a triumph for James III in that it removed once and for all the menace of the disinherited, it was probably accepted with mixed feelings by Richard III. Obviously, he no longer had to pay a pension to Douglas, nor give material aid to Albany. The latter had shown himself to be an awkward ally; on 12 March 1484, one of his ships seized two wine ships of his benefactor's ally, the Duke of Burgundy, bound for the port of London, and robbed them of £375 worth of wine, goods, and merchandise.[23] This was not the sort of act calculated to endear the exiled duke to Richard III, who had to make restitution to the wine merchant involved, Anthony Kele of Antwerp. Consequently, King Richard's armed support for Albany in the summer of 1484 amounted to a few hundred men at most; and he had probably reduced his predecessor's annuity to Douglas by some £300. On the other hand, it is likely that he appreciated having men like Albany and Douglas in his employ, if only to create trouble on the Scottish border and keep the Scots occupied; and although he can have had no great hopes of a substantial success on Albany's part in July 1484, he was doubtless alarmed at the total rejection of the duke by the Scots at Lochmaben.

The alternative to force was negotiation; and as early as 21 July, the day before Lochmaben, James III wrote a letter to Richard from which it appears that an English squire named Edward Gower had already approached the Scots proposing a truce and marriage alliance. Jamed declared himself well inclined towards the proposals and named his commissioners to conclude a treaty of 'lufe, friendship, aliaunces, and marriage to be had betuix your maist noble blude and oures'. The Scottish commissioners, who were to arrive in Nottingham on 7 September 1484, were named as Chancellor Argyll, William Elphinstone, bishop of Aberdeen, Robert Lord Lyle, Laurence Lord Oliphant, John Drummond of Stobhall, and the royal secretary, Archibald Whitelaw, archdeacon of Lothian.[24] Richard III replied promptly through his messenger Edward Gower on 7 August, agreeing to James's proposals and announcing that he had ordered letters of safe-conduct to be issued to the Scottish ambassadors. In fact he had done this the previous day.[25] His speed in replying, and his complete willingness to negotiate at once, must surely be explained by his just having received news of the failure and rout of Albany and Douglas at Lochmaben.

In addition to the six Scottish ambassadors named above, Lyon King of Arms and Duncan of Dundas accompanied the embassy to Nottingham, and all eight had arrived at the castle there by 12 September. Richard III was there in person to meet them, and on the same day James's secretary, Archibald Whitelaw, addressed a long oration in Latin to the English king. This purports to be a declamation in praise of peace; but it is liberally sprinkled with quotations from Virgil's *Aeneid* and with praises of Richard III's martial exploits.[26] With men of political importance like Argyll and Elphinstone on the Scottish embassy, it seems at first sight curious that the Archdeacon of Lothian should deliver a long address on behalf of the Scots to the English king; but Whitelaw was probably the senior member of the embassy, having been a determinant at St. Andrews University in 1437 (the year Elphinstone was born) and a Master of Arts in 1439. In 1484, therefore, he was probably about sixty-four years of age; as the king's tutor, royal secretary for twenty-two years, and in this capacity a constant attender of parliaments and sittings of the Lords of Council, Whitelaw possessed a knowledge second to none of the inner workings of royal government, an expertise which was to ensure him employment as secretary until 1493.[27] Yet his political views, if he had any, are impossible to ascertain; and his oration to Richard III at Nottingham is the only example of his emergence from the relative obscurity, routine, and drudgery of his position.

On 14 September 1484, the commissioners on both sides abandoned rhetoric and got down to the serious business of negotiations;[28] and a week later a truce and marriage alliance had been agreed upon. The truce, which was drawn up on 20 September, was to last for three years from 29 September 1484; Berwick was included in it; as for Dunbar castle, still in English hands, it was stipulated that it should be included in the truce unless James III were to write to the English king signifying his intention to recover it after six months had elapsed. On the English side the principal conservators of the truce were John, earl of Lincoln, and Henry, earl of Northumberland. The Scottish conservators numbered two earls, Crawford and Huntly; six lords of parliament, Darnley, Kennedy, Lyle, Hailes, Oliphant and Borthwick; and twelve lairds, John Ross of Halkhead, John Lundy of that ilk, James Ogilvy of Airlie, Robert Hamilton of Fingalton, William Bailie of Lamington, John Kennedy of Blairquhan, John Wemyss of that ilk, William Ruthven of that ilk, Gilbert Johnstone of Elphinstone, John Dundas of that ilk, John Ross of Montgrenan (the Lord Advocate), and Edward Crichton of Kirkpatrick (one of the victors of Lochmaben) — a total of twenty in all; and the Admirals and Wardens of the Marches were also to be included amongst the conservators. On 20 September seven of the eight Scottish ambassadors signed the agreement (Duncan of Dundas was the exception).[29] The following day, all eight Scots signed the marriage contract, which provided for an alliance between James III's eldest son James and Anne de la Pole, only daughter of the Duke of Suffolk, and niece to Richard III; the marriage was to be solemnised within the period of the truce, that is within three years.[30]

The entire transaction, however, is less convincing than its predecessor of 1474, and the intentions of both kings rather more suspect. It was, after all, only a truce; and James III was bound to attempt to recover Dunbar as soon as possible. Similarly, the Scottish king was unlikely to accept the loss of Berwick for any length of time. No sum was specified for Anne's dowry; Richard III, more cautious than his brother, seems to have had no intention of advancing any money to James before the marriage was accomplished. The example of the Cecilia dowry was not encouraging from an English standpoint. Finally, there was undoubtedly the problem of personal animosity between the two men, going back, on James's side, to 1482 when Richard, as Duke of Gloucester, had captured Berwick and led an English army unopposed into Edinburgh; and Richard, as king, was undoubtedly aware of the very recent Franco-Scottish alliance of March 1484. There seems no reason to doubt, however, that the Scottish king was sincere about the marriage proposals; such schemes were a major part of his policy towards England during the reigns of Edward IV, Richard III and Henry VII. On 21 October 1484 he ratified the truce.[31]

Seven months later, the three estates meeting in parliament at Edinburgh gave a high priority to pushing forward the marriage plans for Prince James, now a youth of twelve. On 26 May 1485 it was agreed that an embassy numbering six should be sent to York to settle the details of the marriage; these six were to include a bishop, an earl, a lord of parliament, a clerk, and two barons, one a knight and the other a squire, with their servants to a total number of fifty-two. The estates were to pay them £500 Scots for their expenses, £200 each from clergy and barons, £100 from the burghs. It was stipulated that this tax should at once be collected for the ambassadors 'sa that in defalt thirof thai be nocht tarijt as the last ambassat was', another possible explanation of James III's delay in concluding a truce with Richard III the year before.[32]

The proposed embassy, however, was never sent. Indeed, the last reference we have to negotiations between England and Scotland during Richard III's reign occurs on 18 April 1485, a month before the May parliament at Edinburgh; and this was no more than a Scottish safe-conduct granted to Sir Richard Ratcliffe and three other Englishmen to come to Lochmabenstone with a retinue of a hundred to treat of peace and other matters.[33] As the truce was already in force, this is presumably a reference to breaches of the peace committed on the borders. Thereafter, however, there would appear to have been a complete breakdown of negotiations between the two countries for the remainder of Richard III's short reign. The explanation for this could be the simple one of finance; it would take time to raise £500. The grant was made in the Scottish parliament only on 26 May, and the English king was killed at Bosworth less than three months later, on 22 August. It is surprising, however, that no active steps had been taken to implement the provisions of the marriage contract of 1484 before this time, because it was very much in James III's interest to do so. Perhaps he was swithering between the English and the French alliance, or was aware of Henry Tudor's plans to attempt another landing in England. James had, after all, sent some troops to assist Henry Tudor's invasion. Nevertheless, Richard III's defeat and death at Bosworth must have come as a complete surprise; Henry Tudor had embarked from Harfleur as late as 1 August, and at the battle of Bosworth, fought exactly three weeks later, he was commanding a force which was numerically much inferior to that of the English king. Only a combination of apathy and treachery in the royal army lost the battle for Richard III; and it seems unlikely that James III was so wholeheartedly committed to the French connection and to Henry Tudor that he would sever negotiations with King Richard in the summer of 1485.

There is, however, some evidence of Scottish support for Henry Tudor at the time of Bosworth. Pitscottie, whose account of the reign is normally either suspect or wrong on points of detail, states that Henry came over from France in thirty ships containing 3,000 English, 6,000 French, and 1,000 men-at-arms 'callit the Scoittis cumpanie quha had to thair captaine ane nobill knicht quhilk was callit Schir Alexander bruce of Erlshall'. According to Pitscottie, this Scots company, led by Bruce of Earlshall and 'ane borne man of hadingtoune', formed Henry Tudor's vanguard at Bosworth.[34] The numbers are undoubtedly much exaggerated; Polydore Vergil states that Henry left France with only 2,000 men and a few ships.[35] As regards the part played by Bruce of Earlshall, however, Pitscottie may well be correct. Bruce's eldest son, Sir William Bruce of Earlshall, was Pitscottie's neighbour in Fife, and is quoted by Pitscottie as one of the sources for his history.[36] Evidence of a more tangible character of Sir Alexander Bruce's participation in the battle is provided by both English and Scottish records. On 24 November 1485, three months after Bosworth, Bruce was granted a safe-conduct to come to England;[37] and also in 1485, he was described by Henry VII as 'valectus Camere nostre'.[38] On 9 February 1486 James III granted Bruce some of Albany's forfeited Berwickshire lands 'pro eius fideli et gratuito servitio regi tam infra regnum quam extra idem impenso';[39] and on 7 March 1486 Henry VII gave an annuity of £20 to Bruce 'in gracious remuneration of his good, faithful, and approved services, and his great labours in various ways heretofore, and lately done in person, by the king's command, and still continued to the king's certain knowledge'.[40]

These gifts to Bruce by both kings for services rendered suggest that he was the leader of a Scottish contingent at Bosworth; furthermore, this is an event for which Pitscottie's narrative should be treated with a certain amount of respect, as for once the account of what had happened reached him at second hand. Although always vague as to detail, he described Henry Tudor's campaign and victory at length, which suggests that he had a great deal of oral information on the subject; Bosworth is, after all, almost the only event which Pitscottie describes between 1482 and 1488, and it is not strictly relevant to the history of Scotland which he is writing.

However, it is likely that his source for Bosworth, quite apart from information passed on by Sir William Bruce of Earlshall, was the history of John Major, which was published in 1521. Major relates that 'inasmuch as the Earl of Richmond had been long a dweller in France, Charles VIII granted him an aid of 5,000 men (of whom 1,000 were Scots, but John, son of Robert of Haddington, was chief and leader of the Scots)'.[41] Here, surely, is the origin of Pitscottie's 'borne man of hadingtoune'; Pitscottie lifted him out of Major's history; and Major, himself a native of Haddington, acquired his information from the same kind of source as Pitscottie's, namely a local one. Altogether, this provides an interesting case study of the interaction of local oral sources and printed history.

Thus there were Scotsmen fighting for Henry Tudor at Bosworth; but there is no evidence that Henry received any direct assistance from the Scottish government. No English writer mentions a Scottish contingent on Henry's side at Bosworth, probably because, as Major points out, the Scots were in the service of the King of France, and had sailed from Harfleur with Henry's expedition. Presumably James III had little or no control over the men he sent to France with Stewart of Aubigny in the summer of 1484; and the figure of a thousand quoted by Major seems rather high. All these things considered, it seems likely that James III was grateful for Henry Tudor's success after the event, but that he was only very indirectly concerned in promoting that success.

The Scottish king was quick enough to try to take advantage of the accession of Henry VII — a usurper, the founder of a new dynasty who was vulnerable in the north, where Richard III had been popular — to try to recover Berwick. Within a month of Bosworth an English commission of array was issued to the northern counties, ordering them to be in readiness for an invasion of the Scots.[42] In October a similar commission was issued to the officers of the Duchy of Lancaster; mention is made of 'divers the subgettes of our cosyne James, Kyng of Scottes . . . entendying to leaye seege to our town and castel of Berwick'.[43] Conway suggests that these 'divers subgettes' were 'in all probability the Border Lords; Angus Bell the Cat, the Humes, Hepburns, etc., who in 1482 had allied themselves with Albany and Richard, duke of Gloucester'.[44] This argument, however, seems curiously inconsistent. Men like Angus and his adherents had been in alliance with the English in 1482, and were at least partly responsible for the surrender of Berwick to Albany and Gloucester at that time. It seems unlikely that they would later, of their own volition and at considerable risk, stir themselves to attempt to recapture it. However, in view of what is known of the king's constant desire to recover Berwick — an attitude which was to hold up negotiations with Henry VII on more than one occasion — the projected siege mentioned in the commissions of array is much more likely to have been planned by James III himself.

In any event, nothing came of plans for an attack on Berwick in the autumn of 1485. Indeed, on 22 September English safe-conducts were issued to George Browne, bishop of Dunkeld, William Elphinstone, bishop of Aberdeen, Robert Blacader, bishop of Glasgow, Robert Bellenden, abbot of Holyrood, John Ramsay, Lord Bothwell, Sir William Murray of Tullibardine and John Murray of Touchadam, to come to England with a train of eighty attendants. These were the Scottish ambassadors who attended Henry's coronation on 30 October.[45]

If Berwick remained inaccessible, the same was not true of Dunbar castle, recaptured by the Scots in the winter of 1485 or spring of 1486. The fall of Dunbar brought to an end a long and unsatisfactory siege which had continued spasmodically for more than two-and-a-half years. Occasional references to it are to be found in the exchequer records. During the period 1483–6, £42 11/- was paid to a carpenter named William Anderson 'pro factura unius instrumenti bellici vocati le sow' — a bombard of some kind, which may have been used against Dunbar when the six months' truce in which the castle was included had elapsed. There are also charges for gunpowder, for a mould for making bombards, and for artillery.[46] The projected Scottish attack on Berwick, which the English feared in September and October, may indeed have been turned against Dunbar; the siege was renewed about 6 December 1485[47] and brought to a successful conclusion before the end of June 1486, when John Ramsay, Lord Bothwell — who may have conducted the siege on behalf of James III — was given custody of Dunbar.[48]

Henry VII, like Richard III before him, had made no attempt to raise the siege of Dunbar; and negotiations with a view to an Anglo-Scottish peace were probably in progress when the castle fell. On 2 February 1486 English safe-conducts were issued to twelve unnamed ambassadors of the Scots, to be chosen by James III, to come to England with a train of two hundred persons to treat for peace and a settlement of border disputes.[49] There followed a gap of over three months before negotiations were resumed, possibly as a result of Henry VII's preoccupation with Lovell's rebellion in the north of England. Then, on 6 May 1486, Bishop Elphinstone, Abbot Bellenden of Holyrood, John Ramsay, Lord Bothwell, John Lord Kennedy, John Ross of Montgrenan and Secretary Whitelaw were named as James's ambassadors to conclude a truce with Henry VII;[50] and after negotiations a three year's truce was agreed upon by both parties on 3 July. Henry VII confirmed the truce on 26 July,[52] and it was finally ratified by James III on 25 October.[53]

The 1486 truce was to last exactly three years, until sunset on 3 July 1489. Agreements were made that traitors, fugitives from justice, or convicted criminals would not be received by either party to the truce. However, the problem of Berwick prevented a more rapid understanding between the two monarchs; an agreement provided for a meeting of Scottish and English commissioners in the town itself on 8 March 1487, to delimit the ancient boundaries of town and castle, or to fix new ones. If negotiations regarding the actual possession of Berwick broke down, the truce would end on 3 July 1487. However, it was arranged that at the same time as the Berwick commissioners were meeting, English ambassadors would be sent to Edinburgh to negotiate for a longer truce, and also for a marriage alliance between James, marquis of Ormonde, James III's second son, and Katherine, Edward IV's sixth — and fourth surviving — daughter.[54] This last proposal was the forerunner of an elaborate series of marriages which the Scottish king was to suggest in the following year, and was part of a consistent policy towards England which James III had pursued since 1474. It is perhaps significant that he is found on this occasion seeking a royal marriage in England for his second son, who was aged about ten, rather than for his first, James, duke of Rothesay and heir to the throne, a youth of thirteen. It seems rather as though the king was deliberately elevating his second son James, marquis of Ormonde, with a view to weakening the position of the young Duke of Rothesay, for whom both earlier marriage alliances — with Cecilia in 1474 and Anne de la Pole in 1484 — had been arranged. It is possible, though no more than speculative, that James III had begun to mistrust his eldest son who had been brought up, probably since birth, in the queen's household at Stirling, and who continued to live at Stirling, apart from his father, after her death.

For in July 1486 Margaret of Denmark died at Stirling.[55] Her career as James's wife and queen of Scotland, particularly during her last three or four years, is obscure and enigmatic. There can be no doubt that, whatever her motives, she had taken some part in the government at the time of her husband's imprisonment in 1482, and she had probably been in alliance with Albany for a time. Sabadino, in his brief 1492 biography of Margaret, suggests that after his release the king 'reposed more hatred than previously in the Queen, because of her consent to his arrest; as a result . . . he was unwilling even to see her again, either in life or in death — a period of three years'.[56] In spite of inaccuracies, there is a measure of truth in this, for Margaret lived continuously in Stirling for the last three years of her life, with her eldest son in her custody.[57] Throughout the same period, as the Great Seal Register proclaims again and again, the king was to be found in Edinburgh. It follows from this that James and Margaret regularly lived apart, but not that they were estranged. It is impossible to compile a complete royal itinerary for the period, as the Treasurer's accounts are lacking; but it seems likely that King James, together with the papal legate, James Pasarella, bishop of Imola, visited Queen Margaret at Stirling in the late spring of 1486.[58] Probably there were many such visits on the part of the king; and after Margaret's death, the long-delayed mission to Rome, headed by Archbishop Scheves, was entrusted by James with a supplication requesting the canonisation of his wife.[59] This is an indication of more than conventional piety, suggesting that, contrary to Sabadino's belief, relations between James III and Queen Margaret were reasonably good between 1483 and 1486. In spite of the later tales of Lesley and Buchanan, James III had no known mistresses and no illegitimate children; like his grandfather, he appears to have enjoyed a happy marriage at least until the birth of his third son, John, in July 1480. Thereafter, during the crisis of 1482–3, he had at least cause to be grateful to Queen Margaret for helping to secure his release from Edinburgh castle;[60] and the physical separation of king and queen from 1483 onwards may well have been a matter of security, a concern for the safety of the young Duke of Rothesay and his succession to the throne. When James I was murdered at Perth in 1437, the fact that his only son was not in his company ensured his survival, and his separation from his father may indeed have been a matter of royal policy. Such may also have been the case with the Duke of Rothesay; because of his value as heir, he lived apart from his father; and the queen probably located her household at Stirling in order to be with her son. Maternal love may also explain her negotiations with Albany in the autumn of 1482, as his claim to be 'Alexander King of Scots' obviously threatened her son's position as future king. In the end, however, it is impossible to be sure about the character of Margaret of Denmark. Like Mary of Gueldres in the previous reign, she played an important political role; her face on the Van der Goes portrait is hardly the face of a saint; and there is a grim irony in the fact that her efforts to guarantee the security of her eldest son finally resulted in the defeat and death of her husband.

Whatever his personal feelings about the queen, James III was soon making use of the opportunity provided by her death to enter the English marriage market himself. The three years' truce of July 1486 — the very month of Margaret of Denmark's death — contained a clause providing for a further meeting of commissioners in March 1487, to attempt to prolong the peace by means of a threefold marriage alliance.[61] In February 1487, Henry VII duly gave a commission to the Bishop of Carlisle and others to make arrangements for the March meeting;[62] but it did not take place. The rebellion associated with the pretender Lambert Simnel, which came close to losing the English king his throne, occupied Henry VII fully until he defeated the rebels at the battle of Stoke on 16 June 1487. Thereafter negotiations were resumed, and in the autumn Henry's commissioners Richard Fox, bishop of Exeter, and Sir Richard Edgecombe arrived in Edinburgh to discuss the proposed marriage alliances and a prolongation of the truce. James III's commissioners were Bishop Elphinstone of Aberdeen and John Ramsay, Lord Bothwell. On 28 November 1487 an indenture was drawn up between these parties which began by reciting the moves already made towards a permanent peace, and continued by expressing the hope that the existing truce, which had partly expired, might be extended. This was to be achieved by the marriage, already agreed upon in 1486, between James, marquis of Ormonde and earl of Ross, James II's second son, and 'a right noble lady Katerine the thride dothtir of umquhile the ritht noble prince Edward the ferd late king of England sister to the ritht hie and mithti princes Elizabeth nowe quene of Ingland'. In addition to this marriage, it was thought expedient by the commissioners 'for the incressing of mare love and amite betuix the said princis and for the sure observacion of the trewis' that marriages should also be arranged between James III and Elizabeth Woodville, widow of Edward IV, and between 'the richt hie and mithi prince James prince of Scotland duc of Rothissay erle of Carrik and the firste begoten son of the said king of Scottis and ane of the said Edward the ferde umquhile king of England dothtris'.[63]

The marriage between the Marquis of Ormonde and the Princess Katherine, therefore, was the first and most definite of these proposals. Katherine was not, as the indenture states, Edward IV's third daughter, but his sixth, of which six four had survived. The problem of determining which of the late king's remaining daughters was intended for Prince James, the heir to the throne, is more difficult.

Two of them, Mary and Margaret, had died; the eldest, Elizabeth, married Henry VII in January 1486, and Anne, the fifth daughter, had married Thomas Howard, earl of Surrey, in 1475. Thus if Katherine — set aside for Prince James's younger brother — is excluded, there remain only two possible choices — Cecilia, the third, and Bridget, the seventh daughter of Edward IV.

At first sight, Cecilia would appear to be the more likely of the two candidates. After Elizabeth, she was the eldest surviving daughter of Edward IV; and she had been betrothed to the infant Prince James at the time of the Anglo-Scottish marriage alliance of October 1474. Now that the wars which had interrupted negotiations between the two countries had come to an end, the fulfilment of the long-delayed scheme would seem a logical step to take. But there are serious objections to this view. At some time between 25 November and Christmas 1487, Cecilia was married to John, Viscount Welles.[64] It is true that the Anglo-Scottish negotiations which ended in the indenture of 28 November had been going on since August; it may have been Henry VII's intention at the outset to marry Cecilia to the Scottish heir to the throne, and he could have changed his mind during the three-month period of the talks. It is highly unlikely, however, that he was deliberately trying to deceive his fellow sovereign by offering him Cecilia for his eldest son, and then, when the indenture had been drawn up, giving her instead to Viscount Welles. Such an action would hardly lay a secure foundation for future negotiations towards peace in Scotland. It would seem, therefore, that James III was not concerned to have specified which of Edward IV's daughters his eldest son was to marry. On the other hand, it is twice stipulated — in the provisions of the truce of July 1486, and again in the November 1487 indenture — that his second son, James, marquis of Ormonde, should marry Princess Katherine; so this alliance would appear to have been foremost in King James's thoughts. The marriage of Cecilia to Viscount Welles meant that only one of Edward IV's daughters remained available for James III's eldest son — Bridget, who was a year younger than Katherine. The conclusion is inescapable that the Scottish king was deliberately slighting his heir to the benefit of the latter's younger brother James, marquis of Ormonde.

Despite the elaborate marriage proposals of 1487, the three years' truce was extended at this time by less than three months, to expire on 1 September 1489. The reason for the commissioners' failure to negotiate a long peace and alliance is almost certainly to be found in the contention over Berwick, 'of the quhilk castell and town . . . the said king of Scottis desiris alwais deliverance'.[65] James III was extremely determined in his attitude towards Berwick. He was prepared to negotiate in order to obtain it, but may have considered the use of force while the peace negotiations were going on in Edinburgh in the autumn of 1487. On 15 October, Henry VII gave a commission to Lionel Bell, a merchant of North Shields, to provide the town and castle of Berwick-upon-Tweed with wheat, barley, malt, and all other necessary provisions, an indication that an attack from Scotland was expected.[66] However, no Scottish force appeared and the indenture of November 1487 secured Berwick, at least temporarily, from the danger of attack by including it in the extended truce. But this was clearly no long-term solution; for at the same time provision was made for another meeting between English and Scottish commissioners in May 1488, to discuss the proposed marriages at greater length 'togiddir with the appeasing of the said mater of Berwik'; and in July the two kings were to meet.[67]

This was not, however, the end of the matter, for where Berwick was concerned, James III was clearly prepared to ignore the provisions of the truce without waiting for further negotiation. Thus in January 1488 there were further alarms and excursions in north-east England; the Earl of Northumberland was ordered by Henry VII to have ready two hundred men to augment the Berwick garrison, as the Scots intended to lay siege to it within thirty days.[68] At about the same time James III was instructing Scottish ambassadors to England, appointed in parliament at Edinburgh, to demand that the town and castle of Berwick should either be surrendered to the Scots or else 'distroyit and castin doune'.[69] This remarkable statement reveals James III's real attitude to Berwick. The burgh was not of particular value as an economic proposition — indeed the expense of defending it adequately was huge — and the Scots lieges showed little interest in recovering it after 1482. But to the king, Berwick was a symbol of royal prestige, acquired during his minority and lost while he was a prisoner. Unlike his subjects, James III had been prepared to pay to defend the burgh in 1482; now that it was lost, the chances of recovering it by direct assault, in view of general Scottish apathy or downright hostility towards such a venture, seemed remote. Even the siege of Dunbar, a target which from a Scottish point of view was both uncontroversial and much more accessible, had been unduly protracted. So King James may have seen his best chance in making alarming noises about Berwick to put pressure on Henry VII, while at the same time salving his own pride by offering a compromise solution — the destruction of the fortifications.

Before negotiations with England were pursued any further, James III was overtaken by the internal events of 1488. Unquestionably he had shown considerable skill in restoring the diplomatic climate in which a further alliance might be achieved. Much of this was fortuitous, the exploitation of political instability in England which had produced two usurpers in as many years; but the policy itself was forward-looking and would indeed be widely praised in Scotland less than two decades later. In the 1480s, however, alliance with England was unpopular not so much because of the policy itself, but because of the character of the king. A permanent peace on the borders, achieved by a king whose reputation for interference in the localities was already established, would undoubtedly be followed by the intrusion of royal officials into areas where the Earls of Angus, the Hepburns, the Humes and their like enjoyed an authority which generally went unchallenged. There were already signs of royal interference in James III's running battle with the Humes over the revenues of Coldingham, and in his efforts to win the support of Douglas of Cavers, sheriff of Roxburgh, to offset the power of his kinsman, the Earl of Angus, in the Middle Marches. Thus Polydore Vergil, admittedly writing with the benefit of knowledge of the events of 1488 in Scotland, may well have been expressing accurately the view of James III held by his subjects in the south-east when he stated that the Scottish king's name was 'hateful' to them; and there is a ring of truth about James's supposed admission to Henry VII that his desire for amity with England was not shared by his subjects.[70]

As in diplomatic affairs, so also in ecclesiastical policy, the king faced an uphill struggle in the 1480s. The deaths in quick succession of Bishops Laing of Glasgow and Livingston of Dunkeld, the two Chancellors of the 1482–3 crisis period, produced vacancies which posed problems for James III, largely because he was unable to have his own candidate accepted in the case of Dunkeld, while in Glasgow — in so far as he could influence the election at all — his choice merely added to friction amongst the higher clergy.

The Glasgow vacancy followed Bishop John Laing's death on 11 January 1483. The king had not yet recovered full control of government, and probably had nothing to do with the cathedral chapter's nomination for the vacant bishopric, George Carmichael. This man, who had been Treasurer of Glasgow cathedral since 1474, a frequent member of both the Lords of Council and Lords Auditors, and who had attended the parliament of April 1481, must have been elected very soon after Laing's death, for on 18 February 1483 he is described as 'elect of Glasgow' in a royal charter witness list.[71] Carmichael seems to have been an associate of Angus, on whose council he appears on 9 July 1483;[72] this would hardly endear him to the king. It is also likely that Carmichael, like Laing before him, had supported Albany during the winter of 1482; for the duke was still nominally in power when Laing died in January, and it would be natural for the Glasgow chapter to elect in his place a man favoured by, or perhaps even suggested by, Albany. In spite of this, James III seems initially to have been indifferent to Carmichael's election rather than antagonistic towards him, for as 'elect of Glasgow', Carmichael appears in the parliament of March 1483 — one which was full of royal supporters — and witnesses a royal charter at Edinburgh on the 22nd of the same month.[73]

However, on 13 April 1483 Pope Sixtus IV declared the election of Carmichael to Glasgow to be null and void, because it had been made contrary to his reservation of the see. The pope went on to denounce all those who did not reject Carmichael and accept Robert Blacader, bishop of Aberdeen, who arrived in Rome the following month.[74] There are two possible explanations for this volte-face. First, it is possible that the king's orator at the papal curia, George Browne, did not press Carmichael's claims with any vigour; he may in fact have been instructed by James III to ask the pope to reject Carmichael and provide Blacader as the king's nominee for the see. If Carmichael was in fact an Albany supporter, such action would be consistent with the king's policy in January 1483, when the duke was beginning to revert to his old treasons. Blacader is quite likely to have been James's choice for the see, as he had already pursued a lengthy career in the royal service. In 1471, he had been James's ambassador to the pope, and perhaps as reward received the abbacy of Melrose on 30 March of that year.[75] In 1474 Blacader, styled clerk of St. Andrews diocese and principal ambassador of the king of Scots to the pope, was provided to the precentorship of Dunkeld. Ultimately, in 1476, he resigned both abbey and precentory on being granted pensions of 120 marks and £20 Scots respectively out of their revenues. In October 1479 he obtained the archdeaconry of Aberdeen;[76] and he sat as 'elect of Aberdeen' with the Lords of Council on two occasions in June 1480.[77] He was provided to the see of Aberdeen on 14 July 1480, three months after the death of the previous bishop, Thomas Spens, a noted royal counsellor; and he sat in parliament on 11 April 1481 as 'Robert, bishop of Aberdeen'[78] (though in fact he does not appear to have been consecrated during his tenure of the bishopric). Thus Blacader's career before 1483 appears to have been that of a loyal servant of the Crown; and as a former ambassador to the pope he was doubtless regarded by the king as a suitable candidate for the see of Glasgow. If so, King James may have instructed George Browne to suggest to the pope that the election of Carmichael by the cathedral chapter should be set aside.

Alternatively, Browne may not have come into the negotiations at all. It has been suggested that, far from supporting the king in pressing the claims of Blacader to the see of Glasgow, Browne was in fact acting for Albany in attempting to secure papal recognition of Carmichael's election.[79] James III's open hostility towards Browne a year later, when the latter was supported by Sixtus IV in claiming the vacant see of Dunkeld, may thus have been of long standing; and as Blacader was in Rome in person in the spring of 1483,[80] he was in an ideal position to press his own claims in spite of the possible opposition of Browne. Also, it is to be presumed that Blacader would have the king's support in his mission to Rome. Thus Sixtus IV, who probably had very little knowledge of the Scottish political or ecclesiastical scene, must have been acting under powerful pressures to annul Carmichael's election so swiftly, and to threaten his supporters with excommunication; and in fact, after Blacader had been consecrated Bishop of Glasgow in Rome, a letter from the pope describes him as having come to the city on the king's business and his own.[81]

Little or no action seems to have been taken to depose Carmichael from the see of Glasgow. On 29 November 1483, still described as 'elect of Glasgow', he received from Richard III a safe-conduct, at James III's request, to act as a commissioner on state affairs.[82] It is possible, of course, that the safe-conduct had been requested a long time before November, and that its issue had been held up by the prevailing unrest in England during and after the usurpation of Richard III. In any event, Carmichael died in the summer of 1485; and Spóttiswoode suggests rather implausibly that his death occurred on a journey to Rome to try to secure confirmation of his election.[83] Blacader had already been consecrated for over a year, and by 20 October 1484 he is to be found sitting with the Lords of Council.[84]

In the end, the promotion of Blacader to the see of Glasgow was to prove a miscalculation on the part of the king; but even more serious was the long wrangle over the other vacant bishopric, Dunkeld. According to Myln, Bishop Livingston died on 28 August 1483, and was buried on the island of Inchcolm.[85] Less than a month after his death, Alexander Inglis, dean of Dunkeld and archdeacon of St. Andrews, Clerk Register and clerk of the king's council, was elected bishop by the Dunkeld chapter on the nomination of James III.[86] Inglis was the obvious choice for the king to make to place Dunkeld in charge of a loyal and experienced ecclesiastic. He had had a long career as an envoy to settle disputes with the English, acting in this capacity at Alnwick in 1473, as a commissioner in 1476, and as the recipient of the fourth instalment of the Princess Cecilia's dowry in 1478.[87] He had been a frequent attender at parliaments, and had sat on the Lords of Council. Clerk Register and royal charter witness from 1475 onwards, Inglis had been displaced at the time of Lauder by Patrick Leich; and after witnessing the bond made with the Duke of Gloucester by the provost and community of Edinburgh on 4 August 1482[88] — while probably still occupying the office of Clerk Register — he took no further part in government for the remainder of the crisis period. This would undoubtedly be a recommendation in the eyes of James III.

By 17 September 1483 Alexander Inglis was Bishop-elect of Dunkeld. But little more than a month later, on 22 October, Sixtus IV provided George Browne to the see.[89] His reasons for opposing the royal candidate, rather than supporting him as in the case of Blacader, are to be found, according to Myln, in Browne's activities in Rome while acting as 'orator regis'. Apparently he became well acquainted with some of the cardinals, particularly Rodrigo Borgia, bishop of Porto, vice-chancellor of the papal curia, the future Pope Alexander VI. With the help of Borgia, Browne managed to persuade Sixtus IV to quash the election of Inglis to Dunkeld and to have himself appointed to the vacant see. According to Myln, Browne was consecrated in 1484 in the church of St. James of the Spaniards in Rome — probably on Sunday 13 June.[90] However James III, as might have been expected, refused to accept Browne as Bishop of Dunkeld; he complained at length that by acts of the Scottish parliament anyone promoted in this way was reckoned a rebel and traitor; and the shadow of Patrick Graham fell sharply across the ensuing dispute. Inglis was supported by the king, in defiance of the pope's provision of Browne, for little short of two years. Thus he appears as 'electus Dunkeldensis' in a safe-conduct from Richard III of England in November 1483; as 'the elect of Dunkeld' in the parliaments of May 1484 and March and May 1485; and again as 'the elect of Dunkeld' in sittings of the Lords Auditors in February 1484. In a case called before the Auditors on 22 May 1485, Inglis is described as 'Alexander, elect of Dunkeld and Archdeacon of St. Andrews'.[91]

Finally, on 26 May 1485, the king in parliament protested vigorously against Sixtus IV's elevation of George Browne. The royal commissioners travelling to Rome were directed to remind the new pope, Innocent VIII, how the king had 'divers tymes writin and maid supplicacioun bath to our holy fader and his predecessouris for the promocioun of his tender clerk counsalour maister Alex. Inglis dene and elect of the bischoprik of Dunkeld to the bischopric of the samyn, and do all their diligence possible for his said promocioun, and that thai sal schew and declare determytly to our said haly fader that our soveran lord wil not suffre maister George Broun nor nane utheris that has presumyt to be promovit to the said bischopric of Dunkeld contrar our soveran lordis mind, will and special writing to have only possessioun of the samyn'.[92]

Doubtless the king hoped to have Innocent VIII procure Browne's resignation of the see of Dunkeld; but he was to be disappointed. On 16 August 1485, less than three months after parliament's admonition to the pope, George Browne, described as Bishop of Dunkeld, appears as witness to a royal charter granted at Edinburgh,[93] and thereafter turns up regularly as a charter witness. Clearly James III had been forced to give way over Browne's election at some time during the summer of 1485.

Myln relates a colourful story by way of explaining the king's reconciliation with Browne. According to this account, Robert Lauder of Bass — 'Robert with the borit quhyngar', as he was commonly known — interceded on Browne's behalf with James III. Browne himself, returning to Scotland, prudently landed first on Inchcolm; and he entrusted Lauder of Bass with the task of executing his bulls. Lauder, armed with these, approached the gate of Edinburgh castle, but was forbidden entry by Alexander Inglis, the king's nominee for the bishopric. However, catching sight of James III, who was listening at a window, Lauder replied that if he was refused access to the king, he would summon the English to the walls, with whose assistance he would gain entry easily enough. This remark was apparently treated as a joke by the king who, reconciled, accepted a money payment; in addition, his favourite John Ramsay was granted a tack of the church of Abercorn by Browne for a payment of forty marks. Myln goes on to say that, after James III's death and Ramsay's flight to England, the teinds of Abercorn were resumed by the Bishop of Dunkeld; and they were in fact still in the bishop's hands at the Reformation.[94]

Whatever the truth of Myln's tale, the suggestion that the king was prepared to accept Browne as Bishop of Dunkeld because he was paid to do so seems a highly plausible one. Some sort of a compromise was apparently reached whereby Inglis was allowed to retain the fruits which he had obtained during the long dispute; and in compensation for his failure to obtain the see of Dunkeld he was granted the treasurership of Glasgow.[95] James may also have been influenced in his decision to receive Browne as bishop by the presence in Scotland of a papal legate, James Pasarella, bishop of Imola, from April or May 1485, throughout the summer of that year.[96]

Much more ominous than the Dunkeld election, however, was the continuing struggle between the king and the Humes for control of the revenues of the priory of Coldingham. James III had received Hume assistance during a critical period of the winter of 1482–3; and he had duly rewarded Alexander Hume for his support against Albany.[97] But the real problem was the position of Alexander's uncle, John Hume, who was determined to secure all the revenues of Coldingham for himself. As early as August 1473, and in spite of the king's efforts to suppress the priory the previous year, John Hume had acquired a new provision for himself as prior.[98] James III, who in April of the same year had attempted a compromise solution, the erection of a royal chapel at Coldingham, a collegiate church with dean and prebendaries, did not recognise John Hume's status as prior; instead he lent his backing to Patrick Hume, archdeacon of Teviotdale and John Hume's rival, as dean of Coldingham. This royal interference in what had hitherto been a local struggle produced a continuing crisis which grew to enormous proportions by the end of the reign. The king's choice as dean of Coldingham, Patrick Hume, was dead by 1478; and John Hume, who had 'acquiesced out of fear'[99] in the royal erection of a collegiate church at Coldingham, reverted by the end of the '70s to his original position of calling himself prior, taking the fruits, and defying the king.

The seriousness of his own position in 1482–3 had forced James III to make a virtue of necessity and adopt a more conciliatory policy towards John Hume. While still recovering from the Albany crisis, on 5 May 1483 the Scottish king had been issued by Pope Sixtus IV with bulls commanding his nobles and prelates to obey him;[100] and on 21 February 1484 John Hume is described as 'dean of the chapel of the king of Scots' — clearly James III's new erection at Coldingham.[101] But Hume had no intention of accepting the proffered olive branch; and early in the new pontificate — that is, after 12 September 1484 — he promised the king that he would go to Rome to procure the division of the remainder of the Coldingham fruits into prebends; and on this understanding he was issued with royal letters of recommendation to Innocent VIII. On arriving in Rome, however, he immediately misused his letters to acquire from the pope a revocation of the suppression of Coldingham priory and its erection as a collegiate church; his rights as prior of Coldingham were confirmed by the new pope, who at the same time ordered the suppression of the short-lived and partially erected collegiate church there.[102] John Hume had recovered all the Coldingham revenues at a stroke — and made an implacable enemy of the king.

Thus when parliament assembled in May 1485, much of its foreign business concerned the sending of an embassy to Pope Innocent VIII; and although the ostensible reason for this was to offer the king's obedience to the new pontiff, in fact King James must have been much more concerned to restore his authority in ecclesiastical affairs, undermined as it was by the Dunkeld and Coldingham failures. It was agreed by the Lords of the Articles that the Archbishop of St. Andrews should head the embassy, and the king had apparently written to the pope informing him of this. Scheves, according to the parliamentary records of his own free will, had offered to pay his own expenses, and therefore 'he is maist convenient and maist honerable persoun that can be send'. If the king so desired, he could choose any 'personis of estait' he wanted to join the archbishop on embassy.[103] The ambassadors' business included not only the vexed questions of Coldingham, Dunkeld and royal appointments to vacant benefices, but also the recent Franco-Scottish alliance and the much more remote annexation of Orkney and Shetland.

The fact that Scheves was a member of the Lords of the Articles in May 1485, and that the king, however cynically, had already chosen him to head the embassy, indicates that for political purposes at least, James III and the archbishop were prepared to cooperate. Yet Scheves was hardly the man to plead John Ireland's case at the Roman curia;[104] and this may account for the king's apparent reluctance to let the archbishop go to Rome on his own. An English safe-conduct was issued on 24 May 1485 for Scheves and a train of forty to pass through England en route;[105] but it was not used. On 23 September the new king, Henry VII, issued another safe-conduct for Scheves, but on this occasion John Ireland was to accompany him. Ireland's inclusion, presumably to plead his own case at Rome rather than leave it to Scheves, suggests either that James III had not yet accepted George Browne as Bishop of Dunkeld (and therefore regarded Inglis as bishop and Ireland as Inglis's successor in the archdeaconry of St. Andrews) or that the king still hoped to have the Dunkeld decision reversed in favour of his own candidate.

It is however possible that the long delay in despatching Scheves' mission to

Rome was due in large part to the archbishop's reluctance to set out. Scheves, John of Litster, a Franciscan, and Simon Finlay were the papal collectors in Scotland, and they had rendered no accounts to Rome. In February 1485 Innocent VIII had renewed the constitution of Pius II regarding annates, making deprivation the penalty for defaulters, so that Scheves had reason to worry about his own position. Reports had reached Rome that he was retaining for himself a considerable portion of the annates which should have been paid into the papal treasury, and on 5 August 1485 Innocent VIII commissioned James Pasarella, bishop of Imola, who was already in Scotland, to investigate the matter with full power to take any action necessary — to demand the money due to Rome, to interdict and suspend, or even to call in the aid of the secular arm.[106]

Pasarella's general brief from the pope was to restore order in the Scottish church. 'Lately, when he was a cardinal, the pope was grieved to learn that many discords . . . had arisen between James, king of Scots, and the prelates, princes, and inhabitants of the realm, which upon becoming pope he has heard have been almost appeased by the prudence of the said king, prelates, and princes'; nevertheless, in order to restore peace fully throughout Scotland, Innocent thought it as well to send Pasarella with full powers as a legate a latere. In the same month the more material concerns of the curia were included in further commissions to Pasarella, not only making the bishop papal collector in Scotland, but giving him power to proceed by interdict, suspension, excommunication and deprivation against obstinate debtors of the papal camera in respect of annates of benefices obtained by papal authority, and of the crusade.[107]

If the legate's visit was unwelcome to Archbishop Scheves, the king may have viewed it with mixed feelings. Undoubtedly he had sought papal assistance during the 1482–3 crisis to bolster up his own authority by having ecclesiastical censures hurled at his enemies. But this was a double-edged weapon, for it meant revealing his own weakness to the curia, and his subsequent failures over the Dunkeld and Coldingham disputes were in part the result. It is also highly unlikely that James III welcomed Pasarella's commission as papal collector in Scotland; and he probably collaborated with his archbishop in impressing on the legate the poverty of the country and its inability to pay out large sums to the papal treasury. Thus there was a further delay in the departure of Scheves' embassy to Rome, for the archbishop was no doubt required to be in Scotland during the legate's visit, and Pasarella, after spending about three months in the country from March 1485, did not return until early the following year.[108]

In spite of the delay, the business which the Scottish ambassadors were ordered to transact before the Roman curia remained much the same as that put forward by the parliament of May 1485. Some of it was straightforward; the pope was asked to confirm the Franco-Scottish alliance of 1484, and also 'the convencions confederacions and bandis maid betuix our souueran lord and the king of denmark that last decessit' (Christian I, who had died in 1481) 'of the donacioun and Impigneracioun of the landis of orknay and scheteland and of perpetuale exoneracioun Renunsacioun and discharge of the contribucioun of the Ilis eftir the forme of the said convencions'.[109] It is curious to find James, almost seventeen years after the event, seeking the pope's blessing for a contract made with the former king of Denmark in September 1468. It suggests either pressure on the part of the Danish king to recover Orkney and Shetland, of which there is no evidence at this time, or more probably a desire on the part of James III to improve his relations with the papacy. The king's failure over the bishopric of Dunkeld, and his obstinate defence of his own candidate for two years, were after all legacies of the pontificate of Sixtus IV. King James may well have decided to behave in a more statesmanlike way with the new pontiff in order to secure his gratitude and have clarified his position regarding bishoprics and other important benefices. Hence his embassy was given instructions to behave in the most correct way to Innocent VIII, intimating to him the Scottish king's obedience and asking for papal confirmation of treaties already made with foreign princes. In return for all this, the pope was asked to consider the great distance from Scotland to Rome and, on vacancies in important benefices occurring, 'to supercede and delay the disposicioun . . . for the space of sex monethis that our souuerane lordis writing and supplicacioun may be send for the promocioun of sic personis as is thankfull to his hienes sa that thir be na personis promovit to prelaciis nor digniteis without avise of his hienes sen all the prelatis of his Realme has the first vote in his parlment and of his Secrete counsale'.[110]

This last request, clearly made with the Dunkeld conflict in mind, also had a strong bearing on the king's plans for Coldingham; for James III, furious at John Hume's abuse of his letters, ordered his ambassadors to Rome to exhort Innocent VIII to grant 'ane ereccioun of coldingham to our souueran lordis chapell' — that is, to reverse the recent revocation granted to Hume and return to the king's original scheme of suppression of the priory. In the long run, King James's diplomacy achieved the desired result. On 28 April 1487 Innocent VIII reversed his decision in favour of Hume, and reverted to the arrangement of 3 April 1473, by which his predecessor Sixtus IV had accepted the suppression of Coldingham and the reallocation of its revenues, in part to the Chapel Royal at St. Andrews, and in part to the erection of a collegiate church at Coldingham itself. Innocent also gave instructions to 'inhibit the executors and subexecutors of the pope's letters granted to the said John Hom to proceed to any further execution of them, decree null and void whatever has been hitherto or in future may be attempted in this behalf by them and others', and to make prebends at Coldingham 'in all respects as if the letters aforesaid had been directed to them from the beginning by the said Pope Sixtus and during his life-time, and as if in virtue thereof they had begun to proceed to their execution'[111] — a clear indication that John Hume had done little or nothing towards the erection of prebends at Coldingham.

Innocent VIII's belated support for King James in the Coldingham struggle was the last in a series of concessions indicating a growing cordiality between the pope and the Scottish king. Other marks of papal favour had begun to be shown in the spring of 1486. Every year, on 5 March, the pope blessed a golden rose and sent it to some Christian prince selected by him. 'Today,' wrote the ambassador of the Duke of Milan at Rome to his master on 5 March 1486, 'he has blessed one and given it to the king of Scotland. I think it right to inform your lordship of this.'[112]

The Golden Rose was brought to Scotland by Pasarella on his second visit; and at the same time the legate was empowered to put into effect his commission of the previous year ordering clerks and laymen of every rank to obey the king. Rebellion by any noble would result in his lands being laid under an interdict and his goods forfeited. Absolution from these penalties could be granted only by the pope himself; and in order that no-one might plead ignorance of the legate's power, copies of Pasarella's commission were to be displayed in every cathedral throughout Scotland. It is clear from this that the legate's second visit was welcomed, and probably prompted, by the king himself.[113]

However, the most important of the papal concessions to King James was the indult of 20 April 1487, which went a long way towards clarifying the problem of the right of nomination to important benefices. Innocent VIII declared that when vacancies occurred in cathedral churches or monasteries exceeding in annual value two hundred florins gold of the camera, he would refrain for at least eight months from making provision to them, and meanwhile he would wait for letters from the king (and his successors) petitioning on behalf of candidates of his choice.[114] This indult was clearly a response to the king's request in May 1485 that only persons 'as is thankfull to his hienes' should be promoted to important beneficies. In fact, as Thomson points out,[115] the king on that occasion had requested a delay of only six months in making provisions, and the pope had conceded eight. This concession by Innocent VIII smoothed away areas of friction between the papacy and the Scottish Crown; it brought Scotland into line with England and France in making important church elections more or less a formality; and it meant that struggles such as that between Sixtus IV and James III over Dunkeld were unlikely ever to occur again. The papacy might also reap financial gains from the agreement; for rapid nomination by the Crown to high ecclesiastical posts — a matter now of eight months at the most — would mean that payments for bulls of nomination could be demanded more rapidly by the pope. It is possible, in fact, that the indult was partly inspired by the delay in the consecration of Elphinstone as Bishop of Aberdeen about this time. Elphinstone had been provided to Aberdeen on 19 March 1483; but he was not consecrated until 1488-9.[116] The financial loss to the papacy incurred by a technical vacancy of five or six years at Aberdeen may, as Thomson suggests, have provided an incentive to Innocent VIII to establish a system of appointments which would operate more swiftly than the existing one.[117]

James III's subsequent behaviour suggests that he regarded his negotiations with Innocent VIII with some satisfaction. In theory at least, the indult of April 1487 greatly strengthened his authority over the Scottish clergy; prospective rebels ran grave risk of incurring excommunication; and the gift of the Golden Rose in March 1486 was an indication of papal favour towards King James which became known throughout Europe.

In fact, however, the major ecclesiastical problems had not been solved at all, for they had little to do with the papacy. The trouble lay much nearer home, and concerned the character of James III and the attitudes of the Scottish clergy towards him. The indult might well prove a boon to his successors; but of what use was it to James himself, when already on two occasions in the 1480s the bearers of royal letters to the curia — Browne and Hume — had misused them to feather their own nests? If he wanted to secure effective control of appointments to vacant benefices, the king had to make certain of the loyalty of his ambassadors to, or spokesmen in, Rome. Even the long-delayed embassy, headed by Archbishop Scheves and Bishop Blacader in the winter of 1486-7,[118] produced not only the indult but deep rivalry and bitterness between the two ambassadors. Their first business at the curia was their own rather than the king's. Scheves was determined to be recognised as primate and legatus natus of the realm — probably not only to bolster up his flagging reputation and status with the king, but also to avoid a repetition of Pasarella's financial investigations in Scotland — and on 27 March 1487 he had his way; St. Andrews was granted primatial status, and the privileges of the see of Canterbury were extended to that of St. Andrews. James III may well have given his support to the archbishop in this;[119] but the result was simply — and predictably — to antagonise Scheves' fellow ambassador Robert Blacader, who at once acquired privileges for himself within his own diocese by way of compensation — the right to grant absolution for simony, to collate to benefices reserved to the apostolic see, and to visit and correct exempt religious houses. More important, Blacader was granted the right to levy money on the diocese of Glasgow to meet the cost of his translation from Aberdeen; and he began a campaign to secure personal exemption from Scheves' jurisdiction.[120]

The king had failed to restore peace and order in the Scottish church. Perhaps the task was impossible, but if so, King James's creation of Scheves as archbishop in the '70s was the root of much of the trouble. Scheves — like Graham before him — had provoked opposition from other bishops simply by occupying the office of archbishop; and his intimacy with an unpopular king made matters worse. Thus in 1482-3 Bishop Laing of Glasgow had been nominal head of the administration which rejected Scheves; Livingston of Dunkeld throughout resented Scheves' elevation; and Stewart, the elect of Moray, had forced the archbishop to resign in an effort to seize St. Andrews for himself. Thus, by 1483, a tradition of opposition to Scheves had been established which was reflected in the elections to Glasgow and Dunkeld; and even the king, in his anxiety to promote John Ireland, had provided a dangerous precedent for Blacader to follow by securing for Ireland a papal exemption from the archbishop's jurisdiction.[121] In the last analysis, however, James III had no option but to support Scheves as his own choice and former favourite; and in doing so, he helped to foment the hostility of the other major 'political' bishops. Indeed, the only committed royalist amongst the bishops who played an active part in government in the 1480s — apart from Scheves himself — was William Elphinstone, bishop of Aberdeen.

Thus the concessions made to King James by Innocent VIII between 1485 and 1487 were of little practical assistance to the Scottish monarch because he could not command enough effective support — clerical or lay — within Scotland itself. The Golden Rose of 1486 was an empty papal gesture, of no more value to James III than the hat and sword which were to be bestowed on James IV by Julius II in 1502. Likewise Pasarella's visit in 1486, backed by Innocent VIII's injunction to James's lieges to obey the king, proved of little assistance; for though the pope might threaten with excommunication all those who took up arms against James III, within two years the king was dead and Pope Innocent was selling absolutions to the Scottish rebels.

Yet it is unlikely that James III viewed his position in relation to his subjects in a pessimistic light. For him, the embassy to Rome had been a major success, strengthening his hold over the Scottish clergy and at last giving him the means to settle the outstanding problem of Coldingham. Thus in the autumn of 1487, with all the overweening confidence which characterised the royal Stewart family, King James went over to the offensive. Armed with Innocent VIII's bull of 28 April 1487, he had a statute passed in parliament at Edinburgh the following October warning all his lieges spiritual and temporal against resisting the royal scheme to suppress Coldingham priory and reallocate its revenues to the chapel royal; furthermore, any appeals to the Roman curia against the suppression, or the use of the bulls purchased for the same purpose, would be treated as cases of treason.[122] Clearly the royal wishes were initially ignored by John Hume, who continued to regard himself as prior of Coldingham; he had, after all, another set of bulls which he had obtained in 1484–5 from Innocent VIII acknowledging him as prior, and presumably had no intention of obeying the new ones unless he were forced to. Relying on the support of his relatives and the distance of his priory from Edinburgh, he passively defied the papal instructions. None of the Humes — John Hume himself, his brothers George Hume of Aytoun and Sir Patrick Hume of Fastcastle, and their nephew Alexander, second Lord Hume — was present in parliament in October 1487; indeed they may have been aware in advance of the legislation regarding Coldingham which the king intended to introduce. After October, much depended on whether James III would proceed beyond parliamentary threats.

In the event, he decided to do so; he was, after all, being openly defied by the Humes, and he had to maintain royal authority. But in addition, there is at least a possibility that a change of plan in his schemes for beautifying the chapel royal provided an incentive for attempted coercion of John Hume and his relatives. The original plan in 1472 had been to reallocate the Coldingham revenues to the chapel royal of St. Mary of the Rock at St. Andrews; but thereafter St. Andrews is not specifically mentioned. On the other hand, the years 1485–7 saw the foundation and construction of a royal collegiate church at Restalrig, just outside Edinburgh, confirmed by papal bulls on 13 November 1487.[123] James III was clearly very proud of his new foundation; he took Pasarella to see Restalrig, presumably while it was still under construction, in the spring or summer of 1486; and he described the building to the pope as a chapel 'which James, King of Scots, has caused to be sumptuously built at his own expense, and which he has endowed with estates and possessions'.[124] King James's close personal interest in Restalrig suggests that he may have planned to establish his collegiate church there as the chapel royal, replacing St. Mary of the Rock, St. Andrews.[125] The king would require money to endow the new foundation, and it is probably no coincidence that his supplication that Restalrig be made a collegiate church was registered at Rome on 7 May 1487, little over a week after the pope's suppression of Coldingham and the reallocation of the priory's revenues to the chapel royal.

R

To get his money, James III had to attack the Humes and their supporters; and while it is probably going too far to suggest that in attempting to do so the king 'had signed his own death warrant',[126] he had undoubtedly provoked the first phase of the rebellion which in the end would cost him his life.

NOTES

1. *Rot. Scot.*, ii, 461; Gairdner, *Letters of Richard III and Henry VII*, i, 53.

2. B.M. Harl. MS. 433, f. 248 v.

3. *Ibid.*

4. *A.P.S.*, ii, 164-5.

5. *Ibid.*, 164.

6. English safe-conducts were issued for Scottish ambassadors to come south in March and April 1484; but they do not appear to have been used: *Rot. Scot.*, ii, 461, 462.

7. *A.P.S.*, ii, 165.

8. *E.R.*, ix, 432, 433-4.

9. *Foedera*, xii, 235-41.

10. S.R.O. MSS. Treaties with France, Nos. 16-19. A 17th century copy of the 1484 treaty, mistakenly dated 22 May 1483 (on which date Louis XI, not Charles VIII, was king of France) is to be found in B.N. MS. francais 23,023, ff. 244-251 v. Another copy, in an 18th century hand, is in B.M. Add. MS. 12,192 pp. 58-71.

11. B.N. MS. francais 15,889, f. 435 v.

12. Balfour, *Annales*, i, 209; *E.R.*, ix, 573.

13. *Rot. Scot.*, ii, 461-2; *Foedera*, xii, 251.

14. *A.P.S.*, ii, 173.

15. Buchanan, *History*, ii, 152-3.

16. *R.M.S.*, ii, No. 1597; *Scots Peerage*, i, 220; Fraser, *Annandale*, i, pp. xvii, xxiii.

17. Fraser, *Carlaverock*, i, 154.

18. Confirmed by royal charter, 26 January 1492–3; *R.M.S.*, ii, No. 2131.

19. *A.P.S.*, ii, 139; *R.M.S.*, ii, Nos. 1603, 1597, 1594.

20. *E.R.*, ix, Pref., p. lvi.

21. *Cal. Docs. Scot.*, iv, Nos. 1494, 1496, 1497.

22. Buchanan, *History*, ii, 153.

23. P.R.O., E 404, 78/3/26.

24. Gairdner, *Letters of Richard III and Henry VII*, i, 59-61.

25. *Ibid.*, 61-2; *Rot. Scot.*, ii, 464.

26. *Bannatyne Miscellany*, ii, 41-48.

27. *Ibid.*, 36.

28. *Ibid.*, 39-40.

29. *Foedera*, xii, 235-241.

30. *Ibid.*, 242-4.

31. *Ibid.*, 250.

32. *A.P.S.*, ii, 170.

33. *Cal. Docs. Scot.*, iv, No. 1513.

34. Pitscottie, *Historie*, i, 191, 195-6.

35. Polydore Vergil, *Historia Anglica*, 29.

36. Pitscottie, *Historie*, i, 2.

37. *Rot. Scot.*, ii, 469-70.

38. P.R.O., DL 42, no. 21, f. 97 v.

39. *R.M.S.*, ii, No. 1638.

40. *Cal. Docs. Scot.,* iv, No. 1518.
41. Major, *History,* 393.
42. *Cal. Patent Rolls: 1485-94,* 39.
43. Campbell, *Materials,* i, 93-4.
44. Conway, *Henry VII's Relations with Scotland and Ireland,* 9.
45. *Rot. Scot.,* ii, 469.
46. *E.R.,* ix, 434-5.
47. *Ibid.,* 433.
48. *Ibid.,* 523.
49. *Rot. Scot.,* ii, 471.
50. *Cal. Docs. Scot.,* iv, No. 1521.
51. Leland, *Collectanea,* iv, 203.
52. *Rot. Scot.,* ii, 473-7.
53. *Foedera,* xii, 316.
54. *Rot. Scot.,* ii, 473-7.
55. *E.R.,* ix, 408, 468.
56. *S.H.R.,* xxxii, (1952), 52-7.
57. *E.R.,* ix, 251, 327, 495.
58. *Ibid.,* 451.
59. Vat. Reg. Supp. 870, f. 121 r; *C.P.L.,* xiv, 4.
60. *R.M.S.,* ii, No. 1539; *E.R.,* ix, 213; and *see above,* Chapter 8.
61. *Rot. Scot.,* ii, 475.
62. Campbell, *Materials,* ii, 120.
63. *Rot. Scot.,* ii, 480.
64. *Complete Peerage,* xii, pt. 2, 449; Nicholas, *Privy Purse Expenses of Elizabeth of York,* xx.
65. *Rot. Scot.,* ii, 480, 481.
66. *Cal. Docs. Scot.,* iv, No. 1528.
67. *Rot. Scot.,* ii, 481.
68. Scofield, Star Chamber, 20.
69. *A.P.S.,* ii, 182.
70. Polydore Vergil, *Historia Anglica,* 29, 41.
71. *R.M.S.,* ii, Nos. 1169, 1560; *A.P.S.,* ii, 134.
72. Fraser, *Douglas,* iii, 436.
73. *Laing Chrs.,* No. 189.
74. Theiner, *Vetera Monumenta,* Nos, 873, 876.
75. *Ibid.,* No. 850.
76. Dowden, *Bishops,* 128n.
77. *A.D.C.,* 49, 59.
78. *A.P.S.,* ii, 133.
79. Herkless and Hannay, i, 110.
80. Theiner, *Vetera Monumenta,* No. 876.
81. *Ibid.*
82. *Rot. Scot.,* ii, 461.
83. *C.P.L.,* xiv, 56; Vat. Reg. Supp., 850, f. 51 r-v (for Carmichael's death); *Spottiswoode,* i, 224.
84. *A.D.C.,* 85.
85. Myln, *Vitae,* 26.
86. *Laing Charters,* No. 191; Myln, *Vitae,* 26.
87. *Cal. Docs. Scot.,* iv, No. 1408; App. i, No. 27; No. 1449.
88. *Ibid.,* No. 1480.
89. *Eubel,* ii, 163.
90. Myln, *Vitae,* 28; Dowden, *Bishops,* 80.
91. *Foedera,* xii, 207; *A.P.S.,* ii, 166, 167, 168; *A.D.A.,* 127, 136, 141.
92. *A.P.S.,* ii, 171.

93. *R.M.S.*, ii, No. 1623.

94. Myln, *Vitae*, 28-9; J. A. F. Thomson, 'Innocent VIII and the Scottish Church', in *Innes Review*, xix, Part i, (Spring 1968), 25.

95. Myln, *Vitae*, 29.

96. *H.M.C. Rep. xv*, App. viii, Drumlanrig MSS, 59.

97. *See above*, Chapter 8. The entire struggle is discussed in Norman Macdougall, 'The Struggle for the Priory of Coldingham, 1472–88', in *Innes Review*, xxiii, (1972), 102-114.

98. Vat. Reg. Supp. 694, f. 129 v.

99. *C.P.L.*, xiv, 45-6.

100. Herkless and Hannay, i, 123.

101. *C.P.L.*, xiii, 192-3.

102. *Ibid.*, xiv, 47.

103. *A.P.S.*, ii, 170-1.

104. *See above*, Chapter 9.

105. *Rot. Scot.*, ii, 468.

106. *C.P.L.*, xiv, 56-7.

107. *Ibid.*, 51, 52, 56-7.

108. *H.M.C. Rep. xv*, App., 8, 59; Pasarella was in Mainz on 20 October 1485 (*Cal. State Papers (Venice)*, i, 156); in England, January 1486 (Campbell, *Materials*, i, 209; *Foedera*, xii, 313).

109. *A.P.S.*, ii, 171.

110. *Ibid.*

111. *C.P.L.*, xiv, 47-8.

112. *Cal. State Papers (Milan)*, i, 247.

113. Theiner, *Vetera Monumenta*, 496-9; *C.P.L.*, xiv, 51; Boece (*Vitae*, 76) suggests that the purpose of Pasarella's visit in 1486 was to bestow 'several privileges on the nobles and commons', which is the reverse of the truth. He does, however, also record that James III was delighted to see the legate.

114. *C.P.L.*, xiv, 4.

115. J.A.F. Thomson, *op.cit.*, 28.

116. *Eubel*, ii, 87; W. Angus, 'Note on the Consecration of William Elphinstone, Bishop of Aberdeen', in *Aberdeen University Review*, xxiii, (1935–6), 135-6.

117. J. A. F. Thomson, *op.cit.*, 29 and n.40.

118. *Ibid.*, 26-7.

119. *C.P.L.*, xiv, 152; J. A. F. Thomson, *op. cit.*, 27.

120. *C.P.L.*, xiv, 30, 159-60. Blacader was finally granted exemption from Scheves' jurisdiction on 25 May 1488, when the rebellion — in which he sided with Prince James — was at its height: *C.P.L.*, xiv, 220-1.

121. Vat. Reg. Supp. 833, f. 92 r–v.

122. *A.P.S.*, ii, 179.

123. Vat. Reg. Supp. 870, ff. 264 r–v, 265 r; *C.P.L.*, xiv, 211-213.

124. Boece, *Vitae*, 76-7; *C.P.L.*, xiv, 212.

125. This possibility is discussed at length in Macdougall, *op.cit.*, 109-112.

126. Mackie, *James IV*, 39.

11

Disaster at Bannockburn: 1488

THE death of James III, during or after a battle fought near the site of Robert I's famous victory of 1314, and given the name 'Sauchieburn' in the seventeenth century, brought to an end a civil war which had disturbed central and southern Scotland for upwards of four months. It was the surprising and tragic finish to a series of crises provoked by the king himself, and which, up to the very end, he seemed likely to resolve in his favour. Although many problems of interpretation remain, the events themselves are fairly fully described in contemporary sources, notably the parliamentary debate in October 1488 which attempted to fix responsibility for the crisis, and the trials and forfeitures of some of James III's supporters at the same time.

That there should have been a rebellion, or series of rebellions, is in itself easy to understand. The genesis of the turmoil of 1488 is to be found on 15 October 1487, when a short-lived parliament meeting in Edinburgh was prorogued until 11 January 1488, leaving a number of controversial issues unresolved — the English marriages proposed for the king and his sons, the English truce and the related problem of the possession of Berwick; and above all, the suppression of the priory of Coldingham and annexation of half its revenues to the chapel royal.[1] It may be that the king continued parliament until January to allow the English truce to be finalised — as it was on 28 November 1487 — but if so he also gave a breathing space of three months to the Humes and their supporters to prepare resistance. Furthermore, in the January parliament James III threw caution to the winds by adding to the outstanding business some provocative schemes of his own.

The estates assembled in Edinburgh on 11 January — a sizeable gathering of eighty, including a large number of lairds — and it was presumably on that day that the Lords of the Articles were elected. No list of those chosen has survived, but the usual procedure was clearly in operation, as the Lords of the Articles are mentioned in two of the nineteen statutes passed. Clearly there was considerable debate amongst the legislators over the business put before them, for it was not until 29 January that the entire gathering of the estates reassembled and the statutes were approved.[2]

The first business concerned the proposed English marriage alliances, the fulfilment of the terms of the indenture of November 1487. The Lords of the Articles suggested an embassy, whose expenses of £250 Scots were to be paid for by the three estates, and whose members would travel to Newcastle, York 'or quhat uthir place contenit in the said indenturis geif the king of Ingland wil nocht send to Edinburgh'; this body was to consist of a bishop, a lord of parliament, a clerk, and a knight or squire, all of them to be chosen by the king. Their business was not only to organise the proposed May diet for the arranging of two of the marriages, those of the king and his eldest son, but also, as we have seen, to demand that the town and castle of Berwick were either surrendered to James III or else 'distroyit and castin doune'.[3] Such pressure was no doubt intended to impress Henry VII, and it might well have done so in the end; as Nicholson reminds us, 'for the first time in two hundred years the Scottish and English kings were sincere and like-minded in a desire for peace'.[4] But to the Scottish nobility of the south-east, already faced with James's interference at Coldingham and the plight of the Humes, the prospect of permanent peace with England based on the recovery of Berwick must have been alarming in the extreme; and when many of them joined the Humes in defying their intransigent sovereign, they may have done so as a matter of self-defence.

Further alarm was no doubt caused by efforts to extend royal control over the administration of justice. In the field of civil cases, as we have seen, the king reversed the legislation of October 1487 by insisting that litigants should have the right to direct appeal to the Lords of Council, otherwise 'it were deferring of Justice to mony partijs'.[5] His hard-pressed councillors can hardly have agreed with him; and it is likely that some magnates who exercised local jurisdictions, while accepting in theory the principle that the council was the ultimate court of appeal in civil cases, were extremely reluctant in practice to make any concessions to a king whom they feared and distrusted. Nor did James III stop here, for the same parliament of January 1488 produced a spate of legislation on the subject of criminal justice. The existing justice ayres were to be 'dissolvit and disertit', and new ones set both north and south of Forth, to be held 'at sic dayis and tymes as salbe thocht expedient be our Souerane lord and his Secret consale'. The king did not intend to go out on the ayres himself, but employed two loyal and powerful earls — Crawford and Huntly — to undertake the task as Justiciars north of Forth. South of Forth, there would also be two Justiciars, and parliament named four candidates from whom the king would choose two — Lords Bothwell, Lyle, Glamis and Drummond.[6] This legislation is far more precise than any which had preceded it; far more than the piecemeal attempts of the parliaments of 1478 and 1485 to enforce law and order throughout the country, the statutes of 1488 suggest a positive determination on the part of the king to see that it was done effectively. No doubt such legislation pleased royal supporters and some members of the estates who had been urging the king for years to provide firm justice by driving the ayres; but other lords, especially south of Forth, must have found remarkably ominous King James's statement that he would send 'certane wise lordis and persons of his consale' with the Justiciars to act as assessors and give counsel.[7]

James III showed an even more aggressive spirit in his attempt to settle the problem of Coldingham once and for all. On 29 January parliament recalled the statute made three months previously threatening with forfeiture any who attempted to resist the suppression of the priory; since that time, certain unspecified temporal persons had acted in defiance of the statute, and they were to be summoned to answer for their crimes on 5 May. However, as it was difficult to assemble the estates at Edinburgh at that time, many members having a great distance to travel, parliament ordered that a number of representatives be chosen from each estate to sit in judgment on the offenders; in addition, this body was to have 'the hale power of the body of the parliament . . . to avise common and conclude apone sic uthir materis as sal occur in the mene tyme'. This last commission was similar to that given to committees of parliament in 1469, 1471, 1474, 1476 and 1478;[8] but the 1488 committee was larger than any of these, numbering fifty in all, little short of the average attendance at parliament during the reign, and hopelessly cumbrous. Side by side with the king's friends and supporters — Scheves, Elphinstone, the Earls of Crawford, Atholl, Erroll and Marischal, Lords Bothwell and Avandale, and John Ross of Montgrenan — are to be found his future enemies — the Bishops of Glasgow and Dunkeld, the Earls of Angus and Argyll, and Lords Drummond and Lyle. Some of the latter at least would be disinclined to take action against the breakers of the Coldingham statute; and all of them would throw in their lot with the Humes in less than two months. The conclusion must be that James III was taken by surprise by the much more serious rebellion which broke out in February and March; in January, he was totally preoccupied with the coercion of the Humes.

The king was however aware that the Humes — George of Aytoun, Patrick of Fastcastle, and their brother John, who still regarded himself as prior of Coldingham — would resist, and that they would be able to call on a fair amount of local support. To insure against this, King James emulated his father by publicly rewarding those whom he reckoned loyal to the Crown or whose loyalty he hoped to retain. On 29 January he created four new Lords of Parliament. Robert Crichton of Sanquhar, one of the victors of Lochmaben, was made Lord Crichton of Sanquhar; John Drummond of Cargill, whom the king had thrust out of the office of Steward of Strathearn in 1475 and whom he doubtless wished to conciliate, was created Lord Drummond; John Hay of Yester, sheriff of Peebles, an active parliamentarian, and related through his wife to the loyal family of Lindsay of Byres, was created Lord Hay of Yester; and Sir William Ruthven of that ilk, one of the conservators of the truce of September 1484, was made Lord Ruthven. On the same day the king indicated his trust in William Douglas of Cavers, sheriff of Roxburgh — a tenant and kinsman of the Earl of Angus — by confirming Douglas in his regality of Cavers before the assembled estates.[9]

Also on 29 January, James III created three new knights — David Kennedy, son and heir of the loyal John, Lord Kennedy; William Carlyle, son and heir of John, first Lord Carlyle, himself one of the king's own creations; and Robert Cunningham of Polmaise, near Stirling. But by far the most provocative creation of the day was James's raising of his second son, the Marquis of Ormonde, to the dignity of Duke of Ross. (The title of Earl of Edirdale was bestowed on him at the same time; he was already Earl of Ross and Lord of Brechin.)[10] This creation, coming only eighteen months after a projected marriage alliance for the marquis which the king had tenaciously pursued, must have suggested to some of the disaffected that James III was growing mistrustful of James, duke of Rothesay, his eldest son. This belief may have been reinforced by the fact that, though the proposed English marriages of the king and Duke of Rothesay were made conditional on Berwick being restored or 'castin doune',[11] that of the Marquis of Ormonde and Princess Katherine was not mentioned at all. It was the first to be proposed, the match in which James III appears to have been most interested, and this may be why he did not make it, like the others, conditional on Berwick's return or destruction.

At any rate, reaction to the creation was rapid and dramatic. Only four days later, on 2 February 1488, the young Duke of Rothesay, not yet fifteen years of age, left Stirling castle without his father's knowledge and was soon to be found on the side of the disaffected. The keeper of Stirling castle, James Shaw of Sauchie, married his daughter Helen to Patrick Hume of Polwarth about this time,[12] and may have regarded King James's fulminations against temporal persons who supported the Humes as a threat to his own safety. His solution was to remove the prince, and although the boy's exact whereabouts are unknown during the next two months, it seems probable that Shaw of Sauchie took him to join his Hume kinsmen, perhaps first at Linlithgow, and that by the end of March or beginning of April he had been returned to Stirling castle.[13]

The defection of the prince, although widely commented on by the sixteenth century chroniclers, receives scant treatment in contemporary record sources. In the parliament of February 1490 reference is made to 'the secund day of februare quhilk was the day of our souerane lord that now is cuming furth of Strivilin';[14] and that is all. There is no official account of who was involved on the rebel side, and even the later chroniclers are in some doubt about this. Both Lesley and Ferreri give roughly the same list of rebel nobility — the Earls of Angus, Argyll and Lennox (Lord Darnley), Lords Hailes, Hume, Drummond, Lyle and Gray[15] — but neither relates these men specifically to the removal of the prince from Stirling on 2 February 1488. Indeed, at this early stage, the fact that his son had joined the disaffected and that he was therefore facing a very serious threat seems to have been quite unknown to the king. James's ignorance of the true situation for little short of three weeks suggests strongly that there was no abduction of the prince from Stirling, but that he went willingly, or at any rate without protest, with the keeper of the castle, James Shaw of Sauchie.

With benefit of hindsight, the later chroniclers had much to say about the prince's actions and motives; but they were clearly confused as to the order of events, and the location of the main personalities involved, in 1488. Thus Lesley believes that James III was in Stirling and the prince in Edinburgh; the rebels, 'certane noble men', are credited with the laudable — if highly conventional — motive of reforming the government through removal of wicked counsellors; yet in spite of this, they had to compel Prince James to side with them.[16] Ferreri, while praising the prince's benign nature and his reluctance to have anything to do with the rebels, suggests that Shaw of Sauchie was persuaded to hand him over to lend respectability to the revolt.[17] Buchanan follows both these writers in stressing the prince's initial refusal to join the rebels, and their belief that he might be used as a suitable regent once James III had been defeated; but his account is hopelessly confused, placing as it does the prince's defection after the king's departure for the north late in March, and thereby suggesting that King James took the initiative in the ensuing hostilities.[18] Finally, Pitscottie, normally the least reliable of the sixteenth century chroniclers, devotes no fewer than five folios of his *Historie* to 1488, citing as his source his ancestor David, Lord Lindsay of Byres, who was present on the royal side at Sauchieburn. Parts of his account are highly questionable; it seems unlikely that Prince James was moved to defect from Stirling by the news that his father was coming with a large army to imprison him; and James III did not take his son to Stirling after the revolt had broken out, as Pitscottie suggests. But he knows that the key to the ensuing crisis was the prince's defection, and that Shaw of Sauchie was the keeper of Stirling; he suggests very plausibly that the rebels sent a messenger 'quietly' to Shaw, persuading him with some difficulty — and bribery — to deliver the prince to them and thereafter keep the castle in Prince James's name and theirs against the king; and finally he relates that the rebels took the prince to Linlithgow, where they issued proclamations justifying their actions and calling on the lieges to muster to defend the prince against his father, who intended to deal with his son and heir as he had dealt with his brother Albany.[19]

Thus on 2 February Prince James left Stirling castle and joined the disaffected — at this stage probably the Humes and their allies. It was a momentous step which reflects the growing wisdom of those who risked defying an adult Stewart monarch. The crisis of 1482–3 had shown that violent protest, no matter how well supported, could not succeed unless the king were coerced indefinitely or eliminated, and at that time few could have considered going so far. By 1488, however, King James had shown that he had not altered his policies of the previous decade, his unpopularity had spread even into the ranks of his own council, and many more than six years previously must have favoured his removal from government. But though a few of the rebels may have thought to kill the king, to the majority such a course would be unthinkable, the more so because James III was protected by the threat of papal censures against all subjects who took up arms against him. The solution adopted by the rebels of 1488 was twofold — to disguise the fact of rebellion by making the classic complaint against evil counsellors misguiding the king, and — much more constructively — to acquire control of the heir to the throne as an alternative head of state.

Prince James's attitude to all this is difficult to discern. He was of course young, only attaining his fifteenth birthday on 17 March 1488; and the later chroniclers are unanimous in stating that he was initially reluctant to join the rebels and that a measure of coercion was employed to ensure that he did so. Young though he was, however, the Duke of Rothesay may already have been alarmed by his father's mistrust of him, dating back, perhaps, as far as 1486, and jealous of his younger brother's elevation to the dukedom of Ross on 29 January. Furthermore, during the ensuing four-month rebellion, there is no indication whatever that the prince had any desire to rejoin his father. As we shall see, he must have had at least two opportunities to do so, in April and May; but instead he is to be found in arms with the disaffected before and during the battle of Sauchieburn in June. It is probable, therefore, that he had grievances which made him a tool of the rebel nobility at the outset, but that his ambition grew as the rebellion progressed. Even after his father's death and his accession as James IV his remorse, as Nicholson reminds us, 'came late rather than early';[20] although he endowed masses for his mother's soul as early as October 1488, it was not until 1496 that he did the same for his father.

More than a fortnight elapsed between the prince's departure from Stirling on 2 February 1488 and James III's realisation that he was facing a more serious threat than that presented by the Humes. Then, on 21 February, the king 'be the avise of his consale . . . for certane reassonable and gret caus' abandoned the continuation of the January parliament to 5 May; and he dissolved the committee of fifty recently appointed to take action against those who had defied the suppression of Coldingham. Instead, a new 'generale parliament' was to meet in Edinburgh on 12 May, to be convened not only by the issue of the usual general precepts to all lords, prelates, barons, freeholders and burgh commissioners, but also by the despatch of special letters under the signet 'to al the prelates and gret lordis of his Realme' — presumably certain members of the first two estates were to be specially summoned — and these letters would indicate the king's reasons for calling parliament at this time.[21]

On the same day — 21 February — Bishop Elphinstone appears for the first time in witness lists to royal charters as Chancellor, a post which he was to retain until Sauchieburn.[22] It is clear from this appointment, and the dissolution of the proposed committee of parliament at the same time, that the king had received word of his son's removal from Stirling, that he had grown suspicious of Chancellor Argyll, and that he feared — or knew — that other members of the committee of fifty had treasonable intentions. His solution, therefore, was to summon a new parliament, presumably one which he could pack with supporters. In the meantime, an atmosphere of mistrust and suspicion hung over the court at Edinburgh, with Argyll, although no longer Chancellor, witnessing royal charters until 23 March, Angus acting in a similar capacity till 7 March, and Bishops Blacader of Glasgow and Browne of Dunkeld still at court with Argyll until 23 March.[23]

By this time James III clearly recognised the extent of the rebellion and the grave danger to his own position. On 24 March he signed a privy seal letter in Edinburgh;[24] but thereafter, in order to avoid another Lauder, he left the city for the north. Clearly he had been planning his departure for some time. The Comptroller, George Robison, who had handled money for the king during the 1482 crisis, gave up his post of custumar of Edinburgh on 11 March, and on leaving the city took with him £1028 13/2d of the burgh customs, money which had not been recovered by the following November.[25] This would suggest that King James sent Robison north with as much ready cash as he could muster; and on or shortly after 24 March, James himself left Edinburgh. At about the same time he sent John Ramsay south to request aid from Henry VII,[26] and according to Ferreri he also despatched a similar plea for help to Charles VIII of France. Ferreri also suggests that the king asked the pope to send a legate to act as mediator;[27] but as a papal legate was already expected in Scotland, and had been since January,[28] there was no need for such a supplication. In any case, James presumably intended to make use of the legate to inflict ecclesiastical censures on the rebels, not to mediate with them on his behalf.

By 6 April, James III had reached Aberdeen.[29] His route appears to have lain via

Leith, across the Forth in one of Sir Andrew Wood's ships,[30] and subsequently through Fife and Angus. Pitscottie's suggestion that he ordered the sheriffs of Fife, Strathearn and Angus to summon all his lieges spiritual and temporal between the ages of sixteen and sixty is very plausible; rather less so is his description of King James being pursued all the way to Leith by the rebels, in his haste abandoning some of his coffers containing money and clothing.[31] In fact, the king went north with part of the royal household, probably leaving members of it, notably Secretary Whitelaw, in Edinburgh castle; and his action reflects his desire to raise the loyal north on his behalf while still retaining control of his capital's strongpoint and the royal jewel house. The rebel threat came from the south and south-east, and James's response to it appears intelligent and carefully planned. It seems highly unlikely that, as Ferreri suggests, the king sent messengers to Lindores abbey while on his way north, offering the forfeited and imprisoned Earl of Douglas restoration to his lands and titles in return for assistance in crushing the rebels;[32] and Lesley's account, in which the rebel faction offered to restore Douglas if he would lead them, seems equally improbable.[33] Significantly Pitscottie, whose information about events in Fife is often reliable, makes no mention of Douglas being approached by either faction; and the tradition of Douglas's involvement may well have originated in oral tales which Buchanan received, suggesting that the king invited Archibald, earl of Angus — whom Buchanan thereafter consistently calls Douglas — to Edinburgh castle, and there proposed an alliance with a view to exacting revenge on other members of the nobility who had caused offence.[34]

It was on these flimsy foundations — based no doubt on the king's search for allies before he left Edinburgh for the north (including Angus who subsequently defected) — that the seventeenth century writers, Hume of Godscroft and Drummond of Hawthornden, built extensively. Godscroft's aim, to glorify the houses of Douglas and Angus, led him to suggest the alternatives, that Angus consulted Douglas on behalf of the rebels, that the king personally visited Douglas at Lindores, but that neither side was successful in enlisting his support. Indeed, Godscroft puts in Douglas's mouth a speech to the king condemning the bad counsel which caused James to issue black money.[35] The wisdom of the forfeited earl is accepted even by the royalist Drummond of Hawthornden, who claims that Douglas advised the rebels, including Angus, not to take up arms against the king. Also, 'he sent to all such of his Friends whom his disasters had left unruined, to take arms for the king, as the Dowglasses of Kayvers and others'.[36]

Drummond's account, therefore, adds the information that Douglas of Cavers — a former tenant of the Black Douglases and now holding lands of Archibald, earl of Angus — remained a committed royalist in 1488, a fact which can be verified from official records. But his association with the forfeited ninth earl, a man whose power had collapsed more than a generation before, is much more in doubt. Indeed, it is difficult to see why either side in 1488 should wish to enlist Douglas, because he had long ceased to be of any importance either politically or militarily; and it was by this time out of the question that king or rebels would restore him to his lands and titles. Douglas, imprisoned and nearing the end of his life, was doubtless prepared to settle for much less; and it is possible that he is to be identified with the Sir James

Douglas, knight, who received an annual pension of £200 from James IV in 1489, 1490 and 1491, parts of which were paid out of the farms of Kinclaven (nine miles north of Perth and therefore less than twenty miles from Lindores).[37] If these accounts indeed refer to the forfeited ninth earl, they would indicate no more than that the new regime freed the old man and that James IV paid him a modest pension until Douglas's death in 1491. Alternatively, Douglas may simply have been used by James III to reinforce royal progaganda; if the king went to Lindores at all, it can only have been to force his prisoner to give out to any friends he might still have in the south that he was on the royal side. This would account in part for two of Angus's tenants — Douglas of Cavers and Scott of Branxholm[38] — supporting the king in the latter stages of the rebellion. In the last analysis, however, all that can be said with certainty is that Douglas was unacceptable to both sides as a leader, and that if he had any influence on the events of 1488, it was slight.

However ably he reacted to the events of February and March, James III was nevertheless faced by the most serious threat to his regime since 1482. The identities of the rebel leaders may be discovered by consulting the parliamentary record of the initial proposals for a settlement between king and rebels in April 1488, and by studying the various grants of lands and offices made by James IV to his supporters after Sauchieburn. In the former case, those appointed to negotiate on behalf of the rebel nobility were Robert Blacader, bishop of Glasgow, Archibald Douglas, earl of Angus, Colin Campbell, earl of Argyll, the displaced Chancellor, Patrick Hepburn, second Lord Hailes, and Robert, second Lord Lyle.[39] First in the field, and later joining up with these five, was a large gathering of Humes — Alexander, Master of Hume, soon to succeed his grandfather as Lord Hume; his brother John Hume of Earlston; his uncles John Hume, the self-styled prior of Coldingham, George Hume of Aytoun, and Patrick Hume of Fastcastle. To these groups may be added George Browne, bishop of Dunkeld, John, Lord Drummond, Andrew, Lord Gray, and Laurence, Lord Oliphant; and prominent among the lairds who supported the prince were James Shaw of Sauchie, keeper of Stirling castle, Sir William Stirling of Keir, and Walter Ker of Cessford. Finally, William Knolles, preceptor of Torphichen, replaced the Abbot of Arbroath as Treasurer six days after the battle of Sauchieburn,[40] and must thus be accounted sympathetic towards the rebels, if not actually in arms with them.

So much for the participants; individually, their motives for defying the king were extremely diverse, ranging from personal grievances to fears for their future — perhaps for their lives — if James III continued to govern. Even moderates, former royal counsellors like Argyll and Drummond, cannot have looked for anything less than the enforced abdication of the king; for without this at least, they were doomed to a repetition of the events of 1482-3.

Prominent amongst the extremists were the Humes, forced into revolt by King James; indeed, their struggle with the king had been in progress intermittently for sixteen years, and had intensified during the 1480s. Thus in February 1485 Alexander, Master of Hume, was cited before the Lords of Council for 'the violent takin' of royal letters of summons from the king's messenger, John Scot; the summonses related to the wrongful appropriation by Hume of the teinds and fruits of Coldingham.[41] Another branch of the family was involved for a different reason. On 14 January 1485, George Hume of Wedderburn and his brother Patrick — known familiarly as 'Lang Patrick of Pollart' — had been summoned before the Lords of Council to answer for the seizure of the house of Hirdmanstone from John Sinclair of Hirdmanstone, and for disobeying royal letters to restore both house and goods. George Hume had sent procurators to the Council, but Patrick did not appear. The Council duly found against both men, and for disobeying royal letters George and Patrick were ordered to enter their persons in ward in Blackness castle, 'thir to remain on thir avne expens quhil thai be punyst for thir offence and frede be the king'.[42] Here, then, were two more Humes who resented royal interference in the south-east; and after James III's death, Patrick Hume of Polwarth was duly rewarded by the new regime with the office of Chamberlain of Stirlingshire.[43]

The Humes on their own would therefore have presented a significant threat to King James's ambitions in the south-east; together with their allies, they constituted a menace to the king's safety. Prominent amongst the latter was Patrick Hepburn, Lord Hailes, the man who had been forced to surrender Berwick castle to the English in 1482,[44] and who may have been mistrusted by James III as a result. As a neighbour of the Humes, he probably had ties of friendship, if not formal bonds, with that family; and his role on the rebel side in 1488 must have been a major one, for his rewards were considerable. In 1488-9 he was created Earl of Bothwell, Master of the Royal Household and Admiral of Scotland, guardian of the young Duke of Ross, keeper of the castles of Edinburgh and Threave, and Warden of the West and Middle Marches; and by 1492 he was sheriff of Berwick.[45] Hepburn's adherence to the rebel cause in 1488 may well have brought in his near neighbour George, Lord Haliburton and his eldest son Archibald, whose lands lay in and around Dirleton and whose family had intermarried with the Hepburns of Hailes in the previous generation;[46] but a much more formidable rebel was Archibald, earl of Angus, who while sharing Hume and Hepburn concern at growing royal interference in the south-east, also possessed the status which automatically made him one of the principal leaders of the disaffected. In view of the king's harrying of him before the Lords of Council, Angus may well have felt that he had no choice in 1488; both he and Andrew, Lord Gray, formed a special category — men who had neither been pardoned nor punished for their earlier treasons in 1482-3, and who had everything to gain and nothing to lose from organised rebellion.

Lords Drummond and Lyle had the same objectives as Angus, Hailes and the Humes — that is, they aimed at the removal from government of the king — but they joined the rebellion on account of personal injustices for which they held James III responsible. Drummond's adherence to the rebel side seems an act of ingratitude, as he had been created Lord Drummond by the king as recently as 29 January. But this elevation had not healed old wounds, especially the king's arbitrary seizure of the Stewartry of Strathearn in 1475, revoking Drummond's grant of the office in order to confer it on Sir William Murray of Tullibardine. This had made an implacable enemy of Drummond, the more so because the Drummonds and Murrays were at feud and Murray was eventually to be found in James III's army at Sauchieburn. The triumph of the rebels in June resulted in an immediate restoration of the Stewartry of Strathearn to Drummond as its former possessor.[47] Family connections may also have been involved, for Drummond's son and heir William was married to Isabel, second daughter of Colin, earl of Argyll, the king's displaced Chancellor.[48]

At first sight, the adherence of Robert, Lord Lyle to the rebel faction appears more puzzling, for the man had been a loyal supporter of the Crown during and after 1482, employed by James III on embassies to England in 1484, and as one of the conservators of the truce made in that year.[49] The key to his behaviour in 1488 lies in the territorial gains which he had made at the expense of the Earl of Buchan in 1485; for on 19 May of that year, following the apprisal by the Lords Auditors of some of the exiled Buchan's Forfarshire lands, these were bestowed upon Lyle. By April 1488, however, Buchan had not only returned to Scotland but had recovered favour with the king, joining the royalists in Aberdeen. Lyle clearly resented Buchan's return and renewed intimacy with James III; for in April–May 1488, during the tortuous negotiations for a settlement between king and rebels, reference was made to the healing of discords between the rival parties, 'specealy betuix the Erle of Buchain and Lord Lile'.[50] Lyle may bitterly have reflected that Buchan was being rewarded by James III in spite of his former extensive treasons, while his own service to the king in the '80s was ignored; and it is also possible that he was passed over by King James for one of the two Justiciars' posts south of Forth. Certainly he was rapidly rewarded for his part in the rebellion with the Justiciarship of Bute and Arran, on 25 July 1488.[51]

Of the two bishops who joined the rebel faction, Blacader of Glasgow and Browne of Dunkeld, the former played a much more prominent part in the events of 1488. His grievances were directed against Archbishop Scheves, who as we have seen[52] still enjoyed royal and papal favour, and who in March 1487 had achieved his ambition of having St. Andrews erected into a primatial church by Innocent VIII. As Scheves' fellow ambassador, Blacader resented the archbishop's new status and his own failure to have Glasgow made an archbishopric at the same time. Not until 25 May 1488 did Blacader even acquire written ratification from the papacy of Glasgow's exemption from the authority of the primate.[53] Jealousy of Scheves combined with his aspirations for his own see, therefore, probably account for Blacader's defection to the rebels in March 1488. Browne of Dunkeld, who left court to join the disaffected at about the same time, was less actively involved in the events which followed. His antagonism towards James III was doubtless the result of the Dunkeld election struggle of 1483–5 and the necessity of paying off King James and his favourite John Ramsay with bribes in order to obtain possession of his see. Unlike Blacader, Browne was not chosen as a commissioner on behalf of the rebels at the time of the projected negotiations with the king in April.

Of all the defections from court in March 1488, by far the most serious was that of Colin Campbell, earl of Argyll. He had served the king loyally throughout the '70s and '80s as Master of the Household, Chancellor, Councillor, and royal lieutenant in Argyll. Indeed, his record of service was without blemish, even in 1482–3, until his sudden dismissal from the Chancellorship in February 1488. No record evidence, or plausible chronicle evidence, provides us with a clue as to the nature of

Argyll's grievances, but they must have been serious, probably arising out of King James's actions in the parliament of January 1488. Argyll was unlikely to relish the king's reversal of the October 1487 legislation concerning civil appeals; he may well have resented James's choice of Justiciars south of Forth; and as the most powerful magnate in the west, he probably regarded the king's creation of his second son as Duke of Ross and Earl of Edirdale as the prelude to increased royal interference in an area which, since the collapse of John Macdonald's power and the assault on his bastard son and his offspring,[54] he had come to regard more and more as his own. His defection to the rebels may well have been a gradual process, originating in his alarm at royal threats over Coldingham in October 1487, an alarm no doubt increased by James III's belligerence in January 1488 and brought to a head by his dismissal of Argyll as Chancellor by 21 February. There was thus time for the earl to gather support, to involve on his side two lords of parliament, Drummond and Oliphant, whose families were related to his through marriage,[55] and to negotiate with the Humes and Hailes about the best use of Prince James in the coercion and removal of the king.

For it was this objective alone which united the rebel leaders, and there must have been various shades of opinion amongst them about what was to be done with James III. Doubtless many looked back to 1482, when the king had been coerced into changing his entire administration, and it is possible that Argyll wished to acquire for himself what Albany had failed to get, the office of Lieutenant-General, on the ground that the prince was still a minor. Alternatively it may have been hoped that James would abdicate in favour of his son; and a minority group of extremists, who doubtless included Angus and Gray, must have been seeking an opportunity to bring about the king's death. This was a rebellion led by determined, and in some cases desperate, men, whose position in Scotland would be impossible if James III were to continue to reign.

They must also have been extremely worried men, for they were attempting to achieve something unparallelled in Scottish history — the deposition of a sane adult monarch, a man who not only had all the prestige of Stewart kingship on his side, but who in spite of his arbitrary and illegal acts could still muster powerful armed support within Scotland, who had the friendship of Henry VII and the blessing of the pope. Worst of all from the rebel point of view, they had failed to secure the person of King James; and his withdrawal to Aberdeen made it inevitable that the issue would be settled by force of arms.

During the king's absence from Edinburgh, the rebels overran much of the south and south-east of Scotland. Drummond of Hawthornden claims that they surprised Dunbar castle, of which Lord Hailes became keeper, and used the money in the captured royal coffers there to hire troops.[56] This may have happened, because the royal keeper of Dunbar, John Ramsay, had been sent to England as James III's ambassador to Henry VII; and the castle lay in a position which, although very defensible, had the disadvantage of being close to rebel lands, and cut off from Edinburgh by the territories of Angus and Hailes. Although Edinburgh castle was held for the king, the rebels may have uplifted the burgh customs, for there appears to have been no custumar between 11 March and 3 May.[57] A number of laymen and clerks of the dioceses of St. Andrews and Glasgow, who were later to petition the pope for absolution, must have joined the rebels at this time; these included the abbot and entire convent of Jedburgh, and George Shaw, abbot of Paisley, who was present at the final battle of Sauchieburn together with William Crichton, one of his monks.[58] On the other hand, Shaw's neighbour, Sir Thomas Semple of Elliston, sheriff of Renfrew, joined the king.[59]

The escape of James III to the north imposed on the rebels the need to justify their actions both in Scotland and abroad. They must have known that the king had already sent John Ramsay to negotiate on his behalf at the English court; and indeed King James must have been regularly in touch with Henry VII throughout the period of the crisis. Ramsay had gone to England some time after 23 March, and was to be found with the English king at Windsor on 27 April.[60] Together with two of the Stewart half-uncles — Buchan and the Bishop of Moray — and Alexander Lord Forbes, Ramsay had received a commission from James III to deliver to the Earl of Northumberland and Sir William Tyler, governor of Berwick, by virtue of which both men were asked to give pardons to all Scots who might fall into their hands who were prepared to fight against the Scottish king's rebels.[61] This was a recruiting measure; Northumberland was being asked to allow all Scots refugees — mainly fugitive criminals — who undertook to fight for James III to return to Scotland. Criminals in sanctuaries in northern England were always a ready source of soldiers for English armies, and King James now hoped to use them against his rebels in southern Scotland.

Faced with an inaccessible king and the danger of English armed intervention on his behalf, the rebel leaders adopted three courses of action — they produced their own propaganda, they attempted to influence Henry VII in their favour, and they opened negotiations with James III while he was still in Aberdeen. Their propaganda was very conventional: the king, they claimed, was misled by 'dissaitful and perverst counsale', and as a result was guilty of 'the inbringing of Inglismen to the perpetuale subieccione of the realm'. This was the official explanation of the rebellion, given in October 1488 when some of James III's more committed supporters were indicted by the new regime.[62] Both of the charges contain some truth; to the rebels, John Ramsay, Lord Bothwell was the prime example of the upstart counsellor who worked to make a success of the king's Anglophile policies, and whose despatch to England in April 1488 was a threat to them all. Undoubtedly his mission was to convince Henry VII that he must send armed assistance to James III; and so the charge of attempting 'the inbringing of Inglismen' is true, though it was hardly on Ramsay's advice alone that the king had sent to England for aid.

However, in attempting to justify their revolt abroad, the rebels required more specific, and more damning, propaganda. Evidence of this is provided by a letter from Hans, King of Denmark (Christian I's son and successor) to Prince James, in which the Danish king expresses his great sorrow at the news which he has received from Scotland, namely that the late Queen Margaret, his sister, had been murdered 'per quemdam Johannem Ramsa . . . qui ut fertur ipsam veneno pessimo interemit', and that despite this crime Ramsay is still retained as one of the king's most intimate advisers.[63] This charge is clearly a fabrication intended only for the Danes;

it is not to be found in Ramsay's indictment in the parliament of October 1488, and it does not form any part of the criticisms of James III or his familiar either in contemporary sources or in the growing legends which informed the sixteenth century chroniclers. Indeed, the charge that the late queen had been poisoned is to be found only in this letter and is merely a reflection of Ramsay's unpopularity with the rebel faction.

Once committed to securing their aims by military means, the rebels did not scorn attempting 'the inbringing of Inglismen' to assist their own cause. In May 1488 Henry VII issued a safe-conduct to seven of their number — Robert Blacader, bishop of Glasgow, George Browne, bishop of Dunkeld, Colin, earl of Argyll (still described as Chancellor), Patrick Lord Hailes, Robert Lord Lyle, Matthew Stewart, Master of Darnley, and Alexander, Master of Hume — to travel to England.[64] The date of the Scottish request for the safe-conduct is not known, but it is likely to have been after James III went north to rally support late in March or early in April. The only possible motive for the rebels' denuding themselves of important leaders at this juncture would be to enlist the English king's aid, at least to the extent of permitting the recruitment of troops in England. Probably the safe-conduct was not used; certainly one of the rebel leaders named in it, the Bishop of Dunkeld, was at Stirling late in May,[65] and it seems likely that events overtook all of them when the king went over to the offensive in May.

The rebels' third course of action was to open negotiations with the king in Aberdeen. The sheer strength of James III is illustrated by the witness list to his first surviving Aberdeen charter, erecting the town of Alyth in Perthshire into a burgh of barony in favour of Alexander, Master of Crawford, on 6 April. Present were the Chancellor, William Elphinstone, bishop of Aberdeen; Andrew Stewart, bishop of Moray; Andrew Painter, bishop of Orkney; George, earl of Huntly; David, earl of Crawford, the Chamberlain; William, earl of Erroll, the Constable; James Stewart, earl of Buchan; William, earl Marischal; John, Lord Glamis; Alexander, Lord Forbes; Thomas Stewart, Lord Innermeath, son-in-law of the Earl Marischal; and William, Lord Ruthven — a formidable total of three bishops, five earls, and four lords of parliament.[66] Ten days later, on 16 April, also in Aberdeen, King James confirmed a charter made by his father in 1452, granting to the Bishop of Moray the cathedral church of Moray and the barony and burgh of Spynie in free regality. James III's bishop was his half-uncle Andrew Stewart, and the witness list to the charter, with the obvious omission of Stewart's name, is identical with that issued on the 6th.[67]

Some time in April, or at the latest early May, the rebels sent messengers north with proposals for a settlement. They were in an awkward predicament, for the most extreme of their leaders — Angus, Gray and the Humes — could not agree to anything less than pardons for their past and present treasons, and moderates and extremists alike could hardly trust a written promise by the king. Events were to show that his attitude throughout was one of intransigence; the rebels must be crushed by any means possible. As in 1482–3, this included the making of pacts with the insurgents which the king did not regard as binding on himself and which could be revoked when they had served their purpose. The truth was that the

S

confrontation between king and rebels in the spring of 1488 could only be resolved if James III fell into the hands of the prince's party, if Prince James were reunited with his father, or if one or other of them was eliminated. The shadow of 1482 loomed over the ensuing negotiations, and mutual mistrust — fully justified on the rebel side as events were to show — made the articles drawn up at Aberdeen a hollow sham.

As James III was in a stronger position than the insurgents, why did he negotiate with them at all? The probability is that he was hampered, like the rebels, in securing agreement as to what course should be pursued. Some of his supporters, including his half-uncle Buchan — newly restored to favour and perhaps anxious to excuse his past treason through present loyalty — took a hard line and encouraged the king to break the Aberdeen settlement at the earliest possible opportunity.[68] But others, including the northern earls, were clearly in favour of a negotiated settlement, and were appalled when the king, having signed the articles, immediately refused to implement them and broke his word to supporters and insurgents alike.[69] For the present, however, he temporised; time was on his side, English assistance would surely be forthcoming soon, and even in the south of Scotland many would commit themselves openly to the monarchy if the rebels failed to secure a rapid advantage.

The nine Aberdeen articles — which were merely preliminary points for discussion by the commissioners on both sides — were signed by James III, and commissioners were duly proposed, six for the king, five for the prince. Not surprisingly, the royalists were all northerners — Bishop Elphinstone, the Earls of Huntly and Erroll, the Earl Marischal, Lord Glamis, and Sir Alexander Lindsay of Auchtermonzie, the Earl of Crawford's brother. Elphinstone was Chancellor; but surely the others were chosen because they were on the spot in Aberdeen. They were 'to comone, conclude and end' with the Bishop of Glasgow, the Earls of Angus and Argyll, and Lord Hailes and Lyle, all of whom were commissioned by the prince to negotiate in his name and in the names of the insurgent lords.[70]

In content, the nine Aberdeen articles are extremely vague; but they fall broadly into three categories — articles affecting the welfare of the king, of his son, and of the rival factions of the nobility. The first three points concern James III himself. The commissioners are to discuss how 'the kingis hie honour, estate, riale autorite [may] be exaltit, conservit and borne up' so that he may be able to bring justice to all parts of his realm. The following proposal is equally vague; the king is to be surrounded constantly by 'prelatis, erlis, lordis and baronis and utheris personis of wisdome, prudence and of gud disposicioun and unsuspect to his hienes . . . to the gud giding of his realme and lieges'. This is presumably a reference to the composition of the royal council, and may be a stipulation on the part of the king that it should consist only of loyal nobles and clergy chosen by himself; the treason of his former Chancellor, Argyll, had doubtless alarmed him greatly.

The second group of articles — numbers four, five and six — concerns Prince James. It is suggested that 'at the consideracione of the said lordis' — presumably the commissioners on both sides are implied — 'the kingis hienes sall gif honorabill sustentacioun and levin to my lord prince his sone'. Then, in article five, 'wise lordis and honorabill personis of wisdome and discrecioun' are to be with the prince constantly 'for the gud governance of him and securite of his person in his tender age'. Finally, article six stipulates that the commissioners are to discuss 'how my lord prince sall in all tymes tocum be obedient to his faider the king and how that faiderly luff and tenderness sall at all tymes be had betuex thame'. Again, these points are vague in the extreme; but it would seem from article four that the prince's grievances included dissatisfaction with the household and living which had been allotted to him by his father. Article five, leading on from this, was concerned with the choice of lords who would make up the prince's household and have possession of the prince; and this problem alone would have made the task of the royal commissioners extremely difficult, if not wholly impossible. The final article in this category, concerning the means of achieving a reconciliation between the king and the prince, is vague and insubstantial, but betrays lack of trust on both sides. As we have seen, Prince James may have feared that his father intended to supplant him as heir with his younger brother, the Marquis of Ormonde, created Duke of Ross as recently as 29 January, and he may have been seeking assurances that such was not the case.

The final group of articles — numbers seven, eight and nine — are concerned with the nobility on both sides. There is to be an exchange of pardons. Thus, in article seven, 'the lordis and other personis being about my lord prince sall haf our soverane lordis favouris and grace, favouris and hertly forgevinnys'. This article is similar to article three, which requires that 'all the personis being about my lord prince that has in tyme by gane done displessour to his hienes make honorabile and aggreabile amendis to his hienes be the wisdome and discrecione of the said lordis, thar liffis heretage and honouris except'. Article eight complements these two; on the other side, 'my lord prince sal take in hertlie favouris all lordis spirituale and temporale and all uthir personis that has bene with the kingis hienes in consale or uthir service now in this tyme of trouble'.

There is probably an important distinction to be drawn between those persons specified in article seven, and those in article three. Articles seven and eight, which constitute an act of oblivion, are the necessary basis of any agreement. The question arises, however, as to what crime such mutual pardons were intended to cover. If it was treason — which may be interpreted during this crisis as having taken up arms against the winning party — then the winning party would have to assert that the opposition were rebels, and rebellion involves levying war; so long as no fighting had taken place, however, it could be argued by the peacemakers and by those who sought a compromise that there was no rebellion, only disfavour, for which forgiveness was appropriate. On the other hand, article three shows that some of the nobility were in a much more serious case, as they had already done enough to justify forfeiture of their lives and heritages. This could be a reference to Angus or Gray, but much more probably implies the Humes, against whom judicial proceedings had long been going on. It must be doubted whether the Humes — who were not represented amongst the proposed rebel commissioners — would have considered making 'honorabile and aggreabile amendis' as required by article three; and it is unlikely that the king at this late stage would have settled for less than the forfeiture of the entire Hume family.

These articles — three, seven and eight — are the only ones in the proposed agreement which reveal any (likely) substance behind the generalities of which they are composed; and the final article, number nine, is surprisingly specific. It refers to the healing of feuds between individual members of the nobility, 'and specealy betuix the erle of Buchain and Lorde Lile'.[71] Apart from the names of the commissioners, Buchan and Lyle are the only lords specified in the nine articles; and it may be that their names are included because both men were in Aberdeen, which would be the case if Lyle were the rebel ambassador. Article nine is therefore a matter of private business tacked on to the general points for discussion; and it had arisen, as we have seen, because Lyle's advancement in the 1480s was blocked by the return of Buchan from exile.

King James duly signed the articles; but unless he carried the matter further by sending them south and issuing the required commission to Elphinstone and the northern lords, he was not making any substantial concessions. There is in fact no evidence that commissions were issued; and there are indications that the articles were never received by the rebels in the south. Thus in the parliament of October 1488, 'Jhonne, Lord Glammys present and schew certane articulis subscrivit with the forsaid umquhile King James hand'.[72] It may well be asked how Glamis obtained possession of the articles, because he was neither a rebel nor a supporter of the king in the latter stages of the crisis. The answer must be that he was given the document, or a copy of it, by the king while James was in Aberdeen, and waited, together with the other prospective commissioners on the royal side, for his commission to go south and negotiate with the rebel leaders on the basis of what had been laid out in the nine articles. When the king changed his mind and decided to go south himself, Huntly, Erroll, Marischal and Glamis returned to their own lands and the articles became obsolete.

In a sense, they had never been particularly relevant to the situation in 1488. For all the complexities of articles three, seven and eight, enjoining mutual forgiveness as a means of setting the Scottish political world to rights, the truth was that mutual mistrust would have doomed any set of proposals from the start. The rebel cause survived as long as its leaders had possession of Prince James; if they lost him, they were doomed. Likewise the king recognised that the survival of the rebellion depended upon his eldest son, and his aim was to obtain physical control of Prince James at the earliest opportunity. This could not be achieved by negotiating at long distance from Aberdeen; so early in May[73] the king prepared to come south to confront the insurgents. The reaction of the northern lords when their sovereign casually broke the pact which he had just signed and committed them to negotiate is variously reported in the parliamentary records of the following October. One account states that Huntly, Erroll, Marischal and Glamis 'and utheris the kingis trew liegis left him and his dissaitful and perverst counsale and anherdit to our soverane lord that now is' (that is, joined the prince's faction).[74] But the indictment of the Earl of Buchan in the same parliament tells a different story; after James III had broken the agreement on his half-uncle's advice, 'Comites de huntle Erole merschell et dominus de glammis . . . dictum Jacobum et eius opinionem reliquerunt et ad loca propria reddierunt'.[75] The latter statement, that the northern lords returned to their own lands, seems much the more likely of the two. There is no record that they adhered to the rebel cause, and the statement that they did reads like propaganda concocted by the victors of Sauchieburn to give the impression that they had fairly general support at an early stage.

James's decision to depart from Aberdeen was no doubt influenced by many factors, among them concern about the safety of the royal jewel house in Edinburgh castle, still in royalist hands. But as his breaking of the Aberdeen pact involved his being abandoned by the northern earls, he must have reckoned on acquiring armed support from some other quarter before risking his person in the south. Such evidence as we have suggests that he expected English assistance, indeed that he went south to meet it. His half-uncle Buchan, who advised him to break the Aberdeen agreement, was later to be accused of dealings with the king of England, 'pro importacione certorum Anglicorum ad distructionem regni et ligiorum Scocie, et pro instigacione et causacione Regis Anglie in propria persona cum suis armis et copia virorum in regnum Scocie advenisse'; and associated with Buchan in his efforts to secure an English invasion on James III's behalf were John Ramsay, Lord Bothwell — already in England, at Windsor, on 27 April — Andrew Stewart, bishop of Moray, Alexander, Lord Forbes, John Ross of Montgrenan, John Murray of Touchadam, Stephen Lockhart of Cleghorn, and James Hommyl, the royal tailor.[76] With Bothwell as his ambassador in England, Ross of Montgrenan in Edinburgh castle, Buchan in his own army, and lairds like Murray of Touchadam acting, presumably, as messengers, the Scottish king's line of communications with Henry VII was probably very efficient. If James III expected an early response from England, he must have been concerned to find a suitable landing place for the prospective reinforcements. Dunbar castle had fallen, the south-east was hostile, and rebel troops may also have been dangerously close to Edinburgh castle and its port of Leith; so Blackness castle, whose keeper was the loyal John Ross of Halkhead,[77] was clearly the nearest suitable point on the Forth to land reinforcements. Such a scheme would explain James's presence there early in May.

If this was the royal plan, it misfired badly. English aid was not forthcoming, either in May or during the following month; and Bothwell himself did not return from England until after 24 May.[78] It seems likely that the cautious Henry VII had given Bothwell hope of military assistance in the near future, and this message may well have been passed on to James III by his favourite with an optimism which was unjustified. In any event, when the Scottish king arrived at Blackness castle — presumably using the loyal Sir Andrew Wood to ferry him across the Forth — there was no sign either of Bothwell or of English armed assistance. Instead King James was rapidly confronted by a rebel force which had hastened up, possibly from Linlithgow;[79] and the king, unable or unwilling to emerge from the castle, promised to conclude another pact with his enemies. The parliamentary indictments of Buchan and Ross of Montgrenan in October 1488 suggest that a battle seemed likely; for the king, though lacking the support of the northern earls, had with him at Blackness Chancellor Elphinstone, James Stewart, earl of Buchan, Andrew Stewart, bishop of Moray, David, earl of Crawford, Chamberlain and Master of the Household, Alexander Lord Forbes, William Lord Ruthven, Thomas Lord Innermeath, John Ross of Montgrenan, Sir William Murray of Tullibardine, Thomas Fotheringham of Powrie, James Innes of Innes, John Ross of Halkhead, keeper of Blackness castle, and Thomas Turnbull of Greenwood, the royal standard bearer.[80] However, no battle took place, nor does any record survive of an agreement made between the rival parties at Blackness; certainly the new regime was unable to produce any written pact five months later, which suggests that there never was one. James III, caught at a disadvantage, turned for advice to his Lord Advocate, John Ross of Montgrenan, who counselled him to break any agreement with the rebels and return to Edinburgh castle.[81] It may be that the insurgents presented the king with a series of proposals similar to those put forward at Aberdeen and asked him to ratify them, whereupon he suddenly withdrew. Alternatively, it is possible to envisage a situation in which King James, remaining in Blackness castle himself, appointed Buchan, Ruthven, Murray of Tullibardine and Fotheringham of Powrie as his negotiators, and then immediately departed to Edinburgh, leaving all four as hostages. They may indeed have taken an oath on the king's behalf that he would reach an agreement with the insurgents; if this was the case, the absence of a Blackness written settlement would be explained, because any agreement would be rudimentary and verbal.

The king's escape route presumably lay by way of the Blackness sea-gate to Wood's ships in the Forth, and so to Leith and Edinburgh castle, which he had reached by 16 May. He left behind him a frustrated rebel faction, protesting at his second public breach of faith within a month, and as hostages four supporters whose feelings towards their sovereign can be imagined. In the second of the major crises of the reign, Buchan had once again managed to choose the wrong side. Indeed, the royalists lost heavily through the king's breaking of the Aberdeen and Blackness agreements — Huntly, Erroll, Marischal and Glamis in the former case, Buchan, Ruthven, Murray and Fotheringham in the latter. The basic problems posed by the rebellion remained unsolved; the rebels were unable to seize the king, and the king was unable to obtain possession of the prince. The entire crisis was a contest for the control of royalty.

By 16 May, James III had returned to Edinburgh castle and was already making preparations to renew the struggle. On that date he sent a letter under the privy seal to the sheriff of Dumbarton and his deputies, ordering them not to compel the burgesses of Dumbarton to attend shrieval weaponshowings. Instead, the community might hold its own weaponshowings, a privilege which had been accorded to all royal burghs in February 1484. King James's immediate concern in May 1488 was to raise troops as quickly as possible; and the reference in the letter to 'our hoistingis and weris bigane and now of late' suggests an urgency on his part to remove any burghal discontent over the actions of royal officials.[82]

Two days later, on 18 May, James III began to reward those who had supported him at Blackness. David, fifth earl of Crawford, was created Duke of Montrose, thus becoming the first duke in Scottish history who was not a member of the royal family. The terms of the creation make it clear that Crawford was being rewarded for defence of the king's person 'in campo bellico apud Blaknes'.[83] On the same day, for good and faithful service by his familiar Sir Thomas Turnbull of Greenwood — and especially for acting as royal standard bearer at Blackness — James granted Turnbull the lands of Terringzean in Ayrshire.[84] On 20 May, again for services performed at Blackness, the king granted in feu farm to James Dunbar of Cumnock some £44 worth of lands in Morayshire.[85] The following day he issued a confirmation to David Scott of Branxholm of the lands and barony of Branxholm, together with lands in Peeblesshire and Roxburghshire; in the charter it was specified that the regrant was made as reward for services rendered in times past by David Scott, and especially in recognition of the part played by his son Robert Scott, with his followers and friends, under the royal standard at Blackness.[86]

On 24 May the king shifted his ground slightly, making two grants which are indicative of his intention to renew the war. One was to William Douglas of Cavers, sheriff of Roxburgh, and his heirs, a regrant of the regality of Cavers which Douglas had resigned into the king's hands; the recipient, however, was required to promise that he would serve the king faithfully, and go in person together with such friends, kindred and supporters as he could raise, wherever the king might direct. If he failed in this service, the charter confirming his regality was to have no force or effect, for it was specifically granted in return for his continuing faithful service to the king.[87] The other royal grant on 24 May was to James Innes of Innes and his heirs, some £20 worth of land in the lordship of Moray, made in recognition of Innes's support 'in exercitu regis apud Blaknes', with the added proviso that Innes should continue to serve the king loyally 'pro toto tempore instantis discordie'.[88] Finally, on 28 May, James III created Lord Kilmaurs Earl of Glencairn, like Douglas of Cavers and Innes for his support at Blackness, and on condition that he continued to assist the Crown until the rebellion was over.[89] On 3 June, a precept was issued under the quarter seal adding the £30 lands of Drummond and the £10 lands of Duchray, both in the earldom of Lennox, to Glencairn's holdings in the south.[90]

These latter grants suggest that King James's decision to renew the war, and so repudiate any verbal promise he may have given at Blackness about reaching a settlement with the rebels, was made before 24 May. He was probably influenced by the return of his familiar John Ramsay, Lord Bothwell, from his English embassy, by 28 May. Bothwell may have sent messages to Edinburgh in advance of his arrival, assuring King James that armed assistance from the north of England was on the way, and encouraging the king to take the offensive once more. According to his summons for treason the following October, Bothwell was responsible, together with John Ross of Montgrenan, for advising the king to leave Edinburgh castle 'cum armis et copia virorum . . . ad invadendum nos eius filium, tunc Principem, apud Striuelin'.[91] However, his indictment does not accuse him of treasons of later date — unlike Ross of Montgrenan, who was present at Sauchieburn — and it is likely that he was once more despatched to England in search of armed assistance from Henry VII; by the autumn, he had taken refuge at the English king's court.[92]

By the end of May, in spite of setbacks which were partly of his own making, King James had rallied a fair body of supporters to Edinburgh. Some had come south with him from Aberdeen, notably Elphinstone and Crawford, who as Chancellor and Chamberlain respectively were naturally attached to the royal household; the two remaining Stewart half-uncles, John, earl of Atholl, and Andrew, bishop of Moray; and Alexander Lord Forbes. Others had either stayed in Edinburgh during the royal progress to Aberdeen, or now joined the king from outlying parts of the country. James Douglas, earl of Morton, the king's uncle, had arrived at court by 20 May; Robert Colquhoun, bishop of Argyll, had come in by the following day; Lord Kilmaurs, as his elevation to earl on 28 May showed, had been with James III since before Blackness; and other loyal lords of parliament present in Edinburgh at this time were David, Lord Lindsay of Byres, John, Lord Maxwell, William, Lord Graham, William, Lord Borthwick, John, Lord Carlyle, and William, Lord Abernethy. Secretary Whitelaw appears to have remained in Edinburgh throughout, and witnessed all great seal charters made between 18 and 28 May.[93] Clearly, therefore, even after the loss of four of his supporters as hostages at Blackness, and lacking the assistance of the northern earls, the king could still call on a substantial body of support in the south in his preparations for renewing the war.

An important feature of these preparations was James III's elaborate disposition of his money. Thus, after Sauchieburn, it took the victors a long time to accumulate the coffers of money which the late king had distributed amongst his supporters. The Treasurer, David Lichtoun, abbot of Arbroath, was supplanted immediately after Sauchieburn by Sir William Knolles, preceptor of Torphichen; and Lichtoun then had to hand over to the victors three boxes of money and jewels. On 26 June he brought two of them to Perth; the first, a black box, contained 4,340 gold 'demis' — Scottish half-crowns — 428 golden Louis, and 566 French crowns; the second, 'a quhite coffre of irne', yielded 3,988 angel nobles. Probably about the same time, the former Treasurer handed over another coffer which, apart from various oddments and gold chains, contained French gold coins in large numbers — Louis, half-nobles, crowns and ducats.[94] On 21 June the Countess of Atholl delivered up to the victors two coffers, one containing 316 rose nobles and 500 half rose nobles, the other 1,307 angel nobles and 357 half-crowns. The contents of these boxes were described as 'the money takin be the Cuntas of Atholl and Johne Steward'. Presumably the latter name is a derogatory reference by the new regime to the Earl of Atholl, a refusal by the victors less than a fortnight after Sauchieburn to accord him his title. Two days later, on 23 June, another coffer, containing 1,084 Henry nobles and 1,020 rose nobles, was received at Scone by the new Treasurer Sir William Knolles, Robert Blacader, bishop of Glasgow, Lord Lyle, John Hepburn, prior of St. Andrews, Patrick Hume, and Lord Drummond. Three men who had found the box 'quhen it was in the myre' — possibly after the battle — were duly rewarded.[95] Finally, the most valuable find of all was made by one Walter Simson after the battle of Sauchieburn; in 1489, he was rewarded for recovering a box containing £4,000 in gold coins found on the field 'prope Striveling in die sancti Barnabe Apostoli'.[96]

Clearly the object of this elaborate distribution of cash by the king was to pay his troops and, where necessary, to buy support. The greater part of the royal treasure, however, was left in the jewel house in Edinburgh castle, where an inventory of both money and precious ornaments was drawn up by the victors of Sauchieburn six days after the battle, revealing the remarkable total of £24,517 10/-.[97] Thus the removal of large sums of money by James III on his departure from the castle on his last campaign is not to be regarded as the act of a desperate, fleeing man, as Pitscottie suggests,[98] but of a resourceful monarch whose earlier vicissitudes had taught him the necessity of having ready cash in quantity. If only at the end, King James proved the exception to the general rule that Scottish monarchs could not afford a contract army.

Having made his preparations, James III left Edinburgh castle early in June on what was to prove his last campaign. Later writers — Ferreri, Buchanan, and Drummond of Hawthornden — suggest that the king's principal motive in moving towards Stirling was to come in contact with his northern supporters.[99] While in Edinburgh castle, according to Drummond, he was in dangerous proximity to the rebels; but if he moved to Stirling he might secure the passage over the Forth for loyal reinforcements advancing from the north.[100] The king may indeed have thought in this way; but in fact his northern support proved as illusory as the English army feared by the insurgents, for there is no evidence whatever that the northern lords — Huntly, Erroll, Marischal and Lord Glamis — stirred themselves to assist James III after the king had broken the Aberdeen agreement in April. King James's motive in advancing to Stirling, therefore, was surely to seize the person of his rebellious son who, styling himself 'Prince of Scotland' and attended by the Bishop of Dunkeld, Lords Gray, Oliphant and Drummond, was again living in the castle.[101] The remainder of the rebel force was presumably located much nearer Edinburgh, possibly at Linlithgow, certainly close enough to surprise the king at Blackness when he had arrived there early in May. It would seem, therefore, that James III intended to destroy the insurgents'· cause by seizing their nominal leader while their forces were still divided.

At first he appeared successful. Although we do not know for certain what route the royal forces took from Edinburgh to Stirling, it seems likely that, having crossed the river by the Queensferry, they advanced along the north side of the Forth, thus avoiding the rebels in the vicinity of Blackness. The king may well have sailed up the Forth in one of Sir Andrew Wood's ships. Arriving in the Stirling area from the east, and remaining on the north side of the river, James III either sent or led a force to attack and burn the tower and place of Keir, the seat of Sir William Stirling of Keir, one of the prince's supporters.[102] The destruction — much of which was inflicted by the royalist Sir Adam Murray of Drumcrieff, younger brother of Cuthbert Murray of Cockpool — was extensive, so serious in fact that Stirling of Keir was to be found the following year claiming the enormous sum of £1,000 in damages.[103] More immediately, the royal attack on the Keir estates probably precipitated the first of the two battles fought in the Stirling area early in June, at Stirling bridge, only a day or two before the final conflict at Sauchieburn. Presumably the prince or his guardians, realising the danger of allowing James III to adopt an advantageous position, emerged from the castle with as large a force as they could muster, crossed the bridge to the north side of the Forth, and joined battle with the royal army on or about the site of Wallace's victory in 1297. In this skirmish the rebels, including Prince James, were put to flight; as we learn from the indictment of John Ross of Montgrenan the following October, James III's Lord Advocate had been involved in 'fugacione et prosecucione nostre persone [Prince James] extra pontem de Striuelin, ibi incendia, depredaciones et occisiones faciens'.[104]

The royal army was thus left in control of the town — though probably not the castle — of Stirling, while the prince and his adherents fled south-east, in the direction of Falkirk. During this flight, they doubtless came in touch with the main body of the rebel army hastening up from the south. This force must have included many of those who had been present at Blackness the month before, and who had remained south of Forth, in the vicinity of Edinburgh, while James III had been in the castle. On his sudden departure, they must have pursued him as swiftly as possible to Stirling; but it may have taken them some time to muster all their supporters. At any rate, a liaison must have been effected between the prince's party, fleeing south from their defeat at Stirling bridge, and a large rebel force coming up from the south-east. Either the following day or a few days afterwards, on Thursday 11 June, the battle of Sauchieburn was fought.

The king had lost the initiative; he had failed to seize his son, or indeed to prevent Prince James joining up with the main rebel army, and he did not have the support of the northern earls. Thus the commanders in the royal army at Sauchieburn included one duke, David, fifth earl of Crawford, the newly created Duke of Montrose; two earls, Atholl and Alexander Cunningham, created Earl of Glencairn only a fortnight before the battle;[105] one bishop, Robert Colquhoun of Argyll;[106] and five lords of parliament, Forbes, Carlyle, Graham, Lindsay of Byres, and Innermeath. There were present also a number of loyal knights and lairds — John Ross of Montgrenan;[107] Cuthbert Murray of Cockpool and his militant brother Sir Adam Murray of Drumcrieff; John Murray of Touchadam; James Innes of Innes; Sir Alexander Dunbar; Robert Charteris of Amisfield; Stephen Lockhart of Cleghorn; Roger Grierson of Lag;[108] William Douglas of Cavers, sheriff of Roxburgh;[109] David Scott of Branxholm; and Sir Thomas Semple of Elliston, sheriff of Renfrew.[110] This is an approximate list of the principal leaders on the royal side. There may have been others, for example Chancellor Elphinstone, the Bishop of Moray, and James Douglas, earl of Morton, the king's uncle, who was certainly at court in Edinburgh late in May and may have gone to Stirling with his nephew.[111] It is likely, however, that the royal army at Sauchieburn was one of lairds rather than lords.

The rebels had no such problem. Having met the prince's force fleeing south, their army was no doubt at full strength and, according to all the sixteenth century chroniclers except Pitscottie, it was stronger than the king's. It is likely that all the powerful members of the disaffected were present — the Earls of Argyll and Angus, Lords Hailes, Lyle, Drummond, Gray and Oliphant; the entire Hume clan, headed by Alexander, Master of Hume, and including his uncles George of Aytoun, Patrick of Fastcastle and Thomas of Langshaw; and lairds such as Shaw of Sauchie, Ker of Cessford, Stirling of Keir, and possibly also Edmonstone of Duntreath.[112] The clergy were represented by George Shaw, abbot of Paisley, who was present at Sauchieburn with William Crichton, one of his monks;[113] and Bishops Blacader and Browne may also have been in the rebel army. Certainly the latter was in Stirling castle a few weeks before the battle. The superiority in numbers of the rebel army is probably to be accounted for by the fact that, whereas Douglas of Cavers brought a mere twenty-four supporters to fight for the king,[114] the Humes alone, apart from Alexander, Master of Hume, included in their number four lairds and the Prior of Coldingham; and Lord Hailes' supporters and Hepburn relatives provided another four lairds and the Prior of St. Andrews.

Much ink has been spilt by writers trying to determine the exact site of the battle. Contemporaries had no doubt, referring to it as 'the field of Stirling', or suggesting that fighting took place 'apud Strivelin' or 'prope Strivelin';[115] and three of the sixteenth century chroniclers — Abell, Lesley and Ferreri — are in agreement with record evidence on this point. Abell places the battle 'beside striwiling', with the king's death in Bannockburn mill; Lesley claims that King James 'jonit in battell aganis his ennemyeis, at Bannokburn within tua myle to Strivelinge'; and Ferreri locates the king's camp at Bannbckburn village.[116] Not until the publication of Drummond of Hawthornden's history in 1655 was the name 'Sauchieburn' first used to describe the battle; and this name is not really at odds with the other evidence, for Drummond describes 'a small brook named Sawchy-Burn', which he claims is 'not far distant from that Bannockburn, where King Robert the Bruce overthrew the great Army of Edward Carnarvan'.[117] James III was well schooled in the significance of Robert I's victory in 1314, and determined to emulate the hero king in a battle fought on or near the site of Bannockburn. Bruce had borne the Brecbennach of St. Columba with him to the field; James III carried Bruce's sword.[118] Taking all the available evidence into consideration, it seems reasonable to suggest that the battle of Sauchieburn is correctly so called, and that the conflict took place at or near the confluence of the Sauchie and Bannock burns, about two miles due south of Stirling and slightly to the south-west of the 1314 battle.[119]

Contemporary accounts of the battle of Sauchieburn merely mention that it happened, without giving any details beyond the fact that the king was killed. Thus the parliamentary record cryptically dismisses the battle as 'the slauchteris committ and done in the field of striuilin quhar our souerane Lordis faider happinit to be slane'.[120] However, short accounts of the struggle are to be found in all the sixteenth century histories. Lesley states that battle was joined and that 'eftir gryeit slauchter made on baith sides, the king was slane the xj day of Junij 1488'. Before the battle, the prince had given orders that no-one should lay violent hands on his father. Ferreri tells roughly the same story, adding that when the king's supporters saw the battle going against them, they asked James to leave the field. According to the same account, the dead on the royal side included the Earl of Glencairn, Sir Thomas Semple of Elliston, Lords Erskine and Ruthven, and others who are not specified.[121]

Lord Erskine, however, survived the battle — if indeed he was there — to die about 1493, and Ruthven was already a hostage; but there is some evidence to suggest that Glencairn[122] and Semple[123] were killed in the struggle.

For a wealth of circumstantial — and highly dubious — detail, we must however turn to the accounts of the battle given by Buchanan and Pitscottie. Buchanan, followed much later by Drummond of Hawthornden, states that the rebels were beginning to fall back when the men of Annandale put the centre of the king's army to flight by virtue of having longer spears.[124] Pitscottie's description of the battle is the most detailed, though it is seen almost exclusively through the eyes of the king. Having been presented with a large grey charger, the gift of Lord Lindsay of Byres, James III sat astride it watching the approach of the rebel army 'witht his awin baner displayand aganis him'. Thereupon 'he rememberit the wordis of the witche that said to him befoir that he sould be distroyit and put doune be the neirest of his kin'. In Pitscottie's account, this prophecy was made late in the 1470s by a witch brought to court by the royal favourites to alienate the king from his brothers Albany and Mar; but he makes it serve a second turn with reference to 1488.[125] Buchanan includes the same prophecy — that the king should be killed by the nearest of his kin — but attributes it to a Flemish astrologer named Andrews who had come to James's court.[126] He adds that some witches prophesied to the king that the lion should be killed by his whelps. Drummond makes the best of both worlds by including the witches' prophecy and also a tale that James's counsellors suborned an old woman to tell him, while he was out hunting, that he should beware of his nearest kinsmen, who would bring about his ruin.[127]

There was of course nothing new about Buchanan's and Pitscottie's witches and their prophecies, for they are to be found in some of Boece's least likely tales. Thus James III, sitting on his horse watching the approach of his rebellious son and remembering the witch's prophecy, might almost be the Macbeth in Bellenden's translation of Boece, who seeing the approach of Malcolm's army, 'understude the prophecy was completit, that the wiche schew to him; nochtheles, he arrayit his men'. Scarcely had the battle begun when Macbeth, like Pitscottie's James III, took flight and was killed in the pursuit.[128] In essence, Pitscottie is telling the Macbeth story all over again; a tyrant's death is predicted by a witch or witches, and his fears of the fulfilment of the prophecy turn him into a coward on the battlefield. Thus James III 'tuik sic ane waine suspitioun in his mynd that he desyrit and haistalie tuik purpos to flie. In this mean tyme the lordis seing the king tyne curage desyrit him to pase by the ost quhill they had fouchin the battell'.[129] This last statement is a distortion of Ferreri's account, in which the royal commanders asked the king to leave the field only when the battle was clearly going against him.[130]

Not surprisingly, the aspect of Sauchieburn on which contemporary and near-contemporary official sources concentrated was the death of the king; and oral tradition provided the sixteenth century chroniclers with a variety of tales concerning the slaying of James III. The problem lies in reconciling these two very different types of source.

The record evidence on the subject falls naturally into three groups — the parliamentary apologia, and indictment of John Ross of Montgrenan, in October

1488, the accusations made against the new government by the rebels of 1489, and finally, a statute of February 1492 offering a reward for the capture of the slayers of the late king. The parliamentary record of October 1488 suggests that James III was killed in battle, as reference is made to 'the slauchteris committ and done in the field of striuilin quhar our souerane lordis faider happinit to be slane'.[131] However, the indictment of John Ross of Montgrenan, at the same time, states that the king was slain by unknown vile persons after leaving the field.[132] The two statements are not necessarily contradictory. Allowance must be made for a certain amount of caution on the part of the new government. Its members were almost certainly ignorant of the identities of those who had killed James III; but in order to secure themselves against possible papal censures, or the wrath of the new king — who had given orders before the battle that no-one should lay violent hands on his father[133] — it was necessary to dissociate themselves entirely from the vile (that is, lowly) persons who had slain the late king. This could best be done by suggesting that he had left the battlefield before he was killed; but such a statement does not add much to our knowledge. The battle of Sauchieburn was probably brief in duration, and much of it may have been taken up with pursuits of fugitives on the royal side and isolated skirmishes. It is significant that the names of two important royal supporters killed in the battle are known, but that no-one of note appears to have lost his life on the rebel side. Taken together, therefore, the two pieces of parliamentary evidence of October 1488 would suggest that the king 'happinit to be slane' during one of many pursuits which constituted part of the battle.

The second section of contemporary record evidence regarding James's death is drawn from propaganda issued by rebels against the new regime in 1489. These men, a combination of northern lords and disappointed office-seekers from the south, were anxious to represent themselves as the late king's loyal subjects whose principal desire was to avenge his death; and so in their propaganda they made a number of references to James III's demise. The first of these is to be found in a letter written by Alexander, Master of Huntly, to Henry VII of England on 8 January 1489. Huntly asks the English king to 'ramembir of the thresonable and cruel slauthir of my soverane lorde and Kyng, falsly slayne be a part of his fals and untrew legis'; and he goes on to say that he has made alliances with the late king's friends and kinsmen 'to caus the comittars of the said murthir to be punyst acording to justice'.[134] The conscience of the conservative north was again displayed on 12 September 1489, when the provost and burgesses of Aberdeen declared in a public meeting their dissatisfaction that 'no punishment had been imposed on the treasonable vile persons who put their hands violently on the king's most noble person'.[135] At about the same time, those who had actually taken the field against the new regime in the west of Scotland produced their apologia, complaining that 'our Souerane Lorde, quhome God assoilze, wes cruelly slayne be vile and tresonable personis, and na punycioune of justice is done thairfor'; and they made a sharp distinction between 'the said vile treasonable personis that cruelly put hand in his maist noble persoune', and 'thir noble and weilie avisit lordis that intendit to justice and gaif thair writingis for the conservacioune and keping of our Souerane Lordis [i.e. James III's] maist noble persone'.[136] The noble and well advised lords referred to are surely the rebel leaders before Sauchieburn, giving a written pledge that they would not do harm to James III; and that such a procedure took place is implied by Abell, Lesley and Ferreri when they state that Prince James gave orders before the battle that no-one should lay violent hands on his father.[137] Presumably the prince's leading supporters all obeyed this command; and so the reiterated statements, in October 1488, and January and October 1489, that the late king had been slain by vile persons — vile in the sense of lowly, and therefore obscure — are probably the truth.

Concern about the manner in which James III had met his death must however have continued in some quarters, for as late as 15 February 1492 the Lords of the Articles — 'for the eschewin and cessing of the hevy murmour and voce of the peple of the ded and slauchter of vmquhile our souerane Lordis faider and progenitour quham god assolze King James the thrid' — introduced a statute offering a reward of one hundred marks' worth of land to anyone giving information leading to the arrest of those responsible for the slaughter of the late king.[138] Pressure may have been brought to bear on them to make this gesture; 'the hevy murmour and voce of the people' may well be a reference to public meetings similar to that held in Aberdeen in September 1489, demanding punishment to be meted out to those who had slain James III. Whatever the reason, the statute of February 1492 seems to have achieved its purpose, as no more is heard of the death of the late king. The reward of a hundred marks' worth of land offered for the apprehension of his killers was never claimed.

Thus what emerges most strikingly from the record evidence relating to this subject is that all parties — the new government, the rebels of 1489, and the people — were unanimous about the manner of the late king's death; those responsible were vile and treasonable persons whose identities were unknown. In every account but one, James III is described as having been 'slain' rather than 'murdered'. The exception is the letter sent by the Master of Huntly to Henry VII in January 1489, in which the late king's death is described as 'murthir'; but Huntly is not consistent, for earlier in the same letter he states that James III was 'falsly slane be a part of his fals and untrew legis'. Thus the overall impression conveyed by the record evidence is that the late king was slain in battle, perhaps during a pursuit or skirmish following the main engagement.

Broadly, this was the interpretation placed on James III's death by four of the five sixteenth century chroniclers. The first of them to write, Adam Abell of Jedburgh in 1533, is brief but illuminating. In his account, the rebels 'conspirit aganis the king and gaif him batell beside striwiling and thare wes he slane. He was confessit before with maistir Johne Yrland proffessor of theologie'. Subsequently he comments that 'be ewill counsall (the prince) gaif feild to his father bot it is said he forbad to put hands in him. Bot thai did the contra for thai slew him in the mill of bannoburne'.[139] The location of the slaying, in Bannockburn mill, appears for the first time in Abell's chronicle.

It is most unlikely that Abell's work — which was never published — was widely circulated, or that the later sixteenth century chroniclers had the opportunity to use it; but the source from which he acquired his material seems also to have provided

Lesley, Ferreri, Pitscottie and Buchanan with much of their information.[140] Thus Lesley, after remarking that the king was safe throughout the battle because the prince had given orders that no-one was to lay violent hands on his father, goes on to say that 'certane wicked men, quha had him in hatrent of old, awaitit on him and slew him in the mill of Bannokburne, nocht far from the place quhair the field wes strekin'. Ferreri repeats the story about the prince's admonition before the battle, and continues by describing the king's flight and refuge in an unspecified mill. His pursuers recognised his horse standing outside the mill, discovered the king and stabbed him to death; these were men who, according to Ferreri, had borne James III a grudge for a long time, and could not afford to let him live for fear of his taking revenge on them for crimes which they had committed in the past.[141]

George Buchanan, describing the king's death in his history, which appeared in 1582, adds a wealth of circumstantial detail but essentially tells the same story as the others. King James, injured by falling from his horse, took refuge 'in molas acquarias non longe ab loco ubi pugnatum erat'. His intention was to board one of the nearby ships — presumably Sir Andrew Wood's vessels, which Buchanan later mentions as cruising up and down the Forth, taking off the wounded from the battle. However, being overtaken, James III was slain, together with a few attendants, at the mills. Unlike the other chroniclers, Buchanan specifies the supposed assassins by name: Patrick Gray, 'familiae suae princeps' — presumably Lord Gray is indicated — Stirling of Keir, and a priest named Borthicus or Borthwick; and he concludes by recording that the report of James's death stopped the pursuit and slaughter of the fugitives.[142]

Two of Buchanan's assassins — Lord Gray and Sir William Stirling of Keir — are known to have been on the rebel side at Sauchieburn. However, Buchanan also states that the king was attended by some followers; so if there is any truth to his story, James III was not attacked merely by three assassins, two of whom had in any case presumably given a written promise — as leaders in the prince's army — not to lay violent hands on the king. If Gray and Stirling of Keir are to be associated with James III's death at all, it can only be in the sense that they may have been the leaders of the skirmishing party or parties at whose hands the king met his death; and even this cannot be proved.[143]

Thus the only account of the king's death which is really at odds with the record and chronicle evidence is that of Pitscottie, who tells a tale of a king fleeing alone from the battlefield on a large grey horse, the fastest in Scotland (a gift from Pitscottie's ancestor, David, Lord Lindsay of Byres). Thrown from the horse, he was carried wounded into Bannockburn mill by the miller and his wife, and having revealed his identity and asked for a priest to shrive him, he was stabbed to death by an unknown assassin who claimed to be a priest. Thereupon the murderer removed King James's body and no-one ever discovered where it was buried.[144] These statements require a brief examination.

It must be said at the outset that Pitscottie's story of the horse presented to the king by David, Lord Lindsay of Byres, some time before the battle has to be treated with scepticism. Pitscottie states that Lindsay of Byres and his followers joined the royal army at St. Johnston (a remarkable detour for the royalists on their way from

Edinburgh to Stirling!), and that he appeared 'rydand all inairmett upoun ane great gray curser and lychtit doun and maid his obedience to the king; thairefter presentit the said curser to the king, schawand his grace that gif he had ado in his extremitee ether to flie or follow that horse wald war all the horse of Scottland at his plesour, gif he wald seit weill'.[145] This is surely an example of Pitscottie embroidering a good tale. At a time when, according to his account of events, the king was in a strong position at the head of a powerful army, the chronicler makes one of the royal commanders suggest what his narrative later goes on to describe, that James III might have to flee and would only be safe if he managed to avoid falling off his horse. The source of such a story is presumably a tale passed down through the family of Lindsay of Byres — in an effort to exaggerate the importance of their ancestor — that the second Lord had presented a horse to James III. Buchanan, the only other sixteenth century chronicler to mention the king's fall from his horse, omits Pitscottie's colourful story of the miller's wife and states that James was accompanied by some attendants; and it is hardly credible that the king fled alone from the field.

Nor does the tale that James III was stabbed to death by some unknown who claimed to be a priest stand up to examination. It may, in fact, be no more than a confused and distorted expansion of Adam Abell's bald statement about the aftermath of the battle. Abell had stated that the rebels 'conspirit aganis the king and gaif him batell beside striwiling and thare wes he slane. He was confessit before with maistir Johne Yrland proffessor of theologie'.[146] John Ireland was the royal confessor, and what Abell means is that James III made his confession to Ireland before the *battle*. Abell's chronicle was not printed; therefore the distortion of his statement that the king was confessed by Ireland, into Pitscottie's lurid tale of the murderer being asked by King James to shrive him, must be the result of both chroniclers using a common source. This may have been a ballad of some kind, which mentioned that the king did not die unshriven; in Abell's time the confessor's name was still in the ballad, but forty-five years later, when Pitscottie wrote his history, it had presumably dropped out. As for the stabbing, it has been suggested by Graham[147] that Pitscottie adapted Bellenden's account of the murder of Sir John Comyn by Robert Bruce to fit into his tale of the slaughter of James III; and the two narratives are, in fact, very similar. Bellenden had stated that two of Bruce's friends 'went to the Cumin, and inquirit him gif he had ony deidis woundis; or gif he trowit to recovir, gif he had ony gud surrigiane. And becaus he said he micht recover, thay straik him iii or iv othir straikis, mair cruelly; and sone eftir he gaif the gaist'.[148] Pitscottie's adaptation states that the supposed priest 'kneillit doune upoun his knie and speirit at the kingis grace gif he might leif gif he had good leiching, quho ansuerit him and said he trowit he might'. Thereupon the murderer 'pullit out ane quhinger and gif him foure or fyve straikis ewin to the hart'.[149]

Pitscottie's catalogue of errors, misconceptions and deliberate borrowings is completed by his statement that, after the murder, the assassin removed the king's body and that no-one ever discovered where he buried it. James III was buried in Cambuskenneth abbey beside his queen; Buchanan states that his funeral took place on 25 June 1488, a fortnight after the battle; and even Abell's very brief account makes mention of the king's burial in Cambuskenneth.[150]

It is clear from all this that Pitscottie's description of James III's death cannot be accepted as serious history. This being the case, the argument that the king was murdered rather than slain in battle no longer carries any weight, for Pitscottie is its only real advocate. As we have seen, the accounts of the other four sixteenth century historians complement rather than contradict the contemporary record evidence, and the obvious conclusion to be drawn is that this evidence, meagre though it is, presents a valid picture of the king's death. With the rashness which characterised many members of the Stewart dynasty, James III, carrying Bruce's sword and about a third of his annual income in a black box, committed himself to an unnecessary and unequal struggle and was killed in a skirmish at Bannockburn mill.

NOTES

1. *A.P.S.*, ii, 180.

2. *Ibid.*, 181-2.

3. *Ibid.*, 182. The bishop and lord of parliament whom the king would choose for the English embassy in 1488 would presumably be Elphinstone and Bothwell, the men who had negotiated the indenture of November 1487. Bothwell eventually went south, but the outbreak of rebellion in February precipitated Elphinstone into the Chancellorship and presumably prevented his travelling to England.

4. Nicholson, *op.cit.*, 519.

5. *A.P.S.*, ii, 183; and *see above*, Chapter 9.

6. *A.P.S.*, ii, 182. The four candidates for justiciarships south of Forth can hardly have been approved by many of the southern nobility. Two of them — Glamis and Drummond — were northern lords, while the others were — up to this time — committed royalists, Bothwell in particular being resented as the king's favourite.

7. *Ibid.*

8. *Ibid.*, 97, 101, 108, 114, 119.

9. *Ibid.*, 181.

10. *Ibid.*

11. *Ibid.*

12. *E.R.*, x, 2-3; *Scots Peerage*, iv, 336. Shaw's daughter Helen had been married first to Archibald, son and heir of George, third Lord Haliburton of Dirleton. Father and son both died c. 1488.

13. Pitscottie (*Historie*, i, 203-4) suggests that the prince was removed to Linlithgow. Throughout the conflict, the rebel forces appear to have been divided. One army was probably located at Linlithgow in late April or early May, when the king was speedily confronted at Blackness; while another force, including the prince, found it possible to return to Stirling once James III had gone north (24 March – 6 April 1488). For the personnel on the rebel side at Stirling late in May, *see* S.R.O., RH 1/1/3 (photostat).

14. *A.P.S.*, ii, 223.

15. Lesley, *History*, 55; Ferrerius, *Appendix to Boece*, f. 399 r. Lesley omits Lord Lyle from his list.

16. Lesley, *History*, 56.

17. Ferrerius, *Appendix to Boece*, f. 399 r-v.

18. Buchanan, *History*, ii, 157.

19. Pitscottie, *Historie*, i, 203-4. Although Pitscottie's account is all based on hearsay evidence, this part of his narrative contains some interesting and convincing material because his family, the Lindsays of Byres — that is, his grandfather Patrick, fourth Lord Lindsay of Byres, and the fourth Lord's elder brother David, second Lord — had played a part in the crisis. Later in his narrative, however, when he comes to describe the battle of Sauchieburn and its aftermath, Pitscottie is totally unconvincing because his aim is simply to glorify the deeds of his ancestors, the Lindsays of Byres: *ibid.*, 208-9, 219-226.

20. Nicholson, *op.cit.*, 531.

21. *A.P.S.*, ii, 184.

22. *R.M.S.*, ii, No. 1707. This charter does not follow a gap in the Great Seal Register, but is in mid-sequence. Thus the previous charter for which a witness list survives is dated 18 February 1488, three days earlier (*R.M.S.*, ii, No. 1705). This was witnessed by Elphinstone and Argyll, the latter still described as Chancellor.

23. *R.M.S.*, ii, Nos. 1709 – 1722 (for Argyll, Blacader and Browne as witnesses); No. 1717 (for Angus).

24. Fraser, *Wemyss*, ii, 111.

25. *E.R.*, x, 57, 62.

26. Leland, *Collectanea*, iv, 240, quoting B.M. Cotton MS., Julius B. xii. John Ramsay, Lord Bothwell, as ambassador of the king of Scots, was at Windsor on 27 April.

27. Ferrerius, *Appendix to Boece*, f. 399 v.

28. *A.P.S.*, ii, 183.

29. S.R.O. Airlie Charters, Section 12, No. 9.

30. On 21 March 1488, a few days before his departure from Edinburgh, James III confirmed to Sir Andrew Wood, his wife, and their heirs, an earlier grant in feu-farm of the lands and town of Largo in Fife: *R.M.S.*, ii, No. 1720. The king may have crossed the Forth in the 'Yellow Carvel', a ship with which both he and Wood were closely associated: *E.R.*, viii, 293; *T.A.*, i, 54, 66, 68.

31. Pitscottie, *Historie*, i, 202. Pitscottie and Buchanan are nevertheless the only sixteenth century chroniclers to appreciate that the king left Edinburgh and went north to gather support; neither of them mentions Aberdeen as his objective. Bishop Lesley, however, mentions only Stirling and Edinburgh in his account of the crisis, the king being resident in the former, the rebels in the latter: Lesley, *History*, 56-8.

32. Ferrerius, *Appendix to Boece*, f. 400 r.

33. Lesley, *History*, 57-8 (at the very end of his account of the reign).

34. Buchanan, *History*, ii, 156.

35. Hume, *Douglas and Angus*, 206.

36. Drummond, *History*, 169.

37. *E.R.*, x, p. lxvii, 116-7, 183, 253-4.

38. Fraser, *Buccleuch*, ii, 89.

39. *A.P.S.*, ii, 210.

40. *T.A.*, i, 79-80.

41. *A.D.C.*, 113. This may well be the origin of Pitscottie's story that in 1488 a royal herald sent to cite the Humes to appear in parliament for treason 'was evill intreitit in the executioun of his sowmondis . . . and his lettres revin': Pitscottie, *Historie*, i, 201.

42. *A.D.C.*, 46, 93-4.

43. *E.R.*, x, Pref., p. xlii.

44. *Ibid.*, ix, 433.

45. *R.M.S.*, ii, No. 1774; *E.R.*, x, 58-9, 77, 100, 376; *Rot. Scot.*, ii, 485-6.

46. *Scots Peerage*, iv, 335.

47. *A.P.S.*, ii, 181; Atholl Chrs., i, No. 47; Royal Letters, No. 2 (Blair castle); *R.M.S.*, ii, No. 1759.

48. *Scots Peerage*, i, 335.

49. *Cal. Docs. Scot.*, iv, Nos. 1501-5.

50. *R.M.S.*, ii, No. 1617; S.R.O. Airlie Chrs., Section 12, No. 9; *A.P.S.*, ii, 210.

51. *A.P.S.*, ii, 182; *R.M.S.*, ii, No. 1752. Lyle was clearly dissatisfied with his gains in 1488, for he rebelled against the new regime the following year.

52. *See above*, Chapter 10.

53. Theiner, *Vetera Monumenta*, 502.

54. Nicholson, *op.cit.*, 481-2; and *ibid.*, 544-5, for subsequent developments in the west and north in the following reign. Argyll had been a Justiciar south of Forth as early as 1462: *Scots Peerage*, i, 332-3.

55. Laurence Lord Oliphant's son and heir John was married to Argyll's fourth daughter Elizabeth: *Scots Peerage*, i, 335; and there was also a link between Oliphant and the Earl of Angus, as George, Master of Angus, was betrothed to Margaret, eldest daughter of Oliphant, on 20 July 1485: *Scots Peerage*, i, 186. Oliphant's participation on the rebel side is proved by his supplication to the pope in 1490, asking for absolution for having opposed James III 'in pluribus conflictibus' between the prince and his father: Vat. Reg. Supp., 918, f. 17 v.

56. Drummond, *History*, 167.

57. *E.R.*, x, 57.

58. Vat. Reg. Supp., 899-948 *passim;* Wilkins, *Concilia,* iii, 634; Vat. Reg. Supp., 947, f. 95 r-v (for Shaw's supplication).

59. *A.D.A.*, 119.

60. *R.M.S.*, ii, No. 1722; Leland, *Collectanea,* iv, 240.

61. *A.P.S.*, ii, 201.

62. *Ibid.*, 210-11.

63. Danske Rigsarkiv, T.K.U.A., Skotland, A.1, 1.

64. *Rot. Scot.*, ii, 485-6.

65. S.R.O., R.H. 1/1/3.

66. S.R.O., Airlie Chrs., Section 12, 9; *Scots Peerage,* v, 4.

67. *Moray Registrum,* 234-6. Further evidence of the king's presence in Aberdeen at this time is to be found in two entries in the exchequer records relating to two chalders of wheat sent from Moray to James III in Aberdeen: *E.R.*, x, 85, 192; in the reference to 'the wyrkingis maid at Abirdene' in the indictment of John Ross of Montgrenan the following October: *A.P.S.*, ii, 205; and in the use of Aberdeen as the location of the royal mint at the end of the reign.

68. *A.P.S.*, ii, 201.

69. *Ibid.*

70. *A.P.S.*, ii, 210. These proposals for a settlement, which were produced by Lord Glamis in the parliament of October 1488, are sometimes incorrectly described as the Blackness agreement, presumably because the king was confronted by the rebels at Blackness castle in May 1488, and because the parliamentary record of October 1488 refers to agreements made by the prince and his father 'apud blaknes et alubi' (*A.P.S.*, ii, 202). But this statement implies that other places were involved. Significantly, the indictment of John Ross of Montgrenan, James's Lord Advocate, who was not apparently at Aberdeen, accuses him of counselling the king at Blackness, and arraying the royal army against the prince at Stirling, but acquits him of 'the wyrkingis made at Abirdene' (*A.P.S.*, ii, 205). Not only were the royal commissioners all northerners, but the issuing of commissions to treat for peace on both sides makes it clear that this was a settlement negotiated at a distance, not the work of representatives of two opposing armies at Blackness.

71. *A.P.S.*, ii, 210 (for all nine articles).

72. *Ibid.*

73. He was in Aberdeen on 6 and 16 April (S.R.O. Airlie Chrs., Section 12, No. 9; *Moray Registrum,* 234-6); and back in Edinburgh by 16 May (Dumbarton Burgh Records, No. 6). Allowing time for the appointment of commissioners to negotiate with the rebels, and indeed for the drawing up of the nine articles, it seems most likely that James III left Aberdeen about the end of April.

74. *A.P.S.*, ii, 210-11.

75. *Ibid.*, 201.

76. *Ibid.*, 201, 202. In addition to Buchan, Bothwell and Ross of Montgrenan were subsequently accused of attempting to induce the King of England to enter Scotland 'to the perpetual subjection of the realm': *A.P.S.*, ii, 202, 204.

77. *E.R.*, x, 33.

78. He is known to have advised the king to leave Edinburgh castle on his last campaign in June: *A.P.S.*, ii, 202; but he does not appear at Edinburgh as witness to Great Seal charters during the period 18–24 May: *R.M.S.*, ii, Nos. 1724-30. However, he witnessed a charter at Edinburgh on 28 May: Cunninghame Graham Muniments, GD 22/2/2; his return may therefore be dated 24–28 May.

79. Pitscottie (*Historie,* i, 203-4) places the rebel headquarters at Linlithgow throughout the crisis. Blackness is the port for Linlithgow.

80. Buchan, Ruthven, Murray of Tullibardine and Fotheringham of Powrie were handed over to the rebels as hostages at Blackness: *A.P.S.*, ii, 201. The Bishops of Aberdeen and Moray and Lord Forbes were with the king in Aberdeen on 16 April, and again at Edinburgh on 18 May; so they must have come south to Blackness with King James: *Moray Registrum,* 236; *R.M.S.*, ii, No. 1724. Innes of Innés and Turnbull of Greenwood were later rewarded by the king for their services at Blackness: *R.M.S.*, ii, Nos. 1730, 1723. Thomas Lord Innermeath was charged with treason on 12 August 1488 (*T.A.*, i, 92), which makes it probable that he came south from Aberdeen with the king and was present at Blackness.

81. *A.P.S.*, ii, 204.

82. Dumbarton Burgh Records, No. 6; *A.P.S.*, ii, 165. Freedom from shrieval jurisdiction was a privilege claimed more and more by burghs at this time. The most striking example of this development during James III's reign occurred in November 1482, when the king granted to the burgh of Edinburgh the right to appoint its own sheriff: *Edinburgh City Chrs.*, 157.

83. *R.M.S.*, ii, No. 1725.

84. *Ibid.*, No. 1724.

85. *Ibid.*, No. 1727.

86. Fraser, *Buccleuch*, ii, 89.

87. *H.M.C. Rep. vii*, App., 729.

88. *R.M.S.*, ii, No. 1730 (the last registered charter of the reign).

89. S.R.O. Cunninghame Grahame Muniments, GD 22/2/2.

90. *Laing Chrs.*, No. 198.

91. *A.P.S.*, ii, 202.

92. Leland, *Collectanea*, iv, 243. It is significant that no real evidence can be produced to show that Henry VII gave James III any material assistance at all during the 1488 crisis. Yet the prospect of such assistance was clearly feared by the insurgents; and their belief that Henry VII would come north in person was perhaps based on the terms of the 1487 truce, which provided for a meeting between the two kings in July 1488: *Rot. Scot.*, ii, 481.

93. *R.M.S.*, ii, Nos. 1724-30; Fraser, *Buccleuch*, ii, 91; *H.M.C., Rep. vii*, App., 729.

94. *T.A.*, i, 86-7.

95. *Ibid.*, 85-7.

96. *E.R.*, x, 82.

97. *T.A.*, i, 79-87, 97, 166-7; *E.R.*, x, 82. The accumulation of the royal hoard, apparently in the 1480s, may be attributed partly to income from profits of justice, especially remissions, from forfeitures and from trading ventures, but above all to the profits of royal debasement (1480–82). This case is ably argued by Joan Murray in 'The Black Money of James III', in *British Archaeological Reports 45* (1977), 115-130.

98. Pitscottie, *Historie*, i, 202.

99. Ferrerius, *Appendix to Boece*, f. 440 r–v; Buchanan, *History*, ii, 158-9.

100. Drummond, *History*, 173.

101. S.R.O., RH 1/1/3.

102. *R.M.S.*, ii, No. 1811; *T.A.*, i, 96.

103. *A.D.A.*, 130.

104. *A.P.S.*, ii, 204. Pitcairn (*Criminal Trials*, i, 8), suggests that the battle of Stirling bridge took place on 10 June, the day before Sauchieburn; but he cites no authority for this statement.

105. *Scots Peerage*, iv, 233.

106. Vat. Reg. Supp., 903, f. 162 r.

107. *A.P.S.*, ii, 204.

108. *Lag Chrs.*, No. 36.

109. *H.M.C., Rep. vii*, App., 729.

110. *Scots Peerage*, vii, 530.

111. The participation of some of the royalists in the above list is inferred from the fact that they were with James III at or after the confrontation at Blackness, or from their subsequent indictments for treason at the start of the new reign: *R.M.S.*, ii, Nos. 1724, 1725, 1727; Fraser, *Buccleuch*, ii, 89; *T.A.*, i, 92-3. The difficulty of compiling an accurate list lies in the fact that there were only ten summonses for treason under the new regime, and only two forfeitures — Lord Bothwell and John Ross of Montgrenan.

112. The presence in the rebel army of all these men — with the exception of Lord Oliphant — is inferred from the grants of lands and offices which they received on the accession of James IV. Oliphant received a papal absolution for his part in the rebellion: Vat. Reg. Supp., 918, f. 17 v.

113. Vat. Reg. Supp., 947, f. 95 r–v.

114. *H.M.C., Rep. vii*, App., 729.

115. *A.P.S.*, ii, 204, 210, 211; *E.R.*, x, 82; *R.M.S.*, ii, No. 1755.

116. N.L.S. MS. 1746 ff. 111 r, 112 r; Lesley, *History*, 57; Ferrerius, *Appendix to Boece*, f. 400 r.

117. Drummond, *History*, 174. Drummond's geography is admittedly weak; for example he describes Falkirk as 'a little town six miles eastward from Stirling'.

118. G.W.S. Barrow, *Robert Bruce*, 321-2; *E.R.*, x, 82. James III's hoard in the jewel house at Edinburgh castle contained another relic of 1314, 'King Robert Brucis serk': *T.A.*, i, 83.

119. Ordnance Survey 2½in. maps, Sheets NS 78, 79, 88, 89. An alternative site for the battle is suggested by Angus Graham, 'The Battle of "Sauchieburn"', in *S.H.R.*, xxxix (Oct. 1960), 95-6. Graham ingeniously suggests — following Pitscottie and Drummond — that 'Sauchieburn' is to be identified with the Sauchinford burn; but such a site would place the battle about seven miles south-east of Stirling, which clashes with the contemporary evidence.

120. *A.P.S.*, ii, 211.

121. Lesley, *History*, 57; Ferrerius, *Appendix to Boece*, f. 400 v.

122. *A.P.S.*, ii, 216. Glencairn's son Robert (*Scots Peerage*, iv, 234) was described simply as 'Lord Kilmaurs' in the parliament of February 1490.

123. *Archaeological Collections relating to the County of Renfrew*, ii, p. xiv; *A.D.A.*, 119 (20 October 1488).

124. Buchanan, *History*, ii, 159.

125. Pitscottie, *Historie*, i, 166, 205, 207.

126. Andrews or Andreas appears to have been a courtier during the period 1471-4, a doctor prescribing medicines for the king and receiving a present of a French gown from James in 1474: *E.R.*, viii, 124; *T.A.*, i, 48, 69. No references to Andreas are to be found in Scottish official records after 1474; yet Buchanan credits the man with predicting the death of Charles the Bold in 1477, an event which he claims brought Andreas to James III's notice: Buchanan, *History*, ii, 140.

127. Drummond, *History*, 135.

128. Bellenden, *Chronicles*, ii, 173-4.

129. Pitscottie, *Historie*, i, 207. In spite of the presence of his ancestor Lindsay of Byres on the royal side, and therefore acting as a somewhat remote source, Pitscottie appears to have had no idea of what happened at Sauchieburn. He gives an impossible list of participants, suggests that the royal forces numbered thirty thousand, the rebels eighteen thousand, and is concerned above all to glorify the Lindsay name. Thus David, second Lord Lindsay of Byres, not only plays a key role at Sauchieburn, but his brother Patrick, fourth Lord, is to be found — as Chancellor — late in the reign of James IV advising the king against the folly of underestimating the English at Flodden: Pitscottie, *Historie*, i, 267-8.

130. Ferrerius, *Appendix to Boece*, f. 400 v.

131. *A.P.S.*, ii, 211.

132. *Ibid.*, 204.

133' Ferrerius, *Appendix to Boece*, f. 400 v.

134. Pinkerton, *History*, ii, App. i, quoting B.M. Cotton, Caligula B III 19.

135. *Aberdeen Council Register*, 45; Boece, *Vitae*, 154. Buchanan (*History*, ii, 164) claims that Alexander, Lord Forbes, rode through Aberdeen and the neighbouring towns carrying James III's torn and bloodstained shirt on a spear in a recruiting drive to enlist support for the rebels.

136. Lennox Chrs. No. 85; printed in Fraser, *Lennox*, ii, 128-131.

137. N.L.S., MS. 1746, f. 112 r; Lesley, *History*, 57; Ferrerius, *Appendix to Boece*, f. 400 v.

138. *A.P.S.*, ii, 217.

139. N.L.S. MS. 1746, ff. 111 r, 112 r.

140. A detailed evaluation of the sixteenth century histories and their probable sources is given *below* in Chapter 12.

141. Lesley, *History*, 57; Ferrerius, *Appendix to Boece*, ff. 400 v, 401 r.

142. Buchanan, *History*, ii, 159, 161; Buchanan, *Rerum Scoticarum Historia*, lib. xii (edn. 1582), f. 142 v.

143. Even Pitscottie is more cautious than Buchanan when he describes a *single* assassin — 'sum sayis he was the lord Grayis servand': Pitscottie, *Historie*, i, 209.

144. Pitscottie, *Historie*, i, 208-9.

145. *Ibid.*, 205.

146. N.L.S. MS. 1746, f. 111 r.

147. *S.H.R.*, xxxix, (1960), 93.

148. Bellenden, *Chronicles,* ii, 380.
149. Pitscottie, *Historie,* i, 209.
150. *James IV Letters,* No. 542; Buchanan, *History,* ii, 162; N.L.S. MS. 1746, f. 111 r.

12
Images of a King: The 1480s to the 1980s

PUBLIC criticism of James III had continued unchecked throughout the years of his personal rule. The three estates had continually reminded the king of his duty to provide justice by driving the ayres, had pleaded with him to abandon the practice of making money out of remissions and respites, and had exhorted him to advance his reputation abroad not through impractical military adventures but by showing himself to be a ruler of consequence who had won the love of his own people. To much of this King James had turned a deaf ear, and he reacted strongly against criticism of his policy of peace and alliance with England following 1474. His death in battle against some of his own subjects produced, as we have seen, two further generalised indictments of his rule by the winning party of 1488, namely that he had followed the advice of wicked counsellors — a conventional complaint about rulers in all rebel literature — and that he had been guilty of the inbringing of Englishmen, a charge which could be levelled at the insurgents as well as the king. But however justified these complaints may have been, they go only a small part of the way towards explaining the growth in the sixteenth and subsequent centuries of a remarkable legend surrounding the character and policies of James III. By the end of the sixteenth century King James was widely portrayed as a recluse who could not or would not govern, who offended his brothers and his nobility by giving ear to low-born favourites, above all Cochrane the stonemason, the man largely instrumental in bringing about the ruin of Albany and the death of Mar. Acquisitive and lazy, James III was no leader in war, and he was contrasted to his disadvantage with his manly brothers Albany and Mar. This view of the king was further embellished in the seventeenth, eighteenth and nineteenth centuries, and much of it is still current today. The steady growth of such a legend over the centuries requires further examination.

Fortunately the literary sources of the period provide us with contemporary glimpses of the king's character and the problems which James III had to face; and these may be compared with the record evidence, especially the parliamentary acts, to see how far they present a credible picture of royal government during this reign. Three contemporary or near-contemporary works are relevant — Hary's *Wallace*, written in the 1470s, with its implied criticism of the king's foreign and domestic policies, *The Thre Prestis of Peblis*, completed in the 1480s or early 1490s and containing much more direct condemnation of royal weaknesses; and one of Robert Henryson's moral fables, 'The Lion and the Mouse'.

Good internal evidence, unconnected with James III, exists to suggest a date for Hary's *Wallace*. In Book XI of the poem, the author quotes as authorities two southern knights, Sir William Wallace of Craigie in Ayrshire and Sir James Liddale of Halkerston in the sheriffdom of Edinburgh. Both men were knighted about 1471–2,[1] and Wallace was killed at the siege of Dunbar in April or May 1479;[2] as both men are referred to by Hary as being alive and as knights, the poem must therefore have been written between 1471–2 and May 1479. More precisely, McDiarmid suggests that its composition should be attributed to the years 1476–8, and he has two grounds for this view: first, that *The Wallace*, being violently anti-English and containing in its opening lines a condemnation of alliance with 'our ald ennymis', was written after the conclusion of the Anglo-Scottish marriage treaty of October 1474; and secondly, that in his opposition to the royal policy and his association with Sir James Liddale, who was the Duke of Albany's steward,[3] Hary was a supporter of Alexander, duke of Albany, whose hostility towards the king must have been growing in the years before his imprisonment and ultimate flight from Dunbar in 1479.

The implied criticism of James III in Hary's *Wallace* is wholly concerned with the king's pro-English policies, and McDiarmid has even suggested that the hero of the poem is to be identified with the Duke of Albany, who in April 1474 had been prepared to resist a projected English invasion and who had certainly been opposed to the alliance.[4] This is possible; but McDiarmid goes much further when he suggests that 'discontented nobles regarded him (Albany) as the natural leader of any opposition to the procedures of James's Council and the favourites who composed it; and it seems to me certain that Hary's statement that Wallace wore the crown for a day in order to provoke battle from the English has a reference to a possible role for Albany in the kind of national emergency for which James would be unsuited as a leader'.[5] Here McDiarmid begs the question by accepting the later legend of James's lack of warlike qualities; and his ready acceptance of Albany as a national hero rather than a disillusioned conspirator reflects Hary's own bias in the 1470s, the starting point of the James III myth.

More explicit criticism of James III is to be found in *The Thre Prestis of Peblis*, a poem dating from the 1480s or early 1490s[6] and consisting of three tales told by three Peebles priests in order to entertain each other. The first two of these are satires on the Scottish king, in the first case for his misgovernance of Church and State, in the second for his frivolity in consorting with young counsellors instead of his nobility. The main complaint in the first tale is that the administration of justice is corrupt; but the second attacks the king personally for taking gifts and granting remissions for serious crimes. In character he was mercurial, changing swiftly from levity to 'greit hauines and thocth', fickle in friendship, quickly tiring of favoured officials, and false to his queen. Most of these characteristics are to be found in a story contained within the second tale, in which the principal role is played by the king's wise fool Fictus. Shortly before Christmas the king was attracted by the beauty of the daughter of a burgess named Innes, and he ordered Fictus to fetch the lady to the royal bed that night. However, the fool approached the queen in secret, told her of her husband's infidelity and advised her to slip into the king's bed in place of the burgess's daughter. The queen agreed, and for three nights shared her husband's bed. On the king's declaring to Fictus that he was well satisfied with the new arrangement, the fool revealed to him that he had been sleeping with his wife. Thereafter the king asked the queen for forgiveness and a reconciliation followed.

The story should not of course be taken literally, nor is it original; it may have been adapted from Boccaccio by the Scottish poet, and its most famous appearance in literature came later when it supplied the plot of Shakespeare's *All's Well that Ends Well.*[7] In the context of the Scottish court in the 1480s, it probably drew its relevance from the temporary estrangement of James III and Margaret of Denmark during the crisis of 1482. It is not a stern indictment of the king; the wise fool points a moral, and all ends happily. At no time did the vicious rebel propaganda of 1488 — the charge that the queen had been poisoned on her husband's instructions — become part of the legend; this story was purely for Danish consumption, and was quite unknown in Scotland.

Apart from criticism of the king's personal characteristics, the main charges brought against him by the author of the *Thre Prestis* are corrupt administration of justice and reliance on young counsellors. The former grievance is the theme of the first tale. The nobles explain to the king why they are no longer 'full of freedom, worship and honour, hardy in heart to stand in every stour'. The king's justices are so full of arrogance, greed and avarice that they diminish the prestige of the lords; they indict lords and pillage smaller men, and all for greed, so that husbandmen are unable to arm themselves and lords have to marry their sons to the daughters of rich peasants. The cost of trumped-up charges seems to be the bone of contention in this strained argument. The solution proposed is that the king's justice be accompanied by a doctor of laws who would see both the thief punished and the innocent acquitted. It is difficult to relate this to any of the known complaints about James III's justice in criminal affairs. The poem suggests that the justices were too harsh, while other complaints are to the effect that they were not diligent enough and were too free with remissions. On the other hand, the 'doctor of laws' points unmistakably to Dr. John Ireland, who from 1480 appeared frequently in the sederunts of the king's council in civil causes. All this suggests that the author has no very clear idea of what specifically was wrong with the king's justice, and has confused the justiciar with the Lords of Council.

As regards the king's household, the poet is more explicit; and the second tale opens with a description of the royal character and associates:

> The king was fair in persoun, fresh and fors,
> Ane feirie man on fute or zit on hors;
> And neuertheless feil falts him befell:
> He luifit ouer weil yong counsel;
> Yong men he luifit to be him neist;
> Yong men to him thay war baith Clark and Priest.
> He luifit nane was ald or ful of age,
> Sa did he nane of sad counsel nor sage.
> To sport and play, quhyle up and quhylum doun,
> To al lichtnes ay was he redie boun.[8]

This theme of young counsellors about the king is touched upon again when the writer states that 'the Cuntrie throw him was misfarne, throw yong counsel . . .'[9]

Finally, earlier in the same tale the complaint about lack of wise counsel is linked
with the failure of the king to administer firm justice throughout the land.
According to the story, the king while out hunting came upon a wounded man who
had been attacked by thieves and reivers. This individual complained that

> The falt is yowris, Sir King, and nathing myne:
> For and with yow gude counsal war ay cheif,
> Than wald ye stanche weill baith reuer and theif.[10]

Thus the complaint is not that the 'yong counsel' about the king had an evil
influence on his actions, but rather that they led him to neglect his duties, and that
as a result justice was not being properly administered. The 'young' members of the
royal household are never described as favourites by the author of the *Thre Prestis*;
and they are mentioned only in the second tale, in the three instances quoted above.
Despite being led astray, the king is portrayed sympathetically from the outset,
rather as Rex Humanitas is treated in Lindsay's *Three Estates*.

   Thus *The Thre Prestis of Peblis* may be said to make four criticisms of James III —
that justice was not being properly administered, that royal justice was corrupt, that
the king used young counsellors, and that he became estranged from the queen.
(There is, however, no complaint that the king was personally covetous.) The first
two criticisms are conventional ones which are reflected in the parliamentary
records, but little understood by the poet; in the case of the others, the 'young
counsel' may be a veiled reference to John Ramsay, while as we have seen, there is
record evidence to show that the queen took some part in the government during
her husband's imprisonment in the autumn of 1482. These criticisms in particular
provided material for the later legend.

   A comparison may be made between the *Thre Prestis* and Robert Henryson's
moral fable 'The Lion and the Mouse', in which contemporary politics are also
reflected. The lion, the king of beasts (and obviously also the King of Scots), lay
asleep while the mice played over him. When he awoke he seized the mouse which
pleaded for its life. The lion 'put the case' that if he had been dead and stuffed with
straw, it still behoved the mice 'becaus it [the corpse] bair the prent of my persoun'
to fall on their knees in dread.[11] The renewed pleas of the mouse were for justice
tinged with mercy; it was no matter for credit for a lion to overcome a mouse.
Eventually the lion granted a remission and released the mouse. Later the lion went
hunting, slaying both tame and wild until the people set a trap with nets into which
he fell. Tied up with ropes, he lamented the prospect of an early death: 'Quhay sall
thir bandis breik? Quha sall me put fra pane of this presoun?'. However, the mouse
reappeared and with the aid of its fellows released the lion. In the 'moralitas'
Henyrson explains that the lion is a ruler who sleeps and does not govern his land;
the mice are the 'commonty'; lacking effective rule by their lords and princes, they
do not fear to rebel.[12]

   In a fascinating study of Henryson's major narrative poems,[13] Professor
MacQueen draws attention to possible connections with James III in the symbolism
of 'The Lion and the Mouse'. He suggests that the lion's hunting when he 'slew
both tame and wild' may refer to confiscations and executions of Lowlanders and

Highlanders during the reign, and the imprisoning of the lion to events after Lauder Bridge. It might be added, to strengthen this argument, that the 'bandis' referred to might be written bonds. MacQueen further suggests that 'although Henryson does not say so, it is fairly clear that the hunters who trap the lion are the Scottish nobility whose general hostility to James III is notorious'.[14] In fact, the 'moralitas' and the poem are not in complete accord. In the former the lion represents slothful government, and it might be expected that the hunting lion would be sympathetically portrayed; yet in the poem, when the lion hunts he becomes 'the cruel lion'. Complete consistency, an accord between the poem and the politics of James III's reign, is not to be looked for.

The passage in the poem in which the lion claims that the mouse should have bowed the knee even to a stuffed lion-skin 'may even be a caricature of Stewart ideas on the divine right of kings', according to MacQueen.[15] Although somewhat anachronistic, this view reflects accurately James III's exalted notion of his 'majesty' which may be caricatured here. But if Henryson saw the king as sleeping while disorder raged, it seems strange that he should continue the caricature when the king awakes and seizes the rebel. The poem's moral content is in the main the argument by the mouse that the lion's justice should be tempered with mercy, but it is scarcely arguable that by this Henryson meant to favour the granting of remissions by the king. It is also difficult to point to the widespread executions which are said to mar James's reign and to be reflected in the poem. It is however noteworthy that Henryson, in the 'moralitas', does comment on those who imprisoned the lion:

> Thir crewall men, that stentit hes the nett,
> In quhilk the lyone suddanely wes tane,
> Waitit alway amendis for till get . . .

The captors of the cruel lion are now, somewhat inconsistently, cruel men, but it is difficult to see why the poem requires this condemnation in the 'moralitas'. The explanation may lie in the next few lines:

> Moir till expone as now I latt allane,
> Bot king and lord may weill wit quhat I mene;
> Fegour heirof oftymes hes bene sene.[16]

These cryptic and allusive remarks suggest that Henryson is making reference to recent events about which it was wiser not to be explicit. The cruel men are surely not a generalised Scottish nobility, as MacQueen suggests, but specifically the captors of the king, presumably in 1482. The poem is not after all hostile to James III, but criticial of him; it is also critical of the unruly 'commonty'. Most clearly, it condemns the imprisonment of the king.

Thus this tale by Henryson and the *Thre Prestis* alike reflect the politics of the time in which they were written. Neither is a political tract, an exact allegory of James III and his nobles; neither is a clear and consistent criticism either of the king or the nobility. If either reflects the politics of James III's reign, it does so only in highly conventional terms. The satire in both is very muted or even wholly absent.

As evidence of opinion in James's reign, both poems suggest sympathy with his difficulties and commendation of his attempts to overcome them. Such sympathy is in marked contrast to the attitude of the anonymous author of the final chapter of the *Liber Pluscardensis*. This takes the form of a vernacular poem of forty-one stanzas entitled 'The Harp'.[17] It is addressed to a king and urges that he should govern well, above all in the administering of royal justice. The principles set forth are detailed and explicit; the king should reward the worthy, punish wickedness, expel the wicked, love them that are wise, and 'cheis the counsal at war wyss, Be al thi thre estatis ordinance'. No man should be chosen for his high birth,[18] but rather men of great prudence, neither wretched, greedy nor partial, should be appointed to serve on the council. The poet goes on to complain that the royal treasure inherited by the king in the minority has now gone, though he does not explain how or where. He emphasises the need for a justice who would be made auditor of complaints to the poor and so relieve the 'grete counsale' of the heavy burden of dealing with complaints not strictly its business. The king's judges are further criticised for abusing their jurisdiction for love, friendship, or feud, and ought to be punished; and royal authority is undermined when dissidents are able to defy royal officials in the localities and escape scot-free. Finally the king himself is criticised:

> Quhen grete counsale, with thine awn consent
> Has ordanit strate justice na ma to spair
> Within schort tym thou changis thine entent
> Sendand a contrar lettir incontinent . . .
> Than al the warld murmuris that thou art bocht.[19]

When the king in the sphere of justice gives a remission where the full rigour of the law is required, the poet concludes that he offends both against God and the office of kingship.[20]

It is unlikely that 'The Harp' was written after 1461. It belongs to a work which in effect stops in 1437 with the death of James I, but which has occasional references to events up to 1453 and a note on the death of James II; and if Skene is correct, it may be dated to the 1450s or, at the latest, 1461.[21] In either case the poem cannot refer to James III, and it seems most likely that it was addressed to his father, who had faced similar problems, above all those accruing from a long minority. Some of the criticisms in the poem are echoed in acts of parliament under James II, James III and James IV. To take an example from the final stanza of the poem, directed against remissions: in the parliament of March 1504 James IV admitted that his over-hasty granting of remissions had been responsible for 'the gret invonvenientis of slauchter movit and happinit ilk day mair and mair', and promised that he would give no more remissions for 'slauchter to be committitt upone forthocht fellony'. This was a repetition, couched in even stronger language, of a promise made by James III in a statute of 1484.[22]

However, the text of the poem cannot be taken to refer to James III simply because his reign ended in failure and failures evoke widespread criticism. In fact, it provides valuable evidence that a 'successful' king was subject to the same criticisms as an 'unsuccessful' one, that the evils complained of were endemic in society, and that all kings succumbed to them in some degree. Finally, 'The Harp' is a warning against selecting from the evidence for James II's reign only those points which redound to his credit and assist in explaining his 'success', and against doing the reverse for James III. For the truth is that in contemporary literature James III is criticised only in conventional terms. The complaint about ineffectual and corrupt justice, as we have seen, was levelled at every king from James II to James V. Similarly, the indictment of James III for acceptance of 'yong counsel' may be regarded as a conventional complaint of the period, and may have been greatly exaggerated by reference to the Scottish king's contemporaries in England and France, Edward IV and Louis XI. In England, the elevation of the Woodville clan, following Edward IV's marriage to the widow of a former Lancastrian, was much resented by the loyal Yorkist nobility, especially the king's younger brothers Clarence and Gloucester;[23] while in France, Louis XI's reliance on low-born counsellors — including his barber Oliver le Dain, who was made a count and used as a royal envoy and justiciar — produced a sharp reaction by the nobility on Louis' death, one of its first expressions being the hanging of le Dain in May 1484.[24] Much nearer home, James III's two successors would be attacked for their more modest elevations of John Damien de Falcusis and Oliver Sinclair of Pitcairns.

Evidence that events outside Scotland influenced Scottish historiography is to be found in a short chronicle appended to the earliest manuscripts of Andrew Wyntoun's *Orygynale Cronykil of Scotland*. A mere ten folios, it nevertheless bears the imposing title 'Heir is assignt the cause quhy our natioun was callyt fyrst the Scottys', and endeavours to cover the history of Scotland from its legendary beginnings down to 1482, when tantalisingly it breaks off.[25] Only the last two folios cover the fifteenth century, but in this short space the writer contributes significantly to the growth of the James III legend.

Most interesting are his comments on the years 1479 and 1482, for it is at this point that the legend begins to appear. Under 1479, the chronicler accurately describes the siege of Albany's castle of Dunbar by the royal forces; but he then passes directly on to the death of John, earl of Mar, who in this account was slain because he was in sympathy with witches and warlocks recently burned on 'crag gayt'. We have already seen that the death of Mar is explicable without recourse to such stories, which are simply borrowed from the accusations for which another royal brother, George, duke of Clarence, had been executed in England the year before. No doubt the story of Clarence's conspiracy with necromancers spread rapidly to Scotland;[26] and the fact that Mar's execution probably took place in private must have raised doubts as to the manner of his death which could be explained away by citing the bizarre Clarence story of the previous year. Perhaps significantly, the writer does not blame the king openly for Mar's death, remarking cautiously that 'thai said' Mar favoured witches and warlocks.

The last portion of the chronicle is an extensive treatment of the crisis of 1482. The writer talks of hardship caused by the Anglo-Scottish war, especially the destruction of corn and cattle, but claims that 'gret hungyr and deid' were mainly the responsibility of the king, who had introduced black money into the realm. He goes on to relate that in July James III intended to invade England, whereupon 'the lordis of scotland' held a council in Lauder Kirk, cried down the black money, slew one part of the royal household and banished another. Thereafter, they took the king and put him in Edinburgh castle 'in firm kepyng', where he remained until Michaelmas. His principal fault — apart from debasement — was that he took counsel from members of his household, 'at war bot sympill', rather than his lords. The writer concludes by claiming that economic recovery followed the crying down of the black money.[27]

In character, the chronicle is remarkably unbiased against either the king or Albany. Thus the king's 'simple' counsellors are not associated with Mar's death or the introduction of black money, while on the other hand the fact that no mention is made of Gloucester's invasion of southern Scotland in July 1482 — instead James III is held responsible for planning to invade England — disguises Albany's treasonable designs on the Crown. It is of course possible that the chronicler had no idea what had happened in the summer of 1482; but his concentration on Albany's career, following the duke's progress from 1464 through to his banishment in 1479 and beyond, suggests that he may have been one of Albany's supporters.

The chronicler is also sympathetic towards the Lauder rebels, who are described as 'the lords of scotland'; and this would suggest that he was writing during the period when Albany and the rebel lords were attempting to reach a settlement — that is, from October to December 1482. Two earlier comments would appear to support this dating. Describing Albany's capture at sea by the English, the writer goes on to say that, when the duke was freed, he was 'honorabilly deliverit' to his brother King James. Then, under the date 1469, James III was married to Margaret of Denmark 'in gret dignite'.[28] Complimentary remarks about Albany, the queen and the rebel lords would be included in the chronicle if it were written at the time when all of them were associated in carrying on the government — that is, from early October until late December 1482. On the other hand, it would be extremely difficult to write any completion of the version of 1482 given in this chronicle after Albany's fall in December, and the subsequent recovery of authority by the king.

Thus this short fragment established the existence of the legend of Mar's slaying because he was in league with witches and warlocks, and it reinforced the complaints in contemporary literature about the king's reliance on 'simple' or base-born counsellors. However, none of these individuals is named, and referring to the parliamentary indictments of James's supporters in October 1488 does not help us much, for while one of them — Ross of Montgrenan — was a laird, and another — John Ramsay, Lord Bothwell — could be regarded as an upstart lord of parliament, the third was the king's half-uncle, the Earl of Buchan, by no stretch of the imagination a 'simple' or 'yong' counsellor. The parliamentary complaint was not however designed to indict these men because of their age or birth, but because they had given bad counsel to the king on a specific occasion; in other words, they were on the losing side in 1488.

After 1488, however, it might have been expected that legends concerning James III would rapidly die out, for there was no political motive for continuing to blacken the late king's name. The parliamentary apologia of October 1488, claiming that James III had brought his fate upon himself through acceptance of bad counsel, but insisting that he had 'happened' to be slain, said all that needed to be said. Once the new government had weathered the rebellion of 1489, made pious noises about discovering the vile persons who had laid violent hands on the late king, and — more prosaically but equally unsuccessfully — made inquiries about what had befallen the residue of James III's enormous hoard,[29] it remained only for those directly involved at Sauchieburn to pay for their absolutions from Rome and for the young king to endow masses for the soul of his father in 1496. Even former friends of James III had no cause once their master was dead; they might dislike the new regime, but they had to live with it. So after histrionic gestures by Lord Forbes — carrying the late king's bloody shirt on a lance through Aberdeenshire — had signally failed to rouse the conservative north, and after the burgesses of Aberdeen had dutifully recorded in their council register their displeasure at the manner of King James's death, both sides in the recent civil war were happy to draw a veil over the immediate past and settle down to a relatively peaceful co-existence, easing the collective conscience of the nation by consigning James III and all his works to a convenient oblivion.

Thus for two generations after 1488 we find no obvious extensions of the legend of James III enshrined in contemporary public records or literature; indeed, the histories of the period, by John Major and Hector Boece, demonstrate clearly that the legend had not been absorbed at all, and that the writers of the 1520s had no clear picture of the character and failings of the king. Thus Major, whose *History of Greater Britain* was published in 1521, confined himself to the non-committal remark that 'you shall find many a king, both at home and abroad, who was worse than James the Third'.[30] Such a remark is perhaps not surprising coming from a man whose principal themes included glorification of the Stewart monarchy and the desirability of Anglo-Scottish friendship; but it is perhaps significant that James III is mentioned at all in a work which does not cover the reign. Only a year later, in 1522, Hector Boece published his Latin *Lives of the Bishops of Mortlach and Aberdeen*, and once again we find sympathetic treatment of the king and his policies. James III, according to Boece, had subdued the Highlanders and brought the whole country to a well-established peace. Later in the same work, Boece praises the king as a devout and merciful man.[31] In fact, he says nothing about James III which could not have been said, arguably with greater force, about James IV, and the reason is clear. Much of the work is a hagiography of Bishop Elphinstone of Aberdeen, who as James's principal counsellor (according to Boece) could only be responsible for wise advice; so by association with Elphinstone, James III receives conventional praise, rather than conventional criticism, from Boece. The same is true of Boece's *Scotorum Historiae*, published in Paris in 1526; although James III's reign is not covered in the main body of the work, Boece includes in an appendix, which takes the form of a catalogue of Scottish kings, a thumbnail sketch of the king which is broadly sympathetic towards James and anti-baronial in character.[32] This is a remarkable afterthought in a work which makes much of the right of nobility and people to depose tyrants, and follows the careers of forty mythical kings in order to display the process in operation. The explanation may lie in Boece's earlier commitment to praise of James III as Elphinstone's sovereign. In any event, his fabulous *Scotorum Historiae* showed that it was possible to make a theme of deposed kings; but they were all mythical monarchs like Culenus, Evenus III and Ferchard. James III was not numbered amongst them.

In 1530, however, there occurred a striking change. Sir David Lindsay's 'Testament of the Papyngo' made a dramatic contribution to the legend of James III because the poet enlarged on and extended the theme of bad counsel which had laid dormant for two generations, and in so doing established a pattern of complaint which thrust King James and his familiars from comparative obscurity on to a pinnacle of notoriety. For the first time in any commentary on the reign, the leader of the favourites is named as Cochrane, and he and his 'catyue companye' are credited with alienating King James from 'prudent Lordis counsall', causing the exclusion from court of Albany and Mar,

> Tyll, in the Kyng, thare grew sic mortall feid,
> He flemit the Duke and patt the Erle to dede.

The sequel was the hanging of Cochrane and the rest from Lauder Bridge and the capture of the king, though Lindsay does not say by whom; and in the next stanza he deplores the civil war of 1488:

> How that the Sonne, with baner braid displayit,
> Agane the Fader, in battell, come arrayit.

The poem concludes with a stanza in which Lindsay laments the death of James III, the poet regretting the king's rashness in giving battle without sufficient strength:

> Wald God that prince had bene, that day, confortit
> With sapience of the prudent Salomone,
> And with the strength of strang Sampsone supportit,
> With the bauld oste of gret Agamenone.
> Quhat suld I wys, remedie wes thare none:
> At morne, ane king with sceptour, sweeird, and croun;
> Att ewin, ane dede deformit carioun.[33]

Thus Lindsay, forty-two years after James III's death, adds substantially to the legend. Cochrane is not only named for the first time, but directly associated with the destruction of Albany and Mar; and the executions at Lauder are described as hangings. Lindsay has clearly also some source for the battle of Sauchieburn and Prince James's part in it, though he has nothing to say about the causes of the break between father and son. Indeed, four of the poem's six stanzas are taken up with Cochrane and the favourites, whose demise might have been expected to benefit the royal government; instead, Lindsay immediately passes on to 1488 and the death of James III. He is — perhaps judiciously — unbiased throughout, heavily critical of the favourites and yet sympathetic towards the king at the end. Unquestionably, however, the sufferers in the poem are the Scottish nobility, above all Albany and Mar.

This last fact provides us with the answer to the main problems posed by the relevant six stanzas of Lindsay's poem, namely his reasons for portraying the reign in this way and the nature of the sources upon which he was able to draw. It was necessary to specify much more precisely than before the evils perpetrated by James III's low-born counsellors in order to rescue the reputation of the king's younger brother Alexander, duke of Albany; for Albany's son John had arrived from France in May 1515 to take up his duties as Governor of the Realm in the minority of James V. Long before his arrival, James IV had restored the Albany title; and in February 1511 he also commended his cousin's authority in France and his political sagacity.[34] John, duke of Albany, a man of about thirty when he arrived in Scotland for the first time, was rapidly recognised as the second person in the realm by the estates in November 1516, following the death of the infant James V's younger brother Alexander.[35] As heir presumptive to the throne for many years, Albany built up a large following of pro-French Scotsmen and became the protagonist of Franco-Scottish alliance, a policy which was to be followed by James V throughout his short life. Even after Albany's final departure from Scotland in 1524, he continued to play an active part in Scottish foreign policy until his death in 1536. He was, for example, closely involved in the abortive marriage negotiations between James V and Marie of Bourbon in 1535.

The importance of John, duke of Albany, throughout the generation following 1511 undoubtedly revived considerable interest in the career of his father Alexander, whose reputation was now rescued, his English treasons forgotten, and his actions praised as those of a nobleman who consistently advocated Franco-Scottish friendship and condemned his royal brother's Anglophile policies. These were themes which would be popular with the supporters of John, duke of Albany, and might even provide useful propaganda for James V. Thus Duke Alexander, more than a generation after his death, was finally accorded the heroism which he had never exhibited during his lifetime; and it is striking that all the sixteenth century histories which cover the reign of James III — Abell, Lesley, Ferreri, Pitscottie and Buchanan — are unanimous in their praise of Alexander, duke of Albany, and therefore critical of King James. Even when Albany's obvious treasons are cited — for example his claim to be 'Alexander King of Scotland' in 1482 was known to Lesley — the duke is not criticised by any of the commentators on the reign. This remarkable rescue operation is arguably the biggest single contribution to the James III legend, for praise of Albany inevitably involved, to a greater or lesser degree, condemnation of the king; and myths about his character and policies were pressed into service to justify the actions of various sixteenth century political power groups.

Literary sources would provide little practical help — beyond the reiterated and conventional complaint about young or low-born counsellors — and so the writers of the 1530s and thereafter must have turned to oral evidence, popular tales or ballads describing the dramatic events of James III's reign — the banishment of Albany and death of Mar, the Lauder crisis, and 1488. A great deal of information was doubtless purveyed by lesing-makars, individuals who uttered 'false and slanderous accusations calculated to prejudice the relations between the sovereign and the lieges', and against whose activities parliament passed acts, gradually increasing in severity, in 1318, 1424 and 1540.[36] These professional slanderers of

U

the Crown would be able to supply tales about Lauder which concentrated on the favourites — for whom careers required to be invented — and which lost sight of the manifest treasons of those involved in seizing the king; and Albany, who was not physically present at Lauder, could simply be praised as the man who freed his brother from Edinburgh castle. A few names of royal servants who had been in attendance on the king at Lauder filtered down to those at court in 1530 — Lindsay and Ferreri in particular — and these writers, distanced almost half-a-century from 1482, incorporated them uncritically into their texts, and understandably included amongst the favourites the names of those who had actually perished at Lauder — Cochrane, Preston and possibly Roger — together with others — Ireland and Hommyl — who had undoubtedly survived.[37] Likewise the mysterious death of the Earl of Mar could be turned to Albany's advantage as a further instance of James III's tyranny when he trusted in evil counsellors; and it is not surprising that it figures prominently in all subsequent histories.

In 1533, three years after the appearance of Lindsay's 'Testament of the Papyngo', Adam Abell, an Observantine friar of Jedburgh, completed a chronicle which he described as 'The Roit or Quheill of Tyme'; this contains a short section relating to James III, part of a larger work, owing much to Boece, which carries Scottish history from its fabulous beginnings down to the writer's own time, with occasional references to contemporary events in England and Europe.[38] The first two sentences, a thumbnail sketch of the king, are immediately reminiscent of other sources. According to Abell, 'Scottis kyng 104 wes James 3 sone of forsaid James (II). He wes ane dewot man bot he wes gretumlie gevin to carnale pleasure by his halie quene and privat consall of sympill men'.[39] There is nothing really new here. The story of James's devotion is to be found in Boece's *Lives of the Bishops of Mortlach and Aberdeen*[40], which Abell is unlikely to have seen; but both authors must have drawn on a common tradition of James's piety. The statement about 'carnale pleasure' and the queen, so strongly reminiscent of *The Thre Prestis of Peblis*, likewise shows the existence of a well-established account of James III's philandering. Finally, the reference to 'privat consall of sympill men' recalls the short chronicle of 1482, in which the royal counsellors are also described as 'sympill', and Lindsay's poem of 1530, which condemns them as low-born. These, then, are three motifs found independently in Abell's narrative and in other sources, with the variations which time and oral transmission would introduce.

Even Abell's statement that 'the herll of Mar wes slane be consall of ane trucur callit cochrene'[41] is not wholly original, for the notorious favourite is credited by Lindsay with counselling the king to banish Albany and put Mar to death. In Abell's account, Cochrane appears as one of the 'sympill men' about the king, though his trade, or position in James's service, is not specified.

The remainder of Abell's account of the reign is little more than a biography of Alexander, duke of Albany, who is consistently praised. On the other hand, Abell condemns throughout a group which he describes as the 'lordis coniuratouris', who are held responsible for Gloucester's invasion in 1482, the Lauder hangings, and the final rebellion of the reign. Remarkably, Albany is praised for bringing an English army to Edinburgh — Gloucester is conveniently omitted at this point —

and delivering James III from the castle, whereupon 'the lordis coniuratouris fled in argile. Notwithstanding soyn efter the king tuke thame to grace. And soyn eftir the duke wes flemyt agane to ingland'. Throughout his description of the 1482 crisis, Abell seems to have a common body of information with the author of the short chronicle of 1482, but he lacks the latter's chronological accuracy, giving the date 1480 'or thare about' for all these events. He treats the crisis at Lauder in isolation from the English invasion, describing it as 'the raid of lawdir', which is neither part of an incursion into England by James III nor yet an invasion of Scotland by Gloucester and Albany. The crisis, according to Abell, appears to have arisen when 'be consall of forsaid cochron wez cunzet the blak copir quhar throw raiss gret darth and mortalite in the realm'. Accordingly, at Lauder, 'cochren and the laif of his privat consall wes tane and iustifiit to be hangit'.[42]

Abell then follows Albany's career into the '80s. Under the year 1486 he describes the Albany-Douglas invasion of 1484 which ended in the skirmish at Lochmaben. This is a reasonably accurate account, including the date of the fight by saint's day, 'the magdalene day', 22 July. Thereafter, however, Abell's account is extremely confused. He has Albany return to Scotland 'to his brodir', which suggests that a reconciliation took place. However, 'suyn eftir be iniurious consall he wes tane and put in the castell of edinburgh'. He escaped by slaying his keeper and making bedclothes serve as a rope with which he lowered himself to the ground from a window 'and salit to france'.[43] The story that James and Albany were reconciled is appropriate to the crisis of 1482–3, but not to any later date; and the tale that the duke was thereafter imprisoned 'be iniurious consall' seems out of place, for Abell has already described the hangings of Cochrane and other members of the household who might be expected to give such advice. Also, it is not known for certain that Albany was ever a prisoner in Edinburgh castle, or that he escaped from it, though he fled abroad twice — in 1479 and 1483 — from his own castle at Dunbar. It seems clear, therefore, that Abell or his source had received a good tale, much garbled in oral transmission, about a daring prison break by Albany, but that they were unable to provide any clear motivation or context for it.

Nevertheless Abell presses on with Albany's career; after the duke's final flight to France, he married 'ane gret lady of heretage this dukis modir'. This reference to John, duke of Albany, who had been absent from Scotland for nine years when Abell completed his chronicle, suggests that either Abell himself, or his source, was a supporter of the pro-French Governor of Scotland; and Abell's description of Alexander duke of Albany's career significantly ends with the statement that 'eftirwert wnhappelie in iusting he wes slane'.[44]

With Albany dead, Abell now disposes of James III in three sentences: 'Than the forsaid coniuratouris his [the king's] bredir slane thai conspirit aganis the king and gaif him batell beside striwiling and thare wes he slane. He wes confessit before with maistir Johne Yrland proffessor of theologie. He wes berist in cambuskynnith the 29 yere of his ring of god 1489'.[45] The implication is that, with Albany dead, James III had lost his principal supporter and was therefore easy prey for the 'coniuratouris'.

Abell's source, therefore, is pro-Albany, sympathetic towards James III though critical of his counsellors, and highly critical of the unspecified conspiratorial lords. Apart from Boece, whose history Abell is clearly following, another source must have provided him with a string of tales about Albany, prefaced by general comment on James III, mentioning the death of Mar and the ascendancy of Cochrane, and concluding with a version of the king's final battle and death in 1488.[46] Parts of the legend — particularly the distortion of Albany's true character and Cochrane's part in Mar's death — were now firmly established. Abell's information, based as much of it must have been on oral transmission, produced many garbled stories; for example the statement by Abell that the conspirators fled to Argyll after Albany had freed the king in 1482 reappears in a much more accurate version in Lesley's history, from which it appears that the men who fled were in fact King James's supporters Scheves, Avandale and Argyll.[47]

Thus Abell's 'Roit and Quheill of Tyme' provides us with a few stories about the more dramatic events of James III's reign, but there is little more — no chronological framework worth the name, no apparent motivation in the actions of the principal characters. But Albany's good character is established beyond doubt. If the king himself is still treated sympathetically, this is merely because he is not held directly responsible for the crimes described. Abell, like Lindsay before him, has nothing to say about royal policies between 1482 and 1488; and until this was attempted, the final rebellion remained inexplicable.

The 1530s proved a fruitful decade for extensions of the James III legend. At about the same time as Abell completed his chronicle, John Bellenden's translation and amplification of Boece's *Scotorum Historiae* — a work commissioned for James V[48] — was published in Edinburgh. Although the reign of James III is not of course covered, Bellenden adds a genealogy of the Stewarts at the end of Book XII, and this includes the statement that the Earl of Mar 'was slane in the Cannongait, in ane baith fatt'.[49] Bellenden does not say who was responsible for this bizarre execution; but the suggestion that Mar was killed in a bathing vat — similar to, or identical with, a brewer's or dyer's vat — indicates a borrowing from the story of the death of the Duke of Clarence, who was currently said in England to have been drowned in a butt of Malmsey wine in 1478.[50] Tales of the death of Mar in a remarkably similar fashion were clearly already widespread when Bellenden wrote, and were rapidly incorporated into the legend.

A full generation passed between the comments of Lindsay, Abell and Bellenden and the appearance of the first full-scale account of the reign of James III, a vernacular history covering the period from 1437 to 1561 written by Bishop John Lesley, who presented the completed work to Mary Queen of Scots in 1570.[51] The ensuing twelve years produced a spate of histories covering the reign. Lesley himself published a Latin history, including Boece's mythical kings, at Rome in 1578;[52] Giovanni Ferreri, a Piedmontese monk who had come to Scotland in 1528, spent some time at court, and was employed as a teacher at Kinloss between 1531 and 1537, added an appendix to the second edition of Boece's *Scotorum Historiae* — published at Paris in 1574 — in which he covered the reign of James III;[53] Robert Lindsay of Pitscottie, whose *Historie and Cronicles of Scotland* were written between January 1576 and April 1579, produced the most colourful and least accurate account;[54] and George Buchanan's *Rerum Scoticarum Historia* — an extensive history published in 1582 though sections of it were written up to a generation earlier — devotes Book XII to James III.[55]

This remarkable group of histories might be expected to add substantially to our knowledge of the reign, for they were written by men who were poles apart in their political outlook — Lesley the staunch defender of Mary Queen of Scots, Buchanan her implacable enemy — or geographical location — Ferreri a cosmopolitan figure whose travels embraced Scotland, France and Italy, Pitscottie a Fife laird who did not even consult the public records of his own country. Yet their accounts of the character and policies of James III are in fact remarkably similar. To a certain extent this may be explained by borrowings from each other; Ferreri, for example, relied heavily on Lesley's history and was anxious to consult that of Buchanan. But much more important is the undoubted fact that all four had absorbed the legend of James III established by the 1530s, and that they were bound to build on this tradition. This involved all of them in praising Albany at the expense of King James and his counsellors, though by the later sixteenth century this had no political purpose whatever, John duke of Albany having died in 1536 and the Franco-Scottish alliance being long since a thing of the past. But the Albany legend, firmly rooted in popular tradition and enshrined in the works of Sir David Lindsay and Adam Abell, persisted and coloured all later accounts of the reign. Above all, the histories of the 1570s — especially those of Lesley and Ferreri — appear more impressive than they are, for their authors were able to draw on the parliamentary records, first published in 1566, which gave the legend — that is, the death of Mar on the advice of low-born favourites, above all Cochrane, the unsullied career of Alexander duke of Albany, the Lauder hangings, and the débâcle at Stirling in 1488 — a framework of authenticity which it ill deserves. As the first to write, Bishop John Lesley suffered particularly from the impossible problem of reconciling the sources which he consulted — English histories of Polydore Vergil, Fabyan, and Hall, Scottish public archives and monastic cartularies[56] — with the popular legend, established for more than a generation.[57]

However, the works of Lesley, Ferreri, Pitscottie and Buchanan do rather more than simply embellish the legend. In one important respect — their view of James III's character — they add to it. As we have seen, Boece and Abell had taken a sympathetic view of King James as devout and merciful, if badly counselled; but by the time Buchanan's history appeared in 1582, James had degenerated into 'a most insatiable tyrant'.[58] This is the most extreme view; but it is worth asking the question why the king's reputation should suffer at all almost a century after his death. The answer lies not so much in the publication in 1566 of the parliamentary records — which three of the four chroniclers consulted and which would contain the official justification of the rebels of 1488 — as in two apparently unrelated events, the wide circulation of Boece's *Scotorum Historiae* and the deposition of Mary Queen of Scots.

Lesley, Ferreri, Buchanan and Pitscottie all regarded themselves in some sense as continuators of Boece. The preface to Lesley's Latin history is quite explicit on this point, and Ferreri's study of James III is simply an appendix to the second edition

of the *Scotorum Historiae*. Pitscottie produced a manuscript which is pure Boece up
to and including the reign of James II; and although Buchanan claimed to be giving
his own version of Scottish history, he nevertheless devotes some sixty pages to
Boece's forty mythical kings. All four writers were however also writing in the
aftermath of the enforced abdication of Mary Queen of Scots in 1567, and this
inevitably coloured their views of the reign of James III, for here, it appeared, was a
comparatively recent example of the deposition of a tyrant by his oppressed people.
Such a precedent was a godsend to Buchanan, whose history develops the themes of
Queen Mary's adultery and conspiracy to murder at considerable length in order to
justify her deposition. To make this argument more convincing, however,
Buchanan felt it necessary to refer to precedents in Scottish history for the
deposition of tyrants by their subjects; so he quoted instances from Boece's
legendary kings, and he quoted 1488. In 1572, however, as Trevor-Roper has
shown, the Welsh antiquary Humphrey Lluyd had 'blown up all Boece's extra 700
years of Scottish history, all those forty kings whose vertiginous alternations of
election, fornication and deposition had provided the historical basis of the alleged
ancient Scottish constitution'.[59] It does not appear that the ageing Buchanan, or
indeed any of the other chroniclers of the period, took Lluyd's findings seriously;
indeed a triumphant rejection of them was the publication of the second edition of
the *Scotorum Historiae*, with Ferreri's appendix, at Paris in 1574. But Buchanan
was nevertheless left with only one recent precedent for what appeared to be a
deposition with which to press his view of popular sovereignty, for the legend of
James III was still circulating widely.

Buchanan was however a protestant revolutionary, concerned to justify the
deposition of Queen Mary; the same could not be said of the others, above all
Bishop Lesley, the Queen's champion. But Lesley like the others was trapped by
the existing legend of James III and his determination to produce a continuation of
Boece's history. Thus, having failed in his consultation of public and private
archives to discover any convincing reasons for James III's unpopularity and
ultimate overthrow, he turned not only to the legend, but to Boece's mythical kings.
Approximately one-third of these were tyrants whose vices included the taking of
evil counsel and voluptuous living, both themes which were already established in
the legend of James III; and by exaggerating both, Lesley could explain what
otherwise must have seemed to him inexplicable — the crises of 1482 and 1488.
Thus the former is explained in terms of King James excluding his nobility from his
presence, living voluptuously, and above all ignoring the queen in the pursuit of a
whore called Daisy; while 1488 is treated in almost exactly the same way, with the
king once more surrounded by 'men of meane and sobre estate', and 'taking his
plesour of wemen'.[60]

In the event, therefore, it mattered little whether the chroniclers were concerned
to uphold the sanctity of monarchy, as Lesley was, or committed like Buchanan to a
justification of popular sovereignty and the deposition of tyrants; by the late
sixteenth century, one's view of James III, thanks to the legend and to the
popularity of Boece, would be roughly the same irrespective of contemporary
political attitudes. Thus although Boece himself had stopped short of James III's

reign and only briefly described the king in sympathetic terms, two generations later the tyrants among the mythical kings in his history were being used in conjunction with oral tales to provide a kind of identikit picture of James III; and his character as a tyrant was firmly established. Indeed, in Buchanan's prose the king, with his early fall from grace 'into every species of vice' — worst of all his supposed incestuous relationship with his younger sister Margaret — takes on the character of a Scottish Caligula.[61]

For the revolutionaries of the late sixteenth century, however, the feature of James III's reign which provided the greatest propaganda value was the Lauder crisis. As early as 1566, in the first book of his *History of the Reformation in Scotland,* John Knox suggested that James V might have had to face a crisis, similar to that of 1482, at the end of October 1542, when he was leading an army south to resist English invasion. According to Knox, 'while the King lies at Fala, abiding upon the guns, and upon advertisement from the army, the Lords begin to remember how the King had been long abused by his flatterers . . . It was once concluded, that they would make some new remembrance of Lauder-Brig, (which is not far to the S. of Fala Muir) to see if that would, for a season, somewhat help the estate of their country. But, because the Lords could not agree amongst themselves upon the persons that deserved punishment (for every man favoured his friend), the whole escaped'.[62] Knox clearly regarded the nobility of 1542 as acting out of patriotic motives in their desire to remove unpopular royal counsellors, and he thereby implies that their predecessors of 1482 were similarly high-minded. He had assimilated the legend of Lauder — presumably from the same sources as informed Lindsay and Abell — as just retribution for evil familiars, a proper constraint laid on an errant king by his 'natural' counsellors, the nobility.

A generation later, the target of protestant critics was not James V but his grandson James VI, struggling to assert himself against the kirk radicals, above all Andrew Melville. Melville, called upon to defend remarks critical of the king and court in an aggressive sermon, drew upon the legend of James III for justification: 'But if now a dayes' said I, 'a minister would release in the court the example that fell out in King James the Thrid's dayes, who was abused by the flatterie of his courteours, he would be said to vaig frome his text, and perchance accused of treasoun'.[63] The neurotic Francis Stewart, earl of Bothwell, in a belated effort to excuse his dealings with the Catholic earls, went further in a letter to the Presbytery of Edinburgh in September 1594. To justify his behaviour, Bothwell remarked that the Papist lords 'began to lay before my eyes the injuries which ill advised councillors about his Majesty have induced him to execute against us, craving that I, as one specially interested, even more than they, would concur to put in practice the lovable custom of our progenitors at Lauder, where unto I most willingly assented'.[64] Remarks like this make it clear that, by the end of the sixteenth century, the Lauder crisis — reduced in popular literature to the seizure and hanging of the royal favourites — had become a stick with which dissidents of any political complexion might beat the counsellors of James VI; and Lauder must have seemed highly relevant in the years following the Ruthven raid of 1582, a useful precedent to justify the seizure of the king and expulsion of his friends Lennox and Arran.

James VI himself must have been familiar with the Lauder story; indeed, according to Sir George Mackenzie, the king was thrashed by George Buchanan, then his tutor, for abusing Buchanan when ordered to write an essay justifying the Lauder Bridge hangings.[65]

A British Museum manuscript which consists of miscellaneous transcripts of documents relating to various aspects of late sixteenth century Scotland — religion, church discipline, blood feuds — includes a tale relating to James III which is not to be found in any other source, either contemporary or sixteenth century. This occurs in the section of the manuscript entitled 'The General State of the Scottish Commonwealth with the cause of their often mutinies and other disorders' — an English view of late sixteenth century Scottish politics.[66] Here we see the other side of the coin: the Scottish nobility have the power to coerce the king, but are not praised as the saviours of their country for doing so. Indeed, the writer stresses the consistent weakness of the Scottish monarchy, which he attributes mainly to the strength of the nobility. Thus there is no hint of cooperation between king and magnates in this account, but rather an echo of John Major's condemnation of the over-mighty subject. We are told that the monarch simply ratifies the decisions of the nobility and commons in parliaments; that he lacks the power to bestow many public offices, as many of these are hereditary; that the power of many nobles within their jurisdictions is as absolute as that of the king; that the king cannot afford a contract army; and that no appeal to the royal courts from local magnate judgments is admissible. Altogether this is a very distorted picture of Scottish politics, but one which an English commentator, viewing events north of the border in the late sixteenth century, might understandably be expected to have.

It is in the context of appeals that the James III story appears. The writer, having stressed that some of the nobility held the power to execute justice absolutely within their jurisdictions, without appeal to the king, by virtue of their hereditary charters, goes on to cite as an example 'the Earle of Morton's charter, which James the 3rd tore openly, being offended with the absoluteness thereof, especially with this part of no appellation to the Prince . . . but before he removed from the place where he tore it, he was forced by the nobility to sit down, and sow it up again with his own hand; and for that cause it is called yet the sewed charter'.[67] This tale can hardly be taken literally as an event which actually occurred during James III's reign; in a general sense, however, it reflects the spreading beyond Scotland of the legend of his confrontations with the Scottish nobility. If the writer was able to consult a collection of Scottish state papers, the tale might be held to draw its relevance from the crisis of 1482–3 when James III, a prisoner of magnate factions, lost the support of the Earl of Morton's son and heir, a man who occupied the important office of sheriff of Edinburgh and whom the king names as an Albany supporter in the indenture of March 1483.[68] In view of the chronicler's woeful ignorance of the workings of the Scottish state, however, it seems much more likely that the Earl of Morton is named in the tale because of English familiarity with the power of the Regent Morton, whose reputation as a tough and unscrupulous diplomat, effectively controlling the royal government of James VI during the minority years before 1581, suggested to the writer that an Earl of Morton was an obvious choice as a representative of the overmighty Scottish nobility in an earlier age.[69]

By the end of the sixteenth century, therefore, oral tradition and political necessity had combined to swell the legend of James III to immense proportions. The writers of later histories, building on their sixteenth century predecessors, could only embellish what was already there. Thus David Hume of Godscroft, whose *History of the Houses of Douglas and Angus* was published in Edinburgh in 1644, appears mainly to have followed Buchanan's *Historia* in describing the career of Archibald, fifth earl of Angus;[70] while Drummond of Hawthornden, whose history was first published in 1655, who must have made use of Lesley, Ferreri and Buchanan, and have seen one of the manuscripts of Pitscottie's *Historie*, falls victim to the legend when he states that James III 'resolved and dispatched all matters by his Cabinet Counsel: where the Surveyor of his Buildings was better acquainted with the affairs of the State than the gravest of his Nobility'.[71]

Yet both Godscroft and Drummond made their own significant contributions to the legend of James III by including information which cannot be traced to any earlier period. Godscroft, whose aim was to glorify the house of Angus, naturally emphasises the statesmanlike and patriotic motives of Archibald, fifth earl of Angus, at Lauder. Indeed, he describes the hanging of the royal familiars as 'a very remarkable and rare example of the carefulness of the commonwealth, joyned with all modestie, love, and dutifulnesse towards their king'.[72] This statement is in itself a remarkable extension of the legend; but it is perhaps to be explained by Godscroft's inclusion in his description of the Lauder crisis of the fable in which the mice, in order to receive advance warning of the approach of their enemy the cat, choose a leader to hang a bell round its neck. According to Godscroft, when the nobles were holding their conference in Lauder Kirk to decide what could be done to remove the royal favourites, Lord Gray told the story of the mice, the cat, and the bell, whereupon Archibald, earl of Angus, volunteered to bell the cat.[73] This fable, which is not to be found in any of the sixteenth century histories, does not seem appropriate to the hangings which followed; however, in the form in which Godscroft tells it, it was current in fourteenth century England, where it forms part of the second version of William Langland's great alliterative poem *Piers Plowman*, which was completed in 1377. According to Jusserand, the fable was not new even then, being famous both in England and France during the Middle Ages.[74] In Langland's work, however, the fable may probably be related to English political events of the years 1376-7. Jusserand has suggested that the 'parliament of mice' in the poem are the Commons of the 'Good' Parliament of April–July 1376. The objects of their displeasure were Alice Perrers, mistress of the senile Edward III, and the old king's familiars, notably Richard Lyons, who were accused of various corrupt practices. The solution to the Commons' problems — which Jusserand relates to belling the cat — was to insist on the appointment of a council of a dozen lords who were to keep a close watch over State business, half of them always in the vicinity of the king 'in such a manner that no important affairs should pass or be delivered without the assent and advice' of the entire council.[75] However, this resolution had no sooner been taken, and the new counsellors appointed, than parliament was dissolved, John of Gaunt declared its acts null, and the Commons' Speaker, Sir Peter de la Mare, the 'raton of renon' in the poem, was imprisoned.

These events bear some resemblance to the fable as related by Langland. The mice and rats, gathered together in parliament, were all agreed that they should bell the cat; however, 'there ne was ratoun in alle the route for all the rewme of Fraunce, That dorst have ybounden the belle aboute the cattis nekke, Ne hangen it aboute the cattes hals al Engelonde to wynne'.[76] In the poem, as in the contemporary crisis to which it referred, no action was taken by the disaffected because they lacked an effective leader. It is possible, therefore, that Hume of Godscroft, knowing the fable as it appeared in *Piers Plowman* and its reference to the Good Parliament of 1376, realised how it could be made to redound to the credit of his hero Archibald, earl of Angus, at the council of war held by the Lauder lords in 1482. Angus would supply the lead in belling the cat, that is in removing the royal familiars and reforming the council, the objects also of the English Commons of 1376, but in the case of Lauder carried through to a successful conclusion. This use of Langland's version of the fable would help to explain Godscroft's remarkable bias in his description of Lauder Bridge.

Drummond of Hawthornden's viewpoint was very different. As the staunch defender of Stewart divine right, he was appalled by the Lauder Bridge episode, which he found quite unjustifiable. Nevertheless, he understood it in terms of the king's allowing himself 'to be governed by mean Persons, and Men of no Account, to the Contempt of the Nobility'; and as Dr. Rae reminds us, 'in Drummond's view, Kings who rejected or attacked the aristocracy were as guilty of disturbing the divinely-ordained natural society as those who rebelled against the Crown'.[77] Thus the section of his history which Drummond found most difficult to write was that relating to James III; appalled by the successful rebellion against King James in 1488 and by the fact that the rebels not only went unpunished but obtained high office in the new government, Drummond was nevertheless trapped by his sources — including probably Lesley, Ferreri, and a borrowed manuscript of Pitscottie[78] — into accepting much of the already established legend. But if the sanctity of monarchy were to be upheld, Drummond had to discover virtues in James III to offset his faults. Thus he wrote and rewrote this section of the history, correcting and amending it several times until, as Rae convincingly shows, the character of the king changed from being outright evil to showing an almost excusable weakness, while the opposition is more and more condemned in each succeeding draft.[79]

Part of this metamorphosis involved rescuing the principal familiar, Cochrane, from the lowly status which had been assigned to him by the sixteenth century chroniclers. The writers of that period had on the whole been agreed on the subject of Cochrane's profession or trade. Abell had referred to him simply as a 'trucur', an abusive term meaning rogue, rascal, or villain; but Lesley, followed by Ferreri, had improved on this by suggesting that he was a mason. George Buchanan, it is true, uses the word 'architectus' to describe Cochrane,[80] and this is erroneously translated as 'a common stone-mason' by Aikman.[81] Pitscottie, as usual, gives the fullest description: Cochrane 'at his beginning was bot ane printis to ane maisonne and withtin few yeiris become werie ingeneous into that craft and bigit money stain house witht his hand into the realme of Scottland: and becaus he was conning in that craft nocht efterlang thai maid him maister maisone'.[82] Thus Buchanan alone elevates Cochrane to the status of architect; and Drummond of Hawthornden, seizing his chance to find Cochrane a respectable court position and so partially rescue James III from the charge of taking advice from lowly favourites, describes him as a surveyor of the royal buildings.[83] At the end of the eighteenth century, John Pinkerton more cautiously referred to Cochrane as 'a mason or architect'.[84]

This distinction would not be an important one were it not that it gave rise to further legends regarding James III and Cochrane which have persisted down to the present day. The use of the term 'architect' rather than 'mason' in referring to Cochrane's supposed profession suggests that he might well have been a refined and artistic man rather than a mere tradesman; and on this view he fits well into the picture of James III as an 'artistic' monarch who had no taste for his kingly duties but who surrounded himself with the ablest men of the day in the spheres of architecture and music, and so enriched Scotland with beautiful buildings, above all the Great Hall at Stirling Castle. This is still a popular view. As recently as 1938 it was suggested that the execution of Cochrane in 1482 'abruptly put a term to one of the most oustanding careers connected with British architecture. For this Cochrane had (almost undoubtedly) designed for his royal friend the stately hall of Stirling Castle, the first building as it appears, in the whole of the British Isles, that displays any Renaissance influence'.[85] Even more recently, in 1958, R. L. Mackie stated that, of the royal familiars, 'the most dear to the king and the most detested by his subjects was Robert Cochrane the master mason, in whom men saw, not the artist who had designed the Great Hall of Stirling Castle . . . but the King's evil genius'.[86]

This is one of the later legends. None of the sixteenth century chroniclers links Cochrane with the building of the Great Hall at Stirling; and in fact there is architectural evidence to suggest that the hall, like the Chapel Royal, was a James IV creation.[87] But even if one follows the Pitscottie legend, which emphasises James III's great love of Stirling and his supposed residence there supervising the building of the Great Hall and Chapel Royal during the last winter of his life, it must be said that Pitscottie never associates Cochrane — in his account hanged at Lauder in 1482 — with this enterprise. The conversion of Cochrane from a hated low-born familiar into an eminent architect is thus a seventeenth century extension of the legend, probably originating with Drummond and gradually adopted by later historians.

Two writers who ignored Cochrane's rehabilitation are to be found conducting a short pamphlet war in London in 1735. The first of these produced a 52-page work entitled 'The Life of Sir Robert Cochran, Prime Minister to King James III of Scotland', heavily based on Buchanan, Godscroft and Pitscottie (whose *Historie* had been published for the first time the previous decade, in 1724). Unfortunately, the title's promise is hardly borne out by the text, which is little more than an attempt to fill out the shadowy career of Cochrane as it was portrayed by the sixteenth century chroniclers. Thus 'Sir Robert' is duly vilified for his many supposed crimes, to which the writer adds the persecution and imprisonment of Archbishop Patrick Graham. Sir Andrew Wood is brought into the tale to provide an example of the sort of loyal subject whose advice James III should have been accepting. But the real purpose of the pamphlet is revealed by the anachronisms contained in it; the writer describes the rebels as 'the country Party' and the government as 'Sir Robert's Ministry', and it is clear that these late seventeenth and early eighteenth century terms refer not to Cochrane at all but to Sir Robert Walpole, whose government is being criticised obliquely through use of a suitably obscure allegory.[88]

The second pamphlet bears an even more impressive title: 'A Detection of the Falshood, Abuse, and Misrepresentations in a late Libel, intitled, The Life of Sir Robert Cochran, Prime Minister in Scotland to James the Third'; and the writer slightly exceeds his rival in length. He makes it clear from the outset that he is an Englishman, and expresses surprise that no Scot had thus far seen fit to challenge the 'Life of Cochran'. But his sources are very similar to those of the man he is attacking, with a heavy reliance on Buchanan (supplemented by brief references to Crawfurd's *Officers of State*, Spottiswoode's history, Balfour's *History of Scots Statesmen*, Sibbald's *Lives of the Chancellors of Scotland*, Godscroft and Pitscottie). Once again anachronisms abound — terms like 'Cabals' and 'Prime Ministers', 'Court', and 'Country' parties — and the author appears most concerned to refute the statements made by the writer of the 'Life' and to exonerate Lord Hume, whom the earlier pamphleteer had described as 'abject, haughty, selfish and illiterate'. Praise of Hume suggests that the author of the 'Detection' may have been a supporter or relative of his descendant William, eighth earl of Hume, who was to fight at Prestonpans on the government side ten years later, and distinguish himself by attempting to rally his troop of Churchill's dragoons.[89] It may therefore be the eighteenth century earl rather than the fifteenth century lord to whom the pamphleteer is referring when he describes Hume as 'a Person of great Parts and Abilities, who came very early to make a Figure, and to have a large Share in the Administration of Affairs whilst he was but young'. In the process of praising Hume, the author of the 'Detection' almost loses sight of Cochrane; but he is as convinced of his villainy as his fellow pamphleteer, and appears concerned only to modify what he regards as the exaggerated statements made in the latter's 'Life of Cochran'. Yet he appears to have no clear attitude to Cochrane. His main point is that Cochrane was never a knight; and he condemns the author of the 'Life' for describing Thomas Preston — according to Buchanan Cochrane's father-in-law — as a nobleman on the sole authority of Buchanan's expression 'Praestonus honesto loco natus', continuing contemptuously: 'The World might have rather imagined, that the Father-in-Law of Cochran was a Dust-man, or a Glass-man, or any thing mean and contemptible'. He goes on to assert that this kind of infamous behaviour should not be written about at all, out of respect for the 'illustrious descendants' of men like Cochrane (which is surely inconsistent with his denigration of Cochrane) or Alexander, Lord Hume.[90] These confused remarks did not go unchallenged, for in the same year the writer of the original 'Life of Cochran' produced yet another pamphlet, 'A Letter to the Detector of the Pretended Falshoods, etc., in the Life of Sir Robert Cochran', in which Cochrane's (that is, Walpole's) reputation is somewhat belatedly rescued. We may be forgiven for failing to penetrate these obscure and confused allegories; presumably Sir Robert Walpole did so with ease.

It is however refreshing to turn from such inspired lunacies as these to the scholarship of Father Thomas Innes, principal of the Scots College at Paris, whose *Critical Essay on the Ancient Inhabitants of Scotland* was published in 1729, effectively demolishing Buchanan's *Rerum Scoticarum Historia* as serious history. But, as a Jacobite, Innes was prepared to use his scholarship to serve the cause; and in October 1729 we find him writing a letter to the Old Pretender — 'James III' of Great Britain — in which the illegality of the rebellion of 1488 plays a prominent part. Thus Innes complains that 'Boece and Buchanan continue still without being examined into and controlled, to be lookt upon as the common standard of the history of Scotland in ancient times . . . but the principles they are built upon, and the practices that they authorise and command, have been the chief source of all the rebellions that have happened in that kingdom within these last two hundred years: that is, since A.D. 1488, which is the date as well of the first successful rebellion in Scotland, to wit, that against King James III, as of the first Act against the right of monarchy which was designedly made by the authors of that rebellion to screen themselves from the punishment due to their crime'.

Innes then lends himself to the conspiracy theory of history when he describes the appearance in Scotland — 'no doubt by the contrivance of some of the adherents of those conspirators' — of historical forgeries containing the story of the forty mythical kings; 'and in this new invented history of the Scots, these kings are made accountable to their subjects; and, accordingly, of these forty kings, about a third part are arraigned, or condemned, or punished by their subjects for pretended maladministration'. These tales were used by the 'very credulous' Hector Boece, whose history, according to Innes, could be used together with the successful rebellion of 1488 to justify the deposition of Queen Mary in 1567. Thereafter, 'to justify further that attempt', George Buchanan, 'a zealous Calvinist and the best orator of the times', was employed to write what Innes describes as a libel, *De jure Regni apud Scotos,* based on the precedents for the deposing power contained in the story of the first forty kings, and subsequently written up more fully in Buchanan's history.

After this lengthy preamble, Innes at last comes to the point when he claims that 'it was upon the same principles and pretended right to call the sovereign to account, that the factious party in the Scottish convention, A.D. 1689, proceeded to that height of insolence, as to declare that your royal father (James II and VII) had forfeited the crown'.[91] Here we find the final instance of the shade of James III being invoked to serve a specific political purpose; together with the other examples which he quotes, Innes denies the legality of the rebellion of 1488 against James III of Scotland in order to bolster up the claims of 'James III' of Great Britain and the Jacobite cause. It is a sad reflection of the impact of scholarship that Innes's skills saved neither the reputation of James III nor the Jacobites.

Some time after 1815, however, George Chalmers, an Edinburgh antiquary who was clearly dissatisfied with the legend of James III, began to prepare a new history of the reign. He did not complete it, but over a hundred pages of notes survive. The title page reads: 'The History of the Life and Reign of James the Third, the King of

Scots, 1460–1488: with an Appendix of Documents, ascertaining its dates, and illustrating its obscurities' — a bold claim, but one which Chalmers did his best to justify by drawing up tables of officers of state, by consulting family archives for original charters of the period, and above all by referring to the state archives — the Great Seal Register, the parliamentary registers and the Treasurer's Accounts. Chalmers' manuscript, even in its incomplete state, illustrates that the author had a clear idea of the problems of the reign — for example, the complicated political manoeuvres of the autumn of 1482, and the reasons for the prince's defection in 1488 — and had gone some way towards solving them. Above all, Chalmers clearly understood that the chronicle narratives were frequently at odds with the record evidence, and was attempting to evaluate these two very different types of source. It is a matter for regret that he did not publish the results of his researches; if he had done so, he would have provided the first scholarly attempt to clarify the problems of the reign.[92]

Chalmers' true successors were the host of nineteenth century editors who undertook the colossal task of printing the vast bulk of Scottish public records, together with the publishing clubs who made available a huge quantity of unpublished material, family archives, original charters, and monastic cartularies, and infinitely eased the labours of later Scottish historians. But work of this kind is rarely newsworthy, and the attention of the general reader was caught instead by Sir Walter Scott's *Tales of a Grandfather,* one of the most influential popular histories ever written.[93] Not surprisingly, it contains the standard sixteenth century view of James III, with all the popular stories and dramatic tableaux. The favourites loom large, as do the Lauder hangings and the king's murder after Sauchieburn.[94] There is nothing new in all this; but it was undoubtedly Scott's example which called forth at least three of four historical plays on James III, all based on the legends extensively embellished by the imaginations of their authors. Fortunately, only one of these plays appears to have been performed, a fact which is surely a tribute to nineteenth century taste.

The first to appear was *James III, King of Scotland: A Tragedy in Five Acts,* by the author of *Catherine de Medicis*. It was printed in London in 1820, follows the legend implicitly and runs to only 53 pages.[95] Its brevity may explain its failure to reach the stage; but in 1847 Chapman and Hall of London printed *Feudal Times; or, The Court of James the Third,* described as 'A Scottish Historical Play by the author of "The Earl of Gowrie", "The King of the Commons", etc.' (one James White). Although only ten pages longer than its predecessor, this work had the distinction of being performed in the Theatre Royal, Sadlers' Wells. More interesting than the 1820 play, it is concerned solely with the crisis of 1482, above all with the villainy of the royal favourite Walter Cochrane.[96]

The worst doggerel on the subject had already been penned by Sir David Erskine, who completed two plays on James III in 1827–8. Erskine, a natural son of David Steuart Erskine, eleventh earl of Buchan (1742–1829), was a neighbour of Sir Walter Scott, and responsible for such literary gems as 'Love amongst the Roses', described as a military opera in three acts, and plays on James I, James II, and —

inevitably — Mary Queen of Scots. His two James III plays may well be regarded as the final Buchan revenge on that unfortunate monarch.

The first to be completed was 'Latter Days of King James III of Scotland: A tragedy in five acts', which Erskine wrote at Dryburgh some time before July 1827. Then, presumably realising that there was scope for another work covering the early years of the reign, he wrote 'King James the Third of Scotland, An Historical Drama ['a tragedy', erased] in five acts', completing this at Dryburgh in January 1828. The action of the drama runs from shortly before the death of James II to the marriage of James III and Margaret of Denmark in 1469. No doubt the fact that the play ends happily caused Erskine to have second thoughts about describing it as a tragedy; he should certainly have called it an opera or musical, for there appears to be more singing than speaking. But Erskine carries it all off with a command of verse and metre which McGonagall would certainly have envied:

> (Voluntary, accompanied by the Holyrood Abbey organ):
> Once more we behold a lov'd Scottish Queen
> to us a great blessing not quite unforseen,
> Rich dower she has brought to bless our lov'd land
> And Orkney and Shetland she brings with her hand.
> O Bless her all people assembled now here
> O Bless her all people some far and some near
> To honor the Queen Let Loud Cannon roar
> She's landed at last on Scotland's lov'd shore.
>
> (Castle guns fire in the distance).

As the chorus roars out the first four lines once more, Skene, described in the cast list as Colonel of the Corps of Guides, comes forward and sings; and his song is in itself a remarkable rejection of the legend in the interests of providing a happy ending:

> Here's God bless the King, King James is the boy
> To rule our brave land, our troops to employ,
> He grows up to manhood, he now does excell
> In all martial feats will bear off the belle.
> His soldiers are staunch, his coffers are stor'd
> He knows how to wield a two edged sword
> And ev'ry man here, O well I do know
> Will fight bravely by him when to war he does go.[97]

Erskine's most substantial contribution to the legend is however to be found in his 'Latter Days of King James III', in which the battle of Sauchieburn is described with a detail which even Pitscottie would have envied:

> (Enter Lord Hume's March men and the Highlandmen. They skirmish with lances and broadswords. Flourish of trumpets, Bugles, Kettle Drums, and the March men are beat off).
> Lord Maxwell: 'Well done, my brave highland men,
>   Donal Doo the Piper there, play them
>   brose and batter'.
> (Donal Doo plays as described).

(Enter the Annandale men, the Rank Riders of the Borders, and the Bathgate miners, and skirmish. The Bathgate miners are beaten back on the king's main battle).

Lord Erskine: 'See, your Majesty
    The Annandale Rank riders of the borders
    Have beat our Bathgate miners and they are
    Falling back on our Main body'.

James III: 'Sir Lewis Stuart
    Go and Rally those Bathgate miners
    They know you, Sir Lewis, you are their
    Neighbour — let's see if they're made of rallying stough'.

Sir Lewis: 'Immediately your Majesty;
    And if I do not bring them back into
    The fight I'm much mistaken for braver
    Fellows never was, than the Bathgate miners
    Since Adam was a boy'.

                                         (Exit Sir Lewis).[98]

Fortunately not all writers of popular literature produced doggerel like this. In 1855 the prolific novelist James Grant brought out a historical romance entitled *The Yellow Frigate*, the ship in the title being James III's *Yellow Carvel*. Not surprisingly, Sir Andrew Wood figures prominently in the story as the king's admiral and the kind of man whose advice James ought to follow — a curious echo of the 1735 pamphlet — and there is an extended character study of James III, based largely on Scott and the familiar legend. The favourites are present in force, and the king is eventually dispatched by George Buchanan's three assassins in a dramatic scene.[99]

This combination of romantic literature and eccentric drama kept legends of James III well to the fore throughout the nineteenth century; and in spite of the labours of the publishing clubs and the editors of the public records, serious histories were still producing much the same tales in the early twentieth century. Thus in 1902 Hume Brown repeats the classic legend when he says of James that 'by his love of seclusion, his distaste for all the activities of a feudal king and knight, James alienated the sympathies of every class of his subjects. To the commons a ruler of this type was as repugnant as to the nobility. It was in the choice of his immediate followers and advisers, however, that James most sorely tried the loyalty of his people . . . Most notable of them was Thomas Cochrane, by profession an architect, whose ascendancy over James was the main cause of the disasters of his reign'.[100] Much more recently, in 1958, R.L. Mackie tried to attribute virtues to the king without really altering the legend. James, he claimed, was 'an enlightened, keen-witted Renaissance prince, delighting more in the company of men as clever as himself, however lowly they might be, than in that of his illiterate and arrogant nobles'.[101] Even Dickinson, in a perceptive and stimulating analysis of late medieval Scottish politics, could still say in 1961 that James III, 'in his contempt of warlike exercises and manly sports . . . was contrasted, to his disadvantage, with his brothers the Duke of Albany and the Earl of Mar'.[102] It was left to Professor Duncan in the 1970s to demolish much of the legend in a brilliant revision of Dickinson's work;[103] and in 1974 Dr. Nicholson, while continuing to regard the royal favourites as important, laid a number of old ghosts in a painstaking survey of the reign.[104]

However, there is still life in the legend, and the 1970s and early 1980s witnessed what may be the final embellishments of tales already five centuries old. In 1971 A. M. Kinghorn simply repeated the sixteenth century legend of James's 'low-class cronies', with a combination of Lesley's and Ferreri's lists and Robert (*sic*) Cochrane upgraded to architect;[105] but in the same year came the remarkable revelation, by a lady claiming to be the reincarnation of James IV, that Cochrane was responsible for modernising the urinals in the banqueting hall of Edinburgh castle, a statement which, if true, somewhat reduces the notorious favourite's artistic stature. Furthermore, the same unchallengeable authority tells us that many of James III's troubles were caused by his homosexuality, a view advanced by no other writer.[106] Then, on Christmas Eve 1975, Professor Duncan wrote a short story in which James III and the Earl of Mar attempt simultaneously to poison each other, with Archbishop Scheves, locked in the privy, a horrified onlooker.[107] However, the most recent contribution to the legend was made in 1980, when Caroline Bingham published a book of Scots poetry to which she contributed a poem on the battle of Sauchieburn. For the first time in any account, John Ramsay, Lord Bothwell, is credited with advising the king to fight rather than flee[108] — a difficult task, as Ramsay was in England at the time. Future years may yield further extensions of these stories; for the present it would be as well to consign them to the coffee table — or to the groaning shelf weighed down by popular 'modern' histories of Scotland — where they properly belong.

NOTES

1. *A.D.A.*, 23; *R.M.S.*, ii, No. 1031; *E.R.*, viii, 100.

2. *E.R.*, viii, pp. lxx-lxxi.

3. *Yester Writs*, No. 170.

4. *Hary's Wallace*, i, p. xxiv; *T.A.*, i, 44.

5. *Hary's Wallace*, i, p. xxiv.

6. *See* T. D. Robb, *Thre Prestis*, ix-xi, for the dating of the poem and identity of the king. For a stimulating discussion of the author's sources, *see* R. D. S. Jack, *The Italian Influence on Scottish Literature* (Edin., 1972), 15-20.

7. *Thre Prestis*, p. xxvi.

8. *Ibid.*, lines 453-462.

9. *Ibid.*, lines 567-8.

10. *Ibid.*, lines 542-544.

11. *Poems of Robert Henryson*, ii, 309, lines 132-3.

12. *Ibid.*, 313-4.

13. MacQueen, *Henryson*, 170-3 and Preface.

14. *Ibid.*, 171.

15. *Ibid.*, 172.

16. *Poems of Robert Henryson*, ii, 315, lines 292-4.

17. *Liber Pluscardensis*, i, 392-400.

18. This is a unique departure from the conventionally expressed view that the nobility were the 'natural' counsellors of the king, to be found — for example — in the Short Chronicle of 1482; B.M. Royal MS. 17 Dxx, f.308r; and *see* Wormald, *Court, Kirk, and Community*, 67.

19. *Liber Pluscardensis*, i, 399.

20. *Ibid.*, 400.

21. *Ibid.*, (Bk. xi, ch. xii), 381

22. *A.P.S.*, ii, 165, 250.

23. Scofield, *Edward IV*, i, 332-3.

24. *Lettres de Louis XI*, iv, 160-1.

25. B.M. Royal MS. 17 Dxx, ff.299r-308r. For a discussion of the dating of this chronicle, and the full text of the last two folios (307r-308r), *see below*, Appendix A.

26. The chronicler has a fair amount of information about Yorkist England, including the defeat and death of Warwick the Kingmaker at Barnet, the death of the 'saintly' Henry VI and the miracles which followed his demise; and it seems likely that he was also familiar with stories about the death of Clarence.

27. B.M. Royal MS. 17 Dxx, f. 308r.

28. *Ibid.*, f. 307r.

29. *A.P.S.*, ii, 230.

30. Major, *History*, 368.

31. Boece, *Vitae*, 73, 76-7. There is only a hint of the legend purveyed by the author of the 1482 Chronicle when Boece remarks in passing that it was said that James took counsel from men of obscure origin; but he does not develop this statement: *ibid.*, 56-7.

32. Boece, *Scotorum Historiae, Regum Scotorum Catalogus* (Paris edn., 1526).

33. The poem is printed in Pitscottie, *Historie*, i, 211-12 (at the end of Pitscottie's account of the reign of James III).

34. *James IV Letters*, No. 347.

35. *A.P.S.*, ii, 283.

36. *A.P.S.*, i, 112; ii, 8, 360. For the definition of 'lesing-makars', *see* W. A. Craigie and A. J. Aitken (edd.), *A Dictionary of the Older Scottish Tongue from the Twelfth Century to the end of the Seventeenth*, (Chicago and Lond., n.d.), iii, 694. 'Lesing' is defined as 'the action of telling lies, lying, falsehood'.

37. Ferrerius, *Appendix to Boece*, f. 391 r-v.

38. N.L.S. MS. 1746, ff. 110v-112r. The section relating to James III is printed in full in Appendix B.

39. *Ibid.*, f. 110v.

40. Boece, *Vitae*, 73.

41. N.L.S. MS. 1746, f. 110v. 'Trucur' is a Middle Scots abusive term, roughly translated as rogue, rascal, or villain.

42. *Ibid.*, f. 110v.

43. *Ibid.*, f. 111r.

44. *Ibid.*

45. *Ibid.*

46. It may be significant that Abell's stated object in writing 'The Roit and Quheill of Tyme' was to praise his order and his monastery. In 1491 the abbot and convent of Jedburgh received an absolution from Pope Innocent VIII for having taken the part of James III's rebels in the civil war of 1488: Wilkins, *Concilia*, iii, 634. Tales of 1488 may therefore have been passed on to Abell directly, or at second-hand, by those Jedburgh monks who had been involved on the rebel side.

47. Lesley, *History*, 50.

48. Bellenden, *Chronicles*, i, p. xxxix.

49. Bellenden, *Boece*, bk. xii, f.lxxv (r-v).

50. Mancini, *Usurpation of Richard III*, 76-7.

51. Written while Lesley was Queen Mary's ambassador in England, between 1568 and 1570: Lesley, *History*, 7-9.

52. John Lesley, *De Origine, Moribus et Rebus Gestis Scotorum Libri Decem* (S.T.S., 1888).

53. Hector Boece, *Scotorum Historiae* (second edn., Paris, 1574), appendix by Giovanni Ferreri (terminal date 1488).

54. Robert Lindsay of Pitscottie, *The Historie and Cronicles of Scotland* (S.T.S., 1899–1911), i, 152-210.

55. George Buchanan, *Rerum Scoticarum Historia*, bk xii (Edin., 1582). As early as 1555 Ferreri had written from Paris to Bishop Reid, his former patron at Kinloss, asking Reid to obtain for him a copy of George Buchanan's Scottish History 'for the work on which I am now engaged': *Papal Negotiations with Mary Queen of Scots, 416*.

56. Lesley, *De Origine*, i, pp. xx-xxi.

57. A full discussion of the problems faced by Lesley, Ferreri, Pitscottie and Buchanan is to be found in: Macdougall, 'The Sources: A Reappraisal of the Legend' in J. M. Brown (ed.), *Scottish Society in the Fifteenth Century*, 25-32.

58. Buchanan, *History*, ii, 138-9.

59. 'George Buchanan and the Ancient Scottish Constitution', *E.H.R.*, Suppl. 3, (1966), 27.

60. Lesley, *History*, 48, 55. The origins of 'Daisy' are discussed above in Chapter 8; it should also be noted that the legend had become further garbled in transmission since Abell's time. Thus Abell had described the favourite Cochrane as being responsible for the death of the Earl of Mar. By the time Lesley wrote, the story had developed so that Cochrane was *made* Earl of Mar by the king: Lesley, *History*, 48.

61. Buchanan, *History*, ii, 152.

62. Knox, *History*, i, 32. I am indebted to Mr. Roger Mason for drawing my attention to this reference. Later in the same work (i, 221) Knox refers explicitly to Cochrane as the classic example of the Scottish royal favourite, and compares him with the 'evil' counsellors influencing Mary of Guise in August 1559.

63. *Bruce Collections* (Wodrow Society), 55.

64. *Scottish Papers XI*, no. 349. I am indebted to Mr. Chris Upton for this reference.

65. Mackenzie, *Writers*, iii, 179-180. Mackenzie is a late authority (early eighteenth century) for the statement that Archibald, earl of Angus, acquired the nickname 'Bell-the-Cat' for his part in the Lauder crisis. According to Mackenzie, Buchanan knew the 'Bell-the-Cat' story; but if he did, and related it to Lauder, it is remarkable that he did not include it in his *Historia*, where he manages to find room for a lengthy fictitious speech by the Earl of Angus. It seems likely therefore that the 'Bell-the-Cat' story — which is related by none of the sixteenth century chroniclers — is of seventeenth century origin, a view which I take below.

66. B.M. Add. MS. 35, 844, ff.193r-198r.

67. *Ibid.*, f. 194 r.

68. S.R.O. State Papers No. 19 (discussed above in Chapter 9).

69. I am indebted for this suggestion to Dr. Jenny Wormald.

70. Mistakenly described as the sixth earl by Hume, *Douglas and Angus*, 219-236.

71. Drummond, *History*, 143.

72. Hume, *Douglas and Angus*, 227. This is one of Godscroft's purple passages. But the entire work abounds with praise, not only of Angus, but of the entire magnate class in late medieval Scotland, stressing the nobles' concern to protect the commonwealth against the crimes committed by misguided or tyrannical rulers. This feature of the work is discussed at length by Roger Mason in an unpublished paper, Secular Historiography and the Political Culture of early seventeenth-century Scotland (1977), 16-25.

73. *Ibid.*, 226.

74. Jusserand, *Piers Plowman*, 39-40. The fable of the mice, the cat, and the bell had appeared in England in the Latin collection of Odo de Cheriton in the early thirteenth century; and in France, in a series of moralising tales written about 1320 by the Franciscan Nicol Bozon.

75. *Ibid.*, 45-6.

76. *Ibid.*, 225.

77. Thomas I. Rae, 'The Historical Writing of Drummond of Hawthornden', *S.H.R.*, liv, (1975), 40.

78. *Ibid.*, 32-3.

79. *Ibid.*, 43.

80. Buchanan, *Rerum Scoticarum Historia* (edn. 1582), f. 138r.

81. Buchanan, *History*, ii, 141.

82. Pitscottie, *Historie*, i, 176.

83. Drummond, *History*, 143-4.

84. Pinkerton, *History*, i, 289.

85. I. C. Hannah, 'Triumphant Classicism,' in *The Stones of Scotland* (ed. Scott-Moncrieff, Lond., 1938), 103-4.

86. Mackie, *James IV*, 15-16.

87. *R.C.A.M.S., Stirlingshire,* i, 182-3.

88. N.L.S. Pamphlets: 3/2367..

89. *Scots Peerage,* iv, 480.

90. N.L.S. Pamphlets: 1.593/NLS.

91. *Spalding Miscellany,* ii, 353-5.

92. N.L.S. Adv. MS. 16.2.20.

93. Sir Walter Scott, *Tales of a Grandfather* (1st series, 3 vols, Edin., 1828-9).

94. *Ibid.,* vol. ii, 161-202. It is, of course, doing Scott a grave injustice to regard him simply as a writer of historical romances, for his influence on nineteenth century archivists and historians — above all Thomas Thomson and Patrick Fraser Tytler — was considerable. The most recent analysis of nineteenth century Scottish historical developments — albeit a controversial one — is in Marinell Ash, *The Strange Death of Scottish History* (Edin., 1980).

95. N.L.S. Pamphlets 3.2857.

96. N.L.S. Pamphlets 2.492(1).

97. N.L.S. Adv. MS. 5.1.16., ff. 185-266.

98. N.L.S. Adv. MS. 5.1.17.

99. James Grant, *The Yellow Frigate* (Edin. 1855).

100. Hume Brown, *History,* i, 269.

101. Mackie, *James IV,* 11.

102. Dickinson, *Scotland from the Earliest Times to 1603* (First edn. 1961), 227.

103. Dickinson/Duncan, *op.cit.,* Chapter 21.

104. Nicholson, *Scotland: The Later Middle Ages,* Chapters 14-16.

105. Kinghorn, *The Chorus of History,* 198.

106. A. J. Stewart, *Falcon: The Autobiography of His Grace James the 4 King of Scots* (Lond., 1971), 5-6, 19-20. Shortly before going to press, I was presented by Miss Lindsay Beaton with a copy of a historical novel entitled *Gentle Eagle* by Christine Orr (London 1937). This is a fanciful life of James IV which strikingly anticipates *Falcon* and delicately hints at James III's supposed homosexuality (pp. 6, 8).

107. Printed in the Weekend Scotsman, 10 Jan. 1976. This short story, entitled 'The Professor's Tale', reflects Professor Duncan's fascination with the death of the Earl of Mar, an event for which he supplies a brilliant, if controversial, interpretation in Dickinson/Duncan, *op.cit.,* 247.

108. Bingham, *The Voice of the Lion* (Edin. 1980), 38-41.

Conclusion

'IT is unfortunate,' remarks Professor Duncan, 'that James III's very real failings have been obscured by fictitious embellishments.'[1] Yet the sixteenth century legend, if it obscured the royal faults by inventing or emphasising others, also allowed the king some sympathy: he was a devout and merciful man, misled by bad counsellors. The record evidence hardly supports such a view; rather we are presented with a fairly clear portrait of an aloof, overbearing and vindictive ruler whose dangerously exalted concept of Scottish kingship confounded his friends and eventually proved a godsend to his enemies.

Some of James III's faults, notably in the spheres of justice, finance and early foreign policy, are obvious and were much commented on by contemporaries. The parliamentary complaint that royal justice was not being vigorously administered by the king in person occurs again and again — in 1473, 1478, 1484 and 1485; and in October 1488 one of the young James IV's first promises was to ride in person to all the ayres accompanied by the justices.[2] Clearly James III had not done this. He delegated the responsibility by appointing justices — Sir David Guthrie served in this capacity in 1473-4[3] — and ayres were duly held; the Exchequer accounts (particularly in 1471, the only year for which the sheriffs' accounts survive) provide evidence of ayres held at Ayr, Cupar, Edinburgh, Haddington, Peebles, Perth, Selkirk and Stirling.[4] But the king does not appear to have been present, unlike his predecessor and two successors, so that royal justice in criminal actions was probably slack, and was attended also by the much criticised practice of granting remissions to those convicted of serious crimes such as slaughter or premeditated theft. James IV would continue the practice and be censured for it in the parliament of 1503;[5] but James III was criticised by the estates for giving remissions in 1473, 1478, 1484, 1485 and 1487,[6] a clear indication that the effective administration of justice was being undermined in order to acquire cash for the Crown. Doubtless the reprieved murderer in Boece's famous story of James III's clemency paid a tidy sum for his life and freedom.[7]

In the field of civil justice the reign saw changes, though not necessarily improvements. After May, 1471 there are no further references in the records of this reign to the appointment of Sessions — judicial committees of parliament which met three times a year at Edinburgh, Perth and Aberdeen (and latterly only twice, at Edinburgh and Perth), when parliament was not sitting, to hear appeals from the ordinary courts. Each Session had normally consisted of three members of each estate, and in the reign of James II many such bodies were appointed in parliament or general council. Yet the demise of the Sessions after 1471 was not accompanied by any form of parliamentary protest, presumably because thereafter the Council held sessions, the Lords of Council records beginning in 1478. These show that the judges were often the same men who served as Lords Auditors during sessions of parliament; and many of them were also royal councillors.[8] They met in Edinburgh because the king was there; and though their records are incomplete — the gaps occurring when we would most like to know what was going on, from 1480 to 1483, and again from 1485 to 1488 — it would appear that the institution was such a success that long before the end of the reign the Council was becoming overburdened with appeals. How far the statutes of 1469 and 1471, encouraging appeals from the ordinary courts to the Council, were resented by local lords — or indeed by the overworked councillors — must remain a matter for speculation; but it is surely significant that James III reaffirmed the subject's right of direct appeal to the Council in January 1488, at a time when he was deliberately adopting an extremely belligerent attitude towards recalcitrant members of his nobility. The successful rebels of that year retaliated by trying and forfeiting *in absentia* John Ross of Montgrenan, the king's Advocate, a man with a better record of attendance at Lords of Council meetings than anyone else, with the exception of two successive Chancellors, Avandale and Argyll.[9] Ross was one of only four people tried and forfeited by the new regime, which suggests that his commitment to James III in 1488 had been such as to cause great offence, far greater than simply being present in the royal army at Sauchieburn. His indictment also makes much of his journeys to England to obtain armed support from Henry VII; but underlying these charges, which were also levelled at others who were acquitted,[10] is Ross's work as an administrator and lawyer; and it is tempting to see in his prominence on the Council part of the reason for the deep divisions which existed in that body towards the end of the reign, and for the defection to the rebel side of Argyll and his relatives by marriage, Lords Oliphant and Drummond. Ross was after all only an Ayrshire knight with no known university training; clearly influence with the king had acquired for him his prominence in judicial affairs, and it was this influence, rather than the man's ability, which was resented by those who feared the king.[11] In civil as in criminal justice, therefore, the personality of James III exercised a baleful influence; and to this we must return.

Complaints also abounded about the king's devices throughout the reign for raising money. To some extent his actions in this respect are understandable. The royal income, as Dr. Murray reminds us,[12] is not strictly calculable because many exchequer accounts are missing, and these are not in any case simple statements of revenue and expenditure. But the king's ordinary revenue was made up of three components: the farms of burghs and sheriffs, which were haphazard and accounted only for a small proportion of the whole; customs on the exports of wool and hides, in which field receipts fluctuated according to the availability and size of foreign markets;[13] and finally Crown lands. James III may well have been concerned about the uncertainty and inadequacy associated with the first two; but in the case of Crown lands, in spite of falling rents from the early years of the century, the vast increase in the territorial wealth of the monarchy since 1424 meant that his financial position was no worse, and probably much better, than that of his two predecessors.

James I had annexed the earldoms of Mar, March, Strathearn, Fife, Menteith and Lennox to the Crown; the Act of Annexation of 1455 added important Douglas lands, including Galloway, Ettrick Forest, and Ardmannoch (Black Isle); while James III's marriage brought in Orkney and later Shetland, the forfeiture of the Boyds produced the lordship of Kilmarnock and smaller properties in Forfarshire, Perthshire and Dumfriesshire, and in 1476 the Lord of the Isles forfeited Knapdale, Kintyre and the earldom of Ross. Mary of Gueldres' early death in 1463 ensured that her dower lands reverted to the Crown, and the forfeitures of Albany and Mar later in the reign took care of the problem of making adequate territorial provision for the members of the royal family. Further forfeitures in the 1480s, including Lord Crichton, Sir James Liddale and James Gifford of Sheriffhall, suggest that revenue from this source was steadily growing. Inevitably portions of lands thus acquired were distributed amongst royal supporters; but over the reign the king made considerable gains, as he did also from his right to the temporalities of vacant bishoprics. He does not however appear to have been concerned to attack at the roots the problem of making the most out of the extensive and increasing Crown lands — that is, by following parliament's advice to James II in 1548 to 'begyne and gif exempill to the laif' by letting royal lands in feu-farm[14] — and it was not until the following century, especially after 1508, that James IV adopted the practice on a large scale. It may be that in the reign of James III conditions were not suitable for extensive feuing; possibly the Scottish lairds and peasantry on Crown lands in the '70s and '80s were unable to pay high compositions and farms.[15]

There can be little doubt, however, that the key factor in financial policy throughout the reign was the attitude of the king, who in spite of the territorial benefits produced by forfeitures and Crown annexations still regarded the royal income as inadequate. Thus he indulged in that most unpopular of devices to bring in ready cash, the levying of extraordinary taxation in parliament. On six occasions — 1472, 1473, 1479, 1482, 1485 and 1487 — he attempted to tax the estates; and in 1473-4 he negotiated with Louis XI of France in an attempt to secure a large pension from the French king. With the sole exception of 1482, when the money demanded was for the justifiable cause of defending the borders against English invasion, these schemes brought in little or no return, as the taxations of 1473 and 1479 do not appear to have been collected, and no money was forthcoming from the king of France. In fact, King James's only success in raising money abroad was in extracting 8,000 marks sterling from Edward IV, over five years, as part of Princess Cecilia's dowry, though her proposed marriage with Prince James was never accomplished.

It would appear that, by the end of the '70s, the king felt himself acutely embarrassed by his poverty in relation to other European rulers; in the spring of 1479, he had had to agree that the dowry of 8,000 Scots for the proposed marriage of his sister Margaret to Anthony, earl Rivers, should be deducted from the annual payments being made by the English towards Cecilia's dowry. The iron may have entered King James's soul when the taxation of 1479 towards Margaret's marriage failed to come in in any quantity; and within a year we find that the king had embarked on a new financial policy of debasement of the coinage and hoarding of money. Thus in subsequent crises James III carried large sums about the country with him; at Lauder he was robbed of £146,[16] and in the spring of 1488 he made elaborate dispositions of his money, not only sending it to supporters throughout the country but ultimately carrying with him to Stirling more than £4,000 in gold coin in a black box. The greater part of the royal hoard, however, was left in Edinburgh castle jewel house, and the inventory of it made after James III's death makes it clear that, financially, his position had improved immeasurably since 1479.[17]

Acting on the principle that bad money drives out good — that is, that the worst form of currency in circulation regulates the value of the whole currency and drives all other forms of currency out of circulation — James III introduced the notorious 'black money', a combination of very base billon and copper, between 1479 and 1482, and hoarded 'good' money from about 1480 onwards. Such a policy could not solve the long-term financial problems of the Crown, and debasement may only have been introduced by James III as a means of clearing foreign debts. But it surely also provided the profits which made up much of the royal treasure.

As we have seen, criticism of the king extended beyond his judicial and fiscal policies to include his very personal foreign policy. His early years of adult rule had seen his advancement of wild schemes of conquest on the continent, including invasions of Brittany, Gueldres and Saintonge; and he had also intimated to Louis XI his intention of making a pilgrimage to Rome. Faced, however, with almost total lack of enthusiasm for these schemes both at home and abroad, he had ultimately come round to the policy which he was to pursue tenaciously for the remainder of his life, namely peace and alliance with England. In the course of thirteen years, between 1474 and 1487, he attempted to negotiate English marriages for his son James (on three occasions), his second son James, his younger sister Margaret, and himself. None of these efforts was successful; but the policy itself was wise and forward-looking. Fifteen years after James III's death, his son married an English princess to great popular acclaim. But in the 1470s, as works like Hary's *Wallace* clearly illustrate, a policy of close alliance with England encountered widespread popular hostility in southern Scotland; for it meant an end to border warfare and its pickings, increased interference on the Marches by royal officials, and in general the extension of Stewart power to include an area where it had rarely been effective in the past. The long-drawn out Coldingham dispute is the classic example of a powerful border family's resentment of royal interference during this reign; and it is probably significant that the only occasion on which James III and the Humes were able to cooperate was during the crisis of 1482–3, when the English alliance had temporarily collapsed.

Although not the first Scottish king to appreciate that the French alliance was an encumbrance rather than a help — latterly James I had held similar views — James III was the first to cultivate friendship with England so assiduously. Thus his renewal of the Franco-Scottish alliance in 1484 may be regarded as part of a device — probably successful — to put pressure on Richard III to treat for peace with Scotland; it was not a change of policy. At the same time, Scottish foreign policy was gradually becoming broader in scope as successive monarchs attempted to break out of the triangular pattern of alliances which tradition and geography tended to impose upon the country. James II had married as part of a Burgundian alliance, and sought to play the role of European mediator towards the end of his short life. James III inherited and extended this policy, for his marriage to Margaret of Denmark brought him immediate and very substantial territorial gains; and subsequently he behaved as though Scotland were a European power of immense strength rather than a poor country at the north-western extremity of the continent — 'in finibus orbis', as the Duke of Milan remarked to Louis XI in 1474. King James's public expressions of the Stewart monarchy's international status — the concept of 'empire' first mentioned in 1469, the expulsion of imperial notaries, the silver coinage on which the king appears wearing an imperial crown, the proposed continental adventures of the early '70s — can hardly have impressed his European contemporaries; they certainly alarmed his own subjects, and this at a time when James III was attempting to achieve a major shift in Scottish diplomatic attitudes towards England. Arguably, as in other areas of royal concern, it was as much the king's personality as the policy he advocated which produced internal resistance.

At home, James III may be regarded as an innovator in that, to a greater extent than any previous king, he ran his administration from Edinburgh. James II had held parliaments and general councils at Stirling, Perth and Edinburgh; sessions had met at Aberdeen, Perth and Edinburgh; and royal charters were granted at Stirling, Edinburgh, Crichton, Dalkeith, Methven, Linlithgow, Perth, Falkland, Melrose, Ayr, Lanark, Lochmaben and Jedburgh. Under James III, there is a striking change; all parliaments (with the exception of the Boyd parliament of January 1468 at Stirling) met in Edinburgh. At the outset, this may not have been a conscious effort at centralisation; in the autumn of 1474 it was intended to hold a parliament at St. Andrews, but it was transferred to Edinburgh. The Lords of Council held sessions in Edinburgh; and during James III's active rule — that is, from 1469 onwards — apart from five isolated charters, two granted at Stirling in November 1470 and April 1472 respectively, one at Perth in June 1472, and two in April 1488 at Aberdeen (where the king had retired during the crisis),[18] all traceable royal charters under the great seal — some 650 — were granted at Edinburgh. As we have seen in discussing the 1482 crisis, it seems likely that the royal administrative seals were kept permanently in Edinburgh, at least during the '80s. This policy of centralisation is perhaps also reflected in James's preoccupation in his last years with the building and endowment of his new collegiate church at Restalrig, which he may have planned to replace St. Mary of the Rock, St. Andrews as the Chapel Royal. The king himself described Edinburgh as his favourite burgh; and he may have had a powerful practical motive for siting his administration there on a permanent basis. The Edinburgh wool exports had not fallen sharply like those of other Scottish burghs because the Edinburgh merchants had managed to concentrate in their own hands most of the Flanders contracts. This was already the case in the 1450s, when James II was borrowing from them.[19] A generation later James III also relied on them, notably Walter Bertram, Patrick Baron and George Robison in 1482, and Robison again in 1488; and a future provost of Edinburgh, Richard Lawson, is to be found serving on the Lords of Council from 1483.[20]

Because of its continuing prosperity, Edinburgh was the only place in Scotland where there were any financiers, and common sense would therefore suggest the burgh as a permanent home for the royal administration.

Throughout the reign, as we have seen, James III held sessions of council at Edinburgh, a contrast with his father's concept of itinerant sessions of parliamentary nominees visiting Aberdeen, Perth and Edinburgh for forty days each. Perhaps significantly, James III's sittings of the Lords of Council at Edinburgh often went on for periods of more than three months at a time, an indication of considerable pressure of business. But they were not an innovation. James I had chosen his session which sat wherever he might command; and after 1498 James IV's sessions were regular sessions of council, not of parliamentary nominees. It may be that too much is made of the distinction between the two, and of the question of who chose the sessions in each case. But it is clear from the evidence that in so far as there is a distinction, the 'parliamentary' sessions of James II and those of the minority of James III were abnormal, not the norm; and James III, on taking over the government himself, reverted to the system of council sessions introduced by his grandfather and eventually restored by his son.

The king's use of Edinburgh as the only legislative centre was continued by his successors, for all the parliaments of James IV and James V met there, and all but two of Queen Mary's. But this fixing of the legislature in one place was not paralleled, in subsequent reigns, by attempts on the part of the monarch to run the entire administration from Edinburgh. In the sphere of civil justice, it was possible for the king to stay in one place and order plaintiff and defendant to appear before the council; and this was doubtless efficient enough, because the winning party in a civil case had an interest in seeing that the decision of the court was carried out, and it was therefore unnecessary to have the Lords of Council travelling all over the country. However, the administration of criminal justice was quite another matter, for only the king had an interest in punishing crime; and in Scotland it was probably necessary for him to supervise personally the enforcement of the law. Both James IV and James V were very active in travelling about the realm on justice ayres, and like James II they granted charters in many other towns besides Edinburgh.

In the face of this renewed activity, it may be doubted whether the static administration introduced by James III was really effective. In general, the king seems to have left too much to others; he sent out justices into the localities but did not attend the ayres in person; and although he may have gone north to make his authority felt during the suppression of the Ross rebellion in the spring of 1476, he cannot have been absent from Edinburgh for much longer than a month, and relied on the effective use of the commissions of lieutenancy which he had issued to Argyll, Atholl, Crawford and Huntly. The contrast with James II in his latter years, and even more, with James IV, is very striking; for it is arguable that much of the success of both was due to the king's personal contact with officials in the localities.

To many if not most of his subjects, however, James III remained a remote figure in Edinburgh, a ruler whom they never saw; and this fact may have led the later chroniclers to suggest that he lived apart as a recluse. This is an over-simplification, for there is evidence to illustrate that the king travelled about the country during his majority. When he left Edinburgh, however, it was not to administer justice in person in the localities, but often merely to hunt at Falkland. This is in sharp contrast to the minority years; as a youth, the king had hunted in Strathearn, in the forest of Mamlorne, in Glenfinglas or near Balquhidder, he had spent much time in the royal castles of Stirling and Doune and in the palace of Falkland, celebrated Christmas of 1466 at Perth, and visited Peebles and Kirkcudbright in the south. The first royal progress, in 1464, had included visits to Dundee, Aberdeen, Elgin and Inverness, while the second brought James III and his new queen to Aberdeen, Fyvie, Banff and Inverness in the summer of 1470.[21] Thereafter, for the remainder of his life — some eighteen years, in fact almost the entire period of his active rule — the king appears to have remained in Edinburgh or in close proximity to it, allowing himself only comparatively short excursions to Stirling, Linlithgow or Falkland, and in the final crisis about a month's stay in Aberdeen.[22] This feature of James's government does not however imply a lack of interest in travel on the part of the king, only that it was the prospect of foreign travel which preoccupied him from the early '70s — Brittany, Saintonge, Gueldres, Amiens and Rome, but not, as the estates pointed out with reasonable justification in July 1473, journeys throughout Scotland doing his job.[23]

It is clear from all this that the central problem of the reign concerns the personal character of James III. Arguments can be advanced in support of his pro-English foreign policy, or — rather more tentatively — his positive ideas about centralisation of the royal administration. It can even be argued that the king was endowed with considerable political ability — witness his recovery from the grave crisis of 1482–3 — and possessed the skill or cunning to gain a short-term advantage over his enemies. But there, surely, his virtues as a ruler end. At close quarters, for the politically active, for the civil servants in the royal administration, above all for a large proportion of the Scottish nobility, James III was a frightening example of a ruler who did not recognise the responsibilities of power, who refused to learn from his mistakes, and whose ability to ignore or alienate potential supporters was quite staggering.

These fatal character flaws manifested themselves in a number of ways. First, and in some ways most damaging of all, King James failed to provide adequate rewards for those who served him loyally. To take only two examples: in the '70s the Earl of Huntly was fobbed off by the king with a gift of a mere hundred marks in return for the earl's vitally important military service in Ross; and in the '80s the leader of the southern lairds who had fought the king's battle for him at Lochmaben, Robert Crichton of Sanquhar, had to wait almost four years until January 1488 before James III rewarded him with a lordship of parliament, and then only because growing opposition forced him to bid for support. We cannot be sure what role Crichton of Sanquhar played in the crisis of 1488; but in Huntly's case it is significant that whereas the first Earl of Huntly had been able to gather a sizeable force to fight for James II at Brechin in 1452, a generation later the second earl sat in the north and left his sovereign James III to perish at Sauchieburn.

Secondly, like his grandfather, King James acted rashly and on occasions illegally against certain members of his nobility. The most striking example of this arbitrariness is to be found in May 1471, when James not only gave Chancellor Avandale the life-rent of the Lennox — an illegal act, as the earldom was not in the royal gift and Avandale was illegitimate — but subsequently issued his Chancellor with letters of legitimation. John Stewart, Lord Darnley, the frustrated candidate for the Lennox, suffered the further indignity of being recognised briefly as earl by James III and then having his brieves of service to the earldom revoked for no apparent reason. A similar lack of any sense of justice is to be found in the king's arbitrary suppression of Coldingham priory in 1472, a curious response to the Prior of Durham's appeal to promote the reoccupation of the priory by Durham monks, one which produced a protracted 'cold war' in the south-east and ended only at Sauchieburn. Finally, the king made another enemy — quite unnecessarily — when in 1475 he thrust John Drummond of Cargill out of the office of Steward of Strathearn, replacing him with Murray of Tullibardine.

Thirdly, King James, although not extravagant according to the records, failed to provide, in Duncan's words, 'court life and its perquisites'.[24] Instead, for at least eight years, he hoarded money. He seems to have spent little on two of the most costly projects of the period, the acquisition of artillery and construction of warships, and the building of castles or palaces. The surviving Treasurer's Accounts for 1473–4 reveal a number of small payments to smiths for the forging of guns; but this does not seem to have amounted to much in terms of hard cash.[25] On the whole King James was content to use his father's stock of artillery; and when he required more, he appealed both to Louis XI of France and Archduke Sigismund of Austria. As regards the building of a navy, James III may have been responsible for the construction of the 'Yellow Carvel', though it is by no means clear that this vessel was a warship rather than merely an armed merchantman; but his expenditure on this or other vessels can hardly have matched that of his son, whose fleet numbered nine to a dozen warships. Similarly, in his outlay on architecture, James III must have been extremely frugal, for no sizeable building can be attributed to him. By contrast, James I built Linlithgow, James II was mainly responsible for Holyrood, James IV had halls constructed at Edinburgh and Stirling castles, and also the Chapel Royal at Stirling, and James V's palaces at Stirling, Falkland, Holyrood and Linlithgow were all vastly extravagant undertakings.

The records do not reveal evidence of such magnificent ostentation, or of a glittering Renaissance court, in the reign of James III. Small pensions to courtiers travelling to Bruges to learn the lute are hardly proof that the king was an artist or a patron of the arts on a large scale. He was clearly obsessed not with spending money but with hoarding it, an aspect of his character which must have caused great resentment. Indeed, the king's miserly nature was so well known that the new regime in 1488 refused to believe that his enormous hoard recovered after Sauchieburn — £24,000 in money alone — was more than the tip of the iceberg, and ten years later they were still intent on bringing civil actions against those who had made off with the remainder.[26]

Fourthly, the king appears to have been acutely mistrustful of his kin. We will probably never know who took the initiative in James's protracted struggle with Albany in the late '70s and early '80s; but the results of the conflict are clear enough. Albany was driven out of the kingdom, and ultimately forfeited; Mar died in unknown circumstances after being arrested, and was forfeited.[27] Of James's two sisters the elder, Mary, was imprisoned on returning to Scotland in 1471 seeking a pardon for her forfeited Boyd husband, Thomas, earl of Arran, with whom she had fled to Bruges. The king married her off to James, Lord Hamilton, in 1474; but in the crisis of 1482–3 she reverted to her Boyd allegiance. Margaret, the younger sister, finally evaded her brother's marriage schemes for her by having an affair with William, Lord Crichton, one of the rebels of 1482–3. James's Stewart half-uncles Atholl and Buchan, fearing that the king intended to attack them for past treasons, took the initiative by striking first at Lauder;[28] and they were subsequently joined by their younger brother Andrew Stewart, bishop-elect of Moray. Although Margaret of Denmark's influence on this major Stewart crisis was ultimately benign, she was certainly prepared to negotiate with both Stewart kin groups who shared power in the autumn of 1482; and her eldest son, the future James IV, was ultimately so afraid of his father's actions that he became the indirect instrument of James III's death. This is an appalling catalogue of internecine treachery and mistrust which may be explained mainly in terms of the neurotic suspicions of an exceedingly unpleasant king.

Fifthly, this unpleasantness is reflected in James's public breaches of faith. The most striking examples of this trait are to be found during the major crises of 1482 and 1488. In the former case, James's elaborate letter to John Stewart, Lord Darnley, in October 1482, absolving Darnley and his associates of any blame for holding him captive in Edinburgh castle during the early autumn, quite openly reveals that the king had allowed Darnley to 'sele and subscrive ... certane endenturis' with the rebel lords, 'to eschew that tha Lordis suld tak na suspicioun again the said Lorde Dernele be refusing thareof'.[29] Yet these same lords — the Stewart half-uncles and their supporters — were still in power, together with the Albany faction, when James wrote his letter to Darnley inviting him to simulate acceptance of their authority, and implying that any bonds made with them could easily be annulled once the king had recovered power. This letter, with its cynical disregard for written bonds, reveals more in three pages about James III's shifty character than one can find in the parliamentary records for the entire reign. Even worse was the king's total repudiation of the Aberdeen articles of April 1488, a written agreement providing for negotiations with the rebels which he himself had signed and which his supporters in the north clearly hoped might lead to a settlement.[30] Their immediate desertion of the royal cause thereafter reflects what they thought of a king who broke his word to friend and enemy alike, displaying a lofty contempt for both.

Such a character inevitably provoked a sharp magnate reaction, and in political terms the reign may be regarded as a series of confrontations between king and nobility, the most dramatic expressions of which were the rebellions of 1482 and 1488. Many of those who had been involved in coercion of the king on the former occasion attempted to offer their support to him on the latter, a fact which is in itself indicative of James's arbitrary nature and the desperate search for security of those who feared that they had offended him. For these were frightened men. As Dr. Wormald reminds us, 'the history of Crown-magnate relations is strewn with victims of Stewart aggression against those who were vulnerable to the Crown's thirst for land or those who could be regarded as political opponents'.[31] Other Stewarts succeeded in their assaults on sections of the nobility by ensuring that, if they took with one hand, they gave with the other. But James III assailed his magnates on a grand scale in pursuit of his imperial pretensions; in the course of only twenty years he alienated, attacked, killed, forfeited or removed the Duke of Albany, the Earls of Atholl, Buchan, Angus, Mar, Argyll, Lennox, Arran, Ross, Orkney, and possibly Morton; Lords Boyd, Crichton, Oliphant, Drummond, Lyle, Hailes, Hume and Gray; and amongst the clergy, the Bishops of Glasgow, Moray and Dunkeld and the first Archbishop of St. Andrews, not to mention the abbots and convents of Paisley and Jedburgh. Naturally these assaults were not simultaneous, and at no time of crisis did James III find himself, like Richard II of England in 1399, wholly devoid of support. But if we include the northern lords who remained neutral after James's breach of faith at Aberdeen in 1488, then the total number of earls coerced by, or alienated from, the king during his adult rule is thirteen. Indeed, amongst the politically active earls the only one to retain consistent royal favour throughout was Crawford.[32]

Thus it was that when James III fought his last battle he did so with the minimum of magnate support — Crawford having been elevated to the rank of duke for his loyalty, the Earl of Atholl hoping to recover some of the prestige he had lost in 1482, Alexander Cunningham, Lord Kilmaurs, made Earl of Glencairn three weeks before Sauchieburn on condition that he continued to support the king throughout the rebellion, and a handful of southern lairds and knights, some of whom had been similarly coerced into service. It was a poor return on two decades of adult rule, and more immediately, a striking commentary on collective magnate mistrust of a ruler who lost the support of no fewer than four earls within weeks of Sauchieburn.

In the last analysis, therefore, James III failed not because of his policies — many of which would rapidly be adopted by his popular son — but because of his personality. Perhaps he deserved better at the hands of the chroniclers, for he did fulfil at least one of the classic duties of a medieval king, that of leader in war. He wanted to go in person to Brittany, Gueldres and Saintonge, and he turned out at the head of his troops in 1476, 1481, 1482 and 1488, on the last occasion at Blackness, Stirling Bridge and Sauchieburn. However, in only two of these instances — 1481 and 1482 — was King James attempting to defend his country against foreign invasion; on the other occasions he was embroiled in war with his own subjects. He combined the ruthlessness and acquisitiveness of his grandfather and father with the unpleasantness of his grandson; and perhaps his true legacy was not his Anglophile policy — speedily repudiated by the new regime — but simply his money, the thousands in gold spilling out of Avery's box into the Sauchieburn mud.

NOTES

1. Dickinson/Duncan, *op.cit.*, 239.

2. *A.P.S.*, ii, 208.

3. *T.A.*, i, 66, 68.

4. *E.R.*, viii, *passim.*

5. *A.P.S.*, ii, 250.

6. *Ibid.*, 104, 118, 165, 170, 176.

7. Boece, *Vitae*, 76-7.

8. *A.D.A.*, 34-5. The best analysis of Lords of Council personnel during the reign is A. L. Brown, 'The Scottish "Establishment" in the Later 15th Century', in *Juridical Review*, xxiii (1978), 89-105.

9. Brown, *op.cit.*, 99. Avandale died in 1488; and Argyll was of course one of the most prominent rebels of that year.

10. *A.P.S.*, ii, 200-205.

11. In spite of his forfeiture in 1488, Ross had been restored within two years — largely through the intercession of Henry VII and the pope — and he is once more to be found serving on the Council in 1490: Brown, *op.cit.*, 99.

12. A. L. Murray, 'The Comptroller, 1425-1488', in *S.H.R.*, lii, (1973), 1-29, esp. 12-16, 29.

13. This important subject forms part of a forthcoming St. Andrews M.Phil. thesis by Isobel Guy.

14. *A.P.S.*, ii, 49.

15. *See* R. G. Nicholson, 'Feudal Developments in Late Medieval Scotland', in *Juridical Review*, xviii, (1973), 1-21, esp. 4.

16. *E.R.*, xi, 219.

17. Joan Murray, in *B.A.R.* 45 (1977), 115-130, estimates that the king might have made as much as £29,000 from the profits of debasement; A. L. Murray, *op.cit.*, 29, more cautiously states that the sources from which the king could have amassed this treasure are largely unknown, and warns against attempting to write the financial history of the reign from the exchequer rolls alone.

18. *R.M.S.*, ii, Nos. 1010, 1058, 1063; S.R.O. Airlie Chrs., Section 12, No. 9; *Moray Registrum*, 234-6.

19. *E.R.*, vi, 305.

20. *A.D.C.*, 81-118 *passim.*

21. These itineraries are based on the Great Seal Register, the Exchequer Rolls, and the Treasurer's Accounts, and are discussed in detail above in Chapters 3-5.

22. The records from which a royal itinerary may be compiled, notably the Exchequer Rolls and the Treasurer's Accounts, are incomplete — in fact the latter only supplies information for 1473-4; and the fact that the king considered holding a parliament in St. Andrews in 1474 (*T.A.*, i, 52) suggests that his travels may have been more extensive than the records reveal. But they cannot have been on anything like the scale of his predecessor or successor.

23. *A.P.S.*, ii, 104.

24. Dickinson/Duncan, *op.cit.*, 244.

25. A typical entry is that of 23 April 1474: 'Item, gevin at the Kingis commande to the goldsmyth that makis the gun . . . £3': *T.A.*, i, 49. It was only in the crisis of 1482 that King James paid out a substantial sum, £214 4/- 'for expensis . . . in a hunder and aucht wall of irne to the makin of serpentynis and gunnys': *E.R.*, ix, 218-9.

26. A. L. Murray, *op.cit.*, 29.

27. For a brilliant — though very debatable — interpretation of these events, *see* Dickinson/Duncan, *op.cit.*, 247-8.

28. In considering the motives of Atholl and Buchan in the period leading up to 1482, I have benefited greatly from discussions on the subject with Miss Lindsay Beaton.

29. Fraser, *Lennox*, ii, 121-3.

30. *A.P.S.*, ii, 210-11.

31. Wormald, *Court, Kirk, and Community*, 11.

32. This fact must surely raise serious doubts as to the validity of Professor Brown's comment that 'an earl at court may often have achieved more in five minutes than Alex Inglis' (the clerk register and James III's candidate for the bishopric of Dunkeld in the 1480s) 'at umpteen meetings of the council': Brown, *op.cit.*, 105. This could be regarded as fair comment on the early years of James IV's reign; but no earl, at court or anywhere else, achieved much of permanence under James III unless his name was Crawford. On the other hand, Inglis is an example of a man who was close to the king in the '80s, like John Ireland and Ross of Montgrenan, all of them councillors whose advice the king clearly valued.

Appendix A.
The Short Chronicle of 1482

Part of the short Chronicle appended to the Royal Manuscript of Andrew Wyntoun's 'Orygynale Cronykyl of Scotland'.

(B.M. Royal MS. 17 DXX ff 299-398)

This is entitled 'Heir is assignt the cause quhy oure natioun was callyt fyrst the Scottys'. It runs to some ten folios, in which the history of Scotland is described from its mythological beginnings down to 1482. The portion of this chronicle which deals with the fifteenth century has been printed by Pinkerton (*History*, i, 502-4), but with two passages from the time of James III omitted. The full text of the Royal MS. for that reign is given below:

f. 307 r. The zere of god a m iiii^c and lx and thrid day of August deit king James the secund at roxburgh be the brekyn of his awyn gunnis at straik him to deid at the secund sege of roxburgh and he was erddit in haly rudhouss on the sanct laurence day nixt folowand the decess of James the secund was king James the thride his sone crownyt in Kelso he beand aucht zeris of eld and ane half the zere of god a m iiii^c lxiii zeris Jhone of Dowglace was slayne in Edynburgh and erle James his brother was chasyt in Ingland Anno domini m° cccc° lxix° James the Thrid of Scotland the xiii day of Julij was maryit in haly rudhouss in gret dignite with margaret with the kingis douchter of norway dasie and swasie and demmerk and that sammyn zere was banysyt the lord bowde and schir alexander lord and knycht was hedyt in edynburgh Anno domini m° cccc° lxiii° Alexander duke of Albany was tane on the se be the inglissmen and honorabilly deliverit for the instance of his brother King James be king edward in ingland. Anno domini m° cccc° lxx° king edward of ingland was banysyt be the erle of warwick and passyt in flandriss and was resawit be the duk of burgunze for the dukis wyf was his sister and king hary at was befor banysyt in scotland be edwardis fadir was than restoryt to the crown of ingland Anno domini m° cccc° lxxi° the said edward come again (307 v) in Ingland with gret power of the duke of burgunzhe and straik ane batell with the erle of Werwyk be syd lundoun and slew the erle and all his complices wincust And deprivyt king hary and tuke the croune and efterwart slew hary the quhilk was callit ane sanct and mony miraclis kythit in Ingland That ilk zere was sene ane marvalouse stern in the firmament And that ilk zere drownyt the bischoipis of Sanct Androis barge and sum juge that the stern seyne aperit for caus of the drownyn of that schip and others say for cause of the depriwyn and murtyryng of the haly man king hary Anno domini m° cccc° lxxix° King James the thred banysit Alexander his brother duke of abbany and passyt in france and was maryit thar and eftir that he come in Ingland and maid his residence with king edward of Ingland And than the king of scotland gart sege dunbar the dukis castell and the lord of bunterdaill was capitane and he and his stall away be the se and so the king gat the castell and that zere was mony weches and warlois brint on crag gayt and Jhone the erle of mar the kingis brothir was slayne becaus thai said he faworyt the weches and warlois Anno domini m° cccc° lxxx° thair raise ane gret were betwix Ingland and Scotland and that zere the erle of Anguys with gret power of Scottis passyt in Ingland and brynt balmburgh and lay thre nychtis and thre dais in ingland and that zer was gret tempestis of wedder for ane gret storme began at new zeir day and lestyt quhill the xxvi day of Marche (308 r) the morn eftir our lady day in lenterin the storme brak

311

And nixt beltyn day eftir was ewill beltyn day Anno domini m° cccc° lxxxii° thir was ane gret
hungyr and deid in Scotland for the boll of meill was for four pundis for thir was blak cunzhe in the
relame strikkin And ordinyt be king James the thred half pennys and three penny pennys
Innumerabill of coppir And thai yeid twa zere and mair And als was gret were betuix Scotland and
Ingland and gret distructioun throw the weris was of corne and catell And thai twa thyngs causyt
baitht hungar and derth and mony pure folk deit of hunger And that sammyn zere in the monetht
of Julij the king of scotland purposyt till haif passyt in Ingland with the power of scotland and
passyt on gaitwart to lawdyr and thar the lordis of Scotland held thair consaill in the kirk of lauder
and cryit downe the blak silver and thai slew ane part of the kingis housald and other part thai
banysyt and thai tuke the king him self and thai put him in the castell of Edynburgh in firm kepyng
for he wrocht mair the consaell of his housald at war bot sympill na he did of thame that was lordis
And he was haldyn in the castell of Edinburgh fra the magdalyne day quhill michaelmess And than
the wictall grew better chaip for the boll that was for four punds was than for xxii s. ('xxxi' erased)
of quhyt silver.

It has been suggested in Chapter 12 that the composition of this short chronicle
may be dated to the late autumn of 1482. The only serious objection to this view is a
statement on f.302 r–v: 'Ther fell ane discord betuix ws and the pechtis and we
warrayt on thame lang tyme and put thame out utralye of the land of scotland be our
king kenauche Makalpyn the quhilk was done sewyn hundre zeir syne that is to say
the zeir of our lord auch hunder xxx and od zeiris and so remanyt the Saxons in the
south and we in the north'. Taken literally, this statement indicates that the
chronicle was written about 1530. However, it should be noted that, in describing
early history, the chronicler is vague and notoriously inaccurate about dating. Thus
on f.304 he states that 5,199 years elapsed between the Creation and the birth of
Christ. Between the Creation and the appearance in history of the first Scotsmen
was a period of 4,315 years; and between the first Scots and the writer's own time,
another 1,800 years. Thus, by the chronicler's own dating, the total number of
years which had passed since the Creation was 6,115 (4,315 plus 1,800); and there
were 5,199 years before Christ. Therefore a simple subtraction (6,115 minus 5,199
B.C.) should supply us with the date of the chronicle's composition. But the answer
is 916 A.D.; and the conclusion must be that the chronicler's dating (particularly
when it takes so vague a form as 'sewyn hunder zeir syne') is not to be taken
literally.

Appended to a later, and unfoliated, manuscript of Wyntoun's chronicle (N.L.S.
Adv. MS. 19. 2. 4.) is a short chronicle of eleven folios which bears the title 'Brevis
Cronica'. This is not related to the Royal MS. chronicle but is an independent
summary of Boece's *Scotorum Historiae*. Thus the account of John Balliol, Wallace,
Bruce and David II, following Boece, is much fuller than the Royal MS. chronicle.
No reference is made to Kenneth Macalpin and the destruction of the Picts; and
from the time of Macbeth onwards there are references to Boece's chapters at the
end of most paragraphs. The 'Brevis Cronica' ends in mid-sentence with a
description of the events of Robert II's reign:

Eftir the deith of David, Robert Stewart his sisteris sone was crownit and gouernit his realme in
greit tranquillite he renewit the confideratioun betuix France and Scotland and hade greit Victoryis
vpoun Inglismen at the feild callit Ottirburne the erle of Northumbirland was tane with the Scottis.
This king . . .

It should be stressed that the 'Brevis Cronica' is not in any way related to the Royal MS. Chronicle, as the two have often been confused (most recently in R.L. Mackie, *James IV*, p. 13, n.2).

Appendix B. Adam Abell
'The Roit and Quheill of Tyme':
by Adam Abell of Jedburgh

N.L.S. MS. 1746. 126 ff., small octavo.

A short history of Scotland from its legendary beginnings down to the year 1537. The conclusion (ff. 119v, 120v) contains some information about the author.

f. 119v.   Soli deo honor et gloria.

> Heir endis the rute or quheill of tyme Be ane pure brothir of the brethir minoris of observance in our place of Jedwart the zere of god 1533 in with the act of the nativitie of our lady the mothir of god quene of hewin.

On f. 120v is added:

> The forsaid brothir adam abell continuand his process of the forsaid rute heir he begynis quhair he lewit in the zere of god 1534 zeris and sa procedand for his schort tyme . . . ,

and the manuscript continues to f. 126 and the year 1537. Thus the work was written by Adam Abell, a friar of the Observant Franciscan house at Jedburgh in 1533 with a continuation by him to 1537. It is dedicated to St. Francis of Assisi.

The section of the work relating to the reign of James III is to be found on ff. 110v–112r:

f. 110v.   Scottis kyng 104 wes James 3 sone of forsaid James. He wes ane dewot man bot he wes gretumlie gevin to carnale pleseure by his halie quene and privat consall of sympill men Be the quhilk consall he destroeit his awne bredir maist necessair to him. For the herll of Mar wes slane be consall of ane trucur callit cochrene.

> Alexander the Duke of Albany wes banest diverss tymis the zere of god 1480 or thare about. The forsaid duke brocht the inglis men in Scotland with duke of glossistir the kingis brodir and that be proditioun of the scottis lordis quhem fra the king of ingland had 26 selis. Thre zere eftir or thare about be the consall of forsaid cochron wes cwnzet the blak copir quhar throw raiss gret darth and mortalite in the realm. Eftir that the zere of god 1480 wes the raid of lawdir quhar the king wes tane be the lordis and put in the castell of edinburgh als cochren and the laif of his priwat consall wes tane and iustifit to be hangit. Suyn eftir the duke brocht the inglis men to edinburgh and deliuerit the king bot the lordis coniuratoris fled in argile. Notwithstanding

f. 111r.   soyn eftir the king tuke thame to grace. And soyn eftir the duke wes flemyt agane to ingland. The zere of god 1486 the forsaid duk and the herll of dowgless with the inglis men straik batell on the magdalene day quhare thai wer wincust be the lordis of the west bordour. And mony inglis men wes slane. The erll of dougless wes tane. The duke wes lattin awa and passit agane to ingland quhare he wes accusit be the king of ingland for the slauchtir of the inglis men. Bot be the help of Johne Liddaill Schir James of Liddalis son quietlie he staw out of ingland and come in Scotland to his brodir. Suyn eftir be iniurious consall he wes tane and put in the castell of edinburgh. Bot first he slew the lard of Manerstone his kepar and syne be lynnyng clathis he passit awa downe at ane

314

windo and salit to france and wes gratuislie thare be the king resaifit and mareit ane gret lady of heretage this dukis modir. But eftirwert wnhappelie in iusting he wes slane. Than the forsaid coniuratoris his bredir slane thai conspirit againis the king and gaif him batell beside striwiling and thare wes he slane. He wes confessit before with maistir Johne Yrland proffessor of theologie. He wes berist in cambuskynnith the 29 zere of his ring of god 1489.

The chronicler then turns to English history, beginning with the date 1461. He also gives a brief summary of contemporary European events before reverting to Scottish history on f. 112r:

f. 112r. 1489. Scottis king 105 wes James fourt, forsaid James sone. He wes crownit the xvi zere of his age on Sanct Johne the baptist day. He be ewill consall gaif feild to his fathir bot it is said he forbad to put hands in him. Bot thai did the contra for thai slew him in the mill of bannoburne. Notwithstanding he wes ane nobill prince and pecebillie gidit the kinrik for he wsit wismennis consall ('and principallie of brothir minoris of observance', erased). He did gret penance for the being aganis his fadir. He punist thewis and roweris . . . he fundit owr place of striwiling and dowrit with reliks mony ethir halie places.

Sources and Bibliography
I. Manuscript Sources

A. *Edinburgh*

Scottish Record Office

Registrum Magni Sigilli Regum Scotorum, vols. vi-xi.
Acta Dominorum Concilii.
Treaties with France, Nos. 16-19.
State Papers No. 19.
Ailsa Muniments.
Airlie Charters.
Boyd Papers, Inventory.
Breadalbane Charters.
Cunninghame Graham Muniments.
Duntreath Muniments.
Erroll Charters.
Lord Forbes papers.
Glencairn Muniments.
Hay of Yester Writs.
Lennox Charters.
Seafield Charters.
Swinton Charters.

National Library of Scotland

MS. 73 (Morton Royal Letters).
MS. 1746 (Adam Abell).
Dundas Charters, B 73, 83, 102, 108, 109, 110.
Wigtown Charters No. 47.
Advocates MSS. 16.2.20. (MS. of George Chalmers).
          18.2.8. (John Ireland's 'Meroure of Wyssdome').
          19.2.3. (Andrew Wyntoun's 'Orygynale
          19.2.4. Cronykil')
          34.5.10. (History of the See of St. Andrews).
          A.1.32. ('The buk callyt Regiam Majestatem' — 15th cent.).
          A.3.22. (The Malcolm MS.).
          A.7.25. (John Bannatyne MS.).

Edinburgh University Library

MS. Borland 208 (Colvil MS.).

B. *London*

Public Record Office
E 39 (Scots Docts.).
E 404, 77/2/64, 71; 77/3/21, 41, 45, 59, 73; 78/3/26.

British Museum

Additional Charters, 1247, 1518, 19561, 19562.
Additional MSS. 12192, 21505, 35844, 43496.
Cotton MS. Vespasian C xvi.
Harleian MSS. 433, 543.
Royal MS. 17 Dxx.

C. *Other Scottish Sources*

Argyll Muniments at Inveraray castle, Argyllshire.
Atholl Muniments at Blair castle, Perthshire.
Glamis Charters and Writs at Glamis castle, Angus.
Moray Muniments at Darnaway castle, Morayshire.
Dumbarton Burgh Records.

D. *Paris*

Bibliothèque Nationale
MSS. français 4331, 6981, 12065, 15889, 20685, 23023.
MSS. français nouv. acq. 6214, 7025.
MS. Lat. 10187.

Archives Nationales

J 677, J 678, J 679 (Treaties between France and Scotland, 1295-1557).

E. *The Vatican*

Registra Supplicationum (cited in footnotes as Vat. Reg. Supp.)

F. *Innsbruck*

Landesregierungs-Archiv, Sigismund iv c/180/9 (Letter from James III to Archduke Sigismund of Austria).

G. *Copenhagen*

Danske Rigsarkiv, T.K.U.A., Skotland, A1, 1.

II. *Printed Works*

Wherever possible the contractions used in the text to describe these are drawn from: *List of Abbreviated Titles of the Printed Sources of Scottish History to 1560, S.H.R.*, Supplement, Oct. 1963.

A. *Primary*

Abbotsford Misc.	*Miscellany of the Abbotsford Club.* (Abbotsford Club, 1837).
Aberdeen Council Register	*Extracts from the Council Register of the Burgh of Aberdeen* (Spalding Club, 1844-48).
A.D.A.	*The Acts of the Lords Auditors of Causes and Complaints*, ed. T. Thomson (Edinburgh, 1839).
A.D.C.	*The Acts of the Lords of Council in Civil Causes*, ed. T. Thomson and others (Edin., 1839 and 1918).
A.D.C. (1496-1501)	*Acta Dominorum Concilii: Acts of the Lords of Council in Civil Causes.* vol. ii, A.D. 1496-1501; with some Acta Auditorum et Dominorum Concilii, A.D. 1469-1483, edd. G. Neilson and H. Paton (Edinburgh, 1918).

A.P.S.	The Acts of the Parliaments of Scotland, edd. T. Thomson and C. Innes (Edinburgh, 1814-75).
Arbroath Liber	*Liber S. Thome de Aberbrothoc* (Bannatyne Club, 1848-56).
Archaeological Collect-	*Archaeological and Historical*
ions relating to the	*Collections relating to the County*
County of Renfrew	*of Renfrew*, ed. A. Gardner (Paisley, 1885-90).
Asloan MS	*The Asloan Manuscript*, ed. W. A. Craigie (S.T.S., Edinburgh 1923), vol. i.
Auctarium	*Auctarium Chartularii Universitatis Parisiensis*, edd. H. Denifle and A. Chatelain (Paris, 1894-1942).
Bannatyne Misc.	*The Bannatyne Miscellany* (Bannatyne Club, 1827-55).
Bellenden, *Boece*	Hector Boece's *Chronicles of Scotland*, translated into Scots by John Bellenden (edn. Thomas Davidson, Edin., n.d. but about 1536).
Bellenden, *Chronicles*	*The Chronicles of Scotland* compiled by Hector Boece, translated into Scots by John Bellenden 1531 (Edin., 1821; not so full as Bellenden, *Boece*).
Boece, *Scotorum*	Hector Boece, *Scotorum Historia*.
Historiae	In hac in Scotorum Historiam Isagoge continentur: Tabella literaria in ea contentorum; Scotorum Regni descriptio et mores; Regum Britanniae quae nunc Anglia, series; Regum Scotorum Catalogus. Quae impressa sunt Typis Iodoci Badii; et impensis Hectoris Boethii (Paris, 1526).
Boece, *Vitae*	*Hectoris Boetii Murthlacensium et Aberdonensium Episcoporum Vitae* (New Spalding Club, 1894).
Buchanan, *History*	G. Buchanan, *The History of Scotland*, translated J. Aikman (Glasgow and Edinburgh, 1827-29).
Buchanan, *Rerum*	George Buchanan, *Rerum Scoticarum*
Scoticarum Historia	*Historia*, bk. xii (Edin., 1582).
Cal. Docs. Scot.	*Calender of Documents relating to Scotland*, ed. J. Bain (Edinburgh, 1881-8).
C.P.L.	*Calendar of Entries in the Papal Registers relating to Great Britain and Ireland: Papal Letters*, vols. xiii, xiv. ed. J. A. Twemlow (H.M.S.O., 1955, 1960).
Cal. Patent Rolls	*Calendar of the Patent Rolls*, Edward IV vol. iii, 1476-85 (London, 1901); Henry VII vol. i, 1485-94.
Cal. State Papers	*Calendar of State Papers and*
(Milan)	*Manuscripts existing in the Archives and Collections of Milan* vol i, ed. A. B. Hinds (London, 1912).
Cal. State Papers	*Calendar of State Papers and*
(Venice)	*Manuscripts, relating to English affairs, existing in the Archives and Collections of Venice*. Vol. i, 1202-1509, ed. Rawdon Brown (London, 1864).
Cameron, *Apostolic*	*The Apostolic Camera and Scottish*
Camera	*Benefices* 1418-88, ed. A. I. Cameron (Oxford, 1934).
Campbell, *Materials*	William Campbell, *Materials for a History of the Reign of Henry VII* (Rolls Series, 1873 and 1877).
Davies, *York City*	*Extracts from the Municipal Records of*
Records Extracts	*the City of York during the Reigns of Edward IV, Edward V, and Richard III*, ed. R. Davies (London, 1843).
Devon, *Issues of the*	*Issues of the Exchequer: being a*

Exchequer	collection of payments made out of His Majesty's Revenue, from King Henry III to King Henry VI inclusive. Extracted and translated from the original rolls of the Ancient Pell Office. By Frederick Devon, of the Chapter House Record Office, Poet's Corner, Westminster (London, 1837).
Drummond, *History*	William Drummond of Hawthornden, *History of Scotland from the year 1423 until the year 1542* (London, 1681).
Edinburgh City Chrs.	*Charters and Other Documents relating to the City of Edinburgh* (S.B.R.S., 1871).
Eubel	*Hierarchia Catholica medii Aevi 1198-1600*, 3 vols., (vols i and ii ed. Eubel, vol. iii by Van Gulik and Eubel).
E.R.	*The Exchequer Rolls of Scotland*, edd. J. Stuart and others (Edinburgh, 1878-1908).
Fasti	*Fasti Ecclesiae Scoticanae Medii Aevi ad annum 1638* (ed. D. E. R. Watt, St. Andrews, 1969).
Ferrerius, *Appendix to Boece*	*Appendix to Hector Boece, Scotorum Historiae*, second edition, by Giovanni Ferreri (Paris, 1574).
Ferrerius, *Historia*	*Ferrerii Historia Abbatum de Kynlos* (Bannatyne Club, 1839).
Foedera	*Foedera, Conventiones, Litterae et Cuiuscunque Generis Acta Publica*, ed. T. Rymer, Record Commission edition (London, 1816-69).
Fraser, *Annandale*	W. Fraser, *The Annandale Family Book* (Edinburgh, 1894).
Fraser, *Buccleuch*	W. Fraser, *The Scotts of Buccleuch* (Edinburgh, 1878).
Fraser, *Carlaverock*	W. Fraser, *The Book of Carlaverock* (Edinburgh, 1873).
Fraser, *Colquhoun*	W. Fraser, *The Chiefs of Colquhoun and their Country* (Edinburgh, 1869).
Fraser, *Douglas*	W. Fraser, *The Douglas Book* (Edinburgh, 1885).
Fraser, *Keir*	W. Fraser, *The Stirlings of Keir* (Edinburgh, 1858).
Fraser, *Lennox*	W. Fraser, *The Lennox* (Edinburgh, 1874).
Fraser, *Menteith*	W. Fraser, *The Red Book of Menteith* (Edinburgh, 1880).
Fraser, *Wemyss*	W. Fraser, *Memorials of the Family of Wemyss of Wemyss* (Edinburgh, 1888).
Gairdner, *Letters of Richard III and Henry VII*	*Letters and Papers illustrative of the Reigns of Richard III and Henry VII*, ed. James Gairdner (London, 1861-3).
Glasgow Registrum	*Registrum Episopatus Glasguensis* (Bannatyne and Maitland Clubs, 1843).
Hall, *Chronicle*	Edward Hall, *Chronicle*, ed. Henry Ellis (London, 1809).
Hary's Wallace	*Vita Nobilissimi Defensoris Scotie Wilelmi Wallace Militis*, ed. M. P. McDiarmid (Edinburgh, S.T.S., 1968).
Poems of Robert Henryson	*The Poems of Robert Henryson*, ed. G. Gregory Smith, vol. ii (S.T.S., 1906).
Hist. Croy. Cont.	*Historiae Croylandensis Continuatio* (Rerum Anglicarum Scriptores, vol. i, Oxford, 1684).
H. M. C.	*Reports of the Royal Commission on Historical Manuscripts* (London, 1870-).
Hist. Chapel Royal	*History of the Chapel Royal of Scotland* (Grampian Club, 1882).
Hume, *Douglas and Angus*	David Hume of Godscroft, *The History of the Houses of Douglas and Angus* (Edinburgh, 1644).
James IV Letters	*The Letters of James the Fourth 1505-13*, edd. R. K. Hannay and R. L. Mackie (S.H.S., 1953).
Jusserand, *Piers*	*Piers Plowman: A Contribution to the*

Plowman	*History of English Mysticism*, ed. J. J. Jusserand (London, 1894).
Family of Kilravock	*The Family of Kilravock 1290-1847* (Spalding Club, 1848).
Knox, *History*	John Knox, *History of the Reformation in Scotland*, ed. W. C. Dickinson (Edinburgh, 1949).
Lag Chrs.	*The Lag Charters 1400-1720*, ed. A. L. Murray (S.R.S., 1958).
Laing Chrs.	*Calendar of the Laing Charters 854-1837*, ed. J. Anderson (Edinburgh, 1899).
Leland, *Collectanea*	John Leland, *De rebus Britannicis Collectanea*, ed. Hearne (London, 1770), vol. iv; from B. M. Cotton MS. Julius B xii, 4-11.
Lesley, *De Origine*	J. Lesley, *De Origine, Moribus et Rebus Gestis Scotorum Libri Decem* (S.T.S., 1888).
Lesley, *History*	J. Lesley, *The History of Scotland from the Death of King James I in the Year 1436 to the Year 1561* (Bannatyne Club, 1830).
Lettres de Louis XI	*Lettres de Louis XI, roi de France*, edd. J. Vaesen and others (Paris, 1883-1909).
Liber Pluscardensis	*Liber Pluscardensis*, ed. F. J. H. Skene (Edinburgh, 1877).
Lindsay, *Three Estates*	Sir David Lindsay, *A Satire of the Three Estates*, ed. M. P. McDiarmid (London, 1967).
Major, *History*	John Major, *A History of Greater Britain* (S.H.S., 1892).
Mancini, *Usurpation of Richard III*	Dominic Mancini, *The Usurpation of Richard III*, ed. C. A. J. Armstrong (Oxford, 1936).
MRHS	D. E. Easson, *Medieval Religious Houses in Scotland* (London, 1957).
Meroure	Johannes de Irlandia, *The Meroure of Wyssdome*, vol. i (S.T.S., 1926).
Moray Registrum	*Registrum Episcopatus Moraviensis* (Bannatyne Club, 1837).
Morton Registrum	*Registrum Honoris de Morton* (Bannatyne Club, 1853).
Myln, *Vitae*	A. Myln, *Vitae Dunkeldensis Ecclesiae Episcoporum* (Bannatyne Club, 1831).
Nicolas, *Privy Purse Expenses*	*Privy Purse Expenses of Elizabeth of York:* Wardrobe Accounts of Edward IV, ed. Sir H. Nicolas (1830).
Origines Parochiales	*Origines Parochiales Scotiae* (Bannatyne Club, 1851-5).
Papal Negotiations with Mary Queen of Scots	*Papal Negotiations with Mary Queen of Scots during her reign in Scotland 1561-1567*, ed. J. H. Pollen (S.H.S., 1901).
Paston Letters	*Paston Letters*, ed. J. Gairdner (London, 1904).
Perth Blackfriars	*The Blackfriars of Perth*, ed. R. Milne (Edinburgh, 1893).
Pitcairn, *Criminal Trials*	*Criminal Trials in Scotland from 1488 to 1624*, ed. R. Pitcairn (Edinburgh, 1833).
Pitscottie, *Historie*	Robert Lindesay of Pitscottie, *The Historie and Cronicles of Scotland* (S.T.S., 1899-1911).
Prot. Bk. Young	*Protocol Book of James Young 1485-1515*, ed. G. Donaldson (S.R.S., 1952).
R.M.S.	*Registrum Magni Sigilli Regum Scotorum*, edd. J. M. Thomson and others (Edinburgh, 1882-1914).
Robertson, *Concilia*	*Statuta Ecclesiae Scoticanae*, ed. J. Robertson (Bannatyne Club, 1866).
Rot. Scot.	*Rotuli Scotiae in Turri Londinensi et in Domo Capitulari Westmonasteriensi Asservati*, edd. D. Macpherson and others (1814-19).
St. Andrews Acta	*Acta Facultatis Artium Universitatis Sancti Andree 1413-1588*, ed. A. I. Dunlop (S.H.S., 1964).

Spalding Misc.	*Miscellany of the Spalding Club* (Spalding Club, 1841-52).
Theiner, *Vetera Monumenta*	A. Theiner, *Vetera Monumenta Hibernorum et Scotorum Historiam illustrantia* (Rome, 1864).
Thre Prestis	*The Thre Prestis of Peblis,* ed T. Robb (S.T.S., 1920).
T.A.	*Accounts of the Lord High Treasurer of Scotland,* edd. T. Dickson and Sir J. Balfour Paul (Edinburgh, 1877-1916).
Polydore Vergil, *Historia Anglica*	Polydore Vergil, *Historia Anglica* (Camden Society, 1844).
Wilkins, *Concilia*	*Concilia Magnae Britanniae et Hiberniae,* ed. D. Wilkins (London, 1737).
Yester Writs	*Calendar of Writs preserved at Yester House 1166-1503,* edd. C. C. H. Harvey and J. MacLeod (S.R.S., 1930).
York Civic Records	*York Civic Records,* ed. A. Raine (Yorkshire Archaeological Society, 1939).

B. *Secondary*

Abercromby, *Martial Achievements*	Patrick Abercromby, *Martial Achievements of the Scots Nation* (1711-15).
Balfour, *Annales*	Sir James Balfour of Kinnaird, *Annales of Scotland in Historical Works,* ed. James Haig (London, 1824-5).
Beaucourt, *Histoire de Charles VII*	G. du Fresne de Beaucourt, *Histoire de Charles VII* (Paris, 1881-1891).
Brown, *Scottish Society in the Fifteenth Century*	J. M. Brown (ed.), *Scottish Society in the Fifteenth Century* (London, 1977).
Conway, *Henry VII's Relations with Scotland and Ireland*	Agnes Conway, *Henry VII's Relations with Scotland and Ireland 1485-1498* (Cambridge, 1932).
Crawfurd, *Officers*	G. Crawfurd, *The Lives and Characters of the Officers of the Crown and of the State in Scotland* (Edinburgh, 1726).
Dempster, *Historia*	*Thomae Dempsteri Historia Ecclesiastica Gentis Scotorum: sive De Scriptoribus Scotis* (Bannatyne Club, 1829).
Dickinson, *Scotland from the Earliest Times to 1603*	W. C. Dickinson, *Scotland from the Earliest Times to 1603,* A New History of Scotland vol. i (Edinburgh, 1961).
Dickinson/Duncan	W. C. Dickinson, *Scotland from the Earliest Times to 1603,* revised by A. A. M. Duncan (3rd edn., Oxford, 1977).
Donaldson, *Scottish Kings*	Gordon Donaldson, *Scottish Kings* (London, 1967).
Dowden, *Bishops*	J. Dowden, *The Bishops of Scotland* (Glasgow, 1912).
Dunlop, *Kennedy*	Annie I. Dunlop, *The Life and Times of James Kennedy, Bishop of St. Andrews* (Edinburgh, 1950).
Dupuy, *Histoire de la Réunion*	A. Dupuy, *Histoire de la Réunion de la Bretagne à la France* (Paris, 1880).
Ferguson, *Relations with England*	W. Ferguson, *Scotland's Relations with England: A Survey to 1707* (Edinburgh, 1977).
Hannay, *Early History of the Scottish Signet*	R. K. Hannay, *The Early History of the Scottish Signet* (Edinburgh, n.d.).
Herkless and Hannay	J. Herkless and R. K. Hannay, *The Archbishops of St. Andrews* (Edinburgh, 1907).
Hume Brown, *History*	P. Hume Brown, *History of Scotland* (Cambridge, 1902).
Kingsford, *English Historical Literature*	C. L. Kingsford, *English Historical Literature in the Fifteenth Century* (Oxford, 1913).
Lang, *History*	Andrew Lang, *A History of Scotland,* vol. i (Edinburgh, 1900).

Macfarlane, *Nobility*   K. B. Macfarlane, *The nobility of later medieval England* (Oxford, 1953).

Mackenzie, *Writers*   G. Mackenzie, *The Lives and Characters of the most eminent Writers of the Nation* (Edinburgh, 1708-22).

Mackie, *James IV*   R. L. Mackie, *King James IV of Scotland, a Brief Survey of his Life and Times* (Edinburgh, 1958).

MacQueen, *Henryson*   John MacQueen, *Robert Henryson, A Study of the Major Narrative Poems* (Oxford, 1967).

Mitchison, *History*   Rosalind Mitchison, *A History of Scotland* (London, 1970).

Menzies, *The Scottish*   Gordon Menzies (ed.), *The Scottish*
Nation   *Nation* (London, 1972).

Maitland Thomson,   J. Maitland Thomson, *The Public*
Public Records of   *Records of Scotland* (Glasgow,
Scotland   1922).

Napier, *Memoirs of John*   Mark Napier, *Memoirs of John Napier of*
Napier of Merchiston   *Merchiston* (Edinburgh, 1834).

Nicholson, *Scotland:*   R. G. Nicholson, *Scotland: The Later*
The Later Middle Ages   *Middle Ages, 1286-1513* (Edinburgh, 1974).

Nisbet, *Heraldry*   A. Nisbet, *A System of Heraldry*, new edition (Edinburgh, 1816).

Pinkerton, *History*   J. Pinkerton, *The History of Scotland from the Accession of the House of Stuart to that of Mary, with Appendices of Original Papers* (London, 1797).

Ramsay, *Lancaster*   Sir James H. Ramsay, *Lancaster and*
and York   *York* (Oxford, 1892).

Ross, *Edward IV*   Charles Ross, *Edward IV* (London, 1974).

Scofield, *Edward IV*   Cora L. Scofield, *The Life and Reign of Edward the Fourth* (London, 1923).

Scofield, *Star Chamber*   Cora L. Scofield, *A Study of the Court of Star Chamber* (Chicago, 1900).

Spottiswoode   J. Spottiswoode, *History of the Church in Scotland to the end of the reign of King James VI* (3 vols., Edinburgh, 1847-51).

Stewart, *The Scottish*   I. H. Stewart, *The Scottish Coinage*
Coinage   (2nd edn., London, 1967).

Thompson and Campbell,   Colin Thompson and Lorne Campbell,
The Trinity Panels   *Hugo van der Goes and the Trinity Panels in Edinburgh* (Edinburgh, 1974).

Wormald, *Court, Kirk,*   Jenny Wormald, *Court, Kirk, and*
and Community   *Community: Scotland 1470-1625* (London, 1981).

C. *Works of reference*

Dictionary of the Older   *A Dictionary of the Older Scottish*
Scottish Tongue   *Tongue from the Twelfth Century to the end of the Seventeenth,* edd. Sir William A. Craigie and A. J. Aitken (Chicago and London, n.d.).

Scots Peerage   *The Scots Peerage,* ed. Sir J. Balfour Paul (Edinburgh, 1904-14).

D. *Articles and Notes*

Angus, W.,   'Note on the Consecration of William Elphinstone, Bishop of Aberdeen', *Aberdeen University Review,* xxiii, (1935-6), 135-6.

Angus, W., and Dunlop, A. I., 'The Date of the Birth of James III,' (conflicting views), *S.H.R.,* xxx, (Oct. 1951), 199-204.

Armstrong, C. A. J.,   'A Letter of James III to the Duke of Burgundy,' *S.H.S. Misc.* viii, 19-32.

Brown, A. L.,	'The Scottish "Establishment" in the later Fifteenth Century,' *Juridical Review*, xxiii, (1978).
Burns, J. H.,	'John Ireland and "The Meroure of Wyssdome",' *Innes Review*, vi, part ii, (1955), 86.
Chandler, S. B.,	'An Italian Life of Margaret, Queen of James III', *S.H.R.*, xxxii, (1953), 52-7.
Dickinson, W. C.,	'The Administration of Justice in Mediaeval Scotland,' *Aberdeen University Review*, xxxiv, (1952).
Dickinson, W. C.,	'Oure Signet of the Unicorn', *S.H.R.*, xxvi, (1947), 147-8.
Dobson, R. B.,	'The Last English Monks on Scottish Soil,' *S.H.R.*, xlvi, (April, 1967), 1-25.
Durkan, J.,	'The Beginnings of Humanism in Scotland,' *Innes Review*, iv, (1953), 5.
Finlayson W. H.,	'The Boyds in Bruges,' *S.H.R.*, xxviii, (1949), 195-6.
Graham, A.,	'The Battle of "Sauchieburn",' *S.H.R.*, xxxix, (Oct. 1960).
Grant, A.,	'The Development of the Scottish Peerage,' *S.H.R.*, lvii, (1978), 1-27.
Hannay, R. K.,	'On "Parliament" and "General Council",' *S.H.R.*, xviii, (April, 1921), 157-170.
Lyall, R. J.,	'Politics and Poetry in Fifteenth and Sixteenth Century Scotland,' *Scottish Literary Journal*, vol. 3 No. 2 (Dec. 1976), 5-29.
McDiarmid, M. P.,	'The Date of the "Wallace",' *S.H.R.*, xxxiv, (April, 1955), 26-31.
Macdougall, N.,	'The Struggle for the Priory of Coldingham, 1472-88', *Innes Review*, xxiii, (1972), 102-114.
Macfarlane, L. J.,	'The Primacy of the Scottish Church, 1472-1521,' *Innes Review*, xx, 111-129.
Madden, C.,	'Royal Treatment of Feudal Casualties in late medieval Scotland,' *S.H.R.*, lv, (1976), 172-194.
Murray, A. L.,	'The Comptroller, 1425-1488,' *S.H.R.*, lii, (1973), 1-29.
Murray, Joan,	'The Black Money of James III,' *British Archaeological Reports* 45 (1977), 115-130.
Nicholson, R. G.,	'Feudal Developments in Late Medieval Scotland,' *Juridical Review* (April 1973), pt. i, 1-21.
Rae, T. I.,	'The historical writing of Drummond of Hawthornden,' *S.H.R.*, liv. (1975), 22-62.
Stewart, I. H.,	'Some Scottish Ceremonial Coins,' *P.S.A.S.*, xcviii, (1964-6), 256-61.
Thomson, J. A. F.,	'Some New Light on the Elevation of Patrick Graham,' *S.H.R.*, xl, (April, 1961), 83-88.
Thomson, J. A. F.,	'Innocent VIII and the Scottish Church,' *Innes Review*, xix, part i, (Spring, 1968), 23-31.
Trevor-Roper, H. R.,	'George Buchanan and the Ancient Scottish Constitution,' *E.H.R.*, Supplement 3, (1966).

Index